THE ROYAL NAVY
DAY BY DAY

This book is dedicated to all those who have
contributed to the naval service and to those who have helped them.
but especially to those who in various ways have paid the price of Admiralty.

THE ROYAL NAVY
DAY BY DAY

Edited by
Lieutenant-Commander R.E.A. Shrubb, Royal Navy
and
Captain A.B. Sainsbury, VRD, MA, Royal Naval Reserve

CENTAUR PRESS

Copyright©1979 Portsmouth Royal Naval Museum Trading Company Ltd.
First published in 1979 by Centaur Press Ltd., Fontwell, Sussex BN18 0TA to whom all correspondence concerning the text and its sale should be sent.

ISBN 0 900000 91 0

Designed and printed by Coasbyprint Ltd., Portsmouth, Hampshire, PO3 5NH.

FOREWORD

By Admiral Sir Terence Lewin, GCB, MVO, DSC, ADC, *First Sea Lord.*

Such is the richness of our Naval Heritage that every day is an anniversary not just of one, but of a whole series of events stretching back in time to the beginnings of our Nation. Some of these events changed the course of history, some may have involved just one or two men in a boat, but each has made its contribution to the tradition and reputation of the Royal Navy of today.

It is the nature of sea warfare that glory belongs to all, as much to the cook as to the coxswain; all are literally in the same boat. The battle is won as much in the preparation and training as in the heat of the action. Our Naval Heritage is an ever growing tapestry to which every man and woman now serving is adding his or her contribution. To serve the Royal Navy as a regular or a reservist or as a civilian is not just to have a profession or a job, but to be part of a Service which occupies a unique place in the history of our country and the world.

The idea for this book was born from the need to find inspiration for a particular speech, and a need to fill the gap left by the demise of the old Admiralty Desk Diary, which showed the major naval anniversaries. The initial research, undertaken by Lieutenant-Commander R. E. A. Shrubb, Royal Navy, produced enough material to fill six booklets which were published for a naval readership. This in turn attracted further interest and it was decided to expand it into a more comprehensive and illustrated book for a wider readership, and the task of continuing this work was generously undertaken by Captain A. B. Sainsbury, VRD, Royal Naval Reserve.

The book provides the bare outline of the picture on the tapestry canvas; the fuller stories of the great victories and of the myriad of minor actions provide the detail, and the light and shade which go to complete the masterpiece. "The Royal Navy Day by Day" deserves a place on the bookshelves not only of every naval ship and establishment, but in the home of anyone who has the sea in his blood. In our country that must include most of us. If your interest is stimulated and you are encouraged to delve deeper, I promise you will be well rewarded.

Terence Lewin

PREFACE

People interested in naval history are well aware of the main dates in the Navy's calendar. But the professionalism and style, the tradition and history that characterise the service today come far less from a few big events than from a much more intricate mosaic of happenings, some of them of a seemingly everyday nature, that covers periods of peace as well as of war, and reflects social and organisational changes as well as feats of arms and courage. We have chronicled samples of them all. We trust (Nelson would have said 'confide') that you will want to follow up something that catches your interest, such as an anniversary, the name of a ship or an individual, or a reference to a place or an event.

The keys to the book are its indexes: one thing leads to another. We are not entirely sorry that we have not been able to index separately all the ships that have borne the same name. That would have given you a clearer course but it would have deprived you of some fascinating, if accidental, excursions, which is partly why we persist in regarding history as provocative and as fun. The contents are a sample distilled from the whole history of the navy. They tell of adventure and courage, of endurance and tedium, of hardship and achievement. But the history of the Royal Navy, which like our postage stamps has no need to identify itself with the country's name, and which for many years was brought up on the maxim Fisher had displayed at Osborne, "there is nothing the navy cannot do", is not entirely a story of battleships and bloodshed. The administrative side of the service is as important as the military. And the service is never off duty: it has to contend with the elements, in peace and in war, and its operational and diplomatic activities in peacetime are often as important as its tasks in war which, by its ready presence, it has sometimes prevented.

Nor is naval history all about ships, either at war or in peace: "it is sailors, not ships, that constitute a Navy", said Admiral Napier (6th November). So we have included some dates of human as well as of material significance and if we have included the birth and death days of some more famous men we have not forgotten the more numerous if less illustrious. We are conscious of our obligations to our ancestors and of our debts to the dead, for "if anyone would understand any great work, he must not look at the dead without thinking of the living in them, nor at the living without thinking of the dead."

We have tried to balance various interests and factors. We have had in mind young people in the service or still at school, whose interest we hope to kindle, just as much as Flag Officers (or their Secretaries) seeking a peg on which to hang a speech. We have tried to combine the peacetime and the wartime work of the service with its full-time and its part-time members, be they men or women. We have pointed to some themes — the development of the capital ship and the submarine, and the changing role of the Royal Marines. We have not left out the less happy moments. We shall not have pleased everyone by including every historical detail but we hope that the chosen mix is about right. If you care to suggest corrections or enrichment we shall be glad to hear from you through our publisher, Michael Packard, to whose efforts and expertise the book and we owe so much.

So many people have helped us, by supplying information and photographs, that it would be unrealistic to list them individually and invidious to select only some. We must thank the Naval Historical Branch of the Ministry of Defence (Navy), the National Maritime Museum, Greenwich, the Portsmouth Royal Naval Museum and the Controller of Her Majesty's Stationery Office; the service museums of HMS *Dolphin* (Gosport), HMS *Vernon*, RNAS Yeovilton and the Royal Marines at Eastney; the Imperial War Museum, the Royal Army Museum in Chelsea and the Royal Air Force Museum at Hendon. We acknowledge with great and genuine gratitude all other sources and supporters.

A.B.S.
R.E.A.S.

TABLE OF CONTENTS

Abbreviations and Initials

AA	Anti-Aircraft
AB	Able Seaman
A/C	Aircraft or Aircraft Carrier
ADC	Aide de Camp
AFO	Admiralty Fleet Order
AM	Albert Medal
AMC	Armed Merchant Cruiser
A/S	Anti-Submarine
Asdic	Allied Submarine Detection Investigation Committee
BCF	Battle Cruiser Force
BCS	Battle Cruiser Squadron
BH	Battle Honour: [bh] in text
BPF	British Pacific Fleet
BS	Battle or Battleship Squadron
Ben Mar	Bengal Marine
BYMS	British Yard Mine Sweeper
Cdr	Commander
Cdre	Commodore
CinC	Commander-in-Chief
CMB	Coastal Motor Boat
CPO	Chief Petty Officer
CS	Cruiser Squadron
CTL	Constructive Total Loss, i.e. written off
DBR	Damaged Beyond Repair
DEMS	Defensively Equipped Merchant Ship
DF	Destroyer Flotilla, or Direction Finding
DNC	Director of Naval Construction
DSC	Distinguished Service Cross
DSO	Distinguished Service Order
EGM	Empire Gallantry Medal
Enigma	German encyphering machine
ERA	Engine Room Artificer
ESM	Electronic Support Measures
FAA	Fleet Air Arm
Fr	France, French
FF	Free French forces in WWII
FOAC	Flag Officer Aircraft Carriers
FOCAS	Flag Officer Carriers and Amphibious Ships
FOF3	Flag Officer Flotillas 3
GC	George Cross
GCB	Knight Grand Cross of the Order of the Bath
GM	George Medal
GMD	Guided Missile Destroyer
GOC	General Officer Commanding
HFDF	High Frequency Direction Finding
HNL	Netherlands
Hon EI.Co	Honourable East India Company
HDML	Harbour Defence Motor Launch
IN	Indian Navy
KDG	King's Dragoon Guards
LCS	Light Cruiser Squadron
LCT	Landing Craft, Tanks
L/S	Leading Seaman
LSH	Landing Ship, Heavy
LSI	Landing Ship, Infantry
Lt	Lieutenant
Lt-Cdr	Lieutenant-Commander
M	Naval General Service medal awarded, for ship or for boat action
M*	Gold medal awarded, 1794-1815
MAS	Motorbarea Armartta SVAN (Society Veneziano Automobile Nautica) in short, an Italian motor torpedo boat

MCD	Minewarfare and Clearance Diving branch
MgB	Motor Gun Boat
ML	Motor Launch
MN	Merchant Navy
MS	Minesweeper
MT	Motor Transport
MTB	Motor Torpedo Boat
MVO	Member of the Royal Victorian Order
NATO	North Atlantic Treaty Organisation
Neth	Netherlands
NID	Naval Intelligence Division
Ord	Ordinary Seaman
OTU	Operational Training Unit
Pinch	An operation planned to capture a specific piece of equipment, usually an intelligence operation
PO	Petty Officer
PWO	Principal Warfare Officer
QARNNS	Queen Alexandra's Royal Naval Nursing Service
QR&AI	Queen's Regulations and Admiralty Instructions
Q.ship	A merchant ship converted to attack enemy submarines by decoying them into attacking her
Radar	Radio detection and ranging
RAAF	Royal Australian Air Force
RAFVR	Royal Air Force Volunteer Reserve
RAN	Royal Australian Navy
RANVR	Royal Australian Navy Volunteer Reserve
RCAF	Royal Canadian Air Force
RCN	Royal Canadian Navy
RD	Reserve Decoration
RDF	Radio Direction Finding
RFC	Royal Flying Corps
RIN	Royal Indian Navy
RM	Royal Marine, Royal Marines
RMA	Royal Marine Artillery
RMLI	Royal Marine Light Infantry
RMR	Royal Marine Reserve, formed from the
RMFVR	Royal Marine Forces Volunteer Reserve
RNAS	Royal Naval Air Service
RNAY	Royal Naval Aircraft Yard
RNB	Royal Naval Barracks
RNC	Royal Naval College
RND	Royal Naval Division
RNEC	Royal Naval Engineering College
RNH	Royal Naval Hospital
RNR	Royal Naval Reserve
RNVR	Royal Naval Volunteer Reserve
RNVSR	Royal Naval Volunteer Supplemental Reserve
RNZN	Royal New Zealand Navy
ROK	Republic of Korea
SAAF	South African Air Force
SANF	South African Naval Force
SM, s/m	Submarine
SONAR	Sound Navigation Ranging
Sq	Squadron
Sub-Lt	Sub-Lieutenant
TB	Torpedo Boat
TBD	Torpedo Boat Destroyer
TF	Task Force
TG	Task Group
USS	United States Ship
VC	Victoria Cross
VRD	Volunteer Reserve Decoration
VSTOL	Vertical Short Take-Off or Landing
WRNR	Womens Royal Naval Reserve
WRNS	Womens Royal Navy Service
WRNVR	Womens Royal Naval Volunteer Reserve

Day by Day Summary of the
History of the Royal Navy

1586	Sir Francis Drake captured San Domingo *(Bonaventure, Tiger, Primrose)*.
1653	Pay set at 24 shillings per month for Able Seamen (fixed until 8th May 1797).
1693	Appointment of first officers at Dock (now Plymouth Dockyard).
1758	*Adventure* captured the Dunkirk privateer *Machault* close off Dungeness.
1807	Capture of Curaçoa by *Anson, Arethusa, Fisgard, Latona* and *Morne Fortunee*. [m*, m, bh]
1809	*Onyx* captured the Dutch *Manly* 60 miles N.W. by W. of the Texel. [m]
1859	*Britannia* became cadet training ship.
1892	Gambia River expedition: *Sparrow, Widgeon* and *Thrush*.
1906	*Dryad* commissioned in Naval Academy Buildings, Portsmouth Dockyard.
1915	*Formidable* sunk by U24, 21 miles East of Start Point.

HMS *Scylla* in 1942

1915	Engineers became part of military branch with executive curl on their stripes.
1943	*Scylla* homed by Coastal Command aircraft onto German blockade runner *Rhakotis* and sank her in Bay of Biscay.

Intelligence reports indicated an inward bound ship approaching the Bay: she was sighted by a Sunderland aircraft and the light cruiser *Scylla* was detached from escorting a convoy to intercept. The *Scylla* was guided by the Sunderland dropping flares along the course to be steered, and after 20 hours steaming at 28 knots through a gale sighted the *Rhakotis* just before sunset. She was sunk by gunfire and torpedo 140 miles from the French coast, having left the Far East on 5 November with a valuable cargo for the German war effort. On board were two survivors from the torpedoed merchantman *City of Cairo* who had been rescued by the *Rhakotis* after 36 days in the Atlantic in an open boat: both survived.

1952	RNR and RNVR stripes finally straightened, with R in curl.
1956	Seamen, Engineer, Electrical and Supply Officers combined on the General List, Branch Officers becoming Special Duties Officers.
1971	Naval Pay computerised.
1975	Operations Branch formed.
1979	FOCAS became FOF 3.

2nd JANUARY

1757 Capture of Calcutta by Vice-Admiral Charles Watson *(Kent)* and troops under Colonel Robert Clive. Ships: *Bridgewater, Kent, Kingfisher, Tiger.*

1779 Chapel of Greenwich Hospital destroyed by fire; rebuilt by 'Athenian' Stuart and reopened in 1789.

1783 *Magicienne* fought the French *Sibylle* and *Railleur* 500 miles to the eastward of Grand Bahama Island.

1807 Boats of *Cerberus* cut out a French privateer from under a battery near the Pearl Rock, Martinique. [m]

1858 *Shannon's* Naval Brigade at the action at the Kali Nadi bridge. Indian Mutiny Medal.

1879 Rifled muzzle-loading gun (38 ton) in *Thunderer* burst, precipitating return to breech-loading.

1941 *Terror, Aphis* and *Ladybird* provided harassing fire in support of assault on Bardia.

1943 *Alarm* severely damaged by aircraft at Bone, and written off.

1944 Helicopters first used in sea warfare (Sikorski R4 in Atlantic Convoy).

1947 *Royal Arthur* commissioned: first Petty Officers' training at Corsham.

The Fleet Air Arm family of Helicopters,
From humble beginnings as an observation platform, the helicopter has developed into one of the main striking weapons of the Navy.
Sea King (front) fully equipped to hunt and attack submarines. Greatly feared by submariners since it has the capabilities of a frigate, except in endurance and reload ability.
Wessex 1 and *3.* The *Wessex 3* was the forerunner of the *Sea King.* It has much less endurance when loaded with torpedoes, but can seek out and kill submarines using similar techniques.
Whirlwind For a long time the work-horse of the Fleet Air Arm helicopters; used in anti-submarine role for dunking sonar.
Wasp (rear) Carried by almost all frigates for use as a weapon carrier and launch platform in anti-submarine and surface role. Also valuable for 'over the horizon' surveillance, load carrying etc. It is being replaced by the *Lynx.*

3rd JANUARY

1670	George Monck, Duke of Albemarle, died.
1695	*Nonsuch* taken by the French *Français* 200 miles to the westward of the Scilly Islands.
1707	*Fowey, Milford* and *Romney* destroyed the French *Content* in Almeria Bay, Spain.
1793	*Childers* fired on by French batteries at Brest: first shots in the French wars.
1799	*Wolverine* fought the French luggers *Furet* and *Ruse* 5 miles N.N.E. of Boulogne.
1801	Boats of *Melpomene* in the Senegal River, West Africa, cut out the French *Sénégal* which was wrecked while being brought out.
1807	*Pickle* captured the French *Favorite* 20 miles S.S.W. of Lizard Head. [m]
1864	*Haughty* sank two pirate junks, one inside and one outside Pinghai Bay, China.
1919	*Kent* arrived at Vladivostok.
1941	*Barham, Valiant* and *Warspite* bombarded Bardia, captured by British troops on 5th January.
1943*	"Chariot" human torpedo sank the Italian light cruiser *Ulpio Traiano* in Palermo harbour. The first successful employment of these weapons, in World War II, by the RN.
1945	Assault on Akyab, Burma. Operation Lightning. Ships: *Napier, Nepal, Shoreham.* Bombardment force: *Newcastle, Nigeria, Phoebe; Pathfinder, Raider, Rapid.*

*The Chariot, referred to as a Pig (Maiale) by the Italians

During the Second World War, diving technology was such that divers could only operate at very shallow depths (approx 5 fathoms) using an oxygen breathing apparatus which did not leave a trail of bubbles. Enemy harbours were heavily defended with anti-submarine nets, smaller mesh anti-torpedo nets, and boom defence vessels. It took great courage to venture into a defended harbour in a diving suit to attack enemy ships. The chariot used was battery powered, with a range of 20 miles at 3½ knots. It had a crew of two, one of whom was employed cutting through net defences. It carried a 700 lb charge attached to the front of its 25 foot long body, and the charge could be slung beneath an enemy ship. With a speed of only 3½ knots it was mainly employed in the Mediterranean and Far East. The Italians scored the first success with one at Alexandria, when they disabled two British battleships. The Germans made a number of successful attacks off the Normandy beaches, and a Japanese cruiser was sunk by a British chariot at Singapore. At a cost of only £2200 it was a cheap way of attacking enemy shipping, in material terms. The risk to the crew was enormous.

4th JANUARY

1761	*Trent* captured the French *Bien-Aimé* 30 miles S.S.E. of Cape Tiburon, Haiti.
1781	*Courageux* captured the French *Minerve* 30 miles to the westward of Ushant.
1807	Landing party from *Imperieuse* destroyed Fort Roquette, Arcachon on West coast of France.
1915	C. 31 lost off Belgian coast.
1916	Start of operations for the relief of Kut-al'Amara, Mesopotamia, River gunboats: *Gadfly, Butterfly, Cranefly, Dragonfly*; from 10th Jan. *Flycatcher* (ex-Turkish patrol boat). British War Medal: clasp 'Mesopotamia' approved but not issued.
1945	Air strike on oil refineries at Pangkalan Brandan, Sumatra, by Rear-Admiral Sir Philip Vian *(Indomitable)* Operation Lentil. *Indefatigable[1], Indomitable[2], Victorious[3], Argonaut, Black Prince, Ceylon, Suffolk* and 8 destroyers of 25th and 27th D F. FAA Sq:

Avenger	849[3], 857[2],
Corsair	1834[3], 1836[3].
Firefly	1770[1].
Hellcat	888[1], 1839[2], 1844[2].
Seafire	887[1], 894[1].

5th JANUARY

1795 *Blanche* captured the French *Pique* 3 miles to the westward of Marie Galante, West Indies. [m, bh]

1798 *Pomone* captured the French privateer *Chéri* 280 miles to the south-westward of Ushant.

1814 *Blazer, Desiree, Hearty, Piercer, Redbreast, Shamrock* and gunboats at the capture of Glückstadt, Holstein. [m, bh]

1814 *Bacchante* and *Saracen* captured Cattaro (Kotor), Yugoslavia. [bh]

1942 *Upholder* sank the Italian s/m *Ammiraglio Saint-Bon* off the Lipari Islands (38° 22'N., 15° 22'E.).

1943 US Task Force, including *Achilles*, bombarded Munda and Kolombangara Island (Guadalcanal campaign). *Achilles* damaged by Japanese aircraft.

1951 Evacuation of Inchon, Korea.

The Chinese offensive in Korea began on 31st December 1950, and military forces were pulled South in the face of heavy enemy action. In the Inchon area, the cruisers *Kenya* and *Ceylon* and Australian destroyers *Warramunga* and *Bataan* together with *USS Rochester* and *Evertsen* (Dutch) formed the Gun Fire Support Group, providing interdiction for the Army, who reported Inchon as completely evacuated by 5th January. A total of 68,913 personnel, 1,404 vehicles and 62,144 tons of cargo were lifted from Inchon to Taechon and Pusan. In December, 105,000 US and ROK military personnel and 91,000 civilian refugees had been lifted by sea from Hungnam.

Chain Shot

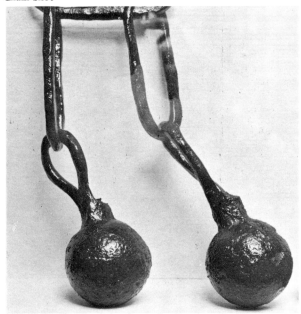

6th JANUARY

Grape Shot
This particular type consisted of three tiers of cast iron balls, separated by parallel iron discs and connected by a central pin. The whole was enclosed in a canvas bag, bound tightly round with rope.

1745 *Captain, Dreadnought, Hampton Court* and *Sunderland* fought the French *Fleuron* and *Neptune* 250 miles to the westward of Ushant. *Captain* recaptured the British privateer *Mars*.

1801 Boats of *Mercury* captured fifteen sail of a French convoy between Sète and Marseilles.

1813 Boats of *Bacchante* and *Weazle* captured five French gunboats 15 miles S.E. of Cape Otranto, Calabria. [m]

1814 *Niger and Tagus* captured the French *Cérès* 240 miles to the southward of Cape Verde Islands.

1900 *Powerful's* Naval Brigade at the repulse of the Boers on Waggon Hill, Ladysmith. South Africa Medal: clasp 'Defence of Ladysmith'.

1916 E.17 wrecked off Texel.

1916 *King Edward VII* sunk by mine 25 miles 080° from Cape Wrath; her namesake had said at her launch that she should always be a flagship and she was lost on her first voyage as a private ship.

1945 Operations in Lingayen Gulf, Phillipines, by U.S. forces from the 5th to the 9th, when troops landed. [bh]. Present: *Arunta, Australia, Warramunga, Gascoyne, Shropshire, Warrego* (all RAN).

1945 *Wallasea* sunk by the German E-boat S. 138 South of Mounts Bay, Cornwall. (Convoy WP.457)

1945 *Walpole* mined in N Sea: CTL.

7th JANUARY

1730   Royal approval given to 'Regulations for the Naval Service': predecessor of QR and AI.

1746   George Keith Elphinstone born.

1779   Court-martial of Admiral Keppel began.

1804   Commodore Samuel Hood *(Centaur)* seized, fortified and commissioned the Diamond Rock, West Indies.

1806   Boats of *Franchise* cut out the Spanish *Raposa* at Campeche, Mexico.

1841   Capture of the Chuen pi and Tai kok tau forts in the Boca Tigris, Canton River. (Chuen pi) — *Calliope, Hyacinth, Larne;* Bengal Marine steamers *Enterprise, Madagascar, Nemesis, Queen.* (Tai kok tau) — *Samarang, Druid, Modeste, Columbine.* Seamen and Marines of *Blenheim, Melville* and *Wellesley.* Troops: Royal Artillery, 26th and 49th Regiments; 37th Madras Native Infantry, Bengal Volunteer Regiment. China, 1841-2, Medal.

The First Chinese War, 1841-2

Napoleon's description of Britain as a 'nation of shopkeepers' was not far from the truth, and it was the wealth she accrued from her trade which subsidised the coalitions which eventually led to his downfall. It is not surprising therefore that unimpeded trade should be one of the main considerations in Britain's foreign policy. China's exports were very attractive to the West and when the Chinese began to interrupt the opium trade, as well as failing to discourage the piracy which was endemic in the Far East, relations with other trading powers began to deteriorate. Further ill-treatment of British residents and traders followed, and a punitive expedition was mounted. In a series of joint Army and Navy operations, the Chinese were defeated and agreed to British terms.

1841   *Nemesis* and boats of *Calliope, Hyacinth, Larne, Starling and Sulphur* destroyed 13 war junks in Anson's Bay. China, 1841-2, Medal.

1862   Landing party from *Falcon* destroyed Robene, Sierra Leone.

1883   Andrew Browne Cunningham born.

1900   Blockade of Laurenço Marques, Mozambique, by *Forte, Thetis, Magicienne.* First use of wireless to co-ordinate action.

1917   Sea Lions in A/S experiments in Gareloch.

1918   *S.S. Braeneil* rammed and sank U.93 in SW Approaches.

1940   *Undine* and *Seahorse* scuttled after depth charge attacks by the German M.1201, M.1204 and M.1207, and by the German 1st M/S Flotilla respectively in the Heligoland Bight.

1941   *Anemone* sank the Italian s/m *Nani* off Faeroes.

1944   *Tweed* sunk by U.305 in N Atlantic. Operation Stonewall.

1945   Operations in the Kaladan River, Burma. Ships: *Jumma* and *Narbada* (both RIN); M.L. *381, 829.*

Nemesis **attacking war junks in Anson's Bay — First Chinese War, 1841**

Swabbing the decks, HMS *Calliope,* **1895**

8th JANUARY

1758   *Hussar* captured the French privateer *Vengeance* 60 miles West of Lizard Head.

1761   *Unicorn* captured the French *Vestale* 30 miles S.W. of Belle Île. [bh]

1780   Admiral Sir George Bridges Rodney *(Sandwich)*, with 18 sail of the line, captured a Spanish convoy and its escort (22 sail) 300 miles to the westward of Cape Finisterre. (See 16th January)

1798   *Kingfisher* captured the French privateer *Betzy* 150 miles to the westward of Burling Island, Portugal.

1806   Body of Vice-Admiral Lord Nelson taken from Greenwich to Whitehall by river.

1862   Landing party from *Falcon* and a detachment of the 2nd West India Regiment destroyed Robaga, Sierra Leone.

1916   Evacuation of Gallipoli Peninsula completed.

1918   *Cyclamen* sank the German UB.69 off Bizerta.

1942   *Aphis* bombarded Halfaya Pass in support of the Army advance from Egypt.

1944   *Bayntun* and *Camrose* (RCN) sank U.757 in SW Approaches. (Convoy OS.64/KMS.38)

1944   Sunderland U/10 (RAAF) sank U.426 in Bay of Biscay.

*John Jervis (Admiral of the Fleet Earl St. Vincent) (1734-1823)

Jervis joined the navy at the age of 14, was a Lieutenant at 20 and by 1795 was Admiral in command of the Mediterranean fleet blockading Cadiz. In 1797 he defeated 21 Spanish ships with 15 of his own off St. Vincent. For this he was created an Earl. He was known as a firm disciplinarian, particularly in handling mutineers in the fleet during 1797 and 98. In 1801 he was appointed First Lord of the Admiralty and during the Peace of Amiens concentrated his efforts on reforming the dockyards. His actions aroused much enmity, but succeeded in exposing the corruption that was rife. Inevitably at that time, there were political repercussions and he was obliged to resign from the Admiralty in 1804. By 1806, after a change of government, St Vincent returned to become acting Admiral of the Fleet, but finally retired because of ill-health in 1807. At the Coronation of King George IV in 1821 he was promoted Admiral of the Fleet.

9th JANUARY

1734*   John Jervis born.

1744   Battle of Toulon (see 5th April).

1781   *Fairy* taken by a French privateer 30 miles S.S.W. of the Scilly Islands.

1801   *Constitution* taken by two French cutters off Portland. Recaptured by the Revenue cutter *Greyhound.*

1806   Funeral of Vice-Admiral Lord Nelson in St. Paul's Cathedral.

1810   *Plover* recaptured the British brig *Pomona* — prize to the St. Malo privateer *Saratu* — 70 miles W.S.W. of the Scilly Islands.

1811   *Princess Charlotte* captured the French privateer *Aimable Flore* 210 miles W.S.W. of Ushant.

1918   *Racoon* wrecked on NW coast of Ireland.

1940   *Starfish* scuttled after depth charge attack by the German minesweeper M.7 in the Heligoland Bight.

1942   *Vimiera* sunk by mine in the Thames Estuary. (Convoy FS.693)

1942   Sunderland X/230 sank U.577 off Mersa Matruh.

1761 Admiral Edward Boscawen, 'Old Dreadnought', died. When his wife, an admirable correspondent, lamented his absence from home during the harvest, he replied 'To be sure I lose the fruits of the earth, but I am gathering the fruits of the sea'. To an officer of the watch who sighted two French ships and then called his Captain to ask what he should do, Boscawen replied 'Do? Do, dammit; fight 'em!' and appeared on deck in his nightshirt.

1761 *Seahorse* fought the French *Grand* 100 miles S.W. of Start Point.

1761 *Juno* and *Venus* captured the French *Brune* 170 miles to the westward of Ushant.

1797 *Phoebe* captured the French *Atalante* 60 miles to the northward of the Scilly Islands.

1806 Cape Town and its defences capitulated to the forces under Major-General Sir David Baird and Commodore Sir Home Riggs Popham *(Diadem)*. A Naval Brigade was landed. [bh]. Ships: *Belliqueux, Diadem. Diomede, Encounter, Espoir, Leda, Protector, Raisonnable. Narcissus* was cruising 30 miles to the southward of the Cape and did not arrive in Table Bay until after Cape Town had capitulated.

1810 Boats of *Armide* and *Christian VII* captured six French coasters in Basque Roads.

1810 *Plover* captured the St. Malo privateer *Saratu* 20 miles S.S.W. of the Scilly Islands. The British brig *Brothers —*

prize to the *Saratu* — was recaptured earlier in the day.

1854 *Illustrious* became cadet training ship.

1912 First aircraft launch from British warship (Short S27 Box Kite from *Africa* — at anchor).

1915 *Greenfly* sunk by mine in N Sea.

1924 *Resolution* rammed and sank H.42 off Portland Bill.

1941 *Gallant* severely damaged by mine S.E. of Pantellaria. (Towed to Malta: bombed 5th April 1942 and sunk as breakwater in September 1943.)

1941 *Hereward* sank the Italian t.b. *Vega* off Malta. *(Bonaventure, Jaguar* and *Southampton* also engaged). Operation Excess.

At the start of 1941, convoys were being run to Piraeus and Malta in Operation Excess, involving all naval forces in the Mediterranean. The carrier *Illustrious* formed part of the escort of a convoy from Alexandria to Malta.
On 10 January the situation was dramatically challenged with the unexpected attack on the carrier *Illustrious*, and the battleships *Warspite* and *Valiant* by the Luftwaffe. Thirty aircraft of Flieger korps X of the Luftwaffe attacked *Illustrious*, and ten engaged the other ships.
The flying was brilliant, with the aircraft diving from 12,000 feet at angles of 65^0 to 80^0, releasing bombs at 800 feet and following with gun attacks on the carrier. There were 6 aircraft in the dive at any one time throughout the 6 minute attack.
Illustrious was badly damaged but limped into Malta. There, despite continuous Luftwaffe attack, she was repaired sufficiently in 13 days to sail for Alexandria. She had lost 30% of her aircrew and was withdrawn from the Mediterranean for repairs, leaving the Luftwaffe in control of the central Mediterranean air space.

1943 GC (ex-AM): Able Seaman E. Hawkins, for saving life on burning and sinking ship in N Atlantic.

HMS *Illustrious* under heavy bombing attack

11th JANUARY

1782   Capture of Trincomalee by Vice-Admiral Sir Edward Hughes (*Superb*) and the Hon. East India Company's troops. Ships: *Burford, Eagle, Exeter, Monarca, Superb, Worcester*. Frigates, etc.: *Combustion, Nymph, Seahorse*.

1783   *Cyclops* captured the French *Railleur* 80 miles to the eastward of Cape Henry, Virginia.

1794   Escape of *Juno* from Toulon harbour.

1810   *Cherokee* captured the French privateer *Aimable Nelly* at Dieppe. [m]

1829   Boat of *Alacrity* captured a Greek piratical mistico under Cape Palipuri, Gulf of Kassandra.

1846   Capture of Kawiti's pah at Ruapekapeka, New Zealand, by Naval Brigade and troops. Ships: *Calliope, Castor, Elphinstone* (Indian Navy), *North Star, Racehorse*. Troops: Royal Artillery, Royal Sappers and Miners, 58th and 99th Regiments. New Zealand, 1845-47, Medal.

1917   *Ben-my-Chree* sunk in action off Asia Minor.

1917   *Cornwallis* sunk by U.32, 62 miles S.E. of Malta.

1941   *Southampton* sunk by German aircraft East of Malta. Operation Excess.

1944   *Tally Ho* sank the Japanese Cruiser *Kuma* in Malacca Strait.

H.M. Submarine *Tally Ho,* **1943**

Ward Room HMS *London,* **1895**

12th JANUARY

1797   *Spitfire* captured the French *Allerger* 90 miles West of Ushant.

1798   *Gorgon* recaptured the *Ann* brig off Dartmouth and captured the French privateer *Henri* 170 miles to the south-westward of Ushant next day.

1810   *Scorpion* captured the French *Oreste* off Basse Terre, Guadeloupe. [m, bh]

1915   Capture of Mafia Island, German East Africa. Ships: *Fox, Kinfauns Castle.* Seaward support: *Weymouth, Adjutant, Duplex.* Troops: King's African Rifles (4 coys.) British War Medal: clasp 'German East Africa' approved but not issued.

1918   *Narborough* and *Opal* wrecked in gale outside Scapa Flow.

1922   *Victory* moved into No.2 Dock in Portsmouth Yard, the oldest dry dock in the world.

1942   *Unbeaten* sank U.374 off Cape Spartivento.

1945   *Regulus* (m/s) sunk by mine off Corfu.

1945   Assault on Myebon, Burma. Operation Pungent. Ships: *Jumna, Napier, Narbada;* (all RIN), HDML *1248*, ML *854.*

In January 1945 the Japanese were being driven from Burma and 3rd Commando Brigade, Royal Marines was sent by sea to land and secure Myebon. This was achieved with some opposition. They were then relieved by Army units and launched an attack by landing craft along 27 miles of river to Kangaw. They achieved surprise and captured the hills overlooking the beaches, cutting off the Japanese army. On 31st the Japanese attacked and kept up the attacks on Hill 170 for 36 hours with waves of Banzai charges.

At the end of the battle the ground was thick with Japanese dead, but the hill was still held by 1 and 42 Commandos. Special order of the day: "The Battle of Kangaw has been the decisive battle of the whole Arakan campaign, and that it was won was largely due to your magnificent courage on Hill 170," by GOC XV Corps.

1950   *Truculent* sank after collision with S.S. *Dvina* in Thames estuary.

1952   Royal Naval Mine Watching Service instituted.

1971   Admiral of the Fleet Lord Tovey died.

'Lull before the Storm'—the landing at Myebon behind Japanese lines by 42 Commando.

13th JANUARY

1794	*Sphinx* captured the French *Trompeuse* 120 miles to the south-eastward of Cape Clear.
1797	*Amazon* and *Indefatigable* (Captain E. Pellew) drove ashore and wrecked the French *Droits de l'Homme* in Audierne Bay, Brittany. [m, bh]. *Amazon* also wrecked.
1855	*Bittern* and her boats destroyed two pirate junks off Flap (Flat) Island, near Foochow.
1915	*Roedean* sunk at Longhope.
1942	*Aphis* bombarded Halfaya Pass in support of the Army.
1943	*Ville de Québec* (RCN) sank U.224 off Cape Tenez. (Convoy TE.13)
1944	Wellington L/172 sank U.231 in NW Atlantic.
1968	NATO Standing Naval Force Atlantic formed. (STANAVFORLANT)

One of the strengths of the NATO alliance is that it demonstrates from day to day that the Western democracies have the resolve to defend their way of life jointly if it is threatened by force. Although NATO has common tactical doctrines and NATO forces are part of a unified command in war, constant exercise and testing of procedures is necessary to keep NATO's Naval fighting edge honed. The NATO Standing Naval Force Atlantic, under the command of the NATO Supreme Allied Commander, Atlantic, helps to achieve this.

Ships (top to bottom) Portuguese *Almirante Magalhaes Correa*, Danish *Herluf Trolle*, Netherlands *Van Speijk*, HMS *Londonderry*, USS *Barney*. Federal German ship *Hessen* is not included in the photograph.

14th JANUARY

1676	Boats of Commodore Sir John Narbrough's squadron destroyed four Algerine men-of-war at Tripoli. Ships: *Harwich, Henrietta, Portsmouth*.
1694	*Conquest* merchantman fought a French 26-gun ship off the mouth of the Tagus.
1809	Capture of Cayenne in French Guiana by Captain James Lucas Yeo (*Confiance*) and Portuguese troops. [m, bh]
1848	Boats of *Philomel* captured the slaver *Wandering Jew* off the Gallinas (Kife) River, Sierra Leone.
1917	*Penshurst (Q.7)* sank UB.37 20 miles off Cherbourg.
1918	G.8 lost in N Sea.
1918	German destroyer raid on Yarmouth.
1941	GC: Pro. T/Sub-Lieut. John Bryan Peter Miller, RNVR, Pro. T/Sub-Lieut. William Horace Taylor, RNVR, Able Seaman Stephen John Tuckwell. (*Gazette* date). Bomb and mine disposal.
1942	*Triumph* sunk by mine in the South Aegean.
1943	*Hursley, Pakenham* and Beaufort aircraft sank the Italian s/m *Narvalo* S.E. of Malta. (Convoy ME. 15)

11

1704   *Lyme,* escorting a convoy, fought off a French 46-gun ship 6 miles S.W. of Dodman Point.

1743   *Sapphire* sank two and severely damaged three Spanish privateers at Vigo.

1815   *Endymion* defeated the American *President* 70 miles S.E. by S. of Montauk Point, Long Island; she actually surrendered to *Pomone* and *Tenedos,* who came up at the end of the action whilst *Endymion* was bending fresh sails. [m*, m, bh]

1822   Establishment of HM Coastguard by Treasury minute, putting under the Board of Customs the Preventive Water Guard, the Riding Officers and the Revenue Cruisers.

1922   Reconstitution of HM Coastguard.

1942   *Hesperus* sank U.93 off Cape St. Vincent.

1942   GC: Lieutenant George Herbert Goodman, MBE, RNVR for dismantling Italian self-destroying torpedo.

1945   *Thane* torpedoed by U.482 off the Clyde lightvessel. Towed in by *Loring,* but found to be damaged beyond repair.

Merchant Ship Losses in Second World War

Total of Allied Merchant shipping lost	6439 ships
	24,390,000 tons
of this total Britain lost	3194 ships
	12,251,000 tons

(54% of total British merchant shipping tonnage at opening of hostilities).

Causes for loss:		
	Submarines	2775 ships
	Air attack	753 ships
	Surface attack	237 ships
	E-Boat attack	99 ships
	Other	411 ships
	Mined	521 ships
	Marine causes	1643 ships

German U-boat Losses in World War II

No. of U-Boats built		1162
No. of U-Boats lost		782
Causes of loss:	Surface ship attack	246
	Air attack	288
	Joint air/surface	50
	Submarine	21
	Mines	26
	Other	93

(Of these, 521 were sunk by British forces; 166 by U.S. forces; 12 shared).

HMS *Churchill,* later the Russian *Deiatelnyi* (see 16th January 1945)

16th JANUARY

Admiral Lord Rodney (1718 - 1792)

George Bridges Rodney was the son of a Captain in the Marines, and joined the Navy at the age of twelve. By 1742 he was a Captain and saw action under Hawke at Finisterre (14 Oct) in *Eagle*. He reached Flag rank in 1759 and was active in the West Indies until 1762. In 1779 he relieved Gibraltar, capturing a Spanish convoy and destroying a squadron of Spanish warships en route for the West Indies. After a series of drawn battles against the French in 1780, he eventually brought them to the battle off the Saints on 12th Apr., when he broke the enemy's line of battle and achieved a conclusive victory. However, he had many enemies in the troubled political arena at home, and even as he was winning the victory, orders were on the way relieving him of his command. By the time he arrived home he was a hero and was elevated to the peerage.

1636   *Sovereign of the Seas* laid down.

1780   Admiral Sir George Bridges Rodney (*Sandwich*) defeated 11 Spanish sail of the line under Admiral Don Juan de Langara (*Fénix*) 12 miles South of Cape St. Vincent [bh]. Captured: *Diligente, Fénix, Monarca, Princesa.* Captured, but wrecked: *San Eugenio, San Julian.* Blew up: *Santo Domingo.* Ships: *Ajax, Alcide, Alfred, Bedford, Bienfaisant, Culloden, Cumberland, Defence, Edgar, Invincible, Marlborough, Monarch, Montagu, Prince George, Resolution, Royal George, Sandwich, Terrible.* Frigates: *Andromeda, Apollo, Hyena, Pegasus, Triton.*

The Moonlight Battle 1780.

The Royal Navy entered a more offensive phase during the War of American Independence when Admiral Rodney was sent with a strong squadron to escort a convoy to relieve Gibraltar and Minorca, and then to reinforce the West Indies station. Off Cape Finisterre he encountered a Spanish convoy of 17 merchant and 5 warships, which he captured. (8 Jan). Eight days later he sighted a squadron of 11 Spanish warships, off Cape St Vincent. The result was a British victory which resulted in an easing of the pressure on Gibraltar. From the Mediterranean, Rodney sailed for the West Indies, where two years later he was to transform the Royal Navy's battle tactics at the Battle of the Saints.

1798   Boats of *Babet* captured the French schooner *Désirée* between Dominica and Martinique.

1799   *Flora* recaptured the British merchant brig *Nymph* 120 miles N.N.E. of Cape Ortegal, N.W. Spain.

1808   *Linnet* captured the French privateer *Courrier* 30 miles East of Cape Barfleur.

1809   *Melampus* captured the French *Colibri* 160 miles N.E. of Barbuda, West Indies.

1814   *Venerable* and *Cyane* captured the French *Alemène* and *Iphigénie* 200 miles SSW of Madeira. [m]

1873   RN College, Greenwich established by Order in Council.

1894   *Havoc*, first torpedo boat destroyer, accepted into service.

1914   S/m A7 lost in mud in Whitesand Bay.

1917   Zimmermann telegram – decoded by NID and helped to bring USA into war. The authenticity of this telegram is the subject of controversy.

"BERLIN TO WASHINGTON. W158. 16 Jan 1917.
"Most secret for your excellency's personal information . . . We propose to begin on 1st February unrestricted submarine warfare. In doing this however we shall endeavour to keep America neutral . . . if we do not succeed in doing so we propose to Mexico our alliance upon the following basis:
Joint conduct of war, joint conclusion of peace . . . your excellency should for the present inform the President secretly that we expect war with the USA (possibly Japan) . . . tell the President that . . . our submarines . . . will compel England to peace within a few months."

1943   Fortress G/206 sank U.337 in N Atlantic. (Convoys DNS.160 and ON.161)

1945   *Amethyst, Hart, Loch Craggie, Peacock* and *Starling* sank U.482 six miles off Macrihanish.

1945   The Russian *Deiatelnyi* (ex-*Churchill*) sunk by German submarine off Murmansk.

1945   *Porpoise* lost, possibly to Japanese aircraft, in Malacca Straight – the seventy-sixth and last British submarine to be sunk in World War II.

17th JANUARY

1682	*Adventure* and *James Galley* drove ashore and burnt the Algerine *Flower Pot* near Mazagran, Algeria.
1773	Captain Cook made first crossing of the Antarctic Circle.
1794	*Pigot* East Indiaman beat off the French privateers *Vengeur* and *Résolu* at Benkulen, Sumatra.
1799	*Flora* recaptured the American merchant ship *Six Sisters* 80 miles N.N.E. of Cape Ortegal, N.W. Spain.
1805	*Pitt* launched, first RN ship built at Bombay.
1862	Boats of *Falcon* and a detachment of the 2nd West India Regiment destroyed Mafengbi and Majohn up the Kate (Ribbi) River, Sierra Leone.
1871	David Beatty born.
1885	Battle of Abu Klea, Sudan. Naval Brigade from *Helicon, Iris, Monarch.* Egyptian Medal: clasp 'Abu Klea'.
1904	Admiral of the Fleet Sir Harry Keppel, Queen Alexandra's "beloved little admiral," died.

1912*	Captain Scott reached the South Pole.
1942	*Gurkha*, second of the name in World War II, sunk by U.133 off Mersa Matruh. (Convoy MW.8B)
1942	*Matabele* sunk by U.454 off Murmansk. (Convoy PQ.8)
1942	*Jupiter* sank the Japanese s/m I.160 in Sunda Strait, between Sumatra and Java. (See 26th October for illustration)
1943	*United* sank the Italian destroyer *Bombardiere* off Marettimo, W of Sicily.
1944	*Glenarm* and *Wanderer* sank U.305 in Atlantic (49° 39'N., 20° 10'W).

* Robert Falcon Scott was born in Devonport and entered the Navy in 1882. In 1900-04 he led the National Antarctic Expedition and in 1911 he commanded a second expedition in an attempt to reach the South Pole. Beset by many misfortunes, defective equipment and ill-health, he made the final assault on foot in the company of "Birdie" Bowers, "Titus" Oates, Edgar Evans and "Doc" Wilson. Enduring tremendous hardship in sub-zero temperature they pressed on towards the Pole. On 17 January 1912 as they approached their goal they saw a flag fluttering in the cold wind — Amundsen the Norwegian explorer had got there first. Bitterly disappointed the party set off back in appalling conditions and despite self-sacrifice and bravery, they perished only 11 miles from a depot. When Scott's diaries were found the whole tragic story was told and it elevated Scott and his men to a high place in British heroism.

Captain Scott (standing centre) and his party at the South Pole

14

18th JANUARY

1695 *Adventure* and *Falmouth* captured the French *Trident* 30 miles N.W. of Pantellaria. *Plymouth* (Captain James Killigrew) also engaged. Killigrew, who was in command of the squadron, was killed whilst engaging the other French ship *Content*.

1801 *Garland,* assisted by boats of *Cyane, Daphne* and *Hornet,* captured the French *Éclair* in Trois Rivières Bay, Guadeloupe.

1806 The whole of the Dutch Settlement at the Cape of Good Hope, with all its Dependencies, surrendered (See 10th January).

1816 Boats of *Bann* captured the slaver *Rosa* off the mouth of the Gallinas (Kife) River, Sierra Leone.

1915 E.10 lost in N Sea.

1916 H.6 stranded on Dutch coast and interned.

1918 *Campanula* sank the German UB.66 off Sicily (35° 35'N., 14° 39' E.)

1972 First plastic warship *(Wilton)* launched.

HMS *Wilton*

Although modern mines are activated in a number of different ways, the magnetic signature which is inherent in all iron hulls remains one of the most significant. The Royal Navy's Coastal Minesweeper class were built of wood, and have lasted well. However, wood still requires a large amount of maintenance, so the modern technology of glass-reinforced plastics was employed in the building of the minehunter HMS *Wilton*. She was launched in 1972, completed in 1973 and is 153 feet long with a beam of 28 feet. She carries a crew of 37. Her displacement is 450 tons. She is equipped with the most modern detection and neutralisation devices for clearing minefields.

19th JANUARY

1695 *Carlisle* captured the French *Content* 70 miles W.N.W. of Marettimo, Sicily. *Southampton* also engaged on the previous day.

1759 *Ripon* engaged the St. Pierre forts, Martinique.

1762 Harrison's fourth chronometer passed first Board of Longitude test *(Deptford)* at Jamaica.

1826 Capture of Melloon (Minhla) by the Irrawaddy flotilla and troops. Flotilla: *Diana* steamer,[1] boats of *Alligator* and others and Hon E.I. Company's gunboats. Troops: 13th, 38th, 41st, 47th, 87th and 89th Regiments; Bengal and Madras Artillery, Bengal Engineers, Madras Pioneers. 18th, 28th and 43rd Madras Native Infantry. [1] During the operations connected with this First Burmese War a steam vessel was employed for the first time in military operations.

1839 Capture of Aden. [bh]. Ships and vessels: *Cruizer, Volage.* Indian Navy: *Coote, Mahe.* Troops: Bombay Artillery, 1st Bombay European Regiment, 24th Bombay Native Infantry.

1875 *Nassau* and *Rifleman* captured Fort Mozambique, Mombasa.

1917 E.36 lost in N Sea.

1918 UB.22 sunk by mine off Heligoland.

1918 H.10 lost in N Sea.

1940 *Grenville* sunk by mine off the Kentish Knock, in the Thames estuary.

1941 *Greyhound* sank the Italian s/m *Neghelli* off Phalconera.

1943 *Port Arthur* (RCN) sank the Italian s/m *Tritone* off Bougie. (Convoy MKS.6)

1944 *Violet* sank U.641 in N Atlantic (50° 15'N., 18° 49'W.). (Convoy OS.65/ KMS.39)

1960 *Bulwark* commissioned as first Commando carrier.

20th JANUARY

A Swordfish torpedo aircraft

1615 Nicholas Downton *(New Year's Gift)*, with three other East Indiamen, repulsed a Portuguese armada off Surat.

1801 *Mercury* captured the French *Sans-Pareille* 20 miles N.W. of Minorca.

1814 *Venerable* captured the French *Iphigénie* 300 miles W.S.W. of Palma Island, Canary Islands. [m]. *Cyane* was also awarded the medal, having engaged and hung on to the French frigate since the 16th.

1918 *Raglan* and M.28 sunk by the German *Goeben* off Imbros, outside the Dardanelles, *Breslau* sunk by mine; *Goeben* mined and beached. *Lizard* and *Tigress* engaged.

1921 K5 lost on exercise off Torquay.

1925 Embarrassingly unsuccessful attacks on *Marlborough* by aircraft, cruisers and battleships.

1942 *Deloraine, Katoomba, Lithgow*, (all RAN), and the USS *Edsall* sank the Japanese s/m I.124 in the Timor Sea off Port Darwin.

1943 MTB 260 sank the Italian s/m *Santorre Santarosa* off Tripoli, Libya.

MTB 347 of same class as MTB 260

21st JANUARY

1807 Boats of *Galatea* captured the French *Lynx* 10 miles East of La Guaira, Venezuela. [m, bh]

1810 Boats of *Freija* cut out three French vessels and destroyed two batteries in Mahault Bay, Guadeloupe.

1810 *Amazon* captured the St. Malo privateer *Général Perignon* 25 miles S. by E. of Belle Île.

1857 Boxer's Metal Time Fuse adopted for RN.

1866 Parachute light balls design approved (fore-runner of starshell).

1920 *Espiegle, Topaze, Clio* and *Odin*, with subsequently *Ark Royal*, in start of a three-week classic combined operation of all three Services against the 'Mad Mullah' of Somaliland.

1940 *Exmouth* sunk by U.22 off Wick.

1941 *Gnat, Ladybird* and *Terror* bombarded Tobruk.

1943 P.212 (later *Sahib*) sank U.301 W of Corsica.

1945 *Icarus* and *Mignonette* sank U.1199 off the Wolf Rock. (Convoy TBC.43)

1945 Assault on Ramree Island, Burma. Operation Matador. Ships: *Ameer, Flamingo, Kistna* (RIN), *Llanstephan Castle, Napier, Pathfinder, Phoebe, Queen Elizabeth, Rapid, Redpole, Spey.*

HMS *Exmouth*, 1938

22nd JANUARY

1617   *Dolphin* merchantman fought five Barbary corsairs off Sardinia.

1782   *Hannibal* surrendered to d'Orvres in Indian Ocean.

1783   *Hussar* captured the French *Sibylle* 120 miles S.E. by E. of Cape Henry, Virginia.

1794   *Britannia* and *Nonsuch* East Indiamen captured the French privateers *Vengeur* and *Résolu* a few miles to the northward of Thwartway Island, Sunda Strait.

1809   *Cleopatra* and *Jason* captured the French *Topaze* close off Pointe Noire, Guadeloupe.

1849   The Indus flotilla (Indian Navy) at the siege and capture of Multan. An I.N. Naval Brigade served in the siege batteries as a complete unit.

1879   Colonel Charles Pearson's column defeated the Zulus on the Inyezane River. Naval Brigade from *Active*. South Africa, 1877-79, Medal: clasp '1879'.

1913   Launch by Vickers at Elswick of a battleship for Brazil which sold her to Turkey from whom the Admiralty confiscated her, so she had three nationalities in one year. As *Agincourt,* carried largest number of heavy guns in any warship afloat: last vessel in RN to carry 12 in: her seven turrets were named after the days of the week.

1943   GC (ex-AM): Leading Seaman W. Goad, *Somali,* for saving life at sea in Arctic Convoy (*Gazette* date).

1944   Anzio Landing. Operation Shingle [bh]. Ships: *Albacore, Barmond, Barndale, Beaufort, Boxer, Bruiser Bude, Bulolo, Cadmus, Cava, Circe, Crete, Delhi, Dido, Espiegle, Faulknor, Fly, Glengyle, Grenville, Hornpipe, Inglefield*, Janus*, Jervis, Kempenfelt, Laforey, Loyal, Mauritius, Orion, Palomares, Penelope*, Prinses Beatrix, Rinaldo, Rothesay, Royal Ulsterman, St. Kilda, Sheppey, Spartan*, Tetcott, Thruster, Twostep, Ulster Queen, Ultor, Urchin, Waterwitch.* MLs: 121, 134, 295, 307, 338, 443, 554, 558, 565, 567, 569, 575, 581. *Sunk.

1945   Assault on Kangaw, Burma, Ships: *Jumna* and *Narbada* (RIN), MLs: 416 843, 854, 885, 892. 3rd Commando Brigade: 42 and 44 RM Commandos 1 and 5 Army Commandos (see 31st January).

The Zulu Wars 1879

HMS *Spartan*, 1943

17

23rd JANUARY

1759 Bombardment of Basse Terre, Guadeloupe, by Commodore John Moore *(Cambridge)*. Ships: *Berwick, Burford, Cambridge, Lion, Norfolk, Panther, Ripon, St. George.* 50's and smaller: *Amazon, Bonetta, Bristol, Ludlow Castle, Renown, Roebuck, Spy, Winchester, Woolwich.* Bombs: *Falcon, Granado, Infernal, Kingfisher.*

1761 *Minerva* captured the French *Warwick* 90 miles N. by W. of Cape Penas, North coast of Spain.

1798 *Melampus* captured the French *Volage* 100 miles to the Westward of the Scilly Islands.

1801 *N.S. De Los Dolores,* ex-Spanish felucca, (one gun) captured the Spanish guardacosta *Santa Maria* (six) near Cape Rosario, South America.

1814 *Astraea* and *Creole* fought the French *Étoile* and *Sultane* close off English Road, Mayo Island, Cape Verde Islands.

1833 Admiral Edward Pellew, Viscount Exmouth, died.

1861 A gun's crew of *Pelorus* at the defence of No. 3 Redoubt in front of Huirangi, New Zealand. New Zealand, 1860-61, Medal.

1877 Naval Intelligence Division established.

1917 Harwich Force fought the German 6th Destroyer Flotilla off the Schouwen lightvessel. *Simoom,* torpedoed by the German S50, sunk by *Matchless.* Ships: *Centaur, Conquest, Aurora, Penelope, Cleopatra, Undaunted, Grenville, Radstock, Sorceress, Rigorous, Rob Roy, Meteor, Melpomene; Nimrod, Moorsom, Morris, Matchless, Phoebe, Manly, Mansfield; Simoom, Starfish, Surprise, Milne.*

1935 *Hood* collided with *Renown.*

1942 Four Swordfish aircraft of 830 Sq., Malta, under Lieutenant F H E Hopkins, in bad weather, torpedoed an escorted Italian storeship making for Tripoli, Libya.

1943 Bombardment of Zuara, Libya. Ships: *Cleopatra, Euryalus; Javelin, Jervis, Kelvin, Nubian.*

1944 *Janus* sunk by German torpedo aircraft off Anzio. Operation Shingle.

1945 45 Commando RM in action.

Memorable Date of 45 Commando RM — Montforterbeek, 23rd January 1945.
In January 1945 Allied Forces were advancing NE against the Germans in Holland. 1 Commando Brigade was given the task of clearing the area of the left flank of the 7th Armoured Division between the Division and the River Maas. The Montforterbeek was a small stream running across the front and taking its name from the village of Montfort. A fine action was fought in this area by 45 Commando.

Royal Marines in Arctic kit being inspected by Admiral Sir Terence Lewin and Major-General E.G.D. Pounds RM, 1975

One of NATO's flanks is the North of Norway. Although the border with the USSR lies in the Actic regions, the coastline of Norway gives easy access to the North Atlantic across which any NATO reinforcements would have to pass. An invasion of Norway could be undertaken at an early stage in any future conflict. In this case, Norway's forces would need reinforcement, and this task is given to the Royal Navy and Royal Marines. They undertake regular training in warfare under Arctic conditions and have developed great expertise at this special form of combat.

1708 Admiral of the Fleet Sir George Rooke died.

1761 *Granado, Hound* and *Richmond* destroyed the French *Félicité* 3 miles N.E. of the Hook of Holland. Action on the 24th, when she ran ashore; found abandoned on the 25th, and burnt on the 26th.

1915 Action of the Dogger Bank. [bh]. Vice-Admiral Sir David Beatty *(Lion)* fought Rear-Admiral Hipper *(Seydlitz)*. *Blücher* sunk. Ships: *Lion, Tiger, Princess Royal; New Zealand, Indomitable.* 1st LCS: *Southampton, Birmingham, Nottingham, Lowestoft.* 1st DF: *Arethusa, Aurora; Acheron, Attack, Hydra, Ariel; Ferret, Forester, Defender, Druid; Hornet, Tigress, Sandfly, Jackal; Goshawk, Phoenix, Lapwing.* 3rd DF: *Lookout, Lysander, Landrail; Laurel, Liberty, Laertes, Lucifer; Laforey, Lawford, Lydiard, Louis; Legion, Lark; Undaunted.* 10th DF: *Meteor, Miranda, Milne, Mentor, Mastiff, Minos, Morris.* British War Medal: clasp "Dogger Bank, 24 Jan. 15," approved but not issued.

German ships bombarded Yarmouth, (3rd Nov 1914), Scarborough, Whitby and Hartlepool (10th Dec) and sailed again on 24th Jan 1915 for a third raid. The squadron consisted of 3 battle cruisers, 1 armoured cruiser and lighter forces. They were engaged by Vice-Admiral Sir David Beatty's battle cruiser squadron. The heavy cruiser *Blücher* was hit and slowed down. At the same time Admiral Beatty believed himself under attack by submarine. He therefore ordered a turn to port, away from the submarine. Shortly after that he ordered close action. However, since the order for the turn to port was still extant the squadron believed that his wish was for close action against *Blücher* who had dropped behind the other German ships. *Blücher* was therefore destroyed while the remainder of the squadron escaped.

1945 Air strike on oil refineries at Palembang, Sumatra by Rear-Admiral Sir Philip Vian *(Indomitable)*. [bh]. Carriers: *Indefatigable(1), Indomitable (2), Illustrious(3), Victorious(4). King George V; Argonaut, Black Prince, Euryalus;* 10 destroyers of 25th and 27th DF* Oiler escort: *Ceylon, Urchin.* Operation Meridian I. FAA Sq.: Avenger 820(1), 849(4), 854(3), 857(2). Seafire 887(1), 894(1). Firefly 1770(1). Corsair 1830(3), 1833(3), 1834(4), 1836(4). Hellcat 1839(2), 1844(2). *25th D.F.: *Grenville (D.25), Undaunted, Undine, Ursa, Whirlwind.* 27th DF.: *Kempenfelt (D.27), Wager, Wakeful, Wessex, Whelp.* Reconnaissance s/ms: *Sturdy, Tantivy.* Air/Sea Rescue s/m: *Tantalus* and Walrus aircraft.

HMS *Tiger*, World War I.

25th JANUARY

1747   *Grand Turk* captured the St. Malo privateer *Tavignon* 10 miles South of Lizard Head.

1782   Rear-Admiral Sir Samuel Hood *(Barfleur)*, at anchor at Basse Terre, St. Kitts, repulsed an attack by Vice-Admiral Comte de Grasse *(Ville-de-Paris)* with 29 sail of the line. [bh]. Ships: *St. Albans, Alcide, Intrepid, Torbay, Princessa, Prince George, Ajax; Prince William, Shrewsbury, Invincible, Barfleur, Monarch, Belliqueux, Centaur, Alfred; Russell, Resolution, Bedford, Canada, Prudent, Montagu, America.* Frigates, etc.: *Champion, Eurydice, Expedition, Gros Islet, Nymphe, Sibyl, Solebay.* Regiments: 13th, 28th, 69th.

1783   *Fox* captured the Spanish *Santa Catalina* a few miles off Havana.

1788   Founding of Australia; marines hoisted flag at Sydney Cove, New South Wales.

1798   *Mercury* captured the French privateer *Constance* 80 miles to the north-westward of Burling Island, Portugal.

1841   John Arbuthnot Fisher born.

1915   *Repulse* and *Renown* laid down — an appropriate date, it being their progenitor's seventy-fourth birthday.

1917   German destroyer raid on Southwold and Wangford, Suffolk.

1917   *Laurentic* sunk by mine two miles 070° from Fanad Point, Lough Swilly.

1943   *Corncrake* foundered in N Atlantic.

HMS *Hood* and *Repulse,* 1937

26th JANUARY

1782 Hood again repulsed de Grasse. (See 25th January)

1800 *Penelope* captured the Spanish privateer *Carmen* 30 miles West of Alboran Island, Western Mediterranean.

1804 *Cerberus* captured the French *Chameau* and drove another gunboat ashore close to Cap de la Hogue.

1826 *Sulphur* launched at Chatham: last bomb vessel in RN.

1841 Hong Kong formally occupied by Commodore Sir James Bremer (*Wellesley*).

1918 *Leven* sank UB.35 in Channel, and U.109 mined.

1918 P.62 rammed and sank U.84 in S.W. Approaches.

1932 M.2 (ex K.19) sank on exercises off Portland.

1942 *Thanet* and *Vampire* (RAN) fought a Japanese cruiser and 3 destroyers off Endau, E coast of Malaya. *Thanet* sunk.

1945 *Aylmer, Bentinck, Calder* and *Manners** sank U.1172 off Liverpool. *Damaged.

1945 Assault on Cheduba Island, Burma. Operation Sankey. Ships: *Ameer, Kenya, Newcastle, Nigeria, Norman, Paladin, Phoebe, Raider, Rapid, Spey, Teviot.*

27th JANUARY

1799 *Flora* captured the French privateer *Intrépide,* and *Caroline* recaptured the British letter of marque (privateer) *Jane* 170 miles N. by W of Cape Ortegal, N.W. Spain.

1805 *Amazon* captured the Spanish *Gravina* 140 miles to the westward of Cape St. Vincent.

1807 *Jason* captured the French *Favorite* 30 miles off the coast of Dutch Guiana.

1807 *Caroline* captured the Spanish register-ship *San Rafael* (alias *Palas*) in Albay Gulf, Phillipines.

1807 *Lark* captured the Spanish guarda-costas *Carmen* and *Postillon* 5 miles N.E. by E. of Point San Blas, Panama.

1816 Admiral Samuel, Viscount Hood died.

1866 Electric firing cartridges introduced.

1918 Arab camelry seized the Turkish Dead Sea Flotilla at El Mezraa.

1944 *Mauritius* and *Kempenfelt* bombarded the coast road and town of Formia, Italy.

1945 *Bligh, Keats* and *Tyler* sank U.1051 off Cahore Point, Ireland.

Royal Marines on their way to assault Cheduba Island off Burma, 1945.

Sir Francis Drake (c 1540 - 1596)

Blue jackets hauling the guns in Africa, late 19th Century.

Seamen were often employed as expert gunners during the Victorian colonial wars — firstly, because they were usually excellently trained and secondly because their guns usually had a greater range than the lighter Army pieces. The classic use of naval artillery was at Lady-smith in 1899 (Second Boer War) when the British were completely outgunned by the Boers' fine 6 inch "Long Toms". It is likely that the town would have fallen had not a naval brigade from *HMS Powerful* arrived just in time with two naval 4.7 inch guns on improvised carriages. Exploits such as these so captured the public imagination that they were re-enacted in England at various naval displays. From these re-enactments have come the modern competitions that are now such a popular feature of every Royal Tournament.

1596	Death of Sir Francis Drake off Porto Bello, West Indies.

"It matters not, man! God hath many things in store for us".
Sir Francis Drake died of fever off Porto Bello on the Caribbean Coast and was buried at sea from his ship the *Defiance*. Born near Tavistock, he was the first English Admiral to achieve international fame. He claimed Nova Albion (San Francisco) for the Queen in 1579, and on this 3 year voyage the dividend paid to investors was £47 for every £1 invested — probably the most successful voyage in history. With a group of English Seamen, he was probably one of the founders of the Chatham Chest for the relief of wounded Seamen. He was Mayor of Plymouth, its MP and arranged the supply of water to the town from the Moor. Buckland Abbey, which was his, and also Sir Richard Grenville's home, is now a Museum.

1744	*Fly* captured the Spanish privateer *N.S. Del Rosario* 80 miles to the westward of Ushant.
1801	*Oiseau* and *Sirius* captured the French *Dedaigneuse* 2 miles off Cape Belem (Veo), N.W. Spain.
1806	*Growler* captured the French privateer *Voltigeur* 40 miles N.N.E. of Ushant.
1806	*Attack* captured the French privateer *Sorcier* 40 miles N.N.W. of Ushant.
1881	Reverse at Laing's Nek, Transvaal. Naval Brigade from *Boadicea*. Troops: RA, KDG, 21st, 58th and 60th Regiments; Natal Military Police.
1915	British Government decided to make a naval attack on the Dardanelles.
1915	*William P Frye* (US) sunk by the German a.m.c. *Prinz Eitel Friedrich*. First U.S. vessel sunk by a belligerent warship in World War I.
1918	*Hazard* lost in collision in Channel.
1918	VC: Lieutenant-Commander Geoffrey Saxton White (E.14) (Posthumous). E.14 destroyed by Turkish depth charges and gunfire near Nagara Pt., Dardanelles in pursuit of *Goeben*.
1927	*Sylph* stranded at Aberavon and broken up there.
1944	Sunderland D/461 (RAAF) sank U.571 off Blacksod Bay, Ireland. (Convoy ON.221 and SC.151)

29th JANUARY

1780 *Surprise* captured the French privateer *Duguay-Trouin* 40 miles S. by W. of Dodman Point.

1801 *Bourdelois* captured the French *Curieuse* 200 miles East of Barbados. Sank whilst prisoners were being shifted.

1810 Boats of *Jalouse* and *Phoenix* captured the French privateer *Charles* 270 miles W. by S. of Ushant.

1856 VC instituted by Royal Warrant, to be worn on a blue ribbon by naval recipients

1876 Admiralty decision to found Engineering College.

1915 Walney Island airship shed (Barrow-in-Furness) shelled by U.21. First operation by a German submarine in the Irish Sea.

1917 K.13 foundered in trials in Gareloch: salvaged and recommissioned as K.22.

1925 *Elphinstone* (RIN) (ex-*Ceanothus*), wrecked on Nicobar Island.

1941 GC (ex-AM): D.G.M. Hay, Cadet RNR, SS *Eurylochus* for saving life in shark infested sea after ship sank.

1943 *Kiwi* and *Moa* (both RNZN) sank the Japanese s/m I.1 off Guadelcanal.

1944 *Spartan* sunk by German glider bomb off Anzio. Operation Shingle.

1945 Air strike on oil refineries at Palembang, Sumatra. For ships see 24th January. Operation Meridian II.

The Victoria Cross was instituted during the Crimean War to honour acts of extreme valour carried out in the presence of the enemy. The first presentations were made by Queen Victoria in Hyde Park on 26th June 1857; twelve naval personnel and two Royal Marines were among the sixty-two decorated.

23

30th JANUARY

1761   *Amazon* and *Solebay* captured the French privateer *Chevrette*, which had run ashore a few miles to the westward of Calais.

1797   *Andromache* captured an Algerine frigate 15 miles S.S.W. of Cape de Santa Maria, Portugal.

1814   *Fylla* captured the French privateer *Inconnu* 30 miles S.E. by S. of Guernsey.

1855   Royal Marines designated a Light Corps and became RM Artillery and RM Light Infantry until 1923: the Blue and the Red Marines.

1857   Uniform introduced for POs, seamen and boys.

1867   *Captain* laid down (full rigged turret ship) see 7 September.

Introduction of the Turret Mounting

Around 1860, the RN introduced the rifled, breech-loading gun; its Armstrong breech mechanisms proved unreliable and unsafe, and the Navy therefore reverted to muzzle-loading for its larger guns until 1881. At the same time, advances in technology were enabling bigger guns to be manufactured. A few large rifled pieces able to deliver massively destructive blows came to be preferred to the broadside tiers of numerous smaller cannon. To permit fewer guns to cover a wide arc of fire, the old guncarriages were replaced by pivot mountings. The idea of enclosing the gun, or a pair of them, in armoured turrets revolving with the gun, was developed leaving only the muzzles exposed. Controversy arose between proponents of the new turret idea and the advocates of the old fixed battery system. Certainly a combination of turret system and a full rig of sail (which the RN continued to supply along with a steam propulsion plant), was of little advantage, because of the maze of standing rigging. The proponent of the turret system in England was Captain Cowper Coles whose efforts to combine this form of armament with a full rig of sails ended in disaster when his ship, the *Captain*, capsized in a squall because of her low freeboard. Coles went down with her.

1918   Wellholme ketch *(Danton)* sunk by U.55 in the English Channel.

1940   *Fowey*, *Whitshed* and Sunderland Y/288 sank U.55 off Ushant. (Convoy OA.80G) — a coincidental anniversary.

1942   *Thorn* sank the Italian s/m *Medusa* South of Brioni Island in the Adriatic.

1943   *Samphire* sunk by the Italian s/m *Platino* off Bougie. (Convoy TE.14)

1944   *Meteor* and *Whitehall* sank U.314 off North Cape. (Convoy JW.56B)

1944   Wellington K/172 sank U.364 in Bay of Biscay.

1944   *Hardy*, second of the name in World War II, torpedoed by U.278 and sunk by own forces off Bear Island. (Convoy JW.56B)

1952   First NATO Supreme Allied Commander Atlantic appointed.

Sir Winston Churchill's funeral cortege, Whitehall, 30th January 1965.

Although Sir Winston Churchill's service career was spent in the Army, he was twice First Lord of the Admiralty. His coffin was hauled on a gun carriage by a party of sailors, a practice normally carried out only at royal funerals since 1901 when the horses at Queen Victoria's funeral became unmanageable, whereupon the seamen present stepped forward and picked up the traces.

24

31st JANUARY

1748 *Nottingham* and *Portland* captured the French *Magnanime* 250 miles W.S.W. of Ushant. [bh]

1779 *Apollo* captured the French *Oiseau* in the Baie de St. Brieuc, Brittany.

1824 *Cameleon* and *Naiad* captured the Algerine *Tripoli* in Algiers Bay.

1874 Defeat of the Ashantis at Amoaful. [bh]. Naval Brigade from *Active, Amethyst, Argus, Beacon, Bittern, Coquette, Decoy, Druid, Encounter, Merlin, Tamar, Victor Emmanuel.* Ashantee Medal: clasp "Coomassie".

1918 E.50 lost on active service and K.17 and K.4 on exercise in N Sea. K.17 rammed by *Fearless* and K.4 by *Inflexible* or by K.6.

1941 *Huntley* sunk by Italian torpedo aircraft off Sidi Barrani, Libya.

1942 *Belmont* sunk by U.82 S.E. of Nova Scotia. (Convoy NA.2)

1942 *Culver* sunk by U.105 in N Atlantic. (Convoy SL.98)

1943 GC (ex-AM): Lt-Cdr W.H.D. McCarthy for trying to save life off Benghazi.

1944 *Magpie, Starling* and *Wild Goose* sank U.592 in Western Approaches.

1945 Memorable Date of 42 and 44 Commandos RM – Kangaw (see 12th January).

HMS *Captain* **in 1870**

1st FEBRUARY

1806* Naval Academy at Portsmouth renamed Royal Naval College at request of King George III.

1807 *Lark* captured a Spanish gunboat in Puerto Cispata, Colombia.

1829 *Black Joke* captured the Spanish slaver *Almirante* 200 miles S.E. by S. of Lagos, Nigeria.

1858 *Teazer* and boats of *Ardent, Childers, Pluto, Spitfire* and *Vesuvius* destroyed nine towns up the Great Scarcies River, Sierra Leone.

1873 RN College Greenwich opened.

1917 German "unrestricted" submarine warfare began.

1926 RN Shore Wireless Service instituted by Order in Council.

1937 GC(ex-EGM): C.G. Duffin, Senior Shipwright Diver, HM Dockyard, Portsmouth. (*Gazette* date)

1943 *Welshman* sunk by U.617 off Tobruk.

1949 WRNS became a permanent and integral part of the Naval Service though not subject to Naval Discipline Act.

1952 WRNVR established.

Sailor: a Rowlandson print of 1799

***The Royal Naval College (now Staff Officers' Mess, Portsmouth)**

2nd FEBRUARY

1747   *Edinburgh* and *Nottingham* captured the French privateer *Bellone* 100 miles N.W. by W. of Ushant. *Eagle* also in company.

1780   *Defiance* wrecked in operations at Charleston (see 11th May).

1811   *Theban* engaged a French lugger privateer, and her boats recaptured the latter's prize from under the batteries near Dieppe. *Skylark* covered the latter operation.

1813   Boats of *Kingfisher* captured one trabaccolo and destroyed five others near Cape Agia Katerina, Corfu.

1859   *Pearl's* Naval Brigade returned on board from operations in the Gorakhpur District. (See 12th September)

1867   Writer rating introduced.

1941   *Ark Royal* aircraft attacked power plant (Tirso Dam), Sardinia. Operation Picket. FAA Sq.: 800 (Skua), 810 (Swordfish).

HMS *Westcott*

1941   *Formidable* aircraft attacked Mogadishu, Italian Somaliland. Operation Breach. FAA Sq.: 826, 829 (Albacore).

1942   *Westcott* sank U.581 S.W of the Azores.

1944   *Orion* and *Soemba* (Neth.) bombarded the Formia area, NW of Naples.

Members of an FAA training Squadron and Seafox aircraft, 1939

1781 Admiral Sir George Bridges Rodney *(Sandwich)*, with 12 sail of the line, captured St. Eustatius, West Indies, 6 Dutch men-of-war and over 150 merchantmen. The islands of Saba and St. Martin were seized at the same time. The Dutch were practically defenceless and surrendered on being summoned.

1807 Capture of Montevideo by Brigadier-General Sir Samuel Auchmuty and Rear-Admiral Charles Stirling *(Diadem)*. Ships: *Ardent, Diadem, Lancaster, Raisonnable, Charwell, Daphne, Encounter, Howe* (Storeship), *Leda, Medusa, Pheasant, Staunch, Unicorn.* A Naval Brigade was landed.

1809 *Aimable* captured the French *Iris* 110 miles E. by S. of Aberdeen.

1810 *Valiant* captured the French armed merchantman *Confiance* 30 miles S. by W. of Belle Île.

1812 *Southampton* captured the Haitian *Améthyste* (also called *Heureuse Réunion*) 3 miles South of Rochelois Bank, Haiti.

1814 *Majestic* captured the French *Terpsichore* 300 miles N.N.W. of Madeira.

1839 Capture of Karachi by *Algerine* and *Wellesley; Constance* (Indian Navy); the 40th Regiment and 2nd Bombay Native Infantry.

1885 Captain Lord Charles Beresford *(Safieh)* rescued Colonel Sir Charles Wilson's party on River Nile; unsuccessful in attempt to relieve General Gordon at Khartoum.

1915 Repulse of the Turkish attack on the Suez Canal. [bh]. Ships: *Swiftsure, Ocean, Clio, Minerva, Proserpine, Himalaya,* T.B.043. R.I.M. *Dufferin, Hardinge.* Armed Tugs: *Fanny, Lubeck, Mainstay, Mansoura, Prompt, Virginia.* French: *D'Entercasteaux, Requin, Robuste, Sylphe.* British War Medal: clasp "Suez Canal" approved but not issued.

1940 *Sphinx* bombed by German aircraft off Kinnairds Head, Aberdeen; sank next day.

1942 GC: Lieut-Commander William Ewart Hiscock DSC, for torpedo disposal at Malta. (*Gazette* date).

1943 Fortress N/220 sank U.265 in Atlantic.

1945 *Bayntun, Braithwaite* and *Loch Eck* sank U.1279 in Shetland/Faeroes gap.

1945 *Arley* damaged by mine off Sheringham buoy, Norfolk; sank in tow.

Instruction in the preparation of the electro-mechanical mine in HMS *Vernon*, c 1886

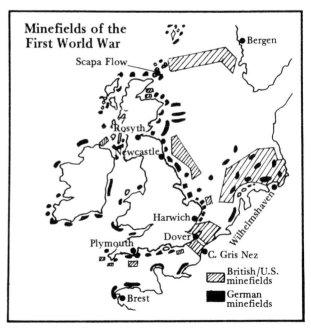

The extent of offensive and defensive mining in home waters, World War I.

MK 17 MINE

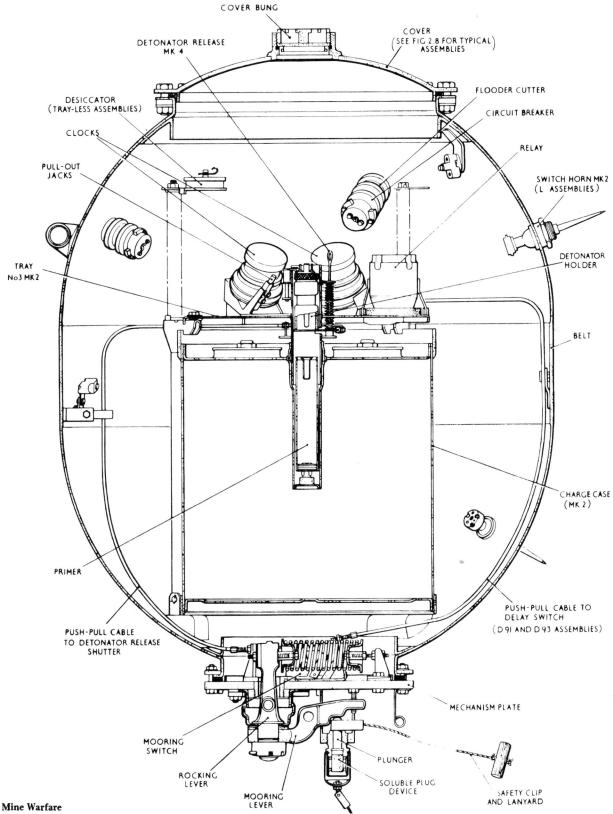

COVER BUNG

COVER
(SEE FIG 2.8 FOR TYPICAL
ASSEMBLIES)

DETONATOR RELEASE
MK 4

FLOODER CUTTER

CIRCUIT BREAKER

DESICCATOR
(TRAY-LESS ASSEMBLIES)

RELAY

CLOCKS

SWITCH HORN MK2
(L ASSEMBLIES)

PULL-OUT
JACKS

DETONATOR
HOLDER

TRAY
No3 MK2

BELT

PRIMER

CHARGE CASE
(MK 2)

PUSH-PULL CABLE
TO DELAY SWITCH
(D 91 AND D 93 ASSEMBLIES)

PUSH-PULL CABLE
TO DETONATOR RELEASE
SHUTTER

MECHANISM PLATE

MOORING
SWITCH

ROCKING
LEVER

PLUNGER

MOORING
LEVER

SOLUBLE PLUG
DEVICE

SAFETY CLIP
AND LANYARD

Mine Warfare

As a weapon both of blockade and defence, the mine has been used extensively in both World Wars. Even the basic moored mine is a very complex mechanism designed to prevent any risk of explosion before it is laid, but to ensure that it is 'live' when required. The Mk 17 (above) was developed in 1919-20 and was the basic British war stock mine of the Second World War.

29

4th FEBRUARY

1695	*Dartmouth* taken by two French ships in the Channel.
1781	*Monarch, Panther* and *Sibyl* captured the Dutch *Mars* and a convoy of 24 sail 30 miles W. by N. of St. Martin, West Indies.
1804	Boats of *Centaur* cut out the French *Curieux* in Fort Royal harbour, Martinique. [m, bh]
1805	*Acheron* and *Arrow* (in defence of a convoy of 32 sail, of which 3 only were captured) taken by the French *Hortense* and *Incorruptible* 30 miles to the northward of Cape Tenez, Algeria. [m, bh]
1853	Repulse by the Burmese of a combined British force near Donabew (Danubyu) and capture of Prome. Landing party from *Fox, Sphinx* and *Winchester; Phlegethon* (Bengal Marine) and 67th Bengal Native Infantry.
1858	*Pelorus'* Naval Brigade (Captain F.P.B. Seymour) left the ship at Rangoon to garrison the fort at Meaday (Myede), Burma.
1874	Capture of Coomassie(Kumasi).[bh]. (See 31st January)
1915	Drifter *Tarlair* fitted with prototype A/S Hydrophones.
1918	*Zubian* (½ *Nubian* ½ *Zulu*) sank the German UC.50 off Essex Coast. *Zulu* had been mined off Dunkirk 8th November 1916, and *Nubian* torpedoed 27th October 1916. Both reached home and the undamaged halves were combined in *Zubian*, at suggestion of Admiral Bacon.
1919	*Penarth* mined off Yorkshire coast.
1943	*Beverley* and *Vimy* sank U.187 in N Atlantic. (Convoy SC.118)
1945	*Loch Scavaig, Loch Shin, Nyasaland* and *Papua* sank U.1014 in NW Approaches.
1949	*Royal Sovereign* returned by USSR after five years service as *Archangelesk*.

5th FEBRUARY

1722	*Swallow* captured the pirate *Ranger* (James Skyrm) 30 miles N. by W. of Cape Lopez, French Equatorial Africa.
1800	*Danae, Fairy, Harpy, Loire* and *Railleur* captured the French *Pallas* close off Les Sept Îles, Brittany. [m]. The medal was awarded only to *Fairy* and *Harpy*.
1804	*Eclair* fought the French *Grand Décide* 200 miles North of Tortola, West Indies.
1809	*Loire* captured the French *Hébé* 80 miles N.W. of Burling Island, Portugal.
1810	Capture of Guadeloupe by Lieutenant-General Sir George Beckwith and Vice-Admiral the Hon. Sir Alexander Cochrane *(Pompee)*. [m, bh]. Ships and vessels: *Abercrombie, Achates, Alcmene, Alfred, Amaranthe, Asp, Attentive, Aurora, Bacchus, Ballahou, Bellette, Blonde, Castor, Cherub, Cygnet, Elizabeth, Fawn, Forester, Freija, Frolic, Gloire, Grenada, Guadeloupe, Hazard, Laura, Loire, Melampus, Morne Fortunee, Netley, Observateur, Orpheus, Pelorus, Perlen, Plumper, Pompee, Pultusk, Ringdove, Rosamond, Savage, Sceptre, Scorpion, Snap, Star, Statira, Superieure, Surinam, Thetis, Vimiera, Wanderer.*
1888	Bruce Fraser born.
1940	*Antelope* sank U.41 in SW Approaches (49° 21'N., 10° 04'W). (Convoy OA.84)
1942	*Arbutus* sunk by U.136 in N Atlantic (55° 05'N., 19° 43'W). (Convoy ON.63)

HMS *Royal Sovereign* at Vigo, 1922.

6th FEBRUARY

1799   *Argo* captured the Spanish *Santa Teresa* 30 miles North of Minorca.

1806*   Battle of San Domingo. [m*, m, bh]. Vice-Admiral Sir John Duckworth *(Superb)* beat the French squadron of five sail of the line under Rear-Admiral Leissegues *(Impérial)* in San Domingo Bay. Captured: *Alexandre, Brave*, Jupiter,* Destroyed: *Diomède, Impérial,* Ships: *Agamemnon, Atlas, Canopus, Donegal, Northumberland, Spencer, Superb.* Frigates, etc: *Acasta, Epervier, Kingfisher, Magicienne.*
*Foundered on passage to England.

1845   *Terrible* (sixth of the name) launched at Deptford: first four-funnelled ship in RN.

1865   *Hector* fitted with first armour-piercing steel shot.

1915   *Erne* wrecked off Rattray Head, Aberdeen.

1942   *Rochester* and *Tamarisk* sank U.82 in N Atlantic. (Convoy OS.18)

1943   *Louisburg* (RCN) sunk by aircraft off Oran. (Convoy KMS.8)

1947   *Wellington* became HQ Ship of the Worshipful Company of Master Mariners.

7th FEBRUARY

1602   Capture of Puerto Bello by *Pearl* and *Prudence* privateers.

1794   *Pigot* (East-Indiaman) taken by the French *Prudente, Cybèle, Duguay-Trouin* and *Île-de-France* at Benkulen, Sumatra.

1811   *Hawke* captured the French privateer *Furet* 20 miles S.W. by W. of Beachy Head.

1813   *Amelia* repulsed by the French *Aréthuse* 40 miles W.N.W. of Tamara, Îles de Los, French Guinea.

1919   *Erin's Isle* mined off the Nore.

1941   Western Approaches command shifted from Plymouth to Liverpool.

1943   Fortress J/220 sank U.624 in N Atlantic (55° 42'N., 26° 17'W). (Convoy SC.118)

*Battle of San Domingo

Although Trafalgar had marked the end of Franco-Spanish hopes of gaining command of the seas, the French resolved upon a "guerre de course" to prevent the flow of trade which gave Britain the wealth to continue to oppose Napoleon on the continent. One squadron was sent on this mission to the West Indies. A squadron under Sir John Duckworth destroyed the main French squadron, and only the frigates escaped. The French had driven two ships ashore in an endeavour to escape, but they were destroyed by boats of the British squadron.

Battle of San Domingo

8th FEBRUARY

1794   *Fortitude* and *Juno* bombarded Mortella Tower, Gulf of St. Floren, Corsica.

1799   *Daedalus* captured the French *Prudente* 120 miles South of Cape Natal, S.E. Africa.

1805   *Curieux* captured the French privateer *Dame Ernouf* 60 miles to the eastward of Barbados.

1813   Boats of *Belvidera, Junon, Maidstone* and *Statira* captured the American *Lottery* in Lynnhaven Bay, off Chesapeake Bay.

1916   British Government requested naval assistance from Japan.

1917   *Liberty* sank UC.46 in Dover Strait.

1917   *Thrasher* sank UC.39 4½ miles South of Flamborough Head.

1917   *Gurkha* sunk by mine 4 miles S.W. of Dungeness.

1918   *Boxer* sunk in collision with S.S. *St. Patrick* in Channel.

1918   UB.38 sunk by mine off Dover.

1942   *Alysse* (French) sunk by U.654 off Newfoundland, having left Convoy ONS.60.

1943   *Regina* (RCN) sank the Italian s/m *Avorio* off Philippeville, Algeria. (Convoy KMS.8)

1943   *Bredon* sunk by U.521 off the Canary Islands .(Convoy Gibraltar II)

1944   *Woodpecker* and *Wild Goose* sank U.762 in SW Approaches .(Convoy SL.147/MKS.38)

1963   First experimental touch-and-go by VTOL P.1127 on *Ark Royal* off Portland.

Elia-type mines which were produced in large quantities in 1914, seen here on the cruiser HMS *Ariadne,* converted in 1917 for mine laying operations in the Heligoland Bight.

9th FEBRUARY

1746   *Portland* captured the French *Auguste* 80 miles S. by E. of the Scilly Islands [bh].

1748   John Thomas Duckworth born.

1808   Boats of *Meleager* cut out the French privateer *Renard* at Santiago de Cuba.

1916   *Mimi* and *Fifi* (ex-German *Kingani*) sank the German *Hedwig von Weissman* on Lake Tanganyika, thereby securing command of the lake.

1941   Bombardment of Genoa by Force H, under Vice-Admiral Sir James Somerville *(Renown)*. Operation Result. Ships: *Malaya, Renown, Sheffield.* Screen: *Duncan, Encounter, Fearless, Firedrake, Foresight, Foxhound, Fury, Isis, Jersey, Jupiter.* Simultaneous attack by FAA from *Ark Royal* on Spezia, Pisa and Leghorn. FAA Sq.: 800; 808; 810; 818; 820. (Skua, Fulmar, Swordfish).

1943   *Erica* sunk by British mine between Benghazi and Derna.

1944   *Kite, Magpie* and *Starling* sank U.238 and *Starling* and *Wild Goose* sank U.734 in S W Approaches (Convoy SL. 147/MKS.38). This was a furious and prolonged encounter: 150 depth charges were used in three hours, one counter-mining a torpedo from the U-boat only a few yards off *Starling's* quarter deck.

1944   *Relentless* sank the German tanker *Charlotte Schliemann* in southern Indian Ocean.

1945   *Venturer* sank U.864 off Bergen.

HMS *Starling* — This ship was one of the most successful anti-submarine vessels of the Second World War. In her, Captain Walker led his group in the destruction of a large number of U-Boats.

10th FEBRUARY

Admiral of the Fleet Lord Fisher of Kilverstone (1841-1920)

Admiral "Jacky" Fisher joined the navy in 1854 and became First Sea Lord in 1904. During his term of office he undertook far reaching and forceful reforms in many aspects of naval life. He is most famous for his ideas on the building of capital ships. His battle ships were called "Dreadnoughts" and they were heavily armoured, with 10 x 12in guns. They so transformed naval ship building that all capital ships were hence forward termed "Dreadnoughts" or "Pre-dreadnought". Fisher was famous for the enthusiasm he brought to everything. Typical messages of his were "the Essence of war is Violence; Think in Oceans; Shoot on Sight, Moderation in war is Imbecility". Fisher resigned over the Dardanelles campaign in 1915 and, although he never commanded a fleet in action, he was considered one of Britain's greatest naval admistrators.

1582   Sir Francis Drake captured Cartagena.

1715   First diving equipment demonstrated in Thames and accepted into Service (**Andrew Becker**).

1722   *Swallow* captured the pirate *Royal Fortune* (Bartholomew Roberts) 30 miles West of Cape Lopez, French Equatorial Africa.

1809   *Horatio* and *Superieure* captured the French *Junon* 90 miles N.E. by N. of Virgin Gorda, West Indies, [m] *Driver* and *Latona* also engaged, but not awarded the medal.

1810   *Thistle* captured the Dutch *Havik* 480 miles S.E. by S. of Bermuda. [m, bh]

1846   Charles Beresford born.

1906   *Dreadnought* launched having been built in a year and a day. Last vessel built with ram for the Navy; first major vessel driven by turbines.

1916   German Government informed U.S. Government that all defensively-armed merchant ships would be treated as belligerents from 1st March onwards.

1940   *Salve* and *Servitor* swept first magnetic mine with LL sweep off Sunk light-vessel.

1944   Wellington 0/612 sank U.545 in NW Approaches.

1944   Swordfish A/842 *(Fencer)* sank U.666 in W Approaches.

HMS *Dreadnought*

11th FEBRUARY

Pay Day c.1900

1744   Admiral Thomas Mathews *(Namur)* fought the Franco-Spanish fleet of 28 ships of the line under Vice-Admiral de Court *(Terrible)* and Rear-Admiral Don Juan Jose Navarro *(Real Felipe)* off Toulon (20 miles S.S.W. of Cape Sicie). The Spanish *Poder* was captured (by Edward Hawke leaving the line) then retaken; abandoned later and burnt by the British on the following night. Ships: *Stirling Castle, Warwick, Nassau, Barfleur, Princess Caroline, Berwick, Chichester, Boyne, Kingston, Dragon, Bedford, Somerset, Princessa, Norfolk, Namur, Marlborough, Dorsetshire, Essex, Rupert, Royal Oak, Dunkirk, Cambridge, Torbay, Neptune, Russell, Buckingham, Elizabeth, Revenge.*

1747   *Enterprise* captured the French *Vestale* 24 miles West of Cape Tiburon, Haiti.

1778   Admiral Keppel's honourable acquittal of 'malicious and ill founded charges' after Admiral Palliser's battle off Ushant led to court martial of the latter, who received a 'censorious acquittal'.

1797   Commodore Horatio Nelson *(Minerve)* hove to and lowered a boat to pick up a man, when closely pursued by two Spanish ships-of-the-line in Gibraltar Bay. "By God I'll not lose Hardy: back the mizzen topsail".

1916   *Arethusa* sunk by mine off the North Cutler buoy, Harwich.

1916   *Arabis* sunk by three German destroyers 95 miles East of Whitby.

1918   *Westphalia (Cullist)* sunk by U.97 in the Irish Sea.

1941   *Erebus* bombarded Ostend.

1942   *Spikenard* (lent to RCN) sunk by U.136 in N Atlantic. (Convoy SC.67)

1944   Wellington D/407 (RCAF) sank U.283 in NW Approaches.

1944   *Wild Goose* and *Woodpecker* sank U.424 in W Approaches.

1944   *Launceston* and *Ipswich*(RAN) and *Jumna* (RIN) sank the Japanese s/m RO.110 in Bay of Bengal.

1964   GC: Chief Petty Officer Jonathon Rogers, DSM, RAN for gallantry at sinking of *Voyager* in collision with *Melbourne*. (Posthumous)

Recreation on HMS *Hannibal* c. 1900

35

12th FEBRUARY

1756 Rear-Admiral Charles Watson *(Kent)*, with some East India Company's ships and troops under Colonel Robert Clive, destroyed the pirate stronghold of Tulagi Angria at Geriah (Vijaydurg). West coast of India. Ships and vessels: *Bridgwater, Cumberland, Kent, Kingfisher, Salisbury, Tiger.* E.I.Co.: *Bombay, Drake, Guardian, Protector, Revenge, Triumph, Viper, Warren.*

1811 Boats of *Active* and *Cerberus* cut out eleven Venetian vessels and burnt two military storehouses at Ortona, East coast of Italy.

1844 Boats of *Harlequin* and *Wanderer* burnt the villages on the Merdoo (Morodu) River, Sumatra.

1848 Boats of *Alarm* and *Vixen,* with a detachment of the 38th Regiment, destroyed a fort at Serapaqui, River San Juan de Nicaragua.

1918 *Roxburgh* rammed and sank U.89 off N Donegal (55° 33'N., 7° 32'W).

1940 *Gleaner* sank U.33 in the Firth of Clyde.

1940 *Glasgow* captured the German trawler *Herrlichkeit* off Tromsö (69° 56' N., 16° 49' E.).

1940 *Hasty* captured the German *s.s.Morea* in Atlantic (41° 42' N., 15° 03' W.). Operation V.O.

1941 *Snapper* sunk by unknown cause in the Bay of Biscay.

1942 *Maori* sunk by aircraft at Malta.

1942* Unsuccessful attack on the German *Gneisenau, Scharnhorst* and *Prinz Eugen* during their escape up Channel. Ships: *Campbell* (D.21)., *Vivacious, Worcester; Mackay* (D.16), *Whitshed,* MGB.: 41, 43. MTB.: 44, 45, 48, 219, 221; 32, 71. FAA.: 825 Sq. — Swordfish V.4523, W.5907, W.5978, W.5983, W.5984, W.5985 (all lost). RAF.: 28 Beaufort aircraft of 42, 86 and 217 Sq. VC: Lieutenant-Commander(A) Eugene Esmonde (W.5984/825). (Posthumous).

1943 Hudson F/48 sank U.442 in Atlantic (37° 32'N., 11° 56'W.).

1944 *Paladin* and *Petard* sank the Japanese s/m I.27 in Indian Ocean (1° 25'N., 72° 22'E.).

The Channel Dash 1942
The two German battle cruisers *Scharnhorst* and *Gneisenau* and the cruiser *Prinz Eugen* were under regular air-attack at their base at Brest, and Hitler wanted them back in the relative safety of German home ports.
They slipped out on the night of 11 February to make a dash up-Channel, with a strong aircraft umbrella and E-boat escorts.
At 1055 Lieutenant-Commander Esmonde (below) with 825 squadron of Swordfish torpedo bombers learnt of the German dash. In spite of heavy snow the squadron was airborne at 1230 to attack the Germans 23 miles away. Ten Spitfires only arrived to cover the attack and these had to weave to fly slowly enough to remain in touch with the "string bag" bi-planes.
The Spitfire cover was hopelessly inadequate and by the time Esmonde started his run in, he had half a wing shot away. Still he kept on until a FW190 shot him down. All the other aircraft were also shot down and not one hit on the enemy was recorded.
Esmonde was posthumously awarded the VC, and 4 DSOs and one CGM were awarded. Of the aircrew taking part in the attack there were only 5 survivors, 4 of whom were wounded.
Sub-Lieutenant Lee (one of the aircrew) wrote of the attack "... I think myself that we all realised before take-off that even with fighter escort our chances were very slim, certainly of getting back, but we were confident that they would enable us to make a decent run onto the target. Certainly under the circumstances there was no alternative and some attack by torpedo bombers had to be made, and I think Esmonde's action was justified and the whole squadron were behind him ..."
"There can, in the history of forlorn hopes, be few more moving stories than that of the last flight of No. 825 Squadron. Its leader — the same officer who had led the Swordfish from the *Victorious* to attack the *Bismarck* in May 1941 — typified all that was finest in the newest branch of the naval service and the junior members of her squadron followed him faithfully to the end" — S.W. Roskill.

Lt-Cdr Eugene Esmonde VC

36

13th FEBRUARY

1719   George Bridges Rodney born.

1801   *Success* taken by the French squadron under Rear-Admiral Ganteaume in the western half of the Mediterranean.

1805   *St. Fiorenzo* captured the French *Psyche* 4 miles E.S.E. of Ganjam, Bay of Bengal. [m, bh]

1810   Boats of *Armide, Christian VII* and *Caledonia* captured a French gunboat and burnt three chasse-marees in Basque Roads. [m]

1812   *Apollo* captured the French *Merinos* off Corsica.

1814   *Boyne* and *Caledonia* fought the French *Adrienne* and *Romulus* close off Cape Brun, outside Toulon.

1878   Vice-Admiral Phipps Hornby took his squadron through the Dardanelles to Constantinople.

1941   *Shropshire* bombarded Mogadishu, Italian Somaliland

The Battle of Cape St Vincent. The melee after Nelson's turn (see 14th February)

1941   Albacore aircraft of 826 and 829 Sq. *(Formidable)* attacked Massawa, Eritrea. Operation Composition.

1942   *Scorpion* sunk by Japanese ships off Singapore.

1942   *Tempest* torpedoed by the Italian t.b. *Circe* in the Gulf of Taranto. Sank later in tow.

1943   *Pozarica* capsized after damage by aircraft off Bougie on 29th January.

1945   *Denbigh Castle* torpedoed by U.992 off Kola Inlet. Beached in Bolshaya Volokovaya Bay and capsized later. (Convoy JW.64)

February 1830

Disease remained by far the greatest killer of seamen until the First World War. Throughout the nineteenth century, surgeons struggled to overcome the most common killers. How heroically they struggled is illustrated by the story of Dr McKinnel of *HMS Sybille* off Lagos.

The ship's company had contracted Yellow Fever from *HMS Eden,* and 101 men had died out of a complement of 160. Morale was so low that McKinnel believed many were dying of sheer fatalism when they perceived a symptom. He therefore took a pint of black vomit from a patient who was dying of disease, publicly drank it down and walked around the deck until it was clear to all that it was no trick. The improvement in morale had a dramatic effect on the death rate.

14th FEBRUARY

1779   Captain James Cook *(Resolution)* murdered by natives of Hawaii during his third voyage of exploration.

1797   "A victory is very essential to England at this moment" — Jervis. Battle of Cape St. Vincent. 24 miles W. by S. of Cape St. Vincent. [m, m*, bh]. Admiral Sir John Jervis *(Victory)* defeated 27 Spanish sail of the line under Vice-Admiral Don Jose de Cordoba *(Santissima Trinidad)*. Four captured: *Salvador Del Mundo, San Ysidro, San Jose, San Nicolas*. Ships: *Culloden, Blenheim, Prince George, Orion, Colossus, Irresistible, Victory, Egmont, Goliath, Barfleur, Britannia, Namur, Captain, Diadem, Excellent,* Frigates, etc.: *Bonne Citoyenne, Fox, Lively, Minerve, Niger, Raven, Southampton.* Regiments: 2/1st 11th, 18th, 50th, 51st, 69th, 90th. The 69th, now the Royal Regiment of Wales, have the Naval Battle Honour "St. Vincent, 1797".

Battle of Cape St. Vincent. Sir John Jervis leading a fleet of 15 ships of the line encountered a Spanish fleet (28 of the line) which was sailing from Cartagena to Cadiz as a first step towards combination with the French. Jervis led his close-hauled line through the scattered formations of the enemy, intending to reverse course and attack the main body which was to leeward. Soon after the leading ship *(Culloden)* had turned, Nelson in the *Captain* (third from the rear) realised the enemy might escape. He therefore wore ship and headed straight for the enemy, supported by Collingwood and others. As a result of this bold but risky manoeuvre the Spanish fleet was thrown into confusion. Warned of the danger of colliding with two enemy ships, Troubridge in the *Culloden* made the matter-of-fact but memorable reply, "Let the weakest fend off."

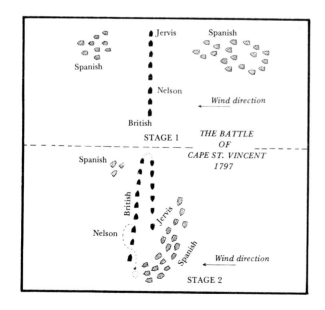

THE BATTLE OF CAPE ST. VINCENT 1797

1805   *San Fiorenzo* took the French *Psyche.* [m]

1807   *Bacchante* captured the French *Dauphin* 80 miles N. by E. of Cape Rafael, Santo Domingo.

1807   *Ajax* destroyed by fire off Tenedos. (Blew up on 15th).

1808   Boats of *Confiance* cut out the French *Canonnier* in the mouth of the Tagus. [m]

1813   Boats of *Bacchante* captured by the French *Alcinous* and a convoy of eight vessels 20 miles E.N.E. of Otranto.

1858   *Pelorus'* Naval Brigade arrived at Meaday, Burma.

1942   VC: T/Lieutenant Thomas Wilkinson, RNR (Li Wo). (Posthumous). Action with an escorted Japanese convoy off Singapore.

The *Li Wo*, a small auxiliary patrol vessel armed with one old four inch gun, met the advance force of the Japanese invasion fleet South of Singapore. She turned towards and engaged despite the odds, and finally rammed a transport before being sunk. They were 10 survivors of her crew and passengers, and her Captain, Lieutenant T.S. Wilkinson RNR, was posthumously awarded the VC.

1942   *Dragonfly* and *Grasshopper* sunk by Japanese aircraft off Sumatra.

1943   Catalina J/202 sank U.620 off Portugal. (Convoy KMS.9)

1944   *Tally Ho* sank the German U-It.23 (ex-Italian s/m *Reginaldo Guiliani*) off Penang, Malaya.

1945   *Bayntun, Braithwaite, Loch Dunvegan* and *Loch Eck* sank U.989 N of Shetlands.

1956   Admiral Sir Walter Cowan died.

1979   *Ark Royal*, fourth of the name and the RN's last fixed-wing carrier, paid off.

15th FEBRUARY

1783   *Magnificent* captured the French *Concorde* 30 miles to the south-westward of Nevis, West Indies.

1797   *Lapwing* captured the Spanish privateer *San Cristobal* 30 miles S.W. of St. Kitts.

1807   Nathaniel Dance *(Earl Camden)*, in charge of an unescorted merchant convoy of 27 ships, beat off an attack by 5 French warships under Rear-Admiral Durand-Linois *(Marengo)* at the southern entrance to Malacca Strait. Ships engaged: *Earl Camden, Royal George, Ganges* (Brig).

1809   *Belle Poule* captured the French *Var* from under the batteries at Valona, Albania.

1857   *Auckland* (I N) and *Eaglet* destroyed five mandarin junks and captured a 30-gun battery in Tung Chung Bay, near Hong Kong. A detachment of Bombay Artillery was serving in *Auckland* as Marines.

1892   Admiral of the Fleet Sir Provo Wallis died.

Underwater Polaris Missile Firing
To call the Polaris submarines the capital ships of today is an understatement of their awe-inspiring military power. The Royal Navy maintains constant Polaris patrols which, in terms of range and striking power, far exceed the Fleets of the last war. The photograph shows a missile as it emerges from the sea.

1918   German destroyer raid in Dover Strait, on the Folkestone-Gris Nez Barrage. Ships: *Swift, Marksman; Termagant, Melpomene, Zubian, Amazon;* M 26, *Syren, P.50, Racehorse;* + *Newbury, Lingfield; Sabreur, Viernoc, Colleague,* * *James Pond, Laroone, St. Germain, Erna;* ML *12*, ML *272*. Drifters: *Feasible, Reaper, City of Glasgow, Silver Line, Acceptable, City of Edinburgh, Achievable; Chrysanthemum II, Marys,* *Christina Craig, Our Friend, B.T.B., Test, Holmsgarth;* *Cosmos, + Golden Gain, + Golden Rule, *Silver Queen, Conifer, Paragon II; Shipmates, Cyclamen, I.F.S., Rosemma, Condor II,* * *W. Elliot, Fearless; Begonia II, Crescent II, Azarael, Scotch Girl, Arndilly Castle, Regain, Angeline;* *Cloverbank, Fragrant, John & Norah,* + *Vera Creina; Tessie,* *Veracity, Courage, Supporter, Radiant II, Lustre Gem, Implacable;* * *Jennie Murray,* + *Treasure, Vigilant,* + *Violet May, Hope II, Edith; Ocean Roamer, Young John, Bien Venu, Lord Leitrim, Herring Seeker, Kessingland.* Recalled and took no part: *Attentive, Murray, Nugent, Crusader.* * Sunk + Damaged.

1930   GC (ex-EGM: Able Seaman George Willet Harrison, *(Hood)* for gallantry in rescuing a trapped shipwright.

1940   Germany announced that in future all British merchant ships would be treated as warships.

1940   *Exeter* reached Plymouth from Falkland Islands: First Lord first on board.

1942   Singapore capitulated to Japanese land forces.

1943   Liberator S/120 sank U.529 in N Atlantic. (Convoy SC.119).

1944   *Upstart* sank the German *Niedersachsen* (ex-Italian *Acqui*) off Toulon.

1968   First British Polaris missile fired, by *Resolution* submerged 30 miles off Cape Kennedy.

16th FEBRUARY

1762 Capture of Martinique by Major-General the Hon. Robert Monckton and Rear-Admiral George Bridges Rodney (*Marlborough*). [bh] Ships: *Alcide, Devonshire, Dragon, Dublin, Foudroyant, Marlborough, Modeste, Nottingham, Raisonnable, Stirling Castle, Temeraire, Temple, Vanguard, Culloden.* 50's and smaller: *Antigua, Barbados, Basilisk, Crescent, Crown,* (Storeship), *Dover, Echo, Falkland, Granado, Greyhound, Levant, Lizard, Nightingale, Norwich, Penzance, Repulse, Rochester Rose, Stag, Sutherland, Thunder, Virgin, Woolwich, Zephyr, Amazon.*

1782 Vice-Admiral Sir Edward Hughes (*Superb*) and squadron captured six sail of a French convoy 10 miles to the south-eastward of Sadras. (See 17th February).

1783 *Argo* taken by the French *Amphitrite* and *Nymphe* off Sombrero, West Indies.

1798 *Alfred* captured the French privateer *Scipion* at Basse Terre, Guadeloupe.

1854 *Barracouta* and two boats of *Winchester* captured seven pirate junks off the Lema Islands, near Hong Kong.

1858 Boats of *Bloodhound* captured a 6-gun battery in the Benin River.

1916 War Office took over from the Admiralty the anti-aircraft defence of United Kingdom.

1918 Dover shelled by a German submarine.

1940 *Cossack* released British prisoners from the German *Altmark* in Jossing Fjord. Operation D.T.

The cruiser *Arethusa* and the 4th Destroyer Flotilla (Captain Vian) were searching the Norwegian coast for enemy shipping, including the *Altmark*, one of *Graf Spee's* supply ships and believed to be carrying British merchant seamen captured by the raider. *Arethusa* sighted the *Altmark*, but two Norwegian destroyers frustrated attempts of parties from *Intrepid* and *Ivanhoe* to board her. *Altmark* then entered Jossing Fjord, followed by *Cossack*. Again, a Norwegian destroyer prevented boarding, claiming *Altmark* was in neutral waters, was unarmed and carried no prisoners of war. That evening *Cossack* re-entered the fjord, went alongside and released 299 prisoners to the cry of 'The Navy's here'.

HMS *Cossack;* **launched 1937, sunk 1941**

PO Gould VC

Lt Roberts VC

When the submarine *Thrasher* attacked a ship off Suda Bay in Crete, she was counter-attacked heavily. She surfaced two hours after dark to find two unexploded bombs in the casing. Although the submarine would have to dive immediately if detected by the enemy forces in the area, which would inevitably drown the men in the casing, Lieutenant P.S.W. Roberts and Petty Officer T.W. Gould volunteered to go out and dispose of the bombs. Both were awarded the Victoria Cross.

1942   VC: Lieutenant Peter Scawen Watkinson Roberts, P.O. Thomas William Gould, for removing two bombs from external hull of *Thrasher*.

1944   *Mauritius* bombarded the Formia area.

1945   *St. John* (RCN) sank U.309 off Shetlands.

1945   Assault on Ruywa, Burma. Ships: *Flamingo* and *Narbada,* (RIN).

Life below decks, HMS *Doris*, c 1900

17th FEBRUARY

1782 First battle between Vice-Admiral Sir Edward Hughes *(Superb)* and 12 ships under Commodore Chevalier de Suffren *(Héros)* 9 miles S.E. of Sadras. [bh] Ships: *Monmouth, Burford, Eagle, Worcester, Superb, Hero, Isis, Monarca, Exeter.* Frigate: *Seahorse.* Fireship: *Combustion.* Detachments of the 98th Regiment served as Marines. *Exeter* badly damaged. On being asked by the master what was to be done, Captain King replied "There is nothing to be done except to fight her until she sinks".

1794 Capture of the Convention Redoubt, San Fiorenzo (St. Florent), Corsica, by Lieutenant-General David Dundas and Commodore Robert Linzee *(Alcide).* Ships: *Alcide, Egmont, Fortitude.* Frigates: *Juno, Lowestoffe.* Seamen from the squadron were landed.

1805 *Cleopatra* taken by the French *Ville-de-Milan* 240 miles to the south-eastward of Bermuda.

1810 Capture of Amboina, Moluccas, South China by *Cornwallis, Dover, Samarang* and a detachment of the Madras European Regiment. [bh]

1855 *Curacoa, Furious, Valorous* and *Viper* assisted in repelling a Russian attack on the Turkish entrenchments at Eupatoria, Crimea. Crimean Medal.

1858 *Pearl's* Naval Brigade, with detachments of the 1st Bengal Military Police Battalion and Gurkha allies, destroyed the fort at Chandipur, Gogra River. Indian Mutiny Medal.

1886 Ranks of Fleet and Staff Paymasters and Engineers created.

1912 P.O. Evans died in the Antarctic on Captain Scott's expedition.

1917 VC: Commander Gordon Campbell (Q.5) which, as *Farnborough*, sank U.83 67 miles West of the Fastnet.

1943 *Paladin* and Bisley W/15 (SAAF) sank U.205 off Derna (32° 56'N., 22° 01'E.)

1943 *Fame* sank U.201 and *Viscount* sank U.69 in N Atlantic. (Convoy ONS.165)

1943 *Easton* and *Wheatland* sank the Italian s/m *Asteria* off Bougie.

1945 *Bayntun* and *Loch Eck* sank U.1278 N.N.W. of Shetlands.

1945 *Bluebell* sunk by U.711, and *Alnwick Castle* and *Lark* sank U.425, off Kola Inlet. (Convoy RA.64) *Lark* torpedoed by U.698 and beached at Murmansk, salvaged by Russians and taken into service as *Nepsun*.

HMS *Fearless* fights a fire on a Greek Ship, 1976

A Royal R.N. *Seaking* Helicopter about to rescue crewmen of the U.S.S. *Steel Vendor*, October 1971.

18th FEBRUARY

Robert Blake (1599 – 1657)
Although Blake is not so well known as Nelson or Drake, he certainly merits the same acclaim. He was the son of a merchant and was noticed by Cromwell as a competent soldier and an able MP. He was an ardent parliamentarian but in 1649 at the age of 50 went to sea as one of the three "generals at sea". Not only did he achieve eventual victory over the Dutch and place Britain in a leading position of maritime power, but his 'Fighting Instructions' formed the basis of fleet tactics at sea for the next century. He was also responsible for the first Articles of War, which form the basis of naval discipline. With Samuel Pepys he was one of the founding fathers of the modern navy.

1653*   First day of battle between the Joint Admirals Robert Blake and Richard Deane *(Triumph)* with about 85 ships, and Admiral Marten Tromp with a large convoy, off Portland. 5 Dutch ships destroyed, 1 captured, as well as many of the convoy. [bh]
Red Squadron: *Triumph, Fairfax, Laurel, Lion, President, Foresight, Adventure, Nonsuch, Pelican, Tiger, Happy Entrance, Amity, Satisfaction, Cygnet, Old Warwick, Discovery, Eagle, Roebuck, Nicodemus, Angel, Ruth.*
Blue Squadron: *Speaker, Victory, Assistance, Advice, Convertine, Ruby, Dragon, Success, Assurance, Waterhound, *Sampson, Nightingale, Merlin, Providence, +Expedition.* White

Squadron: *Vanguard, Rainbow, Diamond.* Unspecified: *Worcester, Prosperous, Sapphire, Oak, Martin, Fortune, Sussex, @Centurion, Kentish, Katherine, Raven, Princess Maria, Welcome, @Arms of Holland, Gilliflower, (Gilly Flower), Tulip, @Dolphin, Guinea, Advantage, Convert, Gift, Plove, Duchess, Pearl, Falmouth, @Tenth Whelp, Paradox, Ann and Joyce, Ann Piercy, Charles, Chase, Elizabeth and Ann, Exchange, Giles, Hannibal, Mary Ketch, Paul, Reformation, Richard and Martha, Speaker's Prize, Thomas and Lucy, Thomas and William, William and John, @Brazil Frigate, @Cullen, @Lisbon Merchant.* *Sank after action damage. +Not before the 19th. @ Doubtful if engaged.

* The First Dutch War. By 1650, the Dutch were outstripping the English in the race for maritime power. Their merchant and fishing fleets were far more numerous than the English. However the main artery of their trade was the English Channel. The English claimed a salute at sea whenever they met a foreign warship in the channel. In 1652, Tromp refused to salute Blake off Dover. The sea battles of the Kentish Knock, the Thames, Dungeness, and the Downs ensued; in this last battle Tromp won, having lashed a broom to his masthead to show that he swept the English off the seas. The last sea battle of the first war was the battle of the Gabbard, when the English fleet under Monck and Deane won a definite victory. The Dutch coast was blockaded. Tromp was killed.

1797   Capture of Trinidad by Lieutenant-General Sir Ralph Abercromby and Rear-Admiral Henry Harvey *(Prince of Wales).* Ships: *Bellona, Invincible, Prince of Wales, Scipio, Vengeance.* Frigates, etc: *Alarm, Arethusa, Favourite, Terror, Thorn, Victorieuse, Zebra, Zephyr.*

1800   *Alexander, Foudroyant, Northumberland* and *Success* captured the French *Généreux* 10 miles W.S.W. of Cape Scalambri, Sicily. The French *Ville-de Marseilles* was captured earlier in the day by *Alexander.*

1807   *Bacchante, Dauphin* and *Mediator* captured a fort, two French schooners and their prizes in Samana Bay, San Domingo.

1852   Boats of *Cleopatra, Semiramis* (Indian Navy) and *Pluto* (Bengal Marine) destroyed a pirate stronghold in the Tungku River, Borneo.

1861	Landing parties from *Arrogant* and *Torch*, with detachments of the 1st and 2nd West India Regiments, burnt two towns up the Gambia River.
1897	Capture of Benin, Nigeria. [bh]. Naval Brigade under Rear-Admiral Sir Harry Rawson from *Alecto, Barrosa, Forte, Magpie, Philomel, Phoebe, St. George, Theseus, Widgeon.* Ashantee Medal: clasp 'Benin 1897'.
1910	Bunga-Bunga hoax on *Dreadnought.*
1915	German submarine blockade of Great Britain began.
1916	Allied forces completed the conquest of the Cameroons. [bh]. Ships:

Cumberland and *Challenger*. British War Medal: clasp 'Cameroons' approved but not issued.

1940	*Daring* sunk by U.23 off Duncansby Head (Convoy HN.12).
1944	*Penelope* sunk by U.410 off Anzio. Operation Shingle.
1944	*Spey* sank U.406 in Atlantic (48° 32' N., 23° 36' W.).(Convoy ONS.29)
1944	*Mauritius* and *Laforey* bombarded the Formia area.
1952	Greece and Turkey joined NATO.

"A sketch of the scene shortly before the attack was launched on Benin"

44

19th FEBRUARY

1653 — Second day of the battle between Blake and Tromp off the Isle of Wight.

1667 — *Pearl* fought a Dutch 50-gun ship in the North Sea.

1743 — Unsuccessful attack on La Guaira, Venezuela. Ships and vessels: *Advice, Assistance, Burford, Comet, Eltham, Lively, Norwich, Otter, Scarborough, Suffolk.* Lieutenant-General Robert Dalzell's Regiment was present at this action.

1783 — *Invincible* recaptured *Argo* 55 miles to the northward of the East end of Puerto Rico.

1794 — Occupation of San Fiorenzo (St. Florent), Corsica and capture of French *Minerve* (See 17th February).

1801 — *Phoebe* (36) captured the French *Africaine* (40) a few miles off Ceuta, N. Africa. [bh]. Captain Barlow knighted.

1807 — Vice-Admiral Sir John Duckworth *(Royal George)* forced the passage of the Dardanelles; eleven sail of the Turkish squadron destroyed and remaining two taken by the division under Rear-Admiral Sir Sidney Smith *(Pompée)*.
Ships: *Canopus, Repulse, Royal George, Windsor Castle, Standard, Pompée, Thunderer* and volunteers from *Ajax.*
Frigates: *Active, Endymion.*
Bombs: *Meteor, Lucifer.*

1915 — British and French bombardment of the outer forts of the Dardanelles begun. [bh] Ships: *Agamemnon, Cornwallis, Inflexible, Triumph, Vengeance.* French: *Bouvet, Gaulois, Suffren.* British War Medal: clasp 'Dardanelles' approved, but not issued.

1915 — The Norwegian *Belridge* torpedoed without warning by the German U.16 in Channel. First neutral ship so attacked. (The Germans stated later that the ship was attacked "in error").

The Dardanelles. This narrow passage is the only outlet from Russia to the Mediterranean. It is therefore of vital strategic importance, and was especially so in the last three major wars. Both February bombardments were tactical errors since they gave the Turks warning of impending attack and caused them to strengthen their defences. The resultant minefields repulsed the Allied Fleet in 1915 and led to the disastrous Gallipoli campaign.

Hoisting aircraft aboard in the First World War

1915 — *Goldfinch* wrecked in fog on Sandoy Island, Orkneys.

1917 — *Lady Olive* (Q.18) sank the German UC.18 12 miles West of Jersey. *Lady Olive* was also sunk.

1943 — *Hursley, Isis* and Wellington aircraft of 38 Sq. sank U.562 off Benghazi. (Convoy XT.3)

1943 — Wellington B/172 sank U.268 off Ushant.

1944 — *Starling* and *Woodpecker* sank U.264 in N Atlantic. (Convoy ON.224)

1944 — *Spey* sank U.386 in N Atlantic. (Convoy ONS.29)

1979 — First appointment of a WRNS Officer as First Lieutenant of an RN establishment — *Mercury.*

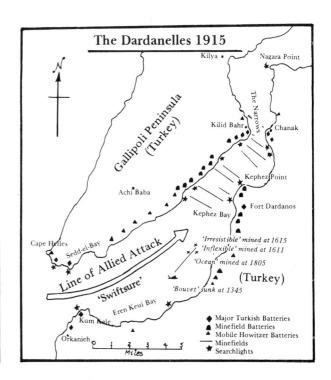

The Dardanelles 1915

Kilya •   Nagara Point
Gallipoli Peninsula (Turkey)
The Narrows
Kilid Bahr   Chanak
Kephez Point
Achi Baba
Fort Dardanos
Kephez Bay
Cape Helles
Sedd-el-Bahr
'Irresistible' mined at 1615
'Inflexible' mined at 1611
'Ocean' mined at 1805
Line of Allied Attack
(Turkey)
'Swiftsure'
'Bouvet' sunk at 1345
Eren Keui Bay
Kum Kale
Orkanieh
Miles

◆ Major Turkish Batteries
▲ Minefield Batteries
▲ Mobile Howitzer Batteries
— Minefields
★ Searchlights

45

20th FEBRUARY

1653   Third day of the battle between Blake and Tromp between Beachy Head and Calais.

1807   *Carrier* captured the French privateer *Ragotin* 60 miles North of Goeree, Netherlands.

1815   *Cyane* and *Levant* taken by the American *Constitution* 180 miles W.S.W. of Madeira.

1858   *Pearl's* Naval Brigade, with a detachment of the 1st Bengal Military Police Battalion and Gurkha allies, defeated the Indian rebels at Phulpur. Indian Mutiny Medal.

1907   Opening of Prince of Wales Basin.

The Prince of Wales Basin in Devonport Dockyard was opened by the Prince of Wales who came up harbour for the ceremony in the Admiralty Yacht *Vivid*. The size of the 10 years work can be estimated by the materials used: 2,500,000 cu ft of granite (1½m from Cornwall, 1m from Norway), 170,000 cu ft of limestone, 220,000 tons of cement from the Thames. 114 acres were turned into a fitting-out yard with docks, basins, etc. The cost was £6 million. The giant cantilever crane was one of the items completed after the opening, in 1909.

1941   *Ouse* sunk by mine at Tobruk.

1944   *Warwick* sunk by U.413 off Trevose Head.

1944   *Woodpecker* torpedoed by U.764 in N Atlantic. Sank in tow on the 27th.

1945   *Vervain* sunk by U.1208 off Waterford, Eire and *Amethyst* sank U.1208 in SW Approaches. (Convoy HX.337)

H.M. Submarine *M2* flying off a seaplane c 1928. The recovery crane is shown above the hangar entrance. The three *M* class submarines were experimental boats. Two were lost in accidents; *M2* foundered in 1932 probably due to the hangar hatch becoming opened while partially submerged. The aircraft is a Parnall Peto.

21st FEBRUARY

1729   Order in Council established the Naval Academy and abolished King's Letter Boys (see illustration 1st February).

1759   *Vestal* captured the French *Bellone* 600 miles S.W. of Lizard Head. [bh]

1779   Remains of Captain Cook buried at sea.

1790   *Guardian* (Lieutenant Edward Riou) arrived at Table Bay after having sustained very severe hull injuries by striking an iceberg on 24th December, 1789 on route to Australia.

1810   *Horatio* captured the French *Nécessité* 400 miles S. by E. of Flores, Azores.

1861   Naval Brigade from *Arrogant, Falcon* and *Torch* with the 1st and 2nd West India Regiments, destroyed the stockades at Saba, Gambia River.

1916   German Government informed U.S. Government that defensively armed merchant ships would henceforth be regarded as cruisers.

A Bosun's Call, 1812
(Still in use in RN today)

1940   *Manchester* and *Kimberley* (Northern Patrol) captured the German *s.s. Wahehe* in N Atlantic. Operation W.R.

1941   Albacore aircraft of 826, 829 Sq. *(Formidable)* attacked Massawa.

1943   Liberator T/120 sank U.623 in the North Atlantic. (Convoy ON.166)

1952   Admiral Sir Arthur Power appointed first NATO C-in-C Channel.

Captain James Cook (1726 — 1779)

Cook began his life at sea as an apprentice to ship-owners at Whitby. He volunteered for the King's service in 1755 and by 1759 was a Master in HMS *Mercury* employed in surveying the St. Lawrence River and in piloting ships of the fleet. He published four highly accurate volumes of sailing directions (1766 — 68) after surveying operations off the coasts of Newfoundland and Labrador. In 1768, he was commissioned Lieutenant in command of HMS *Endeavour,* and carried-out astronomical observations with other scientists for the Royal Society in the Pacific, where he also sailed round, examined and charted the coast of New Zealand and explored the west coast of Australia. He returned in 1771. He sailed again as Commander of HMS *Resolution* in July 1772, accompanied by HMS *Adventure,* heading for the Pacific. He sailed close to the ice, passing the Antarctic Circle for the first time in January 1773. He reached Easter Island by January 1774 after exploring several of the South Pacific islands and not having seen land for 104 days. He returned to England in July 1775. In 1776 the Royal Society honoured him with the Copley Gold Medal for his paper on ship's hygiene. During his long voyage, only 1 man had died and his crew was remarkably free from scurvy and had no fever. He was promoted to Captain in August 1775 and appointed to Greenwich Hospital. He sailed again in July 1776 for the North Pacific, to discover a passage round North America. He again visited New Zealand and discovered the Sandwich Islands (Hawaii) on his way to the west coast of America in March 1778. He conducted a running survey of the west coast north until turning back and west at the end of August to the Sandwich Islands for the winter months. On 14th February 1779 he was tragically killed by islanders on Hawaii.

22nd FEBRUARY

1692	Captain Wren *(Norwich)*, with *Antelope*, *Diamond*, *Mary* and *Mordaunt* escorting a convoy, repulsed a superior French force under Captain Comte de Blenac when off Desirade, West Indies.
1797	French force landed in Fishguard Bay. Surrendered on the morning of the 24th.
1799	*Espoir* captured the Spanish *Africa* 9 miles S.S.E. of Marbella, South coast of Spain.
1812	*Victorious* and *Weazle* captured the French *Rivoli*, and destroyed *Mercure* 14 miles N.W. by W. of Cape Salvore, in the Gulf of Trieste. [m*, m, bh]
1895	Destruction of Nimbi, Brass River, by Naval Brigade from *Barrosa*, *St. George*, *Thrust*, *Widgeon* and Niger Coast Protectorate Forces. Ashantee Medal: clasp 'Brass River 1895'.
1941	*Shropshire* bombarded Brava, Italian Somaliland.
1941	*Montgomery* sank the Italian s/m *Marcello* off Skerryvore.
1943	*Weyburn* (RCN) sunk by mine off Cape Spartel. (Convoy MKS.8)
1945	*Trentonian* (RCN) sunk by U.1004 off Dodman Pt. (Convoy BTC.76)
1945	*Pincher*, *Recruit* and *Evadne* sank U.300 off Portugal. (Convoy Appian Flight F)

23rd FEBRUARY

1633*	Samuel Pepys born.
1674	*Tiger* captured the Dutch *Schakerloo* in Cadiz Bay.
1695	*Centurion* engaged four Dunkirk privateers, capturing one, 15 miles E.N.E. of the North Foreland.
1805	*Leander* captured the French *Ville-de-Milan* and recaptured *Cleopatra* 300 miles S.E. by S. of Bermuda.
1810	*Royalist* captured the Boulogne privateer *Prince Eugène* off Dungeness. [m]
1854	Admiral Napier appointed to command the North Sea Fleet in the Russian war, and Rear-Admiral Dundas the Mediterranean.
1858	*Algerine* and two boats of *Calcutta* destroyed four pirate junks in Long Harbour, Mirs Bay.
1915	Royal Marines occupied Lemnos.
1940	*Gurkha* sank U.53 S. of the Faeroes.
1942	*Trident* torpedoed the German cruiser *Prinz Eugen* off Norway.
1942	P.38 sunk by the Italian t.b. *Circe* off Tripoli.
1942	*La Combattante* (French) sunk by mine in N Sea.
1943	*Bicester*, *Lamerton* and *Wheatland* sank U.443 off Algiers.
1943	*Totland* sank U.522 in Atlantic. (Convoy UC.1)

Samuel Pepys (1633 - 1703)

Pepys was the epitome of a man for all seasons. His life spanned England's only excursion from monarchy: it began when Charles I was on his throne, and he was nine when the Civil War began. His career began during the Protectorate, blossomed with the Restoration of Charles II and soared through the Dutch Wars, the Plague and the Fire of London. Religion nearly cost him his life: ironically the Glorious Revolution cost him his career.

Even so, it was a memorable one, and his Diary ensures his imperishable reputation, not only as a man with a perpetually enquiring mind, who became a Fellow and President of the Royal Society, Master of the Clothmaker's Company, an elder brother and twice Master of Trinity House and a governor of Christ's Hospital as well as the first Secretary of the Board of Admiralty, but also as an avaricious but adorable, ambitious but endearing man about town and citizen of the world.

24th FEBRUARY

1809   Capture of Martinique by Lieutenant-General George Beckwith and Rear-Admiral the Hon. Sir Alexander Cochrane *(Neptune)*. [m, bh].
Ships and vessels: *Acasta, Aeolus, Amaranthe, Bacchus, Belleisle, Bellette, Captain, Cherub, Circe, Cleopatra, Cuttle, Demerara, Dominica, Eclair, Ethalion, Eurydice, Express, Fawn, Forester, Frolic, Gloire, Goree, Haughty Hazard, Intrepid, Liberty, Mosambique, Neptune, Pelorus, Penelope, Pompee, Port d' Espagne, Pultusk, Recruit, Ringdove, St. Pierre, Snap, Star, Stork, Subtle, Superieure, Surinam, Swinger, Ulysses, Wolverine, York.*
The Military General Service Medal was bestowed on the Army, and the French eagles sent home were the first seen in England.

1809   *Defiance, Caesar, Donegal* and *Amelia* drove ashore the French *Calypso, Cybèle* and *Italienne* at Sables d'Olonne, West coast of France. *Cybèle* became a total wreck.

1813   *Peacock* taken by the American *Hornet* off the mouth of the Demerara River, British Guiana.

1841   Repulse of boats of *Termagant* by a Spanish brig 15 miles W.N.W. of Cape Mount, Sierra Leone.

1855   *Leopard* and the French *Fulton* destroyed ten guns and other Russian Government property at the estuary of the Kuban River, Black Sea.

1917   Re-occupation of Kut-al' Amara. River gunboats: *Butterfly, Mantis.* Supports: *Gadfly, Moth, Snakefly, Tarantula.*

1941   *Dainty* sunk by German aircraft off Tobruk.

1941   *Terror* sank off Derna after being bombed by German aircraft off Benghazi on the 22nd and off Derna on the 23rd.

1943   *Vandal* failed to surface during trials in Kilbrennan Sound: never salvaged.

1944   *Keppel* sank U.713 off Narvik. (Convoy JW.57)

1944   *Waskesiu* (RCN) sank U.257 in N Atlantic.(Convoy SC.153)

1944   *Anthony, Wishart,* Catalina G/202 and U.S. aircraft sank U.761 off Gibraltar.

1945   *Duckworth* and *Rowley* sank U.480 and Warwick K/179 sank U.927 in SW Approaches. (Convoy BTC.78)

HMS *Royal Sovereign,* **1895**

25th FEBRUARY

1744	*Solebay* captured the Spanish *Concordia* 30 miles West of Cadiz.
1744	William Cornwallis born.
1781	*Cerberus* captured the Spanish *Grana* 60 miles West of Cape Finisterre.
1814	*Eurotas* engaged the French *Clorinde* 180 miles W.S.W. of Ushant. [m, bh]
1915	Bombardment of Dardanelles forts resumed. Outer forts partially destroyed by the 26th.
1917	German destroyer raid on Margate and Westgate. Drifter *John Lincoln*.
1917	*Laconia* sunk by U.50 124 miles West of Valentia Island, Ireland.
1918	*Onslow* sank UB.17 in Channel.
1936	GC(ex-EGM): Edwin Crossley, HM Dockyard, Chatham. *(Gazette* date)

Clearance Diving

1940	*Escort, Imogen, Inglefield* and *Narwhal* sank U.63 off NW Scotland. (Convoy HN.14)
1941	*Exmoor* sunk by the German S.30 off Lowestoft. (Convoy FN.417)
1941	*Upright* sank the Italian cruiser *Armando Diaz* off Kerkenah Bank, Mediterranean.
1942	RAF bombed *Gneisenau* in Kiel. She was never repaired, and was sunk as a blockship at Gdynia.
1942	Formation of Royal New Zealand Navy.
1944	*Mahratta* sunk by U.956 off N Norway; Catalina M/210 sank U.601 (Convoy JW.57)
1944	*Inglefield* sunk by glider bomb off Anzio. Operation Shingle.
1944	*Affleck, Gore* and *Gould* sank the German U.19 in N Atlantic.
1966	MCD Branch formed.

The Minewarfare and Clearance Diver Branch was formed in response to the increasing complexity of minewarfare, which makes minesweeping in the old sense impractical. Clearance divers are highly qualified and often work at the limits of modern technology. Their tasks include all the more complex underwater operations as well as mine countermeasures and training teams of ships divers for the less complex diving tasks.

1970	Concept of the Military Salary approved in Parliament.

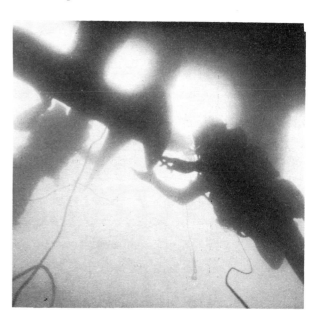

26th FEBRUARY

1813 *Furieuse* and *Thames* with the 2nd Bn. 10th Regiment, captured Ponza Island, West coast of Italy.

1814 *Dryad* received the surrender of the French *Clorinde*. *Eurotas* was fast coming up under jury rig, having been dismasted in the action on the previous day.

1841 Capture of the Wantong and Anung Hoi forts in the Boca Tigris, Canton River. Ships: *Alligator, Blenheim, Calliope, Druid, Herald, Melville, Modeste, Samarang, Wellesley;* Bengal Marine Steamers *Madagascar, Nemesis, Queen.* Troops: Royal Artillery, 26th and 49th Regiments; Madras Artillery, 37th Madras Native Infantry, Bengal Volunteer Regiment. China, 1841-2, Medal.

1852 Loss of *Birkenhead* (ex-*Vulcan*) off Point Danger, Simons Bay, South Africa. The discipline observed so impressed the German Emperor that an account was read to every unit in the Imperial Army.

1891 Launch of the seventh *Royal Sovereign,* first ship to carry all main armament on weather deck and secondary in casemates, to exceed 12,000 tons and to have steel armour. This class "presented a proud, pleasing and symmetric profile, initiating a new era of volcanic beauty after twenty years of misshapen misfits." (Parkes) (See 24th February)

1915 VC: Lieutenant-Commander Eric Gascoigne Robinson *(Vengeance)* at Gallipoli for charging two 4in guns in turn under heavy fire.

1916 Completion of evacuation of Serbian Army by RN and Italian force.

1917 Operations following the re-occupation of Kut-al'Amara. Recaptured: *Firefly, Sumana.*

1935 First British radar tested.

1948 GC (ex-AM): Chief Petty Officer J. Lynch *(Nigeria)* for saving life of rating lost overboard in gale at Port Stanley, Falkland Islands.

27th FEBRUARY

1806 *Hydra* captured the French *Furet* 30 miles S.E. by S. of Cape de Santa Maria, Portugal.

1841 Capture of the Whampoa forts, Canton River, and destruction of the Chinese Cambridge. Ships: *Alligator, Calliope, Herald, Modeste, Sulphur.* Bengal Marine Steamers: *Madagascar, Nemesis.* China, 1841-2, Medal.

1847 Senior Engineers became commissioned officers.

1859 No 4 Detachment, Indian Navy, with the 1st Assam Light Infantry and Assam Local Artillery, stormed and captured Romkong (Rengging) and Passi, Assam.

1881 Defeat of the British by the Boers at Majuba Hill, Transvaal. Naval Brigade from *Boadicea* and *Dido.* Troops: 58th, 3/60th and 92nd Regiments.

1900 Capture of Cronje's final laager at Paardeberg. Naval Brigade from: *Barrosa, Doris.* South Africa Medal: clasp Paardeberg.

1941 *Leander* sank the Italian disguised raider *Ramb I* in Indian Ocean.

1942 *Electra* and *Jupiter* sunk by Japanese surface forces in the Java Sea. Also sunk: Dutch: *De Ruyter* (Rear-Admiral K Doorman), *Java, Kortenaer* and *Evertsen* (beached, destroyed on the 28th). Damaged: *Exeter* and the USS *Houston. Jupiter* sank early on the 28th.

1945 *Loch Fada* sank U.1018 in SW Approaches. (Convoy BTC.81)

1966 *Lowestoft* began the Beira patrol off Mozambique as a result of Rhodesian UDI - maintained for nine years.

The Monitor HMS *General Wolfe,* with 18in gun, 1918

28th FEBRUARY

1579 Francis Drake *(Golden Hind)* captured the Spanish *Cacafuego* off Cape San Francisco, Ecuador.

1758 *Monmouth* captured the French *Foudroyant*; *Revenge* and *Berwick* captured the French *Orphée* 20 miles to the southward of Cartagena; *Monarch* and *Montague* drove *Oriflamme* ashore at Monte Cope. [bh]

1760 *Aeolus, Brilliant* and *Pallas* captured the French privateers *Blonde, Maréchal de Belle-Île* and *Terpsichore* 6 miles to the Southward of the Mull of Galloway.

1797 *Terpischore* (32) fought the Spanish *Santissima Trinidad* (120) 70 miles W. by S. of Cape Spartel, Morocco.

1810 Sea Fencibles disbanded: 61 Captains, 245 Lieutenants and 23,455 men.

1866 Grape shot declared obsolete in RN.

1940 Launch of *King George V*; first ship to carry 14in gun since 1915, to have quadruple mounting for main armament and to be designed to carry aircraft.

1942 *Perth* (RAN) and USS *Houston* sunk by Japanese surface forces in the Java Sea (5 45' S., 106 13' E.).[bh]

HMAS *Perth* and USS *Houston* left Batavia at 2100 to slip through the Sunda Strait. They had been under strain and hazard for the previous three months as the Japanese attacked the area, and the *Houston* had been damaged in the Battle of Java Sea. At 2300, just as they arrived at the entrance to the straits, they encountered a Japanese invasion force. They engaged the enemy at once, and fought until their magazines were empty and even the practice rounds had been fired. They did much damage to the invasion force, but were finally overwhelmed and sunk.

1945 *Labuan, Loch Fada, Wild Goose* and *Liberator* H/112 (USN) sank the U.327 off Scilly Islands (49° 46'N., 5° 47'W.).

When morale was at a low ebb in 1758, the capture of *Foudroyant* (80 guns) by the smaller *Monmouth* (64 guns) delighted the nation.

29th FEBRUARY

1812 Boats of *Menelaus* cut out the French *St. Joseph* a little to the east of d'Agay Roads, near the Gulf of Fréjus, South coast of France.

1812 *Semiramis* captured the St. Malo privateer *Grand Jean Bart* 80 miles S. by W. of the Scilly Islands.

1884 VC: Captain Arthur Knyvet Wilson (*Hecla*) for fighting off a fierce attack on gun single handed and carrying on although wounded. Naval Brigade at the (second) battle of El Teb, Sudan. Ships: *Euryalus, Carysfort, Hecla, Briton, Dryad, Sphinx*. Egyptian Medal: clasp 'El-Teb.'

Captain Arthur Wilson commanded HMS *Hecla* during the Egyptian and Sudanese Wars of 1882 and 1884-5. On 29th February 1884, he marched out to the battle of El-Teb with an infantry square, purely as a spectator — but the square broke under enemy attack. Springing into the gap, he beat off the Dervishes singlehanded and, when his sword broke, fought on using his bare fists although he had been wounded in the head. His action saved the day and he was recommended for the Victoria Cross though remained unmoved by what he had done. Returning to his ship he wrote home: "I have just returned from a very pretty little fight . . ." A typical entry in his diary reads "Docked ship. Awarded VC". He went on to become a most successful and much admired Admiral who, by rigorous training and realistic battle-practice, did more than any other sea-going officer to prepare the Navy for war in the years leading up to 1914. During the First World War, he was brought back from retirement to be **First Sea Lord**.

Captain Arthur K. Wilson VC, RN. (1842 - 1921)

1916 *Alcantara* fought the German raider *Greif* 70 miles N.E. of the Shetlands. *Alcantara* torpedoed and sunk: *Greif* abandoned, being finally sunk by *Andes*.

1940 *Despatch* intercepted the German *s.s. Troja* which scuttled herself off Aruba.

HMS *King George V*

53

1st MARCH

1799   *Sybille* captured the French *Forte*
        in Balasore Road, Bay of Bengal.
        A detachment of the Scotch Brigade
        was present. [m, bh]

1814   *San Domingo* captured the American
        letter of marque *Argus* 370 miles
        S.W. of Bermuda.

1864   RNR Officers' uniform instituted.

1881   RN Medical School, Haslar, opened.

1916   German extended submarine campaign
        begins.

1916   *Primula* torpedoed by U.35 in E
        Mediterranean.

1917   *Pheasant* sunk by mine one mile West
        of the Old Man of Hoy, Orkneys.

1941   Albacore aircraft of 826 Sq. *(Form-
        idable)* attacked Massawa.

1942   *Exeter* and *Encounter* sunk by Japan-
        ese surface forces in the Java Sea (5°
        00'S., 111° 00' E.).

1944   *Affleck, Garlies, Gore* and *Gould* sank
        U.358 in Atlantic (45° 46'N., 23°
        16'W.). *Gould* sunk in the action.
        (45° 45'N., 23° 10'W.).

A Wren servicing aircraft during World War II

The longest continuous U-Boat hunt.
The First Escort Group of Captain class frigates was on
patrol in the Western Approaches and detected and sank
U.91 on 25th Feb, 1944. On 29th *Garlies* gained an
asdic contact with U.358 and the group attacked with
hedgehog and depth charges. All through the night and
next day contact was maintained and a total of 104
depth charges expended. On 2nd, *Gore* and *Garlies*
returned to Gibraltar, while *Affleck* and *Gould* maintained asdic contact. At 1920, *Gould* was hit by an
acoustic homing torpedo. The submarine surfaced in
desperation.
Affleck opened fire at 1500 yards, and then attacked
with depth charges. One survivor was picked up from
U.358.

HMS *Gore*

2nd MARCH

1709   *Assistance, Assurance* and *Hampshire*, with a convoy, fought a French squadron of five ships under Captain René Duguay Trouin (*Achille*) 24 miles S.S.W. of Lizard Head. Five of the convoy were taken.

1783   *Resistance* captured the French *Coquette* 8 miles to the north-westward of Grand Turk Island, West Indies.

1795   *Lively* captured the French *Espion* 40 miles N.W. of Ushant.

1800   *Nereide* captured the French privateer *Vengeance* 180 miles to the westward of Rochefort.

1808   *Sappho* captured the Danish *Admiral Jawl* 20 miles N.E. of Flamborough Head. [m]

1808   Capture of Marie Galante Island, West Indies, by *Cerberus*, *Circe* and *Camilla*.

1858   *Pearl's* Naval Brigade made an unsuccessful attack on the fort at Belwa, India.

1940   *Berwick* intercepted the German *s.s. Wolfsburg* in Denmark Strait: *Wolfsburg* scuttled herself.

1940   *Dunedin* intercepted the German *m.v. Heidelberg* 60 miles W.S.W. of the Mona Passage, West Indies: *Heidelberg* scuttled herself.

1945   A raiding force of 500 men, supported by *Liddesdale*, captured Piskopi, N.W. of Rhodes.

Agadir 1960

When two earth tremors struck Agadir on the night 1st/2nd March 1960, *HMS Tyne* was despatched from a visit in Spain to assist. *Tyne* arrived 6 days after the tremors had struck, with many extra supplies she had embarked at Gibraltar, and with some 60 wooden huts prefabricated onboard during the passage by the shipwrights. She was allowed to land this equipment, but was not allowed to land personnel. The Bay in which she anchored was unsafe as the earth tremor, believed to have been centred out to sea, had raised the sea bed, and the harbour was out of action. The temperature was 105 in the shade, and flies abounded. The final death toll was reported as 12,000, and over 20,000 were left homeless — but exact figures will never be known.

The C in C Naval Home Command, Admiral Sir David Williams, leaves his command in HMS *Apollo*, Portsmouth 1st March 1979

3rd MARCH

1807   The squadron under Vice-Admiral Sir John Duckworth engaged the Dardanelles forts on the return passage from Constantinople. (See 19th February)

1811   *Nymphen* captured the French privateer *Vigilante* 40 miles East of Yarmouth.

1940   *York* intercepted the German S.S. *Arucas* off Iceland (63° 30'N., 15° 13'W.) *Arucas* scuttled herself.

1945   *Rapid, Rocket, Roebuck* and *Rotherham* (Force 68) bombarded Port Blair, Andaman Islands.

Cabin-Boy: a Rowlandson print of 1799

Boat deck, HMS *Good Hope,* **1895**

56

4th MARCH

1653 *Leopard* and three hired merchant-men, *Levant Merchant, Peregrine* and *Samson,* taken by the Dutch squadron under Captain Johan van Galen off Leghorn. *Samson* was burnt by a fireship; a fourth hired ship, *Bonaventure,* blew up, and a fifth, *Mary,* escaped.

1709 *Portland* fought the French *Coventry* and *Mignon* 40 miles N. by W. of Puerto Bastimentos, Colombia. A detachment of Brigadier-General Thomas Handasyd's Regiment was present.

1806 *Diadem* captured the French *Volontaire* in Table Bay, South Africa.

1807 Boats of *Glatton* cut out a Turkish treasure-ship in Port Sigri, Lesbos.

1842 Arthur Knyvet Wilson born.

1850 *Medea,* with a party from *Hastings,* captured 13 pirate junks in Mirs Bay.

1872 First warship model test (*Greyhound*) at Admiralty Experimental Works, Torquay.

1915 *Gurkha* and *Maori* destroyed U.8 near the Verne lightvessel (50° 56'N., 1° 15'E.) by modified sweep. First success with indicator nets.

1941 Transportation of Imperial troops from Egypt to Greece. Ended on 24th April, when the evacuation began. Operation Lustre.

1941* Successful raid on the Lofoten Islands, Norway. Operation Claymore. Ships: *Bedouin, Eskimo, Legion, Somali* (D.6)*, Tartar; Sunfish, Prinses Beatrix, Queen Emma,* Close support: *Edinburgh, Nigeria.* Troops: R.E., Commandos, Norwegian forces.

1942 *Stronghold* and *Yarra* (RAN) sunk by Japanese surface forces 300 miles S of Java.

1943 *St. Croix* and *Shediac* (both RCN) sank U.87 in N Atlantic. (Convoy KMS.10)

Coaling - at the turn of the century

1943 Hudson V/500 sank U.83 in W Mediterranean (37° 10'N., 0° 05'E.).

1944 *Onslaught* and Swordfish B/816 (*Chaser*) sank U.472 off North Cape (73° 05'N., 26° 40'E.) (Convoy RA.57).

1944 *Shropshire* bombarded Hauwei Island, Admiralty Islands.

*Raid on the Lofoten Islands

On 1st March a force of five destroyers under Captain C. Caslon in *Somali* and two cross channel steamers, carrying 500 men of 3 and 4 Commando, 50 Royal Engineers and some Norwegian troops sailed from Scapa Flow on Operation Claymore. The objective was to destroy the Norwegian oil factories on the Lofoten Islands, which were valuable to the Germans. A submarine was used as a navigational beacon, and the force achieved complete surprise with a first landing at 0500 on 4th March. All the objectives including a fish factory ship were destroyed. By 1300 the troops had re-embarked with 200 German prisoners, and the force returned on 6th March. This was a good example of the exploitation of sea power as a flexible aid to military force, where a small force can strike where and when required, and keep large numbers of enemy troops employed guarding many places. Most important was the acquisition from the trawler *Krebs* of a set of Enigma rotors.

5th MARCH

1800	*Phoebe* captured the French privateer *Heureux* 200 miles W.S.W. of Cape Clear.
1804	Boats of *Blenheim* repulsed in an attempt to cut out the French *Curieux* at St. Pierre, Martinique.
1804	Boat of *Eclair* cut out the French privateer *Rose* at Deshayes, Guadeloupe.
1858	*Pearl's* Naval Brigade, with the Bengal Yeomanry, a detachment of the 1st Bengal Military Police Battalion and Gurkha allies, Baruk and Gorakhnath Regiments, completely defeated the 14,000 Indian rebels at Amorha, thereby preventing a second extensive rising in the Trans-Gogra district. [bh]. Indian Mutiny Medal.
1915	Bombardment of the Smyrna forts. (continued for five days). Ships: *Euryalus, Swiftsure, Triumph; Anne Rickmers* (seaplane carrier). Minesweepers: 285 and four others. Sunk: M/S 285.
1942	VC: Commander Anthony Cecil Capel Miers. (*Torbay*). Attack on shipping in Corfu Roads.
1944	Swordfish F/816 (*Chaser*) sank U.366 off N Norway. (Convoy RA. 57)

Commander Miers, VC with his family at Buckingham Palace. Under his command *Torbay's* exploits in the Mediterranean included landing an attack on Rommel's shore headquarters.

6th MARCH

1709	*Portland* captured the French *Coventry* 40 miles N. by W. of Puerto Bastimentos. (See 4th March).
1740	Vice-Admiral Edward Vernon (*Strafford*) bombarded Puerto Cartagena — ineffectively.
1797	*Phaeton* captured the French privateer *Actif* 120 miles to the Southward of Ushant.
1811	Landing parties from Rear-Admiral Sir Richard Keats' squadron destroyed French batteries between Rota and Puerto de Santa Maria on Spanish coast. Ships: *Milford, Implacable, Warrior*. Bombs: *Hound, Thunder*.
1866	*Pallas,* sixth of the name, completed: first HM ship designed and built as a ram.
1902	Queen Alexandra's Royal Naval Nursing Service constituted by Order in Council.
1918	H.5 lost by collision in Irish Sea.
1918	GC (ex-AM): Flight Lieutenant V.A. Watson for saving life in a blazing naval airship (*Gazette* date).
1940	Corton and Cross Sands lightvessels bombed and machinegunned by German aircraft.
1941	"We must assume that the Battle of the Atlantic has begun" — Winston Churchill.
1943	XE11 rammed and sunk by boom vessel *Norina* in Loch Striven.
1944	Swordfish X/816 (*Chaser*) sank U.973 off N Norway. (Convoy RA.57)
1944	*Icarus, Kenilworth Castle,* and *Chaudiere, Chilliwack, Fennel, Gatineau* and *St. Catherines,* (all RCN), sank U.744 in N Atlantic (52° 01'N., 22° 37'W.). (Convoy HX.280)

7th MARCH

Vice-Admiral Cuthbert Lord Collingwood (1748-1810)

1665   *London* blown up by accident at the Nore.

1762   *Milford* captured the French letter of marque *Gloire* 400 miles S.W. by S. of Cape Finisterre.

1778   *Yarmouth* sank the American *Randolph* (blew up) 150 miles to the eastward of Barbados.

1795   *Berwick* taken by the French *Alceste*, *Vestale* and *Minerve* in San Fiorenzo Bay (Gulf of St. Florent).

1797   *Alcmene* captured the French privateer *Surveillant* and her prize 30 miles to the South-westward of Mizen Head.

1804   Boats of *Inconstant* cut out a French vessel at Goree, which place surrendered on the 9th.

1810   Vice-Admiral Lord Collingwood died at sea on his way home after eventually being granted sick leave — "Then I may yet live, to meet the French once more".

1885   John Tovey born.

1915   *Winifred* and *Kavirondo* drove the German *Mwanza* ashore at S end of Lake Victoria, thus establishing local naval supremacy.

1916   *Coquette* mined off E Coast.

1916   E.5 lost in N Sea.

1916   Second attempt to relieve Kut-al 'Amara. River gunboats: *Mantis*, *Dragonfly*, *Gadfly*, *Mayfly*, *Sawfly*.

1918   King George V designated the King's Squad and instituted King's Badge for Royal Marines under training.

1918   Start of naval operations against Murmansk and Archangel. Ships: *Glory*, *Cochrane*, *Attentive* and *Nairana*.

1941   *Arbutus* and *Camelia* sank a U. 70 (after ramming by *m.v. Mijdrecht*) in NW Approaches. (Convoy OB. 293)

1943   Fortress J/220 sank U.633 in N Atlantic

1945   *La Hulloise*, *Strathadam* and *Thetford Mines*, (all RCN), sank U.1302 in Irish Sea.

1952   Clearance Diver branch (later MCD) formed. (See 25th February).

Fleet Clearance Divers at a wreck in the Suez Canal, 1974

8th MARCH

1297 First recorded use of the word 'Admiral' in English.

1689 Office of Lord High Admiral of England effectively removed from the Monarch (James II) by the appointment of Lords Commissioner for executing the office, a procedure first used on the death of the Duke of Buckingham in 1628 and reversed in 1964 when the Monarch (Her Majesty Queen Elizabeth II) resumed the title upon the Board of Admiralty becoming the Admiralty Board of the new Defence Council.

1748 Capture of Port Louis (St. Louis), Hispaniola (Haiti), by Rear-Admiral Charles Knowles *(Canterbury)*. Ships: *Canterbury, Cornwall, Elizabeth, Oxford, Plymouth, Strafford, Warwick, Worcester*. Sloops: *Merlin, Weazle*.

1796 Capture of Neira Island, Banda group of the Moluccas, by Rear-Admiral Peter Rainier *(Suffolk)*. Ships and vessels: *Amboyna, Centurion, Orpheus, Resistance, Suffolk, Swift*.

1801 Landing of seamen, under Captain Sir Sidney Smith *(Tigre)* and troops, in Aboukir Bay. [m]

1808 *St. Fiorenzo* captured the French *Piemontaise* to the Southward of Cape Comorin, India. [m, bh]

1855 *Viper* destroyed a Russian Martello tower at Djimiteia near Anapa, Black Sea.

1940 *Dunedin* captured the German *m.v. Hannover* in the Mona Passage, West Indies.

1941* *Wolverine* sank U.47 in N Atlantic (60° 47'N., 19° 13'W.). (Convoy OB. 293)

1944 *Tenacious* and *Troubridge* bombarded Pupnat and Blato, Korcula Island, off Yugoslavia.

*Battle of the Atlantic

U.47 commanded by Gunther Prien, who sank *Royal Oak*, sighted outward bound convoy OB.293 and called other U-boats to the area. After dark, the U-boats closed and attacked in the normal way. However, the escorts were gaining new skills and UA (Eckermann) was damaged by a depth charge attack and had to return to base; U.70 was forced to the surface by 2 corvettes and sunk; U.99 (Otto Kretschmer) was forced to withdraw with half his torpedoes remaining. Only 2 merchant ships were sunk. U.47 shadowed the convoy and was caught coming out of a rain squall by the veteran destroyer *Wolverine*, and after several attacks by depth charges and cunning shadowing, *Wolverine* sank her.

A few days later U.110 (Lemp, who sank the liner *Athenia* on the first day of the war) homed U-boats onto a homeward bound convoy South of Iceland. U.99 came, and U.100 (Schepke, who was rivalling Kretschmer for first place in tonnage sinkings). A strong escort of 5 destroyers and 2 corvettes kept the U-boats at long range on the first night and only one merchant ship was sunk. More U-boats attacked the next night, and 5 ships were sunk. But the convoy system worked as it lured the U-boats to the escort, and the escort held on. U.100 was sighted on the surface by the destroyer *Walker*, which brought the destroyer *Vanoc* in to ram and sink the submarine. U.99, out of torpedoes, was going round the stern of the convoy to return to base. Her CO left a junior officer on the bridge who sighted the *Vanoc* recovering survivors from U.100 and dived. But *Walker*, covering *Vanoc*, attacked and forced U.99 to the surface before sinking her.

4 U-boats had been sunk in one fortnight, with three of Germany's most successful Captains.

Mustering bedding c. 1900.

Albacore Aircraft

9th MARCH

Aircrew briefing on board *Furious* before a raid on the *Tirpitz*, 3 April, 1944

1741 Partial reduction of the batteries at Puerto Cartagena, Colombia, by Vice-Admiral Edward Vernon (*Princess Caroline*). Ships: *Princess Amelia, Windsor, York, Norfolk, Russell, Shrewsbury, Ripon, Litchfield, Jersey, Tilbury; Orford, Princess Louisa, Worcester, Chichester, Princess Caroline, Torbay, Strafford, Weymouth, Deptford, Burford; Defiance, Dunkirk, Lion, Prince Frederick, Boyne, Hampton Court, Falmouth, Montague, Suffolk.* Frigates etc: *Experiment, Sheerness, Vesuvius, Terrible, Phaeton, Goodley; Squirrel, Shoreham, Eleanor, Seahorse, Strombolo, Success, Vulcan, Cumberland, Alderney, Pompey; Astraea, Wolf, Etna, Firebrand, Virgin Queen.*

1797 *St. Fiorenzo* and *Nymphe* captured the French *Resistance* and *Constance* 10 miles S.W. of Brest. [m, bh]

1778 *Ariadne* and *Ceres* captured the American *Alfred* 200 miles North of Barbados.

1806 Boats of *Egyptienne* cut out the French privateer *Alcide* at Muros, N.W. Spain.

1860 *Niger's* landing party in defence of New Plymouth: start of second New Zealand war.

1914 Lieutenants of eight years seniority became Lieutenant-Commanders.

1941 *Southdown* and *Worcester* repulsed an attack by German E-Boats on Convoy FS.429A.

1942 Albacore aircraft of 817 and 832 Sq. (*Victorious*) made an unsuccessful attack on the German battleship *Tirpitz* off Norway.

1944 *Asphodel* sunk by U.575 in SW Approaches (45° 24'N., 18° 09'W.). (Convoy SL.150/MKS.41)

1976 Sir Michael Cary died, last Secretary of the Board of Admiralty.

1705 Leake's second relief of Gibraltar. [bh]. Allied fleet under Vice-Admiral Sir John Leake *(Hampton Court)* captured or destroyed the French squadron under Commodore Baron de Pointis *(Magnanime)* 9 miles S.W. of Marbella, Spain. Ships: *Antelope, Bedford, Canterbury, Expedition, Greenwich (?), Hampton Court, Lark, Leopard, Newcastle, Nottingham, Pembroke, Revenge, Swallow, Tiger, Warspite* and 9 others, with 4 Dutch and 8 Portuguese. Captured: *Ardent*, Arrogant, Marquis**. Destroyed: *Magnanime, Lys*. *Captured by Dutch ships.

1761 *Ripon* fought the French *Achille* 60 miles West of Ushant.

1796 *Phaeton* captured the French *Bonne-Citoyenne* 120 miles W.S.W. of Cape Finisterre.

1810 *Owen Glendower* captured the French privateer *Camille* 10 miles North of Cape Barfleur.

1823 Admiral George, Viscount Keith died.

1842 Repulse of the Chinese attacks on Ningpo and Chinhai. Ships: *Blonde, Columbine, Hyacinth, Modeste*. Steamers: *Sesostris* (I.N.), *Phlegethon, Queen* (Ben. Mar.). Regiments: 18th, 26th, 49th and 55th; Madras Artillery. China, 1841-42, Medal.

Admiral George, Viscount Keith (1746-1823)

1915 *Acheron, Ariel* and *Attack* sank U.12 off the Firth of Forth.

1917 G.13 torpedoed and sank UC.43 off Shetlands.

1917 VC: Lieutenant Archibald Bisset Smith, RNR (*Otaki*) (Posthumous). Gallantry in *Otaki's* action with the German disguised raider *Mowe*. (37° 50'N., 18° 00'W.).

1918 UB.58 sunk by mine off Varne lightvessel.

1943 *Tigris* sunk by mine in the Gulf of Tunis.

1944 *Blankney, Blencathra, Brecon* and *Exmoor* sank U.450 off Anzio. Operation Shingle.

1944 *Mull* sank U.343 North of Bizerta.

1944 *Forester* and *Owen Sound, St. Laurent* and *Swansea* (RCN) sank U.845 in N Atlantic (48° 20'N, 20° 33'W.). (Convoy SC.154)

1944 Sunderland U/422 (RCAF) sank U.625 in Atlantic (52° 35'N., 20° 19'W.).

1945 U.275 sunk by mine off Beachy Head.

1957 Air branch of RNVR disbanded after ten years' existence.

The photograph shows the origin of "Make and Mend", the traditional phrase for time-off.

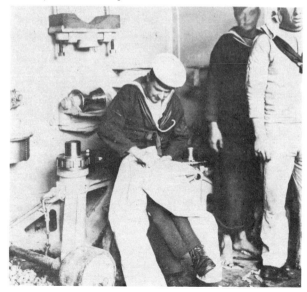

Equity or a Sailor's Prayer before battle.

1708 The Cruiser and Convoys Act allocated prize money to captors at the Crown's expense; a great incentive to captains and crews.

Prize Money (Cruisers and Convoys) Acts
The interdiction of enemy trade in the eighteenth and nineteenth centuries was an essential part of maritime war. The Prize Money Acts ensured that much of the value of any enemy merchant vessels and their cargoes captured was paid to the ships' companies of the captor ship. This prize money was a major inducement to service in the Royal Navy, at a time when basic pay was very low compared with the Merchant Navy. However prize money became so sought after that particularly in small ships the main business of attacking and sinking enemy warships sometimes took second place.
"Head Money" was therefore introduced, which amounted initially to £10 per gun in every enemy ship sunk. This rate became too low; (£740 for a 74 gun ship). The amount was therefore increased to £5 per head of the enemy crew (£3,000 for a 74 gun ship). Both prize money and head money were shared according to laid down proportions amongst the whole ship's company.

1727 *Royal Oak* captured the Spanish *N.S. del Rosario* 60 miles N.W. of Cape Spartel, Morocco.

1756 *Warwick* taken by the French *Atalante* and *Prudente* off Martinique.

1757 James Saumarez born.

1810 *Echo* captured the French privateer *Capricieux* 5 miles N.W. of Dieppe.

1812 *Phipps* captured the French privateer *Cerf* in Dover Strait.

1815 *Acasta*, *Leander* and *Newcastle* recaptured *Levant* at Porto da Praia, Cape Verde Islands; escape of the American *Constitution* and her other prize, *Cyane*.

1845 *Hazard* and a detachment of the 96th Regiment at the defence of Port Russell, New Zealand, which was abandoned to Heke and the Maoris. New Zealand, 1845-7, Medal.

1854 First RN steam fleet sailed for operations — fifteen ships left Spithead for the Baltic under Admiral Napier.

1915 *Bayano* sunk by U.27 off Corsewall Point.

11th MARCH

King George V with Admiral Beatty at Scapa Flow, 1917

1917 British forces captured Baghdad, Mesopotamia. River gunboats: *Butterfly, Firefly, Gadfly, Mantis, Moth, Snakefly, Tarantula.*

1918 *Retriever* sank UB.54 in N Sea.

1927 AFO 626 recognised 'Heart of Oak' and 'A Life on the Ocean Wave' as the marches of the RN and RM, 'Nancy Lee' for the advance in review order and 'Iolanthe' as a Flag Officer's salute.

1936 Admiral of the Fleet Earl Beatty, Viscount Borodale of Wexford and Baron Beatty of the North Sea, died.

1940 Bomber Command aircraft sank U.31 in Schillig Road, Jade River. (Salvaged by enemy.)

1942 *Naiad* sunk by U.565 off Sidi Barrani.

1943 Convoy HX 228 in NW Atlantic attacked by U-Boat pack. *Harvester* and *Aconit* (Fr French) sank U.444 (51° 14' N.,29° 18' W.). *Harvester* sunk by U.432 in 51° 23'N, 28° 30'W. *Aconit* sank U.432 in 51° 23'N., 28° 30'W.

1944 Catalina D/279 and P/262 (SAAF) sank the German U-It 22 (ex-Italian s/m *Alpino Bagnolini*) off Cape of Good Hope (41° 28'S., 17° 40'E.).

Squid projectiles exploding

12th MARCH

1672   Captain Sir Robert Holmes *(St. Michael)* fought the Dutch Smyrna fleet (50 convoy and 6 escort) off the Isle of Wight. Ships: *Cambridge, Diamond*[1] *Fairfax, Gloucester*[1], *Resolution, St. Michael, Success*[1], *York*. [1] Joined on the 14th.

1704   Rear-Admiral Thomas Dilkes *(Kent)* captured the Spanish *Porta Coeli, Santa Teresa* and the armed merchantman *San Nicolas* 20 miles W. by S. of Cape Spartel, Morocco. Ships: *Antelope, Bedford, Kent, Panther, Suffolk.*

1917   U.S. Government announced the arming of all merchant vessels in the war zone.

1917   E.49 mined off Shetlands.

1917   *Privet* (Q.19) sank U.85 24 miles S. by E. of Start Point. *Privet* sank on 13th in Plymouth Sound; salvaged.

1943   *Turbulent* sunk, by A/S craft, off Bastia, Corsica.

1943   *Lightning* sunk by German E-Boat off Bizerta.

1943*   *Bayntun* fitted with early Hedgehog A/S weapon.

1945   *Loch Ruthven* and *Wild Goose* sank U.683 in SW Approaches.

* Anti-Submarine Weapons
The depth charge, a cannister of explosive designed to explode at a variable depth and crush a submarine, is an effective weapon against all but the fastest submarines.
Its great disadvantage during the Second World War lay in the fact that a ship had to steam over a submarine to drop it, and the place where asdics are least effective is dead astern, where propeller noise and water disturbance make sound-wave detection impossible.
Two weapons were invented to solve the problem — both ahead-firers. The Hedgehog fired a large number of small bombs ahead of the ship as indicated by asdic echoes. See 7th August. They only exploded on contact and so had no deterrent power. The Squid (below) fired 3 large depth bombs ahead of the ship, set at a depth predicted by the asdic and these proved highly effective.

Squid

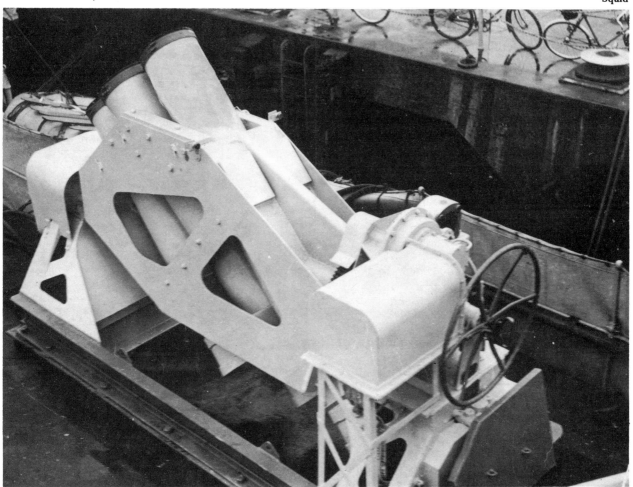

13th MARCH

1672 Continuation of Holmes' action. Capture of the Dutch *Klein Hollandia* and five merchantmen. (See 12th March).

1708 *Leopard* captured the French *Salisbury* in the Firth of Forth.

1761 *Vengeance* captured the French *Entreprenant* 200 miles to the southward of Ushant.

1762 *Fowey* captured the Spanish *Ventura* 24 miles W.N.W. of Cape Tiburon, Haiti.

1762 RNH Stonehouse, Plymouth opened.

1780 *Courageux* captured the French privateer *Monsieur* 140 miles S.W. by S. of the Scilly Islands.

1795 *Lively* captured the French *Tourterelle* 40 miles to the northward of Ushant. [m]

1795 Action off Genoa between Vice-Admiral William Hotham and a French fleet under Rear-Admiral Pierre Martin. *Agamemnon* and *Inconstant* fought the French *Ça-Ira*. (See 14th March).

1801 "I hate your pen and ink men; a fleet of British ships of war are the best negotiators in Europe"; Nelson to Lady Hamilton, on his way to Copenhagen.

1804 *Fort Diamond,* with a party from *Emerald,* captured the French privateer *Mosambique* in Ceron Cove, Martinique.

1806 *London* captured the French *Marengo,* and *Amazon* captured *Belle-Poule,* 640 miles W. by S. of the Canary Islands. [m, bh]

1808 *Emerald* destroyed the French *Apropos* in Ria de Vivero, North coast of Spain. [m]

1811 Captain William Hoste's frigate action, close off the North point of Lissa (Vis) in the Adriatic. [m*, m, bh]. Capture of the Franco-Venetian *Bellona* and *Corona* and destruction of *Favorite.* Ships: *Active, Amphion, Cerberus, Volage.*

Hoste made only one signal beyond the minimum executive orders — "Remember Nelson".

1823 Death of Admiral of the Fleet the Earl St. Vincent — "We must not expect too much of men; we are too apt to over-rate the services we render them."

1841 Capture of the Macao Passage fort, Canton River (defending the channel between Gough and Honam Islands). Ships: *Modeste, Starling.* Steamer (Bengal Marine): *Madagascar.* Boats of *Alligator, Blonde, Calliope, Conway, Cruizer, Herald, Hyacinth, Nimrod, Pylades.* China, 1841-2, Medal.

1841 *Nemesis* (Bengal Marine), with boats of *Atalanta* (Indian Navy) and *Samarang,* destroyed Mo To fort and several other forts and junks during a three days' passage up the Broadway Estuary and through various inland waterways to the Canton River. China, 1841-2, Medal.

1855 Bombardment of Soujak Kale, Novorossisk Bay, Black Sea. Ships: *Highflyer, Leopard, Swallow, Viper,* and the French *Fulton.* Crimean Medal.

1858 VC: Able Seaman Edward Robinson, (*Shannon*), at the siege of Lucknow. He was gravely injured when exposing himself to heavy fire at 50 yards to put out a fire.

1859 *Clown, Janus* and boats of *Niger* destroyed a village, 20 pirate junks, 11 fast boats and a 36-gun stockade in the neighbourhood of the Broadway Estuary. (Operations lasted for three days).

The Naval Prayer
O Eternal Lord God who alone spreadest out the heaven and rulest the raging of the seas; who hast compassed the waters with bounds until day and night come to an end; be pleased to receive into Thy almighty and most merciful protection, the persons of us Thy servants, and the fleet in which we serve. Preserve us from the dangers of the sea, and from the violence of the enemy, that we may be a safeguard to our Sovereign Lady Queen Elizabeth and her dominions, and a protection for such as pass on the seas upon their lawful occasions, that the inhabitants of our island may in peace and quietness serve Thee our God, and that we may return in safety to enjoy the blessings of the land with the fruits of our labours and with a thankful remembrance of all Thy mercies to praise and glorify Thy holy name.

Amen

13th MARCH

1869　*Druid* launched, last vessel built at Deptford Yard.

1884　Battle of Tamaai, Sudan. Naval Brigade from *Euryalus, Hecla, Briton, Carysfort, Dryad* and *Sphinx.* Egyptian Medal: clasp Tamaai.

1917　*Warner* (Q.27) sunk by U.61 in SW Approaches.

1940　*Maloja* intercepted the German *s.s. La Coruña,* which scuttled herself in the Iceland-Faeroes Channel.

1941　*Scarborough* intercepted two captured Norwegian whale catchers off Cape Finisterre, which were scuttled.

1944　*Prince Rupert,* Fortresses J/220 and R/206, Wellington B/172 and the USS *Haverfield, Hobson* and aircraft from USS *Bogue* sank U.575 in Atlantic.

1945　Amphibious assault on Letpan (E. of Ramree Island, Burma) Operation Turret. Covering force: *Eskimo, Roebuck, Cauvery, Jumna* (both RIN).

1945　U.260 abandoned after being mined off Galley Head, SW of Ireland.

"Hands to perform Divine Service", 1895

Recapture of the guns at Tamaai.

14th MARCH

1757   Admiral Byng executed onboard *Monarch* after being court martialled for dereliction of duty.

"On Monday, March 14th, 1757, all the men-of-war at Spithead were ordered to send their boats with the captains and all the officers of each ship, accompanied with a party of marines under arms, to attend the execution of Mr. Byng. Accordingly they rowed from Spithead, and made the harbour a little after 11 o'clock, with the utmost difficulty and danger, it blowing prodigiously hard at N.W. by N., and the tide of ebb against them. It was still more difficult to get up so high as the *Monarch* lay, on board which ship the admiral suffered. Norwithstanding it blew so hard and the sea ran very high, there was a prodigious number of other boats round the ship, on the outside of the ship's boats, which last kept all others off. Not a soul was suffered to be aboard the *Monarch*, except those belonging to the ship. Mr. Byng, accompanied by a clergyman who attended him during his confinement, and two gentlemen of his relations, about 12 came on the quarterdeck, when he threw his hat on the deck, kneeled on a cushion, tied a handkerchief over his eyes, and dropping another which he held in his hand as a signal, a volley from six marines was fired, five of whose bullets went through him, and he was no more. He died with great resolution and composure, not showing the least sign of timidity in the awful moment."

1779   *Rattlesnake* captured the French privateer *Frelon de Dunkerque* 12 miles to the North westward of Le Havre.

1795   Vice-Admiral William Hotham *(Britannia)* fought a French fleet of 15 sail of the line under Rear-Admiral Pierre Martin *(Sans Culotte)* 20 miles S.W. of Genoa. [m, bh]. Capture of the French *Ça-Ira* and *Censeur.* Ships: *Captain, Bedford, Tancredi, Neapolitan, Princess Royal, Agamemnon: Illustrious, Courageux, Britannia, Egmont, Windsor Castle; Diadem, St. George, Terrible, Fortitude.* Frigates, etc: *Fox(1), Inconstant, Lowestoffe, Meleager, Minerva*[1]*, Moselle, Palade*[1]*, Poulette, Romulus, Tarleton.* Regiments: 11th, 25th, 30th, 50th, 69th.

1808   *Childers* fought the Danish *Lougen* off Lindesness, Norway. [m]

1915   *Kent. Glasgow* and *Orama* found the German *Dresden,* the last survivor of the German Pacific squadron, at Juan Fernandez: she scuttled herself.

1921   New Zealand division of the RN formed.

*HM Submarine *Thunderbolt*, so renamed after sinking on trials before the war when named *Thetis*.

1942   P.34, later *Ultimatum,* sank the Italian s/m *Ammiraglio Millo* in Ionian Sea.

1943   *Moravia* sunk by mine off Orfordness.

1943*   *Thunderbolt* (ex-*Thetis*) sunk by the Italian corvette *Cicogna* off C. St. Vito.

1943   *Hadleigh Castle* fitted with first Squid A/S weapon. (See 12th March).

1945   *Natal* (SANF) sank U.714 off the Farnes.

HMS *Glasgow,* 1915.

1360   Winchelsea burnt by the French. Cinque ports ships captured thirteen of the enemy.

1793   Three gunboats, manned from *Syren*, at the defence of Willemstadt, Netherlands. [m]

1798   *Kingfisher* captured the French privateer *Lynx* 120 miles N.W. by W. of Oporto.

1842   Defeat of the Chinese on the heights of Segaon, near Mingpo. Steamers: *Sesostris* (I.N.), *Nemesis, Phlegethon, Queen* (Ben. Mar.). Boats of: *Blonde, Cornwallis.* Naval Brigade from: *Blonde, Columbine, Cornwallis, Hyacinth, Modeste.* Regiments: 18th, 26th and 49th; Madras Artillery, Madras Sappers and Miners, 36th Madras Native Infantry. China, 1841-2, Medal.

1915   *Blonde* attacked by German aircraft. First merchant ship to be so attacked.

1917   *Foyle* sunk by mine in Straits of Dover.

1918   *Michael* and *Moresby* sank U.110 in NW Approaches.

First midget submarine launched.

1918   D.3 accidentally sunk by French airship in Channel.

1942   *Vortigern* sunk by the German S.104 off Cromer. (Convoy FS.749.)

1942   *Dido, Euryalus* and 6 destroyers bombarded Rhodes. Operation M.F.8.

1943   First RN X-craft, midget s/m, launched.

1944   *Starling, Wild Goose* and Swordfish A/825 (*Vindex*) sank U.653 in Atlantic.

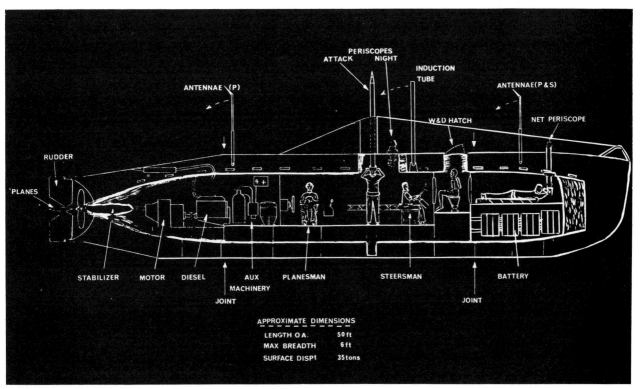

Diagram of midget submarine

16th MARCH

1757   *Greenwich* taken by the French *Brune, Diadème* and *Éveille* 30 miles off Cape Cabron, San Domingo.

1781   Vice-Admiral Arbuthnot *(Royal Oak)* beat the French squadron under Captain Sochet Des Touches *(Duc-de-Bourgogne)* 40 miles N.E. by E. of Cape Henry, Virginia thus regaining control of Chesapeake Bay.[bh]. Ships: *Robust, Europe, Prudent, Royal Oak, London, Adamant, Bedford, America.* Frigates: *Guadeloupe, Iris, Pearl.*

1782   *Success* and *Vernon* captured the Spanish *Santa Catalina* 50 miles W.S.W. of Cape Spartel.

1858   *Shannon's* Naval Brigade at the capture of Lucknow by the forces under General Sir Colin Campbell. [bh]. Naval Brigade manned all the breaching artillery on one side of the Gumti River. Indian Mutiny Medal: clasp 'Lucknow'.

1889   *Calliope* weathered a hurricane at Apia, Samoa in which three American and three German warships sank. She became the first drillship of Tyne Division RNVR in 1907 and wore the flag of Flag Officer, Tyne in World War II.

1917   *Achilles* and *Dundee* sank the German disguised raider *Leopard* 240 miles N. by E. of the Shetland Islands. [bh]. British War Medal: clasp 'Leopard 16 March 17' approved but not issued.

1940   *Iron Duke* and *Norfolk* damaged in German air raid on Scapa Flow.

1944   *Affleck, Vanoc* and three U.S. Catalina aircraft sank U.392 in Straits of Gibraltar.

Depth Charges exploding

HMS *Calliope*, **1889**

17th MARCH

A Ship's Carpenter: a Rowlandson print of 1799

1794 Boats of Vice-Admiral Sir John Jervis's fleet captured the French *Bienvenue* in Fort Royal harbour Martinique. (Abandoned temporarily — see 20th March), [m, bh]. Ships: *Asia, Assurance, Avenger, Beaulieu[1], Blonde, Boyne, Dromedary, Experiment, Irresistible, Nautilus, Quebec, Rattlesnake, Roebuck[1], Rose, Santa Margarita, Seaflower[1], Spiteful, Tormentor, Ulysses[1], Vengeance, Venom, Vesuvius, Winchelsea, Woolwich, Zebra.* [1] Awarded the medal, though not present on this day.

1796 *Aristocrat, Diamond* and *Liberty* destroyed the French *Étourdie*, seven other vessels and a battery at Port Erqui, North coast of France. [m]

1800 *Queen Charlotte* blew up at Leghorn.

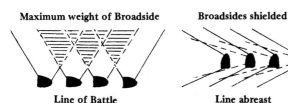

Maximum weight of Broadside	Broadsides shielded
Line of Battle	Line abreast

Battle tactics: The line of battle where a fleet sailing in line-ahead could keep both broadsides available.

1800 Mutineers handed *Danae* over to the French, having taken her into Brest on the 14th.

1804 *Loire* captured the French privateer *Brave* to the south westward of Cape Clear.

1814 *Ajax* captured the French *Alcyon* 90 miles to the southward of the Scilly Islands.

1858 Boats of *Calcutta* and *Starling* captured or destroyed five pirate junks in Deep Bay, and recaptured *Heather Bell* yacht.

1869 RM Fourth Division ("The Household") at Woolwich disbanded after Order in Council.

1912 Captain L.E.G. Oates, 5th Royal Iniskilling Dragoons, died in Antarctic, voluntarily walking into a blizzard in a a vain affort to improve the chances of Captain Scott's party surviving: "I am just going outside and I may be a little time".

1917 German destroyer raid in Dover Strait. Ships: *Laertes, Laforey, Llewellyn[1], Paragon[2]*. [1] Torpedoed and [2] sunk by the German S.49 and G.86.

1917 *Mignonette* sunk by mine 1½ miles S.31°E. of Galley Head, S.W. of Ireland.

1941 *Walker* sank U.99 and, with *Vanoc*, sank U.100 off Faeroes. (Convoy HX.112). First operational detection of U-Boat by radar.

1942 *Unbeaten* sank the Italian s/m *Guglielmotti* off Scilly.

1945 *Rapid, Saumarez* (D.26) and *Volage* bombarded Sigli, Sumatra.

1945 *Guysborough* (RCN) sunk by U.878 off Ushant.

1948 Brussels Treaty signed (Belgium, France, Luxembourg, Netherlands, and United Kingdom).

After the Second World War, the USSR moulded its 'area of influence' into a virtual empire. The Brussels Treaty was an attempt to restore the balance of power. However, the democracies of Western Europe were so weakened by the war, that the balance could only be restored by forming the wider, North Atlantic Alliance. This now secures the North Atlantic Area (including Europe) by the declaration that an attack on one of the partners is an attack upon them all.

18th MARCH

1799   *Tigre* captured six French gunvessels and recaptured *Torride* off Cape Carmet, Syria. [m]

1799   *Telegraph* captured the French *Hirondelle* 30 miles N.W. of Île de Bas, Brittany. [m]

1813   Boats of *Undaunted* cut out a French tartan and stormed a battery at Carry, near Marseilles.

1841   Destruction of the last forts in the approaches to Canton. Ships and vessels: *Algerine, Herald, Hyacinth, Louisa, Cutter, Modeste, Starling, Young Hebe.* Bengal Marine Steamers: *Madagascar, Nemesis.* Boats of *Blonde, Conway.* China , 1841-2, Medal.

1882   Launch of fourth *Edinburgh*, first RN ship to carry breech-loading gun and to have compound instead of iron armour. Last of the Victorian Citadel ships.

1904   Submarine A1 sunk in collision: salvaged.

1915   Repulse of allied naval attack on the Narrows, Dardanelles. Sunk: *Irresistible* and *Ocean;* French *Bouvet.* Damaged: *Inflexible.* All mined and fired on.

1915   Maiden flight of non-rigid naval airship SS (Submarine Scout) No.1 at Kingsnorth on Medway.

1915   *Dreadnought* rammed and sank U.29 in N Sea (58° 21'N., 1° 12'E).

1917   German destroyer raid on Ramsgate and Broadstairs. Vessels: T.B.4, *Redwald* and five other drifters.

1917   *Paragon* sunk in action with German destroyers off Dover.

1917   *Alyssum* sunk by mine 3 miles S.31° E. of Galley Head, S.W. of Ireland.

1917   *Duchess of Montrose* mined off Dunkirk.

1942   *Upholder* sank the Italian s/m *Tricheco* off Brindisi.

1945   *Lookout* and *Meteor* sank the German TA29 (ex-Italian *Eridano*) (43° 46'N. 9° 18'E.,) and TA24 (ex-Italian *Arturo*) (43° 49' N., 9° 24' E.,) off Spezia. A third enemy escaped.

The Forecastle HMS *Victorious*, 1895

19th MARCH

1725   Richard Howe born.

1759   *Aeolus* and *Isis* fought the French *Blonde; Aeolus* captured the French *Mignonne* off Yeu Island, France.

1779   *Arethusa* wrecked on Île Molène, near Ushant, after engaging the French *Aigrette.*

1813   Boats of *Apollo* and *Cerberus* destroyed four vessels, a battery and a tower three miles N.W. of Porto di Monopoli.

1857   Boats and landing party of *Hornet* destroyed 17 pirate junks at St. John Island, S.W. of Macao.

1943   GC: Chief Officer George Preston Stronach, MN for rescue work in S.S. *Ocean Voyager* at Tripoli.

1945   *Rapid, Saumarez* (D.26) and *Volage* bombarded Port Blair, Andaman Islands.

1949   Admiral of the Fleet Sir James Somerville died.

1977   RM rigid raiding craft from *Vigilant* captured 5 terrorists off Warrenpoint (Ireland). *Vigilant* engaged shore positions.

HMS *Vigilant* with Royal Marine rigid raiding craft off Irish Coast

20th MARCH

1707	*Resolution* attacked by six French ships and run ashore near Genoa. Burnt by her own people on the following day to avoid capture.
1780	*Lion* (Captain the Hon. William Cornwallis), *Bristol, Janus,* and *Kingston* and *Gayton* privateers fought the French *Annibal* (Commodore La Motte-Picquet), three others of the line and a frigate 25 miles to the northward of Monte Cristi, Haiti.
1794	Landing party from *Zebra* captured Fort Louis, Martinique. *Bienvenue* retaken. [m]
1796	*Pomone, Anson, Artois* and *Galatea* captured the French *Étoile* and four vessels of a convoy off Pointe du Raz, Brittany.
1805	*Renard* destroyed the French privateer *Général Ernouf* 100 miles N.E. of Cape Haitien. Enemy blew up.
1940	*Fortune* sank U.44 off Norway, SW of Narvik.
1941	*Malaya* torpedoed by U.106 in Mid-Atlantic. (Convoy SL.68)
1941	*Helvellyn* sunk by German aircraft in Thames.
1942	*Heythrop* sunk by *Edridge*, having been torpedoed by U.652 off Bardia.
1943	Sunderland T/201 sank U.384 in N Atlantic (54° 18'N 26° 15'W). (Convoy HX.229 and SC.122)
1944	*Graph* (ex-U.570) wrecked on the West coast of Islay: salvaged but scrapped 1947.
1944	*Stonehenge* sunk by unknown cause in Malacca Strait.
1945	*Lapwing* sunk by U.716 at the entrance to Kola Inlet (N Russia).
1945	*New Glasgow* (RCN) rammed and sank U.1003 in NW Approaches.
1945	Liberator B/86 sank U.905 off N of Scotland.
1953	First naval helicopter lift of troops into combat (RN Sikorskis in Malaya).

21st MARCH

1800	*Peterel* captured the French *Ligurienne* and two vessels of her convoy close off Cape Couronne, near Marseilles. [m, bh]
1807	Capture of Alexandria, Egypt. Ships: *Tigre; Apollo, Wizard.*
1813	Boats of *Brevdageren* and *Blazer* cut out the Danish *Liebe* and *Jonge Troutman* in the Elbe River. [m]
1855	*Bittern* destroyed eight pirate junks at Brig Island, near Swatow.
1862	The Royal Marines divided into two separate corps, Royal Marine Artillery (RMA) and Royal Marines Light Infantry (RMLI), until 1923.
1890	Formation of RM Depot Band.
1918	Destroyer action between Allied and German flotillas off Dunkirk. Ships: *Botha, Matchless, Morris, Myngs, North Star, Swift; General Craufurd, M.25, Terror; C.M.B.20A.* French: *Bouclier, Capitaine-Mehl, Magon, Oriflamme.* German sunk: A.7.
1940	*Ursula* sank the German *s.s. Heddernheim* 8 miles East of The Skaw.
1944	Sixteenth and last chaplain to be killed on active service in World War II: death in Arakan of the Rev. H.C.W. Mauger, RNVR, of 42 RM Commando.

Royal Marines of 40 Commando returning to HMS *Albion* in a Wessex Mk V after shore patrol in Sarawak, April 1963.

22nd MARCH

1794 Capture of Fort Bourbon and the whole of Martinique by General Sir Charles Grey and Vice-Admiral Sir John Jervis *(Boyne).* [bh] The Naval Brigade manned several of the breaching batteries on shore. Ships: see 17th March.

1797 Boats of *Hermione* cut out three French privateers and their twelve prizes from a bay at the West end of Puerto Rico.

1808 *Nassau* and *Stately* captured the Danish *Prinds Christian Frederik.* The prize went ashore immediately afterwards on Sjaellands Odde, Kattegat, and was burnt next day. [m]

1885 Action at Tofrek (McNeill's Zareba), Sudan. Naval Brigade from *Carysfort, Condor, Coquette, Dolphin* and *Sphinx.* Egyptian Medal: clasp 'Tofrek'.

A Zareba was an improvised but major entrenchment, fortified by thorn bushes. General Sir John McNeil VC constructed one as an intermediate supply post in the desert outside Suakin. The work was unfinished, and the troops were eating a meal when they were suddenly attacked by 5000 tribesmen, The British squares were at first overrun by stampeding animals and tribesmen, but in twenty minutes had reformed and killed 1000 tribesmen and 900 camels.

1911 Royal Fleet Auxiliary Service established by Order in Council.

The Royal Fleet Auxiliary Service, usually known as the RFA, is the branch of the RN Supply and Transport Service which provides a logistic support force for the Navy in the form of ships that carry and provide to the fleet at sea its requirements of fuel, food, ammunition and stores of all kinds; in addition it carries out other support tasks for the armed services. The ships are painted grey but they are not warships and are not manned by naval personnel. They fly the blue ensign defaced (an heraldic term not so offensive as it sounds) by a vertical gold anchor in the fly. Nearly all their officers and petty officers and a proportion of the ratings are career service personnel who remain with the RFA throughout their sea-going careers. The remainder are drawn from the Merchant Navy and all are on MN pay and conditions. RFAs normally form part of naval task groups and accompany the warships on their normal peacetime deployment and whenever emergencies occur. The RFA comprises 34 ships, half of which are tankers and the remainder stores support ships, store carriers, logistic landing ships and a helicopter training ship. There are: fleet tankers and freighting tankers. A fleet tanker can carry four or five different grades of oil required by warships and naval aircraft, and can issue them simultaneously. She can refuel up to three other ships at a time, one either side at a distance of between 80 and 150 feet with the third steaming astern.

1916 *Farnborough* (Q.5) sank U.68 off coast of Kerry.

1918 *Gaillardia* sunk by mine in Northern Barrage, off Orkney.

1942 Second Battle of Sirte (34° 10'N 18° 10'E). Rear-Admiral Philip Vian *(Cleopatra)* repulsed an attack by a superior Italian force on Convoy MW.10. [bh]. Ships: *Breconshire,*

A convoy sailed for Malta from Alexandria, with a heavy escort of four cruisers and ten destroyers, which was joined later by another cruiser and seven destroyers. Italian naval forces sailed from Taranto and Messina to intercept the convoy, which was also subject to heavy air attacks. On 22nd March at 1427 part of the enemy force was sighted. The four British light cruisers, together with the fleet destroyers, turned towards the enemy, leaving the convoy, which was under air attack, in the keeping of an AA cruiser and the smaller destroyers. The British force were to windward, and used smoke to cover the convoy and their approach to the Italian force, which included heavy cruisers. The enemy were driven off, but returned at 1640 having been reinforced by more ships, including a battleship. Once again, the light cruisers and fleet destroyers closed, and attacked with torpedoes and gunfire, using smoke and the weather gauge to close to effective range. Three British destroyers *(Havock, Kingston and Lively)* were hit by 15in shells but the enemy were held at bay and finally driven off. This was a brilliant victory by Admiral Vian, in command of the 15th Cruiser Squadron, which was marred only by the loss of half the convoy to air attack the next day as they neared Malta.

Carlisle, Cleopatra, Dido, Euryalus, Legion, Penelope. 5th D F : *Avon Vale, Beaufort, Dulverton, Eridge, Hurworth, Southwold.* 14th D F : *Jervis, Kelvin, Kingston, Kipling.* 22nd D F : *Hasty, Havock, Hero, Lively, Sikh, Zulu.*

1942 GC : Lieutenant Dennis Arthur Copperwheat, *Penelope*, for ammunition disposal in Valetta Harbour.

1943 *Aphis* bombarded Gabes in support of the 8th Army.

1943 Wellington G/172 sank the German U.665 in SW Approaches.

1945 Liberator M/120 sank U.296 in NW Approaches.

1946 *Dawson* (RCN) foundered off Hamilton, Ontario.

1950 Hansard, Column 1973 No 148 "The Royal Marine establishment being closed down at Chatham will be replaced by a naval establishment, HMS *Serious*, the training establishment of the Supply and Secretarial Branch . . ."

23rd MARCH

1742	Victualling yard on Tower Hill transferred to Deptford by Order in Council.
1757	Capture of Chandernagore by Vice-Admiral Charles Watson *(Kent)* and Colonel Robert Clive. Ships: *Kent, Tiger, Salisbury, Bridgwater.*
1791	*Pandora* arrived at Tahiti in search of *Bounty* mutineers.
1804	*Osprey* fought the Bordeaux privateer *Egyptienne* 200 miles East of Barbados.
1805	Boats of *Stork* cut out the Dutch privateer *Antilope* under Cape Roxo, Puerto Rico.
1806	Boats of *Colpoys* cut out three Spanish luggers at Aviles, North coast of Spain.
1815	*Penguin* taken by the American *Hornet* off Tristan da Cunha.
1830	RNH Bighi, Malta founded.
1859	Boats of *Heron, Spitfire, Trident* and *Vesuvius,* a Colonial gunboat, and the 1st West India Regiment captured Kambia, Great Scarcies River, Sierra Leone.
1917	*Laforey* mined in Channel.
1918	*Arno* lost in collision off Dardanelles.
1922	*Versatile* accidentally rammed and sank H.42 off Europa Point.
1941	*Visenda* sank U.551 in NE Atlantic.
1941	*Shoreham* intercepted the German *s.s. Oder* near Perim, Red Sea: *Oder* scuttled herself.

*Admiral Edward Vernon (1684 - 1775)

Having joined the Navy in 1701 Vernon received a special award of 200 guineas from the Queen in 1704 for conspicuous gallantry at Gibraltar. He became a Member of Parliament and an opponent of Walpole. He had a fiery temper and was tempted by Walpole to make a statement that he could take Portobello in Panama with 6 ships of the line. This unfortunate challenge was taken up by the government and he was given his 6 ships, although hopelessly ill-equipped and ill-manned. By brilliant planning he captured Portobello losing only 7 men doing it. The government reinforced him and sent him to attack Spanish strongholds in the West Indies. These expeditions were not a success. Vernon's nickname was "Old Grogram" because of the material of which his boat cloak was made. He insisted on the rum ration being diluted and henceforth watered down rum was known as 'grog'. See 21st August.

24th MARCH

1387	The Earl of Arundel captured nearly the whole of a Franco-Burgundian merchant fleet.
1740*	Bombardment and capture of Chagres by Vice-Admiral Edward Vernon *(Strafford).* Ships: *Alderney, Falmouth, Norwich, Princess Louisa, Strafford; Goodley* and *Pompey* tenders *(? Greenwich* and *Windsor).* Bombs: *Cumberland, Terrible.* Fireships: *Eleanor, Success.*

Edward Vernon

1804	*Wolverine* taken by the French privateer *Blonde* 600 miles N. by E. of the Azores. (Of the *Wolverine's* convoy, two were taken and six escaped.)
1878	*Eurydice* (training ship) lost in storm off Ventnor. 330 trainees lost: two survivors.
1916	E.24 mined in Heligoland Bight.
1942	*Southwold* sunk by mine off Malta.
1942	*Sharpshooter* sank U.655 off N Cape (73° 00'N., 21° 00'E.). (Convoy QP.9)

76

25th MARCH

1675   *Mary*, first Royal Yacht, wrecked off Skerries.

1797   *Suffisante* captured the French privateer *Bonaparte* 30 miles S.S.W. of Start Point.

1800   *Cruizer* captured the French privateer *Flibustier* to the eastward of Smiths Knoll, North Sea.

1804   *Penguin* destroyed the French privateer *Renommée* at Senegal. (Driven ashore on the 17th).

1806   *Reindeer* fought the French *Phaeton* and *Voltigeur* to the south-eastward of San Domingo.

1855   Boats of *Hornet*, *Spartan*, *Sybille* and *Winchester* destroyed nine pirate junks in Port Shelter, near Hong Kong.

1915   The Dutch *Medea* sunk by U.28 after visit and search. First neutral ship to be so sunk.

1916   *Cleopatra* rammed and sank the German G.194, 55 miles West of Horns Reef lightvessel.

1916   *Medusa* foundered after collision off Danish Coast.

1943   Fortress L/206 sank U.469 S of Iceland.

1944   Mosquito I/248 and L/248 sank U.976 off Bordeaux.

*Operation Iceberg — British Pacific Fleet

In March 1945 the British Pacific Fleet was employed on attacks on Sakishima Gunto, an operation which did much to restore the position of the Royal Navy in the Pacific. The carrier force flew 5,335 sorties, dropping almost 1,000 tons of bombs and firing 1,000 rockets. Half a million rounds of ammunition were fired and 57 enemy aircraft were destroyed in combat. The same number were destroyed on the ground.

26th MARCH

1806   *Pique* captured the French *Phaeton* and *Voltigeur* 10 miles S.W. by S. of Saona Island, San Domingo. [m]

1814   *Hannibal* captured the French *Sultane* 30 miles S.S.E. of Lizard Head.

1857   Capture of Khorramshahr, Persia. Ships and vessels: *Ferooz, Semiramis, Ajdaha, Assage, Victoria, Falkland, Berenice, Clive, Comet.* (All Indian Navy). With the exception of a few Bombay Artillery, "the gentlemen in blue had it all to themselves, and left us naught to do". (Private letter of Brigadier-General Henry Havelock).

1875   William Wordsworth Fisher born.

1898   Capture of Shendi, River Nile. Gunboats: *Fateh, Nasr, Zafir.*

1917   *Myrmidon* lost in collision with SS *Hamborn* in Channel.

1918   P.51 sank U.61 in Bristol Channel. (51° 48' N., 5° 52' W.)

1941   *York* torpedoed by Italian explosive motor-boat in Suda Bay, Crete.

1942   *Jaguar* sunk by U.625 N of Sollum whilst escorting the *Slavol*, oiler, to Tobruk. *Slavol* sunk later by U.205.

1942   *Legion* and P.39 sunk by German aircraft at Malta. *Penelope* damaged.

1945   *Duckworth* sank U.399 off Land's End. (49° 56'N., 5° 22'W.)

1945*   Aircraft of Task Force 57, under Vice-Admiral Sir Bernard Rawlings *(King George V)*, attacked the airfields on Myako and Ishigaki Islands (Sakishima group). Operation Iceberg. [bh]. Carriers: *Illustrious*[1], *Indefatigable*[2], *Indomitable*[3], *Victorious*[4]. Ships: *Howe, King George V; Argonaut, Black Prince, Euryalus, Gambia, Swiftsure.* Destroyers: 11 and 3 with Fleet train. FAA Sq.: Avenger 820[2]; 849[4], 854[1], 857[3], Corsair 1830[1], 1833[1], 1834[4], 1836[4]. Firefly 1770[2]. Hellcat 1839[3], 1844[3]. Seafire 887[2], 894[2].

1964   Last meeting of Board of Admiralty.

Firefly aircraft on board a carrier.

1680	*Adventure* engaged the Algerine *Citron Tree* wrecked later off Arzila, Morocco.	1943	*Dasher* sunk by internal explosion five miles South of Cumbrae Island, Firth of Clyde.

1680   *Adventure* engaged the Algerine *Citron Tree* wrecked later off Arzila, Morocco.

1759   *Windsor* engaged four French East Indiamen, capturing *Duc de Chartres* 200 miles W.N.W. of Cape Finisterre.

1759   *Southampton* and *Melampe* captured the French *Danae* off Westkapelle. *Harmonie* engaged, but escaped.

1804   *Hippomenes* captured the Bordeaux privateer *Egyptienne* 180 miles to the eastward of Barbados.

1811   Royal Marines at Anholt beat off a Danish attack on the island which was commissioned as one of HM ships. [m]. Ships: *Tartar, Sheldrake, Anholt*. *Sheldrake* only awarded the medal.

1812   *Rosario* and *Griffon* defeated twelve French brigs of the 14th Division of the Boulogne Flotilla off Dieppe, capturing two and driving two others on shore. [m]

1814   *Hebrus* captured the French *Étoile* off the Nez de Jobourg. [m*, m, bh]

1918   *Kale* mined in N Sea.

1942   *Aldenham, Grove, Leamington* and *Volunteer* sank U.587 SW of Ireland (47° 21'N., 21° 39'W). (Convoy WS.17)

1943   *Dasher* sunk by internal explosion five miles South of Cumbrae Island, Firth of Clyde.

1943   Fortress L/206 sank U.169 in N Atlantic (60° 54'N., 15° 25'W).

1943   *Laforey* and *Blyskawica* (Pol) carried out a feint landing and bombardment near Cape Serrat.

1945   *Conn* sank U.965 off Hebrides (58° 34'N., 5° 46'W.).

1942 Russian Convoy PQ13

A gale scattered this convoy as it was bound for Russia. By 27th March not one merchant ship was in sight of the escort. Enemy aircraft sighted and on 28th sank two merchant ships. Three German destroyers sailed from Kirkenes to attack and early on 29th they caught a Panamanian freighter. From her crew they learned where the rest of the convoy might be, and altered their sweep. Just before 0900 they came across the cruiser *Trinidad* and the destroyers *Fury* and *Eclipse*. There was a sharp action in low visibility, snow and freezing spray. One German destroyer was sunk, but *Trinidad* was hit by a torpedo. After she had reached the Kola Inlet on 30th, it was found that it was one of her own torpedoes that had circled back at her. The *Eclipse* was also badly hit, but the *Fury* managed to sink U.585. This was the first Russian convoy to suffer large casualties (5 out of 19 merchantmen).

The *Trinidad* sailed for UK on 13th May, and suffered heavy air attack. Late on 14th she was hit by a bomb and was flooded by near misses blowing off repair patches. Despite a 14 degree list she continued at 20 knots and manoeuvred to avoid torpedoes. At 0120 the next morning she was abandoned, and sunk by British forces.

RFA Fleet Tanker *Blue Rover* **refuelling (left), HMS** *Triumph* **and (right) HMS** *Minerva.*

1760   *Penguin* taken by the French *Malicieuse* and *Opale* near the Isles Cies, at the entrance to Vigo Bay.

1779   *Kite* fought a French frigate off Portland.

1795   *Cerberus* and *Santa Margarita* captured the French *Jean-Bart* off Brest.

1806   *Niobe* captured the French *Nearque* off Lorient.

1814   *Phoebe* and *Cherub* captured the American *Essex* and *Essex Junior* off Valparaiso. [m, bh]

1860   VC: Leading Seaman William Odgers, *(Niger)*. First to enter the pah and haul down enemy's colours at Omata. New Zealand, 1860-6, Medal.

1868   ERAs established.

1903   Engineers given military rank, but not status.

1915   *Falaba* sunk by U.28, 38 miles West of the Smalls lighthouse.

1940   *Transylvania* intercepted *Mimi Horn* in Denmark Strait: latter scuttled herself.

1941*   Battle of Cape Matapan (35° 25' N., 21° E.). Admiral Sir Andrew Cunningham *(Warspite)* beat the Italian fleet under Admiral Angelo Iachino *(Vittorio Veneto)*. [bh]. Ships: *Ajax Barham, Formidable, Gloucester, Orion, Perth, Valiant, Warspite.* 2nd D.F.: *Hasty, Hereward, Ilex, Vendetta.* 10th D.F.: *Greyhound, Griffin, Havock, Hotspur, Stuart, Defender.* 14th D.F.: *Janus, Jervis, Mohawk, Nubian, Jaguar, Juno.* FAA Sq.: 700 (ships) Swordfish, Walrus. 803, 806; 826; 829 (carrier). (Fulmar, Albacore and Swordfish). 815 (Maleme). (Swordfish). RAF Sq.: 84, 113, 211 and 201 Group (flying-boats). Sunk: *Fiume, Pola, Zara* (cruisers); *Vittorio Alfieri, Giosue Carducci* (destroyers).

*Battle of Matapan

British convoys were being run to support fighting in Greece. The C-in-C received warning of sorties by the Italian fleet against them. He cleared the area of convoys, and sent 4 cruisers and 3 destroyers to be off Gavdo Island by first light 28th March. At noon on 27th, an RAF reconnaisance aircraft sighted 3 enemy cruisers 320 miles West of Crete. That evening the British main force of 3 battleships, an aircraft carrier and 9 destroyers sailed. The original force of cruisers and destroyers under Vice-Admiral Light Forces (VALF) was ordered to join them. At dawn on 28th, air searches revealed the enemy force near VALF's force. Shortly afterwards, VALF sighted them, as well as another enemy force, which included a battleship, to the North. At 1230 the two British forces joined in pursuit of the enemy, whose forces were all proceeding Westward at speed. Air strikes were unsuccessful until 1530 when a torpedo hit slowed the enemy battleship *(Vittorio Veneto)*. A further strike brought the cruiser *Pola* to a standstill. There were a total of 9 air strikes from RAF and FAA aircraft (shore and sea based) and these 2 hits were the only successes.

continued on next page

HMS Warspite

28th MARCH

At 1830 the Italian Admiral detached the cruisers *Zara* and *Fiume* with destroyers to escort the *Pola*, believing the British to be further East. VALF had been detached to chase the main force and passed the *Pola* at 2100, leaving her to the slower battle fleet. It was a dark and cloudy night, with visibility 2½ miles. At 2200 *Valiant* detected *Pola* on radar, and the battle fleet closed. At 2220 the battle fleet detected the returning Italian force, and opened fire at 3000 yards range, sinking the *Zara* and *Fiume*. The destroyers *Stuart* and *Havock* sank 2 Italian destroyers and the *Jervis* and *Nubian* sank the *Pola* after taking off many of the ship's company.

Contact with the enemy's Main Force was not regained, and the convoys were restarted. The Italians lost 3 cruisers and 2 destroyers with one battleship damaged; the British lost one aircraft. The action took place 100 miles SW of Cape Matapan.

1942*   VC: Commander Rupert Edward Dudley Ryder (MGB314). Lieutenant-Commander Stephen Halden Beattie *(Campbeltown)* Able Seaman William Alfred Savage, (MGB314). Lieut-Colonel Augustus Charles Newman (Essex Regiment). Sergt. Thomas Frank Durrant, RE (ML306). (Posthumous). Attack on St.Nazaire by Light Forces under Commander R.E.D. Ryder (MGB314) and Commandos under Lieut-Colonel A.C. Newman. Destruction of lock gates of the Normandie dock. Operation Chariot. [bh]. Ships: *Atherstone, Campbeltown*[1], *Tynedale.* MGB314[4] MTB 74[2]. ML: 156[4], 160, 177[2], 192[2], 262[2], 267[2], 268[2], 270[4], 298[2], 306[3], 307, 341[5], 443, 446[4], 447[2], 457[2], RAF.: Aircraft from No 19 Group. [1] Blockship; expended. [2] Sunk in action. [3] Captured [4] Sunk by own forces. [5] Broke down: did not take part.

Admiral Sir Andrew Cunningham (1883 –1963)

Cunningham was a highly successful and popular senior naval officer in the Second World War. As CinC of the Mediterranean fleet, he was faced with overwhelming enemy forces when France surrendered to the Germans and Italy entered the war. He succeeded in persuading the French at Alexandria to immobilise their ships. He then won decisive victories over numerically superior Italian forces, and by his offensive use of sea power he kept Malta supplied and available as a base against Axis sea lanes to North Africa. He made the short sea passage from Greece and Italy to North Africa impassable to Axis merchant shipping, and thereby prevented Rommel from receiving the supplies he needed to complete his North African victories. In September 1943 he received the surrender of the Italian fleet at Malta. When the First Sea Lord, Admiral of the Fleet Sir Dudley Pound died, in October 1943, Cunningham succeeded him for the remainder of the war. He died in 1963, with the title Admiral of the Fleet Viscount Cunningham of Hyndhope.

1943   Hudsons L/48, V/48 and L/233 attacked U.77 in W Mediterranean (37° 42'N., 0° 10'E). (she sank on the 29th).

1943   *Breconshire* sunk by air attack at Malta.

1944   *Syrtis* sunk by mine off Bodo, Norway.

1945   *Byron, Fitzroy* and *Redmill* sank U.722 off Hebrides (57° 09'N., 6° 55'W.).

*   St Nazaire had the only dock on the Atlantic seaboard in German hands where the battleship *Tirpitz* could be docked. It was 1148 feet by 164 feet and had been built for the liner *Normandie*. A surprise attack was mounted to damage this dock in case the Germans should decide to use *Tirpitz* on commerce raiding as they had with the *Bismarck*. An ex-USN destroyer, the *Campbeltown*, was modified to cross shallow sandbanks and to ram the dock caissison. She was escorted by an MGB, an MTB, (in case the *Campbeltown* failed to make the caisson) and 16 MLs with Commandos. A U-boat was attacked on passage, and the force temporarily altered course to the South West. The U-boat reported the force, and torpedo boats were sent to investigate; this reduced the opposition met when the force reached St Nazaire that night. The RAF raid to divert the enemy's attention had only alerted them, as low cloud made their bombing inaccurate. The force, however, crossed 400 miles of open sea, and were 3 miles up the estuary before the alarm was given, and a false identity signal allowed them more time for their last 2 miles before the enemy opened fire. *Campbeltown* rammed the lock gate at 0134 and the Commandos were landed. At 0250 the force withdrew to seaward and were met by the returning German torpedo boats. Only 4 MLs reached home safely. The explosives in the *Campbeltown* went up late, just as a large party of German Officers had boarded her. By contrast to Zeebrugge in the first World War, the objectives at St Nazaire were achieved. A working model of the raid can be seen at the Imperial War Museum, London.

80

29th MARCH

1681 *Adventure* and *Calabash* engaged the Algerine *Golden Horse* 25 miles S.W. of Cape de Gata, South coast of Spain: she surrendered to *Nonsuch*. [bh]

1745 *Anglesea* taken by the French *Apollon* off Kinsale.

1779 *Kite* fought a French 20-gun privateer 30 miles S.W. of Needles Point.

1797 *Kingfisher* captured the French privateer *Général* 40 miles W.S.W. of Oporto.

1843 Two boats of *Nimrod* with *Assyria* (Hon. East India Co. steamer), in the Indus River during the conquest of Sind.

1883 Completion of *Agamemnon*, (third of the name) and, next day, of the fifth *Ajax*, last battleships to be armed with rifled muzzle-loading guns and first to have a specific secondary armament.

1942 German attack on Convoy PQ.13: *Trinidad* and *Eclipse* sank the German Z.26 off Murmansk (72° 15' N., 34° 22'E). *Fury* sank U.585 in Arctic, NE of Vardo.

1943 *Unrivalled* sank the German UJ.2201 and 2204 at Palermo.

1944 *Starling* sank U.961 E.S.E. of Faeroes (64° 31'N., 3° 19'W). (Convoy JW.58)

1945 *Duckworth* sank U.246 in Channel (49° 58'N., 5° 25'W.).

1945 Liberator O/224 sank U.1106 off Shetlands (61° 46'N., 2° 16'W.).

1945 *Teme* torpedoed by U.246 off Falmouth; CTL.

The transition from sail to steam: HMS *Alexandra* at Malta, c1880

30th MARCH

1798   *Cambrian* captured the French privateer *Pont-de-Lodi* 400 miles S.W. of the Scilly Islands.

1800   *Foudroyant, Lion, Penelope* and *Vincejo* captured the French *Guillaume Tell*. Action begun by *Penelope* and *Vincejo* just outside Valetta harbour, Malta, and ended 20 miles S.½ W. of Cape Passero, Sicily. [m, bh]. Only *Penelope* and *Vincejo* were awarded the medal.

1811   *Arrow* engaged the battery at St. Nicholas, to the northward of Île-de Ré, and captured the French chasse-marees *Frederick* and *Paix Desirée*. [m]

1837   Original Royal Naval College, Portsmouth, closed.

1912   Captain Scott and the remainder of his party died in the Antarctic. (See 17th February and 17th March). "It seems a pity but I do not think I can write more". "For God's sake, look after our people."

1943   *Glasgow* intercepted the German blockade runner *Regensburg,* from Rangoon, which scuttled herself in N Atlantic.

1944   *Blencathra, Hambledon, Laforey* and *Tumult* sank U.223 off Sicily, *Laforey* being sunk by the U-boat.

1945   *Conn, Rupert* and *Deane* sank U.1021 off Point of Stoer, Hebrides (58° 19'N., 5° 31'W.).

1959   HM Dockyard Malta passed into civilian hands.

1971   First Fleet Chief Petty Officers appointed, by warrant.

31st MARCH

1804   Boats of *Beaver* and *Scorpion* cut out the Dutch *Athalante* in Vlie Road, Netherlands. [m, bh]

1813   Boats of *Redwing, Undaunted* and *Volontaire* captured 11 and destroyed 3 sail of a French convoy at Morgiou, between Marseilles and Toulon, and also destroyed 2 batteries.

1823   Boats of *Thracian* and *Tyne* cut out the pirate *Zaragozana* in Puerto de Mata, Cuba.

1941   *Bonaventure* sunk by the Italian s/m *Ambra* off Crete. (Convoy GA.8)

1941   *Rorqual* sank the Italian s/m *Pier Capponi* in the Mediterranean, S of Stromboli.

1942   Allied shipping losses in March reached ½ million tons, mostly from U-boat attack.

1951   RNR, RNVR and other reserves granted straight stripes with, for a short time, distinguishing buttons.

1961   Closure of the Nore Command.

1964   Her Majesty assumed the title of Lord High Admiral of the United Kingdom, when the Board of Admiralty became the Admiralty Board of the new Defence Council.

1979   Final withdrawal of RN from Malta completed by midnight; F O Malta sailed in *London* a.m. 1st April.

The Lord High Admiral inspects Her Royal Marines

1st APRIL

1761   *Isis* captured the French *Oriflamme* off Cape Tres Forcas.

1779   *Delight* captured the French privateer *Jean Bart* off Dunnose.

1857   Boats of *Auckland* (IN) captured a mandarin junk and stormed a battery in Tung chung Bay, near Hong Kong.

1857   Occupation of Ahwaz, Persia, by an Indian Navy flotilla and detachments of the 64th Regiment and 78th Highlanders. Vessels (IN): *Assyria, Comet, Planet,* Gunboats Nos. 5, 6 and 9, and boats of *Assaye, Falkland* and *Ferooz.*

1885   Naval Nursing Service formed: became QARNNS in 1902.

1892   Royal Naval Artillery Volunteers disbanded.

1916   East coast of England attacked by German airships. L.15, first Zeppelin brought down by shore gunfire, landed in the Thames Estuary and surrendered to *Olivine.*

1916   U.37 sunk .

1918   *Falcon* lost in collision in N Sea.

1918   RFC and RNAS amalgamated as the RAF.

1923   Naval responsibility for H.M. Coastguard, accepted in 1856, transferred to Board of Trade.

1924   *Caroline* became drillship of Ulster Division, RNVR: last survivor of Jutland.

1924   Shipborne element of RAF recognised as Fleet Air Arm.

1941   Swordfish of 824 Sq. disembarked from *Eagle,* wrecked the Italian destroyer *Leone* off Massawa.

1942   *Pandora* and P.36 sunk by aircraft at Malta.

1942   *Urge* sank the Italian cruiser *Giovanni delle Bande Nere* in the Mediterranean.

1944   *Beagle* and Avenger H/846 *(Tracker)* sank U.355 off N Norway. (Convoy JW.58)

1945   *Indefatigable* (Task Force 57) damaged by Japanese Kamikaze air strikes on Myako and Ishigaki Islands (Operations continued on the 2nd and 6th).

1958   RN Supply School, *Ceres,* moved from Wetherby to Chatham (*Pembroke*).

HMS *Formidable* after Kamikaze attacks

83

2nd APRIL

1801 First Battle of Copenhagen. [m, bh]. Vice-Admiral Lord Nelson's attack on the Danish hulks and batteries. *Holsteen* captured, 12 hulks burnt. Ships and vessels: *Arrow, Dart, Otter, Alcmene, Zephyr, Blanche, Amazon, Defiance, Monarch, Ganges, Elephant, Glatton, Arden, Edgar, Bellona, Isis, Russell, Polyphemus, Desiree, Harpy, Cruizer, Agamemnon, Jamaica, Discovery, Explosion, Hecla, Sulphur, Terror, Volcano, Zebra.* Ships in support: *Defence, London, Raisonnable, Ramillies, St. George, Saturn, Veteran, Warrior.* Troops: Royal Artillery (bomb vessels). The 49th Foot, the Hertfordshire Regiment (now the Duke of Edinburgh's Royal Regiment) and one company of the Corps of Riflemen (now the Royal Greenjackets) were awarded a naval crown, superscribed "2nd April 1801, Copenhagen", on their colours.

In 1800, at Napoleon's instigation, the Baltic states of Russia, Sweden and Denmark revived their Armed Neutrality to resist the activities of the British fleet interrupting trade with the continent. After a number of minor incidents the Tsar of Russia confiscated all British ships and properties within his dominions. On the 12th March 1801 Admiral Sir Hyde Parker with Vice-Admiral Nelson as his second in command sailed for Denmark. The Danes continued with acts close to war and Nelson therefore forcefully persuaded Parker that an attack on Copenhagen should be undertaken. Copenhagen had been prepared for an attack and was heavily fortified with shore batteries, forts, moored ships and floating batteries. Parker finally agreed to allow Nelson 12 ships of the line for the close attack, while he himself stood away in deep water to the north. During the approach to Copenhagen 3 of Nelson's ships were grounded and as a consequence only 5 frigates were available to take on the mighty Trekroner Fort. At 1.30 pm when the action had been going on for 3 hours Parker, who could only see the frigates being worsted by the Trekroner Battery hoisted the signal to discontinue the engagement. The frigates seeing the signal withdrew and Captain Riou of the *Amazon* was killed exclaiming "Whatever will Nelson think of us?". Nelson in great agitation said "Leave off the action! . . . now damn me if I do . . . you know, Foley, I have only one eye. I have a right to be blind sometimes and I really do not see the signal!", placing his telescope to his blind eye.

Shortly afterwards the fire from shore slackened and Nelson offered a truce to the Danes. Denmark eventually agreed to suspend her participation in the confederation.

A view of the Battle of Copenhagen from astern of the line of attack (see plan opposite)

2nd APRIL

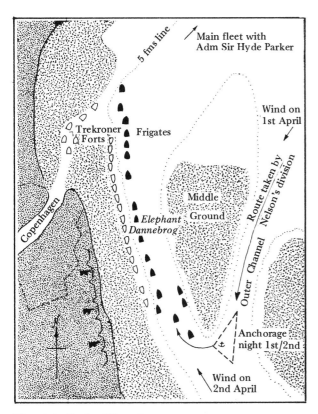

Plan of the Battle of Copenhagen

1809   Boats of *Mercury* cut out the French *Leda* in Porto di Rovigno, Istria.

1825   Capture of Donaby, Burma by Brigadier-General Sir Archibald Cameron and the Irrawaddy Flotilla under Captain Thomas Alexander *(Alligator).*

1879*   Major-General Lord Chelmsford's column defeated the Zulus at Gingindlovu. Naval brigade from *Boadicea, Shah* and *Tenedos.*

1889   Cordite patented for British Service.

1943   *Black Swan* and *Stonecrop* sank U.124 off Oporto (41° 02' N., 15° 39' W.).(Convoy OS.45)

1944   *Keppel* sank U.360 in N Norwegian sea (73° 28' N., 13° 04' E). (Convoy JW.58)

1945   VC: Corporal Thomas Peck Hunter, RM killed in action at the battle of Commachio, Italy. 2nd April is the Memorable Date of 43 Commando RM.

Naval Brigades

Naval Brigades were a familiar feature of the Victorian colonial wars. Britain's possessions were too numerous and too scattered for her to maintain garrisons in each and so, at the first sign of rebellion, Royal Naval ships were diverted to the troublespots. The mere presence of the White Ensign was often sufficient to stop the fighting but usually parties of seamen and Royal Marines were landed to deal with the trouble or to keep it in check until a proper expedition could be organised. Some Victorian bluejackets saw more action ashore in the brigades than at sea in their ships.

The seamen seemed to be capable of almost any task which was required of them. Eyewitnesses constantly paid tribute to their willingness and adaptability and these qualities soon became legendary. Jack could dig trenches; march across Indian deserts or through African swamps; man-handle guns over very difficult terrain; man rocket batteries; "board" an enemy fort; ferry a full-scale expedition up the cataracts of the Nile and even run an armoured train in Egypt. To the Victorians, he was known simply as "The Handyman."

However, the sailors' most constant contribution to the wars, was their effect on morale. Their cheerfulness was infectious and they amused successive generations of soldiers by their refusal to abandon their nautical habits. In the Crimea, they raised the spirits of the besieging army during the terrible winter of 1854; in Abyssinia, in 1867-8, they organised dances with the Sikhs of the Punjab Volunteers, with whom they were great friends and in the Punjab in 1848, a Brigadier reported that the sailors ". . . looked upon their batteries as ships, their 18 pounders as so many sweethearts and the embrasures as portholes . . ."

The days of colonial wars have gone, but this gift for amphibious warfare remains as strong a part of the tradition of the Royal Navy as ever.

*Naval Brigade from HMS *Shah* at Gingindlovu

3rd APRIL

1680   *Hampshire* engaged four Algerine men-of-war off Tarifa, capturing one — *Calabash*. The prize crew were put on board in *Adventure's* boat.

1762   *Hussar* captured two French privateers and destroyed two others under Fort Tiburon, Haiti.

1801   Boats of *Trent* cut out two French vessels off Brehat, in Gulf of St. Malo.

1813   Boats of *St. Domingo, Marlborough, Maidstone, Statira, Fantome* and *Mohawk* cut out four American privateers in the Rappahannock River, Virginia.

1847   A combined force, under Major-General George Charles D'Aguilar and Captain John McDougall *(Vulture)*, spiked the guns of the forts in the Canton River and appeared before Canton to enforce British terms. Ships: *Vulture, Espiegle, Pluto* (Ben. Mar.), *Corsair* (hired). Troops: Royal Artillery, Royal Sappers and Miners, 18th Regiment, 42nd Madras Native Infantry.

1862   A party from *Centaur* (in *Vivid* lorcha) destroyed a pirate lorcha off Friendly Island (Nilo shan), near Ningpo.

1915   Dover Strait mine barrage completed.

1917   *Jason* sunk by mine off Coll Island.

1917   Arthur Lucius Michael Cary born.

1917   VC: Major Frederick William Lumsden, CB, DSO and three bars, RMA — shore service with the Army.

1918   Seven British submarines destroyed at Helsingfors to avoid capture: E.1, E.8, E.9, E.19, C.26, C.27, C.35.

A Barracuda torpedo bomber

1941   *Worcestershire* torpedoed by U.74 in Atlantic (58° 16' N., 27° 22' W.).(Convoy SC.26)

*1941   Swordfish aircraft of 813 and 824 Sq. (disembarked from *Eagle*) attacked four Italian destroyers, sinking *Nazario Sauro* and *Danieli Manin* off Port Sudan. Wellesley aircraft (RAF) attacked the other two, *Pantera* and *Tigre*, at Jeddah, where they scuttled themselves after one of them was torpedoed by *Kingston*.

1944   Aircraft from *Tracker* (Avenger G/846, Wildcat Y/846) and *Activity* (Swordfish C/819) sank U.288 in the Barents Sea (73° 44' N., 27° 12' E). (Convoy JW.58)

1944   FAA attacked the German battleship *Tirpitz* in Altenfjord. Operation Tungsten. Carriers: *Emperor, Fencer, Furious, Pursuer, Searcher, Victorious.* F A A Sq.: 800, 804 (Hellcat), 842 (Wildcat and Swordfish). 827, 830 (Barracuda); 801, 880 (Seafire). 881, 896 (Wildcat). 882, 898 (Wildcat). 829, 831 (Barracuda); 1834, 1836 (Corsair), Ships: *Anson, Belfast, Jamaica, Meteor, Milne, Onslaught, Royalist, Sheffield, Undaunted, Ursa, Verulam, Vigilant, Virago, Wakeful* and *Algonquin* and *Sioux* (RCN).

1945   Liberator U/224 sank U.1276 off Shetland Islands (61° 42' N., 0° 24' W.).

Fleet Air Arm Attack on the Tirpitz
The Admiralty had assessed that damage to the *Tirpitz* caused by the X-craft attack in September 1943 had probably been repaired. It was therefore planned to use two strikes each of 21 Barracudas protected by 40 fighters to attack the *Tirpitz*, which was a threat to the Northern convoys. A force led by the battleship *Anson,* comprising the carriers *Victorious, Furious, Emperor, Searcher, Pursuer* and *Fencer* with a screen of 4 cruisers and 14 destroyers sailed. A part of the Home Fleet covered this force and convoy JW58. Because the convoy escort seemed to be coping with enemy attacks, and the weather was good, the CinC decided to advance the operation by 24 hours. This proved fortunate as, when the first attack took place at 0529 on 3rd, the *Tirpitz* was weighing anchor for sea trials. The enemy was caught unawares, and AA fire did not start until the first attack had begun. The second attack took place an hour later, and the enemy were alert and had started a smoke screen. Each attack lost only one bomber, and one fighter was lost. 4 hits were obtained with 1600 lb bombs and 10 with 500 lb bombs causing 438 casualties and putting *Tirpitz* out of action for another 3 months. Unfortunately the FAA attacks were pressed home with such determination that the bombs were dropped too low to pierce the enemy's armour and inflict greater damage.

4th APRIL

1655 Admiral Robert Blake *(George)* destroyed the forts and nine Algerine warships at Porto Farina, Tunisia. [bh] Ships: *Newcastle, Kent, Foresight, Amity, Princess Maria, Pearl, Mermaid, Merlin, Andrew, Plymouth, George, Worcester, Unicorn, Bridgwater,· Success.*

1680 *Adventure* drove ashore and wrecked the Algerine *Orange Tree* near Cape Spartel, Morocco.

1759 *Achilles* captured the French privateer *Comte de St. Florentine* 180 miles to the westward of Cape Finisterre.

1760 *Bideford* and *Flamborough* fought the French *Malicieuse* and *Opale* 100 miles N.N.W. of Cape Roxent (da Roca), Portugal.

1806 *Renommée* captured the Spanish *Vigilante* under Fort Corralete, close to Cape de Gata, South coast of Spain.

1808 *Alceste, Grasshopper* and *Mercury* defeated twenty Spanish gunboats and captured seven of their convoy off Rota, near Cadiz. [m]

1812 Boats of *Maidstone* captured the French privateer *Martinet* 30 miles S. by E. of Cape de Gata. [m]

1854 Landing parties of *Encounter, Grecian* and the USS *Plymouth* defeated Chinese Imperial troops at Shanghai.

1918 *Bittern* lost in collission with s.s *Kenilworth* off Portland Bill.

1928 Court-martial of Captain K. G. B. Dewar, *Royal Oak*.

1941 *Voltaire* sunk by the German merchant raider *Thor* (Schiff 10) in Atlantic (14° 25' N., 40° 40' W).

1942 *Lance* and *Penelope* damaged during air raid on Malta.

1949 North Atlantic Treaty signed and NATO set up, by Belgium, Canada, Denmark, France, Iceland, Italy, Luxembourg, the Netherlands, Norway, Portugal, the United Kingdom and the United States of America all subscribers then to the doctrine that an attack on one member was an attack on all.

A hit on *Tirpitz*

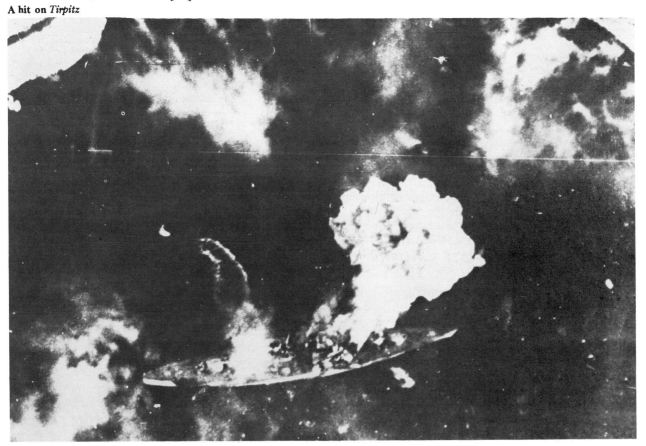

87

5th APRIL

1387 Sir Hugh Spencer defeated by the Flemish Jean de Bucq off Cadzand, Netherlands.

1755 50 independent companies of Marines raised, and divided into three Grand Divisions at Chatham, Portsmouth and Plymouth.

1758 Admiral Sir Edward Hawke *(Ramillies)* prevented the sailing to America of a French convoy from Île d'Aix. Ships: *Alcide, Chichester, Intrepid, Medway, Newark, Ramillies, Union.* Frigates: *Coventry, Hussar, Southampton.*

1797 Boats of *Magicienne* and *Regulus* destroyed thirteen privateers and two batteries at Cape Roxo (Rojo), Puerto Rico.

1800 *Emerald* and *Leviathan* captured the Spanish *Carmen* and *Florentina* with cargoes of quicksilver, 80 miles W.S.W. of Cape Spartel, Morocco.

1804 *Swift* taken by the French privateer *Espérance* 10 miles East of Palamos, S.E. coast of Spain.

1809 *Amethyst* captured the French *Niemen* 12 miles to the northward of Cape Machichaco, North coast of Spain. [m, bh]

1852 Pursers designated Paymasters by Order in Council.

1852 Capture of Martaban, Burma by *Hermes, Rattler, Salamander* and the Bengal Marine steamer *Proserpine;* the 18th and 80th Regiments, 26th Madras Native Infantry, Bengal Artillery and Madras Sappers and Miners.

1852 *Fox, Serpent,* the Bengal Marine steamers *Phlegethon* and *Tenasserim* and the 18th Regiment destroyed the Danot and Da Silva stockades below Rangoon.

1916 Third and final failure to relieve Kut-al'Amara. River gunboats: *Dragonfly, Gadfly, Mantis, Mayfly, Sawfly;* later − *Greenfly, Waterfly.*

1916 Le Havre Drifter flotilla and the French *Le Trombe* forced UB.26 to surrender: she sank later off Cape de la Heve. Drifters: *Endurance, Welcome Star, Stately, Comrades, Pleiades, Pleasance.*

1917 C.7 sank UC.68 in N Sea.

1918 British and Japanese Marines landed at Vladivostok.

Sir Edward Hawke

Edward Hawke was born in 1705 and became a Captain at the age of 29. At the Battle of Toulon in 1744 (9 Jan) he bestowed some glory on an otherwise drawn battle by breaking out of the Line of Battle (still a grave offence) to seize the *Poder.* He was almost dismissed for this. However, he was promoted Rear-Admiral in 1747 and served with distinction. His most famous battle was the annihilation of the French Fleet at Quiberon Bay in 1759. When the pilot protested as he sailed in a November gale in the shoals, Hawke showed his mettle by replying: 'You have done your duty in pointing out the risk. Now, lay me alongside the French Admiral'. Hawke became Admiral of the Fleet in 1768 and died in 1781.

1941 *Scarborough* and *Wolverine* sank U.76 in Atlantic (58° 35' N., 20° 20' W.).(Convoy SC.26)

1942 *Abingdon* sunk by Italian aircraft at Malta.

1942 *Cornwall* and *Dorsetshire* sunk by Japanese carrier-borne aircraft off the Maldive Islands, and *Hector* and *Tenedos* at Colombo.

1943 Hudsons L/233 and W/233 sank U.167 off Canary Islands (27° 47' N., 15° 00' W.).

1949 Warrant Officers became Branch Officers.

1957 *Centurion* commissioned at Haslemere as Central Drafting authority. (St Matthew Ch.8, v.9)

6th APRIL

1776   *Glasgow* fought five American ships under Commodore Esek Hopkins (*Alfred*) 24 miles S.E. of Block Island.

1806   *Pallas* drove ashore the French *Garonne, Gloire* and *Malicieuse* at the mouth of the Gironde River; her boats cut out *Tapageuse* 20 miles upstream.

1811   *Persian* captured the French privateer *Embuscade* off Cape d'Antifer.

1909   *Blackwater* sunk in collision with S.S. *Hero* off Dungeness.

1919   *Kent* landed guns' crews at Vladivostok to support White Russians 4,500 miles W on the Kama River in S. Urals.

1941   *Comorin* destroyed by fire in Atlantic (54° 34' N., 21° 20' W.).(Sunk by *Broke*).

1941   VC: Kenneth Campbell, Flying Officer RAFVR for torpedoing *Gneisenau* in Brest (posthumous).

1942   *Havoc* wrecked off Kelibia light, Tunis. (Blown up by own forces).

1942   *Indus* (RIN) sunk by Japanese aircraft at Akyab.

1943   *Tay* sank U.635 in N Atlantic (58° 25' N., 29° 22'W.) and Liberator R/86 sank U.632 (58° 02' N., 28° 42' W.). (Convoy HX.231)

1944   *Swale* sank U.302 in Atlantic (45° 05' N., 35° 11' W.). (Convoy SC.156)

1945   *Watchman* sank U.1195 in Channel (50° 33' N., 0° 55' W.).(Convoy VWP.16)

Evacuation of Greece (Operation Demon)

The Germans attacked Greece on 6 April, 1941, and that night an air attack on Piraeus hit the *Clan Fraser*, full of ammunition. The resulting explosion destroyed 10 other ships and put that port (the only one reasonably equipped to supply the Army) out of action. By 21st the withdrawal of the Army was approved, and on 24/25 April it started. The enemy had practically uncontested air superiority and land communications were difficult. Withdrawal had to be made from minor ports and over open beaches in the short hours of darkness. Unlike Dunkirk, the trips were long, over 1000 miles round trip, and base support non-existent. The evacuation went on for 7 nights, and 50,732 troops were rescued, 80 percent of those carried there earlier in Operation Lustre, for the loss of 4 transports and 2 destroyers.

(Right) An H2 mine. Developed in 1940, such mines had fixed moorings which were adjusted periodically

7th APRIL

1496   First Dry Dock opened at Portsmouth (cost £193.0s.6¾d).

1694   *Ruby* captured the French privateer *Entreprenant* 80 miles West of the Scilly Islands.

1799   Sortie from Acre to destroy a mine under the walls of that town, led by Major John Douglas, Marines, and Acting Lieutenant John Wesley Wright (*Tigre*). The operation was covered by *Theseus;* a diversion was made by the Turkish troops.

Vice-Admiral Sir William Sidney Smith (1764-1840)

Sidney Smith's brilliance was such that he was considered mad by many. He joined the navy at the age of 11 in 1775 and 5 years later was promoted Lieutenant for gallantry. He was a Post-Captain at the age of 18 in HMS *Fury*. In 1796 he received a 38 gun frigate, the *Diamond*, but was captured by the French whilst leading a boat attack on Le Havre. He escaped by stealing a small boat and rowing across the Channel in 1798. He was then appointed to the 80 gun *Tigre*. In 1799 Napoleon, having conquered Egypt marched to attack Turkish forces at St Jean D'Acre. Commodore Smith arrived at Acre before Napoleon and found the town's defences hopelessly weak.
He stiffened the Turkish garrison with guns and a naval brigade and strengthened the fortifications. Smith then captured Napoleon's siege train with the help of his own squadron, and withstood the French siege from March until May 1799, eventually driving them off.

1875   Launch of *Alexandra*, the first ironclad to be launched by a member of the Royal Family, the first whose launch was celebrated by a religious ceremony and the only one to serve as a flagship throughout her entire active service.

1917   CMBs 4, 5, 6 and 9 attacked four German destroyers off Zeebrugge, CMB 9 sinking G.88: first RN success with coastal craft.

1943   *Tuna* sank U.644 off Jan Mayen Island (69° 38' N., 5° 40' W.).

8th APRIL

1740 *Kent, Lenox* and *Orford* captured the Spanish *Princesa* 120 miles N.W. of Cape Ortegal, N.W. Spain.

1814 Boats of *Boxer, Endymion, Hogue* and *Maidstone* destroyed 27 American vessels and a quantity of naval stores at Pettipague Point (Essex), in the Connecticut River. [m]

1835 *Skipjack* captured the slaver *Marte* 40 miles S.W. of Little Cayman, to the southward of Cuba.

1898 Battle of the Atbara, Sudan. Gunboats not engaged, but landed a rocket party under Lieutenant David Beatty.

1927 *Veteran* returned Chinese fire off Hankow. C-in-C made "I strongly approve of your action".

1940 VC: Lieutenant-Commander Gerald Broadmead Roope (*Glowworm*). *Glowworm* sank after ramming the German cruiser *Admiral Hipper* off the coast of Norway. [bh]

1940* Start of combined operations (which lasted until 8th June) in Norway under Admiral of the Fleet the Earl of Cork and Orrery and General Sir Claude Auchinleck. [bh]. Ships: *Acasta*, Acheron, Afridi*, Amazon, Arab, Ardent*, Arethusa, Ark Royal, Arrow, Ashanti, Aston Villa*, Auckland, Aurora, Basilisk, Beagle, Bedouin, Berwick, Birmingham, Bittern*, Black Swan, Bradman*, Brazen, Cairo, Calcutta, Campbell, Cape Chelyuskin*, Cape Passaro*, Cape Siretoko*, Carlisle, Clyde, Codrington, Cossack, Coventry, Curacoa, Curlew*, Delight, Devonshire, Diana, Echo, Eclipse, Effingham@, Electra, Ellesmere, Encounter, Enterprise, Escapade, Esk, Eskimo, Fame, Faulknor, Fearless, Firedrake, Flamingo, Fleetwood, Forester, Foxhound, Furious, Galatea, Gaul*, Glasgow, Glorious*, Glowworm*, Grenade, Greyhound, Griffin, Gurkha*, Hammond*, Hardy*, Hasty, Havelock, Havoc, Hero, Hesperus, Highlander, Hostile, Icarus, Imperial, Impulsive, Inglefield, Ivanhoe, Jackal, Janus, Jardine*, Javelin, Juniper*, Kelly, Kimberley, Kipling, Larwood*, Loch Shin*, Manchester, Maori, Margaret, Mashona, Matabele, Melbourne*, Mohawk, Northern Gem, Nubian, Pelican, Penelope, Protector, Punjabi, Ranen, Renown, Repulse, Resolution, Rhine*, Rodney, Rutland-shire*, St. Goran*, St. Magnus, St. Sunniva, Seal*, Sealion, Severn, Sheffield, Sikh, Snapper, Somali, Southampton, Spearfish, Sterlet*, Stock, Suffolk, Sunfish, Tarpon*, Tartar, Thirlmere, Thistle*, Triad, Trident, Triton, Truant, Ursula, Valiant, Vandyck*, Vanoc, Vansittart, Veteran, Vindictive, Walker, Wanderer, Warspite, Warwickshire*, Westcott, Whirlwind, Wistaria, Witch, Witherington, Wolverine, Wren, York, Zulu.* Polish: *Blyskawica, Burza, Grom*, Orzel*.* Royal Marine and seamen detachments: *Barham, Hood, Nelson.* FAA Sq.: 800, 801, 803 (Skua); 810, 820 (Swordfish) *Ark Royal.* 701 (Walrus), 816, 818 (Swordfish) *Furious*; 802 (Gladiator) 804, 823 (Swordfish) *Glorious*; 700 ships' flight (Swordfish, Walrus).

* Lost due to enemy action. @ Wrecked.

1941 *Capetown* torpedoed by the Italian MAS 213 off Mersa Kuba; towed by *Parramatta* (RAN) to Port Sudan.

1943 *Moa* (RNZN) sunk by Japanese aircraft at Tulagi, Solomon Islands.

1944 *Crane* and *Cygnet* sank U.962 in N Atlantic (45° 43' N., 19° 57' W.).

1945 *Byron* and *Fitzroy* sank U.1001 (49° 19' N., 10° 23' W.) and *Bentinck* and *Calder* sank U.774 in SW Approaches (49° 58' N., 11° 51' W.).

HMS *Glowworm* **on fire**

9th APRIL

1782   Rear-Admiral Sir Samuel Hood *(Bar-fleur)* fought the division under Commodore the Marquis de Vaudreuil *(Triomphant)* off Dominica. Ships: *Royal Oak, Alfred, Montagu, Yarmouth, Valiant, Barfleur, Monarch, Warrior, Belliqueux, Centaur, Magnificent, Prince William.* Frigates: *Champion, Zebra.* (A few ships of the centre division — see 12th April — were also engaged).

1810   *Drake* captured the French privateer *Tilsit* 60 miles to the westward of the Texel.

1826   Boats of *Alacrity* captured two Greek pirate misticoes at Psara Island, Grecian Archipelago.

1853   Launch of *Malacca* at Moulmein, Burma: first warship fitted with high pressure steam engine (60 psi).

1855   Second bombardment of Sevastopol by the Allied siege batteries, including those of the Naval Brigade.

1915   Contract signed for first American MLs.

1940   *Renown* fought the German battlecruisers *Gneisenau* and *Scharnhorst* 50 miles West of the Lofoten Islands.

The battlecruiser *Renown* with 9 destroyers was off Northern Norway when the modern German Battle-cruisers *Scharnhorst* and *Gneisenau* were sighted. The *Renown* opened fire at 0405 at 9 miles range, and soon hit the *Gneisenau*, putting her main armament out of action. The enemy withdrew, but *Renown* increased to 29 knots and continued the action in a rising sea and through snow sqalls. The destroyers could not keep up, and were diverted to cover the entrance to Vestfjord. *Renown* hit *Gneisenau* on her forward turret and again aft during the chase before losing sight of the enemy at 0630. The older, slower and more lightly protected *Renown* had ousted the enemy by vigorous and immediate pursuit.

1940   *Gurkha* sunk and *Rodney* damaged by German aircraft off Karmo Island, W of Bergen.

1942   *Hermes, Hollyhock* and *Vampire* (RAN) sunk by Japanese aircraft off Trincomalee.

1942   *Lance* severely damaged by German aircraft at Malta. Towed to Chatham in 1943: CTL and scrapped.

1945   Mosquito aircraft of 143, 235 and 248 Sq. sank U.804 and U.843 and Mosquito A/235 sank U.1065 in Kattegat (57° 58' N., 11° 26' E.).

1945   *Admiral Scheer* sunk at Kiel by RAF.

HMS *Hermes* sinking 1942.

HMS *Hermes* between the Wars.

91

10th APRIL

1703   *Salisbury* and the hired armed ship *Muscovia Merchant* together with four of their convoy, taken by a superior French squadron 50 miles to the westward of Goeree, Netherlands.

1746   *Alexander* privateer captured the French *Solebay* close off St. Martin, Île de Ré.

1786   Vice-Admiral the Hon. John Byron died: "Foul weather Jack".

1795   *Astraea* captured the French *Gloire* 150 miles W. by S. of the Scilly Islands. [m, bh]

1826   Boats of *Alacrity* captured two Greek pirate misticoes at Andros Island, Grecian Archipelago.

1855   VC: John Sullivan, boatswain's mate, for heroism in approaching a concealed Russian battery and placing a flag nearby to mark its position for the artillery.

1940   VC: Captain Bernard Armitage Warburton Warburton-Lee *(Hardy)*. First battle of Narvik. Second DF sank two German destoyers *(Anton Schmidt* and *Wilhelm Heidkamp*)* and damaged five more at Narvik; seven merchant ships also sunk including the ammunition ship *Rauenfels*. Ships: *Hardy, Havock, Hostile, Hotspur, Hunter.* [bh]. Losses: *Hardy, Hunter.* * Sank on the 11th.

First Battle of Narvik

In early April 1940, the Germans were invading Norway, and action was fast moving, with intelligence having to be gained on the spot. Captain Warburton-Lee, with 4 destroyers, was ordered to prevent the enemy taking Narvik. Whilst on passage he learnt that the enemy had landed there in some force, but decided to enter the fjord and attack the enemy shipping. He was joined by another destroyer just before arrival, and then made a dawn attack. The element of surprise allowed him to sink two large German destroyers and damage 3 others, but five other German destroyers joined in the action, and the *Hardy* and *Hunter* were sunk, and *Hotspur* damaged. However, two more German destroyers were severely damaged, and seven merchant ships sunk, including an ammunition ship, before the British force withdrew. Captain Warburton-Lee, who was killed, was awarded the Victoria Cross posthumously.

1940   *Truant* torpedoed the German cruiser *Karlsruhe* in the Skagerrak, 10 miles South of Kristiansand: sunk by own forces next day.

Sinking of the Karlsruhe

The submarine *Truant* (Lt-Cdr C. H. Hutchinson) was off Kristiansand at 1830 on 10th, when she sighted a *Köln* class cruiser escorted by 3 destroyers. *Truant* fired a salvo of 10 torpedoes. Although they were sighted, the cruiser *Karlsruhe* was unable to avoid them, and was hit aft: sinking, she was abandoned and sunk by torpedoes from an escorting destroyer, the *Greif*. *Truant* was counter-attacked, and some machinery was badly damaged and leaks caused, but she was able to surface after 19 hours under water and returned to base. Lt-Cdr Hutchinson was awarded the DSO.

1940   Skua aircraft of 800 and 803 Sq. sank the German cruiser *Königsberg* at Bergen. The first occasion on which a major German warship was sunk by air attack in the Second World War.

1940   *Hero* sank U.50 N.NE of Shetlands.

1940   *Thistle* sunk by U.4 off Skudenaes, N.W. of Stavanger.

1943   Wellington C/172 sank U.376 in the Bay of Biscay.

1943   *Adventure* intercepted the German blockade runner *Silvaplana* (ex-*Nor*). from Saigon off Finisterre (43° 18' N, 14° 26' W.) whereupon she was scuttled.

1945   *Tintagel Castle* and *Vanquisher* sank U.878 in SW Approaches. (Convoy ON.295)

A Skua divebomber

11th APRIL

1795   *Hannibal* captured the French *Gentille* to the W.S.W. of the Scilly Islands.

1796   *Ca Ira* burnt out by accident at San Fiorenzo.

1804   *Wilhelmina* fought the French *Psyche* 100 miles to the eastward of Trincomalee.

1809   Captain Lord Cochrane's fireship attack on the French fleet in Basque Roads, under the general direction of Admiral Lord Gambier *(Caledonia)*. Four French ships burnt. [m*, m, bh] . Ships and vessels: *Aetna, Aigle, Beagle, Bellona, Caesar*, Caledonia*, Conflict, Contest, Donegal, Doterel, Emerald, Encounter, Fervent, Foxhound, Gibraltar*, Growler Hero, Illustrious, Imperieuse, Indefatigable, Insolent, King George, Lyra, Martial, Mediator, Nimrod, Pallas, Redpole, Resolution*, Revenge*, Theseus*, Thunder, Unicorn, Valiant, Whiting.* *Provided crews for fireships. An inconclusive action, after which Gambier applied for a court-martial and Cochrane, as an MP, opposed a Parliamentary vote of thanks to his Admiral.

1866   *Bellerophon* (third) completed: served a record 14 years as flagship on the West Indies station.

1918   UB.33 sunk by mine S.W. of Varne lightvessel.

1940   *Spearfish* torpedoed the German pocket battleship *Lützow* North of The Skaw.

The submarine *Spearfish* (Lt J. H. Forbes) was on patrol off the Skaw. She had drawn the attention of A/S vessels on the evening of 10th April, and between 1730 and 1840, 66 depth charges were dropped near her. More charges caused some damage, but by midnight the enemy had withdrawn and the *Spearfish* surfaced. Just after midnight the Officer of the Watch sighted the wake of the German Pocket Battleship *Lützow* on passage to Kiel. Five minutes later, the *Spearfish* fired 6 torpedoes by eye. At least one torpedo hit the *Lützow* aft, removing both her propellers, jamming her rudder and causing her to sink slowly by the stern. It took over 21 hours to tow her to Kiel where repairs took a year to complete. The achievement in getting the *Lützow* back to harbour at all was assessed as being due to the Damage Control Officer's knowledge of the ship.

1940   *Sealion* sank the German *s.s. August Leonhardt* 10 miles South of Anholt, Kattegat.

1941   *Aphis* and *Gnat* bombarded the coast road near Bomba.

1942   *Kingston* sunk by German aircraft at Malta: hull used as blockship.

1943   *Beverley* sunk by U.188 in mid-Atlantic after collision with s.s. *Caimiord.* (Convoy ON.176)

1945   Force 63, under Vice-Admiral H.T.C. Walker *(Queen Elizabeth)*, bombarded Sabang and Oleheh, Sumatra. Operation Sunfish.
Sabang: *Queen Elizabeth, London, Richelieu* (Fr.). Oleheh: 26th D F *Saumarez, Venus, Verulam, Vigilant, Virago,* with *Cumberland, Emperor, Khedive.* FAA Sq.: (Hellcat) 808.

H.M. Submarine *Sealion*

93

12th APRIL

1779   Court-martial of Admiral Palliser.

1782*   Battle of The Saintes. 20 miles off
        the North end of Dominica. [bh].
        Admiral Sir George Bridges Rodney
        (*Formidable*) defeated the French fleet
        of 30 sail of the line under Vice-Admiral
        Comte de Grasse (*Ville-de-Paris*). Cap-
        tured: *Ardent, César, Glorieux, Hector,
        Ville-de-Paris*. Ships: *Marlborough,
        Arrogant, Alcide, Nonsuch, Conqueror,
        Princessa, Prince George, Torbay, Anson,
        Fame, Russell; America, Hercules,
        Prothee, Resolution, Agamemnon,
        Duke, Formidable, Namur, St. Albans,
        Canada, Repulse, Ajax, Bedford, Prince
        William, Magnificent, Centaur, Belli-
        queux, Warrior, Monarch, Barfleur,
        Valiant, Yarmouth, Montagu, Alfred,
        Royal Oak*. Frigates, etc.: *Alarm,
        Alecto, Alert, Andromache, Champion,
        Endymion, Eurydice, Flora, Triton,
        Zebra*. Troops: 69th Regiment, now the
        Royal Regiment of Wales, awarded the
        battle honour of a naval crown, super-
        scribed "12 April 1782" on its colours,
        and the 87th Regiment.

1782   Second battle between Vice-Admiral
        Sir Edward Hughes (*Superb*) and 12
        ships under Commodore Chevalier de
        Suffren (*Héros*) 12 miles N.E. by E. of
        Providien Rock (Elephant Rock, Clarke
        Point), Ceylon. [bh]. Ships: *Exeter,
        Sultan, Eagle, Burford, Monmouth,
        Superb, Magnanime, Monarca, Isis,
        Hero, Worcester*. Frigates: *Combustion,
        Seahorse*. Troops: 98th Regiment.
        See 17th February, 6th July and
        3rd September.

1796   *Revolutionnaire* captured the French
        Unité 60 miles S. by W. of Belle Île.

The Battle of the Saintes ("Saints")

Throughout the Seven Years war the Fighting Instructions had been substantially the same as those written
during the Dutch Wars 100 years earlier. Battles were
fought by fleets sailing in line ahead on parallel course,
and were generally indecisive. Rear-Admiral Sir Samuel
Hood, second in command on the station, was keen to
break the deadlock, but no opportunity offered until
12 April 1782 when an English fleet under Rodney and
a French fleet under de Grasse met off a group of
islets called Les Saintes. At the outset of the battle the
wind did not favour the English fleet and the French
gained the weather gauge. However, as the English van
drew clear of the French rear the wind shifted, enabling
Rodney and Hood to pass through gaps in the French
line and force many of the French ships to close action.
Nelson wrote of this battle "the greatest victory, if it
had been followed up, that our country ever saw".
However, to Hood's fury, no signal for general chase

was hoisted by Rodney, and it was only 5 days later
that Hood was allowed to follow up the victory.

1918   GC (ex-AM): Lieutenant A.G. Bagot,
        DSC, RNVR (ML 356) for saving life
        after fire at sea.

1918   Grand Fleet base moved from Scapa
        Flow to Rosyth.

1918   CMB 33A destroyed by German shore
        battery at Ostend during the cancelled
        blockship operation at that port.

1924   *Australia* (RAN) ceremoniously
        scuttled off Sydney.

1939   WRNS reformed.
The Women's Royal Naval Service was formed in 1917
to replace men required for active service. In the two
years before it was disbanded it grew to almost 7,000,
its members having shown their ability to carry out not
only domestic and clerical duties, but also such work as
boat's crew and wireless telegraphist.
    In April 1939 the King gave permission for the
Service to be reformed and by September 1939 there
were 1,000 Wrens employed as communicators, writers,
drivers, cooks and stewards and a small number of
WRNS Officers. The number of personnel and their
duties expanded considerably to include skilled work
concerned with maintenance of aircraft, weapons and
small craft until by 1944 there was a total force of 74,620.
    At the end of the war the WRNS rapidly reduced in
number but many officers and ratings were still required
to serve an extended service. On 1 Feb 1949 the Service,
first created to meet the Navy's need in wartime, became
an integral and permanent part of the Royal Navy.
Today it numbers some 270 officers and 2,700 ratings.
Although the Women's Services are exempt from the
Sex Discrimination Act, the WRNS are becoming in-
creasingly integrated with the Royal Navy. In September 1976 the WRNS Officers' Training Course moved
from the Royal Naval College Greenwich to the Britannia Royal Naval College, Dartmouth and, in 1978, the
Diamond Anniversary of its formation, the Women's
Royal Naval Service became subject to the Naval Discipline Act for the first time, thereby accepting commitment with equal opportunity.

1941   Landing party from *Mansfield* destroyed
        all essential machinery in the fish oil
        factory at Oyfjord, near Hammerfest.

1945   *Tapir* sank U.486 off Bergen.

1945   *Loch Glendhu* captured U.1024 off
        Isle of Man: the U-boat sank in tow
        off Holyhead on the 13th. (Convoy
        BB.80)

1945   Task Force 57 including *Indefatigable*
        attacked the airfield at Shinchiku
        and harbour at Kiirun, Formosa.
        Operation Iceberg Oolong. FAA Sq.:
        820 (Avenger). 1770 (Firefly). 887
        (Seafire).

13th APRIL

1665	*Mermaid* captured a Dutch private 6-gun ship in the North Sea.
1665	*Diamond* and *Yarmouth* captured the Flushing Directory Ships *Eendragt* and *Jonge Leeuw* in the North Sea.
1748	Officers' uniform introduced by Admiralty Order.
1749	*Namur, Pembroke* and *Apollo* lost in hurricane.
1758	*Prince George,* on passage from England to the Mediterranean, caught fire 180 miles West of Ushant and was totally destroyed.
1783	*Sceptre* captured the French *Naiade* 70 miles N.E. by E. of Cuddalore.
1797	*Viper* captured the Spanish privateer *Piteous Virgin Maria* 20 miles N.N.W. of Alboran Island, Western Mediterranean.
1800	Boat of *Calypso* cut out the French privateer *Diligente* off Cape Tiburon, Haiti.
1868	Naval Brigade at the capture of Magdala, Abyssinia, by Lieutenant-General Sir Robert Napier. [bh]. Ships: *Argus, Daphne, Dryad*[1], *Nymphe, Octavia*[1], *Satellite*[1], *Spiteful, Star, Vigilant.* Medal: Abyssinia, 1867-8. [1] Landed Naval Brigade.
1899	Landing party from *Porpoise* and *Royalist* under Lieutenant Guy Gaunt (*Porpoise*) repulsed a Maatafan attack at Samoa.

A WRNS despatch rider gets mechanical assistance from a Naval rating. Despatch riders drove through blitzes to deliver messages, Second World War.

1940	Second battle of Narvik. Vice-Admiral W.J. Whitworth *(Warspite)* sank 8 German destroyers[2] at Narvik. [bh]. Ships: *Bedouin, Cossack, Eskimo, Forester, Foxhound, Furious, Hero, Icarus, Kimberley, Punjabi, Warspite.* [2] Sunk: *Bernd Von Arnim, Diether Von Roeder, Erich Giese, Erich Koellner, Georg Thiele, Hans Lüdemann, Hermann Künne, Wolfgang Zenker.* Swordfish of 700 Sq. (*Warspite*) sank U.64 in Herjangsfjord.

Following the action on 10 April, it was decided to clear the fjord of enemy shipping. The battleship *Warspite* and 9 destroyers entered on 13 April, using *Warspite's* aircraft to detect enemy positions. The aircraft sank U.64, and warned of destroyers hidden in creeks. 8 large enemy destroyers were sunk by 15in gunfire from the *Warspite*, and in action with British destroyers, with only two British destroyers — *Eskimo* and *Cossack* — being seriously damaged. Advantage of this action could not be taken by the British as no military forces were available.

1941	*Rajputana* sunk by U.108 in Denmark Strait.
1945	MTBs sank the German TA 45 (ex-Italian t.b. *Spica*) in Gulf of Fiume.
1945	Task Force 57 including *Indefatigable* attacked the airfields at Matsuyama and Shinchiku, Formosa. Operation Iceberg Oolong. FAA Sq.: 820 (Avenger) 887 (Seafire); 1770 (Firefly).

HMS *Warspite* seen through a shell hole in *Cossack*

14th APRIL

1293   Sir Robert Tiptoft defeated Charles, Count of Valois, in mid-Channel.

1781   *Roebuck* captured the American *Confederacy* 170 miles S. by E. of Sandy Hook.

1842   Repulse of fire raft attack at Tinghai, S. of Shanghai. Boats of: *Bentinck, Cornwallis, Hyacinth, Starling; Nemesis, Phlegethon* (Ben.Mar.); *Jupiter* transport.

1852*   Capture of Rangoon by Rear-Admiral Charles John Austen *(Rattler)* and Major-General Jeremy Godwin. Ships: *Fox, Hermes, Rattler, Salamander, Serpent.* Indian Navy: *Berenice, Ferooz, Medusa, Moozuffer, Sesostris, Zenobia.* Bengal Marine: *Enterprize, Fire Queen, Mahanuddy, Phlegethon, Pluto, Proserpine, Tenasserim.* Troops: 18th, 51st and 80th Regiments; Bengal Artillery, Madras Sappers and Miners, 40th Bengal Native Infantry, 9th and 35th Madras Native Infantry.

1857   *Raleigh* (fourth of the name) wrecked on Raleigh Rock, off Macao, but fired salute to passing French warship while sinking.

1858   *Pelorus'* Naval Brigade returned on board. (See 4th February).

1861   Boat of *Lyra* captured a slave dhow in Chake Chake Bay, Zanzibar.

1912   RFC with Naval Wing constituted by Royal Warrant.

1915   *Hyacinth* destroyed German *Kronburg* off E. Africa, preventing her from supplying *Konigsberg.*

1916   RNAS from Mudros bombed Constantinople and Adrianople.

1940   Naval force landed from 18th C.S. at Namsos. Operation Henry.

1940   *Tarpon* sunk by the German trawler M.6 off the coast of Norway.

1941   *Gnat, Griffin* and *Stuart* (RAN) bombarded enemy positions at Sollum.

1942   *Stork* and *Vetch* sank U.252 in N Atlantic. (Convoy OG.82)

1942   *Upholder* sunk by Italian t.b. *Pegaso* in 34° 47' N, 15° 55' E., after attacking a convoy 100 miles S.E. of Malta.

1943   *Eskdale* (Nor) sunk by the German S.90 off Lizard Head. (Convoy PW.323)

1944   *Pelican* and *Swansea* (RCN) sank U.448 in N Atlantic.

1944   X.24 laid two charges under the floating dock at Bergen: dock undamaged, but the German *s.s. Barenfels* lying alongside was sunk.

*Attack on Rangoon. *Sesostris* (Steamer) *Fox* and *Moozuffer* in action as a magazine is blown up by shell fire, 1852

96

15th APRIL

1759 *Favourite* captured the French *Valeur* 30 miles East of Cape de Santa Maria, Portugal.

1795 *Artois* captured the French *Jean-Bart* 15 miles West of Île de Ré.

1821 Professor Inman of the Royal Naval Academy published his "Treatise on Navigation and Nautical Astronomy", including his celebrated tables.

1918 Raid by British light forces in the Kattegat. Ships: Force A — *Cardiff, Cassandra, Ceres; Vanoc, Vega, Vehement, Vimiera, Violent.* Force B — *Calypso, Caradoc; Vendetta, Verulam, Wakeful, Winchelsea.* Force C — *Angora, Princess Margaret; Urchin, Venetia, Vesper, Viceroy.* Force D — *Lion, Renown, Repulse, Tiger; Champion, Gabriel, Nerissa, Oriana, Penn, Ulster, Ursa, Ursula. Courageous; Tower, Tristram. Caledonia, Galatea, Inconstant, Phaeton Royalist.* Cover — 5th B.S. *Barham, Malaya, Valiant* and destroyers.

1940 *Fearless* sank U.49 off N Norway.

1941 *Ladybird* bombarded Gazala airfield, Cyrenaica.

1945 *Grindall* and *Keats* sank U.285 in SW Approaches, and *Loch Killin* sank U.1063 off Land's End.

1942 GC: The Island of Malta. (The only award of the GC that was not gazetted).

By 1942 Malta was surrounded on all sides by Axis forces. The existence of Malta was proving a major thorn in the side of Axis forces in North Africa, and it

Convoy gets through to Malta.

An RAF Gloster Gladiator aircraft

was essential to maintain the British presence there. In mid-June two convoys attempted to resupply the island, one from Gibraltar and the other from Alexandria (Operations Harpoon and Vigorous). These convoys failed. Axis airpower covered the approaches to Malta, and Italian submarine and surface ships bases were close to the sea lane. In spite of very severe rationing (10½ oz of bread per day, 3½ oz lard or margarine and 1¾ oz cheese) a careful estimate of the Governor revealed that the island would be obliged to surrender in mid-September. Fuel supplies were almost exhausted and only three Sea Gladiator aircraft (affectionately called 'Faith' 'Hope' and 'Charity') were available for the defence of the island. King George VI sent the following message to the Governor: "To honour her brave people I award the George Cross to the island fortress of Malta to bear witness to a heroism and devotion that will long be famous in history".

Malta Convoys 1942
Ships sunk

	Feb	March	June	Aug
Carriers	nil	nil	nil	1
Cruisers	nil	nil	1	2
Destroyers	nil	3	5	3
Submarines	nil	1	nil	nil
Merchantmen	3	1	6	9
Merchantmen to arrive	nil	*3	2	5

* All sunk at Malta, many more were damaged.

1695   *Hope* taken by a French squadron of five ships 150 miles W.N.W. of Ushant. *Anglesey* and *Roebuck* escaped.

1781   Commodore George Johnstone *(Romney)*, escorting a large convoy of East Indiamen and transports, repulsed the French squadron under Captain Chevalier de Suffren *(Héros)* at Porto da Prai, Cape Verde Islands. Ships: *Active, Diana, Hero, Isis, Jason, Jupiter, Monmouth, Porto, Rattlesnake, Romney.* Armed ships: *Royal Charlotte, San Carlos.* Bomb: *Terror.* Cutter: *Tapageur.* Fireship: *Infernal.* Transport: *Pondicherry.*

1797   *Boston* captured the French privateer *Enfant-de-la Patrie* 50 miles West of Cape Ortegal, N.W. Spain.

1810   Capture of Santa Maura (Levkas), Ionian group, by Brigadier-General John Oswald and Captain George Eyre *(Magnificent)*. Ships and vessels: *Belle Poule, Imogen, Leonidas, Magnificent, Montagu.*

1861   Masters' mates re-styled "Sub-Lieutenant". Captains' insignia increased to 4 stripes.

1918   Submarine HB1 inadvertantly sank Italian s/m H5 in S Adriatic.

1940   *Porpoise* sank the German U.1 off S Norway.

1941   14th D.F. (Captain Mack) destroyed an Axis convoy of five ships and its Italian destroyer escort off Sfax, Tunis. [bh]. Ships: *Janus, Jervis, Mohawk, Nubian, (Mohawk* sunk by *Janus* after being torpedoed). Enemy sunk: *Baleno, Luca Tarigo* and 4 of the convoy. *Lampo* driven ashore and left burning; salvaged, recommissioned and sunk by aircraft on 30th April 1943.

1941   *Gloucester* bombarded the Fort Capuzzo-Bardia area.

1942   Royal Marines from *Kelvin* and *Kipling* landed on Kuphonisi, Crete, to destroy the W/T Station. Operation Lighter.

1943   *Pakenham* and *Paladin* engaged Italian t b. *Cassiopea* and minesweeper *Cigno* at night off Marettimo, sinking the former and damaging the latter. *Packenham* damaged and taken in tow, but was bombed at daylight: sunk by *Paladin* (37° 26'N., 12° 30'E.).

1945   *Esquimalt* (RCN) sunk by U.190 off Halifax.

1945   *Viceroy* sank U.1274 off the Farnes. (Convoy FS.1784)

1945   Air strike on Emmahaven, Padang, Sumatra, by Force 63, under Vice-Admiral H.T.C. Walker *(Queen Elizabeth)*. Ships: *Cumberland, London, Queen Elizabeth, Richelieu* (Fr), *Saumarez* (D.26), *Venus, Verulam, Vigilant, Virago.* Carriers: *Emperor, Khedive.* FAA Sq.: 808 (Hellcat). Operation Sunfish.

1945   *Ekins* mined: CTL.

HMS *Royal Sovereign*, **Portsmouth 1922.**

17th APRIL

1746   *Defiance*, *Ruby* and *Salisbury* captured the French *Embuscade* 170 miles to the southward of the Scilly Islands.

1780   Admiral Sir George Bridges Rodney (*Sandwich*) fought Vice-Admiral Comte de Guichen (*Couronne*), with 23 ships of the line, 30 miles W.S.W. of the North end of Martinique. Ships: *Stirling Castle, Ajax, Elizabeth, Princess Royal, Albion, Terrible, Trident, Grafton, Yarmouth, Cornwall, Sandwich, Suffolk, Boyne, Vigilant, Vengeance, Medway, Montagu, Conqueror, Intrepid, Magnificent, Centurion.* Frigates, etc.: *Andromeda, Deal Castle, Greyhound, Pegasus, Venus.*

1806   *Sirius* captured the French *Bergère* off the mouth of the Tiber. [m]

1809   *Castor*, *Pompee* and *Recruit* captured the French *D'Hautpoul* 30 miles S.W. by S. of Cape Roxo (Rojo), Puerto Rico. [m]. A detachment of the 63rd Regiment was on board *Pompee*.

1813   *Mutine* captured the French privateer *Invincible* 700 miles W. by S. of Cape Finisterre.

1858   *Pearl's* Naval Brigade at Thamowlee (Jamauria), with the 13th Light Infantry, Bengal Yeomanry, 1st Bengal Military Police Battalion and Gurkha allies.

1862   British and French forces captured Tserpoo. Naval Brigade from *Pearl*, *Vulcan, Imperieuse, Flamer, Coromandel.* Troops: R.A., 99th Regiment; 5th Bombay Native Light Infantry, 22nd Bengal Native Infantry; Ward's Chinese troops.

1915   E.15 grounded near Kephez Pt., Dardanelles; damaged by Turkish gunfire and obliged to surrender, later blown up by picket boats of *Triumph* and *Majestic*.

1917   Two Japanese destroyer flotillas joined the Allied forces in the Mediterranean.

1918   *Pilot Me* and *Young Fred* sank UB.82 in NW Approaches.

1940   Naval force landed at Aandalsnes. Operation Primrose. *Suffolk* damaged by German aircraft after bombarding Stavanger airfield. Operation Duck.

1941   GC: Lieutenant Ernest Oliver Gidden, GM, RNVR for mine disposal on Hungerford Bridge, London.

1941   Admiralty building, Whitehall, damaged by German aircraft.

1944   Canso S/162 (RCAF) sank U.342 in N Atlantic.

1951   *Affray* lost in Channel.

Portsmouth Dockyard Church after an air attack, 17 April 1941

A swordfish with floats.

18th APRIL

1782   *Aeolus* captured the French privateer *Aglae* 30 miles to the northward of Cape Cornwall.

1797   Boats of *Dido* and *Terpsichore* cut out the Spanish *Principe Fernando* at Santa Cruz, Tenerife.

1797*   Spithead mutineers petitioned the Board of Admiralty.

1813   *Unicorn* and *Stag* captured the American letter of marque *Hebe* 100 miles S.W. of Ushant.

1814   Capture of Genoa. Ships: *America, Aboukir, Caledonia, Boyne, Iphigenia, Furieuse, Cephalus, Edinburgh, Berwick, Curacoa, Pembroke, Prince of Wales, Rainbow, Pylades, Swallow, Union* and a Sicilian flotilla.

1940   *Sterlet* sunk by the German UJ.125, 126 and 128 in the Skagerrak.

1941   *Fiona* sunk by aircraft off Sollum.

1941   *Gloucester* bombarded the Bardia area.

1943   P.615 sunk by U.123 South of Freetown.

1943   *Regent* sunk by mine off Monopoli, in the S Adriatic.

*Extract from petition by the Spithead mutineers to Admiral of the Fleet Earl Howe . . .

"It is now upwards of 2 years since your petitioners observed with pleasure the augmentation which had been made to pay of the army and militia, and the provision that took place with the respect of their wives and families, of such soldiers as were serving on board, naturally expecting that they should in their turn experience the same munificence, but alas no notice has been taken of them, nor the smallest provision made for their wives and families except what they themselves sent out of their pay to prevent them being burdensome to the parish.

That your petitioners humbly presumed that their loyalty to their sovereign is as conspicuous and their courage as unquestionable as any other description of men in His Majesty's Service as their enemies can testify, and as your Lordship can witness who so often led them to victory and glory and by whose manly exertions the British flag rides triumphant in every quarter of the globe.

And your petitioners humbly conceive that at the time when their wages were settled in the reign of Charles II it was intended as a comfortable support both for themselves and families, but at present by the considerable rise in the necessaries of life, which is now almost double, and an advance of 30% on slops, your Lordship will plainly see that the intentions of the legislature is counteracted by the before mentioned causes and therefore most humbly pray for relief . . ."

HMS *Diamond* in action with French Gunboats off Cap Le Havre, 17 April 1796: the action in which Captain Sir Sidney Smith was captured. (See 7th April)

19th APRIL

1587 "Singeing of the King of Spain's beard" by Sir Francis Drake (*Elizabeth Bonaventure*) at Cadiz. Ships: *Dreadnought, Elizabeth Bonaventure, Rainbow* and about 30 merchant ships.

1757 Edward Pellew born.

1770 Captain James Cook started to survey Eastern Australia.

1781 *Resource* captured the French *Unicorne* 20 miles S.W. by W. of Cape Blaise (San Blas) Gulf of Mexico. Detach ment of the loyal American Rangers and of Artillery were present.

1782 Rear-Admiral Sir Samuel Hood (*Barfleur*) captured four French ships in the Mona Passage, between Puerto Rico and San Domingo. Ships: *Alfred, Barfleur, Belliqueux, Magnificent*[1], *Monarch, Montagu, Prince William, Valiant*[2], *Warrior, Yarmouth.* Frigates: *Alecto, Champion*[3].
[1] Captured *Aimable*. [2] Captured *Caton* and *Jason*. [3] Captured *Cérés.*

1917* Peak of Merchant Ships sinkings by U-boats.

*First World War: The Convoy System

By the beginning of 1917 Germany had about 100 U-boats operating and with their numbers increasing rapidly there was a dramatic increase in the damage they inflicted. Losses to shipping were

Month	Ships Sunk	Tonnage
January	181	298,000
February	259	468,000
March	325	500,000
April	423	849,000

On one day alone (19th April) 11 British Merchant ships and 8 fishing vessels were sunk by submarines and mines. These losses could not have been sustained for more than about 5 months without totally crippling Britain. The convoy system was accordingly introduced in May. (See 10th May).

1941 *Glengyle* landed a raiding party of 460 men to attack Bardia.

1944 *Ula* (Nor) sank U.974 off Stavanger.

1944 Air raid on Sabang. Operation Cockpit. Carrier Force (70): *Renown* (Vice-Admiral Sir Arthur Power), *Illustrious* (Rear-Admiral C. Moody), *Saratoga* (U.S.); *Ceylon, Gambia, London; Quillam* (D.4), *Queensborough, Quadrant; Cummings, Dunlap, Fanning* (all U.S.). Covering Force (69): *Queen Elizabeth* (Admiral Sir James Somerville), *Valiant, Richelieu* (Fr); *Newcastle* (Rear-Admiral A.D. Read — C.S.4), *Nigeria, Tromp* (Neth); *Tactician, Napier Nepal, Nizam; Rotherham* (D.11), *Racehorse, Penn, Petard, Van Galen* (Neth), *Quiberon.* (RAN) FAA Sq.: 810, 847 (Barracuda), 1830, 1833 (Corsair) (*Illustrious*).

Assault on Sabang

On 16th April, a force under Admiral Somerville sailed from Trincomalee, and arrived off the SW of Sabang by 19th. At 0530 aircraft from the carriers *Illustrious* and *Saratoga* (USN) attacked the port from different directions at once and achieved complete surprise. The first AA fire rose after the first bombs had landed. Three of the four oil tanks were destroyed and extensive damage was done to installations, but there was no shipping to be hit. 24 enemy aircraft were destroyed on the ground, and one Allied aircraft was shot down, but its pilot was rescued by the submarine *Tactician* which came under fire from shore batteries during the rescue. It was the first raid by the Eastern Fleet, which comprised three battleships (1 French), a battlecruiser, two carriers (1 USN), six cruisers (1 RNZN, 1 Dutch), and 15 destroyers (4 RAN, 2 USN and 1 Dutch).

1945 Mosquito aircraft of 143, 235 and 248 Sq. and 333 Sq. (Nor) sank U.251 in the Kattegat (56° 37'N., 11° 51'E.).

Marines in America 1775.

20th APRIL

1657   Admiral Robert Blake *(George)* destroyed sixteen Spanish ships at Santa Cruz, Tenerife. [bh]. Ships: *Bridgwater, Bristol, Centurion, Colchester, Convert, Fairfax, Foresight, George, Hampshire, Jersey, Langport, Lyme, Maidstone, Nantwich, Newbury; Newcastle, Plymouth, Ruby, Speaker, Swiftsure, Unicorn, Winsby, Worcester.* He died on the voyage home, just off Plymouth.

1667   *Princess* fought seventeen Dutch men-of-war on the Dogger Bank. [bh]

1807   Boats of *Richmond* cut out the Spanish privateer *Galliard* 18 miles to the northward of Peniche, Portugal. [m]

1810   *Firm, Sharpshooter* and *Surly* captured the French privateer *Alcide* at Pirou, Granville Bay, North coast of France. [m]

1814   *Orpheus* captured the American *Frolic* 15 miles N.N.W. of Puerto Matanzas, Cuba.

1837   Captain Robert Contart McCrea, with boats of *Zebra*, captured the ex-Rajah of Kedah at Bruas, Perak.

1917   *Nepaulin* mined near Dyke lightvessel.

1940   *Rutlandshire* bombed and driven ashore, and *Auckland* damaged at Namsos, by German aircraft.

Mr. Winston Churchill boarding Maurice Farman seaplane, Portsmouth Harbour.
Pilot: Lt A.M. Longmore, RN, later Air Chief-Marshal Sir Arthur Longmore,
one of the first four naval pilots trained.

102

21st APRIL

1702   Overseer and Inspector of naval chaplains first appointed, by Order in Council.

1782   *Foudroyant* (Captain J Jervis; made KB) captured the French *Pégase* 30 miles N.N.W. of Ushant. [bh]

1796   *Indefatigable* (38) captured the French *Virginie* (44) 80 miles W.S.W. of the Scilly Islands. [m, bh]

1798   *Mars* captured the French *L'Hercule* in the Passage du Raz (Raz de Sein), Brest. [m, bh]

1848   *Erebus* and *Terror* abandoned in Arctic Ice.

1904   Capture of Illig, Somaliland. Ships: *Fox, Hyacinth, Mohawk* and the Italian *Volturno*. Regiment: 1st Bn. The Hampshire Regt. General African Medal, clasp 'Somaliland 1902–1904'.

1917   German destroyer raid in Dover Strait. Dover shelled just before midnight on 20th/21st. [bh]. Ships: *Swift, Broke, Sabreur*. German destroyers G42 and G85 sunk. British War Medal: clasp "21 April 1917" approved for *Broke* and *Swift* but not issued.

1918   ML413 sank UB.71 W of Gibraltar.

1941   Bombardment of Tripoli by Admiral Sir Andrew Cunningham (*Warspite*). Ships: *Barham, Gloucester, Valiant, Warspite; Hasty, Havock, Hereward, Hero, Hotspur, Jaguar, Janus, Jervis, Juno*. Mark ship: *Truant*. Albacores of 826 and 829 Sq and Fulmars of 803 and 806 Sq (*Formidable*).

1943   *Splendid* scuttled after depth charge attack by the German-manned destroyer *Hermes* (Z.G.3)*. Finally sunk by gunfire 2 miles S.S.E. of Capri. *Ex-Hellenic *Vasilefs Georgios I*.

1945   *Bazely, Bentinck* and *Drury* sank U.636 in NW Approaches.

1945   *Retalick* engaged several German explosive motor boats 210° Ostende 28m, sinking four.

Battle of the Atlantic March to May 1943

912 ships sailed in North Atlantic convoys during this period. March 1943, East Bound Convoy HX 228 was escorted by an experienced mixed British, Free French and Polish Escort Group. The destroyer *Harvester* detected a U-boat on the surface by radar and rammed it. *Harvester* and the U-boat were damaged, the French corvette *Aconit* sinking the latter. *Harvester* then came to a standstill as a result of action damage and was torpedoed as *Aconit* returned to assist. *Aconit* sank the U-boat by depth charging and ramming. U.121 also attacked the convoy, was hit by debris from an exploding ship, was blinded and just escaped being sunk by the escorts in a counter attack. Five merchant ships were lost.

HX 229 which followed had a weak escort and was set upon by 38 U-boats in all. There was no air cover or rescue ship, and 13 merchant ships were sunk. SC122

Bridge of a Destroyer, World War 2.

Bridge of a Cruiser.

21st APRIL

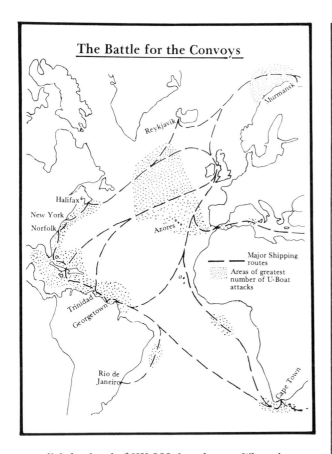

The Battle for the Convoys

Major Shipping routes

Areas of greatest number of U-Boat attacks

lost. One U-boat was sunk, and the battle ended when aircraft from Iceland were able to assist the escorts. Although on the face of it a German victory, German records revealed that 2 U-boats were severely damaged and nearly all other U-boats received bomb or depth charge attacks.

In April HX231 lost only 3 ships with 2 U-boats sunk; then HX233 lost one ship for 1 U-boat sunk.

The turning point came with convoy ONS5, escorted by Commander Gretton's Escort Group. Forty ships sailed on 22nd April with 6 escorts. After 5 days of gales one merchant ship had detached to Iceland for repairs, and one fallen behind. At one time 8 were showing Not Under Command Lights. U-boats converged on 28th, and the escorts followed HFDF bearings to keep the 'homing' U-boats down. That night the escorts forced U-boats down 6 times, using radar to detect them in a rising gale.

The next day one merchant ship was sunk, but most U-boats went ahead to join another group and lie in wait. Five days of bad weather followed and the convoy was scattered by gales, and low visibility. On 5th and 6th May the U-boats struck: 11 ships were sunk. One U-boat was sunk by RCAF aircraft, another by a corvette escorting a group of 11 stragglers. Fog on 6th gave the escort the chance to use their radar to advantage, and 24 attacks were detected and beaten off: U.638 sunk by *Loosestrife* and U.125 by *Vidette*; U.531 was rammed by *Oribi* and U.438 sunk by depth charges from *Pelican* (just joining with the First Escort Group). A total of 60 U-boats attacked, 6 were sunk for 12 merchantmen lost. Two other U-boats collided and were lost, others were badly damaged. In all, 27 U-boats were sunk during this period.

U-boat command morale sank, and there was a reluctance to attack future convoys.

On 24th May 1943. U-boats were withdrawn from the North Atlantic routes, and the Battle of the Atlantic had been largely won.

was slightly ahead of HX 229, but slower. When the two convoys joined, the U-boats attacked and SC122's regular escort was overwhelmed, and 8 more ships were

HMS *Harvester*

22nd APRIL

1773   All Captains entitled to half-pay.

1813   *Weazle* destroyed four French gunboats and eight vessels of a convoy in Boscaline (Marina) Bay, Yugoslavia. [m, bh]

1847   Detachment of North American and West India squadron — *Alarm, Daring, Hermes, Vesuvius* and *Persian* — protected British interests in Gulf of Mexico during American — Mexico War.

1854   Bombardment of Odessa. British ships: *Arethusa, Furious, Retribution, Sampson, Terrible, Tiger.* French: *Caton, Descartes, Mogador, Vauban.* Rocket boats of *Agamemnon, Britannia, High-*

flyer, Sans Pareil, Trafalgar. Arethusa, the only purely sailing ship in the squadron, operated separately. This was the last occasion when a sailing ship in action was manoeuvred under sail.

1918   *Jackall* and *Hornet* drove off Austrian attack on Otranto defences.

1918   UB.55 sunk by mine North of Varne lightvessel.

1940   *Pelican* damaged by German aircraft off Norway (62° 49' N., 4° 20' E.).

1941   *York,* aground in Suda Bay, near-missed by German aircraft.

The Bombardment of Odessa, 1854. A magazine hit by a shell from HMS *Retribution* (2nd from left)

23rd APRIL

1697   George Anson born.

1794   *Arethusa, Concorde, Flora* and *Melampus* captured the French *Babet, Engageante* and *Pomone* 25 miles to the south-westward of Guernsey.

1797   *Magicienne* and *Regulus* repulsed a French attack on Fort Irois, Haiti.

1809   Boats of *Amphion, Mercury* and *Spartan* captured thirteen vessels at Porto Pesaro, East coast of Italy.

1895   *Vernon* shifted to Portchester Creek.

1915   Burial of Sub-Lt. Rupert Brooke, RNVR on Scyros, off Troy.

1916   *Bluebell* intercepted German *Aud* in effort to support Irish rebellion: She scuttled herself off Queenstown (Cork).

1918   VC: Acting Captain Alfred Francis Blakeney Carpenter *(Vindictive)*. * Lieutenant-Commander George Nicholson Bradford *(Iris)*. *Lieutenant-Commander Arthur Leyland Harrison *(Vindictive)*. Lieutenant Richard Douglas Sandford (C.3) Lieutenant Percy Thompson Dean RNVR (M.L. 282). Captain Edward Bamford DSO, RMLI *(Vindictive)*. Sergeant Norman Augustus Finch, RMA *(Vindictive)*. Able Seaman Albert Edward MacKenzie *(Vindictive)*. * Posthumous.

Block ship operations at Zeebrugge and Ostend. [bh]. Ships: *Afridi, Attentive, Brilliant-, Daffodil, Erebus, Faulknor-, General Craufurd-, Intrepid, Iphigenia, Iris, Lightfoot-, Lingfield, Lord Clive-, Manly, Mansfield, Marshal Soult-, Mastiff-, Matchless-, Melpomene, Mentor-, Moorsom, Morris, Myngs, North Star, Phoebe, Prince Eugene-, Scott, Sirius-, Stork, Swift-, Teazer, Tempest-, Termagant, Terror, Tetrarch-, Thetis, Trident, Truculent, Ulleswater, Velox, Vindictive, Warwick, Whirlwind, Zubian-*, Monitors: M.21, M.24, M.26, Submarines: C.1 C.3. CMB.: 2, 4, 5, 7, 10, 12, 15A, 16A, 17A, 19A, 20A, 21B, 22B, 23B, 24A, 25BD, 26B, 27A, 28A, 29A, 30B, 32A, 34A, 35A. ML.: 11, 16, 17, 22, 23, 30, 60, 79, 105, 110, 121, 128, 223, 239, 241, 252, 254, 258, 262, 272, 274, 276, 279, 280, 282, 283, 308, 314, 345, 397, 416, 420, 422, 424, 429, 512, 513, 525, 526, 532, 533, 549, 551, 552, 555, 556, 557, 558, 560, 561, 562. 4th Battalion RM. The ships marked - took part in the unsuccessfull Ostend operation. *Intrepid, Iphigenia* and *Thetis* sunk as block ships, C.3 expended; *Iris* and *Daffodil*, Mersey ferries, renamed *Royal Iris* and *Royal Daffodil* by command of King George V.

Captain Carpenter VC., Commander Osborne and Ship's Company, HMS *Vindictive*.

The damaged brows used for landing on the Mole, *Vindictive*

23rd APRIL

A Memorable Date observed by the Royal Marines

HMS *Vindictive* showing damage.

Zeebrugge and Ostend

In the First World War these ports were used by the Germans as submarine bases with easy access to the British sea lanes. Admiral Sir Roger Keyes planned the raids which were launched on 23rd April 1918, intended to block them. They were scarcely successful.

The Zeebrugge attack was carried through with great heroism under heavy enemy fire. Three old minelayers, *Intrepid, Iphigenia* and *Thetis*, filled with concrete, were sunk in the canal. The old cruiser *Vindictive* landed an assault party of seamen and Marines on the Long Mole, held in position by two Mersey Ferries *Iris* and *Daffodil.* The obsolete submarine C3 was driven in under the shoreward end of the Mole and blown up, cutting the Mole's defenders off from reinforcements. Motor launches were used in the attack and to take off blockship crews.

The battle on the Mole was ferocious and the crews of *Vindictive* and *Iris* as well as the assault parties carried out the attack with remarkable resolution, although their ships were shot full of holes and their casualties were terrible. There are dozens of tales of heroism and of the 8 VC's awarded, some were allocated by ballot under Rule 13 of the Royal Warrant since it would have been impossible to choose between them. 50% of the Royal Marines were casualties, and as a special honour no other RM battalion has ever again been numbered the 4th.

The Ostend operation did not succeed since the blockships were sunk before reaching their target. *Vindictive* sailed again, this time as a blockship for Ostend. Her bows are now a War Memorial in that port.

1940 Troops and naval base staff landed at Molde, Norway.

1943 *Hesperus* sank U.191 in N Atlantic (56° 45'N., 34° 25'W.). (Convoy ONS.4)

1943 Liberator V/120 sank U.189 in N Atlantic (59° 50'N, 34° 43'W.). (Convoy HX. 234)

1945 Liberator U/86 sank U.396 off Hebrides (59° 29'N, 5°22'W.).

1947 *Warspite* ran ashore in Prussia Cove, Cornwall on her way to breakers: broken up there instead.

HMS *Thetis* on her way to Zeebrugge.

24th APRIL

1546 Navy Board established.

1590 Ten English merchantmen beat off an attack by twelve Spanish galleys near Gibraltar. Ships: *Ascension, Centurion, Crescent, Elizabeth, Margaret and John, Minion, Richard Duffield, Samuel, Solomon, Violet.*

1709 *Bristol* taken by the French *Achille* and *Gloire* 330 miles S.W. by S. of Lizard Head. *Chester* captured *Gloire* and recaptured *Bristol.*

1778 *Drake* taken by John Paul Jones in the American *Ranger* off Carrickfergus, N Ireland.

1808 *Grasshopper* and *Rapid* captured two Spanish vessels and two gunboats, and wrecked two more gunboats off Faro, Portugal. [m]

1916 VC: Lieutenant Humphrey Osbaldeston Brooke Firman and Lieutenant-Commander Charles Henry Cowley, RNVR (both posthumous) for attempts to relieve Kut-al' Amara with 270 tons of supplies in *Julnar*, which was sunk.

1940 *Curaçoa* damaged by German aircraft at Aandalsnes.

1941 Evacuation of Imperial troops from Greece. Operation Demon. Ended 29th April. [bh]. Ships: *Ajax, Auckland, Calcutta, Carlisle, Coventry, Decoy, Defender, Diamond, Flamingo, Glenearn, Glengyle, Griffin, Grimsby, Hasty, Havock, Hereward, Hero, Hotspur, Hyacinth, Isis, Kandahar, Kimberley, Kingston, Muroto, Nubian, Orion, Perth+, Phoebe, Salvia, Stuart+, Ulster Prince, Vampire+, Vendetta+, Voyager+, Waterhen+, Wryneck.* +RAN.

1943 Fortress D/206 sank U.710 South of Iceland (61° 25'N. 19° 48'W.). (Convoy ONS.5)

1943 *Sahib* scuttled after depth charge attack by the Italian corvettes *Gabbiano* and *Euterpe* and t.b. *Climene* North of Cape Milazzo (38° 25' N. 15° 20' E).

1944 Sunderland A/423 (RCAF) sank U.311 in Western Approaches (50° 36'N, 18° 36'W.).

The visit of HRH The Prince of Wales to Hong Kong, 6th-8th April, 1922

25th APRIL

<table>
<tr><td>1513</td><td>Sir Edward Howard defeated by Chevalier Pregent de Bidoux off Brest.</td></tr>
<tr><td>1725</td><td>Augustus Keppel born.</td></tr>
<tr><td>1758</td><td>Battle of Sadras [bh]: see 29th April.</td></tr>
<tr><td>1796</td><td>Boats of Agamemnon, Diadem, Meleager and Peterel captured four French store-ships at Loano, Italian Riviera.</td></tr>
<tr><td>1825</td><td>Capture of Prome: see 2nd April.</td></tr>
<tr><td>1831</td><td>Black Joke captured the slaver Mariner-ito 18 miles E.S.E. of Cape Horacio, Fernando Po.</td></tr>
<tr><td>1858</td><td>Pearl's Naval Brigade at Pachawas, with the 13th Light Infantry, Bengal Yeomanry, 1st Bengal Military Police Battalion and Gurkha allies.</td></tr>
<tr><td>1868</td><td>Launch of the eighth Repulse: last wooden capital ship, and last major ship launched at Woolwich; completed at Sheerness.</td></tr>
<tr><td>1908</td><td>Gladiator sunk in collision with S.S. St.Paul off Isle of Wight.</td></tr>
<tr><td>1915</td><td>VC: Commander Edward Unwin (Hussar). Sub-Lieutenant Arthur Walderne St. Clair Tisdall RNVR. Midshipman Wilfred St. Aubyn Malleson (Cornwallis). Midshipman George Leslie Drewry RNR (Hussar). William Charles Williams, Able Seaman RFR (Hussar). George McKenzie Samson,</td></tr>
</table>

<table>
<tr><td></td><td>Seaman RNR (Hussar). Landing at Gallipoli — V. Beach. (River Clyde).</td></tr>
<tr><td>1915</td><td>UB.13 mined and sunk off Zeebrugge.</td></tr>
<tr><td>1916</td><td>German battle cruiser raid on Lowestoft and Yarmouth.</td></tr>
<tr><td>1916</td><td>E.22 torpedoed and sunk by UB.18 off Yarmouth.</td></tr>
<tr><td>1918</td><td>Jessamine sank U.104 in South Irish sea (51° 59'N, 6° 26'W.).</td></tr>
<tr><td>1918</td><td>St. Seiriol mined off Shipwash light vessel.</td></tr>
<tr><td>1918</td><td>Cowslip torpedoed off Cape Spartel.</td></tr>
<tr><td>1918</td><td>Willow Branch (Bombala) sunk by U.153 and U.154 East of the Cape Verde Islands (20° 50' N, 17° 20' W.).</td></tr>
<tr><td>1940</td><td>Bradman and Hammond sunk by German aircraft at Aandalsnes.</td></tr>
<tr><td>1941</td><td>Pennland, transport, sunk by German aircraft off Megara. Ulster Prince, supply ship, destroyed by aircraft at Nauplia after grounding on the 24th. Operation Demon.</td></tr>
<tr><td>1943</td><td>Pathfinder and aircraft of 811 Sq (Biter) sank U.203 in NW Atlantic (55° 05'N, 42° 25'W). (Convoy ONS.4)</td></tr>
</table>

V Beach seen from HMS *River Clyde.*

Trawler with troops passing HMS *Implacable.*

26th APRIL

1796   *Niger* destroyed the French *Écureuil* under Penmarc'h Point, Brittany.

1797   *Emerald* and *Irresistible* captured the Spanish *Elena* and *Ninfa* in Conil Bay, near Cadiz.

1809   *Thrasher* fought forty French gunboats off Boulogne.

1810   *Sylvia* captured the Dutch *Echo* and two small transports 10 miles North of Batavia. [m, bh]

1810   First appointments to Milford Haven dockyard.

1861   *Brune* and *Fideliter*, with boats of *Alecto, Arrogant, Espoir* and *Ranger*, destroyed Porto Novo, Dahomey.

1876   *Vernon*, established in 1872 as torpedo instruction ship in Fountain Lake, and as tender to *Excellent*, became an independent command.

1928   First Admiralty production order for multiple pom-pom AA guns.

1940   *Arrow* rammed by German minelaying trawler (under Dutch colours) off Kristiansund (63° 15' N, 6° 10' E.). *Birmingham* later sank the trawler.

1940   *Griffin* captured the German Schiff 26 (ex-*Julius Pickenpack*) U-boat supply and depot ship – in Norwegian Sea (62° 37' N, 4° 00' E).

1944   Air strikes on German convoy off Bodö and on shipping there. Operation Ridge (Able). Carriers: *Furious, Victorious, Emperor, Pursuer, Searcher, Striker*. Ships: *Anson* (Vice-Admiral Sir Henry Moore), *Jamaica, Royalist* and 14 destroyers. FAA Sq.: 804 (Hellcat) *Emperor*, 827 (Barracuda) *Furious*, 880 (Seafire) *Furious*, 1834, 1836 (Corsair) *Victorious*.

1944   *Black Prince* and *Ashanti*, with *Athabaskan, Haida* and *Huron* (RCN) engaged 3 German destroyers off Île De Bas. Operation Tunnel. *Haida* sank T.27 and T.29, 7 miles West of Les Heaux.

27th APRIL

1297   All vessels of 40 tuns or more and all vessels in Cinque ports mobilised by Royal writ to take an expeditionary force to France.

1770   Edward Codrington born.

1799   *Black Joke* captured the French *Rebecca* 18 miles W.S.W. of Ushant.

1813   *Surveillante* and *Lyra* captured the American letter of marque *Tom* 85 miles N.N.W. of Cape Ortegal.

1915   VC: Lieutenant-Commander Edward Courtney Boyle. *(E.14)* and Lieutenant-Commander Martin Eric Nasmith *(E.11)* for work in the sea of Marmora, beyond the Dardanelles.

1916   *Russell* and *Nasturtium* sunk by mines off Malta.

1916   *Firedrake* captured the German UC.5, which had grounded on the Shipwash shoal (52° 03' N, 1° 46' E), and took her into Harwich.

1917   German destroyer raid on Ramsgate. Ships: *Marshal Ney*, TB.4.

1937   National Maritime Museum, Greenwich opened by King George VI. *Wishart* and CMBs 3, 4, 5 and 6.

1941   *Diamond* and *Wryneck* sunk by German aircraft off Crete (36° 30'N, 23° 34'E.). (Operation Demon)

1941   *Patia*, fighter catapult ship, sunk by German aircraft off the Tyne.

1944   *Untiring* sank the German UJ.6075 off Toulon.

1945   *Redmill* torpedoed by U.1105 off Blacksod Bay (54° 23'N, 10° 36'W.). Towed in by *Jaunty* rescue tug, but CTL.

28th APRIL

1789 Mutiny in *Bounty:* Bligh began his epic voyage with nineteen men in a twenty-three foot boat.

1799 *Martin* captured the French *Vengeur* off The Skaw, Denmark.

1813 Boats of *Orpheus* destroyed the American letter of marque *Wampo* three miles up the West River, Narragansett Bay. [m]

1814 Napoleon surrendered to Captain Ussher in *Undaunted* for passage to Elba.

1851 Admiral Sir Edward Codrington died.

1864 VC: Samuel Mitchell, captain of fore-top, *(Harrier)* for entering the Pah and bringing out his Commander who had been mortally wounded. Attack on the Gate Pah, New Zealand. Naval Brigade: *Curaçoa, Esk, Falcon, Harrier, Miranda.* Troops: 43rd Light Infantry, 68th Regiment, Royal Artillery.

1940 *Black Swan* damaged and *Cape Siretoko* sunk by German aircraft in the Aandalsnes area.

1940 VC: Lieutenant Richard Been Stannard, RNR *(Arab)* at Namsos, Norway.

Lt Cdr M. E. Nasmith, VC.

1941 *Gladiolus* sank U.65 in N Atlantic (60° 04'N, 15° 45'W). (Convoy HM.121)

1942 *Urge* sunk by mine off Malta, on passage to Alexandria.

1943 *Unshaken* sank the Italian t.b. *Climene* off Punta Libeccio (37° 45' N, 11° 33' E.).

1944 Wellington W/612 sank U.193 in Bay of Biscay (45° 38'N, 9° 43'W.).

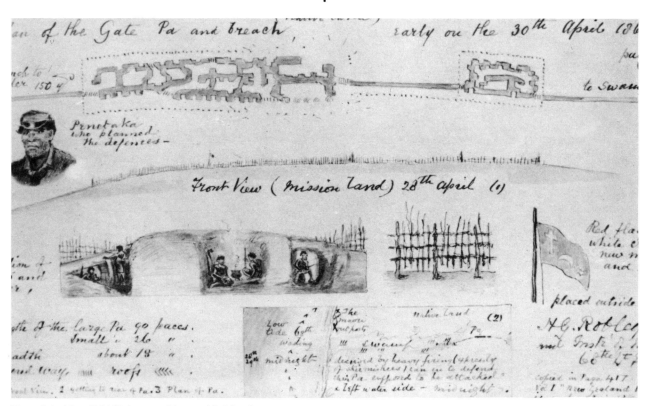

Plan of the 'Gate Pah' (Pah means 'Fortress' in Maori)

1744 *Dreadnought* and *Grampus* captured the French *Medée* 140 miles South of Ushant.

1758 Vice-Admiral George Pocock *(Yarmouth)* fought Commodore Comte d'Ache *(Zodiaque)*, with 9 ships, 12 miles S.E. of Sadras. [bh]. Ships: *Cumberland, Yarmouth, Elizabeth, Weymouth, Tiger, Newcastle, Salisbury,* Frigates, etc.: *Queensborough, Protector.* An inconclusive action like those of 3rd August and 10th September, because of too strict an adherence to the Fighting Instructions.

1758 *Dorsetshire* captured the French *Raisonnable* 20 miles S.S.W. of Ushant. [bh]

1780 Capture of Castillo Viejo, San Juan de Nicaragua. Captain Horatio Nelson *(Hinchinbrook)* had gone in command of the naval force but had been invalided before this date.

1781 Rear-Admiral Sir Samuel Hood *(Barfleur)* fought Vice-Admiral Comte de Grasse *(Ville-de-Paris)*, with 20 ships of the line, a few miles to the westward of Martinique. Ships: *Shrewsbury, Intrepid, Torbay, Prince William, Russell, Centaur, Gibraltar, Montagu, Resolution; Ajax, Princessa, Terrible, Barfleur, Monarch, Invincible, Alcide, Belliqueux, Alfred.* Frigates, etc.: *Amazon, Lizard, Pacahunta.*

1802 Marines styled "Royal Marines" by **George III** "for meritorious service".

1812 *Goshawk, Hyacinth, Resolute* and Gunboat No. 16 captured the French privateers *Brave* and *Napoleon* at Malaga. [m]

1813 Boats of squadron, under the personal command of Rear-Admiral George Cockburn, destroyed American shipping and stores at Frenchtown, Elk River, Virginia. [m]. Ships and vessels: *Dolphin, Dragon, Fantome, Highflyer, Maidstone, Marlborough, Mohawk, Racer, Statira.* A detachment of Royal Artillery took part.

1814 *Epervier* taken by the American *Peacock* 12 miles off the East coast of Florida.

1847 Canned meat added to ships' victualling stores.

1849 *Inflexible* captured six pirate junks off Tamkan, near Hong Kong.

1858 *Pearl's* Naval Brigade at Nagar, with the 13th Light Infantry, Bengal Yeomanry, 1st Bengal Military Police Battalion and Gurkha allies.

1862 *Prince Albert* (first RN turret ship) laid down.

1916 Surrender from starvation of Kut-al 'Amara by Major-General Townshend to the Turkish forces under Major-General Khalil Pasha. Captured: *Sumana* (armed tug).

1921 Mutiny by RNR battalion at Newport (Miners' Strike).

Captain's Cabin HMS *Majestic,* **late 1890's.**

1940   GC (ex-EGM): Lieutenant John Niven Angus Low and Able Seaman Henry James Miller, (both posthumous), for gallantry when *Unity* sank in collision with the Norwegian s.s. *Atle Jarl* off Blyth (55° 13'N, 1° 19'W.).

1941   *Aphis* bombarded enemy positions in the Sollum area.

1941   Evacuation of Imperial troops from Greece completed. [bh]. Operation Demon.

1944   *Haida* and *Athabaskan* (RCN) covering a minelaying operation (Operation Hostile 26), engaged two German destroyers 11 miles N.E. of Ushant, driving them ashore and setting them on fire. *Athabaskan* torpedoed and sunk in 48° 29'N, 4° 09'W.

1945   *Goodall* torpedoed by U.968 off Kola Inlet, N. Russia, and sunk by own forces: *Anguilla, Cotton* and *Loch Shin* sank U.286 and *Loch Insh* sank U.307 in Kola Inlet, just before Convoy RA.66 sailed.

1945   Liberator Q/120 sank U.1017 in NW Approaches.

Mine Clearance

One aspect of warfare which receives constant practice even in peacetime is the clearing of all the unexploded ammunition left lying about after past wars. Full-time teams of clearance divers are still employed making safe or destroying shells, mines and other ordnance which is washed ashore or trawled up around our coasts.

These illustrations show the Far East Fleet Clearance Diving Team in January 1968 working on one of the many mines and torpedo warheads discovered in a secret Japanese ammunition store five miles from Georgetown, Penang. Hundreds of tons of weapons were made safe during these operations.

30th APRIL

1697   *Medway* captured the French privateer *Pontchartrain* 60 miles to the southward of Kinsale.

1704   End of siege of Gibraltar.

1815   *Rivoli* captured the French *Melpomène* 4 miles North of Ischia, West coast of Italy.

1861   Instructor officers first appointed by commission.

1862   Boat of *Ariel* captured a slave dhow at Merka, East coast of Africa.

1863   Indian Marine replaced Indian Navy.

1903   RNB Chatham commissioned as *Pembroke*.

1915   AE.2 (RAN) sunk by the Turkish t.b. *Sultan Hissar* near the island of Marmara.

1917   VC: Acting-Lieutenant William Edward Sanders, RNR *(First Prize-Q.21)* in action with U.93 120 miles SW of the Fastnet.

1917   *Tulip* (Q.12) sunk by U.62 150 miles W by N of Valentia Island. (52° 10'N, 14 ° 20'W.).

1918   *Coreopsis* sank the German UB.85 off Isle of Man (54° 47' N, 5° 27' W.).

1940   *Bittern* damaged by German aircraft at Namsos (64° 28' N, 11° 30' E.). Sunk by *Carlisle*.

1940   *Dunoon* sunk by mine off Great Yarmouth (52° 45' N, 2° 23' E.).

1941   *Parvati* (RIN) sunk by mine near Mocha, Red Sea.

1942*   *Edinburgh* torpedoed by the German U.456 in Barents Sea (73° 08'N, 33° 00' E.). (Convoy QP.11 – cover)

1943   Hampden X/455 (RAAF) sank U.227 N of Shetland (64° 05'N, 6° 40'W.).

1943   Operation Mincemeat landing of the late Major Martin, RM, on Spanish coast by *Seraph* .

1945   *Havelock, Hesperus* and Sunderland H/201 sank U.232 in Irish Sea (53° 42' N, 4° 53' W.).

An Avenger strike aircraft

1945   Bombardment and air strike on Car Nicobar airfields, and bombardment of Port Blair, Andaman Islands, by Force 63. Operation Bishop. Carriers: *Empress, Shah.* Hellcat (804) and Avenger (851). Ships: *Queen Elizabeth* (Vice-Admiral H.T.C. Walker), *Richelieu* (Fr); *Cumberland* (Rear-Admiral W.R. Patterson—CS.5). *Ceylon, Suffolk, Tromp* (Neth); *Rotherman,* (D.11), *Tartar* (D.10), *Nubian, Penn, Verulam.*

1945   *Roebuck* (Cdre. D), *Racehorse* and *Redoubt* (Force 62) destroyed a Japanese troop convoy of 10 vessels proceeding from Rangoon to Moulmein. Operation Gable.

1946   GC: Lieutenant George Gosse, RANVR, for oyster mine detection and disposal.

*Russian Convoy QP. 11.

QP. 11 comprised 13 ships returning to UK from Russia. There was a strong escort and the covering cruiser was the *Edinburgh*. On 30th April, while zig zagging ahead of the convoy, *Edinburgh* was hit by two torpedoes and had her stern blown off. She proceeded to Murmansk at slow speed with two destroyers as escort. The U-boat continued to shadow the convoy, and 3 German destroyers set sail to attack the convoy now that its escort was weakened. On 1st May the German destroyers tried 5 times to attack the convoy. Each time they were foiled by the British escort. The *Amazon* was damaged, which left the escort with only six 4.7 in guns and three 4 in guns against the German ten 5.9 in and five 5 in guns. Only one straggling merchantman was sunk. The Germans then turned their attention to the *Edinburgh*, and the convoy had no more attacks. On 2nd, the *Edinburgh* had been joined by 4 mine-sweepers, and the Germans also arrived on the scene. *Edinburgh* hit and stopped a German destroyer, then the destroyer *Forester* was hit. *Edinburgh* was torpedoed again and almost cut in half. Despite this, she continued extremely good fire. The last destroyer, *Foresight,* was also brought to a standstill by the Germans, who then failed to take advantage of the situation, but took off survivors from their destroyer the *Hermann Schoemann,* sank her and withdrew. The two British destroyers got under way again, but the *Edinburgh* had to be sunk.

1st MAY

1689   Battle of Bantry Bay. Admiral Arthur Herbert *(Elizabeth)* fought the French fleet of 24 ships of the line under Vice-Admiral Comte de Chateaurenault *(Ardent)*. Ships and vessels: *Defiance, Portsmouth, Plymouth, Ruby, Diamond, Advice, Mary, St. Albans, Edgar, Elizabeth, Pendennis, Portland, Deptford, Woolwich, Dartmouth, Greenwich, Cambridge, Antelope, York.* Fireships: *Firedrake, Salamander, Saudadoes.*

1707   *Grafton* and *Hampton Court*, with 22 out of a convoy of 45 sail, taken by 9 sail of the line under Commodore Comte de Forbin *(Mars)* 20 miles S.W. by S. of Beachy Head. *Royal Oak* escaped.

1795   *Boyne* destroyed by fire at Spithead.

1795   Able Seaman Provo Wallis signed on; died as Admiral of the Fleet 15th February 1892.

1797   First Spithead Mutiny ended with issue of Admiralty orders against abuses.

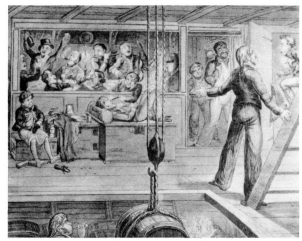

Life below decks – midshipmen's mess c. 1790

1810   Boats of *Nereide* captured the French *Estafette* and stormed two batteries at Jacotet, Mauritius. [m]

1811   *Pomone, Scout* and *Unite* destroyed the French *Girafe, Nourrice* and an armed ship in Sagone Bay, Corsica.

1825   Boats of the Irrawaddy flotilla captured eight Burmese war boats above Prome.

1830   Bombay Marine became Indian Navy.

1838   John Charles Colomb born.

1862   Capture of Kading by Brigadier-General Charles Staveley, with British and Indian troops, and British and French Naval Brigades. Naval Brigade of *Imperieuse, Pearl, Vulcan, Flamer* and *Coromandel.* Troops: RA., RE., 31st, 67th and 99th Regiments; 5th Bombay Native Light Infantry, 22nd Bengal Native Infantry.

1891   Gunnery School on Whale Island commissioned as *Excellent.*

1915   Landing at Gallipoli. VC: Lance Corporal Walter Richard Parker RMLI.

1915   *Laforey, Leonidas, Lawford* and *Lark* sank the German A.2 and A.6 off the North Hinder lightvessel.

1915   *Recruit* sunk by UB.6 off the Galloper lightvessel.

1915   The American *Gulf-light* torpedoed without warning by U.30 off the Scilly Islands. First U.S. merchant ship to be so attacked.

1917   E.54 sank U.81 in SW Approaches.

1918   *Blackmore Vale* mined off Montrose.

1939   Painted Hall Greenwich opened as Mess of the Royal Naval College.

1942   *Punjabi* sunk in collision with *King George V* off Iceland (66° 00' N, 8° 00' W.). (Convoy PQ.15 – cover)

1942   Hudson M/233 damaged U.573 in W Mediterranean (37° 00'N, 1° 00'E.). U-boat reached Cartagena and was later sold to Spain.

1944   Swordfish C/842 *(Fencer)* sank U.277 off N Norway. (Convoy RA.59)

1945   Continuation of Operation Bishop. (See 30th April)

1945   *Catterick* and *Kimberley* provided gun support to Commando raids on Rhodes and Alimnia.

1956   White cap covers put on for last time: ie, not removed on 30th September as usual but worn all the year round.

1970   Start of continuous commissioning of HM ships.

1971   C-in-C Western Fleet became responsible for Far East Fleet.

2nd MAY

1694   *Adventure, Dragon* and *Monck* captured the French privateer *Diligente* 4 miles outside S. Mary's Sound, Scilly Islands.

1781   *Canada* captured the Spanish *Santa Leocadia* 450 miles to the westward of Cape Finisterre.

1809   Boats of *Mercury* and *Spartan* captured twelve vessels and blew up a tower at Porto Cesenatico, East coast of Italy.

1813   Boats of *Redwing, Repulse, Undaunted* and *Volontaire* destroyed the batteries at Morgiou, near Marseilles, and captured six small merchant vessels. [m]

1814   Admiral Alexander Hood, Viscount Bridport, died.

1917   First U.S. Destroyer Flotilla arrived at Queenstown.

1917   *Derwent* sunk by mine 2 cables North of the Whistle buoy, Le Havre.

1918   UB.31 mined in Strait of Dover.

1941   *Jersey* sunk by mine in entrance to Grand Harbour, Malta.

1942   *Wishart, Wrestler* and Catalina C/202 sank U.74 in W Mediterranean.

1942   *Jastrzab* (Pol) (ex-P.551) sunk by *St. Albans* and *Seagull* off N Norway.

1942   *Edinburgh* sunk by *Foresight* in 71° 51' N, 35° 10' E., after being torpedoed by U.456 on 30th April (q.v.) and again on 2nd May by two German destroyers. One of these, the *Hermann Schoemann,* was sunk.

1943   Sunderland M/461 (RAAF) sank U.332 in Bay of Biscay.

1944   *Ajax* bombarded Rhodes.

1944   Swordfish B/842 *(Fencer)* sank U.674 and U.959 off N Norway.(Convoy RA.59)

1945   *Ebor Wyke* sunk by U.979 7 miles North of Skagi, Iceland. Last British warship sunk by U-boat in World War II.

1945   Mosquito aircraft of 143, 235 and 248 Sq., 404 Sq. (RCAF) and 33 Sq. (Nor) sank U.2359 in Kattegat.

1945   First wave of amphibious assault by 26th Indian Div. on Rangoon. Operation Dracula. LSH.: *Largs* (Rear-Admiral B.C.S. Martin — Force W), *Nith, Waveney.* LSI.: *Glenroy, Persimmon, Prins Albert, Silvio.* Depot Ship: *Barpeta.* Support squadron: *Phoebe, Royalist; Emperor, Hunter, Khedive, Stalker; Saumarez* (S.26), *Venus, Vigilant, Virago.* FAA Sq.: 800 (Hellcat) *(Emperor),* 807 (Seafire) *Hunter,* 808 (Hellcat) *(Khedive),* 809 (Seafire) *(Stalker)* and 1700 (Sea Otter).

Seamen's mess in 6-inch battery, **HMS** *Jupiter* c.1900

3rd MAY

1746 Battle in Loch nan Uamh between three British and two French ships, first of six attempts to rescue the Young Pretender. This, not Culloden, was the last battle of the '45.

1747 Vice-Admiral Sir George Anson *(Prince George)* defeated Commodore La Jonquière *(Sérieux)*, with a large convoy, 70 miles N ¾ W. of Cape Finisterre. [bh]. Six of the escorting ships and six merchantmen were captured:- *Diamant, Gloire, Invincible, Jason, Rubis, Sérieux, Apollon, Dartmouth, Modeste, Philibert, Thetis, Vigilant.* Ships: *Bristol, Centurion, Defiance, Devonshire, Falkland, Monmouth, Namur, Nottingham, Pembroke, Prince Frederick, Prince George, Princess Louisa, Windsor, Yarmouth.* Frigates, etc: *Ambuscade, Falcon, Vulcan.*

1810 *Spartan* engaged the Franco-Neapolitan *Achilles, Cérés, Fame, Sparviere* and eight gunboats in Naples Bay. *Sparviere* captured. [m]

1813 Boats of *Undaunted* captured a French ship from under the batteries at Marseilles.

1813 Boats of squadron, under the personal command of Rear-Admiral George Cockburn, destroyed American shipping, military storehouses and a cannon foundry in the Susquehanna River and at Havre de Grace, Virginia. [m]. Ships: *Dolphin, Dragon, Fantome, Highflyer, Maidstone, Malborough, Mohawk, Racer, Statira.* A detachment of Royal Artillery took part in the operation.

1905 Fort Blockhouse, taken over from Royal Engineers, commissioned as *Dolphin*.

1940 *Afridi* sunk by German aircraft NW of Trondheim.

1940 *Aurora, Effingham* and *Resolution* bombarded Beisfjord, Narvik.

1941 *Usk* mined and sunk off Cape Bon.

1941 *Fermoy* sunk by German aircraft in dock at Malta.

1944 Wellingtons E/621 and T/621 drove ashore U.852 at Bandar Bela, Italian Somaliland; blown up by own crew (First attacked on the 2nd).

1945 Allied troops entered Rangoon. Operation Dracula.

1945 Beaufighter aircraft of 236 and 254 Sq. sank the German U.2524 in Kattegat.

1945 Aircraft of 2nd Tactical Air Force sank U.2540, U.3030 and U.3032 in the Belts, Denmark, and U.1210 in Kiel. *Lützow* scuttled at Swinemunde.

The "Through Deck Cruiser", HMS *Invincible,* launched by HM The Queen at Vickers (Barrow), 3rd May, 1977

4th MAY

1786   "Duty is the great business of a Sea-officer. All private considerations must give way to it, however painful it is." Nelson to Frances Nisbet.

1796   *Spencer* captured the French *Volcan* 360 miles N.E. of the Bahama Islands.

1806   Boats of *Nautilus* and *Renommée* cut out the Spanish *Giganta* at Torrevieja, S.E. Spain.

1809   *Parthian* captured the French privateer *Nouvelle Gironde* 150 miles North of Cape Ortegal.

1810   Boats of *Armide, Cadmus, Daring* and *Monkey* destroyed thirteen vessels at Port de Loix, Île de Ré.

1811   Landing party from *Alceste* and *Belle Poule* destroyed a French 14-gun brig at Porto di Parenzo, Istria. [m]

1812   Boats of *Bermuda, Castilian, Phipps* and *Rinaldo* recaptured *Apelles* which had run ashore 3 miles East of Etaples, North coast of France. *Skylark*, which had also grounded in the vicinity, was burnt by her own crew who got away in the boats.

1910   Establishment of Royal Canadian Navy.

1916   *Galatea* and *Phaeton* brought down Zeppelin L.7 10 miles South of Horns Reef lightvessel. E.31 completed her destruction and rescued seven survivors.

1940   *Grom* (Pol) sunk by German aircraft at Narvik.

1942   Battle of the Coral Sea (see 7th May).

The Japanese planned to capture Port Moresby in New Guinea as part of their aim to take the chain of island bases across the supply route from America to Australia and New Zealand. On 20 April they sailed a strong force escorted by cruisers and destroyers from Truk towards the Coral Sea. This force was covered by another force of a carrier and 4 cruisers, while a third force of 2 carriers, 2 cruisers and 6 destroyers approached the Coral Sea from the East, to surprise the Allied forces from the rear. The Allies gained intelligence of these moves and formed 2 powerful task forces of 2 carriers and a third force of 3 cruisers (the USS *Chicago* and HMAS *Hobart* and *Australia)*. On 6 May the invasion fleet was sighted by Allied aircraft, and on the 7th one Japanese carrier was sunk by carrier borne aircraft. The next day both sides attacked each other and one Japanese carrier and both USN carriers were severely hit. The USS *Lexington* exploded later and had to be sunk. The Japanese, however, failed to gain control of Port Moresby or the Coral Sea.

1943   Liberator P/86 sank U.465 in N Atlantic (47° 22'N, 22° 40'W.).

1943   Canso W/5 (RCAF) sank U.630 in NW Atlantic (56° 38'N, 42° 32'W.). (Convoy ONS.5)

1943   *Nubian, Paladin* and *Petard* sank the Italian t.b. *Perseo* off Kelibia, Tunisia.

1944   *Elgin* damaged by mine off Portland.

1944   *Blankney*, USS *Joseph E. Campbell, Pride* and *Sustain,* and *Sénégalais* (Fr) sank U.371 in Mediterranean (39° 49'N. 5° 39'E). (Convoy GUS.38)

1944   Wellington M/407 (RCAF) sank U.846 in Bay of Biscay.

1945   U-boats ordered to cease hostilities.

1945   *Schlelen* mined off Swinemunde.

1945   Beaufighters of 236 and 254 Sq. sank U.236, U.393, U.2338 and U.2503* near Omö, Great Belt. *Scuttled. U.4712 sunk by aircraft in Kiel.

1945   The last air strike by the Home Fleet, on Kilbotn anchorage. Operation Judgement. Carriers: *Queen, Searcher, Trumpeter.* Ships: *Diadem, Norfolk; Carysfort, Opportune, Savage, Scourge, Zambesi; Obedient, Orwell,* R.F.A. *Blue Ranger,* FAA Sq.: 853 (Avenger and Wildcat), 882 (Wildcat), 846 (Avenger and Wildcat). German ships sunk: *Black Watch, Karl von Hering* and U.711.

1973   NATO Standing Naval Force Channel inaugurated at Ostend.

Hellcats and Wildcats over a Carrier, 1945

5th MAY

1794   *Orpheus* captured the French *Duguay-Trouin* 3 miles off the N.E. corner of Mauritius.

1804   Capture of Surinam by Commodore Samuel Hood *(Centaur)* and troops under Brigadier-General Sir Charles Green. Ships: *Alligator, Centaur, Drake, Emerald, Hippomenes, Pandour, Serapis, Unique,* and boats of *Guachapin.* Troops: Royal Artillery, Sappers and Miners, 16th, 2/60th, 64th and 6th West India Regiments.

1861   *Cockchafer, Firm* and *Haughty,* with boats of *Pearl,* destroyed the pirate town of Tsingchow near Swatow, SE China.

1917   *Lavender* sunk by the German UC.75 22 miles S.W. of Waterford harbour.

1918   *Rhododendron* torpedoed by U.70 in N Sea.

1919   *Cupar* mined off Tyne.

1940   *Seal* damaged by mine in the Kattegat, and surrendered to German forces.

1942   Attack on Diego Suarez, Madagascar. (see 7th May). Sunk: Vichy-French: *Bévéziers, Bougainville* by aircraft.

Operation Ironclad — Capture of Diego Suarez
On 18th March 1942, the decision was made to capture Madagascar, which was under Vichy-French control and an excellent base for the Japanese to use to threaten shipping in the Indian Ocean and Middle East. Forces were sailed UK and assembled at Durban. Slow and Fast convoys sailed from Durban on 25th and 28th April respectively, and met 35 miles off Cape Amber on 4th May. Minesweepers swept the way to the first anchorage and then to the assault position, which was reached at 0330 on 5th. The enemy were caught completely unawares as they had regarded the unlit and treacherous channels, which were full of rocks and strong currents, as impassable at night. Aircraft from the *Illustrious* and *Indomitable* attacked the harbour and airfield, the cruiser *Hermione* created a diversion off the East Coast with pyrotechnics, while the *Devonshire* and 4 destroyers covered the landings from 17 ships on the West Coast. By the evening most troops were ashore, but un-expected resistance was met from new defences. The next evening the destroyer *Anthony* took 50 Marines (from the battleship *Ramillies*) in under the Eastern Coastal defences, and landed them at the Naval Base in a heavy sea by coming stern-to the jetty. Their impact was so successful that they were embarrassed by the number of prisoners they took, and by 0300 on 7th the town and its defences were taken. At 1040 the *Ramillies* started a bombardment of the Eastern Coastal defences, which surrendered after 10 minutes. In 60 hours from the first landing the operation was completed for the loss of one corvette. There had been good inter-Service co-operation and the ability to take troops over thousands of miles of ocean and land them with carrier borne air cover was well demonstrated.

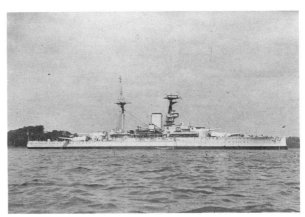

HMS *Ramillies*

1943   *Loosestrife* sank U.638 in NW Atlantic (53° 06'N, 45° 02'W.) and *Pink* sank U.192 (54° 56'N, 43° 44'W.). (Convoy ONS.5)

1944   *Starling, Wild Goose* and *Wren* attacked U.473 which was sunk on the 6th in Atlantic (49° 29'N, 21° 22'W.).

1945   Liberator aircraft sank the following U-boats in the Kattegat:- G/86 sank U.3503; T/206 sank U.534; T/224 sank U.3523; L/311 (Czech) sank U.2365; K/547 sank U.2521.

1945   Bombardment and air strikes (begun on the 4th) on Sakishima Gunto area by Task Force 57. Ships: See 26th March; add *Formidable*[5], and *Uganda,* less *Argonaut* and *Illustrious.* Air strikes continued during May on the 8th, 9th, 12th, 13th, 16th, 17th, 20th, 21st, 24th and 25th respectively. F.A.A. Sq.: Avenger 820, 848[5], 849, 857. Corsair 1834, 1836, 1841[5], 1842[5]. Firefly 1770. Hellcat 1839, 1844. Seafire 887, 894.

1955   West Germany joined NATO.

6th MAY

1673 *St. Helena* recaptured from the Dutch, together with three Dutch East Indiamen. Ships and vessels: *Assistance, Castle, Mary & Martha, William & Thomas.*

1770 Cook discovered Port Jackson (Sydney)

1801* *Speedy* captured the Spanish *Gamo* 15 miles to the south-westward of Barcelona. [m]

*Admiral Thomas Lord Cochrane. (1775 - 1860)

Cochrane was a brilliant sloop and frigate Commander in the Napoleonic Wars, his red head matched his temperament and he was said to be "always holding out his toes to be trodden on and he possessed 10 of them". In 1800, in command of the sloop *Speedy* he gained a great reputation for seizing Spanish prizes. A 32-gun ship, the *Gamo*, was specially commissioned to fight him and in May 1801 the two ships met. The *Speedy* defeated the *Gamo*. Co   ane was appointed to the 32 gun *Pallas* and thence to the 38 gun *Imperieuse*. In 1809 he was in command of the fire-ship raid in the Basque Roads for which he was created a KB. However as a member of Parliament he was constantly attacking the government and he was placed on half pay until 1813. He was fined and sent to prison as a result of stock exchange deals, and from 1817 he commanded the Chilean, Brazilian and Greek navies in turn. He achieved remarkable success with these navies but not without constantly upsetting his superiors. In 1832 he received a free pardon at home and served from 1848 to 1851 as CinC North America and West Indies station. Promoted GCB in 1847. Buried in Westminster Abbey.

1806 *Adamant* captured the Spanish *N.S. de los Dolores* 360 miles N.W. by N. of Tristan da Cunha.

1814 Capture and destruction of the fort at Oswego, Lake Ontario, by ships of the Lake Squadron and troops under Lieutenant-General Gordon Drummond.

Ships: *Charwell, Magnet, Montreal, Niagara, Prince Regent, Princess Charlotte, Star.* Troops: Royal Artillery, Royal Sappers and Miners, De Watteville's Regiment, Glengarry Fencible Light Infantry.

1941 *Camito* sunk by U.97 in Atlantic (50° 40'N, 21° 30'W).

1942 Swordfish aircraft of 829 Sq. *(Illustrious)* sank the Vichy-French s/m *Héros* off Madagascar. (Operation Ironclad)

1943 *Oribi* sank U.531 in Atlantic (53° 00'N, 43° 00'W.) (approx), *Vidette* U.125 (52° 31'N, 44° 50'W.) and *Pelican* U.438 (52° 00'N, 45° 10'W.). (All on Convoy ONS.5)

1944 *Aylmer, Bickerton, Bligh* and Swordfish A/825 and X/825 *(Vindex)* sank U.765 in Atlantic (52° 30'N 25° 28' W.).

1945 Liberator G/86 sank U.1008 in the Skagerrak and Liberator K/86 U.2534 in the Kattegat.

1945 Continuation of Operation Bishop. (See 30th April). Air strikes by aircraft from *Emperor, Hunter, Khedive* and *Stalker,* supported by *Royalist,* on area between Mergui and Victoria Point, Burma. FAA Sq.: Hellcat 800, 808 *(Emperor, Khedive).* Seafire 807, 809 *(Hunter, Stalker).*

HMS *Viper,* 1901

7th MAY

1765 *Victory* launched.

1794 *Swiftsure* captured the French *Atalante* 400 miles to the westward of Cape Finisterre.

1797 Outbreak of second mutiny at Spithead.

1798 British naval garrison from *Badger* and *Sandfly* repulsed a French attack on the Îles de St. Marcouf, North coast of France. Troops: Royal Artillery, Invalids. [m]

1808 *Redwing* captured or destroyed a Spanish convoy and its escort off Cape Trafalgar. Only two of the seven escorts and one of the twelve enemy escaped. [m]

1879 Lieutenants of eight years seniority shipped a half stripe.

1901 *Viper* commissioned: first turbine driven TBD.

1909 Admiralty tender for first airship signed.

1915 *Maori* sunk by mine off the Wielingen lightvessel, near Zeebrugge.

1936 Remains of *Anzac* ceremoniously scuttled.

1940 RNEC opened at Manadon.

1941 *Stoke* sunk by aircraft at Tobruk.

1941 *München*, German weather ship, "pinched" off Iceland.

1942 Capture of Diego Suarez by a combined force under Rear-Admiral E.N. Syfret (*Ramillies*) and Major-General R.G. Sturges, RM. Operation Ironclad. [bh]. Ships: *Active, Anthony, Auricula*, Bachaquero, Cromarty, Cromer, Cyclamen, Devonshire, Duncan, Freesia, Fritillary, Genista, Hermione, Illustrious, Inconstant, Indomitable, Jasmine, Javelin, Karanga, Keren, Laforey, Lightning, Lookout, Nigella, Pakenham, Paladin, Panther, Poole, Ramillies, Romney, Royal Ulsterman, Thyme, Winchester*

Seamen's mess table and gear in HMS *Victory*

Castle, FAA Sq.: Swordfish 810, 829; Wildcat 881, 882 *(Illustrious).* Fulmar 800, 806; Albacore 827, 831; Hurricane 880. *(Indomitable).*
*Mined on the 5th and sank on the 6th.

1942 Battle of the Coral Sea (4th-8th May): south of the Solomon Islands. [bh]. U.S. Task Force 17, under Rear-Admiral F.J. Fletcher, USN, defeated a Japanese force and thus removed the threat of invasion of N Australia. The first major action in which only aircraft carriers were engaged; the heavy surface escorts never sighted one another. RAN ships: *Australia, Hobart.*

1943 *Jervis, Nubian* and *Paladin* bombarded Kelibia, Tunisia.

1943 Hudson X/233 sank U.447 off Portugal (35° 30'N, 11° 55'W.).

1943 Sunderland W/10 (RAAF) sank U.109 (47° 06'N, 10° 58'W) and Halifax S/58 sank U.663 in Bay of Biscay (46° 33' N, 11° 12'W.).

1944 *Valleyfield* (RCN) sunk by U.548 off Cape Race. (Escort Group C.1)

1945 Last British merchantman to be sunk in World War II; torpedoed by U.2336.

1945 Catalina X/210 sank U.320 off Shetlands (61° 32'N, 1° 53'E.).

121

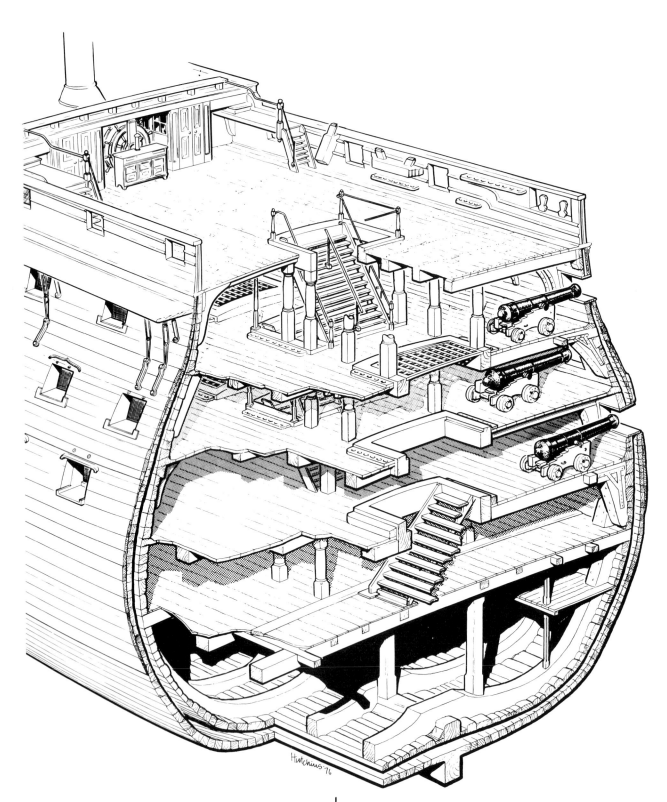

Cut-away of HMS *Victory*

To produce the functional but beautiful ship of the line was a vast, if primitive, industrial undertaking. A basic 'shopping list' for one would be:-

    2500 mature oak trees – weathered after felling,
    17 tons of copper sheets to protect hull below waterline,
    30cwt copper nails,

    7 elm trunks cut to 20 inches square for keel,
    3000 feet of spar timber
    and caulking material for 13 miles of watertight seams.
As an indication of the skill required in construction, each timber was shaped by placing it over a pit with a fire underneath, pouring water over the timber and placing heavy weights in exactly the right place to achieve the correct curvature.

8th MAY

1576   Sir Martin Frobisher *(Gabriel and Michael)* sailed to Baffin Island.

1671   Vice-Admiral Sir Edward Spragge *(Revenge)* destroyed seven Algerine men-of-war and their three prizes at Bougie Algeria. [bh]. Ships: *Advice, Dragon, Garland, Mary, Revenge, Portsmouth.* Fireship: *Little Victory* (expended).

1731   Board of Admiralty first dined in Painted Hall, Greenwich.

1744   *Northumberland* taken by the French *Content* off Ushant.

1797   Sailors' Bill passed to improve service conditions.

1799   *Fortune* taken and *Dame de Grace* sunk by the French *Salamine* off Jaffa.

1804   *Vincejo* taken by 17 French vessels close off La Teignouse Rock, at the entrance to Quiberon Bay.

1807   Boats of *Comus* cut out the Spanish packet *San Pedro* at Las Palmas, Canary Islands.

1811   *Scylla* captured the French *Canonnière* between the Plateau des Triagoz and the Pongaro ledge, off the North coast of Brittany. One of the French convoy she was escorting was also captured, and four more were wrecked.

1861   Board approved Controller's submission that all ships building or to be built should be armoured: end of "Wooden walls".

1863   *Flamer* destroyed ten pirate junks to the northward of Shih pu.

1912   First launch of aircraft from HM ship under way; Short S38 from *Hibernia.*

1918   *Basilisk* and *Lydonia* sank UB.70 off Majorca (38° 08'N, 3° 02'E.).

1918   *Wallflower* sank U.32 between Malta and Sicily

1941   *Ajax, Havock, Hotspur* and *Imperial* bombarded Benghazi.

1941   *Cornwall* sank the German disguised raider *Pinguin* (Schiff 33) in Indian Ocean (3° 27' N, 56° 38' E.).

The tanker *British Emperor* was sunk by the German raider *Pinguin* (6 x 5.9 in guns) north of the Seychelles. She managed to send a distress signal before sinking which was received in the cruiser *Cornwall* 500 miles to the South. *Cornwall* immediately turned and closed at high speed, and used her aircraft to search ahead. Early on 8th May, the raider sighted the *Cornwall* and turned away, but one of the cruiser's aircraft detected her. The raider identified herself as the Norwegian ship *Tamerlane.* The cruiser closed and ordered her to stop, and fired warning shots. The raider then revealed herself and opened fire and hit the cruiser, damaging her steering gear. However, the raider was heavily hit and blew up at 0526. 22 British prisoners and 60 German survivors were rescued.

1942   *Active* and *Panther* sank the Vichy–French s/m *Monge* off Madagascar. Operation Ironclad. (see 7th May)

1942   *Olympus* sunk by mine off Malta.

1945   End of Second World War in Europe.

The First "Aggie Weston's" opened at Plymouth.

Miss Agnes Weston (b 1840) was deeply religious and caring about soldiers. She used to write to her local regiment's soldiers on active service, and one of them asked her to write to a sailor friend. By 1871 she was corresponding with hundreds of sailors and was obliged to have her letters printed.

In 1873 she attended the first meeting of the Naval Temperance Society, and soon found that there was a need for somewhere for the sailors to go in port other than public houses or brothels. After energetic fund raising efforts she opened her first 'sailor's rest'.

"Aggie Weston's" soon became a by-word in the Fleet for comfort and kindness which most of the sailors had never known before. The intention to name a ship *Weston-super-Mare* after a First Lord's birthplace was thwarted by instant lower deck translation to *Aggie-on-Horseback.*

HMS *Hibernia,* with special flying-off track mounted.

9th MAY

1795 Boats of *Diamond, Hebe, Melampus, Niger* and *Syren* captured ten vessels of a French convoy and two of the escort, which had been driven ashore 4 miles to the northward of Cape Carteret, West coast of Normandy.

1810 *Favourite* and *Orestes* captured the French privateer *Dorade* 10 miles W.S.W. of Lands End.

1812 *Decoy* and *Pioneer* captured the French privateer *Infatigable* off Dungeness.

1845 Franklin sailed in *Terror* with *Erebus* to seek the NW Passage.

1917 *Milne* rammed and sank UC.26 in Dover Strait.

1918 *Queen Alexandra*, transport, rammed and sank UB.78 in the Channel (49° 50'N, 1° 40'W.).

1941 GC (ex-AM): Ordinary Seaman A. Howarth for saving life at sea, though injured.

1941 *Aubrietia, Broadway* and *Bulldog* captured U.110 in N Atlantic (60° 31'N, 33° 10'W.). (Convoy OB.318). Sank later in tow, an entire Enigma cyphering machine having been captured.

1943 *Jervis, Nubian* and *Paladin* bombarded Kelibia, Tunisia.

1958 RNEC Keyham closed on completion of move to Manadon.

Surrender of the German heavy cruiser *Prinz Eugen* at Bremerhaven 1945

10th MAY

1694   *Monmouth, Resolution* and *Roebuck* destroyed the French *Jersey* and 25 sail of a convoy in Blancs Sablons Bay, Brittany.

1794   *Castor,* escorting a Newfoundland convoy, taken by the French *Patriote* to the south-westward of Cape Clear. Most of the convoy were also taken by other ships of Rear-Admiral Joseph Neilly's squadron.

1804   *Ethalion* captured the Dutch privateer *Union* 50 miles W.S.W. of Bergen.

1806   Admiral Cochrane launched aerial propaganda attack on France (Kites from *Pallas*).

1812   Boats of *America, Eclair* and *Leviathan* cut out 18 vessels of a French convoy at Laigueglia, Italian Riviera.

1862   Capture of Ningpo by *Encounter, Hardy, Kestrel, Ringdove,* and the French *Confucius* and *Étoile*.

1865   *Haughty* destroyed four pirate junks 40 miles S.W. of Macao.

1870   Reginald Yorke Tyrwhitt born.

1917   Experimental convoy sailed from Gibraltar to the United Kingdom, with *Mavis* and *Rule* (Q.26 and Q.35) as escort.

1918   VC: Lieutenant Victor Alexander Charles Crutchley *(Vindictive)*. Lieutenant Roland Richard Louis Bourke, RNVR (ML.276). Lieutenant Geoffrey Heneage Drummond, RNVR (ML.254).

       Blockship operation at Ostend. *Vindictive* sunk in the harbour. [bh]. Ships: *Faulknor, Prince Eugene, Trident, Velox, Vindictive, Warwick, Whirlwind.* C M B.: 22B, 23B, 24A, 25BD, 26B, 30B. M.L.: 254, 276.

1918   E.34 sank UB.16 in N Sea.

1940   Naval demolition parties landed at Antwerp, Flushing, Hook of Holland and Ijmuiden. Operation X.D.

Antwerp.

The destroyer *Brilliant* sailed from Dover with a demolition party embarked and reached Antwerp on 10 May. Their first and most important task was the sailing of 26 allied ships and 50 tugs, which left on 12th. By noon on 14th some 600 barges, dredgers and floating cranes had been sailed, and by the evening of 17th, 150,000 tons of oil had been made unusable and the entrances to the docks and basins blocked to hinder the advance of the German forces.

Blockships at Ostend

125

11th MAY

1780   Capitulation of Charleston, South
        Carolina, to Vice-Admiral
        Arbuthnot *(Roebuck)* and troops
        under General Sir Henry Clinton.
        Ships: *Blonde, Camilla, Defiance*,*
        Europe*, Fowey, Perseus, Raison-
        nable*, Raleigh, Renown, Rich-
        mond, Roebuck, Romulus, Virginia.
        Armed ships, galleys, etc.: *Assault,*
        Cathcart, Comet, Fidelity, Germain,
        Keppel, Loyalist, Margery, Sandwich,
        Scourge, Squib, Trimer, Vigilant,
        Vindictive, Viper. * Ships not present,
        but landed officers and men to co-
        operate with the Army. *Defiance* was
        wrecked on 2nd February.

1808   *Bacchante* captured the French
        Griffon close off Cape San Antonio,
        Cuba.

1813   *Lyra, Royalist* and *Sparrow* at the
        defence of Castro Urdiales, North
        coast of Spain.

1824   Capture of Rangoon by *Larne, Liffey,*
        H.E.I.Co. cruisers and troops under
        Brigadier-General Sir Archibald Camp-
        bell.

**HMS *Diana* (paddle steamer on right) leading the attack on
stockades on the Rangoon River, 1824**

1853   *Rattler* captured six pirate junks and
        a lorcha in Nam Kwan harbour, near
        Foochow.

1859   Admiralty invited tenders for ironclad
        frigates *Warrior* and *Black Prince.*

1918   E.35 sank U.154 off Madeira.

1941   *Jackal, Kashmir, Kelly* (D.5), *Kelvin*
        and *Kipling* bombarded Benghazi.
        Ladybird bombarded Gazala north
        landing ground.

1942   *Lively, Kipling* and *Jackal* attacked
        by German aircraft in E Mediterranean
        during Operation M.G.2. *Lively* sunk
        in 33° 24' N, 25° 38' E. *Kipling* sunk
        in 32° 38' N, 26° 20' E. *Jackal* damaged
        at same time as *Kipling;* taken in tow
        by *Jervis* but had to be sunk early on
        the 12th in 32° 33' N, 26° 25' E.

1943   *Fleetwood* and Halifax D/58 sank
        U.528 in SW Approaches (Convoy
        OS.47).

1944   *Bicester* bombarded targets in the Ardea
        area, S of Rome.

12th MAY

1652	*Nightingale, President* and *Recovery* fought three Dutch men-of-war with a convoy of seven sail, off Start Point.
1689	*Nonsuch* captured the French *Railleuse* and *Serpente* off the Casquets.
1796	*Phoenix* captured the Dutch *Argo* and recaptured *Duke of York* 30 miles North of the Texel. *Sylph* captured the Dutch *Mercury* off Terschelling. *Pegasus* drove ashore two Dutch brigs, *Echo* and *De Gier,* on Terschelling.
1797	Mutiny at the Nore began in *Sandwich.*
1846	*Fantome* and her boats repulsed Moorish pirates whilst salving the remains of the wreck of the British *Ruth* 6 miles West of Cape Tres Forcas, Morocco.
1854	*Tiger* ran ashore in a fog, 5 miles to the southward of Odessa, and was forced to surrender to the Russians.
1862	British and French forces captured Tsingpu. Naval Brigade from *Imperieuse,*

Pearl, Vulcan, Flamer, Coromandel. French gunboat: No 12. Troops: Royal Artillery, Royal Engineers, 31st and 67th Regiments; 5th Bombay Native Light Infantry, 22nd Bengal Native Infantry.

1865	Two boats of *Wasp* captured an Arab slave dhow off Zanzibar.
1898	*Fox* made punitive raid up Bompol River, Sierra Leone.
1918	D.4 sank UB.72 in Channel.
1918	*Olympic* rammed and sank U.103 in Channel.
1940	*Venomous* and *Verity* landed 200 Royal Marines at the Hook of Holland. Operation Harpoon.
1941	*Ladybird* sunk by aircraft in Tobruk harbour.
1943	*Hesperus* sank U.186 in Atlantic (41° 54'N, 31° 49'W.). (Convoy SC.129)
1943	*Broadway, Lagan* and Swordfish B/811 *(Biter)* sank U.89 in N Atlantic. (Convoy HX.237)

A torpedo being fired from a broadside deck torpedo tube

13th MAY

1731	Hadley presented his Quadrant at the Royal Society.
1757	*Antelope* drove ashore and wrecked the French *Aquilon* in Audierne Bay, Brittany. [bh]
1764	Harrison's fourth Chronometer tested successfully in *Tartar*.
1779	*Cabot, Experiment, Fortune, Pallas* and *Unicorn* captured the French *Danae* and destroyed the rest of the escort to a flotilla of French troops in Cancale Bay, North coast of France.
1787	First convict convoy sailed from Portsmouth to Botany Bay.
1793	*Iris* fought the French *Citoyenne-Française* 200 miles W.S.W. of Cape Finisterre: an indecisive action but the first afloat in the French wars.
1859	Senior chaplain of Greenwich Hospital recognised as "Head of the Naval Chaplains" and "Chaplain to the Fleet".
1915	*Goliath* sunk by the German manned Turkish destroyer *Muavanet-i-Miliet* off Gallipoli.
1916	M.30 sunk by Turkish batteries in Gulf of Smyrna.
1916	*Dulcie Doris* and *Evening Star II* sank the Austrian s/m U.6 12 miles E.N.E. of Cape Otranto.
1937	GC (ex-EGM): Lieutenant Patrick Noel Humphreys *(Hunter)* for gallantry when she was mined off Almeira in Spanish Civil War.
1941	*Salopian* sunk by the German U.98 in N Atlantic (56° 43' N. 38° 57' W.).
1941	*Undaunted* lost in Mediterranean.
1942	Light Coastal forces attacked the escorts to a large German ship off Ambleteuse. M.T.B. 220 missing. Sunk: German t.b. *Iltis* and *Seeadler*.
1943	*Drumheller, Lagan* and Sunderland G/ 423 (R.C.A.F.) sank the German U.456 in Atlantic (48° 37' N, 22° 39' W.). (Convoy HX.237)

14th MAY

1781	*Nonsuch* fought the French *Actif* 50 miles N.W. by W. of Ushant.
1798	Sea Fencibles established by Order in Council.
1806	*Pallas* fought the French *Minerve* off Île d'Aix, Basque Roads.
1807	Defence of Danzig. *Dauntless* grounded on the Holmen.
1829	Admiral Francis Beaufort appointed Hydrographer.
1917	Flying boat 8666 destroyed Zeppelin L.22 18 miles N.N.W. of Texel.
1917	Posts of First Sea Lord and Chief of Naval Staff combined.
1918	*Phoenix* torpedoed in Adriatic.
1940	Royal Marines and demolition parties evacuated in *Malcolm* from the Hook of Holland.
1941	*Puriri* sunk by mine in Hauraki Gulf, New Zealand, whilst clearing minefield laid by the German disguised raider *Orion* (Schiff 36) in June, 1940.
1943	Liberator B/86 sank U.266 in Atlantic (47° 45'N, 26° 57'W.). (Convoy SC.129)
1945	Capture of the Wewak peninsula and airfield, New Guinea, by the 6th Australian Division. Ships: *Newfoundland;* and *Arunta, Colac, Dubbo, Hobart, Swan, Warramunga, Warrego* (all RAN).

Flying boat 8666 - a Curtis Large America

15th MAY

1293 Ships of Cinque Ports defeated French fleet off Cape St. Matthieu, Normandy: sacking of Poitou led to war.

1780 Admiral Sir George Bridges Rodney *(Sandwich)* fought Vice-Admiral Comte de Guichen *(Couronne)*, with 23 ships of the line, 20 miles to the eastward of Martinique. Ships: *Stirling Castle, Ajax, Elizabeth, Princess Royal, Albion, Terrible, Trident; Grafton, Yarmouth, Cornwall, Sandwich, Suffolk, Boyne, Vigilant; Vengeance, Medway, Montagu, Conqueror, Intrepid, Magnificent, Centurion, Triumph, Preston.* Frigates, etc.: *Andromeda, Deal Castle, Greyhound, Venus.* Troops: 5th and 87th Regiments.

1794 *Hebe* captured the French *Maire-Guiton* and recaptured eleven of a recently taken British convoy 130 miles N.N.E. of Cape Villano, N.W. Spain.

1797 End of second Spithead mutiny.

1813 *Bacchante* captured Carlobago (Karlovac), Yugoslavia.

1839 Launch at Portsmouth of Symonds' *Queen;* "the zenith of construction of sailing men o' war".

1917 VC: Skipper Joseph Watt, RNR *(Gowan Lea)* for engaging an Austrian cruiser at 100 yards range with his only gun, refusing to surrender and subsequently rescuing the crew of another drifter. Austrian naval raid in Otranto Strait: 14 British drifters sunk. *Admirable, Avondale, Coral Haven, Craignoon, Felicitas, Girl Gracie, Girl Rose, Helenora, Quarry Knowe, Selby, Serene, Taits, Transit, Young Linnett. Bristol* and *Dartmouth* pursued the three raiders: *Dartmouth* torpedoed.

1918 German submarine raid on St. Kilda.

1940 *Valentine* bombed by German aircraft and beached off Walcheren.

1942 *Trinidad* sunk by *Matchless* off N Cape (73° 37' N, 23° 27' E.) after being set on fire by German bombers late on the 14th.

1943 Halifax M/58 sank the Supply U-boat U.463 in Bay of Biscay (45° 28' N, 10° 20' W.).

1943 *Sickle* sank the German UJ.2213 off the French Riviera.

1944 *Dido* bombarded targets in the Gulf of Gaeta in support of Army attack.

1944 *Blackfly, Kilmarnock* and Catalinas P.1 and P.12 of VP/63 (U.S.) sank U.731 off Gibraltar (35° 55' N, 5° 45' W.).

1973 Second fishing dispute began with Iceland — persisted until 13th November.

HMS *Hunter* in tow after being mined in 1937

A destroyer flotilla entering Gibraltar

1760 Siege of Québec raised. *Diana, Lowestoffe* and *Vanguard* destroyed the French *Atalante, Pomone* and other vessels of the besieging force at Pointe aux Trembles.

1803 Britain declared war on France.

1804 Commodore Sir Sidney Smith *(Antelope)* defeated a division of the Franco-Batavian invasion flotilla off Ostend. Ships: *Antelope, Cruizer, Rattler, Penelope, Aimable, Favourite, Stag.*

1811 *Little Belt* taken by the American *President* 50 miles N.E. of Cape Henry.

1813 Boats of *Berwick* and *Euryalus* captured the French *Fortune* and 15 of a convoy in Cavalaire Roads.

1813 *Shannon* and *Tenedos* captured the American privateer *Invincible* near Cape Ann town, Massachusetts.

DIFFERENT RIGS OF SHIPS USUALLY MET AT SEA.

SHIP.

BARQUE.

TOPSAIL SCHOONER.

FORE AND AFT SCHOONER.

BRIG.

BRIGANTINE.

HERMAPHRODITE BRIG.

TWO TOPSAIL SCHOONER.

Figurehead of HMS *Warrior*

1824 Boats of *Liffey* and the grenadier company of the 38th Regiment captured and destroyed three Burmese stockades near Killyumdine.

1908 D1, first British diesel submarine, launched at Barrow.

1930 RN and RM sports control board established.

1944 Sunderland V/330 (Nor) sank U.240 off Norway (63° 05' N, 3° 10'E.).

1945 *Saumarez* (D.26), *Venus, Verulam, Vigilant, Virago* and *Emperor* (Avenger 851 from *Shah*) sank the Japanese *Haguro* and damaged the destroyer *Kamikaze*, 45 miles S.W. of Penang.

Operation 'Dukedom'

The Japanese heavy cruiser *Haguro* (8 in guns) was attempting to supply the garrison in the Andeman Islands. Having failed at a second attempt, she was returning down the Malacca Straits at high speed with a destroyer when she was sighted by an aircraft. The 26th Destroyer Flotilla, comprising the *Saumarez* (Leader) and 4 V Class destroyers, was off Sumatra and was diverted to engage the enemy. At about 2300 on 15th the *Venus* detected the enemy at 34 miles on radar. The cruiser turned towards the destroyers as they spread out for a torpedo attack, and the *Saumarez* was hit by enemy gunfire as she gained visual contact just after midnight. *Saumarez*, however, managed to fire her torpedoes as the other destroyers also attacked, and it is thought that 8 torpedo hits were achieved. The *Haguro* sank at 0147, and the Japanese destroyer *Kamikaze* was slightly damaged. HM ships lost 2 killed and 3 wounded. See illustration of *Saumarez* 26th October.

From the first page of the *Admiralty Manual of Seamanship,* **1882**

1655   Capture of Jamaica by Admiral William Penn *(Swiftsure)* and troops under General Robert Venables.

1667   *Princess* fought two Danish men-of-war off the coast of Norway, between the Sean and Malshond.

1795   *Hussar* and *Thetis* engaged four French ships, capturing *Prévoyante* and *La Raison*, 60 miles E. by N. of Cape Henry, Virginia. [m]

1862   Capture of Najaor by Brigadier-General Charles Staveley, with British and Indian troops, and British and French Naval Brigades. Naval Brigades repulsed a rebel Chinese attack near Tsiolin (or Cholin). Naval Brigade of *Impérieuse, Pearl, Vulcan, Flamer* and *Coromandel.* Troops: Royal Artillery, Royal Engineers, 31st, 67th and 99th Regiments; 5th Bombay Native Light Infantry, 22nd Bengal Native Infantry.

1917   Admiralty convoy committee set up.

1917   Second experimental use of sea lions against submarines.

1917   *Setter* lost in collision with *Sylph* off Harwich.

1917   *Glen* sank UB.39 in Channel.

1940   *Effingham* wrecked off Norway (67° 17' N, 13° 58' E.).

1941   *Gnat* bombarded Gazala airfield.

1943   *Swale* sank U.640 S. of Greenland (58° 54' N, 42° 33' W.). (Convoy ONS.7)

1943   Hudson J/269 sank U.646 off Iceland (62° 10' N, 14° 30' W.).

1943   Italian s/m *Enrico Tazzoli* sunk by air attack N.N.W. of Cape Ortegal.

1944   Wellingtons A/36, H/36 and X/36, and the USS *Bibb, Ellyson, Emmons, Gleaves, Hambleton, Macomb, Nields* and *Rodman* sank U.616 in W Mediterranean (36° 46' N, 0° 52' E.). (First attacked on the 14th).

1944   Allied air attack on the Japanese naval base at Sourabaya. Operation Transom. Force 66: Carriers — *Illustrious* (Rear-Admiral C. Moody) and *Saratoga* (U.S.), with 27 Avengers, 18 Dauntless, 24 Hellcats and 16 Corsairs. Ships: *Renown* (Vice-Admiral Sir Arthur Power); *Kenya* (Rear-Admiral A.D. Read — C.S.4), *London, Suffolk* and *Tromp* (Neth); *Napier* (Cdre. D), *Quadrant, Quality, Quiberon; Cummings, Dunlap, Fanning* (U.S.); *Van Galen* (Neth). Force 65: *Queen Elizabeth* (Admiral Sir James Somerville), *Valiant, Richelieu* (Fr); *Ceylon, Gambia; Nepal, Queenborough, Quickmatch, Quilliam, Racehorse, Rotherham.* FAA sq.: 832, 851 (Avenger); 1830, 1833 (Corsair).

Corsairs ranged on a carrier's flightdeck

Deck crew fuelling Avengers

18th MAY

1709   *Falmouth*, escorting a convoy, fought a French 60-gun ship 70 miles to the westward of the Scilly Islands.

1759   *Thames* and *Venus* captured the French *Arethusa* in Audierne Bay.

1809   Occupation of Anholt, Kattegat. Ships: *Standard, Owen Glendower, Avenger, Ranger, Rose* and *Snipe* and 120 Royal Marines under Lt Nicholls.

1842   Capture of Chapu by Vice-Admiral Sir William Parker *(Cornwallis)* and Lieutenant-General Sir Hugh Gough. Ships and vessels: *Algerine, Bentinck, Blonde, Columbine, Cornwallis, Modeste, Starling; Jupiter Transport; Sesostris* (Indian Navy); *Nemesis, Phlegethon, Queen* (Bengal Marine). Troops: Royal Artillery, 18th, 26th, 49th and 55th Regiments; Madras Artillery, Madras Sappers and Miners, 36th Madras Native Infantry.

1915   GC(ex-AM): Chief Petty Officer M.S. Keogh (*Ark Royal*) for rescuing pilot of crashed and blazing aircraft.

1940   *Princess Victoria* sunk by mine off the Humber.

1941   VC: Petty Officer Alfred Edward Sephton *(Coventry)* for gallantry in an aircraft attack on *Coventry* during the Crete operations.

1941   *Salvia, Widnes* and *York* damaged by German aircraft at Suda Bay, Crete.

1944   Catalina S/210 sank U.241 off S.W. Norway (63° 36' N, 1° 42' E.).

The mine deck of HMS *Princess Victoria*, a converted LMS Railway ferry, taken into service 1939

19th MAY

1652 First battle of the Dutch Wars started when Blake demanded that Tromp salute the British fleet. Admiral Robert Blake *(James)* fought Admiral Maerten Tromp *(Brederode)*, with 42 ships, off Dover. Ships and vessels: *Garland, James, Martin, Mermaid,* [bh] , *Portsmouth, Reuben(?), Ruby, Sapphire, Speaker, Star, Victory; Adventure, Andrew, Assurance, Centurion, Happy Entrance, Fairfax, Greyhound, Seven Brothers, Triumph, Worcester(?).*

1692 Battle of Barfleur. Admiral Edward Russell *(Britannia)* fought the French fleet of 63 sail under Vice-Admiral Comte de Tourville *(Soleil Royal)*. [bh] . Ships: Red Sq — *Britannia, Chester, Eagle, Elizabeth, Grafton, Greenwich, London, Restoration, Rupert, St. Andrew; Mary Galley, Portsmouth.* Fireships: *Flame, Roebuck, Spy, Vulture* (Russell), *Bonaventure, Burford, Captain, Centurion, Lenox, Royal Katherine, Greyhound, Sovereign, St Michael; Dragon, Falcon.* Fireships: *Extravagant[1], Hound[2], Vulcan, Wolf[2]* (Delaval), *Cambridge, Hampton Court, Kent, Oxford, Royal William, Ruby, St. Albans, Sandwich, Swiftsure;* Fireships: *Fox[1], Hopewell[1], Phaeton[1], Strombolo.* (Shovell). Blue Sq. — *Adventure,*

Berwick, Defiance, Duchess, Edgar, Monmouth, Mountague, Vanguard, Victory, Warspite; Fireships: *Aetna, Blaze[2], Griffin, Speedwell.* (Ashby). *Advice, Albermarle, Expedition, Lion, Monck, Nepture, Northumberland, Resolution, Windsor Castle;* Fireships: *Cadiz Merchant[1], Half-Moon[3], · Lightning, Owner's Love.* (Rooke). *Charles Galley, Crown, Deptford, Dreadnought, Duke, Essex, Hope, Ossory, Stirling Castle, Suffolk, Tiger Prize, Woolwich;* Fireships: *Hawk, Hunter, Thomas and Elizabeth[3], Vesuvius.* (Carter). White Sq. — Admiral van Almonde with 39 Dutch of the line and 9 fireships. [1] Expended at Barfleur. [2] Expended at Cherbourg. [3] Expended at La Hogue.

In 1692 James II, aided by Louis XIV of France, assembled a large army at La Hogue, and a French fleet in the channel under the command of Comte de Tourville. The English fleet drove de Tourville's ships into La Hogue. On the 23rd May 200 boats from the English fleet attacked the ships at anchor. When they left, La Hogue was on fire and 6 French three-deckers were destroyed. Six other French ships, anchored under the Fort of St. Vast, were attacked on the 24th. In spite of assistance from French cavalry the French ships were boarded and the ships and the fort destroyed.

1745 *Mermaid* and *Superb* captured the French *Vigilant* off Louisburg, Cape Breton Island.

The Battle of Barfleur, 1692

133

19th MAY

HMS *Whitley* **picking up survivors under air attack. The blazing sea around a burning oiler became a common but ghastly event.**

1765 Gosport victualling yard established.

1777 *Beaver* captured the American privateer *Oliver Cromwell* 2 miles S.W. of the Sugar Loaf (Gros Piton), St. Lucia.

1780 Second inconclusive action between Rodney and de Guichen, 120 miles to the eastward of Martinique. (See 15th May).

1794 Commodore John Ford (*Europa*) and Brigadier-General John Whyte captured Port au Prince, Haiti. Ships: *Belliqueux, Europa, Hermione, Fly, Iphigenia, Swan, Irresistible, Marie Antoinette, Penelope, Sceptre.* Troops: Royal Artillery, 22nd, 23rd, 41st Regts. and Colonial.

1808 *Virginie* captured the Dutch *Guelderland* 240 miles N.W. of Cape Finisterre. [m,]

1813 *Rattler* captured the American privateer *Alexander* which had run ashore on Wells Beach, 5 miles South of Kennebunkport, Maine. *Bream,* which was in company, helped to refloat the prize.

1821 Boats of *Revolutionnaire* captured two Greek pirate gunboats off Chiarenza Point (Cape Glarentza), West coast of Greece.

1847 Gunboat tender of *Calliope,* with a detachment of the 58th Regiment, repulsed a Maori attack on Wanganui: last naval commitment in first New Zealand war.

1852 Capture of Bassein by Major-General Henry Godwin and Commodore George Lambert *(Fox).* Ships: *Moozuffer* and *Sesostris* (Indian Navy); *Pluto* and *Tenasserim* (Bengal Marine); Royal Marines and a field gun's crew of *Fox.* Troops: 51st Regiment; Bengal Artillery, Madras Sappers and Miners, 9th Madras Native Infantry.

1940 *Whitley* beached off Nieuport, after attack by German aircraft.

1943 *Jed* and *Sennen* sank U.209 in N Atlantic (54° 54'N, 34° 19'W.), *Duncan* and *Snowflake* sank U. 381 (54° 41'N, 34° 45'W.), Hudson M/269 sank U.273 (59° 25' N, 24° 33' W.) and Liberator T/120 sank U.954 (55° 09' N, 35° 18' W.). (Convoy SC.130)

1944 Wellingtons M/36 and U/36, Ventura V/500, *Ludlow* and USS *Niblack* sank U.960 in W Mediterranean (37° 35' N, 1° 39' E.).

1945 *Terrapin* reduced to CTL by depth-charging in Pacific.

20th MAY

1212   King John ordered Portsmouth Dock, built in 1194, to be strengthened.

1625   The Worshipful Company of Barbers & Surgeons fitted out Surgeons' chests and took control of Naval Surgeons.

1665   An English convoy of nine sail and their escort, a 34-gun ship, taken by Admiral Jacob van Wassenaer, Heer van Opdam, on the Dogger Bank.

1692   The chase after the battle of Barfleur. (see 19th May).

1756*   Admiral the Hon. John Byng *(Ramillies)* fought a French fleet of equal force under Admiral the Marquis de La Galissonnière *(Foudroyant)* 30 miles S.S.E. of Port Mahon, Minorca. (see 14th March). Ships: *Defiance, Portland, Lancaster, Buckingham, Captain, Intrepid, Revenge, Princess Louisa, Trident, Ramillies, Culloden, Deptford, Kingston.* Frigates, etc: *Chesterfield, Dolphin, Experiment, Fortune, Phoenix.*

1799   Siege of Acre raised, after a brilliant defence by Captain Sir Sidney Smith *(Tigre),* with *Theseus* and *Alliance.* [m, bh]

1811   *Astraea, Galatea, Phoebe* and *Racehorse* engaged the French *Clorinde, Néréide* and *Renommée,* capturing the last-named ship off Tamatave, Madagascar. [m, bh]

1854   *Arrogant* and *Hecla* engaged the Russian batteries and captured the merchant ship *Augusta* at Ekenas, Finland.

1855   Commodore Elliot *(Sybille)* with *Bittern* and *Hornet* discovered the Russian *Dvina* and *Aurora* in Castries Bay: an inconclusive pursuit ending Crimean war operations in Far East.

*Admiral John Byng.

During the Seven Years War a French force attacked Minorca in order to split Royal Naval Forces and distract them from attention to Canada. Vice-Admiral John Byng, with 10 ships of the line, was sent to the Mediterranean to guard Minorca. Having picked up three more ships at Gibraltar, he remained there longer than he need have done, arriving off Minorca on 17th May 1756 to discover that French troops had invested Port Mahon, which was the last British stronghold on the island. Action was joined on the 20th with the French fleet, but in light winds the battle was indecisive. On 24th May at a Council of War he concluded that it was not practical for the fleet to relieve Port Mahon and that he should guard Gibraltar. Port Mahon surrendered on 28th June. Admiral Byng was later court-martialled, and shot on the quarter-deck of *Monarch.* (see also 14th March and 28th December)

HMS *Arrogant* and *Hecla* engaging shore batteries. Finland, 1854

1858 Anglo-French squadron under Rear-Admirals Sir Michael Seymour *(Calcutta)* and Rigault de Genouilly *(Nemesis)* captured the Taku forts. Ships: *Calcutta, Furious, Fury, Pique, Coromandel* (tender), *Hesper* (store-ship). Gunboats: *Bustard, Cormorant, Firm, Leven, Nimrod, Opossum, Slaney* (flag for attack), *Staunch, Surprise.* French ships: *Nemesis.* French gunboats: *Avalanche, Dragoone, Fusée, Mitraille, Phlegeton.*

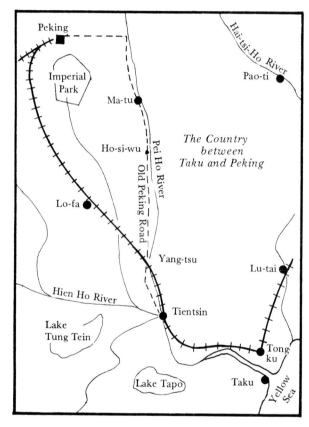

1862 British and French forces captured Tsiolin (or Cholin). (see 17th May).

1917 *Lady Patricia (Paxton,* Q.25) sunk by U.46 S.W. of Ireland.

1917 Flyingboat 8663 sank UC.36 in N. Sea.

1941 Battle of Crete. (Ended 1st June). [bh]. Ships: *Abdiel, Barham+, Formidable+, Queen Elizabeth, Valiant+, Warspite+.* 7th C.S.: *Ajax+, Orion+, Perth+.* 15th C.S.: *Fiji*, Gloucester*, Naiad+, Phoebe.* A/A Cruisers: *Calcutta*, Carlisle+, Coventry.* 2nd D.F.: *Hasty, Havock+, Hereward*, Hero, Hotspur, Ilex+, Imperial*, Isis.* 5th D.F.: *Jackal,*

Kashmir, Kelly*, Kelvin+, Kipling.* 7th D.F.: *Napier+, Nizam+.* 10th D.F.: *Decoy, Defender, Stuart, Vampire, Vendetta, Voyager, Waterhen.* 14th D.F.: *Greyhound*, Griffin, Jaguar, Janus, Jervis, Juno*, Kandahar, Kimberley, Kingston+, Nubian+.* R.A.(D): *Dido+.* Sloops: *Auckland, Flamingo, Grimsby.* Corvette: *Salvia.* Others: *Glengyle, Glenroy, Kos 21, 22* and 23*, Lanner, Rorqual, Syvern*, Widnes*.* M.L.: *1011*, 1030*, 1032.* FAA Sq: 805 (Gladiator, Fulmar and Hurricane (Maleme)), 803, 806 (Fulmar) 826, 829 (Albacore and Swordfish *(Formidable)* MTB: 67*, 213*, 216*, 217*, 314*. *Sunk. + Damaged.

1941 *Widnes* (ex-*Withernsea*) sunk by German aircraft in Suda Bay: salvaged and became UJ.2109: sunk 17th October 1943.

1943 Liberator P/120 sank U.258 in Atlantic (55° 18' N, 27° 49' W.). (Convoy SC.130)

The Taku forts and surrounding country in 1901.

21st MAY

1692 Continuation of the chase after the battle of Barfleur. (See 19th May).

1794 Capture of Bastia, Corsica, after a siege of 37 days, by troops under Lieutenant-Colonel William Villettes (69th Regiment) and seamen under Captain Horatio Nelson *(Agamemnon)*. Ships: *Agamemnon, Fortitude, Princess Royal, St. George. Victory, Windsor Castle.* Frigates, etc: *Imperieuse, Mulette, Proselyte.* Troops: Royal Artillery, Royal Sappers and Miners, 11th, 25th, 30th, 69th Foot.

1800 Boats of blockading squadron, Vice-Admiral Lord Keith *(Minotaur)*, cut out the Genoese *Prima* galley at Genoa.

1858 Admiral Sir Michael Seymour *(Coromandel)* occupied Tientsin.

1941 *Juno* sunk by German aircraft in 34° 35' N, 26° 34' E., during the battle of Crete.

1941 *Urge* sank the Italian t.b. *Curtatone* off Lampedusa.

1941 *Ilex, Jervis* (D.14) and *Nizam* bombarded Scarpanto airfield.

1943 *Sickle* sank U.303 off Toulon (42° 50' N, 6° 00' E.).

1944 *Liddesdale, Tenacious* and *Termagant* sank U.453 off Cape Spartivento (38° 13' N, 16° 38' E.) (First attacked on the 19th).

22nd MAY

1681 *Kingfisher* fought seven Algerine men-of-war off Sardinia.

1692 Vice-Admiral Sir Ralph Delaval *(St Albans)*, with *Ruby* and two fireships, burnt the French *Admirable, Conquerant, Soleil-Royal* and *Triomphant* at Cherbourg. (See 19th May).

1803 *Doris* captured the French *Affronteur* 20 miles S.W. by W. of Ushant.

1812 *Northunberland* and *Growler* destroyed the French *Andromaque, Ariane* and *Mameluk* inshore of Île de Groix. [m]

1841 Boats of advanced squadron destroyed many junks and fire rafts in the approaches to Canton (Nemesis Reach, etc.). Ships: *Algerine, Alligator, Calliope, Columbine, Conway, Cruizer, Herald, Hyacinth, Louisa, Modeste, Nimrod, Pylades, Sulphur.* Steamers: *Atalanta* (I.N.), *Nemesis* (Ben. Mar.). Boats of *Blenheim.*

1917 Mediterranean convoys began as local experiment.

1941 Sunk by German aircraft during the battle of Crete:
Fiji   36° 00' N, 23° 00' E.
Gloucester   35° 44' N, 23° 18' E.
Greyhound   35° 40' N, 23° 15' E.
York abandoned and sunk in Suda Bay.

1943 All U-Boats recalled from Battle of Atlantic.

May 1943 marked a turning point in the Battle of the Atlantic. The last straw for Admiral Doenitz came with the eastward passage of convoy SC130 from Halifax which did not lose a single ship although 5 U-boats were sunk attacking it. Throughout May only 50 merchantmen were sunk for the loss of 41 U-boats, 38 of them in the Atlantic. The introduction of centimetric radar and its fitting in ships and aircraft obliged U-boats to dive during battery charging surface runs and also made surface attack dangerous. In spite of the introduction of a schnorkel, which enabled submarines to charge batteries under the surface, the U-boat menace never again reached the proportions of 1942, in which year nearly 800 million tons of merchant shipping had been sunk.

Walrus flying boat

23rd MAY

1692 Vice-Admiral George Rooke *(Eagle)* with fireships and boats of fleet, burnt the French *Ambitieux, Galliard, Glorieux, Magnifique, Merveilleux* and *St. Phillippe* at La Hogue.

1809 *Melpomene* beat off 20 Danish gunboats at Omö Island, Great Belt.

1811 *Sir Francis Drake* and her boats captured 14 French gunboats and 2 merchant prahus 10 miles N.E. of Rembang, Java. A few of the 14th Regiment were in the boats.

1822 *Comet* launched at Deptford.

"Their Lordships feel it their bounden duty to discourage to the utmost of their ability the employment of steam vessels, as they consider that the introduction of steam is calculated to strike a fatal blow at the naval supremacy of the empire." Obiter of Lord Melville, First Lord in 1828. The first paddle-steamer built for the RN was the *Comet* of 238 tons, launched in 1822, but not armed until 1830. The first real British steam warship was the *Gorgon*, a sloop launched in 1837 and armed with a single cannon at bow and stern. A larger ship, classed as a steam frigate, was the *Firebrand*, launched in 1842.

1918 H.4 sank the German UB.52 in Adriatic (41° 46' N, 18° 35' E.).

1928 GC(ex-AM): Lieutenant R.W. Armytage and Leading Seaman R. Oliver *(Warspite)* for rescuing a trapped stoker.

1934 First performance of Green's setting of Sunset, an evening hymn, by RM band at Malta.

1940 Naval demolition parties landed at Calais, Boulogne and Dunkirk.

On the evening of 23rd May, five V & W Class destroyers rendezvoused off Boulogne to evacuate the troops trapped onshore by the advancing German forces. The *Whitshed* and *Vimiera* went alongside first, and took off detachments of the Welsh and Irish Guards and Royal Marines. Each ship took on 1000 troops, and then withdrew while *Wild Swan, Venomous* and *Venetia* entered harbour. During the embarkation, the shore batteries engaged the ships — the French had not had time to spike them — and tanks were firing at the destroyers along the streets, while they replied over open sights at 100 yards range. While these 5 ships returned to Dover, another destroyer, the *Windsor*, entered and recovered 600 men and a naval demolition party. In the early hours of 24th the *Vimiera* returned and rescued another 1400 troops of the Welsh Guards. A total of 4,360 men were saved by this action.

Admiral of the Fleet Lord Louis Mountbatten
During the early part of the Second World War Mountbatten was in command of *HMS Kelly* and the Fifth Destroyer Flotilla. He gained a reputation for a great offensive spirit; his ship was sunk under him during the fighting off Crete in May 1941. Churchill then appointed him Chief of Combined Operations and as such he was responsible for the highly successful raid on St. Nazaire in March 1942. He also planned the raid on Dieppe which, although it did not achieve many of its objectives, proved a vital training ground for both men and equipment in the great amphibious operations later in the war. As Supreme Allied Commander of South East Asia Command, he was one of the war's most successful allied Commanders. His most notable peacetime appointment was to be the last Viceroy of India, although he became First Sea Lord, and the first Chief of the Defence Staff.

1941 *Kashmir* and *Kelly* sunk by German aircraft in 34° 41' N, 24° 15' E., during the battle of Crete. *KOS 23* beached and abandoned at Suda Bay after damage by German aircraft.

1943 *Active* and *Ness* sank the Italian s/m *Leonardo Da Vinci* N.E. of the Azores (42° 18' N, 15° 53' W.). (Convoy WS.30/KMF.15)

1943 Swordfish B/819 *(Archer)* sank U.752 in N Atlantic (51° 40' N, 29° 49' W.). (Convoy HX.239). First operational success of air to sea rocket projectiles.

24th MAY

1692   Vice-Admiral George Rooke *(Eagle)* with fireships and boats of fleet, burnt the French *Bourbon, Fier, Fort, St. Louis, Terrible* and *Tonant* at La Hogue. (See 23rd May).

1743   Admiral Sir Charles Wager died.

1792   Admiral Lord Rodney died.

1795   *Mosquito* captured the French privateer *National Razor* off Cape Maze (Maysi), Cuba. [m]

1796   Capture of St. Lucia by Lieutenant-General Sir Ralph Abercromby and Rear-Admiral Sir Hugh Cloberry Christian *(Thunderer).* [bh]. A Naval Brigade was landed. Ships: *Alfred, Ganges, Madras, Thunderer, Vengeance.* Frigates, etc.: *Arethusa, Astraea, Beaulieu, Bulldog, Fury, Hebe, Pelican, Victorieuse, Woolwich.*

1814   Boats of *Elizabeth* cut out the French *L'Aigle* from under the guns of Vido Island, Corfu. [m]

1824   Boats of *Naiad* destroyed an Algerine brig of war at Bone, Algeria.

1841   Capture of the British Factory and the remaining river forts and batteries in the eastern approaches to Canton. (Operations ended on the 26th). Ships: *Algerine, Columbine, Cruizer, Hyacinth, Modeste, Nimrod, Pylades.* Steamer (Indian Navy): *Atalanta.* Troops: 26th Regiment; Madras Artillery.

1854   Prince Louis of Battenberg born.

1855   Allied troops landed in Kamish-Burunski Bay, and the fleet obtained possession of the Kerch-Yenikale Strait, at the entrance to the Sea of Azov. *Snake* engaged the batteries and several Russian war vessels, sinking two of them. British fleet of 33 ships under Rear-Admiral Sir Edmund Lyons *(Royal Albert)*; French (of nearly equal force) under Vice-Admiral Bruat *(Montebello).*

1916   E.18 sunk by German Q-ship 'K' off Bornholm in Baltic.

1917   Experimental convoy sailed from Newport News to the United Kingdom, under *Roxborough.*

1940   *Wessex* sunk by German aircraft at Calais.

1941   *Hood* sunk and *Prince of Wales* damaged by the German battleship *Bismarck* in Denmark Strait. Swordfish aircraft *(Victorious)* torpedoed *Bismarck.* FAA Sq.: 825.

The German battleship *Bismarck* (42,500 tons) and cruiser *Prinz Eugen* sailed for commerce raiding in the Atlantic, in May 1941. The Admiralty was aware that German heavy units were at sea, and sailed the Home Fleet from Scapa Flow. The cruiser *Suffolk* sighted the *Bismarck*, and shadowed her in the mist using radar until the battlecruiser *Hood* and the newly completed battleship *Prince of Wales* were able to close. The British capital ships sighted the German force at 0535 on 24th May, and engaged at 13 miles at 0553. The German ships concentrated their fire on the *Hood*, while the British ships could use only their forward turrents. *Bismarck's* second and third salvoes hit *Hood*, and at 0600, she blew up, leaving 3 survivors from her complement of 95 officers and 1324 men. The Germans shifted their fire to the *Prince of Wales,* and she was hit within minutes by four 15 in and three 8 in shells. She broke off the engagement and retired under cover of smoke. *Bismarck*, however, had been hit by two of *Prince of Wales'* 14 in shells, one of which caused an oil leak. As a result *Bismarck* decided to head for St Nazaire.

1941   VC: Lieutenant-Commander Malcolm David Wanklyn for services in command of *Upholder.*

1944   Catalina V/210 sank U.476 off Norwegian Coast (65° 08' N, 4° 53' E.) and Sunderland R/4 OTU sank U.675 off S W Norway (62° 27' N, 3° 04' E.).

HMS *Hood*

25th MAY

1496 First "dry docking" in Portsmouth *(Sovereign)*. Dock infilled in 1623.

1696 *Assistance,* escorting a convoy, repulsed eight French privateers 40 miles S.E. by E. of Southwold.

1794 Admiral Earl Howe's fleet burnt the French *Inconnu* and *Républicaine* to the westward of Ushant.

1795 *Thorn* captured the French privateer *Courrier National* 80 miles N.W. of St. Thomas, West Indies.

1801 Boats of *Mercury* cut out the French *Bulldog* at Ancona, East coast of Italy, but had to abandon her.

1841 Capture of the forts immediately guarding Canton. (Operations concluded on the 30th). Ships: *Algerine, Alligator, Blenheim, Blonde, Calliope, Columbine, Conway, Cruizer, Herald, Hyacinth, Modeste, Nimrod, Pylades, Starling, Sulphur,* and seamen and Royal Marines of *Wellesley* (from Wantong). Steamers: *Atalanta* (I.N.), *Nemesis* (Ben. Mar.). A Naval Brigade was landed. Troops: Royal Artillery, 18th, 26th and 49th Regiments; Madras Artillery, Madras Sappers and Miners, 37th Madras Native Infantry, Bengal Volunteer Regiment.

1841 Boats of *Wellesley* frustrated a fire raft attack in the Boca Tigris.

HMS *Blake* being refueled by the RFA fleet tanker *Olmeda*

1857 Gunboats and boats of squadron destroyed 27 snake boats in Escape Creek, Canton River. Gunboats and tenders: *Bustard, Hong Kong, Sir Charles Forbes, Starling, Staunch.* Boats of: *Fury, Hornet, Inflexible, Raleigh, Sybille, Tribune.*

1893 *Britannia* (Royal Yacht) won her first race.

1915 *Triumph* sunk by U.21 outside the Dardanelles (off Gaba Tepe).

1917 *Hilary* sunk by U.88 60 miles West of the Shetland Islands.

1921 Admiral of the Fleet Sir Arthur Wilson, VC died.

1941 *Grimsby* sunk by German aircraft off Tobruk.

1943 *Vetch* sank U.414 in W Mediterranean (36° 31' N, 0° 40' E.). (Convoy CTX.1)

1943 Liberator S/59 sank U.990 off S.W. Norway (65° 05' N, 7° 28' E.).

1943 VC: Commander John Wallace Linton (*Turbulent*). For services in submarines from 1st Jan 1942 to 1st Jan 1943.

Commander J.W. Linton, VC

26th MAY

| 1585 | *Primrose* merchantman repulsed a Spanish attack at Bilbao. |

1585   *Primrose* merchantman repulsed a Spanish attack at Bilbao.

1703   Death of Samuel Pepys, first Secretary of the Admiralty.

1758   *Dolphin* and *Solebay* fought the French privateer *Maréchal de Belle Île* off Montrose.

1811   *Astraea, Phoebe* and *Racehorse* captured the French *Neréide* and also recaptured *Tamatave*. [m, bh]

1840   Admiral Sir Sidney Smith died.

1845   Boats of *Pantaloon* captured the pirate *Borboleta* 100 miles S.S.W. of Lagos, West coast of Africa.

1855   Boats of Allied light squadron destroyed the Russian shipping at Berdyansk, Sea of Azov. Ships: *Arrow, Beagle, Curlew, Lynx, Medina, Miranda, Recruit, Snake, Stromboli, Swallow, Vesuvius, Viper, Wrangler.* French: *Brandon, Fulton, Lucifer, Megère.*

1918   *Lorna* sank UB.74 in Lyme Bay (50° 32' N, 2° 32' W.).

1940   Evacuation of the B.E.F. from Dunkirk. Operation Dynamo — lasted until 4th June. [bh] . (*Sunk. +Damaged). A/A Cruiser: *Calcutta.* Destroyers: *Anthony+, Basilisk*, Codrington, Esk, Express+, Gallant+, Grafton*, Grenade*, Greyhound+, Harvester+, Havant*, Icarus+, Impulsive+, Intrepid+, Ivanhoe+, Jaguar+, Javelin, Keith*, Mackay, Malcolm+, Montrose+, Sabre+, Saladin+, Scimitar+, Shikari, Vanquisher, Venomous+, Verity, Vimy+, Vivacious+, Wakeful*, Whitehall+, Whiteshed, Wild Swan, Winchelsea, Windsor+, Wolfhound+, Wolsey+, Worcester+.* Sloop: *Bideford+.* Corvettes: *Guillemot, Kingfisher+.* Minesweepers: *Albury, Brighton Belle*, Brighton Queen, Devonia*, Duchess of Fife, Dundalk, Emperor of India, Fitzroy, Glen Avon, Glen Gower, Gossamer, Gracie Fields*, Halcyon, Hebe+, Kellett+, Leda, Lydd, Marmion,*

Medway Queen, Niger, Oriole, Pangbourne+, Plinlimmon, Princess Elizabeth, Queen of Thanet, Ross, Salamander, Saltash, Sandown, Sharpshooter, Skipjack, Snaefell, Speedwell, Sutton, Waverley*, Westward Ho+.* Gunboats: *Locust, Mosquito*.* Trawlers: *Argyllshire*, Arley, Brock, Blackburn Rovers*, Valvi*, Cayton Wyke, Chico, Comfort*, Coniday, Fyldea, Grimsby Town, Gulzar, Inverforth, John Cattling, Kingston Alalite+, Kingston Andalusite, Kingston Olivine, Lady Philomena, Lord Inchcape, Nautilus*, Olvina, Our Bairns, Polly Johnson*, Saon, Sargasso, Spurs+, Stella Dorado*, Thomas Bartlett*, Thuringia*, Westella*, Wolves.* Drifters: *Boy Roy*, Eileen Emma, Fidget, Fisher Boy, Forecast, Gervais Rentoul, Girl Gladys, Girl Pamela*, Golden Gift, Golden Sunbeam, Jacketa, Lord Cavan*, Lord Howard, Lord Howe, Midas, Netsukis,*

Boarding a Destroyer at Dunkirk Pier

26th MAY

The "Little Ships" with Troops, Dunkirk

Paxton*, Shipmates, Silver Dawn, The Boys, Torbay II, Ut Prosim, Yorkshire Lass, Young Mun. Armed Boarding Vessels: *King Orry*, Llanthony, Mona's Isle+.* Special Service Vessels: *Amulree*, Crested Eagle*, Golden Eagle, Grive*, Royal Eagle.* Personnel Ships (Red Ensign): *Archangel, Autocarrier, Ben-my-Chree+, Biarritz+, Canterbury+, Fenella*, Killarney, King George V, Lady of Mann, Loch Garry, Lorina*, Maid of Orleans+, Malines, Maxman, Mona's Queen*, Normania*, Prague+, Princess Maud+, Queen of the Channel*, Royal Daffodil, Royal Sovereign, St. Helier, St. Seiroil+, Scotia*, Tynwald.* Hospital Carriers: *Dinard, Isle of Guernsey+, Isle of Thanet+, Paris*, St. Andrew, St. David+, St. Julian+, Worthing+.* FAA Sq.: 810, 806; 825, 826. (All disembarked). Skua, Swordfish, Albacore). MA/SB: 6, 7, 10, MTBs: 16, 67, 68, 100, 102, 107. Allied Ships:- Neth: Yacht: *Demog I.* (Under French orders). French: *Epervier, Leopard, Bouclier, Bourrasque*, Branlebas, Cyclone+, Flore, Foudroy-* *ant*, Incomprise, Mistral+, Sirocco*.* Avisos: *Amiens, Amiral Mouchez, Arras, Belfort.* Trawlers: *Duperre*, Émile Deschamps*.* Mail Packets *Cote d'Argent, Cote d'Azur*, Newhaven, Rouen.* Drifter: *Pierre Marie*.* Polish: *Blyskawica*, (under British orders).

1940   *Curlew* sunk by German aircraft off Skudesnes, N Norway.

1941   *Formidable* (Rear-Admiral D.W. Boyd) attacked Scarpanto airfield. (Karpathos Is). *Formidable* and *Nubian* damaged by German aircraft (32° 55' N, 26° 25' E.). FAA Sq.: 826, 829; 803, 806. (Albacore, Fulmar).

1941   Swordfish aircraft (*Ark Royal*) torpedoed the *Bismarck*. FAA Sq.: 810, 818, 820.

1943   *Hyderabad* and *Test* sank U.436 in N Atlantic (43° 49' N, 15° 56' W.). (Convoy KX.10)

142

27th MAY

1774 Francis Beaufort born.

1793 *Venus* fought the French *Sémillante* 370 miles N.W. by W. of Cape Finisterre.

1796 *Suffisante* captured the French privateer *Revanche* at the entrance to the Chenal du Four, near Ushant.

1811 Boats of *Sabine* cut out three French privateers at Chipiona, near Cadiz. *Papillon* and *Sabine* sank a French privateer and recaptured her prize.

1855 Landing parties from Allied light squadron destroyed Russian stores and the rest of the shipping at Berdyansk, Sea of Azov. See 26th May.

1857 Boats of *Fury, Inflexible, Raleigh, Sybille* and *Tribune* destroyed 13 war junks at Tungkun, Canton River.

1909 Sir John Colomb died.

1915 *Princess Irene* destroyed whilst priming mines at Sheerness.

1915 *Majestic* sank in seven minutes, torpedoed by U.21 outside the Dardanelles (off Cape Helles).

1916 UC.3 sunk by mine off Zeebrugge.

1916 *Kimberley, Oku, Rodino* and *Searanger* sank U.74 in N Sea (57° 10' N, 1° 20' E.).

1941* Forces under Admiral Sir John Tovey (*King George V*) sank the German battleship *Bismarck* in the Atlantic (48° 09' N, 16° 07' W.), after a chase lasting four days. [bh]. Ships: *Ark Royal+, Aurora, Dorsetshire, Edinburgh Galatea, Hermione, Hood*, Kenya, King George V, Neptune, Norfolk, Prince of Wales, Renown+, Repulse, Rodney, Sheffield+, Suffolk, Victorious*. Destroyers: *Achates, Active, Antelope, Anthony, Cossack, Echo, Electra, Icarus, Inglefield, Intrepid, Maori, Mashona*, Nestor, Punjabi, Sikh, Somali, Tartar, Zulu*. Polish: *Piorun*. FAA Squadrons 800Z (*Victorious*), 808 (*Ark Royal*) — Fulmar. 810, 818, 820; 825 (*Ark Royal; Victorious*). (Swordfish). RAF Squadrons: 10, 201,

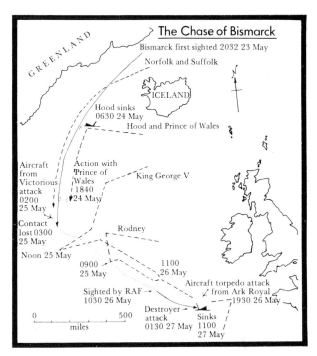

The Chase of Bismarck

Bismarck first sighted 2032 23 May
Norfolk and Suffolk
ICELAND
Hood sinks 0630 24 May
Hood and Prince of Wales
Aircraft from Victorious attack 0200 25 May
Action with Prince of Wales 1840 24 May
King George V
Contact lost 0300 25 May
Rodney
Noon 25 May
0900 25 May
1100 26 May
Aircraft torpedo attack from Ark Royal 1930 26 May
Sighted by RAF 1030 26 May
Destroyer attack 0130 27 May
Sinks 1100 27 May
0 500 miles

206, 209, 210, 221, 240, 269. *Sunk.
+Force H.

Sinking of the Bismarck.

The Home Fleet was joined by other units in the search for the German battleship *Bismarck*, heading for St Nazaire after being damaged by the battleship *Prince of Wales*. A Catalina aircraft sighted her on 26th May, when she was within 24 hours steaming of German air cover. The Home Fleet was 130 miles away. Aircraft from the *Ark Royal*, part of Force H diverted from Gibraltar as a 'long stop', attacked the cruiser *Sheffield* by mistake. From the attack it was discovered that the torpedoes were ineffective, and different firing pistols were fitted for the next attack, in which 2 hits were achieved on *Bismarck*, one of which damaged her steering. Soon afterwards Captain Vian arrived on the scene with 5 destroyers and kept *Bismarck* busy through the night till the main fleet arrived. The weather was too bad for carriers to operate, so the battleships *King George V* and *Rodney* engaged at 8 miles and within 15 minutes *Bismarck* was heavily hit, and within 1½ hours reduced to a burning shambles. The cruiser *Dorsetshire* put 3 torpedoes into her, and *Bismarck* sank at 1036 with flag flying, leaving 110 survivors.

1942 *Fitzroy* sunk by mine off Great Yarmouth.

1944 Liberator S/59 sank U.292 off S.W. Norway (62° 37' N, 0° 57' E.).

1965 Admiral of the Fleet Sir Philip Vian died — twenty five years after the *Bismarck* action.

143

28th MAY

1672   Battle of Solebay. The first battle of the Third Dutch War. Anglo-French fleet of 90 ships under the Duke of York *(Prince)* and Vice-Admiral Comte d'Estrées *(St. Philippe)* fought Admiral de Ruyter *(Zeven Provincien)* with 75 ships. [bh]. Red Sq.: *Bristol, Dartmouth, Diamond, Dunkirk, London, Monck, Old James, Resolution, Sweepstakes, Adventure, Cambridge, Dreadnought, Fairfax, Monmouth, Phoenix, Prince, Royal Katherine, St. Michael, Victory, Yarmouth; Advice, Anne, Charles, Dover, Forester, Greenwich, Rainbow, York.* Blue Sq.: *Antelope, Bonaventure, French Ruby, Gloucester, St. Andrew, St. George, Warspite; Crown, Edgar, Henry, Leopard, Mary Rose, Montagu, Princess, Royal James[3], Rupert, Success; Mary, Plymouth, Ruby, Sovereign, Tiger, Triumph, Unicorn.* White Sq.: (Fr); *Admirable, Alcion, Bourbon, Conquérant, Hasardeux, Illustre, Prince, Téméraire, Terrible, Valiant; Aquilon, Arrogant, Brave, Duc, Éole, Excellent, Foudroyant, Grand, Oriflamme, Saint-Philippe, Tonnant; Fort, Galant, Hardi, Heureux, Invincible, Rubis, Saga, Sans-Pareil, Superbe.* Fireships: *Alice and Francis[1], Ann and Judith [2], Bantam[2], Fountain[3] Katherine [1], Rachel, Robert, Thomas and Edward.* [1] Burnt. [2] Sunk. [3] Blown up.

1673   First action off Schooneveld. 79 ships of Prince Rupert *(Royal Charles)* and Vice-Admiral Comte d'Estrées *(Reine)* fought Admiral de Ruyter *(Zeven Provincien)* with 52 ships. [bh]. Red Sq.: *Anne, Constant Warwick, French Ruby, Happy Return, London, Resolution, Stavoreen, Triumph, Warspite; Crown, Edgar, Gloucester, Henry, Lion, Old James, Princess, Royal Charles, Royal Katherine, Rupert; Assurance, Charles, Mary Rose, Newcastle, Revenge, Victory, Yarmouth.* Blue Sq.: *Foresight, Greenwich, Hampshire, Rainbow, St. Michael, Sweepstakes, York; Advice, Cambridge, Dreadnought, Dunkirk, Henrietta, Prince, St. George, Sovereign, Bonaventure, Diamond, Falcon, Mary, Monck, Ruby, St. Andrew, Unicorn.* White Sq. (Fr): *Aquilon, Conquérant, Oriflamme, Précieux, Prince, Sage, Sans-Pareil, Téméraire, Terrible;*

Aimable, Apollon, Excellent, Fier, Foudroyant, Glorieux, Invincible, Reine, Tonnant, Vailiant; Bon, Bourbon, Duc, Fortune, Grand, Illustre, Maure, Orgueilleux. Fireships: *Providence[1], Rachel[1], Samuel and Anne[1]* [1] Burnt.

1708   Rear-Admiral Charles Wager *(Expedition)* fought twelve Spanish treasure-ships off Puerto Cartagena. Ships: *Expedition, Kingston, Portland.* Detachments of Brigadier-General Thomas Handasyd's Regiment were present. Spanish *Gobierno* captured; *San Jose* blew up.

1781   *Atalanta* and *Trepassey* taken by the American *Alliance* about 120 miles to the south-eastward of Halifax.

1794   *Carysfort* captured the French (ex-British) *Castor* about 390 miles S.W. by W. of Lizard Head. [m]

A Midshipman with his Navigation equipment (see 2nd December): a Rowlandson print of 1799.

28th MAY

1794	Admiral Earl Howe's first action with Rear-Admiral Villaret-Joyeuse, 400 miles W. by S. of Ushant. (See 1st June).
1798	First Sick Bay introduced by Lord St Vincent in the Mediterranean Fleet.
1803	*Albion* captured the French *Franchise* 70 miles W. by S. of Ushant.
1803	*Victory* captured the French *Embuscade* 140 miles N.E. by N. of Cape Ortegal.
1855	Anglo-French squadron bombarded Arabat, Sea of Azov. British: *Ardent, Arrow, Beagle, Lynx, Medina, Miranda, Recruit, Snake, Stromboli, Vesuvius, Viper.* French: *Brandon, Fulton, Lucifer, Mégère.*
1855	*Swallow* and *Wrangler* captured or destroyed several Russian vessels off Genitchi (Genichesk), Sea of Azov.
1941	*Mashona* sunk by German aircraft in SW approaches. (52° 58' N, 11° 36' W.), returning from *Bismarck* action.
1941	Landing party from *Upright* blew up the railway S.W. of Punto Stilo light, S. Italy.
1942	*Eridge, Hero* and *Hurworth* sank U.568 in E Mediterranean (32° 42' N, 24° 53' E.).
1943	Liberator E/120 sank U.304 in N Atlantic (54° 50' N, 37° 20' W.). (Convoy HX.240)
1943	Hudson M/608 sank U.755 off E Spain (39° 58' N, 1° 41' E.).

Naval Gunnery

The first, very primitive naval cannon were used at the Battle of L'Espagnols in 1350 (29th August), but cannon did not become the main weapon at sea until well into the sixteenth century. The basic design of the guns — muzzle-loading smooth-bores firing a solid shot — remained constant throughout the seventeenth and eighteenth centuries, and the only important changes were in methods of casting which enabled safer and heavier guns to be manufactured. Although they had an extreme range of over a mile, such guns were most effective when fired with flat trajectory at close range, and since over such a short distance hitting was assured for both sides, speed of loading rather than accuracy became the crucial factor that won battles.

Throughout the nineteenth century, guns increased in size and the introduction of explosive shells led to the development of armour plating. This in turn led to bigger guns with greater powers of penetration, and above all with greater ranges so that projectiles could be made to plunge onto the target from a great height and therefore with greater energy. Other refinements, such as rifling, breech-loading and high explosives also date from this period. Unfortunately, the implications were not widely realised so that naval tactics did not keep pace with such developments. Naval manoeuvres still tended to take the form of close quarter actions on the Nelsonian model and target practice was conducted at ranges that were measured in hundreds rather than thousands of yards.

Eventually, by the turn of the century, a new generation of senior officers was emerging led by "Jacky" Fisher, Arthur Wilson and Percy Scott who insisted on a more scientific approach to gunnery and other weapons. Practice shoots were conducted at realistic long ranges and human error minimised by the introduction of accurate range-finding instruments together with remote control of the guns from a director placed high above the smoke and noise of the battle. These developments, when linked with the specialised training provided at *Excellent*, revolutionised naval gunnery and led to a tradition of ingenuity and innovation which served the Royal Navy well in two World Wars.

Armour and the Big Gun — Derivation of Jutland Fleets.

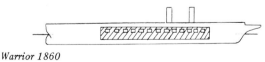

Warrior 1860

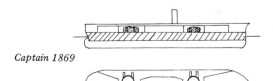

Captain 1869

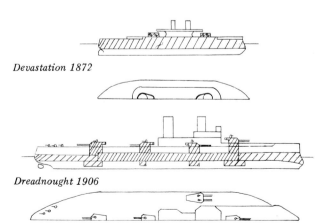

Devastation 1872

Dreadnought 1906

29th MAY

1758   *Dorsetshire* took the *Raisonnable* off the French coast. [bh]

1794   Admiral Earl Howe's second action with the French fleet under Rear-Admiral Villaret-Joyeuse, 400 miles W. by S. of Ushant. (See 1st June).

1797   Boats of *Lively* and *Minerve* cut out the French *Mutine* at Santa Cruz, Tenerife. [m, bh]. A few of the 11th Regiment were in the boats.

1831   Philip Colomb born.

1855   VC: Lieutenant Cecil William Buckley (*Miranda*). Lieutenant Hugh Talbot Burgoyne (*Swallow*). Gunner John Robarts (*Ardent*). Destruction of 73 Russian vessels and food stores at Genitchi (Genichesk), Sea of Azov. Ships: *Ardent, Arrow, Beagle, Lynx, Medina, Miranda, Recruit, Snake, Stromboli, Swallow, Vesuvius, Viper, Wrangler.*

1873   Rifled starshell introduced.

1877   *Shah* and *Amethyst* fought the Peruvian rebel *Huascar* off Ho, Peru. *Shah* fired first British torpedo used in action; also demonstrated poor shooting with her 9 in gun and inadequacy of its ammunition.

1917   First air sea rescue (by flying boat).

1940   *Wakeful* torpedoed by the German S.30 close to the Kwint Whistle Buoy and finally sunk by *Sheldrake*. *Grafton* sunk by U.62 close to wreck of *Wakeful*. *Grenade* and *Crested Eagle* sunk by German aircraft at Dunkirk. Operation Dynamo.

1941   *Hereward* sunk by German aircraft in 35° 20' N, 25° 30' E., during the battle of Crete; and *Imperial* sunk by own forces (*Hotspur*) in 35° 25' N, 25° 20' E., after breakdown of steering gear. *Decoy, Dido* and *Orion* damaged by German aircraft during the same operations.

1942   *Turbulent* sank the Italian destroyer *Emanuele Pessagno* 70 miles N.W. of Benghazi.

30th MAY

1757   *Eagle* and *Medway* captured the French privateer *Duc d'Aquitaine* 100 miles S.W. of Ushant.

1781   *Flora* captured the Dutch *Castor; Crescent* struck to the Dutch *Briel* but was not taken. Both actions 100 miles West of Cape Spartel, Morocco.

1798   *Hydra* drove ashore the French *Confiante* near Beuzeville, Normandy: abandoned and burnt by *Hydra's* boats on the 31st. *Vesuvius* and *Trial* drove ashore the French *Vésuve* near the mouth of the Dives River — refloated and escaped.

1841   Boats of *Dolphin* captured the Brazilian slaver *Firme* a few miles off Whydah, Dahomey.

1859   Chaplain to the Fleet became Chaplain of the Fleet, to rank as a Rear-Admiral.

1862   Landing party of *Centaur* at the defence of Sungkiang, near Shanghai.

1887   Two boats of *Turquoise* captured a slave dhow off Pemba, E Africa.

1906   *Montagu* wrecked on Lundy Island: broken up there. Dummy *Tiger* sunk by UB.8 in Aegean.

1942   *Ramillies* damaged and *Loyalty* (tanker) sunk by Japanese midget submarine at Diego Suarez.

1943   *Untamed* sunk by accident (flooded through log) in the Campbeltown Exercise Area. Salvaged 5th July and renamed *Vitality*.

1944   *Milne* sank U.289 off Norway (73° 32' N, 0° 28' E.).

1951   Admiral of the Fleet Sir Reginald Tyrwhitt died.

The Grand Fleet puts to sea, 1916

31st MAY

1762   *Active* and *Favourite* captured the Spanish treasure-ship *Hermiona* 20 miles S.S.E. of Cape de Santa Maria, Portugal.

1796   *Agamemnon, Meleager, Peterel, Speedy,* and boats of *Blanche* and *Diadem,* captured six French vessels at Porto d'Oneglia, Italian Riviera.

1809   Boats of *Topaze* cut out nine vessels in Demata Bay, near Santa Maura (Levkas), Ionian group.

1825   First "Scuba" type diving device patented.

1910   Reserve Decoration, RD, instituted.

1915   Maiden flight of C1 — first coastal patrol non-rigid airship.

1916*   Battle of Jutland. Admiral Sir John Jellicoe (*Iron Duke*) engaged the German fleet under Vice-Admiral Scheer (*Friedrich der Grosse*). [bh]. British War Medal: clasp 'Jutland 31 May 1916' approved but not issued. Ships: Grand Fleet 1st BS: *Marlborough, Revenge, Hercules, Agincourt, Colossus, Collingwood, Neptune, St. Vincent.* 4th BS: *Iron Duke, Royal Oak, Superb, Canada, Benbow, Bellerophon, Temeraire, Vanguard.* 2ndBS: *King George V, Ajax, Centurion, Erin, Orion, Monarch, Conqueror, Thunderer.* 3rdBCS: *Invincible*, Inflexible, Indomitable.* 1stCS: *Defence*, Warrior+, Duke of Edinburgh, Black Prince*.* 2ndCS: *Minotaur, Hampshire, Cochrane, Shannon.* 4thLCS: *Calliope, Caroline, Constance, Comus, Royalist, Canterbury.* Attached: *Bellona, Blanche, Boadicea, Active, Oak, Abdiel.* 4thDF: *Tipperary*, Broke, Achates, Porpoise, Spitfire, Unity, Garland, Ambuscade, Ardent*, Fortune*, Sparrowhawk*, Contest, Shark*, Acasta, Ophelia, Christopher, Owl, Hardy, Midge.* 11thDF: *Castor (L.C.), Kempenfelt, Ossory, Mystic, Moon, Morning Star, Magic, Mounsey, Mandate, Marne, Minion, Manners, Michael, Mons, Martial, Milbrook.* 12thDF: *Faulknor, Marksman, Obedient, Maenad, Opal, Mary Rose, Marvel, Menace, Nessus, Narwhal, Mindful, Onslaught, Munster, Nonsuch, Noble, Mischief.*

Battle Cruiser Force (Vice-Admiral Sir David Beatty): 1stBCS: *Lion, Princess Royal, Queen Mary*, Tiger.* 2nd BCS: *New Zealand, Indefatigable*.* 5th BS: *Barham, Valiant, Warspite, Malaya.* 1st LCS: *Galatea, Phaeton, Inconstant, Cordelia.* 2nd LCS: *Southampton, Birmingham, Nottingham, Dublin.* 3rd LCS: *Falmouth, Yarmouth, Birkenhead, Gloucester, Chester,* Seaplane Carrier: *Engadine.* 1stDF: *Fearless (L.C.), Acheron, Ariel, Attack, Hydra, Badger, Goshawk, Defender, Lizard, Lapwing.* 9th & 10thDF: *Lydiard, Liberty, Landrail, Laurel, Moorsom, Morris, Turbulent*, Termagant.* 13thDF: *Champion (L.C.), Nestor*, Nomad*, Narborough, Obdurate, Petard, Pelican, Nerissa, Onslow, Moresby, Nicator.*

*Sunk. +Foundered next day. German ships sunk: *Elbing, Lützow, Frauenlob, Pommern, Rostock, Wiesbaden,* S35, V4, V27, V29, V48.

VC: Commander the Hon. Edward Barry Stewart Bingham (*Nestor*). Commander Loftus William Jones (*Shark*) — (posthumous) for heroism during close action with enemy cruiser and destroyers. Although wounded twice (including loss of leg) he kept fighting and then went down with his ship.

Major Francis John William Harvey, RMLI (*Lion*) "whilst mortally wounded and virtually the only survivor after the explosion of an enemy shell in Q Gun House, with great presence of mind and devotion to duty he ordered the magazine to be flooded, thereby saving the ship. He died shortly afterwards;"

John Travers Cornwell, Boy 1st Class. (*Chester*) for devotion to duty.

Jutland Losses	British		German	
	Engaged	Sunk	Engaged	Sunk
Battleships	28	—	22	1
Battle Cruisers	9	3	5	1
Armoured Cruisers	8	3	—	—
Light Cruisers	26	—	11	4
Destroyers	77	8	61	5
Casualties	6748 men		3058 men	

31st MAY

German salvo straddling HMS *Birmingham*.

During World War 1 both the German and British Fleets laid plans to catch the other at a disadvantage in order to obtain supremacy at sea. On 31st May 1916, the German Fleet made a sortie, and the British Fleet sailed in the hope of catching the German Battlecruiser force. At about 1400 both fleets were at sea, and escorts of each closed to investigate a Danish steamer, and so sighted each other.

The British battlecruisers, with the modern *Queen Elizabeth* Class Battleships in company, raced to attack, and sighted the enemy battlecruisers at about 1530. Fire was opened at 1549 at 15,000 yards, and just after 1600, the *Indefatigable* blew up and sank. At 1626, the *Queen Mary* also blew up and sank. However, by now the German ships were being hard hit, and turned away to lead the British towards the main German Fleet.

At 1638, the *Southampton* sighted the main German Fleet. Admiral Beatty in *Lion* realised the trap, and turned to lead the Germans towards Admiral Jellicoe.

At 1817, the Grand Fleet opened fire on the Germans. The battlecruiser *Invincible* blew up just after 1830, but 4 German battlecruisers were badly damaged. The main action was over by 2100.

During the night the German Fleet crossed astern of the British Fleet and reached safety, although they had to sink the battlecruiser *Lützow*. British destroyers sank the battleship *Pommern* with torpedoes.

Although the British lost twice as many men as the Germans and also more ships, the Germans suffered more damaged.

Although inconclusive in itself the engagement was a strategic victory for the British Fleet. As Jellicoe said in a letter to Lady Jellicoe on 6th June, "It is ludicrous for the Germans to claim a victory . . . if they had been so confident of victory they would have gone on fighting instead of legging it for home." Or, as an American journalist put it, "the German fleet has assaulted its gaoler but it is still in prison."

HMS *Lion*, **Admiral Beatty's Flagship.**

31st MAY

The German *Seydlitz* after Jutland.

1918   *Fairy* rammed and sank UC.75 in N Sea (53° 57' N, 0° 09' E.). (Convoy TU.29); UC.75 had just been rammed accidentally by s.s. *Blaydonian*. *Fairy* sank later.

1918   Royal Marine field force landed at Murmansk, North Russia, based at *Glory III*.

1940   *Weston* sank U.13 off Lowestoft. (Convoy FN.184)

1943   *Orion* bombarded Pantellaria.

1943   Sunderland R/201 sank U.440 in E Atlantic (45° 38' N, 13° 04' W.).

1943   Halifax J/58, R/58, Sunderlands X/228 and E/10 (RAAF) sank U.563 in S W Approaches (46° 35' N, 10° 40' W.).

Admiral Sir John Jellicoe saying farewell to officers and men of HMS *Iron Duke*, Scapa November 1916

149

1st JUNE

1360   Establishment of Admiralty court.

1666   The first day of the "Four Days' Battle". The Duke of Albemarle *(Royal Charles)* fought the Dutch fleet of 85 sail under Admiral de Ruyter about 30 miles E.N.E. of the North Foreland. [bh]. Ships: *Antelope, Black Bull, Black Spread Eagle, Breda, Bristol, Clove Tree, Convertine, Essex, Gloucester, Henrietta, Henry, House de Swyte, Lilly, Little Katherine, Loyal George, Plymouth, Portland, Royal Prince, Princess, Rainbow, Royal Charles, Royal Katherine, St. George, St. Paul, Sevenoaks, Swiftsure, Triumph, Vanguard, Victory.* Fireships: *Greyhound, Hound, Little Unicorn, Spread Eagle, Richard, Young Prince* (all expended). Captured: *Black Bull, Little Katherine, Loyal George.*

1705   First pensioners arrived at Royal Hospital Greenwich.

Admiral Earl Howe (Black Dick) 1725 – 1799

It was said of Howe that he "never smiled unless a battle was at hand". In 1765 he was appointed Treasurer of the Navy and in 1776 Vice-Admiral of the North American station. He was a firm disciplinarian but nevertheless very popular with the sailors. He commanded the Channel Fleet in 1794 at the Glorious First of June. In 1797 he returned to Portsmouth to preside over the re-establishment of discipline during the Spithead mutiny.

When his first appointment as a Flag Officer was questioned in Parliament, Lord Hawke "rose up and said, 'I advised His Majesty to make the appointment. I have tried Lord Howe on important occasions; he never asked me how he was to execute any Service but always went and performed it'."

1794   "The Glorious First of June". Admiral Earl Howe *(Queen Charlotte)* defeated Rear-Admiral Villaret-Joyeuse *(Montagne)* to the West of Ushant. [m*, m, bh]. Ships: *Caesar, Bellerophon, Leviathan, Russell, Royal Sovereign, Marlborough, Defence, Impregnable, Tremendous, Barfleur, Invincible; Culloden, Gibraltar, Queen Charlotte, Brunswick, Valiant, Orion, Queen; Ramillies, Alfred, Montagu, Royal George, Majestic, Glory, Thunderer. Audacious* on 28th May only. Frigates, etc.: *Aquilon, Latona, Niger, Pegasus, Phaeton, Southampton, Venus; Charon, Comet, Incendiary, Ranger, Rattler.* Captured: *Achille, America, Impetueux, Juste, Northumberland, Sans-Pareil.* Sunk: *Vengeur-du-Peuple.* Regiments: 2nd, 25th, 29th, 69th. The 2nd Foot, now The Queen's Regiment, and the 29th, now the Worcestershire and Sherwood Foresters Regiment, have as a Battle Honour a Naval Crown, superscribed "1st June, 1794."

Admiral Howe's instructions were to safeguard British trade, to prevent a convoy of grain from America from reaching France, and to defeat the enemy fleet under Villaret-Joyeuse. His tactics were to close the enemy fleet, to break through the line at all points and to engage from the leeward position. He captured 6 ships and sank one but the grain convoy reached France.

1808   *Redwing* captured two Spanish vessels and destroyed another and a battery at Bolonia, S.W. Spain. [m]

1813   *Shannon* captured the American *Chesapeake* 20 miles off Boston, Massachusetts in less than fifteen minutes. [m*, m, bh]

1848   *Scout* captured two pirate junks a few miles off Chimmo Bay.

1857   Destruction of over 70 war junks at Fat Shan Creek by gunboats, tenders and boats of squadron. Gunboats and tenders: *Bustard, Coromandel, Forester, Haughty, Hong Kong, Opossum, Plover, Sir Charles Forbes, Sterling, Staunch.*

1st JUNE

Rear Admiral Sir Philip Broke (1776-1841)
(Broke of the Shannon).

Broke joined the Royal Naval Academy, Portsmouth in 1792. From 1793 to 1795 he served in the Mediterranean and fought in the Battle of Cape St Vincent as a Lieutenant. He was promoted to Captain in 1805 and gained command of 38 gun *Shannon* in 1806. During the period after Trafalgar when there was little sea warfare to be had he fitted the guns of the ship with sights and trained her gunners. This was a new departure, since Nelson's philosophy had always been to close the range and batter the enemy. At a time when many British frigates were being bested by the US navy, the *Shannon* encountered the frigate *Chesapeake* on the 1st June 1813. *Chesapeake* had a new and untrained crew and *Shannon* invited the Captain of the *Chesapeake* to take a month's training before taking on the *Shannon*. *Chesapeake* however sailed to fight the *Shannon* and was defeated within 15 minutes. Broke was severely injured and retired having been made KCB. He died in 1841 after suffering constant pain from his wounds. He declined to hoist additional battle ensigns remarking that "we have always been an unassuming ship".

John Bull taking a luncheon, or British Cooks cramming Old Grumble-Gizzard with Bonne-chere. A Gillray cartoon of 1798.

1st JUNE

1939   *Thetis* foundered in Mersey Bay on acceptance trials. See 14th March.

1940   *Basilisk, Havant, Keith* and *Skipjack* sunk by German aircraft off Dunkirk. Operation Dynamo.

1941   *Calcutta* torpedoed and sunk by German aircraft in Mediterranean (31° 55' N, 28° 05' E.).

1941   Evacuation of Army from Crete ended. [bh]

Evacuation of Crete

On 20th May the enemy bombed Crete and landed by parachute, glider and transport aircraft. The Navy swept the seas, but no attack yet came from that way. The next day the destroyer *Juno* was sunk by bombs, and reconnaisance showed seaborne movement toward Crete. That night a convoy of transports escorted by torpedo boats was intercepted and in a 2½ hour night action many of the enemy craft were sunk and a landing frustrated by the cruisers *Dido, Orion, Ajax* and 4 destroyers.

On 22nd another enemy convoy was turned back, although enemy aircraft bombed the Navy. Many ships were damaged and the cruisers *Gloucester* and *Fiji* sunk rescuing survivors from the destroyer *Greyhound*, which was also lost. That night the Navy evacuated the King of Greece and the British Minister, and the enemy abandoned invasion by sea.

On 23rd the destroyers *Kelly* and *Kashmir* were sunk by bombing. From 21st only destroyers and the fast minelayer *Abdiel* were able to supply the Army, as even the faster merchant ships were too slow to make the 800 mile round trip and enter and leave harbour by night.

On 27th it was decided to evacuate Crete, and the port of Heraklion was chosen together with open beaches, using the hours of 2359 to 0300 because of the unopposed enemy air power. The Navy had been under considerable strain, especially in the recent months with the evacuation of Greece and operations off Crete, but in the next four nights about 18,600 soldiers out of 32,000 were evacuated.

The Navy had prevented any enemy landing by sea until airborne forces had conquered the island. The Army reaction to the Naval support can be summarised by one man's writing at the time: ". . . having reached the sea . . . with a torch we flashed an SOS, and, to our tremendous relief, we received an answer. It was the Navy on the job; the Navy for which we had been hoping and praying all along the route."

Admiral Cunningham declined to stop the evacuation, commenting that while it took three years to build a ship, it would take three hundred to rebuild a tradition.

1942   Attack on Sydney harbour by four Japanese midget submarines: all sunk Sunk: *Kuttabul,* an accommodation ship.

1943   *Starling* sank U.202 in N. Atlantic (56° 12' N, 39° 52' W.).

1943   Beaufighter B/236 sank U.418 in E. Atlantic (47° 05' N, 8° 55' W.).

1943   *Penelope, Paladin* and *Petard* bombarded Pantellaria.

1948   *Reclaim* commissioned: RN's first deepwater diving tender.

HMS *Implacable* (ex-*Duguay-Trouin)* right

2nd JUNE

1653 Joint Admirals George Monck and Richard Deane *(Resolution)*, with 105 ships, fought Admiral Maerten Tromp *(Brederode)*, with 98 ships and 6 fireships, off the Gabbard. [bh]. Red Sq.: *Adventure, Ann and Joyce, Bear, Hannibal, Heart's Ease, Hound, Laurel, London, Mary, Providence, Thomas and William, Triumph; Advice, Diamond, Golden Fleece, Loyalty, Malaga Merchant, Marmaduke, Martin, Mermaid, Pelican, Resolution, Sapphire, Society, Worcester; Fair Sisters, Falmouth, Guinea, Hamburgh Merchant, Phoenix, Sophia, Speaker, Sussex, Tiger, Violet.* Fireships: *Fortune, Fox, Renown.* White Sq.: *Centurion, Exchange, Expedition, Gilly Flower, Globe, Middleboro, Prudent Mary, Raven, Thomas and Lucy, Victory; Anne Piercy, Assistance, Exchange, Foresight, James, Lion, Lisbon Merchant, Merlin, Peter, Portsmouth, Richard and Martha, Ruby, Sarah; Andrew, Assurance, Crown, Duchess, Industry, Pearl, Princess Maria, Reformation, Waterhound.* Fireships: *Falcion (Falcon).* Blue Sq.: *Benjamin, Convert, Crescent, Dragon, Entrance (Happy Entrance), Gift, King Ferdinando, Paul, Roebuck, Samuel Talbot, Vanguard; Adventure, Brazil, Eastland Merchant, George, Great President (President), Kentish, Nonsuch, Oak, Samaritan, Success, Welcome; Arms of Holland, Amity, Blossom, Covertine, Dolphin, Dragoneare, Jonathan, Nicodemus, Rainbow, Tulip, William and John.* Fireship: *Hunter.* (There were two ships each named *Adventure, Exchange* and *Phoenix*).
Flags:

Admiral George Monck

	v*(Triumph*	James Peacock (V.A.).
Red	c*(Resolution*	Monck and Deane (Joint Adms.)
	r*(Speaker*	Samuel Howett (R.A.).
	v*(Victory*	Lionel Lane (V.A.)
White	c*(James*	William Penn (A.)
	r*(Andrew*	Thomas Graves (R.A.).
	v*(Vanguard*	Joseph Jordan (V.A.).
Blue	c*(George*	John Lawson (A.)
	r*(Rainbow*	William Goodson (R.A.).

1666 The second day of the "Four Days' Battle". English — 44 ships; Dutch — 80 ships. Captured: *Black Spread Eagle, Convertine, Essex, Swiftsure.*

1779 *Ruby* captured the French *Prudente* off Île de la Gonave, West Indies.

1805 Boats of *Loire* cut out the Spanish privateer *Esperanza,* and another which could not be brought out, in Camarinas Bay, N.W. Spain.

1805 *Diamond Rock*, (Commander James Maurice), surrendered to a strong French squadron under Captain Cosmao-Kerjulien *(Pluton)*.

1913 C.32 rammed *Prince of Wales.*

1941 *Periwinkle* and *Wanderer* sank U.147 in NW Approaches (56° 38' N, 10° 24' W.). (Convoy OB.329)

1942 Blenheim aircraft of 203 Sq and Swordfish of 815 Sq sank U.652 off Sollum (31° 55' N, 25° 13' E.).

1943 *Jervis* and *Queen Olga* (Greek) attacked an escorted Italian convoy Off Cape Spartivento, Italy. Italian t.b. *Castore* and two of the convoy sunk. Italian destroyer driven ashore.

1970 Tactical school opened in new Woolwich block at *Dryad.*

2nd JUNE

Dutch prints of the Action off Essex, 2 to 3 June 1653, and the Four Days fight, 1 to 4 June 1666. The Print maker clearly thought there was some similarity in the two battles.

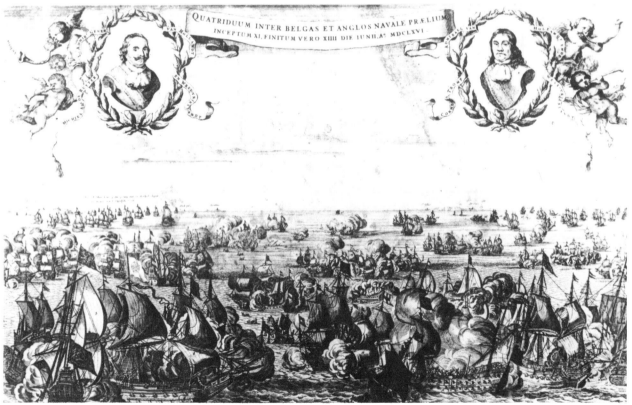

3rd JUNE

1653 Continuation of the action off the Gabbard, ending in the defeat of the Dutch. Additional ships: *Culpepper, Eagle, Employment, Essex,* (Admiral Robert Blake) *Hampshire, Hopeful Luke, John and Abigail, Phoenix, Prosperous, Stork, Swan, Tenth Whelp (Whelp), William* and 5 others. Total Dutch loss: 11 captured, 6 sunk, 3 blown up.

1665 The Duke of York *(Royal Charles),* with 109 ships, defeated the Dutch fleet of 103 ships under Admiral Jacob van Wassenaer, Heer van Obdam *(Eendragt),* 40 miles S.E. of Lowestoft. [bh]. Red Sq.: *Bristol, Coast Frigate, Diamond, Dover, Gloucester, Guinea, Martin, Norwich(?), Royal Exchange, Royal Oak, St. George; Antelope, Blackamore(?), Coventry(?), Fountain, Happy Return, Loyal George, Mary, Mermaid(?), Norwich(?), Old James, Plymouth, Royal Charles, Yarmouth; Amity, Bonaventure, Eagle, Fairfax(?), George, Leopard, Little Mary(?), Portsmouth, Sapphire, Satisfaction, Success, Swiftsure.*
Fireship: *Drake.* White Sq.: *Colchester, Expedition(?), Hector(?), John and Abigail, Katherine, Lion, Monk, Newcastle, Paradox(?), Return, Ruby(?), Triumph; Assurance, Bendish, Exchange(?), Garland, Henrietta, Mary Rose, Merlin(?), Portland, Rainbow, Reserve, Revenge, Royal James; Advice (?), Anne, Bear, Constant Katherine, East India Merchant(?), Kent, Milford, Resolution, St. Andrew, Speedwell(?), Truelove(?).* Fireship: One. Blue Sq.: *Assistance, Castle Frigate, Guernsey, Hambro' Merchant, Hampshire, Henry, Jersey, Lizard(?), Providence, Unicorn, York- Blackamore (Merchant), Breda, Centurion, Dragon, Dunkirk, Good Hope(?), John and Thomas, Maryland (Merchant) (?). Montagu, Oxford Ketch, Pembroke, Royal Prince, Swallow; Adventure, Dreadnought, Essex(?), Forester, Golden Phoenix(?), Marmaduke, Paul(?), Princess, Royal Katherine, Society.* Fireship: One. Other ships possibly present: *Charity[1], Clove Tree, Convertine, Golden Lion, Horseman, John and Katherine, King Ferdinando, London, Loyal Merchant, Maderas, Nightingale, Prudent Mary, Tiger,*

Vanguard, Young Lion. Fireships: *Briar, Dolphin[2], Fame[2], Hound.*
[1] Captured. [2] Expended in action.
Dutch loss: 32 ships, but only 9 prizes were brought in.

1666 The third day of the "Four Days' Battle". Burnt: *Royal Prince, St. Paul.* Captured: *Sevenoaks.*

1711 *Newcastle* fought a French flotilla off St. Pierre, Martinique.

1747 Captains who were not to be employed again when automatically promoted to flag rank became 'Superannuated Rear-Admirals'; nicknamed the Yellow Squadron.

1832 *Speedwell* captured the slaver *Aquila* off the coast of Cuba.

1855 VC: Boatswain Henry Cooper *(Miranda).* Ships and boats of Allied light squadron and launches from the fleet destroyed Russian food stores at Taganrog, Sea of Azov. Ships and tenders: *Ardent, Beagle, Curlew, Danube, Medina, Miranda, Recruit, Snake, Stromboli, Sulina, Vesuvius, Viper, Wrangler.* French: *Brandon, Fulton, Lucifer, Megère, Mouette.* Two launches each from: *Agamemnon, Algiers, Hannibal, Princess Royal, Royal Albert, St. Jean d'Acre* and 8 French launches.

1896 Frederick John Walker born.

1915 British forces captured Kut-al'Amara, Mesopotamia. Ships and vessels: *Clio, Espiegle, Lawrence* (RIN), *Odin; Bahrein, Comet, Lewis Pelly, Miner, Muzaffri, Shaitan, Shushan, Sumana.*

1932 *Implacable* (ex-*Duguay-Trouin*) arrived Portsmouth and exchanged salutes with *Victory,* her Trafalgar adversary. Joined in July 1932 by *Foudroyant* (ex-*Trincomalee*).

1941 First of *Bismarck's* tankers sunk.

1943 *Ilex, Isis, Orion, Paladin* and *Troubridge* bombarded Pantellaria.

1944 Canso T/162 (RCAF) sank U.477 off Shetlands (63° 59' N, 1° 37' E.).

4th JUNE

1666 The last day of the "Four Day's Battle". About 30 miles E.N.E. of the North Foreland. Prince Rupert's squadron (4 June only): ex White Sq.: *Assurance, Breda, Dragon, Leopard, Mary Rose, Plymouth, Royal James.* ex Red Sq.: *Diamond, Essex, Henrietta, Portsmouth, Princess, Revenge, Victory.* ex Blue Sq.: *Amity, Bonaventure, Dreadnought, Expedition, Reserve, Swallow.* Fireships: *Happy Entrance.* Captured: *Clove Tree.* Retaken: *Black Bull.* Albemarle (Monck) defeated by de Ruyter: Admiral Myngs killed.

1673 Second action off Schooneveld. Prince Rupert *(Sovereign)* and Vice-Admiral Comte d'Estrées *(Reine)* fought the Dutch fleet under Admiral de Ruyter *(Zeven Provincien).* [bh]. Red Sq.: *Anne, Constant Warwick, French Ruby, Happy Return, London, Stavoreen, Triumph, Warspite; Crown, Edgar, Gloucester, Henry, Lion, Old James, Princess, Royal Katherine, Rupert, Sovereign; Assurance, Charles, Mary Rose, Newcastle, Revenge, Victory, Yarmouth.* Blue Sq.: *Foresight, Greenwich, Hampshire, Rainbow, St. Michael, Sweepstakes, York; Advice, Dreadnought, Dunkirk, Henrietta, Prince, Royal Charles, St. George, Swiftsure; Bonaventure, Diamond, Falcon, Mary, Monck, Ruby, St. Andrew, Unicorn.* White Sq.: 26 French ships. see 28th May, less *Conquérant.* Fireships: *Trulove, Welcome.*

1742 *Rose* captured a Spanish snow (and her three prizes on the following day) in Exuma Sound, Bahama Islands.

1800 *Cynthia* and *Thames* destroyed the forts at the S.W. end of Quiberon; several small vessels were brought off and some scuttled.

1805 *Loire* captured the French *Confiance* and *Belier,* together with a fort and a battery, in Muros Bay, N.W. Spain. [m]

1844 Boats of *Samarang* destroyed 27 pirate prahus in Patientie Strait, Jailolo Passage.

1846 Anglo-French squadron engaged the San Lorenzo batteries whilst escorting a large convoy down the Parana River, Argentina. British: *Alecto, Dolphin, Fanny, Firebrand, Gorgon, Harpy, Lizard.* French: *Coquette, Fulton.*

1852 Capture of Pegu by Major-General Henry Godwin and Commodore John Tarleton *(Fox).* Boats of: *Fox; Moozuffer* (I.N.) and *Phlegethon* (Ben. Mar.). Troops: Madras Sappers and Miners, one company each of the 80th Regiment and the 67th Bengal Native Infantry.

Capt J. W. Tarleton

1915 E.9 sank a German G. Class destroyer off Danish coast.

1919 L.55 sunk in Baltic by Bolshevik destroyers: salvaged, commissioned into Soviet Navy and used for training until World War II.

1940 Evacuation of the BEF from Dunkirk completed. Operation Dynamo.

The planning for Operation Dynamo was set in hand on 22nd May as German troops were driving the allied armies into the sea. The aim of the exercise was to evacuate 45,000 men in 2 days. Dunkirk itself and its harbour had been totally destroyed, and only 2 breakwaters had enough water alongside them to berth small ships. However, by remarkable effort from all the ports of England a swarm of small craft gathered and in the face of constant heavy bombing, E-boat attacks and mines, they continued evacuating troops until the 4th June. 308,388 men were evacuated in British ships and craft, 29,338 in allied vessels — including 26,175 French troops. Six British and 3 French destroyers had been sunk together with eight passenger ships; 19 destroyers were severely damaged.

1941 Four more of *Bismarck's* supply ships sunk (see 3rd June).

1942 *Cocker* (ex-Kos 19) sunk by the German S.57 between Tobruk and Bardia. (32° 06' N, 24° 14' E.).

1943 *Truculent* sank U.308 off Faeroes (64° 28' N, 3° 09' W.).

1943 Hudson F/48 sank U.594 off Cape St Vincent (35° 55' N, 9° 25' W.).

5th JUNE

1805	*Helena* captured the Spanish privateer *Santa Leocadia* off Cork.
1806	*Vestal* captured the French privateer *Prospero* in Dover Strait.
1807	Boats of *Pomone* captured 13 vessels of a convoy of 27 sail and one of the escorting brigs off Sables d'Olonne and St. Gilles sur Vie. Three more of the convoy were driven ashore.
1812	Boats of *Medusa* cut out the French *Dorade* from Arcachon Basin.
1829	*Pickle* captured the slaver *Boladora* off Puerto Naranjo.
1855	Massacre of several of a boat's crew of *Cossack*, flying a flag of truce, at Hangö (Hanko), Finland.
1855	VC: Thomas Wilkinson, Bombardier RMA, at siege of Sevastopol.
1855	Boats of Allied light squadron destroyed Russian stores at Marianpol, Sea of Azov. See 3rd June.

1915	U.14 sunk by armed trawler, *Oceanic II* off Peterhead.
1916	*Hampshire* sunk by mine West of Marwick Head, Orkneys. Lord Kitchener and his Staff drowned.
1917	First experiments started with ASDIC devices at Harwich.

The principle of asdic is simple. A sound wave is transmitted through the water. If it hits an object, such as a submarine, an echo is heard. The direction from which the echo came and the time it took to return indicate the bearing and range of that object. Refinements have been introduced to make the sound beam more directional, and to go further, but the essential principle is that of today's Sonar: Sound Navigation And Radar. ASDIC stood for Anti-Submarine Detector Investigation Committee.

1917	Sheerness and Naval Establishments in the Medway raided by German aircraft.
1917	*Centaur* sank the German S.20 off Ostend.
1943	*Newfoundland, Paladin* and *Troubridge* bombarded Pantellaria.

A Naval Brigade ashore - 1860's.

1758 Destruction of the shipping and store-houses at St. Malo by Commodore the Hon. Richard Howe *(Essex)* and troops under the Duke of Marlborough. Ships: *Essex, Deptford, Jason, Portland, Rochester.* Frigates: *Active, Brilliant, Flamborough, Maidstone, Pallas, Richmond, Rose, Success, Tartar.* Sloops: *Diligence, Saltash, Speedwell, Swallow, Swan.* Fireships: *Pluto, Salamander.* Bombs: *Furnace, Grenado, Infernal.* Bomb tenders: *Neptune, Nancy, Endeavour.*

1762 Admiral of the Fleet Lord Anson died.

Admiral of the Fleet George Lord Anson (1697-1762)

Anson joined the navy in 1712 and was made post Captain in 1734. In 1737 he was given command of the *Centurion* (60 guns).
In 1740 he was placed in command of 6 small warships, 2 supply ships and 1500 men and ordered to attack Spanish colonies in the Pacific. Although the force sounds quite strong, in fact 500 of the soldiers were Chelsea pensioners and 300 untrained recruits. The ships were in poor condition and his crews in general were of low quality. The expedition suffered fearful losses. Although only 4 were lost in action, 1300 men were lost through disease. All the ships except *Centurion* had to be abandoned. In 1743 off the Phillippines he encountered the Spanish treasure ship *Nuestra Senora de Covadonga.* He captured her and when he returned to England in 1744 he brought a million pound treasure with him. The success of the expedition was almost entirely due to Anson's personal ability. He became so disillusioned at the treatment he had received that he refused to serve further until the government had changed. He ultimately became First Lord in 1751 and was made Admiral of the Fleet in 1761.

1800 Boats of *Impetueux, Thames, Amethyst, Amelia, Cynthia* and 300 of the 2nd Foot burned the French *Insolente* and several smaller vessels; also captured 5 brigs, 2 sloops and 2 gun vessels in the Morbihan, France.

1855 Third bombardment of Sevastopol. (Continued until the 10th.). Naval Brigade and Royal Artillery.

1868 Robert Falcon Scott born.

1940 *Carinthia* sunk by U.46 off W. Ireland (53° 13' N, 10° 40' W.).

1944 Normandy Landing. Operation Neptune. [bh]. Ships: *Abelia, Adventure, Affleck, Ajax, Albatross, Alberni*, Albrighton, Albury, Algonquin+, Apollo, Ardrossan, Arethusa, Argonaut, Aristrocrat, Armeria, Ashanti, Aylmer, Azalea, Bachaquero, Baddeck, Balfour, Bangor, Beagle, Beaumaris, Belfast, Bellona, Bentley, Bickerton, Black Prince, Blackpool, Blackwood*, Blairmore, Blankney, Bleasdale, Blencathra, Bligh, Bluebell, Boadicea, Bootle, Borage, Boston, Braithwaite, Bridlington, Bridport, Brigadier, Brissenden, Britomart*, Bulolo, Burdock, Buttercup, Calgary+, Cam, Camellia, Campanula, Campbell, Camrose+, Cape Breton+, Capel, Capetown, Caraquet, Catherine, Cato*, Cattistock, Celandine, Ceres, Charlock, Chaudiere+, Chelmer, Clarkia, Clematis, Clover, Cockatrice, Cooke, Cotswold, Cottesmore, Cowichan+, Crane, Dacres, Dahlia, Dakins, Danae, Despatch, Deveron, Diadem, Dianella, Dianthus, Domett, Dominica, Dornoch, Douwe Aukes, Drumheller+, Duckworth, Duff, Duke of Wellington, Dunbar, Eastbourne, Eglinton, Elgin, Emerald, Emperor, Enterprise, Erebus, Eskimo, Essington, Fame, Fancy, Faulknor, Fernie, Forester, Fort William+, Fort York, Fraserburgh, Friendship, Frobisher, Fury*, Garlies, Garth, Gatineau+, Gazelle, Gentian, Geranium, Glasgow, Gleaner, Glenearn, Glenroy, Goatfell, Goathland, Godetia, Golden Eagle, Goodson, Gore, Gorgon, Gozo, Grecian, Grenville, Grey Fox, Grey Goose, Grey Owl, Grey Seal, Grey Shark, Grey Wolf, Grou+, Guysborough+, Haida+, Halcyon, Halsted, Hambledon, Hargood, Harrier, Hart, Havelock, Hawkins, Heather, Hilary,*

6th JUNE

Hind, Holmes, Honeysuckle, Hotham, Hotspur, Hound, Huron+, Hussar*, Hydra, Icarus, Ilfracombe, Impulsive, Inconstant, Inglis, Invicta, Isis*, Jason, Javelin, Jervis, Keats, Kellett, Kelvin, Kempenfelt, Kenora, Keppel, Kingcup, Kingsmill, Kitchener, Kite, Kootenay+, Lapwing, Largs, Lark, Larne, Lavender, Lawford*, Lawson, Lennox, Lightfoot, Lindsay, Llandudno, Loch Fada, Loch Killin, Lochy, Locust, Londonderry, Loosestrife, Louisburg+, Loyalty*, Lunenburg+, Lydd, Lyme Regis, Mackay, Magpie, Malpeque+, Matane+, Mauritius, Mayflower, Melbreak, Melita, Mendip, Meon, Meynell, Middleton, Mignonette, Milltown, Mimico, Minas, Misoa, Montrose, Moorsom, Moosejaw+, Mounsey, Mourne*, Narbrough, Narcissus, Nasturtium, Nelson, Nith, Northway, Obedient, Offa, Onslaught, Onslow, Onyx, Opportune, Orchis, Orestes, Oribi, Orion, Orwell, Ottawa+, Outremont+, Oxlip, Pangbourne, Parrsboro, Pelican, Pelorus, Pennywort, Persian, Petunia, Pickle, Pincher, Pink, Pique, Plover, Plucky, Poole, Poppy, Port Arthur+, Port Colborne+, Postillion, Potentilla, Prescott, Primrose, Prince Baudouin†, Prince Charles, Prince David+, Prince Leopold†, Prins Albert†, Prinses Astrid†, Prinses Josephine Charlotte†, Pursuer, Pytchley, Q'Appelle+, Qualicum, Queen Emma, Quorn*, Ramillies, Rattlesnake, Ready, Recruit, Redpole, Regina*+, Restigouche+, Retalick, Rhododendron, Rifleman, Rimouski+, Riou, Roberts, Rochester, Rodney, Romney, Ross, Rowley, Royal Ulsterman, Rupert, Ryde, Rye, St. Helier, St. John+, St. Laurent+, Salamander, Saltash, Sandown, Saskatchewan+, Saumarez, Savage, Scarborough, Scawfell, Scorpion, Scourge, Scylla, Seagull, Seaham, Selkirk, Serapis, Seymour, Shippigan, Sidmouth, Sioux+, Sirius, Skeena+, Southdown, Southern Prince, Speedwell, Spragge, Starling, Starwort, Statice, Stayner, Steadfast, Stevenstone, Stockham, Stork, Stormont+, Strule, Summerside, Sunflower, Sutton, Swansea+, Sweetbriar, Swift*, Tadoussac+, Talybont, Tantaside, Tartar, Tasajera, Tavy, Teme, Tenby, Thames Queen, Thornborough, Torrington, Tracker, Trentonian+, Trollope, Tyler, Ulster, Ulster Monarch, Ulysses, Undaunted, Undine, Urania, Urchin, Ursa, Vanquisher, Vegreville+, Venus, Versatile, Verulam, Vervain, Vesper, Vestal, Vidette, Vigilant, Vimy, Virago, Vivacious, Volunteer, Waldegrave, Walker, Wallflower, Walpole, Wanderer, Warspite, Wasaga+, Waskesiu+, Watchman, Waveney, Wedgeport, Wensleydale, Westcott, Whimbrel, Whippingham, Whitaker, Whitehall, Whitehaven, Whitshed, Wild Goose, Windsor, Woodstock, Worthing, Wren, Wrestler*, X.20, X.23. *Sunk. +RCN. †Belgian. Stord and Svenner* (Norge). Surveying:

Rear-Admiral Creasy, Admiral Sir Bertram Ramsay and Rear-Admiral Sir Philip Vian

Naval Beach Signal Unit

6th JUNE

Astral, Franklin, Gulnare, Scott.
62 A/S Trawlers. 15 LL Trawlers:
42 Danlayers. 95 Mulberries. Blockships: *Centurion, Durban.* F.A.A. Sq.:
819 (Swordfish) 848, 849, 850,
852 and 855 (Avenger).
808, 885, 886, 897. (Seafires). MGB
Flotilla: 1st (6). MTB Flotillas:
1st (8), 5th (7), 13th (8), 14th (12),
21st (7), 22nd (7), 29th (8), 35th (10),
51st (7), 52nd (9), 53rd (7), 55th (12),
59th (8), 63rd (8), 64th (7), 65th (9),
ML Flotillas: 1st (8), 2nd (9), 4th (4),
5th (12), 7th (14), 10th (10), 11th (13),
13th (8), 14th (13), 15th (6), 19th (4),
20th (14), 21st (9), 23rd (8), 33rd
(7), 50th (5), 51st (3), 103rd (8),
150th (9), 151st (9), Unattached (2).
MMS Flotillas: 101st (10), 102nd
(10), 104th (10), 115th (1), 132nd
(10), 143rd (10), 205th (11).
BYMS Flotillas: 150th (10), 159th
(10), 165th (10), 167th (10). SGB
Flotilla: 1st (6) — See Grey Fox, etc.

1944 *Svenner* (Nor) sunk by the German
torpedo boats *Jaguar, Möwe* and T.28
off Normandy (49° 30' N, 0° 01' W.).
Wrestler damaged by mine (49° 36'
N, 0° 28' W.). (Scrapped). Operation
Neptune.

D-DAY

Ships that took part in the Operation:

Warships	1212
Landing Ships and Craft	4026
Ancilliaries	731
Merchant Vessels	864
Total	6833

Of which 78% were British (including Canadian), 17% were American, 5% were French, Norwegian, Dutch, Polish and Greek. Over 10,000 Royal Marines took part, including 5 RM Commandos, an Armoured Support Group, an RM Engineering Commando, Landing Craft Obstruction Units, Signallers, drivers etc. Marines manned no less than two thirds of the assault landing craft. *A Memorable Date observed by 48 Commando RM and by operational RM landing squadrons.*

Gliders with Airborne Division passing over Force S, in Sword area

7th JUNE

1673   *Crown* and *Nightingale* fought three Dutch men-of-war off the Galloper.

1761   Capture of Belle Île by Major-General Studholm Hodgson and Commodore the Hon. Augustus Keppel *(Valiant)*. [bh]. Ships: *Achilles, Buckingham, Burford, Chichester, Dragon, Essex, Hampton Court, Hero, Monmouth, Prince of Orange, Sandwich, Swiftsure, Temeraire, Torbay, Valiant*. Frigates, etc.: *Actaeon, Adventure, Aldborough, Blast, Druid, Escort, Flamborough, Fly, Launceston, Lynn, Melampe, Southampton*. Bombs: *Firedrake, Furnace, Infernal*. Fireships: *Aetna, Vesuvius*. Troops: Royal Artillery, 16th Lt. Dragoons, 2 Bns of Marines, 3rd, 9th, 19th, 21st, 30th, 36th, 67th, 69th Foot; 75th, 76th, 85th, 90th, 97th, 98th Foot. *A Memorable Date observed by the Royal Marines, as the anniversary of their winning the laurels surrounding their badge.*

1777   *Fox* taken by the American *Hancock* and *Boston* off the Banks of Newfoundland.

1780   *Iris* fought the French *Hermione* 90 miles East of Sandy Hook.

1854   Boats of *Vulture* and *Odin* repulsed in an attack on Gamla Karleby, Gulf of Bothnia.

1915   VC: Flight Sub-Lieutenant Reginald Alexander John Warneford, RNAS, for destroying Zeppelin LZ.37 near Ghent.

1915   RNAS aircraft destroyed Zeppelin LZ.38 in her shed at Evere, Belgium.

1917   VC: Lieutenant Ronald Neil Stuart, RNR and Ordinary Seaman William Williams, RNR *(Pargust)* *Pargust* (Q-ship) sank UC.29 55 miles West of Valentia Island (51° 47'N, 11° 40'W.).

1917   Construction of *Zubian* completed.

1942   Sunderland M/202 sank the Italian s/m *Veniero* off Minorca (37° 52' N, 4° 05' E.).

1944   Sunderlands S/201 and R/228 sank U.955 and U.970 respectively in the Bay of Biscay.

Flight Sub-Lt R. A. J. Warneford, VC.

1944   *Memorable Date* of 47 Commando RM; their capture of Port-en-Bessin.

D Day and after, 1944

From D Day to the fall of Le Havre in September, 1944, there were 750 bombardments by warships of cruiser size and above. Destroyers and smaller warships also carried out many bombardments in support of the land forces. Ammunition expended by destroyers and larger warships was:-

16in and 15in	3371 rounds
7.5in to 5.25in	31250 rounds
4.7in and 4in	24000 rounds
Total	58,621 rounds

During this period 609 mines were swept, 28 surface actions took place and the following were landed:— 1,410,600 tons of stores, 152,000 vehicles, 352,570 men. It was estimated during World War 2 that beachhead supplies for 250,000 men for one month would amount to 327,000 tons (tons were measured as approximately 40 cubic feet). To move these supplies 30 to 35 merchant ships and 15 tankers would be needed. The supplies would consist of:- 36,000 tons of food, 100,000 tons of petrol, oil and lubricants, 13,000 tons of other stores, 80,000 tons of building materials for bridges, roads and airfields and demolition work, 50,000 tons of air force parts and replacements, 33,000 tons of weapons and ammunition, 8,000 tons of fighting vehicles, 2,000 tons of medical supplies, 1,000 tons of transport equipment such as steel rails, cranes and locomotives, 1,000 tons of signalling equipment and 3,000 tons of miscellaneous supplies.

8th JUNE

1550 First recorded use of Medway as base for HM ships.

1755 *Dunkirk* and *Torbay* captured the French *Alcide; Defiance* and *Fougueux* captured the French *Lys* in the Gulf of St. Lawrence.

1794 *Crescent, Druid, Eurydice, Valiant* and three others fought the French *Brutus, Scevola* and four others off Guernsey.

1796 *Unicorn* captured the French *Tribune* and *Santa Margarita* the *Tamise,* to the westward of the Scilly Islands. [m, bh]. *La Legère* escaped.

1940* *Acasta, Ardent* and *Glorious* sunk by the German battlecruisers *Gneisenau* and *Scharnhorst* off Norway (68° 45' N, 4° 30' E.). *Acasta* torpedoed *Scharnhorst.* [bh]

The aircraft carrier *Glorious* was returning from Norway, escorted by the destroyers *Ardent* (Lieutenant-Commander J.F. Barker) and *Acasta* (Commander C.E. Glasfurd), when she was caught unawares by the German battlecruisers *Scharnhorst* and *Gneisenau*. The Germans opened accurate fire at 14 miles, and sank the carrier. The destroyers, meanwhile, started to cover her by means of a smoke screen, and attacked with torpedoes. *Acasta* was the last to be sunk, 98 minutes after the action started, but she had succeeded in firing her torpedoes and one hit *Scharnhorst* abreast the after turret damaging her severely. There were only 46 survivors from HM ships.

1940 *Juniper* and *Orama* (transport) sunk by the German cruiser *Admiral Hipper,* (67° 20'N, 4° 10'E.) and (67° 45'N, 4° 00'E.), and *Oil Pioneer* sunk by the *Gneisenau* off Norway (67° 20'N, 4° 10'E.).

1940 *Vesper* and *Wanderer* bombarded the main road between Abbeville and Tréport, N. France.

1941 Allied forces advanced into Syria, supported by naval force under Vice-Admiral E.L.S. King *(Phoebe* – C.S. 15).

1943 Further bombardment of Pantellaria. Ships: *Aurora, Euryalus, Newfoundland* (Rear-Admiral C.H.J. Harcourt – C.S.15), *Orion, Penelope; Jervis, Laforey, Lookout, Loyal, Nubian, Tartar, Troubridge, Whaddon;* MTBs 73, 77, 84.

"Hands may rest at their Action Stations". Royal Marines resting in their 6 inch gun turret, World War 2.

1944 Liberator G/224 sank U.373 (48° 10' N, 5° 31' W.), and U.629 (48° 27' N, 5° 47' W.) off Ushant.

1944 *Lawford* sunk by German aircraft in the Juno area, Seine Bay. Operation Neptune.

1945 *Trenchant* sank Japanese heavy cruiser *Ashigara* in Banka Strait (1° 59' S, 104° 57' E.).

The submarine *Trenchant* (Cdr A. R. Hezlet) was on patrol off the entrance of Banka Strait (off Palembang, Sumatra), with the submarine *Stygian* further out to sea. The *Trenchant* was lying inside an Allied minefield. Early on 8th, a Japanese destroyer was sighted approaching. *Trenchant* was detected, but fired a torpedo and escaped in the darkness. The *Stygian* sighted the destroyer at 1015, and attacked it unsuccessfully, and was counterattacked. At that time, *Trenchant* sighted a *Nachi* Class cruiser (12,700 tons) approaching. The *Trenchant* fired a spread of 8 torpedoes, of which 5 hit and blew off the enemy's bow, set her on fire and made her list to starboard. The cruiser, the *Ashigara*, sank at 1239 in a welter of smoke and foam which removed the only Japanese serviceable heavy cruiser from the area on the eve of the Australian landings in North Borneo. For this brilliant attack, Cdr Hezlet was awarded the DSO and US Legion of Merit.

9th JUNE

1796	*Southampton* captured the French *Utilé* in Hyères Roads. [m]
1799	Boats of *Success* cut out the Spanish *Belle Aurora* from Port Selva. [m]
1801	*Kangaroo* and *Speedy* engaged the shore defences at Oropesa, sank four of the escort to a Spanish convoy and captured three vessels of the convoy.
1836	Royal Marines of *Castor* at the defence of the "ship" *Redoubt* (Carlist War).
1858	*Pearl's* Naval Brigade and troops dispersed a rebel force at Amorha. (2nd action). Troops: 13th Light Infantry; Bengal Foot Artillery, Bengal Yeomanry, 6th Madras Light Cavalry, 1st Bengal; Military Police Battalion.
1860	An initial commission to an officer with subsequent appointments replaced practice of issuing separate commissions for each appointment.
1931	*Poseidon* lost in collision off Wei Hai Wei.
1942	*Mimosa* (F.Fr.) sunk by U.124 in N Atlantic (52° 15'N, 32° 37'W.) (Convoy ONS.100).
1942	Catalina J/240 sank the Italian s/m *Zaffiro* off Majorca (38° 21' N. 3° 21' E.).
1944	*Durban* expended as a blockship during Operation Neptune.
1944	Liberator F/120 sank U.740 in Western Approaches (49° 09' N, 08° 37' W.).
1944	Action off Ile de Bas (48° 59' N, 4° 44' W.) between *Ashanti, Eskimo, Haida* (RCN), *Huron* (RCN), *Javelin, Tartar* with the Polish *Blyskawica* and *Piorun* (10DF) and four German destroyers. Destroyed German Z.32 and Z.H.1 (ex-Neth *Gerard Callenburgh*).

◄ One of HMS *Torbay's* 3 Jolly Rogers, the flags flown by submarines to indicate successes in action. A white bar indicates a merchant vessel sunk; a red bar, a warship sunk; a 'U', an enemy submarine destroyed; stars placed round crossed guns, a vessel sunk by gunfire; aircraft, an aircraft shot down; likewise a barrage balloon; a ram's head, the submarine had rammed a ship; daggers, special operations such as landing agents behind enemy lines.

10th JUNE

1667	Sheerness captured by a Dutch squadron under Admiral van Ghent.
1694	*Portsmouth* captured a French 30-gun privateer about 120 miles to the southward of Ushant. *Canterbury* came up just before the end of the action.
1795	First storekeeper appointed to base at Cape of Good Hope.
1804	*Hunter* captured the French privateer *Liberté* to the north-eastward of Jamaica.
1900	Boxer rebellion threatened Pekin and Admiral Sir Edward Seymour, C in C, left Tientsin with an expeditionary force of 2,129 drawn from eight nations.
1940	*Vandyck* sunk by German aircraft off Ankenes, Norway.
1940	Italy entered World War II.
1941	*Pintail* sunk by mine off the Humber (53° 30' N, 0° 32' E.).
1944	Liberator K/206 and Mosquito W/248 sank U.821 off Ushant (48° 31'N, 5° 11' W.).
1944	*Untiring* sank German UJ.6078 off La Ciotat, W of Toulon.

Sea Slug missile firing, HMS *London*, 1965

1960	*Devonshire* launched (first operational RN Guided Missile ship). See p.179.
1970	*Sheffield* launched by Her Majesty The Queen (first Type 42 destroyer).

Official Submarine losses of World War II

RN	76 lost of 216	35%
USN	52 lost of 288	18%
Germany	782 lost of 1,162	67%
Japan	130 lost of 181	72%
Italian	85 lost of 144	59%

11th JUNE

1593	Return to England (Berehaven) of John Davis *(Desire)*, the Navigator, after most of his crew had died.
1730	First dinner in Painted Hall of Greenwich Hospital.
1779*	Nelson promoted to Post Captain.
1800	Boats of *Renown, Fisgard, Defence* and *Unicorn* cut out eight merchant vessels of a convoy and three of the escort at St. Croix.
1808	Boats of *Euryalus* and *Cruizer* cut out a Danish gunboat and destroyed two troopships in Nakskov Fjord.
1843	Boats of *Dido* destroyed the stronghold of the Saribas Dyaks at Paddi, in the Batang Saribas.
1871	Walter Cowan born.
1917	*Zylpha (Q.6)* torpedoed by U.82 W.S.W. of Ireland (51° 57.5'N, 15° 25'W.). Sank on the 15th.
1935	Classic salvage of *Hastings,* grounded in Red Sea — an accident indirectly attributable to the wardroom cat.
1941	Capture of Assab by, British and Indian troops. Ships: *Dido; Chakdina, Clive, Indus* (RIN).
1943	Surrender of Pantellaria after landing of troops and 25 minutes' bombardment. Ships: *Aphis, Aurora, Newfoundland, Orion, Penelope* and destroyers as on the 8th.
1943	Fortress R/206 sank U.417 in Iceland/Faeroes gap (63° 20'N, 10° 30'W.) but crashed and was lost.
1944	Canso B/162 (RCAF) sank U.980 off Norway (63° 07'N, 0° 26'E.).
1944	Attack on Le Hamel and Rots, *Memorable Date of 46 Commando, RM.*

12th JUNE

1652	Captain Sir George Ayscue *(Rainbow)*, with a squadron of four men-of-war and seven hired merchantmen, captured six ships of the Dutch outward-bound Portuguese trade off Lizard Head.
1667	The Dutch, under Admiral van Ghent, entered the Medway. English ships burnt: *Mathias, Monmouth.* English ships captured: *Royal Charles.*
1685	Boats of *Lark, Greyhound* and *Bonaventure* destroyed two Sali rovers at Mamora.
1745	*Fowey* destroyed the French privateer *Griffon* near Fécamp.
1813	Boats of *Narcissus* cut out the American *Surveyor* up the York River, Chesapeake Bay.
1813	Boats of *Bacchante* cut out ten Neapolitan gunboats and captured a convoy of 14 sail at Guilla Nova.
1869	Completion of *Monarch*; first RN seagoing turret ship and first to carry 12in guns. (see 10th July).
1917	*Sea King* sank UC.66 off the Lizard.
1940	*Calypso* sunk by the Italian s/m *Alpino Bagnolini* off Crete (33° 45'N, 24° 32' E.).
1941	*Bismarck's* sixth tanker sunk (see 3rd and 4th June).
1942	*Grove* sunk by U.77 in the Gulf of Sollum (32° 05' N, 25° 30' E.).
1943	*Aurora, Newfoundland, Orion, Penelope* and six destroyers bombarded Lampedusa, which surrendered.
1963	Admiral of the Fleet Viscount Cunningham of Hyndhope died.

* *"Interest": naval promotion in the Eighteenth Century*
Once an officer was "made post" (appointed to a Captain's command) he took his place at the bottom of a list which was headed by the Admiral of the Fleet. Provided the officer remained alive and was not court martialled, he could be sure of promotion, whether employed or not. It is clear from this that the key to promotion was to be "made post" at the earliest possible moment. To achieve seniority a boy with naval aspirations would be sent to sea at the earliest possible age, and his relatives would go to extraordinary lengths to get him first promoted to Lieutenant and then Captain. Nelson was well placed as nephew of the Comptroller of the Navy and was made "post" aged 20, but, like Collingwood, was only a Vice-Admiral when he died.

13th JUNE

1667	The Dutch in the Medway. *Royal Oak, Loyal London* and *Royal James* burnt by Admiral Van Ghent's squadron.
1761	*Centaur* captured the French *Ste. Anne* off Dona Maria Bay, Haiti.
1796	*Dryad* captured the French *Proserpine* 150 miles to the south-westward of the Scilly Islands. [m, bh]
1797	End of mutiny at the Nore.
1805	Boats of *Cambrian* captured the Spanish privateer *Maria* 240 miles to the south-eastward of Bermuda.
1814	Boats of *Superb* and *Nimrod* destroyed 17 sail of American shipping at Wareham, Mass.
1940	*Scotstoun* sunk by U.25 in NW Approaches (57° 00'N, 9° 57'W.).
1940	*Odin* sunk by the Italian destroyer *Strale* in the Gulf of Taranto.
1940	Fifteen Skua aircraft *(Ark Royal)* attacked the *Scharnhorst* at Trondheim. Only one bomb hit, and that did not explode. Eight Skuas lost. FAA Sq.: 800, 803.
1943	*Nubian* received the surrender of Linosa.
1943	*Ultor* bombarded the D/F station on Salina Islands, Lipari Islands.
1944	*Boadicea* sunk by German torpedo aircraft off Portland (50° 26' N, 2° 34' W.). (Convoy EBC.8)
1944	Canso T/162 (RCAF) sank U.715 off Shetland Is. (62° 45'N, 2°59'W.).

The Torpedo

The Whitehead torpedo, developed in 1870, was the weapon which first gave the submarine a potential as an effective and deadly weapon of war, able to attack targets from a safe distance. Although direct but advanced developments of the diesel-engined, gyro-controlled Whitehead torpedo are still in limited use even today, electro-motor driven, wire-guided homing tor-

14th JUNE

1667	The Dutch withdrew from the Medway, taking with them the *Royal Charles* "at a time, both for tides and wind, when the best Pilot in Chatham would not have undertaken it." (Pepys)
1744	Commodore George Anson *(Centurion)* arrived at Spithead after his voyage around the world.
1789	Captain William Bligh arrived at Kupang, Timor, after his 3618 mile voyage in an open boat following the mutiny in *Bounty*.
1809	Boats of *Scout* cut out seven French storeships and stormed a battery near Cape Croisette.
1809	Harry Keppel born.
1843	Boats of *Dido* destroyed the Saribas town of Pakoo, Borneo.
1917	Admiralty approved scheme for convoy of merchant ships.
1917	*Avenger* sunk by U.69 80 miles West of the Shetland Islands.
1917	Curtis H.12 flying-boat 8677 destroyed Zeppelin L.43 off Vlieland.
1940	Able Seaman R. Tawn rendered safe first German parachute mine, in seven fathoms at Poole.
1943	*Jed* and *Pelican* sank U.334 in N Atlantic (58° 16'N, 28° 20'W.). (Convoy ONS.10)
1943	Whitley G/10 (OTU) sank U.564 in Atlantic (44° 17'N, 10° 25'W.) but crashed and was lost.
1944	*Sickle* sunk, possibly by mine, in the S. Aegean.

pedoes have been in use for some years - particularly for 'three dimension' attacks on submarine adversaries. The latest weapon to enter service with the Royal Navy is known as 'Tigerfish'. Electrically driven and initially wire-guided, it gives the fire control officer complex electronic aids for directing 'Tigerfish' towards its target until its own acoustic homing devices are ready to take over for the final phase.

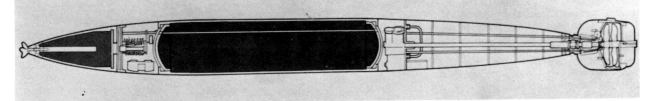

15th JUNE

1780   *Apollo* fought the French privateer *Stanislaus* off Ostend.

1812   *Sandwich* captured the French privateer *Courageux* off Guernsey.

1845   Landing parties from *Conway* and the French *Berceau* and *Zelée* repulsed in an attack on the forts at Tamatave, Madagascar.

1940   *Andania* sunk by the German submarine UA S.E. of Iceland (62° 36' N, 15° 09' W.).

1941   *Bismarck's* seventh and last supply ship sunk: see 3rd, 4th and 12th June.

1942   *Bedouin* sunk by Italian torpedo aircraft off Tunisia (36° 12'N, 11° 38'E.). Operation Harpoon.

1942   *Hasty* torpedoed by the German E-boat S.55 in 34° 10' N, 22° 00' E.: sunk by *Hotspur*. *Airedale* bombed in 33° 50' N, 24° 00' E.: sunk by own forces. *Nestor* (RAN) bombed in 33° 36'N, 24° 30'E.: taken in tow by *Javelin*, but had to be sunk on the 16th. Operation Vigorous.

Operations Vigorous and Harpoon, 1942
These operations were aimed at supplying Malta using two convoys, one from the East (*Vigorous*), and the other from the West (*Harpoon*), with ships arriving at Malta on successive days. The 6 ships in the *Harpoon* convoy passed through the Straits of Gibraltar on the night 11/12 June, escorted by the carriers *Eagle* and *Argus*, battleship *Malaya*, cruisers *Kenya, Liverpool* and *Charybdis* and 8 destroyers. On 14th, in calm weather — which made it difficult for the carriers to operate — the convoy was attacked by high-level, dive and torpedo bombers. One merchant ship was sunk, and the cruiser *Liverpool* badly hit. She had to be towed back to Gibraltar by the destroyer *Antelope*, and arrived there safely despite further air attacks. A U-boat also attacked the convoy, but did no damage.
At 2100 that day the convoy reached 'The Narrows', and the main escort detached, leaving the cruiser *Cairo* and 9 destroyers to escort the convoy and some 10 minesweepers bound for Malta. At 0630 on 15th an enemy force of 2 cruisers and 4 destroyers closed the convoy. The Fleet destroyers of the escort attacked at once, while the *Cairo* (an AA cruiser) and smaller escorts made smoke. The *Bedouin* and *Partridge* were disabled, but one enemy destroyer was hit and the enemy turned away. Meanwhile the convoy was attacked by dive bombers, and the escort had to fight them off whilst the enemy surface force returned to harass the convoy. Three merchant ships were lost during this action. The escort were re-inforced by the fast minelayer *Welshman* that afternoon. She had gone ahead to deliver stores to Malta independently. As the convoy passed through the minefields on the approaches to Malta in the evening of 15th, one of the two merchant ships hit a mine, but was brought to harbour. One destroyer was also lost in the minefield and 3 other escorts damaged. The *Partridge* took the *Bedouin* in tow, but the enemy surface force returned, and while *Partridge* was defending her, the *Bedouin* was sunk by a torpedo bomber.
The *Vigorous* convoy of 11 ships sailed from Port Said on 11th June, with a covering force of 8 cruisers and 26 destroyers, corvettes and minesweepers. On 14th it suffered air and E-boat attacks, and three merchant ships were hit, two being sunk. On 15th, Italian heavy units sailed from Taranto, and that day the convoy changed course several times to avoid enemy surface forces. By 1930 that day, the escort had only one third of its ammunition left, and the convoy had been subject to 'all known forms of attack' — two cruisers had been damaged and the destroyers *Hasty* and *Airedale* sunk. The convoy was recalled, and on the return passage the cruiser *Hermione* and destroyer *Nestor* were lost.
In summary, 2 merchant ships reached Malta out of 17 that set out, and one cruiser and 5 destoyers.

1942   P.35 (later *Umbra*) sank the Italian cruiser *Trento* (previously damaged by Beaufort torpedo aircraft) in Central Mediterranean (36° 07'N, 18° 36'E.).

1944   *Mourne* sunk by U.767 off Penzance (49° 25'N, 5° 30'W.). Operation Neptune.

1944   *Blackwood* torpedoed by U.764 off Portland (50° 07'N, 2° 15'W.): sank on tow on the 16th. Operation Neptune.

1944   *Satyr* sank U.987 off Norway (68° 01' N, 5° 08' E.).

1944   MTBs sank the German TA30 (ex-Italian *Dragone*).

1945   Air strike on and bombardment of Truk, Carolines, by Rear-Admiral E.J.P. Brind (*Implacable*). Operation Inmate. T.G.111.2. Ships: *Implacable, Ruler; Achilles, Newfoundland, Swiftsure, Uganda; Teazer, Tenacious, Termagant, Terpsichore, Troubridge.* Aircraft (*Implacable*): 801, 880 Sq. (Seafire). 828 Sq. (Avenger). 1771 Sq. (Firefly).

1960   RN Hospital Mauritius taken over from the Army. Closed 13th February 1976.

16th JUNE

1745 Capture of Louisburg and the whole of Cape Breton Island by Commodore Peter Warren *(Superb)* and Mr William Pepperell, commanding the Colonial troops. Ships: *Canterbury, Chester, Eltham, Hector, Lark, Launceston, Mermaid, Princess Mary, Sunderland, Superb.*

1797 *Boston* captured the Spanish privateer *St. Bernardo* (alias *Conquestador*) 75 miles N.E. by N. of Cape Ortegal.

1812 *Swallow* fought the French *Renard* and *Goeland* off Île Ste. Marguerita, Gulf of Fréjus.

1842 Capture of Woosung and Paoshan. Ships: *Algerine, Blonde, Clio, Columbine, Cornwallis, Modeste, North Star; Jupiter* Steamers (towing): *Medusa, Sesostris* (IN); *Nemesis, Phlegethon, Pluto, Tenasserim* (Ben. Mar.).

1855 Bombardment of Sevastopol. Ships: *Arrow, Highflyer, Miranda, Niger, Snake, Terrible, Tribune, Viper, Weser* and French steamers. *Danube* and launches of *Royal Albert.*

1871 *Megaera* beached on St. Pauls' Island, Indian Ocean.

1919 *Kinross* mined in Aegean.

1920 *Revenge, Ramillies, Ark Royal* and *Westcott* and destroyers in action against Turks at Istria (until 21st).

1923* X1 launched at Chatham: RNs biggest submarine before the nuclears.

1940 *Grampus* sunk by the Italian t.bs. *Circe* and *Clio* off Syracuse, Sicily.

1940 *Orpheus* sunk by Italian destroyer *Turbine* off Tobruk.

1941 Swordfish of 815 Sq., from Nicosia, torpedoed and sank the French destroyer *Chevalier Paul* off Syria (35° 18' N, 35° 18' E.).

1942 *Hermione* sunk by U.205 South of Crete (33° 20' N, 26° 00' E.). Operation Vigorous.

1942 *Kujawiak* (Pol) sunk by mine off Malta (36° 00' N, 14° 25' E.).

1943 Hudson T/459 (RAAF) sank U.97 off Cyprus (33° 00' N, 34° 00'E.).

1955 *Sidon* sank in Portland Habour after explosion.

*X.1, carried four 5.5in guns and six 21in torpedo tubes. Surface tonnage, 2780 tons.

167

17th JUNE

1693 Vice-Admiral Sir George Rooke *(Royal Oak)* and Rear-Admiral Philips van der Goes *(Admiral General)*, with the famous Smyrna convoy, fought a French fleet of 80 sail under Admiral Comte de Tourville off Lagos. Dutch ships captured: *Wapen van Medemblik, Zeeland.* Convoy was scattered, 92 vessels being taken or destroyed.

1694 *Weymouth* captured the French *Invincible* 140 miles to the westward of Cape Clear. *Dunkirk* was in company, but did little.

1775 *Glasgow* and *Lively* cannonaded the enemy at the Battle of Bunker Hill. Two battalions of Marines engaged ashore: "break and let the Marines pass through you".

1778 *Arethusa* fought the French *Belle-Poule; Alert* captured the French *Coureur.* Both actions took place near Plouescat, Brittany.

1794 *Romney* captured the French *Sibylle* in Mykoni harbour. [m, bh]

1795 Cornwallis' Retreat. Vice-Admiral the Hon. William Cornwallis *(Royal Sovereign)* with 5 ships and 2 frigates fought Vice-Admiral Villaret-Joyeuse *(Peuple)*, with 13 of the line, 14 frigates, 2 brigs and a cutter, off Penmarc'h Point, Brittany. [m, bh]. Ships: *Bellerophon, Brunswick, Mars, Royal Sovereign, Triumph.* Frigates: *Pallas, Phaeton.* Regiments: 86th, 118th.

1813 Admiral Charles Middleton, Lord Barham, died.

1815 *Pilot* fought the French *Égerie* off Cape Corse, Corsica. [m]

1842 Capture of two Chinese batteries six miles above Woosung. Ships: *Clio, Columbine, Modeste.* Steamers (towing): *Phlegethon, Pluto* (Ben. Mar.), *Nemesis.*

1843 Boats of *Dido* destroyed the Saribas town of Rembas, Borneo.

1855 Fourth bombardment of Sevastopol, Crimea. Naval Brigade and Royal Artillery. Sea bombardment by *Princess Royal, Highflyer, Miranda, Sidon, Snake, Viper,* launches of *Royal Albert;* and French steamers.

1900 Bombardment and capture of the Taku forts, China. Ships engaged: *Algerine; Lion* (Fr.); *Iltis* (Ger); *Bobr, Giliak, Koreytz* (Ru). *Fame* and *Whiting* captured four Chinese torpedo boats in the Pei ho, below Tongku, China.

1916 Zeppelin L.48 shot down and yielded German naval signal book.

1918 *Lychnis* sank U.64 off S. Sardinia (38° 07' N, 10° 27' E.).

1919 VC: Lieutenant Augustine Willington Shelton Agar (CMB4) torpedoed and sank the Russian cruiser *Oleg* in Kronstadt.

1940 *La Curieuse* (Fr) sank the Italian s/m *Provana* in the Western Mediterranean, 80 miles off Oran.

1940 Evacuation of BEF from N.W. France (Brest and St. Nazaire) begun. Operation Ariel.

1942 *Wild Swan* sunk by German aircraft off Bantry Bay (49° 52' N, 10° 44' W.).

1944 Mosquito D/333 (Nor) sank U.423 off S.W Norway (63° 06'N, 2° 05'E.).

Captain William Peel VC directing the naval guns outside Lucknow, 1858 (also see 18th June 1855)

18th JUNE

1799 *Centaur, Bellona, Captain, Emerald* and *Santa Teresa* captured the French *Junon, Alceste, Courageuse, Salamine* and *Alerte* 60 miles South of Cape Sicie, S. France.

1806 Hawlbowline naval establishment set up by Order in Council at Queenstown.

1809 *Latona* captured the French *Félicité* 280 miles N. by W. of Puerto Rico.

1812 *Hind* captured the French privateer *Incomparable* 6 miles E.S.E. of Dodman Point.

1826 *Sybille* destroyed two Greek pirate misticoes off Kalo Limniones.

1855 British attack on the Great Redan; French attack on the Malakoff: both attacks repulsed. (Siege of Sevastopol, Crimea). VC: Captain William Peel (*Leander*). When a live shell landed in the magazine, he picked it up and threw it away; he was wounded placing the first ladder for the assault on the Redan. Midshipman Edward St John Daniel was also awarded the VC for

the above actions. Lieutenant Henry James Raby (*Wasp*), Able Seaman John Taylor and Boatswain's mate Henry Curtis awarded VC for a 70 yard dash under heavy and close fire to rescue a wounded soldier.

1858 *Pearl's* Naval Brigade and a company of the 13th Light Infantry defeated the rebel forces at Haraiya, (N of Gogon Rise, India).

1916 *Eden* lost in channel after collision with s.s. *France*.

1941 *Faulknor, Fearless, Foresight, Forester* and *Foxhound* sank U.138 off Cadiz (36° 04' N, 7° 29' W.).

1944 *Fame, Havelock* and *Inconstant* sank U.767 in Channel (49° 03' N, 3° 13' W.).

1944 Wellington A/304 (Pol) sank U.441 off Ushant (49° 03'N, 4° 48'W.).

1944 *Quail* foundered in tow (40° 05' N, 17° 52'E.), after being mined at the entrance to Bari on 15th Nov 1943.

Sevastopol from HMS *Sidon* 1855

1594 *Dainty* fought six Spaniards (including *San Andres*) for three days off San Mateo Bay, Ecuador, and then had to surrender.

1781 *Castor* and *Crescent* taken by the French *Friponne* and another frigate respectively 160 miles S.W. of Ushant.

1793 *Nymphe* captured the French *Cléopatre* 20 miles W. by S. of Start Point. [m, bh]. First decisive action in French wars.

1808 *Seagull* taken by the Danish *Lougen* 20 miles E.S.E. of Lindesnes, S. Norway.

1842 Occupation of Shanghai by a brigade under Lieutenant-Colonel Patrick Montgomerie, Madras Artillery. Ships: *Clio, Columbine, Modeste, North Star.* Steamers (towing): *Nemesis, Pluto, Phlegethon* (Ben. Mar.); *Medusa* (I.N.), *Tenasserim.*

1854 *Eurydice, Miranda* and *Brisk,* with two belated French ships formed White Sea squadron against Russia; main deployments were in Baltic and Black Sea.

A Mosquito aircraft

1917 CMB 1 sunk by German destroyers off the Belgian coast.

1940 *Moonstone* captured the Italian s/m *Galileo Galilei* off Aden (12° 48' N, 45° 12' E.) Latter became X2, then P.711.

The armed trawler *Moonstone*, operating from Aden, detected a submarine by Asdic. She attacked with depth charges, but lost contact. An hour later she gained a new contact, and attacked again. The Italian submarine *Galileo Galilei* surfaced, and the trawler hit the conning tower with a four inch shell. The submarine surrendered, the destroyer *Kandahar* towed her to Aden, and documents captured led to the sinking of another Italian submarine shortly afterwards.

A Naval Brigade in China. 1842

20th JUNE

1743   Commodore Anson *(Centurion)* captured the Spanish *Nuestra Senora de Cova-donga* off Cape Espiritu Santo, Phillipines. [bh]

1747   *Kent, Hampton Court, Eagle, Lion, Chester, Hector, Pluto* and *Dolphin* captured 48 sail out of 170 of a French West India convoy 400 miles N.W. of Cape Ortegal.

1774   John Day lost in first submarine experiment in Plymouth Harbour.

1783   Fifth and final battle between Vice-Admiral Sir Edward Hughes *(Superb)* and Commodore Chevalier de Suffren *(Cleopatre),* with 15 of the line and 3 frigates, off Cuddalore.
Ships: *Defence, Isis, Gibraltar, Inflexible, Exeter; Worcester, Africa, Sultan, Superb, Monarch, Burford, Sceptre; Magnanime, Eagle, Hero, Bristol, Monmouth, Cumberland.* Frigates, etc.: *Active, Minerva, Naiade; Seahorse, Lizard, Medea, Combustion, Juno; Harriott, Pondicherry, San Carlos, Chaser.*

1809   Boats of *Bellerophon* cut out three vessels and stormed a Russian battery at Hango (Hanko), Finland.

1842   *Medusa* (I.N.) and *Phlegethon* (Ben. Mar.), with a boat each from *Columbine* and *Cornwallis,* captured eight war junks and destroyed two batteries in the Yangtze 30 miles above Shanghai.

1849   Boat of *Pilot* captured a pirate junk off Ockseu Island.

1900   Siege of Pekin legations began.

1917   *Salvia (Q.15)* sunk by U.94 in E Atlantic (52° 25'N, 16° 20'W.).

1940   *Beagle* landed a demolition party at Bordeaux.

1940   *Parthian* sank the Italian s/m *Diamante* off Libya (32° 42' N, 23° 49' E.).

1943   *Wallaroo* (RAN) sunk in collision with s.s. *Gilbert Coshin* off Fremantle, Australia.

1944   GC: T/Lieutenant John Bridge GM and bar RNVR for bomb and mine disposal. *(Gazette* date).

1947   GC (ex-AM): Leading Seaman P.R.S. May *(St. Margarets)* for rescuing seven men in fume-filled tank at Malta.

An armed trawler, World War 2

Lord Charles Howard of Effingham.

1596   Capture of Cadiz by the Earl of Essex
(*Repulse*) and Lord Charles Howard
of Effingham (*Ark Royal*), and a Dutch
force under Jonkheer van Duyvenvoorde,
Admiral of Holland. [bh]. Ships: *Ark
Royal, Charles, Crane, Dreadnought,
Lion, Lion's Whelp, Mary Rose, Mere
Honour, Moon, Nonpareil, Quittance,
Rainbow, Repulse, Swiftsure, Tramon-
tana, Truelove, Vanguard, Warspite,
Witness. Alcedo, Amulo, Archangel,
Bark Rowe, Blue Pigeon, Brave, Brown
Fish, Centurion, Chameleon, Cherubim,
Corbett of Ipswich, Darling, Delight,
Desire, Elizabeth of Hampton, Eliza-
beth of London, Experience, George,
Gift of God, Grace of God, Great
Katherine, Golden Dragon, Green
Dragon, Hercules of Rye, Howard,
Hoy of Sandwich, Hunter of Enkhuysen,
Hunter of Schiedam, Jacob of
Enkhuysen, Jacob of Rotterdam,
John and Francis(?), Jonas, Jonathan,
Joshua of Hamburg, Lioness, Mary Ann,
Mary Margaret, Marygold, Mermaid,
Mermaid of Dartmouth, Minion, Peter
of London, Phoenix of Amsterdam,
Pleasure of Bristol, Popinjay, Posthorse,
Primrose, Prudence, Prudence of Ply-
mouth, Roebuck, Roger and Katherine,
Ruben (or Ruby), St. Jacob of Akers-
loot, St. Peter of Enkhuysen, Swan,
Unicorn of Bristol, Vineyard, Violet
of London, Yager of Schiedam.*

1764   William Sidney Smith born.

1782   *Squirrel* captured the French privateer
Aimable Manon 15 miles N. by W. of
Ushant.

1806   *Warren Hastings* (Indiaman) taken by
the French *Piémontaise* 330 miles
S.S.E. of Réunion.

1849   *Pilot* captured a pirate junk off Lam
Yit (China).

1854   VC: A/Mate Charles Davis Lucas (*Hecla*)
for throwing a live shell overboard while
its fuse was burning. *Hecla, Odin* and
Valorous ineffectually bombarded
Bomarsund.

1919   German High Seas Fleet scuttled at
Scapa Flow. 11 battleships, 5 battlecruisers, 5 cruisers and 22 destroyers
sunk: 3 cruisers and 18 destroyers beached.

1940   *Cape Howe* sunk by U.28 in the
Western Approaches (49° 45'N, 8° 47' W.).

1940   Bombardment of Bardia by Vice-
Admiral J.C. Tovey (*Orion*). Ships:
Neptune, Orion, Sydney (RAN),
Lorraine (Fr.); *Dainty, Decoy, Hasty*;
Stuart (RAN).

1942   *Parktown* sunk by the German S.54,
S.56 and S.58 during the withdrawal
from Tobruk (32° 10' N, 25° 05' E.).

1942   P.514 (ex-USS R.19) sunk in collision
with *Georgian* (RCN), escort to Convoy
CL.43, off Cape Race (46° 33'N, 53° 39' W.).

1944   *Fury* damaged by mine in Sword area,
Seine Bay; scrapped. Operation Neptune.

1944   Air strike on Port Blair and Andaman
Islands by Force 60 under Vice-Admiral
Sir Arthur Power (*Renown*). Operation
Pedal. Ships: *Illustrious, Renown, Richelieu*
(Fr.); *Ceylon, Kenya, Nigeria, Phoebe*
and 8 destroyers. Aircraft: 810, 847
Sq. (Barracuda). 1830, 1833, 1837,
Sq. (Corsair).

1944   *Unsparing* sank the German UJ.2106
in the Aegean.

1944   MTBs sank the German TA.25 (ex-
Italian *Intrepido*) off Spezia.

1955   Reopening of chapel at RN College,
Greenwich and its dedication to St.
Peter and St. Paul.

22nd JUNE

1372	Battle of La Rochelle, in which the Earl of Pembroke was defeated by a Castilian fleet under Ambrosio Bocanegra, Admiral of Castille.
1796	*Apollo* and *Doris* captured the French *Légère* 50 miles West of Ushant.
1798	*Princess Royal* packet, carrying mails to New York, beat off the French privateer *Adventurier*.
1813	Boats of *Castor* cut out the French privateer *Fortune* at Mongat, near Barcelona.
1843	Purchase of *Dwarf*: first screw vessel in RN.
1893*	*Victoria* (Vice-Admiral Sir George Tryon) rammed and sunk by *Camperdown* (Rear-Admiral A.H. Markham) off Tripoli, Syria. 1st Div. (Stbd): *Victoria, Nile, Dreadnought, Inflexible, Collingwood, Phaeton.* 2nd Div. (Port): *Camperdown, Edinburgh, Sans Pareil, Edgar, Amphion.*
1900	Capture of the Hsiku Arsenal, China. Naval Brigade from: *Aurora, Centurion, Endymion.*
1923	Amalgamation of RMA (Blue Marines) and RMLI (Red Marines) to re-form the Royal Marines by Admiralty Fleet Order; confirmed by Order in Council 11th October. At the end of July and beginning of August of that year the RMLI's Forton barracks at Gosport was closed (later to become HMS *St Vincent*)

and Eastney barracks became the home of Portsmouth Division, Royal Marines. The ranks of Gunner and Private were replaced by Marine.

1937	*Ajax* from Nassau to Trinidad in support of the Civil Power.
1940	*Campeador V* sunk by mine off Portsmouth.

*1893 — The Price of Blind Obedience

Signal hoisted in Flagship *Victoria*:
"First division alter course in succession 16 points to port preserving the order of the division.
Second division alter course in succession 16 points to starboard preserving the order of the division."
(16 points is 180 degrees).
By semaphore *Camperdown* signalled to *Victoria.* "Do you wish the evolution to be performed as indicated by signal," but before it could be sent, *Victoria* signalled to *Camperdown,* "What are you waiting for?"

BOARD OF INQUIRY
"Markham: It then flashed across my mind that there was only one interpretation of the signal and that was that I was to put my helm down and turn 16 points to starboard and the *Victoria* would ease her helm and circle round outside my division. I was all the more led to believe this as the signal to the second division was hoisted superior to that of the first division. I conferred hurriedly with the flag captain and Captain Johnstone. They were both by my way of thinking, and seeing that was the only safe way of performing the evolution I hoisted the signal . . .
The Court: With the columns at six cables apart, supposing the ships to turn towards each other with their full helm, did the absolute certainty of a collision occur to you?
Markham: Most certainly."

HMS *Victoria*, 10,470 tons, sinking after being rammed by HMS *Camperdown*.

23rd JUNE

1745 *Bridgewater, Sheerness* and *Ursula* captured two Dunkirk privateers and their seven prizes off Ostend.

1795 Admiral Lord Bridport *(Royal George)* fought Rear-Admiral Villaret-Joyeuse *(Peuple)*, with 12 ships, off Île de Groix Brittany. [m, bh] Ships: *Royal George, Queen Charlotte, Queen, London, Prince of Wales, Prince, Barfleur, Prince George, Sans Pareil, Valiant, Orion, Irrestistible, Russell* and *Colossus*, with *Robust, Standard* and *Thunderer* from Captain Sir John Warren's squadron (Quiberon Bay expedition), which did not join up until the action was over. Frigates: *Revolutionnaire, Thalia, Nymphe, Aquilon, Astraea, Babet.* Sloop: *Megaera.* Hospital ship: *Charon.* Fireship: *Incendiary.* Cutter: *Dolly.* Luggers: *Argus, Galatea.* Regiments: 86th, 2/90th, 97th and 118th. French ships captured: *Alexandre, Formidable, Tigre.*

1800 Boats of *Renown, Defence* and *Fisgard* destroyed three batteries at Quimper.

1804 *Fort Diamond* taken by two boats of a French privateer in Roseau Bay, St. Lucia.

1812 *Belvedira* fought the American *President* 100 miles to the southward of Nantucket.

1850 *Sharpshooter* captured the slaver *Polka* at Macahe, Brazil.

1915 C.24 (with *Taranaki*) sank U.40 off Aberdeen (57° 00' N, 1° 50' W.) (first use of a decoy ship by RN against U-Boats).

1918 British Expeditionary Force in *Syren* and *Elope* landed at Murmansk, North Russia.

1925 GC (ex-EGM): Petty Officer Robert Mills Chambers *(Tarantula)* for bravery in support of the civil power in China.

1940 *Pathan* (RIN) mined off Bombay (18° 56' N, 72° 45' E.): sank early on the 24th.

1940 *Falmouth* sank the Italian s/m *Galvani* in entrance to the Persian Gulf (25° 55' N, 56° 55' E.).

Alexander Hood, Viscount Bridport (1726-1814)

Younger brother of Samuel, Viscount Hood (see 12th December). The Hoods are very confusing: the two Viscounts had a pair of younger cousins, brothers with the same Christian names, though in their case, Alexander (1758-1798) who died on active service as a Captain was the elder and Sam (1762-1814), who died as a Vice-Admiral and the first Baronet, the younger.

Son of the rector of Butleigh in Somerset, the elder Alexander was taken to sea in gratitude for the ecclesiastical hospitality enjoyed by a benighted Post captain posting to Plymouth on his way to join his ship in 1741. Promoted Lieutenant in 1746, he was made Post in 1756 and distinguished himself as an aggressive captain in single ship actions. Promoted to the flag list in 1780, he assisted in the relief of Gibraltar in 1782 and two years later was second-in-command to Howe (see 1st June) for which he received an Irish peerage. Temporarily in command in 1795, he routed a stronger squadron off L'Orient and was raised to the English peerage. Succeeded Howe in 1797 but was relieved in 1800 by St. Vincent as a result of a change of Government, a political manoeuvre for which he was consoled by a Viscountcy and the appointments of Vice-Admiral of England and General of Marines. His monument instructs its student:

> "For his bravery, for his abilities,
> For his advancement in his profession,
> For his attachment to his King and Country,
> Consult the annals of the British Navy
>   in which they are written in indelible
>   characters."

1940 *Kandahar, Kingston* and *Shoreham* sank the Italian s/m *Torricelli* off Perim, Red Sea (12° 34' N, 43° 16' E.). *Khartoum* damaged by explosion of torpedo burst by gunfire of submarine and beached at Perim.

1944 *Scylla* mined off Normandy: CTL.

24th JUNE

1340 Battle of Sluys. Edward III *(Thomas)* captured or destroyed the whole of the French fleet of about 200 vessels in the Zwyn, thus pre-empting a French descent on England.

1497 John Cabot *(Matthew)* discovered Newfoundland.

1795 *Dido* (28) and *Lowestoffe* captured the French *Minerve* (38) 150 miles North of Minorca. [m, bh] . *Artemis* escaped.

1801 *Swiftsure* taken by the French *Indivisible, Dix-Aout, Jean-Bart* and *Constitution* 20 miles N.E. of Derna, Libya.

1840 Repulse of landing party of *Favorite* when attacking a stockade at Tongatabu, Friendly Islands.

1869 Moustaches banned and beards permitted in the RN.

1900 VC: Captain Lewis Stratford Tollemache Halliday, RMLI *(Orlando)*. During the Boxer rebellion, when the British legation at Peking was besieged and though wounded, Halliday led a sortie to chase off some attackers.

1917 *Redcar* and *Kempton* mined off Spindle Bay, N of Gravelines.

1919 *Sword Dance* mined in Dvina River, N Russia.

1920 Start of operation against Turks on South coast of Sea of Marmara: *Iron Duke, Marlborough, Benbow, Stuart, Montrose, Shark, Sporty* and *Speedy*.

1937 Admiral Sir William Fisher died.

1941 *Auckland* sunk by German aircraft off Tobruk (32° 15'N, 24° 30'E.).

1942 *Gossamer* sunk by German aircraft in Kola Inlet, N Russia (68° 59' N, 33° 03' E.).

1943 Liberator H/120 sank U.194 in N Atlantic 58° 15'N, 25° 25'W. (Convoy ONS.11)

1943 *Starling* sank U.119 and *Wild Goose, Woodpecker, Wren* and *Kite* sank U.449 in Bay of Biscay (45° 00'N, 11° 59'W).

1944 *Swift* sunk by mine in Sword area, Seine Bay. Operation Neptune.

1944 *Eskimo, Haida* (RCN) and Liberator O/311 (Czech) sank U.971 off Ushant (49° 01' N, 5° 35' W.).

1944 VC: David Ernest Hornell, Flight-Lieutenant RCAF in Canso P/162 (RCAF) sank U.1225 off Norway (63° 00' N, 0° 50' W.).

A patrol of 45 Commando RM in Radfan, an area of Aden, 1963

25th JUNE

1667	Destruction of 20 French ships at Martinique.
1746	Commodore Edward Peyton *(Medway)* fought nine French ships under Commander Mahe de La Bourdonnais *(Achille)* 27 miles off Negapatam, Madras. Ships: *Harwich, Lively, Medway, Medway's Prize, Preston, Winchester.*
1776	Captain Cook sailed on third voyage in *Resolution* with *Discovery.*
1803	*Endymion* captured the French *Bacchante* 600 miles West of Ushant.
1859	Unsuccessful attempt by Rear-Admiral James Hope *(Chesapeake)* to force a passage up the Pei ho. Attack on the Taku forts repulsed. Ships: *Chesapeake, Cruizer, Fury, Highflyer, Magicienne; Assistance, Hesper* (storeships). Gunboats: *Banterer, Cormorant*+, Forester, Haughty, Janua, Kestrel@, Lee+, Nimrod, Opossum, Plover*+, Starling.* French ships: *Duchayla, Norzagaray.* U.S. ships: *Powhatan, Toey-Wan.* *Flag for attack. +Sunk. @Sunk; raised later.
1908	*Indomitable* commissioned: first battle cruiser.
1920	*Revenge, Royal Sovereign, Marlborough* and destroyers with *Kilkis* (Greek) and four transports landed 8,000 Greek troops to occupy Panderma: two RN casualties.
1921	K.15 sank in Portsmouth Harbour; raised and beached: scrapped 1923.
1940	*Fraser* (RCN) sunk in collision with *Calcutta* in the Gironde (45° 44′ N, 1° 31′ W.). (Evacuation from Bordeaux area).
1941	*Lauchberg* (German weather ship) 'pinched' off Iceland with cryptographic material of "inestimable value".
1941	*Parthian* sank the French s/m *Souffleur* off Beirut (33° 49′ N, 35° 26′ E.).
1944	*Affleck* and *Balfour* sank U.1191 (50° 03′ N, 2° 59′ W.) and *Bickerton* sank U.269 off Lyme Bay (50° 01′ N, 2° 59′ W.).
1975	Last Beira patrol completed by *Salisbury.*

26th JUNE

1806	Boats of *Port Mahon* cut out the Spanish letter of marque *San Jose* from Puerto Banes, Cuba.
1809	*Cyane* and *L'Espoir,* with 12 British and Sicilian gunboats, captured or destroyed 22 Neapolitan gunboats in Naples Bay. [m]
1814	Boats of *Maidstone* and *Sylph* destroyed an American turtle (torpedo) boat on Long Island.
1842	*Southampton, Conch* and detachments of the 25th and 27th Regiments quelled the Boer insurrection at Port Natal.
1854	*Prometheus* recaptured the British brig *Cuthbert Young,* taken by Riff pirates, in Zera Bay, 10 miles S.W. of Cape Tres Forcas.
1855	*Racehorse* recaptured the British lorcha *Typhoon* at Lam Yit; her boats captured three pirate junks in Pinghai Bay and the vicinity.
1866	Boxer time fuse adopted for RN shells.
1867	Masters replaced by navigating officers.
1897	*Turbinia* (Charles Parson's experimental turbine vessel) intervened in Jubilee review of the Fleet at Spithead.
1944	*Bulldog* sank the German U.719 in N.W. Approaches (55° 33′ N, 11° 02′ W.).
1944	Liberator N/86 sank U.317 off SW Norway (62° 03′N, 1° 45′E.).

The Submarine K22 at the Spithead Review, 1924. Another interesting phase in the development of the submarine. The K boats were often in collision with other ships and the design was discontinued.

27th JUNE

1756   Surrender of Minorca.

1798   *Seahorse* captured the French *Sensible* 36 miles E.S.E. of Pantellaria.

1806   Capture of Buenos Aires by Commodore Sir Home Riggs Popham *(Diadem)* and Major-General William Carr Beresford. Ships and vessels: *Diadem, Raisonnable, Diomede, Narcissus, Encounter.* Troops: R.A., 71st Regiment, 20th Light Dragoons, St. Helena Artillery, St. Helena Regiment. A Naval Brigade was landed.

1809   *Cyane* fought the Franco-Neapolitan *Ceres* in Naples Bay. [m]

1812   Royal Marines of *Leviathan, Imperieuse, Curacoa* and *Eclair* captured two batteries at Alassio and Laigueglia, Italy; the ships destroyed a convoy of 18 sail.

1829   *Monkey* captured the Spanish slaver *Midas* to the south-westward of Little Stirrup Cay, Great Bahama Bank.

1860   Repulse of a British attack on the Maori pah at Puketakauere. Naval Brigade of *Pelorus,* with the flank companies of the 40th Regiment and detachments of Royal Artillery and Royal Engineers.

1900   Capture of the Chinese Arsenal, Tientsin. Naval Brigade from *Endymion* and *Orlando.*

1940   *Dainty, Defender* and *Ilex* sank the Italian s/m *Console Generale Liuzzi* S of Crete (33° 46' N, 27° 27' E.).

1941   *Triumph* sank the Italian s/m *Salpa* off Mersa Matruh (32° 05' N, 26° 47' E.).

1941   *Wishart* sank the Italian s/m *Glauco* in Atlantic (35° 06' N, 12° 41' W.).

1941   *Celandine, Gladiolus* and *Nasturtium* sank U.556 in Atlantic (60° 24' N, 29° 00'W.). Convoy HX. 133)

1941   Convoy PQ.17 sailed for Russia. 11 of 36 merchant ships arrived.

1941   GC: Lieutenant Geoffrey Gledhill Turner, GM, RNVR, Sub-Lieutenant Francis Haffey Brooke-Smith, RNVR *(Gazette* date). Bomb and mine disposal.

1944   *Pink* mined off Normandy: CTL.

HMS *Endymion*

177

28th JUNE

1550   First appointment of sea victualler.

1762   *Defiance* and *Glasgow* captured the Spanish *Venganza* and *Marte* off Mariel, Cuba.

1776   Bombardment of Fort Moultrie, Charleston. Ships: *Bristol, Experiment, Active, Solebay, Actaeon*, Syren, Sphinx, Friendship, Ranger, Thunder, St. Laurence.* *Grounded and had to be burnt by her own crew.

1803   Boats of *Loire* cut out the French *Venteux* at Île de Bas, France. [m]

1810   Boats of *Amphion, Active* and *Cerberus* cut out 25 gunboats at Porto Grado, Trieste. [m]

1814   *Reindeer* taken by the American *Wasp* 240 miles West of Ushant.

1888   Engineer Cadets introduced, to be trained at Keyham.

1918   D.6 sunk by UB.73 N of Inishtrahull Island, W of Ireland.

1940   7th C.S., under Vice-Admiral J.C. Tovey (*Orion*), chased three Italian destroyers, sinking *Espero* in Central Mediterranean (35° 18' N, 20° 12' E.). Ships: *Gloucester, Liverpool, Neptune, Orion, Sydney.*

1941   *Perth* (RAN), *Carlisle* and 5 destroyers bombarded the Damur area, Syria.

1977   Silver Jubilee review of the Fleet by the Lord High Admiral, Her Majesty Queen Elizabeth II.

A Sea Fury landing on a carrier. The hook has caught the arrester wire which is stretched across the flight deck.

29th JUNE

1417   The Earl of Huntingdon's squadron took four Genoese carracks in the Channel.

1798   *Jason* and *Pique* captured the French *Seine* to the northward of Île de Ré *Mermaid* was in company.

1800   *Anson,* escorting a convoy, captured the Spanish *Gibraltar* and *Salvador* in Gibraltar Strait.

1807   Uniform regulations for masters, surgeons and pursers made by Order in Council.

1940   *Dainty* and *Ilex* sank the Italian submarines *Uebi Scebeli* and *Argonauta* in Central Mediterranean.

1940   Sunderland L/5804 of 230 Sq. sank the *Rubino* in Ionian Sea (39° 10' N, 18° 20' E.). First RAF success on anti-submarine patrol.

1940   *Enterprise* took bulk of bullion from Bank of England to Canada though the Captain did not qualify for Plate Money. Operation fish.

1941   *Waterhen* (RAN) attacked by aircraft off Sollum (32° 15' N, 25° 20' E.). Sank early on the 30th.

1941   *Arabis, Malcolm, Scimitar, Speedwell* and *Violet* sank U.651 in N Atlantic (59° 52' N, 18° 26' W.). (Convoy HX.133)

1942   *Thrasher* sank the Italian fast sloop *Diana.*

1944   *Cooke, Domett, Duckworth, Essington* and Liberator L/224 sank U.988 off the Channel Islands (49° 37' N, 3° 41' W.).

1944   *Tenacious, Terpsichore* and *Tumult* bombarded a look-out station South of Valona (40° 19' N, 19° 23' E.).

Korea 1950–53
On 25 June 1950 the communist North Korean army attacked the South Koreans across the 38th parallel. Within a week the Royal Navy was operating in Korean waters, sinking coastal shipping and attacking communications ashore. The Chinese reinforced the North Koreans and advanced into North Korea during the winter, driving the United Nations Forces back. Allied sea power was used to the full, both in launching sea borne air attacks against North Korean forces, and in evacuating and landing troops as required. Russian built Mig Jet fighters were deployed against the Fleet Air Arm in Korea. Lieutenant P. Carmichael shot down the first Russian Mig to be destroyed.

178

30th JUNE

1690 Battle of Beachy Head. Anglo-Dutch fleet (34 and 22 respectively) under Admiral the Earl of Torrington *(Sovereign)* and Admiral Cornelis Evertsen *(Hollandia)* fought Vice-Admiral Comte de Tourville *(Soleil-Royal)*, with 73 ships and 18 fireships. Ships: Van (Dutch): *Wapen Van Utrecht, Wapen Van Alkmaar, Tholen, West Vriesland, Princes Maria, Castricum, Agatha, Stad En Landen, Maagd Van Enkhuizen, Noord Holland, Maagd Van Dordrecht, Hollandia, Veluwe, Provincie Van Utrecht, Maze, Vriesland, Elswout, Reigersbergh, Gekroonde Burg, Noord Holland, Veere, Cortienne* + 4 fireships: Centre: *Plymouth, Deptford, Elizabeth, Sandwich, Expedition, Warspite, Woolwich, Lion, Rupert, Albermarle, Grafton, Sovereign, Windsor Castle, Lenox, Stirling Castle, York, Suffolk, Hampton Court, Duchess, Hope, Restoration, Constant Warwick.* Fireships: *Dolphin, Hound, Owner's Love, Roebuck, Speedwell, Spy, Vulture, Wolf.* Rear: *Anne, Bonaventure, Edgar, Exeter, Breda, St. Andrew, Coronation, Royal Katherine, Cambridge, Berwick, Swallow, Defiance, Captain.* Fireships: *Cadiz Merchant, Charles, Cygnet, Fox, Griffin, Hawk, Hunter, Thomas* and *Elizabeth.*

1696 Sir Christopher Wren and John Evelyn laid foundation stone of Greenwich Hospital "precisely at 5 o'clock in the evening, Mr Flamsteed the King's Astronomical Professor observing the precise time by instruments."

1707 Rear-Admiral Sir John Norris *(Torbay)* forced the passage of the Var, France.

1797 Nore Mutiny leader Parker hanged.

1803 *Vanguard* captured the French *Créole* off Île Tortuga.

1915 *Lightning* sunk by mine off the Wielingen lightvessel, Zeebrugge.

1917 *Cheerful* sunk by mine 6 miles S.S.E. of Lerwick.

1942 *Medway* sunk by U.372 off Alexandria (31° 03' N, 30° 35' E.).

1944 Canso A/162 (RCAF) and Liberator E/86 sank U.478 in Norwegian Sea (63° 27' N, 0° 50' W.).

1950 *Triumph, Belfast, Jamaica, Cossack, Consort, Black Swan, Alacrity* and *Hart* in first engagement in Korean waters.

1961 Closure of Royal Victoria Yard, Deptford: opened in 1742 and responsible for storing and blending the Navy's rum.

HMS *Devonshire,* RN's first Guided Missile ship, launched 10th June 1960

179

1st JULY

1719   *Grafton, Lenox, Breda* and *Essex* captured two Spanish transports and destroyed a third near Cape San Vito, Sicily.

1731   Adam Duncan born.

1780   *Romney* captured the French *Artois* 100 miles N.N.W. of Cape Ortegal.

1800   Boats of *Renown, Defence* and *Fisgard* destroyed the French *Thérèse* and 19 other vessels at Noirmoutier, France.

1845   A military force, with a gun's crew from *Hazard,* repulsed in the attack on Honi Keke's pah at Ohaeawai, New Zealand. Troops: Royal Artillery, 58th Regiment.

1850   *Cormorant* captured three slave vessels and engaged the fort at Paranagua, Brazil; a fourth slaver was destroyed by her own crew.

1880   RNEC founded at Keyham.

1914   RNAS formed from RFC Naval Wing.

1922   *Insolent* foundered in Portsmouth Harbour.

1940   *Gladiolus* and Sunderland H/10 (RAAF) sank U.26 SW of Ireland (48° 03' N, 11° 30' W.).(Convoy OA.175)

1945   Allied naval and air bombardment of Balikpapan, Borneo, prior to landing by 7th Australian Division. RAN Ships: *Arunta, Hobart, Shropshire; Kanimbla, Manoora, Westralia.*

1946   First nuclear air burst explosion over an unmanned Fleet (Bikini Island, Pacific). Operation Crossroads Able.

1961   Iraq threatened invasion of Kuwait. 42 Commando RM landed from *Bulwark* by 845 NAS (Whirlwinds). 45 Commando RM flown in from Aden by RAF.

1969   C in C Portsmouth (Admiral Sir John Frewen) became first C in C Naval Home Command. (CINCNAVHOME)

1977   WRNS became subject to Naval Discipline Act.

2nd JULY

1667   The Dutch landed at Felixstowe. The Duke of York and Albany's Maritime Regiment of Foot repulsed an attack on Landguard Fort. Ships: *Castle, Virgin.*

1803   *Minerve,* blockading Cherbourg, grounded and had to surrender to the French *La Chiffonne* and *Terrible.*

1805   *Cambrian* captured the French privateer *Matilda* 25 miles S.E. of Tybee Island, Georgia.

1917   First regular convoy of merchant ships sailed from Hampton Roads, Virginia.

1940   Swordfish aircraft of 812 Sq. (disembarked) and Coastal Command aircraft attacked invasion barge concentrations near Rotterdam.

1950   The start of United Nations operations in Korea. [bh].
Commonwealth Task Force: RN. +*Alacrity,* +*Alert,* +*Amethyst,* +*Belfast,* +*Birmingham,* +*Black Swan,* +*Cardigan Bay,* +*Ceylon,* +*Charity,* +*Cockade,* +*Comus,* +*Concord,* +*Consort,* +*Constance,* +*Cossack,* +*Crane,* **Defender,* +*Glory,* +*Hart,* +*Jamaica,* +*Kenya,* **Ladybird,* +*Modeste,* +*Morecambe Bay,* +*Mounts Bay,* +*Newcastle,* **Newfoundland,*+*Ocean,* +*Opossum,* +*St. Brides Bay,* +*Sparrow,* **Tactician,* +*Telemachus,* +*Theseus,* +*Triumph,* +*Tyne,* @+*Unicorn,* **Warrior,* +*Whitesand Bay.* FAA Sq.: 800[1], 801[1], 802[2], 804[2], 807[2], 810[3], 812[3], 821[3], 825[3], 827[3], 898[2]. [1] Seafire. [2] Sea Fury. [3] Firefly. +41st Independent Commando, RM. RFA: +*Brown Ranger,* @**Fort Charlotte,* **Fort Rosalie,* **Fort Sandusky,* **Fort Langley,* **Gold Ranger,* +*Green Ranger,* +*Maine,* (H.M. H.S.), +*Wave Baron,* +*Wave Chief,* +*Wave Duke,* +*Wave Knight,* +*Wave Laird,* +*Wave Premier,* @+*Wave Prince,* **Wave Regent,* +*Wave Sovereign.* RAN: +*Anzac,* +*Bataan,* +*Condamine,* +*Culgoa,* +*Murchison,* +*Shoalhaven,* +*Sydney,* +*Tobruk,* +*Warramunga,* **Arunta.* FAA Sq.: 805[2], 808[2], 817[2]. RCN: +*Athabaskan,* +*Cayuga,* +*Crusader,* +*Haida,* +*Huron,* +*Iroquois,* +*Nootka,* +*Sioux.* RNZN: +*Hawea,* +*Kaniere,* +*Pukaki,* +*Rotoiti,* +*Taupo,* +*Tutira.* +Also United Nations Service Medal. *U.N.S. Medal only. @Fleet Train.

The new generation of bomb; Bikini 1946

HMS *Revenge*, 1968, an RN, nuclear-powered Polaris submarine

3rd JULY

1759 Rear-Admiral George Rodney *(Achilles)* bombarded Le Havre. Ships: *Achilles, Boreas, Brilliant, Chatham, Deptford, Isis, Juno, Norwich, Unicorn, Vestal, Wolfe.* Bomb ketches: *Basilisk, Blast, Carcase, Firedrake, Furnace, Mortar.*

1797 Bombardment of Cadiz. Rear-Admiral Sir Horatio Nelson's boat action with Spanish gunboats at Cadiz. Bombs: *Stromboli, Terror, Thunder.* Covered by: *Emerald, Terpsichore, Theseus.* Troops: Royal Artillery.

1801 *Speedy* taken by Rear-Admiral Durand-Linois' squadron off Gibraltar.

1812 *Raven* defeated 14 French gunbrigs of the Schelde division of the Invasion Flotilla in the Wielingen Channel, driving three ashore.

1840 *Blonde* destroyed two Chinese batteries at Amoy.

J. Trewavas, VC.

1855 VC: Ordinary Seaman Joseph Trewavas, (*Agamemnon* lent *Beagle*), for cutting

hawsers of floating bridge in the straights of Genitchi under heavy fire at close range. Boats of *Beagle* and *Vesuvius* destroyed the ferry at Genitchi, Sea of Azov.

1910 Royal Yacht *Victoria and Albert* heeled in dock: led to resignation of Sir William White as DNC.

1919 *Fandango* mined in Dvina River, N Russia.

1940* Force H, under Vice-Admiral Sir James Somerville (*Hood*), attacked the French warships at Mers-el-Kebir, Oran. Ships: *Hood, Resolution, Valiant; Ark Royal; Arethusa, Enterprise; Escort, Faulknor*(D.8), *Fearless, Foresight, Forester, Foxhound; Active, Keppel*(D.13), *Vidette, Vortigern, Wrestler.* FAA Sq: 800, 803 (Skua), 810, 818, 820 (Swordfish). Operation Catapult. French ship sunk: *Bretagne.* French ships damaged: *Commandant Teste, Dunkerque, Mogador, Provence.*

Admiral Somerville signalled to Admiralty:
After talk with Holland and others I am impressed with their view that use of force should be avoided at all costs. Holland considers offensive action on our part would alienate all French wherever they are.

Admiralty to Somerville:
Firm intention of His Majesty's Government that if French will not accept any of your alternatives they are to be destroyed.

Prime Minister's signal to Somerville on 2nd July:
You are charged with one of the most disagreeable and difficult tasks that a British Admiral has ever been faced with but we have complete confidence in you and rely on you to carry it out relentlessly.

Somerville to Admiral Gensoul:
If one of our propositions is not accepted by 17.30 BST I shall have to sink your ships.

1942 *Le Tigre* (Free French) sank U.215 off New York (41° 48' N, 66° 38' W.).

1943 Wellington R/172 sank U.126 in S.W. Approaches (46° 02' N, 11° 23' W.).

1943 Liberator J/224 sank U.628 in Bay of Biscay (44° 11' N, 8° 45' W.).

First Naval air strikes of Korean War, 1950

Between 0545 and 0615 on 3rd July, aircraft from *Triumph* and the USS *Valley Forge* flew on the first air strikes of the Korean War. 12 Firefly aircraft and 9 Seafires from *Triumph*, armed with rockets, attacked Haeju airfield and damage was done to hangars and buildings. The aircraft all returned safely; flak had been negligible, but slight damage had been caused by small arms fire.

4th JULY

1780   *Prudente* and *Licorne* captured the French *Capricieuse* in the Bay of Biscay.

1803   Boats of *Naiad* cut out the French *Providence* at Île de Sein, Brittany.

1811   Boats of *Unité* cut out the French *St. Francois de Paule* at Porto Ercole. *Cephalus* and boats of *Unite* cut out three French vessels between Civita Vecchia and the mouth of the River Tiber.

1855   Boats of *Racehorse* captured a pirate junk off Ockseu Island.

1915   VC: Lieutenant Frederick Daniel Parslow, RNR (*Anglo-Californian*). (Posthumous). Awarded VC when in command of the unarmed *Anglo-Californian* he was engaged by U.38 South of Ireland (50° 10' N, 9° 00' W.). Although ordered to abandon ship, he continued to signal the presence of the submarine for 2 hours until RN destroyers arrived.

1917   *Aster* mined E of Malta.

1940   VC: A/Ldg. Seaman Jack Foreman Mantle in *Foylebank*, sunk by German aircraft at Portland.

1940   *Pandora* sank the French *Rigault de Genouilly* off Algiers, before orders to suspend further attacks on French ships had been received.

1942 Convoy PQ. 17

PQ. 17 of 36 ships sailed from Reykjavik on 27th June. It was shadowed from 1st July and there were unsuccessful air torpedo attacks that day. There was thick fog on 2nd and 3rd, when it became known that a large German force had sailed from Trondheim. The battleships *Tirpitz*, *Scheer*, *Hipper* and 6 destroyers were heading out, though the *Lützow* and 3 destroyers had run aground near Narvik and returned to harbour. On 4th there were heavy German air attacks, and 3 merchantmen were lost, but the convoy was in good heart. At 2100 however, the threat from the surface raiders was considered greater than that from under the sea or over it, and the convoy was ordered by the Admiralty to scatter. The cruiser escort withdrew westwards and the fleet destroyers joined them. As they left, one British escorting submarine signalled 'intend remaining on the surface as long as possible' ... the destroyer leader *Keppel* replied 'So do I'.

The surface attack did not materialise, and 10 merchant ships were sunk by U-boats, and 11 by aircraft. However, 11 reached Russia, escorted by the AA ships, corvettes etc which had not joined the Fleet. One trawler had escorted 3 merchantmen, been trapped in ice for 3 days and had painted the ships white to avoid detection.

Cargo	Delivered	Lost
Vehicles	896	3350
Tanks	164	430
Aircraft	87	210
Other cargo	57,176 tons	99,316 tons

HMS *Nile* c 1880

183

1695 Bombardment of St. Malo by Admiral Lord Berkeley *(Shrewsbury)* and Vice-Admiral Philips van Almonde. Ships: *Shrewsbury; Charles* (f.s.), *Dreadful*, Carcase* (bombs), and Dutch bombs. *Expended.

1780 *Romney* captured the French *Perle* 50 miles to the westward of Cape Finisterre.

1807 Abortive attack on Buenos Aires by Lieutenant-General John Whitelocke, resulting in the surrender of Brigadier-General Robert Craufurd's force and finally to an armistice and the withdrawal of all British forces from the Rio de la Plata area. Naval forces were under Rear-Admiral George Murray *(Polyphemus)*. Ships: *Africa, Diadem, Polyphemus, Raisonnable.* Frigates: *Medusa, Nereide, Thisbe.* Smaller: *Encounter, Fly, Flying Fish, Haughty, Olympia, Paz, Pheasant, Protector, Rolla, Saracen, Staunch.* A Naval Brigade was landed.

1811 *Cressy, Defence, Dictator, Sheldrake* and *Bruizer,* with a convoy of 108 sail, beat off a Danish flotilla of 17 gunboats and 10 heavy rowboats off Hjelm Island, Kattegat, capturing 4 gunboats and 3 rowboats.

1819 Admiral the Hon. Sir William Cornwallis died. Nicknamed 'Billy Blue' because as soon as bad weather drove him into port he was concerned to resume his blockade as soon as possible, and hoisted the Blue Peter as a preparative signal for sailing as he anchored.

1840 Capture of Tinghai, Chu san, by Commodore Sir Gordon Bremer *(Wellesley)*. Ships: *Algerine, Alligator, Conway, Cruizer, Wellesley, Young Hebe; Rattlesnake* transport. Steamers: *Atalanta* (I.N.); *Queen* (Ben. Mar.).

1916 UC.7 mined and sunk off Zeebrugge.

1920 Landing parties from *Royal Sovereign, Revenge, Venetia* and *Westcott* assisted in occupation of Mudavia by Greek forces, *Ceres, Royal Oak* and *Resolution* having landed troops at Lapsaki, Dardanelles.

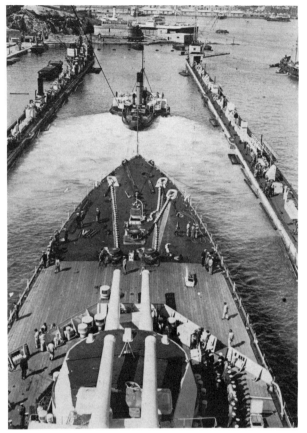

HMS *Repulse* **entering the floating dock at Malta, 1937**

1940 *Whirlwind* torpedoed by U.34 in Western Approaches (50° 17' N, 8° 48' W.): sunk by *Westcott.*

1940 Nine Swordfish aircraft of 813 Sq. *(Eagle)* sank the Italian destroyer *Zeffiro* and a merchant ship at Tobruk.

1940 Swordfish aircraft of 830 Sq. (Malta) attacked Catania airfield, Sicily.

1941 *Torbay* sank the Italian submarine *Jantina* off Izmir (Turkey) (37° 30' 30' N, 25° 50' E.).

1942 *Niger* sunk by British mine off Iceland (66° 35' N, 22° 20' W.). (Convoy QP.13)

1942 Wellington H/172 sank U.502 in Bay of Biscay (46° 10' N, 6° 40' W.).

1943 Liberator G/53 sank U.535 in Bay of Biscay (43° 52' N, 0° 48' W.).

1944 *Wanderer* and *Tavy* sank U.390 in the Channel (49° 52' N, 0° 48' W.).

6th JULY

1779   Vice-Admiral the Hon. John Byron (*Princess Royal*) fought Vice-Admiral Comte d'Estaing (*Languedoc*), with 26 ships, off Grenada. Ships: *Suffolk, Boyne, Royal Oak, Prince of Wales, Magnificent, Trident, Medway; Fame, Nonsuch, Sultan, Princess Royal, Albion, Stirling Castle, Elizabeth; Yarmouth, Lion, Vigilant, Conqueror, Cornwall, Monmouth, Grafton.* Frigate: *Ariadne.* Regiments: 4th, 5th, 40th, 46th.

1782   Third battle between Vice-Admiral Sir Edward Hughes (*Superb*) and Commodore Chevalier de Suffren (*Heros*), with 11 ships and 4 frigates, off Negapatam, Madras. [bh]. Ships: *Hero, Exeter, Isis, Burford, Sultan, Superb, Monarca, Worcester, Monmouth, Eagle, Magnanime; Seahorse.* Regiment: 98th. See 17th February, 12th April and 3rd September.

1801   Rear-Admiral Sir James Saumarez (*Caesar*) fought Rear-Admiral Durand-Linois (*Formidable*) at Algeçiras, S. Spain. Ships: *Audacious, Caesar, Hannibal*[1]*, Pompee, Spencer, Venerable; Calpe.* [1] Captured.

1808   *Seahorse* took the larger Turkish frigate *Badere Zaffer,* and damaged the corvette *Alis Fezan* up the Archipelago. [m*, m, bh]

1809   *Bonne Citoyenne* captured the French *Furieuse* 700 miles E. by S. of Cape Race, Newfoundland. [m*,m, bh]

1812   *Dictator* and *Calypso* destroyed the Danish *Nayaden* between Lyngo and Odden, Denmark, and captured the corvettes *Laaland* and *Kiel,* which had to be abandoned. *Podargus* and *Flamer* were in company, but grounded before the main action though engaged with gunboats and shore batteries. [m]

1841   *Acorn* captured the Portuguese slaver *Gabriel* 300 miles S.W. by W. of Sierra Leone.

1916   E.26 lost in N Sea.

1917   *Itchen* sunk by U.99 70 miles East of Pentland Firth.

1940   *Shark* scuttled after German aircraft attack, assisted by the minesweeping trawlers M.1803, M.1806 and M.1807 off Skudesnaes, Norway (58° 18' N, 5° 13' E.).

1940   Bombardment of Bardia, by *Caledon, Capetown, Ilex, Imperial, Janus, Juno.*

1940   Swordfish aircraft of 810 Sq. (*Ark Royal*) torpedoed and severely damaged the French battle cruiser *Dunkerque* and sank trawler *Terre Neuve* at Oran.

1944   *Cato* and *Magic* sunk by German Marder one-man submarine in Sword area Seine Bay. Operation Neptune.

1944   *Kootenay* and *Ottawa* (RCN) and *Statice* sank U.678 off Brighton (50° 32' N, 0° 23' W.).

1944   *Trollope* torpedoed off French coast: CTL .

HM Submarine *Shark* surrendering to German trawler 1940

185

7th JULY

1777   *Flora* recaptured the American (ex-British) *Fox* 40 miles S. by W. of Cape Sable, N. America.

1805   *Matilda* captured the Spanish privateer *Artrivedo* and her two prizes (*Golden Grove* and *Ceres*) in the St. Mary River, Georgia.

1809   Boats of *Implacable, Bellerophon* and *Melpomene* cut out seven Russian gunboats and twelve merchantmen under Percola Point, Hango Head, Baltic. [m]

1913   Landing party from *Eagle* captured and destroyed a 5-gun fort at Faresina.

1917   *Ettrick* sunk by UC.61 15 miles S. by W. of Beachy Head.

1917   J.2 torpedoed and sank U.99 off Heligoland.

A submarine's crowded quarters.

The Sloop *Bonne Citoyenne* **towing** *La Furieuse.* **(see 6th July)**

8th JULY

1777   *Rainbow* captured the American *Hancock* 170 miles S.S.W. of Cape Sambro.

1778   *Ostrich* and *Lowestoffe's Prize* captured the American *Polly* 10 miles N.N.E. of Galina Point, Jamaica.

1800   *Dart* captured the French *Désirée* in Dunkirk Roads. [m, bh] . Other ships participating: *Ann, Biter, Boxer, Camperdown, Comet, Falcon, Kent, Nile, Rosario, Selby, Stag, Teaser, Vigilant, Wasp* and boats of *Andromeda, Babet, Nemesis* and *Prévoyante.*

1809   Landing party from *Mosquito, Alert* (cutter), *Basilisk, Blazer, Briseis, Bruizer* (gun-vessel), *Centinel, Ephira, Patriot* (schuyt) and *Pincher* captured a battery at Cuxhaven.

1810   Reduction of the island of Bourbon (Réunion). Ships: *Boadicea, Iphigenia, Magicienne, Nereide, Sirius.* Troops: 33rd, 1/56th, 69th, 86th Regiments; Bombay Artillery Pioneers, 1/6th Madras Native Infantry, 2/12th Native Infantry.

1838   Royal Naval College re-established by Order in Council at Portsmouth, under command of *Excellent* until 1905.

1846   Rear-Admiral Sir Thomas Cochrane *(Agincourt)* destroyed the defences of Brunei, Borneo. Ships: *Hazard, Phlegethon* (Ben. Mar.), *Royalist, Spiteful,* (flag for attack). Boats of: *Agincourt, Iris, Ringdove.*

1854   Boats of *Firebrand* and *Vesuvius* destroyed the defences and part of the town of Sulina, Black Sea.

1870   James Reed, Chief Constructor of the Navy, resigned over the issue of fitting full sailing rig in turret ships — see 7th September 1870.

1940   Motor boat of *Hermes* and her Swordfish aircraft of 814 Sq. attacked with depth charges and torpedoes respectively the French battleship *Richelieu* at Dakar.

1943   Liberator R/224 sank U.514 in Bay of Biscay (43° 37' N, 8° 59' W.).

1944   Sunderland H/10 (RAAF) sank U.243 in Bay of Biscay (47° 06' N, 6° 40' W.).

1944   *Dragon* (Pol) and *Pylades* damaged by German one-man submarine in Juno area. Seine Bay. *Dragon* became blockship. Operation Neptune.

HM Submarine *C25* under attack by German aircraft 6th July 1918. She reached port but was never repaired.

9th JULY

1745 *Lion* fought the French *Elizabeth* and *Duteillay* (conveying the Young Pretender) 140 miles to the westward of Ushant.

1782 Boats of *Ripon* captured a French armed boat under the South Foreland.

1803 *Narcissus* captured the French *Alcyon* to the south-westward of San Pietro, near Sardinia.

1810 Boat of *Sirius* captured the French privateer *Edward* off Bourbon (Réunion)

1852 Temporary occupation of Prome, Burma by *Medusa* (Indian Navy), *Proserpine*, *Phlegethon* and *Mahanuddy* (Bengal Marine) and boats of *Fox*.

1863 E. J. Reed appointed Chief Constructor.

1917 *Vanguard* destroyed by internal explosion at Scapa.

1917 RNAS bombed *Goeben* and *Breslau* at Constantinople.

1929 H.47 lost in collision with L.12.

1940 Action off Calabria, Italy (38° 00' N, 17° 30' E.). Operation M.A.5. Admiral Sir Andrew Cunningham *(Warspite)* fought the Italian fleet. Ships: *Dainty, Decoy, Defender, Eagle, Gloucester, Hasty, Hereward, Hero, Hostile, Hyperion, Ilex, Janus, Juno, Liverpool, Malaya, Mohawk, Neptune, Nubian, Orion, Royal Sovereign, Stuart, Sydney, Vampire, Voyager, Warspite.* FAA Sq: Swordfish 813, 824. RAF 201 Group: Flying boats: L.5803, L.5807, L.9020.

1940 *Salmon* sunk by mine S.W. of Stavanger (57° 22' N, 5° 00' E.).

1942 *Hyacinth* captured the Italian s/m *Perla* off Beirut (33° 50' N, 35° 19' E.).

1943 Wellington R/179 sank U.435 in E Atlantic (39° 48' N, 14° 22' W.).

1944 Captain F.J. Walker, CB, DSO and three bars, RN died.

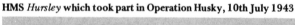

HMS *Hursley* **which took part in Operation Husky, 10th July 1943**

10th JULY

1797 *Santa Margarita* captured the French privateer *Adour* 24 miles S.W. of Cape Clear.

1804 Boats of *Narcissus, Seahorse* and *Maidstone* cut out twelve settees at Le Levandou, Hyeres Road.

1808 Boats of *Porcupine* cut out the Spanish *N.S. Del Rosario* at Porto d'Anzio. [m]

1920 Admiral of the Fleet Lord Fisher of Kilverstone died.

1943 Landing in Sicily. Operation Husky, [bh]. Ships: *Abdiel, Abercrombie, Acute, Albacore, Aldenham, Alynbank, Antwerp, Aphis, Arrow, Atherstone, Aurora, Banff, Bann, Beaufort, Belvoir, Blencathra, Bluebell, Bonito, Boston, Boxer, Brecon, Brissenden, Brittany, Brixham, Brocklesby, Bruiser, Bryony, Bude, Bulolo, Burra, Cadmus, Cairns, Calpe, Camellia, Carlisle, Cava, Cedardale, Cessnock, Chanticleer, Circe, Clacton, Clare, Cleopatra, Cleveland, Cockchafer, Colombo, Convolvulus, Coriolanus, Crane, Cromarty, Cygnet, Dart, Delhi, Delphinium, Derwentdale, Dianella, Dido, Dulverton, Easton, Echo, Eclipse, Eday, Eggesford, Ennerdale, Erebus, Erne, Eskimo, Espiegle, Euryalus, Exmoor, Farndale, Faulknor, Felixstowe, Fishguard, Fly, Formidable, Foxtrot, Fury, Gavotte, Gawler, Geraldton, Glengyle, Grayling, Guardian, Hambledon, Haydon, Hazard, Hebe, Hilary, Holcombe, Honeysuckle, Howe, Hursley, Hurworth, Hyacinth, Hyderabad, Hythe, Ilex, Inchmarnock, Inconstant, Indomitable, Inglefield, Intrepid, Ipswich, Isis, Islay, Jervis, Juliet, Jumna, Keren, Kerrera, King George V, King Sol, Laforey,*
Lamerton, Largs, Lauderdale, Ledbury, Liddesdale, Lismore, Lookout, Lotus, Loyal, Maidstone, Man-o-War, Maryborough, Mauritius, Mendip, Mullet, Mutine, Nelson, Newfoundland, Nubian, Oakley, Offa, Orion, Osiris, Oxlip, Paladin, Panther, Parthian, Pathfinder, Pearleaf, Penelope, Penn, Pentstemon, Petard, Pheasant, Pirouette, Plym, Polruan, Poole, Poppy, Primula, Prince Charles, Prince Leopold, Prins Albert, Prinses Astrid, Prinses Beatrix, Prinses Josephine Charlotte, Protea, Puckeridge, Quail, Quantock, Queen Emma, Queenborough, Quilliam, Raider, Reighton Wyke, Rhododendron, Rhyl, Roberts, Rockwood, Rodney, Romeo, Rorqual, Rothesay, Royal Scotsman, Royal Ulsterman, Rye, Safari, Saracen, Scarab, Seaham, Seraph, Severn, Shakespeare, Sharpshooter, Shiant, Shoreham, Sibyl, Sickle, Simoom, Sirius, Southern Isle, Southern Sea, Sportsman, Starwort, Stella Carina, Stornoway, Stroma, Sutlej, Tactician, Tango, Tartar, Taurus, Templar, Test, Tetcott, Teviot, Thruster, Torbay, Trent, Trespasser, Tribune, Trident, Trooper, Troubridge, Tumult, Tynedale, Tyrian, Uganda, Ulster Queen, Ultor, Unbroken, Unison, United, Universal, Unrivalled, Unruffled, Unruly, Unseen, Unshaken, Unsparing, Uproar, Usurper, Valiant, Venomous, Vetch, Viceroy, Vienna, Vindictive, Visenda, Vulcan, Wallace, Wanderer, Warspite, Wayland, Whaddon, Wheatland, Whimbrel, Whitehaven, Whiting, Wilton, Wishart, Wolborough, Woolongong, Woolston, Wrestler. MGB: 641, 657, 660. M.L.: 1158. MTB: 63, 77, 81, 84, 260, 265, 288, 313, 315, 316, 665. FAA Sq: Seafire 807, 880, 899; Albacore 817 (*Indomitable*); Albacore 820; Seafire 885; Martlet 888, 893 (*Formidable*).

Supply convoy for the landings in Sicily.

10th JULY

Operation Husky — Invasion of Sicily

The invasion started with the landing in the early hours of 10th July. Before nightfall British troops had entered Syracuse and next day the port, capable of taking 5000 tons of stores a day, was in British hands virtually undamaged. During the operation the Navy and Air forces landed 115,000 British troops and 66,000 American troops. Ships involved were:-

	British	American	Other
Warships	199	68	12
Landing Craft, Coastal Craft and Misc.	1260	811	3
Merchant and Troops Ships	155	66	16

In the 3 weeks following the landings 3 German and 8 Italian submarines were sunk for the loss of 4 merchant ships and 2 LSTS, with 2 merchantmen and 2 cruisers damaged. Air attacks caused more problems and dislocations with 13 ships sunk and more damaged.

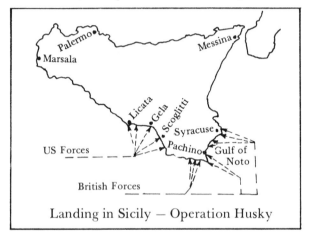

Landing in Sicily — Operation Husky

HM Submarine *Unrivalled* **on Operation Husky, Sicily**

Ships of the 1880's: (front to rear) HMS *Monarch, Alexandra, Temeraire* **and** *Penelope* **at Malta before the siege of Alexandria**

11th JULY

1796 *Melpomene* captured the French *Revanche* 50 miles S.S.W. of Ushant.

1803 *Racoon* captured the French *Lodi* at Leogane, Haiti.

1812 Boats of *Tuscan* cut out a small privateer at Chipiona, Spain; *Encounter* grounded and was taken by the enemy.

1824 Defeat of the Ashantis at Cape Coast Castle. Ships: *Thetis, Swinger, Victor.* Troops: 2nd West India Regiment.

1843 *Helena* launched at Pembroke Dock: served as sloop, coal hulk, police ship and church ship.

1882 VC: Gunner Israel Harding (*Alexandra*) for picking up a live shell and putting it in a bucket of water. Bombardment of Alexandria by Admiral Sir Frederick Beauchamp Seymour (*Alexandra*) [bh] Ships: *Alexandra, Beacon, Bittern, Condor, Cygnet, Decoy, Hecla, Helicon, Inflexible, Invincible, Monarch, Penelope, Sultan, Superb, Temeraire.* Medals: Egypt, 1882: clasp 'Alexandria, 11 July' and Khedive's Bronze Star. "Well done, *Condor.*"

1916 *Era, Nellie Nutten* and *Onward* (trawlers escorting fishing fleet) sunk by U.24, U.46 and U.52 100 miles East of Aberdeen.

1939 Inaugural dinner in Painted Hall, RN College, Greenwich, attended by King George VI.

1940 *Escort* (screening Force H) sank, having been torpedoed on 3rd by the Italian s/m *Guglielmo Marconi*, E of Gibraltar (36° 11' N, 3° 37' W.).

1941 *Defender* damaged by Italian aircraft in the Gulf of Sollum (31° 45' N, 25° 31' E.); 7 miles North of Sidi Barrani. Sunk by *Vendetta* after tow failed.

1942 *Protea* and *Southern Maid* (SANF) and Walrus aircraft of 700 Sq. (FAA) sank the Italian s/m *Ondina* off Beirut (34° 35' N, 34° 56' E.).

1942 *Pelican, Spey* and *Léopard* (Fr) sank U.136 off Madeira (33° 30' N, 22° 52' W.).(Convoy OS.33)

1942 *Beaufort, Dulverton, Eridge* and *Hurworth* bombarded Mersa Matruh area. Albacore aircraft of 820 Sq. drove ships in harbour to sea, an ammunition ship being sunk by the destroyers.

1943 MTBs 640, 651 and 670 sank the Italian s/m *Flutto* off N. Sicily (37° 34' N, 15° 43' E.).

1943 *Howe* and *King George V* bombarded Favignana and Trapani, Sicily; *Dido* and *Sirius* bombarded Marsala. Operation Fracture.

1944 Sunderland P/201 sank U.1222 in Bay of Biscay (46° 31' N, 5° 29' W.).

Sailors of HMS *Monarch* firing rockets during the bombardment of Alexandria.

12th JULY

1346 Edward III destroyed eleven French warships at La Hogue.

1745 *Prince Frederick* and *Duke* (*"Royal Family"* privateers) captured the French *Marquis d'Antin* and *Louis Erasmus* off the Banks of Newfoundland.

1771 Return of Lieutenant James Cook (*Endeavour*) from his first voyage of exploration.

1801 Rear-Admiral Sir James Saumarez (*Caesar*) defeated the Franco-Spanish squadron of Vice-Admiral Don Juan de Moreno and Rear-Admiral Durand-Linois (both in *Sabina*) in the Gut of Gibraltar. [m, bh]. Ships: *Audacious, Caesar, Spencer, Superb, Venerable* and volunteers from *Pompee*. Frigates, etc.: *Calpe, Louisa, Thames* and the Portuguese *Carlotta*. Captured: *St.-Antoine* (Fr). Blew up: *Real Carlos* and *San Hermenegildo* (Sp.).

1871 *Devastation* launched. First capital ship without full sailing rig.

1917 *Patriot* sank U.69 E of Scotland.

1943 *Boston, Cromarty, Poole* and *Seaham* captured the Italian s/m *Bronzo* off Augusta, Sicily (37° 06' N, 15° 24' E.). She became P.714 until given to the French.

Sir James Saumarez (1757 - 1836)

1943 MTB 81 sank U.561 in Messina Strait (38° 16' N, 15° 39' E.).

1943 *Inconstant* sank U.409 in W Mediterranean (37° 12' N, 4° 00' E.).

1943 *Erebus* and 15th C.S. (*Mauritius, Orion, Uganda*) bombarded Augusta, Sicily.

HMS *Devastation*

13th JULY

1795 Admiral William Hotham *(Britannia)* fought Rear-Admiral Pierre Martin *(Orient)*, with 17 ships of the line, off Hyères. Ships: *Victory, Captain, Culloden, Blenheim, Defence, Agamemnon, Britannia, Princess Royal, St. George, Windsor Castle, Gibraltar, Fortitude, Bombay Castle, Saturn, Cumberland, Terrible, Egmont, Bedford, Courageux, Audacious, Diadem.* Frigates, etc.: *Ariadne, Comet, Cyclops, Eclair, Fleche, Meleager, Moselle, Mutine, Resolution.* Regiments: 11th, 25th, 29th, 30th, 50th, 69th, 86th, 2/90th, 97th.

1805 *Melampus* captured the Spanish privateer *Hidra* 500 miles West of Lands End.

1855 VC: Lieutenant George Dare Dowell RMA *(Magicienne)*. George H. Ingouville, capt. of mast *(Arrogant)*. *Ruby* and boats of *Arrogant* and *Magicienne* fought a battery in Trangsund Roads, Gulf of Finland.

1860 Private Dalliger, RMLI, hanged at the yardarm of *Leven* in Yangtse for attempted murder (last hanging at the yardarm).

1900 VC: Midshipman Basil John Douglas Guy *(Barfleur)*, at Tientsin when under intense and close range fire returned with a stretcher to rescue a wounded man. "The ground around him was ploughed up with bullets".

1943 *Unruly* sank the Italian s/m *Acciaio* off Salerno (38° 35' N, 15° 49' E.).

1943 *Echo* and *Ilex* sank the Italian s/m *Nereide* off Taranto (37° 25' N, 16° 07' E.).

1943 Sunderland N/228 sank U.607 in Bay of Biscay (45° 02' N, 9° 14' W.).

1943 Second battle of Kolombangara Solomon Isles, between U.S. and Japanese surface forces. [bh]. *Australia* (RAN) and *Leander* (RNZN) engaged, the latter being badly damaged. First battle private to USN.

Naval Discipline.

The seaman of the days of sail was necessarily tough. His conditions were squalid and the need for instant obedience led to swift discipline. In the First Articles of war in 1652 (see 25th Dec) almost all offences merited death. For lesser offences, the customs of the sea dictated a variety of elaborate, often brutal punishments. The 'cat o' nine tails' was the most common punishment in the first half of the nineteenth century and in ships with martinet captains, a flogging was a routine event. After the reforms of 1832, Parliament began to look closely at Naval Discipline and by 1859 flogging was only allowed without a court martial to men who were not in the 'First Class for Conduct'. By 1871 flogging was only permitted in wartime and it was abolished altogether in 1879.

The 'Second Class for Conduct' is still awarded as a punishment today to deal with persistent offenders.

Hong Kong Harbour, 1901

14th JULY

1612   First record of half-masted flags (*Heartache*); for the dead Captain J.Hall.

1779   *Egmont* taken by the American privateer *Wild Cat* off Cape Spear, Newfoundland. *Surprise* captured *Wild Cat* just before midnight.

1780   *Nonsuch* drove ashore and burnt the French *Légère* on Blanche Bank, off the mouth of the Loire, and captured three vessels of a convoy.

1809   Boats of *Scout* stormed a battery at Carry, near Marseilles. [m]

1869   *Thalia* launched — last ship built in Woolwich Dockyard.

1876   *Thunderer's* box boiler exploded killing 45 men. Last 'box boiler' fitted in HM ships.

1900   Capture of Tientsin native city. Naval Brigade from *Aurora, Barfleur, Orlando, Terrible*.

1909   C.11 sunk by ss *Eddystone* off Cromer.

1916   H.5 sank U.51 off the Weser (53° 55' N, 7° 53' E.).

1942   *Lulworth* sank the Italian s/m *Pietro Calvi* S of the Azores (30° 35' N, 25° 58' W.). (Convoy SL.115)

1974   *Hermes, Andromeda* and *Rhyl* evacuated British subjects from Kyrenia, Cyprus during Turkish invasion.

Cod Wars

One of the long standing tasks of the Royal Navy is to protect the British fishing fleet. Iceland, whose economy depends largely on the fish stocks off her coast has steadily increased her area of exclusive fishing rights. Her gun boats, acting in her best interests but contary to international law, have harassed British trawlers by arresting them or cutting their nets. The incident here shows the gunboat *Baldur* (right) making a run, and being headed off by *HMS Juno*.

194

15th JULY

1796   *Glatton* idiosyncratically armed with carronades fought six French frigates 6 miles N.W. by W. of Schouwen light.

1798   *Lion* engaged four Spanish frigates, capturing *Santa Dorotea,* 90 miles E. by S. of Cartagena, Spain. [m, bh]

1804   *Lily* taken by the French privateer *Dame Ambert* off Cape Romain, S. Carolina.

1815   Napoleon surrendered to Captain Maitland in *Bellerophon,* in Basque Roads in the Bay of Bisquay.

1855   Allied light squadron destroyed Russian stores at Berdyansk, Sea of Azov. Sloops: *Vesuvius, Beagle, Curlew, Swallow, Wrangler* and the French *Milan* and *Mouette.* Gunboats: *Boxer, Cracker, Fancy, Grinder, Jasper.*

1855   VC: Boatswain John Shepherd (*St. Jean d'Acre*), for his two attempts to blow up an enemy battle ship in Sebastopol using a punt full of explosives.

1915   *Severn* and *Mersey* and RN aircraft destroyed the German cruiser *Königsberg* in the Rufiji River, East Africa. [bh]. Support ships: *Challenger, Hyacinth, Laconia, Pioneer, Pyramus, Weymouth.*

1916   H.3 sunk by mine off Cattaro, in Adriatic.

1943   *Sirius* bombarded Catania, Sicily; *Abercrombie* and the USS *Birmingham* and *Philadelphia* bombarded Empedocle and Agrigento.

1943   *United* sank the Italian s/m *Remo* in Gulf of Taranto (39° 19' N, 17° 30' E.).

1943   *Balsam, Mignonette* and *Rochester* sank U. 135 off Canary Islands (28° 20' N, 13° 17' W.). (Convoy OS.51).

1944   Liberator E/206 sank U.319 off S.W. Norway (57° 40' N, 5° 00' E.).

1944   Supply and Secretariat school moved from Highgate School (*President V*) to Wetherby.

1975   Third fishing dispute began with Iceland.

HMS *Glatton* fighting off six French ships 1796

195

1780 *Nonsuch* captured the French *Belle-Poule* 33 miles to the southward of Île d'Yeu, France.

1795 Shutter Telegraphs started to carry signals from Admiralty to Portsmouth in 15 minutes, given clear weather.

1796 *Hazard* captured the French privateer *Terrible* 50 miles N.N.W. of the Scilly Islands.

1806 Boats of *Centaur, Conqueror, Revenge, Achille, Polyphemus, Prince of Wales, Monarch, Iris* and *Indefatigable* cut out the French *César* in the Gironde. [m]

1812 Boats of *Britomart* and *Osprey* captured the French privateer *Éole* off Heligoland.

1855 Allied light squadron destroyed Russian stores and the defences at Petrovskoe, Sea of Azov. Sloops: *Vesuvius, Beagle, Curlew, Swallow, Wrangler* and the French *Milan,* and their boats. Gunboats: *Boxer, Cracker, Fancy, Grinder, Jasper.*

A Corsair's cockpit

1856 Quill Friction Tubes introduced for firing in RN guns.

1918 *Anchusa* torpedoed by U.54 off N coast of Ireland.

1919 *Gentian* and *Myrtle* mined in Gulf of Finland.

1940 *Imogen* sunk in collision with *Glasgow* in a thick fog off Duncansby Head (58° 34' N, 2° 54' W.).

1940 *Phoenix* sunk by the Italian t.b. *Albatros* off Augusta, Sicily.

Model of Shutter Telegraph Hut.

Lieutenant: a Rowlandson print, 1799.

17th JULY

1761   *Thunderer* captured the French *Achille* 57 miles W.½N. of Cadiz. [bh]. *Thetis* captured the French *Bouffonne* in the same locality.

1797   *Anson* and *Sylph* drove ashore and wrecked the French *Calliope* on Penmarc'h Point, Brittany.

1805   *Ariadne* and consorts drove ashore four vessels of the Ostend invasion flotilla off Gravelines.

1812   *Shannon, Belvidera, Guerriere, Africa* and *Aeolus* unsuccessfully chased the American *Constitution* for two days to the eastward of Barnegat, New Jersey.

1855   Destruction of Russian stores on Glofira Spit, Sea of Azov. Sloops and gunboats: *Wrangler, Boxer, Cracker, Fancy, Grinder, Jasper; Curlew.* Boats of: *Vesuvius, Swallow.*

1882   James F. Somerville born.

1942   Lancaster F/61 and Whitley H/502 sank U.751 in S.W. Approaches (45° 14' N, 12° 22' W.).

1943   *Warspite* bombarded Catania, Sicily.

1944   *Telemachus* sank the Japanese s/m I.166 in Malacca Strait (2° 47' N, 101° 03' E.).

1944   Liberator U/86 sank U.361 (68° 36' N, 8° 33' E.) and Catalina Y/210 sank U.347 off Narvik (68° 35' N, 6° 00' E.).

1945   First combined attach on the Japanese mainland (Hitachi area of Honshu) by the British Pacific Fleet and US battleships. Task Force 37. Ships: *King George V, Formidable, Black Prince* and *Newfoundland* with five destroyers.

Corsair aircraft taking off and petrol tank exploding; the aircraft taxied clear, unharmed but for some scorching and the loss of its tank.

1413 Wm. Cotton appointed Keeper of the King's Ships.

1690 *St. Albans* captured a French 28-gun privateer 20 miles S.S.E. of Start Point.

1812 *Spartan* captured the American *Hiram* and *Nautilus* to the southward of Seal Island, and the American privateer *Actress* off Yarmouth, Nova Scotia.

1813 *Havannah* and *Partridge* destroyed a small Neopolitan convoy and its escort near Rodi, Adriatic.

1940 East Coast lightvessels attacked by German aircraft: East Goodwin lightvessel sunk.

A flotilla at exercise, World War 2

1943 Wellington B/221 sank the Italian s/m *Romolo* off Messina (37° 20' N, 16° 15' E.).

1943 *Mauritius* bombarded Catania, Sicily in support of the 8th Army.

1944 Catalina Z/210 sank the U. 742 off Narvik (60° 24' N, 9° 51'E.).

1944 *Balfour* sank U.672 off Portland (50° 03' N, 2° 30' W.).

1944 British 2nd Army broke through in the Caen area. *Enterprise, Mauritius* and *Roberts,* in support, bombarded the German shore batteries.

1961 45 and 42 Commandos, RM relieved on station in Kuwait where they had been landed by 845 NAS (WW) from *Bulwark* (supported by *Centaur** and *Victorious+).* *893 Vixens. +892 Vixens. 42 Commando left on 20th July.

19th JULY

1588	*Golden Hind* sighted the Spanish Armada off Lizard Head.
1745	Lt. Phillips of *Princess Royal* executed for surrendering his ship to French (his Captain, 1st Lt and 60 crew had been killed).
1779	Fruit juice ordered as remedy for scurvy.
1805	Vice-Admiral Lord Nelson reached Gibraltar after pursuing the French to the West Indies, and went ashore for "the first time in two years, wanting ten days."
1806	*Blanche* captured the French *Guerrière* to the southward of the Faeroes. [m]
1837	Engine room branch established by Order in Council.
1854	*Miranda* and *Brisk* bombarded Solovets monastry, White Sea.
1918	Seven Sopwith Camels (from *Furious*) destroyed the Zeppelins L.54 and L.60 in their shed at Tondern, Germany. First Division of 1st Battle squadron with 1st and 7th L C Squadron, and destroyers, in support.
1918	*Garry*, with MLs 49 and 263, rammed and sank UB.110 (raised 4 October) in N Sea (54° 39' N, 0° 55' W.).
1940	*Sydney* (RAN) with 2nd DF, sank the Italian cruiser *Bartolomeo Colleoni* off Cape Spada (35° 43' N, 23° 36' E.) and damaged the Italian cruiser *Giovanni Delle Bande Nere*. [bh]. Ships: *Hasty, Havock, Hero, Hyperion, Ilex, Sydney*.
1941	*Umpire* rammed and sunk by *Peter Hendricks* off the Wash (53° 09' N, 1° 08' E.).
1942	*Dido, Euryalus; Javelin, Jervis, Pakenham* and *Paladin* bombarded Mersa Matruh, N Africa. *Aldenham* and *Dulverton* engaged German E-boats in the same area.
1943	*Laforey, Lookout, Newfoundland* and the Neth. *Flores* engaged nine enemy batteries near Catania, Sicily.

The *Bartolomeo Colleoni* sinking, 1940

199

1545 *Mary Rose* capsized and sank at Spithead through failing to secure for sea when sailing to meet the French.

1588 The Spanish Armada off Plymouth. [bh] . Ships employed during the period: Queen's ships: *Achates, Advice, Aid, Antelope, Ark (Royal), Brigandine, Bull, Charles, Cygnet, Disdain, Dreadnought, Elizabeth Bonaventure, Elizabeth Jonas, Fancy, Foresight, Galley Bonavolia, George, (Golden) Lion, Hope, Mary Rose, Merlin, Moon, Nonpareil, Rainbow, Revenge, Scout, Spy, Sun, Swallow, Swiftsure, Tiger, Tramontana, Triumph, Vanguard, Victory, (White) Bear, White Lion.* (37). Merchant ships under Drake: *Bark Bond, Bark Bonner, Bark Buggins, Bark Hawkins, Bark Manington, Bark St. Leger, Bark Talbot, Bear Yonge, Chance, Delight, Diamond of Dartmouth, Edward Bonaventure, Elizabeth Drake, Elizabeth Founes, Flyboat Yonge, Galleon Dudley, Galleon Leicester, Golden Hind, Golden Noble, Griffin, Hearts-Ease, Hope Hawkyns, Hopewell, Makeshift, Merchant Royal, Minion, Nightingale, Roebuck, Spark, Speedwell, Thomas Drake, Unity, Virgin God Save Her,* and 1 small caravel. (34).
Merchant ships from the City of London: *Antelope, Anthony, Ascension, Bark Burr, Brave, Centurion, Diana, Dolphin, George Noble, Gift of God, Golden Lion, Hercules, Jewel, Margaret and John, Mayflower, Minion, Moonshine, Pansy, Passport, Primrose, Prudence, Red Lion, Release, Rose Lion, Royal Defence, Salamander, Thomas Bonaventure, Tiger, Toby(2)* (30). Merchant ships under the Lord High Admiral: *Anne Frances, George Bonaventure, Jane Bonaventure, Samuel, Solomon, Susan Parnell, Vineyard, Violet,* (8). Merchant ships in Queen's pay: *Black Dog, Edward of Maldon, Katherine, Lark, Marigold, Nightingale, Pippin* (7). Victuallers to the westward: *Bearsabe, Elizabeth Bonaventure, Elizabeth of Leigh, Gift of God, Hope, John of London, Jonas, Marigold, Mary Rose, Pearl, Pelican, Richard Duffield, Solomon, Unity, White Hind* (15). Coasters under the Lord High Admiral: *Aid of Bristol, Bark of Bridgwater, Bark Potts, Bark Webb, Bartholomew of Apsam, Crescent of Dartmouth, Galleon of Weymouth, Gift of Apsam, Handmaid of Bristol, Hart of Dartmouth, Hearty Anne, Jacob of Lyme, John of Chichester, John Trelawney, Katherine of Weymouth, Little John, Minion of Bristol, Revenge of Lyme, Rose of Apsam, Unicorn of Bristol* (20). Coasters under Lord Henry Seymour: *Anne Bonaventure, Bark Lamb, Daniel, Elizabeth of Dover, Fancy, Galleon Hutchins, Grace of God, Grace of Yarmouth, Griffin, Handmaid, Hazard of Feversham, John Young, Katherine of Ipswich, Little Hare, Marigold, Matthew, Mayflower, Primrose of Harwich, Robin of Sandwich, Susan, William of Colchester, William of Ipswich, William of Rye* (23). Voluntary ships: *Bark Halse, Bark Sutton of Weymouth, Carouse, Elizabeth, Elizabeth of Lowestoft, Flyboat, Fortune of Aldborough, Frances of Fowey, Gallego of Plymouth, Golden Ryall of Weymouth, Grace of Apsam, Greyhound of Aldborough, Heathen of Weymouth, John of Barnstable, Jonas of Aldborough, Margaret, Raphael, Rat of Wight, Samaritan of Dartmouth, Sampson, Thomas Bonaventure, Unicorn of Dartmouth, William of Plymouth (23).* Total, 197.

1655 Graving dock built at Portsmouth.

1697 *Weymouth* captured the French *Aurore* 12 miles S.W. of Sables d'Olonne.

1782 *Winchelsea* captured the French privateer *Royal* to the northward of Flamborough Head.

1915 C.27 (with *Princess Marie Jose**) sank U.23 in Fair Isle Channel. *Temporarily renamed *Princess Louise*.

1917 *Queen of the North* mined off Orfordness

1918 *Marne, Milbrook* and *Pigeon* sank UB.124 off Lough Foyle (55° 43' N, 7° 51' W.).

1918 E.34 mined in Heligoland Bight.

20th JULY

1940 *Brazen* sunk by German aircraft off Dover (51° 01' N, 1° 17' E.). (Convoy CW.7).

1940 Six Swordfish of 824 Sq. (*Eagle*) sank the Italian destroyers *Nembo* and *Ostro* at Tobruk.

1941 *Union* sunk by the Italian t.b. *Circe*

off Pantellaria (36° 26' N, 11° 50' E.).

1943 GC: Donald Owen Clarke, Apprentice, MN *San Emiliano* off Trinidad (*Gazette* date).

1944 *Isis* sunk by mine at O buoy, Seine Bay. Operation Neptune.

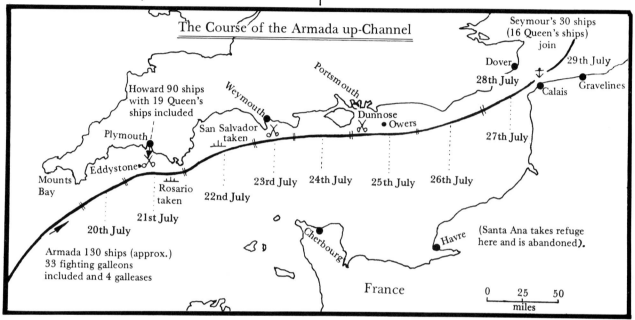

The Course of the Armada up-Channel

Seymour's 30 ships (16 Queen's ships) join

Dover
28th July
29th July
Calais
Gravelines
27th July

Portsmouth

Howard 90 ships with 19 Queen's ships included

Weymouth

Dunnose
• Owers

San Salvador taken

Plymouth

Eddystone

Mounts Bay

Rosario taken

23rd July   24th July   25th July   26th July

22nd July

21st July

20th July

Armada 130 ships (approx.) 33 fighting galleons included and 4 galleases

Cherbourg

Havre

(Santa Ana takes refuge here and is abandoned).

France

0   25   50
miles

An engraving of part of tapestries depicting the running fight with the Spanish Armada, which hung in the old House of Lords

1588	The first engagement with the Spanish Armada off the Eddystone. [bh]
1781	*Charlestown, Allegiance, Vulture, Jack* and *Vernon* escorting a convoy, fought the French *Astrée* and *Hermione* off Sydney, Cape Breton. Captured: *Jack.*
1796	*Aimable* fought the French *Pensée* off Guadeloupe.
1811	*Thomas* and *Cephalus* captured 11 French gunboats and a convoy of 15 sail at Punto Infreschi, Italy.
1812	*Sealark* captured the French privateer *Ville de Caen* 40 miles S.E. of Start Point. [m]
1812	*Nautilus* captured the French privateer *Brave* 15 miles S.E. by S. of Cape Carbonara, Sardinia.
1842	Capture of Chinkiang by Vice-Admiral Sir William Parker *(Cornwallis)* and Lieutenant-General Sir Hugh Gough. Ships: *Apollo, Belleisle, Blonde, Calliope, Childers, Clio, Columbine,*

Cornwallis, Dido, Endymion, Modeste, Plover, Starling, Vixen; Jupiter, Rattlesnake, transports. Steamers (IN): *Auckland, Medusa, Sesostris.* Steamers (Ben. Mar): *Nemesis, Phlegethon, Pluto, Proserpine, Queen, Tenasserim.* Seamen and Marines were landed. Troops: Royal Artillery, 18th, 26th, 49th, 55th, 98th Regiments; Madras Sappers and Miners, Bengal Volunteer Regiment, Madras Native Infantry, 2nd, 6th, 14th, 36th, 41st.

1855	*Arrogant, Cossack, Magicienne* and *Ruby* bombarded the defences of Fredrickshavn, Gulf of Finland.
1917	C.34 sunk by mine laid by UC.74 off Shetlands.
1943	*Aurora, Penelope; Offa, Petard, Quilliam, Troubridge* and the Polish *Piorun* bombarded Cotronei, Italy.
1943	*Erebus* and *Newfoundland* bombarded enemy batteries and troop concentrations in the Catania area, Sicily.
1944	*Curzon* and *Ekins* sank U.212 off Brighton (50° 27' N, 0° 13' W.).

The sail arrangement of a large early nineteenth century frigate:

A jib boom; B flying jib; C outer jib; D inner jib; E fore staysail; F bowsprit; G foremast; H fore course; I fore topsail; J fore topgallant; K fore royal; L main royal staysail; M main topgallant staysail; N main topmast staysail; O main mast; P main course; Q main topsail; R mizzen topgallant staysail; S mizzen royal staysail; T main topgallant; U main royal; V mizzen royal; W mizzen topgallant; X mizzen topsail; Y mizzen mast; Z spanker.

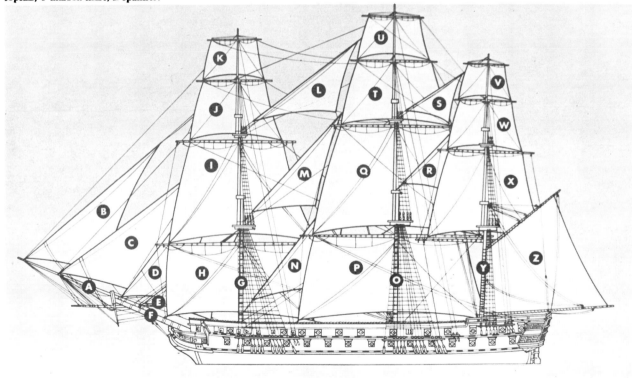

22nd JULY

1588   The Spanish Armada off Torbay. *Revenge* and *Roebuck* captured the Spanish *N.S. Del Rosario.*

1672   *Cambridge* and *Bristol* fought a Dutch East India fleet of 17 sail 30 miles to the westward of Heligoland.

1801   Boats of *Beaulieu, Doris, Robust, Uranie* and *Ville de Paris* cut out the French *Chevrette* in Camaret Bay, France. [m, bh]

1805   Vice-Admiral Sir Robert Calder *(Prince of Wales)* fought Vice-Admiral Pierre Villeneuve *(Bucentaure)*, with 19 French and Spanish ships, 150 miles W.N.W. of Ferrol. Ships: *Agamemnon, Ajax, Barfleur, Defiance, Dragon, Glory, Hero, Malta, Prince of Wales, Raisonnable, Repulse, Thunderer, Triumph, Warrior, Windsor Castle.* Frigates: *Egyptienne, Sirius.* Cutter: *Frisk.* Lugger: *Nile.* Captured: Spanish *Firme* and *San Rafael.*

1811   Boats of *Active* captured a grain convoy of 28 vessels, with their escort, at Ragosniza (Rogoznica), Yugoslavia.

1836   Boats of *Buzzard* captured the Portuguese slaver *Joven Carolina* in the Old Calabar River, Nigeria.

1847   Boats of *Waterwitch* and *Rapid* captured the Brazilian slaver *Romeo Primeiro* off Banda Point, French Equatorial Africa.

1903   Opening of RM School of Music.

The Atlantic Chase 1805

Position	Villeneuve	Nelson
Passes Strait of Gibraltar	9th April	7th May
Arrives in West Indies	14th May (Martinique)	4th June (Barbados)
Leaves Antigua	8th June	13th June
Passes the Azores	30th June (North of)	8th July (South of)
Arrives off Spain	22nd July (Fights Calder off Ferrol)	19th July (Gibraltar)

23rd JULY

1588   The second engagement with the Spanish Armada, off Portland.

1759   Keel of *Victory* laid.

1797   *Seagull* captured the French privateer *Capitaine Thurot* 30 miles S. by E. of Kristiansand. *King George* was in company.

1810   Boats of *Belvidera* and *Nemesis* captured the Danish schooners *Balder* and *Thor* and destroyed Gunboat No. 5 in Vanelvsfjord.

1854   *Miranda* bombarded Kola and then landed an armed party.

1860   *Kestrel* destroyed a pirate junk at the Chain Islands, near Fall Island (Hsiao o Kuan). *Kestrel's* complement was augmented by parties from *Snake* and the French *Dordogne*, and detachments of the 99th Regiment and French Marines.

1940   *Thames* sunk by mine S.W. of Stavanger, Norway (57° 50' N, 3° 10' E.).

1941   *Fearless* damaged by Italian torpedo aircraft off Galita Island (37° 40' N, 8° 20' E.): sunk by *Forester*. Operation Substance.

1943   *Eclipse* and *Laforey* sank the Italian s/m *Ascianghi* off Reggio, (37° 09' N, 15° 22' E.).

Freedom Box awarded to Sir Robert Calder, 1805

24th JULY

A Memorable Date observed by the Royal Marines

1588   The Spanish Armada off St. Alban's Head.

1704   Capture of Gibraltar by Admiral Sir George Rooke *(Royal Katherine)* and the Prince of Hesse-Darmstadt. [bh]. Ships: *Berwick, Burford, Dorsetshire, Eagle, Essex, Grafton, Kingston, Lenox, Monck, Monmouth, Montagu, Nassau, Nottingham, Ranelagh, Royal Katherine, Suffolk, Swiftsure, Yarmouth.* English and Dutch Marines.

After the capture, the Rock was continually besieged by the French and Spanish. The Brigade, which had been reinforced by a further four hundred Marines from the Fleet, held out for nearly six months against repeated attacks until the siege was finally raised.

In one incident during the siege, Captain Fisher of the Marines, with 17 of his men, successfully defended the Round Tower against the continued assaults of 500 French Grenadiers. A contemporary report of this noted defence stated "the garrison did more than could humanly be expected, and the English Marines gained an immortal honour." The Royal Marines wear "Gibraltar" on their badge, and trouble with no other battle honours.

1812   *Acasta* captured the American privateer *Curlew* 70 miles to the south-eastward of Halifax.

1908   *Gala* sunk in collision with *Attentive* off Harwich.

1915   *Prince Charles* sank U.36 10 miles W.N.W. of North Rona. (59° 07' N, 5° 30' W.). First Q. ship success.

1917   Flyingboat 8689 sank UC.1 in N. Sea.

1918   *Pincher* wrecked off Seven Stones.

1942   *St. Croix* (RCN) sank U.90 in Atlantic (48° 12' N, 40° 56' W.). (Convoy ON.113)

1943   Wellington Q/172 sank the supply U-boat U.459 in W Approaches (45° 53' N, 10° 38' W.) but crashed.

1945   *Squirrel* mined off Phuket Island, Malaya, and sunk by own forces. Operation Livery.

1945   FAA attacked targets in the Inland Sea, Japan. [bh]

Operation Substance.
This operation started on 21st July, when a convoy of 6 storeships was sailed from Gibraltar to Malta. Diversions were created in the Eastern Mediterranean, and submarines placed off the Italian ports, to reduce attacks on the convoy. A heavy escort was used, which included Force H, under Admiral Somerville, and the battleship *Nelson* with the cruisers *Edinburgh, Manchester* and *Arethusa.* From the 'Narrows' only the cruisers and destroyers continued to escort the convoy. On 23rd, *Manchester* was torpedoed and had to return to Gibraltar, and later the destroyer *Fearless* was also hit by air attacks and had to be sunk by her consort. In the evening the destroyer *Firedrake* was disabled, but the convoy turned towards Sicily at night to avoid mines and also to shake off the air attacks. At first light the cruisers went ahead and disembarked troops and stores, and the convoy arrived later that day. The convoy returned to Gibraltar safely on 27th July. The opportunity had also been taken to pass the empty 6 merchantmen and auxiliary *Breconshire* from Malta to Gibraltar, and the operation was a complete success.

Wellington aircraft of Coastal Command

25th JULY

1417 The Earl of Huntingdon defeated a Franco-Genoese fleet in the English Channel.

1588 The third engagement with the Spanish Armada, off the Isle of Wight.

1666 Battle of Orfordness. Prince Rupert and the Duke of Albemarle (*Royal Charles*) defeated Admiral de Ruyter (*Zeven Provincien*), with 88 ships, 20 fireships and 10 despatch-vessels, in the Thames Estuary. (Orfordness N.W. by W., 12 or 14 leagues.). [bh]. Red Sq.: (c) *Lion, Jersey, Triumph, Ruby, Fairfax, Swallow, Royal Charles, Antelope, Henrietta, Breda, Sovereign, Foresight, Monck, St. Andrew;* (v) *Greenwich, Portsmouth, Mathias, Diamond, Royal Oak, Crown, East India Merchant, Warspite, Slothany, Charles Merchant;* (r) *Tiger, Newcastle, Revenge, Princess, Henry, Bristol, Cambridge, John and Thomas, Katherine.* White Sq.: (c) *Assurance, Plymouth, Old James, Delft, Dragon, Royal James, Assistance, Leopard, Centurion, Richard and Martha, Montagu;* (v) *Dunkirk, Zealand, St. George, Dover, Royal*

Katherine, Expedition, Guinea, Baltimore, Anne, London Merchant; (r) *Mary Rose, Unicorn, York, Eagle, Rupert, Hampshire, Helverson, Coronation, Kent.* Blue Sq.: (c) *Yarmouth, Bonaventure, Unity, Gloucester, Amity, Loyal London, Portland, Mary, Golden Phoenix, Rainbow, House de Swede;* (v) *Adventure, Sancta Maria, Dreadnought, Rainbow, Victory, Advice, Vanguard, Castle, Guilder de Ruyter, Loyal Merchant;* (r) *East India London, Elizabeth, Resolution*[1], *Providence, Defiance, Happy Return, Turkey Merchant, Welcome, Marmaduke, George, Fanfan.* Fireships: *Abigail*[2], *Aleppine, Blessing*[2], *Briar, Charles, Fortune*[2], *Fox, Great Gift*[2], *Land of Promise*[2], *Lizard, Mary, Paul, Providence*[2], *Richard, St. Jacob, Samuel, Virgin.*
[1] Burnt. [2] Expended in action.

1797 Rear-Admiral Sir Horatio Nelson lost his right arm during the unsuccessful attack on Santa Cruz, Tenerife. Ships: *Culloden, Leander, Theseus, Zealous.* Frigates: *Emerald, Seahorse, Terpsichore.* Cutter: *Fox* sunk.

The Battle of Orfordness, 1666

205

25th JULY

1801 "The moment the enemy touch our coast, be it where they may, they are to be attacked by every man ashore and afloat: this must be perfectly understood. Never fear the event." Nelson, on defence of the Thames.

1803 *Vanguard* and *Tartar* captured the French *Duquesne* to the westward of Haiti. *Bellerophon, Theseus* and *Aeolus* took part in the chase, but were not engaged.

1809 Boats of *Princess Caroline, Minotaur, Prometheus* and *Cerberus,* under Commander Thomas Forrest (*Prometheus*), cut out three Russian gunboats and an armed brig at Frederikshavn, Gulf of Finland. [m]

1810 *Thames, Pilot* and *Weazle* captured or destroyed a convoy of 31 sail and the escort of 7 gunboats and 5 scampavias at Amantea, Italy. [m]

1848 First naval vessel to use Esquimalt — *Constance.*

1860 *Kestrel* destroyed seven pirate lorchas in the Wenchow River (Ou Kiang). (See 23 July).

1887 Golden Jubilee review. "Most of what you see is mere ullage", according to Admiral Hewitt.

1915 British forces captured Nasiriya, Mesopotamia. Vessels *Shushan* (party from *Espiegle*), *Messudieh* (party from *Miner*), *Muzaffri* (party from *Odin*), *Sumana.*

1934 National Maritime Museum Bill received Royal Assent.

1938 *Victory* museum opened in Portsmouth Dockyard.

1938 GC (ex-EGM): Frederick Christie Anderson, Chief ERA for gallantry in support of the Excise Service in Shanghai.

1941 *Newcastle* intercepted the German ss *Erlangen* which scuttled herself in S Atlantic (41° S, 50° W).

1944 Air strike on and bombardment of Sabang, Sumatra. Surface ships of Eastern Fleet engaged Japanese shore defences for the first time since assuming the offensive. Operation Crimson. [bh]. Ships: *Queen Elizabeth* (Admiral Sir James Somerville), Force 62. *Renown* (Vice-Admiral Sir Arthur Power), *Valiant, Richelieu* (Fr); *Illustrious* (Rear-Admiral C. Moody), *Victorious; Ceylon Cumberland, Gambia, Kenya, Nigeria* (Rear-Admiral A.D.Read — CS4), *Phoebe, Tromp* (Neth); *Racehorse, Raider, Rapid, Rocket, Relentless* (Cdre. D), *Roebuck, Rotherham, Quality, Quickmatch, Quilliam* (D.4). *Tantalus* and *Templar* employed on air/sea rescue duty. FAA Sq: Barracuda 831[2]. Corsair 1830[1], 1833[1], 1834[2], 1836[2], 1837[1], 1838[2].
[1] *Illustrious.* [2] *Victorious.*

North Sea Coastal Convoy. World War 2 (see 26th, and 6th September)

26th JULY

1588	The Spanish Armada in the English Channel.
1650	Blake defeated Rupert and John IV.
1666	The battle of Orfordness continued.
1703	Rear-Admiral Thomas Dilkes *(Kent)* captured or destroyed 41 sail of a French convoy of 45 vessels at Granville, France, together with the escort of 3 small warships. Ships: *Kent.* 1 fireship expended.
1758	Capture of Louisburg and the whole of Cape Breton Island by Admiral the Hon. Edward Boscawen *(Namur)* and Major-General Jeffery Amherst. [bh]. Ships: *Bedford, Burford, Captain, Centurion, Defiance, Devonshire, Dublin, Kingston, Lancaster, Namur, Northumberland, Nottingham, Orford, Pembroke, Prince Frederick, Prince of Orange, Princess Amelia, Royal William, Scarborough, Somerset, Sutherland, Terrible, Vanguard, York.* Frigates, etc.: *Aetna, Beaver, Boreas, Diana, Gramont, Halifax, Hawke, Hunter, Juno, Kennington, Lightning, Nightingale, Port Mahon, Shannon, Squirrel, Trent.* Troops: Royal Artillery; 1st, 15th, 17th 22nd, 28th, 35th, 40th, 45th, 47th, 48th 60th, 62nd Regiments. (The 62nd were serving afloat as Marines.
1798	*Brilliant* fought the French *Vertu* and *Regénérée* 20 miles W.N.W. of Grand Canary.
1806	*Greyhound* and *Harrier* captured the Dutch *Pallas* and the Dutch East Indiamen *Batavier* and *Victoria* 25 miles to the westward of Salayer Strait, India.
1809	Admiral Gambier's court-martial began.
1809	Boats of *Fawn* cut out a French cutter and a schooner in St. Marie Bay, Guadeloupe. [m]
1914	Order for dispersal of Fleets, assembled for Royal Review, countermanded by Prince Louis of Battenberg: the first step towards mobilisation for World War I.
1915	E.16 sank the German V.188 50 miles North of Terschelling.
1916	*Grasshopper* sunk in collision in N. Sea.
1917	*Ariadne* sunk by UC.65 3 miles West of the Royal Sovereign lightvessel, off Beachy Head.

Martlet aircraft, later reverted to their original American name Wildcat.

1929	GC (ex-EGM): Midshipman Anthony John Cobham and George Paterson Niven, Able Seaman *(Devonshire),* for gallantry in a turret explosion. GC (ex-AM): Lieutenant-Commander A.H. Maxwell-Hyslop: same incident.
1940	*Swordfish* crippled the German t.b. *Luchs* in N Sea (58° 30' N, 4° 30' E): sunk by own forces.
1941	*Cattistock, Mendip* and *Quorn* bombarded Dieppe. Operation Gideon.
1944	*Cooke* sank U.214 off Start Point (49° 55' N, 3° 31' W.).
1945	*Vestal* sunk by Japanese "Kamikaze" aircraft off Phuket Island, Malaya. Operation Livery.

East Coast and Channel Convoys

The only way of transporting the large quantities of fuel to the Thames and South Coast ports of Britain was by sea. 40,000 tons of coal were required each week. Convoys sailed from the Thames to the Bristol Channel and back, and these had to run within easy range of the enemy airfields in France, and through mined waters. One example was convoy CW 8. 21 ships passed West through the Straits of Dover on 25th July, 1940, and suffered 4 separate dive-bombing attacks that day. 5 ships were sunk and 4 more damaged. 2 escorting destroyers were also damaged. On 26th, E boats attacked and sank 3 more ships, and only 11 ships passed Dungeness. In the last week of July, 1940 alone, 103 ships had to be convoyed through the Straits, and then on 12th August an extra hazard was encountered, when the enemy guns at Cape Gris Nez started firing on convoys. This imposed great strain on the escorts and minesweepers and on the men of the Merchant Navy. East Coast convoys had to run the gauntlet in "E-boat alley" off the Norfolk coast. (see 6th September).

1588 The Spanish Armada off Calais. (33 Spanish ships and 18 lesser craft lost with 27,000 men.).

Augustus Viscount Keppel (1725 – 1786)

Keppel joined the Royal Navy in 1738 and served with Anson, then a Commodore, during his famous voyage round the world, 1740 – 44. He was a Lieutenant in 1744 and rose steadily in command. In 1747 he was captured by the French when his ship ran aground, but was exchanged for French prisoners. When Commodore in the Mediterranean Fleet in 1748, he is reported to have replied to the Dey of Algiers who complained of having to treat with a 'beardless boy': 'Had my Master supposed that wisdom was measured by the length of the beard he would have sent your deyship a he-goat'. He pleaded in vain at Admiral Byng's court martial He commanded the naval squadron at the capture of Gorée in 1758, the leading ship of the line under Admiral Hawke at Quiberon in 1759, the ships at the taking of Belle Ile (Isle) in 1761, and at Havana, where his share of the prize-money was reportedly £25,000. He was promoted to Rear-Admiral in 1762 and was in command at Jamaica till 1764. At home, where he was an MP, he became embroiled in politics, particularly against the Earl of Sandwich, then First Lord of the Admiralty. Despite this antipathy, he was in command of the Channel Fleet in 1776, and by 1778 was Commander of the Grand Fleet as a full Admiral. Due to maladministration only 6 out of 35 ships supposed to be at instant readiness were reputedly 'worthy of a seaman's eye'. Keppel was scarcely able to put to sea with a strong enough force to blockade the French Atlantic ports. He fought D'Orvilliers in July 1778 inconclusively and was court-martialed on politically-motivated charges brought by a junior officer five months after the event. He was unanimously and honourably acquitted and became the hero of the hour. In March 1779, Keppel refused to serve under a naval administration he could not trust, but by 1782 he was First Lord of the Admiralty during Rockingham's new government and was succeeded by Lord Howe. He retired from public life in 1783 and died in 1786. He never married.

1778 Admiral the Hon. Augustus Keppel *(Victory)* fought Vice-Admiral Comte d'Orvilliers *(Bretagne)* 108 miles N.W. by N. of Ushant. Ships: (v) *Monarch, Hector, Centaur, Exeter, Duke, Queen, Shrewsbury, Cumberland, Berwick, Sterling Castle;* (c) *Courageux, Thunderer, Sandwich, Valiant, Bienfaisant, Victory, Foudroyant, Prince George, Vigilant, Terrible, Vengeance;* (r) *Worcester, Elizabeth, Robust, Formidable, Ocean, America, Defiance, Egmont, Ramillies.* Frigates: *Arethusa, Proserpine, Milford, Fox, Andromeda, Lively.* Fireships: *Pluto, Vulcan.* Cutter: *Alert.* Regiments: 50th.
The only significant encounter between the British and French fleets in Home waters in the American War.

1803 *Plantagenet* captured the French privateer *Atalante* 400 miles to the Westward of Ushant.

1809 Landing party from *Aimable, Mosquito, Briseis, Ephira* and *Pincher* destroyed a battery at Gessendorf (Wesermunde). [m]

1914 German High Seas Fleet recalled from Norway to war bases.

1918 *Calvia, Commander Nasmith, Water Priory* and *Vanessa* sank UB. 107 off Scarborough (54° 24' N, 0° 24' W.).

1918 Naval force left Baghdad by road to operate on Caspian Sea.

1921 Second Sea Trial of Asdics (Sonar) analysed.

1940 *Codrington* sunk by German aircraft at Dover.

1940 *Wren* sunk by German aircraft off Aldeburgh (52° 10' N, 2° 06' E.).

1944 *Sunfish* (Russian B.1) sunk in error by Liberator V/86 (RAF) on loan passage to USSR, 240 miles off Norway.

1953 Conclusion of United Nations operations in Korea. Armistice signed.

1588* Fireship attack on the Spanish Armada in Calais Roads. Expended: *Bark Bond, Bark Talbot, Bear Yonge, Elizabeth of Lowestoft, Hope Hawkyns, Thomas Drake.*

1689 Relief of Londonderry. Ships: *Dartmouth; Mountjoy* and *Phoenix* victuallers. Boat of *Swallow.*

1706 Bombardment and storming of Alicante by Vice-Admiral Sir John Leake *(Prince George)* and the Earl of Peterborough. Ships: *Antelope, Berwick, Burford, Canterbury, Dorsetshire, Essex, Falcon, Fubbs Yacht, Grafton, Hampton Court, Leopard, Mary, Medway, Monck, Northumberland, Panther, Prince George, Revenge, Royal Ann, Royal Oak, St. George, Shrewsbury, Somerset, Tiger, Winchester.*

1806 *Mars* captured the French *Rhin* 80 miles North of Cape Ortegal, Spain.

1914 British Fleets ordered to their war bases.

1940 *Alcantara* survived an inconclusive fight with the German disguised raider *Thor* (Schiff 10).

1943 Liberator W/224 and N/4 (USAAF) sank U.404 in the Bay of Biscay (45° 53' N, 9° 25' W.).

1945 FAA attacked targets in the Inland Sea, Japan.

*Armada

The Spanish Armada was a fleet of 160 ships, of which 40 were warships, with 20,000 men (including soldiers) under the Duke of Medina Sidonia. The Admiral who was to have commanded the fleet died just before it sailed. The Armada was sighted off the Lizard on 19th July, and had reached Plymouth by 20th in settled weather making an average speed of 2 knots. The English Fleet, under Lord Howard of Effingham, comprised 27 warships and small vessels, totalling 200. They were able to leave Plymouth ahead of the Armada, and then harass it as it passed up Channel. Gunnery was indecisive; the Spanish ships being larger, the British ships better sailers, and the guns of both having the same effective range of 300 yards. On 27th, the Armada anchored off Calais, and on the night of 28th the English used fireships, which threw the Spanish into confusion. The Spanish fled before a SW wind, and never recovered formation, losing half their ships on the journey home through weather and enemy action. Many sailed completely round the British Isles. The British Fleet retired on 29th after the battle of Gravelines, through lack of food and ammunition but the Armada was shepherded as far North as the Firth of Forth. Sir Francis Drake was the Vice-Admiral of the British Fleet in this action.

HMS *Victory* as she appeared in 1778

1572	Francis Drake attacked Nombre de Dios, Panama. Ships: *Pasha, Swan.*
1588	The final action with the Spanish Armada off Gravelines.
1653	Action between Admiral George Monck (*Resolution*) and Admiral Maerten Tromp (*Brederode*) off Katwijk-aan-Zee. (See 31st July).
1781	*Perseverance* captured the French *Lively* 250 miles N.½ W. of Cape Finisterre; *Narcissus* recaptured a French prize brig.
1782	*Santa Margarita* captured the French *Amazone* 15 miles East of Cape Henry, but had to abandon her next day.
1797	*Aigle* captured the French *Hazard* 50 miles N.N.W. of Cape Finisterre.
1800	Boats of *Viper, Impetueux* and *Amethyst* cut out the French *Cerbère* at Port Louis. [m, bh]
1809	Boats of *Excellent, Acorn* and *Bustard* cut out six Italian gunboats at Duino. [m]

1856	Esquimalt replaced Valparaiso as RN base.
1914	Warning Telegram sent out.
1917	*Halcyon* sank UB.27 26 miles 060° from Great Yarmouth.
1917	Curtis H.12 flyingboats 8676 and 8662 sank UB.20 in N. Sea.
1940	*Delight* sunk by German aircraft off Portland having been detected by new Freya RDF at 60 miles range.
1943	*Trooper* sank the Italian s/m *Pietro Micca* in Otranto Strait (39° 45' N, 18° 25' E.).
1943	Wellington G/172 sank U.614 in S.W. Approaches (46° 42' N, 11° 03' W.).
1945	*King George V, Newfoundland, Undine, Ulysses* and *Urania* and U.S. battleships bombarded Hamamatsu, Honshu.

On the night of 29/30th July, the battleship *King George V* with the destroyers *Undine, Ulysses* and *Urania* shelled works and aircraft factories on South Honshu — the main island of Japan. This was the last occasion on which a British battleship used her guns in action against enemy targets. On 9th August the cruisers *Gambia* and *Newfoundland* together with the destroyers *Terpsichore, Termagent* and *Tenacious* shelled Honshu. The force was present at the formal surrender of the Japanese on 15th August in Tokyo Bay.

A post-war photograph of HMS *Amethyst*

1588   The Spanish Armada in the North Sea.

1775   Return of Commander James Cook (*Resolution*) from his second voyage of exploration in the Pacific. *Adventure* in company for the first half of the voyage. Kendalls K1 Chronometer proved (see also 19th Jan and 13th May).

1782   *Cormorant* captured the French *Téméraire* 25 miles W.S.W. of Cape Clear.

1811   Two boats of *Minden* stormed Fort Marrack, Java. [m]

1811   Boats of *Amazon* cut out four chasse-marees and burnt five more near Penmarc'h Point, Brittany.

1918   VC: Lieutenant Harold Auten, RNR (*Stock Force*) for action with UB.80 in Channel.

1919   Aircraft from *Vindictive* attacked Kronstradt Naval Base.

1938   Virtual abolition of half-pay.

1940   *Narwhal* sunk by German aircraft off Kristiansand.

1941   *Victorious* and *Furious* attack on shipping, at Kirkenes, Norway and Petsamo, Finland respectively. Operation E.F. Ships: *Active, Antelope, Anthony, Devonshire, Echo, Eclipse, Escapade, Furious, Icarus, Inglesfield, Intrepid, Suffolk, Victorious*. FAA Sq: 800, 812, 817 (*Furious*) (Fulmar, Swordfish, Albacore); 809, 827, 828 (*Victorious*) (Fulmar, Albacore).

1941   *Cachalot* rammed and sunk by the Italian t.b. *Generale Achille Papa* off Benghazi.

1943   *Kite, Wild Goose, Woodpecker* and *Wren* sank U.504 and Sunderland U/461 (RAAF), and Halifax S/502 sank the Supply U-boats U.461 and U.462 in Bay of Biscay.

July 30 1943
On 30th a Liberator sighted 3 U-boats crossing the Bay of Biscay; they were U.461 and U.462, both tankers, escorted by U.504. The Liberator's position report was 80 miles in error, but the submarines were resighted by a Sunderland and then by a Catalina operating with the Second Escort Group. A Liberator and a Halifax joined the Catalina and Sunderland, but poor communications between aircraft prevented a co-ordinated attack, even when another Halifax and Sunderland joined the other 4 aircraft. The newly arrived Halifax damaged U.462, but meanwhile the Liberator was hit and had to force land in Portugal, and the other aircraft were also hit by the submarines' gunfire. Sunderland 'U' of 461 Squadron then attacked and sank U.461, whereupon the ships of the Second Escort Group arrived. U.504 dived and was detected on asdic and sunk after 2 hours depth charging, and U 462 scuttled herself as she had been damaged by the aircraft and by the ships of the Second Escort Group. The joint air-sea action had been brought to a successful conclusion despite the initial errors and failures.

1949   *Amethyst* ran the gauntlet of Chinese Communist shore batteries in the Yangtze, from a little below Chinkiang, 150 miles, and rejoined the Fleet on the 31st.

18th April from *Amethyst:-*

Amethyst still aground on Rose Island. Am attempting to make good vital damage to refloat and proceed to Nanking. 60 approx of ship's company including 4 wounded are making way to nearest town. Casualties are about 17 dead including doctor and sick berth attendant. 20 seriously wounded including captain."

23rd April from Admiral:-

"You have my approval to act as you think best if fired on again. I am trying to arrange safe conduct for you to Nanking but doubtful if this will operate quickly. Try to let me know if you have to abandon. I am full of admiration for all in *Amethyst.*

From CinC:-

"I entirely agree your conduct of negotiations and am proud of the spirit and determination of all in *Amethyst.*"

To CinC:-

"I am going to break out at 10 p.m. tonight 30 July."

From *Amethyst* to CinC:-

"Have rejoined fleet south of Woo Sung. No damage or casualties. God Save the King."

HMS *Woodpecker*

30th JULY

In the early 19th century conditions on board ship were appalling; half the deaths in the fleet during the Napoleonic wars were accounted for by disease and a third by accident unconnected with enemy action. The food provided for the sailors was equally unsatisfactory; a weekly ration consisted of 7lb of biscuits, 7 gallons of beer, 6lbs meat, 2 pints peas, 3 pints oatmeal, 6oz sugar, 6oz butter and 12oz cheese. After some months in the hold of a ship these victuals were scarcely consumable: the same could be said of the water supply which was stored in wooden casks. The only palliative available to the sailor was rum, of which he received a half pint daily until 1824. The rum ration survived until 1970, although by that time it had been reduced to one-eighth of a pint per day. By that time too the food in ships had improved beyond all recognition, as had the living accommodation and general conditions of service of the sailors. A daily ration of rum became clearly inappropriate in the highly technical navy of that time. The ration was finally stopped by the Admiralty Board. The First Sea Lord, Admiral of the Fleet Sir Michael Lefanu, who was shortly to retire owing to a terminal illness made a valedictory signal to the fleet:

> "Personal from First Sea Lord:—
> Most farewell messages try
> To jerk a tear from the eye
> But I say to you lot
> Very sad about tot
> But thank you, good luck and goodbye."

Inevitably he was known as Dry Ginger, having hair of that colour.

Quarter deck of HMS *King Edward VII,* **1895**

"Up spirits"; rum being issued to messes in the early part of the 20th century

1653 The last battle of the First Dutch War. Admiral George Monck (*Resolution*) defeated Admiral Maerten Tromp (*Brederode*) off Scheveningen. [bh]. Ships: *Advantage, Andrew, Assurance, Crescent, Diamond, Dragon, Duchess, Exeter Merchant, Expedition, Foresight, Gift, Golden Cock, Great President, Hannibal, Hound, James, John and Katherine, Malaga, Merchant, Mary Prize, Merlin, Norwich, Pelican, Phoenix, Portsmouth, Prosperous, Rainbow, Raven, Recovery, Renown, Resolution, Seven Brothers, Sophia, Tiger, Triumph, Tulip, Vanguard, Victory, William, Worcester.* Fireships: *Hunter* (expended), *Oak* (blew up). (First Meritorious Service Medal).

1718 Admiral Sir George Byng (*Barfleur*) defeated Vice-Admiral Don Antonio de Gastaneta (*San Felipe El Real*) off Cape Passero, Sicily. [bh]. Ships: *Argyll, Barfleur, Breda, Burford, Canterbury, Captain, Dorsetshire, Dreadnought, Dunkirk, Essex, Grafton, Kent, Lenox, Montagu, Orford, Ripon, Rochester, Royal Oak, Rupert, Shrewsbury, Superb.* Fireships: *Garland, Griffin.* Hospital ship: *Loo.*

1801 *Sylph* fought a French frigate off Bilbao, Spain.

1804 Boats of *Centaur* cut out the French privateer *Elizabeth* and a schooner at Basse Terre, Guadeloupe.

1811 Boats of *Procris* captured five French gunboats at the mouth of the Inderamayu River, Java; a sixth blew up. Troops: Detachments of the 14th and 89th Regiments.

1849 *Nemesis* (Ben.Mar.) and boats of *Albatross* and *Royalist* destroyed 88 pirate prahus at the entrance to the Batang Saribas, Borneo.

1942 *Erne, Rochester* and *Sandwich* sank U.213 off the Azores.

1942 *Skeena* and *Wetaskiwin* (both RCN) sank U.588 in N Atlantic.

1942 Hudson of 113 Sq. (RCAF) sank U.754 in W Atlantic (43° 02' N, 64° 52' W.).

1943 July 1943 was the first month of the war when allied shipping construction exceeded losses.

1944 *Loch Killin* and *Starling* sank U.333 in SW Approaches. (First success with the 'squid').

1945 VC: Lieutenant Ian Edward Fraser, RNR and Leading Seaman James Joseph Magennis (XE.3). Midget submarine XE.4 cut the submarine cables between Saigon, and Hong Kong and Singapore. Operation Sabre. XE.1 and XE.3 damaged the Japanese cruiser *Takao* in Johore Strait, Singapore. Operation Struggle.

1951 *Vidal* launched: first HM ship designed and built as surveying ship, and first with cafeteria messing.

Lt. I.E. Fraser, VC, RNR

Ldg/Sea J. J. Magennis, VC

31st JULY

Midget Submarine Operations in the Far East, 1945
Midget submarines in the Far East were based on HMS *Bonaventure*, which in July 1945 was at Brunei Bay. XE1 and XE3 were towed by the *Spark* and *Stygian* to Singapore. XE3 placed her two 4 ton charges under the Japanese cruiser *Takao* (9850 Tons) in the Johore Strait, and LS Magennis swam out of the submarine to place limpet charges on the cruiser. The midget found it difficult to slip away as the cruiser settled down on her, and also because one large charge failed to fall clear. LS Magennis again left the submarine to clear the charge. XE3 then returned to the *Stygian*. XE1, meanwhile, had been delayed, and so did not attack the cruiser *Myoko* but laid her charges by *Takao*. *Takao*

was severely damaged by this attack, and both midget submarines arrived back safely. Lt Fraser and LS Magennis were awarded VCs.

On the same day as this attack, 31 July, XE4 managed to cut the Saigon-to-Hong Kong and Saigon-to-Singapore telegraph cables in 40ft of water despite bad weather and strong tides. She brought back one foot lengths of the cables as evidence.

XE5 spent 3½ days and nights attempting to cut the Hong Kong to Singapore telegraph cable off Hong Kong. She had to make the defended passage 4 times and her divers were working in white mud up to their armpits. She abandoned the attempt on 3rd August, but her efforts had, in fact, been successful.

X-craft with HM Submarine *Selene* near Hong Kong, off to cut sub cables in Singapore, 1945

L'Orient **blowing up at the Nile**

214

1st AUGUST

1295 Dover burnt by the French.

1683 Boats of *Francis* cut out the French pirate *Trompeuse* at St. Thomas, West Indies.

1739 Vernon's orders to his squadron to "take sink, burn or destroy" the enemy: a telling phrase used frequently thereafter.

1740 First performance of "Rule, Britannia!"

1793 *Boston* fought the French *Embuscade* off New York.

1798 Battle of the Nile. [m*, m, bh]. Rear-Admiral Sir Horatio Nelson (*Vanguard*) defeated Vice-Admiral François Brueys (*Orient*) in Aboukir Bay. Ships: *Alexander, Audacious, Bellerophon, Culloden, Defence, Goliath, Leander, Majestic, Minotaur, Orion, Swiftsure, Theseus, Vanguard, Zealous.* Sloop. *Mutine.*

* The Battle of the Nile.
Early in May 1798 Bonaparte and his army, and Admiral Brueys in 13 ships of the line including *L'Orient* (120 guns) and 4 frigates, were able to escape the British blockade and to sail to Malta where they arrived on the 9th June. After a week Bonaparte sailed with the intention of capturing Egypt and interrupting British trade with India. Nelson with a slightly smaller force was in Naples on the 17th June searching for him. He sailed for Alexandria, where he arrived on the 29th June. The French were not there, so Nelson returned to Sicily. Meanwhile the French fleet arrived at Alexandria and Bonaparte defeated the Mameluke army at the Battle of the Pyramids. The French fleet anchored in a strong position in Aboukir Bay. Nelson, after revictualling his ships, returned to Alexandria, and on the 1st August learnt of the location of the French fleet. Despite their strong position and the lateness of the hour Nelson attacked immediately. The French were unprepared for enemy attack from the landward side, and a number of British ships sailed inside the French line at considerable risk from shallow water. In the violent battle that ensued only 2 French ships were able to escape. The French flag ship *L'Orient* blew up with the loss of Admiral Brueys, Commodore Casabianca and his son, 'the boy stood on the burning deck'. "When we ceased firing, I went on deck to view the state of the fleets, and an awful sight it was. The whole bay was covered with dead bodies, mangled, wounded, and scorched, not a bit of clothes on them except their trousers. There were a number of French, belonging to the French Admiral's ship, the *L'Orient*, who had swam to the *Goliath*, and were cowering under her forecastle. Poor fellows! they were brought on board, and Captain Foley ordered them down to the steward's room, to get provisions and clothing. One thing I observed in these Frenchmen quite different from anything I had before observed. In the American

War, when we took a French ship, the *Duc de Chartres*, the prisoners were as merry as if they had taken us, only saying, 'Fortune de guerre — you take me today, I take you tomorrow'. Those we now had on board were thankful for our kindness, but were sullen and downcast as if each had lost a ship of his own.
... The only incidents I heard of are two. One lad who was stationed by a salt-box, on which he sat to give out cartridges, and keep the lid close — it is a trying berth — when asked for a cartridge, he gave none, yet he sat upright; his eyes were open. One of the men gave him a push; he fell all his length on the deck. There was not a blemish on his body, yet he was quite dead, and was thrown overboard. The other, a lad who had the match in his hand to fire his gun. In the act of applying it, a shot took off his arm; it hung by a small piece of skin. The match fell to the deck. He looked to his arm, and seeing what had happened, seized the match in his left hand, and fired off the gun before he went to the cockpit to have it dressed. They were in our mess, or I might never have heard of it. Two of the mess were killed, and I knew not of it until the day after. Thus terminated the glorious first of August, the busiest night in my life." (Recollections of John Nicol, Mariner).

1836 Boats of *Andromache* destroyed six pirate prahus off Pulo Bucalisse, Sumatra.

1861 *Warrior,* first seagoing ironclad, commissioned.

1914 Naval mobilisation ordered.

1915 E.11 raided Constantinople harbour.

1918 Allied Expeditionary Force captured the defences of Archangel. Ships: *Attentive, Nairana, Tay and Tyne.*

1940 *Oswald* rammed and sunk by the Italian destroyer *Ugolino Vivaldi* off Cape Spartivento (37° 46' N. 16° 16' E.).

1940 *Spearfish* sunk by U.34 in North Sea.

1943 Sunderland V/228 sank U.383 in SW Approaches.

1943 Sunderland B/10 (RAAF) sank U.454 in the Bay of Biscay.

1943 *Aurora, Penelope* and 6 destroyers bombarded Cotronei. *Dido, Euryalus, Sirius* and 4 destroyers bombarded the bridge at the mouth of the Oliva River and Vibo Valentia, Gulf of Eufemia, S Italy.

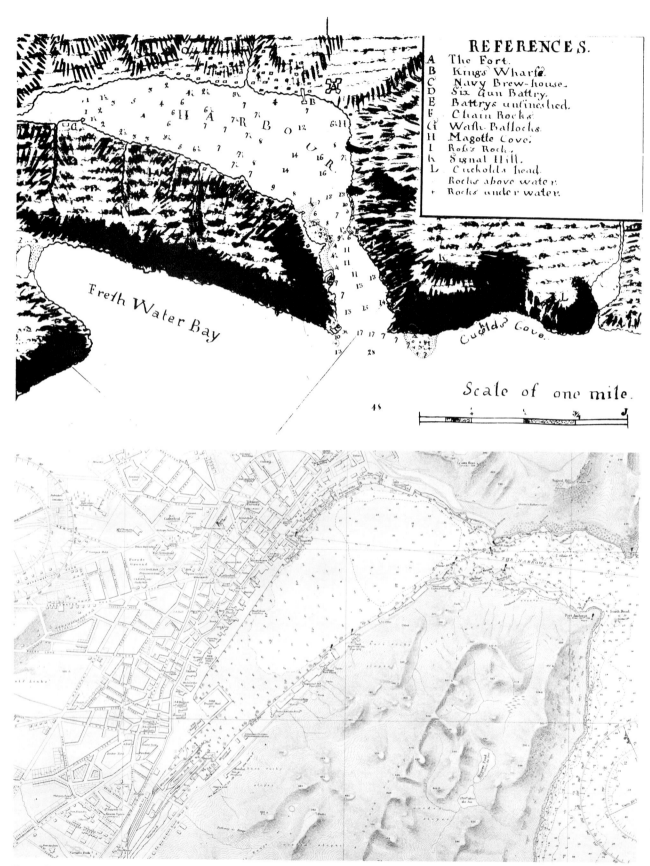

REFERENCES.

A The Fort.
B Kings Wharfe.
C Navy Brew-house.
D Six Gun Battry.
E Battrys unfineshed.
F Chain Rocks.
G Wash Ballocks.
H Magotte Cove.
I Rofes Rock.
k Signal Hill.
L Cucholds head.
Rocks above water.
+ Rocks under water.

Freth Water Bay

Cucholds Cove.

Scale of one mile.

James Cook's survey of St John's harbour, Newfoundland in 1762 compared with the current Admiralty chart

2nd AUGUST

1511 Lord Thomas Howard and Sir Edward Howard killed the Scottish pirate, Andrew Barton and captured his two vessels — *Lion* and *Jannet Perwyn*.

1665 Abortive attack by Rear-Admiral Sir Thomas Teddeman (*Revenge*) on the Dutch shipping at Bergen. Ships: *Breda, Foresight, Golden Lion, Guernsey, Guinea, Happy Return, Norwich, Pembroke, Revenge, Sapphire.* Hired ships: *Bendish, Coast Frigate, Prudent Mary, Society,* Fireships: *Bryer, Hound.* Supports, not engaged: *Bonaventure, Expedition, Martin Galley.* Hired: *Hambro' Merchant.* Ketch: *Edward and Eve, Royal Katherine.* Joined later: *Mary Rose; Constant Catherine, Eagle, Exchange, John and Thomas.*

1745 *Chester* and *Sunderland* captured the French register-ship *Notre Dame de la Délivrance* off Louisburg, Cape Breton Island.

1812 Boats of *Horatio* cut out two Danish vessels and recaptured their prize near Tromso.

1813 *Eagle* and *Bacchante* destroyed the batteries and shipping at Porto di Rovigno, Italy.

1913 Michael le Fanu born.

1917 First deck landing, on *Furious* by a Sopwith Pup.

1918 *Ariel* and *Vehement* mined in N Sea.

1919 *Princess Mary II* mined in Aegean.

1940 Twelve Swordfish (*Ark Royal*), 9 with bombs and 3 with mines, attacked Elmas airfield, Cagliari, and mined the harbour. FAA Sq.: 810, 818, 820 (Swordfish). Operation Crush.

1940 *Cape Finisterre* sunk by German aircraft off Harwich.

1940 GC (ex-EGM): Sub-Lieutenant Alexander Mitchell Hodge RNVR. (*Eagle*) (*Gazette* date).

1941 *Hermione* rammed and sank the Italian s/m *Tembien* off Tunis.

1943 Sunderland M/461 (RAAF) and N/228 sank U.106 in SW Approaches.

Bombardment of Inchon 1950
Inchon was being used as a base by the North Koreans, and the cruisers *Belfast* and *Kenya* carried out a bombardment of key points, such as the power station and railway station, firing over 400 rounds of 6 in shells. 95% of the shots were on target and the remainder were within several hundreds of yards. The destroyers *Cossack* and *Charity* accompanied the cruisers to deal with opposition from ashore, but were not required. Because of the flood stream the *Kenya* carried out the shoot at anchor, while the *Belfast* laid a dan buoy and held position on that. Spotting was carried out by an American Neptune aircraft, carrying RN aircrew from *Triumph* as observers.

First deck landing on HMS Furious by Cdr E. M. Dunning who was killed attempting the same thing two days later.

3rd AUGUST

1666	*Orange Prize* and French *Victory* fought two Flushing capers in the western end of the English Channel.
1758	Vice-Admiral George Pocock (*Yarmouth*) fought Commodore Comte d'Ache (*Zodiaque*) 15 miles S.E. of Negapatam, Madras. [bh]. Ships: *Elizabeth, Tiger, Weymouth, Yarmouth, Salisbury, Newcastle, Cumberland.* Frigate: *Queenborough.* Storeship: *Protector.* See 29th April and 10th September.
1801	*Pomone* captured the French *Carrère* to the southward of the Canale di Piombino, Italy.
1809	*Raven* engaged the batteries at Flushing and Breskens.
1811	*Raven* and *Exertion, Alert* and *Princess Augusta* hired cutters, with boats of *Quebec, Redbreast* and small craft based at Heligoland, captured four French gunboats at Nordeney, Friesland. [m]
1846	Boats of *Royalist* destroyed two pirate prahus off the Mantanani Islands, Borneo.
1901	*Viper,* first turbine-driven destroyer, wrecked.
1916	*Clacton* torpedoed by U-boat off Levant.
1918	Russian *Askold,* of five-funnel fame, taken over at Murmansk as *Glory IV.*
1940	U.25 sunk by mine in N Sea.
1941	First success by Fighter Catapult Ships. Hurricane of 804 Sq (*Maplin*) shot down a Focke-Wulf in Atlantic. (Convoy SL.81)
1941	*Hydrangea, Wanderer* and *St. Albans* (Nor) sank U.401 S.W. of Iceland. (Convoy SL.81)
1942	P.247 (later *Saracen*) sank U.335 off the Faeroes.
1943	GC: Lieutenant Hugh Randall Syme GM and bar, RANVR for bomb and mine disposal (*Gazette* date).
1944	*Quorn* sunk by German one-man submarine in Seine Bay. Operation Neptune.
1953	*Dauntless* commissioned at Burghfield.

4th AUGUST

1800	*Belliqueux* captured the French *Concorde: Bombay Castle* and *Exeter* Indiamen captured the French *Medée* 500 miles N.E. of Rio de Janeiro.
1801	Vice-Admiral Lord Nelson's indecisive bombardment of the Boulogne invasion flotilla.
1804	Admiral Duncan, Viscount Camperdown, died.
1835	*Raleigh* (second of the name) in a typhoon 160 miles S.75° W. of Formosa.
1855	Boats of *Rattler* and the USS *Powhatan,* towed by *Eaglet,* captured ten pirate junks at Kau lan.
1858	*Staunch* destroyed two pirate junks and recaptured their prize off Tau Pung.
1903	King Edward VII opened RN College, Osborne; before it was closed in 1921 it sent 3,967 cadets to RN College Dartmouth.
1914	War declared against Germany.
1915	C.33 lost in N Sea.
1918	British forces arrived at Baku, Caspian Sea.
1921	Promotion of Prince Louis of Battenberg to Admiral of the Fleet.
1940	FAA a/c attacked barges and oil tanks at Rotterdam.
1942	*Croome, Sikh, Tetcott, Zulu* and Wellington M/203 sank U.372 off Jaffa (32° 00' N, 34° 00' E.).
1943	Sunderland G/423 (RCAF) sank the supply U-boat U.489 in Atlantic (61° 11' N, 14° 38' W.).
1943	*Roberts* bombarded the road and railway at Taormina, Sicily.
1943	*Arrow* damaged beyond repair in explosion of ammunition ship in Algiers harbour.
1960	*Discovery* became flagship of Admiral Commanding Reserves until the post was abolished in 1976.

5th AUGUST

1583   First settlers arrived in Newfoundland (*Golden Hind, Delight, Squirrel and Swallow*).

1781   Vice-Admiral Hyde Parker (*Fortitude*) fought Rear-Admiral Johan Zoutman (*Admiraal De Ruyter*) on the eastern end of the Dogger Bank. [bh]. Ships: *Berwick, Dolphin, Buffalo, Fortitude, Princess Amelia, Preston, Bienfaisant.* Frigates etc., with fleet: *Artois, Belle Poule, Cleopatra, Latona, Surprise* cutter, Frigates, etc., with convoy of 200 merchantmen: *Tartar, Alert, Cabot* brigs, *Leith* armed ship; *Busy, Sprightly* cutters. Regiment: 97th.

1781   *Maidstone* captured the American privateer *Montgomery* off Newfoundland.

1798   *Indefatigable* captured the French *Heureux* off Bayonne and wrecked her prize, *Canada*.

1799   Admiral of the Fleet Earl Howe died.

1813   Landing party from *Milford* and *Weazle* destroyed a battery and a signal tower at Ragosniza (Rogoznica), Yugoslavia.

1858   First Atlantic cable laid by *Agamemnon* and the USS *Niagara*.

1864   White ensign allotted to RN, blue to RNR and red to MN.

1864   *Grasshopper* destroyed four pirate junks at Kau lan.

1873   RN Artillery Volunteers formed.

1914   *Lance* and *Landrail* sank the German mine layer *Königin Luise* 30 miles East of Aldeburgh Napes (see 6th August).

1914   *Gloucester* detected *Goeben* in Messina by wireless interception (first RN use of ESM in War).

1917   *Chagford* torpedoed by U.44, 120 miles NW of Tory Island, N Ireland; (abandoned and sunk on 7th August).

1919   GC (ex-AM): Lieutenant E.G. Abbott for saving life after explosion in ex-German *Baden* at Invergordon.

1943   *Red Gauntlet* sunk by the German S86 off Harwich.

1944   *Stayner* and *Wensleydale* sank U.671 off Brighton.

A Sea Hurricane on a merchant ship's catapult. Used for convoy protection in the Atlantic (1941-43). The pilot had to ditch his aircraft close to a ship and be picked up. The aircraft was sacrificed.

Sunderland Flying Boat

6th AUGUST

1497   Cabot (*Matthew*) returned to Bristol after first English voyage of discovery, to Newfoundland.

1798   *Espoir* captured the Genoese pirate *Liguria* 12 miles to the southward of Marbella, Spain. [m]. One officer of the 28th Regiment was present.

1805   *Blenheim,* escorting a convoy, beat off the French *Marengo* and *Belle-Poule* 1,380 miles East of Mauritius.

1826   *Hope* captured the Brazilian slaver *Prince of Guinea* off Wyhdah, Dahomey.

1885   First night gunnery practice by search light — *Alexandra*.

1861   First edition of Queen's Regulations and Admiralty Instructions — "QR & AI".

1914   *Amphion* sunk by German mine laid by *Königin Luise* 35 miles East of Aldeburgh Napes (see 5th August).

1914   *Bristol* fought *Karlsruhe* 250 miles N.E. of Eleuthera Island, Bahamas: *Karlsruhe* escaped.

1915   Suvla landing began in Dardanelles Campaign (ended on 15th August).

1918   *Comet* torpedoed in Mediterranean.

1940   German Type C magnetic mine exploded under examination in mining shed at *Vernon*: 5 killed.

1942   *Thorn* sunk N of Derna by Italian t.b. *Pegaso*.

1942   *Assiniboine* (RCN) sank U.210 in N Atlantic (54° 25' N, 39° 37' W.). (Convoy SC.94)

1944   *Loch Killin* and *Starling* sank U.736 in the Bay of Biscay.

1944   *Bellona, Tartar, Ashanti,* with *Haida* and *Iroquois,* (both RCN) sank all four ships of a convoy and three of the escort off Île d'Yeu, Bay of Biscay.

Coastal Forces in Portsmouth Harbour.

220

7th AUGUST

1657   Admiral Robert Blake died, at sea one hour short of Plymouth, — "at the entering of the Sound, Death seized him".

1781   *Helena*, reinforced by *Repulse* and *Vanguard*, gunboats and boats of ships at Gibraltar, fought fourteen Spanish gunboats in Gibraltar Bay.

1807   *Hydra* bombarded the defences at Bagur, Spain; her boats cut out the Spanish *Prince Eugene*, *Belle Caroline* and *Carmen del Rosario*. [m]

1815   Napoleon sailed from Plymouth in *Northumberland* to exile in St. Helena.

1826   Third class engineer Thomas Brown became first RN Engineer officer.

1844   *Phlegethon* (Ben.Mar.), *Jolly Bachelor* and boats of *Dido* destroyed the Sakarran pirates' stronghold at Patusan.

1864   *Grasshopper* destroyed 20 pirate junks at Kau lan, and burnt the village of Pak shui.

1873   Formation of the Royal Navy Artillery Volunteers.

Convoy SC.94, August 1942

Convoy SC.94 comprised 33 ships escorted by one destroyer and 3 corvettes. It was a slow, East-bound Atlantic convoy, and met problems caused by fog in the first few days. On 5th August, the fog began to clear, and stragglers joined the main body. On that day, a U-boat sank one merchant ship, and then homed other U-boats onto the convoy. On 6th a series of attacks started. The Canadian destroyer *Assiniboine* had a running gun battle with U.210 and sank her after ramming her twice, but was so damaged that she had to return to base. The slower corvettes held off the attackers until late on 8th, when 5 ships were lost in one attack, and another sank later after falling out of the convoy. The *Dianthus*, however, sank U.379 after depth charge attacks and ramming her 5 times.

Two destroyers joined the escort on 8/9th, and the fog cleared sufficiently for air cover to be provided. However, 4 more ships were lost before the air cover arrived on 9th. On 13th the convoy reached British ports, having lost one third of its original strength. However, the sparse escort did well to sink 2 U-boats and damage 4 others, and to hold off the repeated attacks of no less than 18 U-boats without air assistance.

1914   *Gloucester* pursued the German *Goeben* and *Breslau* off Cape Matapan.

1940   Nine Skua aircraft of 801 Sq (Hatston) destroyed petrol storage tanks at Dolvik (Hardangersfjord).

1941   *Severn* sank the Italian s/m *Michele Bianchi* W. of Gibraltar.

The Hedgehog

The clever U-Boat captain early in the war was well aware that a ship could only attack him whilst he was submerged by steaming over his position to drop depth charges. He could plan his avoiding action accordingly. The Hedgehog, an ahead firing weapon, changed the pattern. Not only could he not know when an attack would come, but he did not even know he was being attacked until one of the bombs hit his vessel.

8th AUGUST

1758 Commodore the Hon. Richard Howe *(Pallas)* and Lieutenant-General Thomas Bligh destroyed the port of Cherbourg. Ships: *Essex, Jason, Montague, Portland, Rochester.* Frigates: *Active, Brilliant, Flamborough, Fowey, Maidstone, Pallas, Renown, Richmond, Rose, Success, Tartar.* Sloops: *Diligence, Saltash, Speedwell, Swallow, Swan.* Fireships: *Pluto, Salamander.* Bombs: *Furnace, Grenado, Infernal.* Bomb Tenders: *Endeavour, Nancy, Neptune* and 10 others.

1796 *Mermaid* fought the French *Vengeance* off Basse Terre, Guadeloupe.

1798 *Indefatigable* captured the French *Vaillante* a few miles to the northward of Cape Machichaco, Spain.

1815 *Malta* and *Berwick* at the reduction of Gaeta, Italy. [m]

1914 *Astraea* bombarded Dar-es-Salaam.

1914 U.13 made first submerged attack of World War I, firing a torpedo which missed *Monarch* off Fair Isle.

1915 E.11 sank the Turkish *Barbarousse Hairedene* in the Dardanelles.

1915 *India* sunk by U.22 in the entrance to Vestfjord.

1915 *The Ramsey* sunk by the German *Meteor* off Moray Firth.

1917 VC: Lieutenant Charles George Bonner, RNR and P.O. Ernest Pitcher *(Dunraven)*. *Dunraven* engaged UC.71 off Ushant (48° 00' N, 7° 37' W.). Disabled and taken in tow by *Christopher,* but sank on the 10th in 48° 38' N, 5° 28' W.

1918 Zeppelin L70 shot down by RAF over Immingham: *Scamber* recovered code books.

1918 *Opossum* destroyed UC.49, already damaged by one of her own mines.

1922 *Raleigh,* sixth of the name, wrecked off Pt Amour, Belle Isle Strait, Labrador. Ten lives lost.

1942 *Dianthus* sank U.379 in Atlantic (57° 11' N, 30° 57' W.). (Convoy SC.94)

1944 *Regina* (RCN) sunk by U.667 off Trevose Head. (Convoy EBC.66)

1944 *Valiant* damaged in collapse of floating dock at Trincomalee.

P.O.Pitcher VC with the Royal Family, taken at an exhibition of naval pictures held in London towards the end of World War I — l to r, King George V, Queen Mary, Pitcher, Queen Alexandra, General Sir Dighton Probyn, the oldest VC then living.

9th AUGUST

1573 Drake returned from his first voyage in command.

1666 "Sir Robert Holmes his Bonefire" in Terschelling Roads. Ships: *Advice, Assurance, Dragon, Fanfan, Garland, Edward and Eve, Hampshire, Pembroke, Seaflower, Sweepstakes, Tiger.* Fire-ships (expended): *Fox, Lizard, Richard, Samuel.*

1780 A convoy of 63 sail for the East and West Indies, escorted by *Ramillies, Southampton* and *Thetis* taken by a Franco-Spanish fleet 300 miles N.N.E. of Maderia. 55 of the convoy were captured.

1781 *Iris* captured the American *Trumbull* off the Delaware.

1799 *Speedy* captured three Spanish tartans in a bay to the eastward of Cape de Gata.

1810 *Caroline, Piedmontaise* and *Barracouta* captured Banda Neira Island, Moluccas. [m*, m, bh]. Troops: 2/56th and Madras European Regiment.

1854 VC: Commander J. Bythesea and Stoker W. Johnstone (*Arrogant*) on island of Wardo in the Baltic overcame 5 soldiers with important despatches and brought the latter back.

1855 Bombardment of Helsinki by Rear-Admirals the Hon. Richard Dundas (*Duke of Wellington*) and Charles Penaud (*Tourville*). Ships: *Aeolus, Amphion, Arrogant, Belleisle, Cornwallis, Cossack, Cruizer, Dragon, Duke of Wellington, Edinburgh, Euryalus, Exmouth, Geyser, Hastings, Lighting, Locust, Magicienne, Merlin, Pembroke, Princess Alice, Vulture.* Gunboats: *Badger, Biter, Dapper, Gleaner, Lark, Magpie, Pelter, Pincher, Redwing, Skylark, Snap, Snapper, Starling, Stork, Thistle, Weazel.* Mortar Vessels: *Beacon, Blazer, Carron, Drake, Grappler, Growler, Havock, Manly, Mastiff, Pickle, Porpoise, Prompt, Redbreast, Rocket, Sinbad, Surly.* Rocket boats of: *Arrogant, Cossack, Dragon, Duke of Wellington, Edinburgh, Euryalus, Exmouth, Geyser, Magicienne, Pembroke, Vulture.* French Ships: *Austerlitz, Pelican, Tourville, La Tempête* gunboat.

1856 *Cambridge* commissioned as Plymouth gunnery training ship: ashore in 1907.

1862 *Snake* destroyed four pirate junks in Sandy Bay, St. John Island, Virgin Islands. (Operations lasted three days).

1914 *Birmingham* rammed and sank U.15 120 miles E.S.E. of the Orkneys. (First U-boat sunk by RN).

1914 *Goeben* and *Breslau* passed the Dardanelles despite the Mediterranean Fleet — "the explanation is satisfactory but the result unsatisfactory" (Churchill).

1915 *Lynx* sunk by mine laid in Moray Firth by *Meteor,* sunk on her way home by Harwich Force.

1916 B.10 sunk by Austrian aircraft at Venice, while under repair.

1917 *Recruit* mined in N Sea.

1926 H.29 foundered at Devonport.

1942 Night action off Savo Island (9° 15' S., 159° 40' E.): U.S. and Australian forces fought Japanese surface forces. [bh]. RAN ships: *Australia, Canberra, Hobart. Canberra* damaged and abandoned; sunk by USS *Selfridge.*

Allied amphibious forces were operating off Guadalcanal. The Japanese sent 5 heavy cruisers and 2 light cruisers to attack the transports off shore. Bad air reconnaissance led to inaccurate information being passed to the Amphibious Force, the enemy being reported as 3 cruisers and 2 seaplane carriers. The enemy was able, therefore, to approach without being detected. The Allied cruiser force was scattered around the various entrances to the transports' operation area. The alarm was raised by a US destroyer at 0143 on 9th but the Japanese were then close to the USS *Chicago* and HMAS *Canberra.* The latter was hit by shells and torpedoes and had to be sunk later. No enemy report was made, and the Japanese force was therefore able to come upon another force of Allied cruisers by surprise. Two American cruisers were hit and capsized, the third later blew up. The Japanese failed to take advantage of their success and retired without attacking the transports. Only the US Cruiser *San Juan* and the Australian cruisers *Hobart* and *Australia* and 8 destroyers were undamaged. Faulty intelligence had led to bad dispositions, and this nearly led to a complete disaster. In commemoration of HMAS *Canberra* the USN renamed a *Baltimore* class cruiser the *Canberra,* and she is the only USN ship named after a foreign capital City.

1943 *Aurora* and *Penelope* bombarded enemy targets at Castellamare.

9th AUGUST

1943 *Simoom* sank the Italian destroyer *Vincenzo Gioberti* off Spezia.

1944 *Wren* (second of the name; see 27th July) and Liberator C/53 sank U.608 in Bay of Biscay.

1945 T.F. 37 (BPF) and U.S. 3rd Fleet continue attacks on Japan: Kamaishi bombarded, air strikes along East coast, North of Yokohama.

1945* VC: T/Lieutenant (A) Robert Hampton Gray, DSC, RCNVR (*Formidable* – 1841 Corsair Sq.) at the sinking of the Japanese frigates *Amakusa* and *Inagi* off Japan (38° 26' N, 141° 30' E.).

The citation reads "for great valour in leading from the aircraft carrier *Formidable* an attack on the Japanese destroyers in Onagawa Wan, in the Japanese island of Honshu. In the face of fire from shore batteries and a heavy concentration of fire from 5 warships, Lieutenant Gray pressed home his attack, flying very low in order to ensure success. Although he was hit and his aircraft was in flames, he obtained at least one direct hit sinking the destroyer. Lieutenant Gray has consistently shown a brilliant fighting spirit and most inspiring leadership." The award of the VC was posthumous.

1952 MiG 15 Jet Fighters attacked a flight of RN Sea Furies over Korea. 1 MiG shot down by Lt. Carmichael and 3 damaged. 2 Furies damaged.

1956 Plymouth gunnery range at Wembury commissioned as *Cambridge*.

*Lt. (A) Robert Hampton Gray, VC, DSC, RCNVR

* 9th August 1945

On the day the second atomic bomb was dropped by the Americans on Nagasaki the British Pacific Fleet achieved a record in the quantity of bombs dropped and ammunition fired on any day by the Fleet Air Arm. The four fleet carriers achieved a record for a single day's operational flying with 407 sorties by their Corsairs, Avengers, Fireflies, and Seafires. More than 60 Japanese aircraft were destroyed. Six destroyers, 2 escort vessels, a submarine chaser and a torpedo boat were sunk as well as a number of small craft.

HMS *Formidable* refitting at Cook Dock, Sydney after suffering damage from Kamikaze attacks

10th AUGUST

1512   *Regent* (ex-*Grace Dieu* and the Navy's first two decker) fought the French *Marie la Cordelière* in Camaret Bay, France. Both ships blew up.

1675   Royal Observatory Greenwich founded.

1778   Commodore Sir Edward Vernon *(Ripon)* fought a French squadron of 5 ships under Captain Tronjoly *(Brillant)* off Pondicherry, India. Ships: *Cormorant, Coventry, Ripon, Seahorse; Valentine.* (Indiaman).

1780   *Flora* captured the French *Nymphe* 9 miles to the westward of Ushant.

1794   Capitulation of Calvi, Corsica, to the forces under Lieutenant-General the Hon. Charles Stuart and Captain Horatio Nelson *(Agamemnon)*. Guns were landed from the fleet. The French *Melpomene* and *Mignonne* taken. Ships: *Agamemnon, Britannia, Victory.* Frigates: etc. *Aigle, Aimable, Dido, Dolphin, Fox, Imperieuse, Inflexible, Lowestoffe, Lutin.* Regiments: 18th, 30th, 51st.

1805   *Phoenix* (36) captured the larger French *Didon* (44) 150 miles West of Cape Finisterre. [m, bh]

1813   Commodore Sir James Yeo *(Wolfe)* engaged the American Lake Squadron, under Commodore Isaac Chauncey, on Lake Ontario, capturing the *Growler* and *Julia* schooners.

1855   Continuation of the bombardment of Helsinki. (See 9th August) Additional ship: *Volcano*. Rocket boats of: *Arrogant, Cossack, Dragon, Duke of Wellington, Edinburgh, Euryalus, Exmouth, Pembroke, Vulture.*

1940   *Translyvania* sunk by U.56 off N. Ireland.

1942   *Islay* sank the Italian s/m *Scire* off Haifa.

1942   Pedestal convoy passed Gibraltar on route for Malta.

1942   Wellington H/311 (Czech) sank U.578 in SW Approaches.

1943   *Uganda* and *Flores* (Neth) bombarded enemy positions North of Reposto.

1943   *Parthian* sunk by mine on passage from Malta to Alexandria.

1945   Continuation of operations against Japanese mainland (See 17th July — 9th August). [bh]. Main body of BPF retired after this operation.

HMS *Flora* capturing *Nymphe* **1780**

11th AUGUST

1415   Henry V sailed from Southampton: "fair stood the wind for France".

1673   The last battle of the Third Dutch War. Prince Rupert fought Admiral de Ruyter with 64 ships off the Texel. [bh]. Red Sq: *Sovereign, London, Charles, Royal Katherine, Henry, Victory, French Ruby, Edgar, Warspite, Old James, Triumph, Resolution, Rupert, Monmouth, Mary, Crown, Advice, Pearl.* Blue Sq: *Prince, St. Andrew, Royal Charles, Cambridge, St. George, Unicorn, Henrietta, Dreadnought, Lion, Gloucester, Dunkirk, Monck, Bristol, Bonadventure, Ruby, Success, Guernsey, St. Michael, Swiftsure, Rainbow, York, Greenwich, Hampshire, Portsmouth, Foresight, Sweepstakes.* White Sq: *Fairfax, Plymouth, Anne, Happy Return, Princess, Newcastle, Yarmouth, Leopard, Stavoreen, Mary Rose, Diamond, Swallow, Assurance, Falcon, Nonsuch (or Portland).* Fireships: *Blessing, Friendship, Hopewell, Katherine, Pearl, Leopard, Prudent Mary, Society, Supply, Truelove* (All expended in action). *Laurence.* Yachts: *Henrietta*[1], *Katherine*[2]. Doggers: *Hard Bargain*[2], *Roe*[1], *Rose*[1]. Sloop: *Dolphin*[1]. 1. Sunk. 2. Captured. White Sq: Vice Admiral Comte d'Estrées *(Reine)* with 29 French ships. (See 28th May: Add *Diamant, Pompeux, Royale-Thérèse;* less *Conquérant*).

1782   *Placentia* captured the American privateer *Lord Stirling* off Newfoundland.

HMS *Indomitable, Victorious* and *Eagle* with the Pedestal Convoy

1799   *Courier, Plyades and Espiegle* captured the Dutch (ex-British) *Crash* off Schiermonnikoog. [m]. (Boat of *Juno* also engaged.)

1808   Evacuation by Rear-Admiral Richard Keats *(Superb)* of the Spanish troops from Nyborg, Baltic. Boats of the squadron captured the Danish *Fama* and *Salorman.* [m]. Ships: *Brunswick, Edgar, Superb, Hound, Devastation.*

1808   *Comet* captured the French *Sylphe* 170 miles South of Ushant. [m, bh]

1809   The Walcheren campaign. The Royal Navy escorted and supported a large invasion force that attempted to seize control of the estuary of the River Scheldt, which the French were using as a naval base. After some initial successes, the expedition was forced to withdraw. Over 100 ships of all sizes were involved and a naval brigade was landed. (The campaign began 30th July and lasted until December of that year).

1858   Commodore the Hon. Keith Stewart *(Nankin)* and Major-General Sir Charles Van Straubenzee captured Nam tau, to punish the firing by the Chinese on a flag of truce. Ships: *Nankin, Sampson, Sans Pareil, Canton* (hired P. and O.) *Adventure* (Storeship). Gunboats: *Cormorant, Starling.* Troops: Royal Artillery, Royal Engineers, 59th Regiment; 12th Madras Native Infantry.

1902   Chaplain of the Fleet granted the ecclesiastical dignity of an Archdeacon as well as ranking as a Rear-Admiral.

1918   Flotilla of six 40-ft CMBs sunk or interned after a daylight action with German aircraft off Ameland. Operation No 5. Sunk: CMBs 40, 42, 47. Interned: CMBs 41, 44, 48.

1942   *Eagle* sunk by U.73 South of Majorca. Operation Pedestal.

1943   VC: Flying Officer Lloyd Allen Trigg, RNZAF, in Liberator D/200 sank U.468 off Gambia (12° 20'N., 20° 07'W.), but was shot down and killed.

1944   *Starling* and Sunderland P/461 (RAAF) sank U.385 in the Bay of Biscay.

12th AUGUST

1795 Hydrographer's Department established by Order in Council.

1809 *Monkey* and boats of *Lynx* cut out three Danish lugger privateers off Dais Head (Darsser Ort), Baltic.

1812 Boat of *Minstrel* fought a battery at Benidorm, near Alicante.

1814 Boats of *Star* and *Netley* cut out the American *Ohio* and *Somers* on Lake Erie.

1844 Boats of *Dido* destroyed Seriff Mulah's town in the Sungei Undop, Borneo.

1858 *Shannon's* Naval Brigade (A/Captain F Marten) returned on board from the Upper United Provinces. (See 18th August)

1914 *Minotaur* and *Newcastle* bombarded Yap, Caroline Islands.

1914 U.13 sunk in N Sea.

1915 First enemy ship sunk by torpedo from British seaplane (at the Dardanelles.).

1917 *Oracle* sank the German U.44 12 miles West of Stavanger.

Short 184 Seaplane releasing torpedo, 1915

1941 *Picotee* (RCN) sunk by U.568 in N Atlantic (62° 00'N., 16° 00'W.). (Convoy ON(S).4)

1942 Operation Pedestal. *Cairo* torpedoed by the Italian s/m *Axum* off Bizerta (37° 40'N., 10° 06'E.): sunk by own forces. *Foresight* torpedoed by Italian aircraft off Bizerta (37° 45'N., 10° 10'E.): taken in tow by *Tartar*, but had to be sunk next day. *Ithuriel* and *Pathfinder* sank the Italian s/m *Cobalto* off Bizerta (37° 39'N., 10° 00'E.).

1942 *Wolverine* sank the Italian s/m *Dagabur* off Algiers (37° 12'N., 1° 51'E.).

1943 *Scarab* bombarded the road near Cape Schiso, Italy. *Roberts*, *Uganda* and *Soemba* (Neth) bombarded targets on the right flank of the 8th Army.

1944 Sunderland A/461 Sq. (RAAF) sank U.270 and Halifax F/502 sank U.981 in the Bay of Biscay.

1944 *Findhorn* and *Godavari* (RIN) sank U.198 N.W. of Seychelles (3° 35'S., 52° 49'E.) aided by Avenger of 851 Sq. (*Shah*).

13th AUGUST

1704 Battle of Velez Malaga. Admiral Sir George Rooke *(Royal Katherine)*, with an Anglo-Dutch fleet of 51 sail of the line, fought the Franco-Spanish fleet under Admiral Comte de Toulouse *(Foudroyant)* 25 miles S.S.E. of Marbella. [bh]. Ships: van *Yarmouth, Norfolk, Berwick, Prince George, Boyne, Newark, Garland, Lenox, Tilbury, Swiftsure, Barfleur, Namur, Orford, Assurance, Nottingham, Warspite, Roebuck.* centre *Burford, Monck, Cambridge, Kent, Royal Oak, Suffolk, Bedford, Shrewsbury, Monmouth, Eagle, Royal Katherine, St. George, Mountague, Nassau, Grafton, Firm(e), Kingston, Centurion, Torbay, Ranelagh, Dorsetshire, Triton, Essex, Somerset, Charles Galley, Lark, Newport, Panther, Swallow, Tartar.* Fireships: *Firebrand, Griffin, Hunter, Lightning, Phoenix, Vulcan, Vulture.* Bombs: *Hare, Terror.* Yacht: *William and Mary.* Hosp. Ship: *Princess Anne, Jefferies.* Dutch. *Dort, Ann of Friesland, Lion, Bavaria, (?Batavier), Albermarle, Ann of Utrecht, Flushing; Nymwegen, Gelderland, Unie, Damiaten, Katwijk, Mars.* Fireship: 1. Bombs: 2. Flags: v. *Prince George,* V.A. Sir John Leake. *Barfleur,* Adm. Sir Cloudesley Shovell. c. *Kent,* R.A. Thomas Dilkes. *Royal Katherine,* Adm. Sir George Rooke. *Ranelagh,* R.A. George Byng. r. *Albermarle,* Lt-Adm. Gerard van Callenburgh. *Unie,* R.A. Baron Wassenaer. Captured: French *Cheval-Marin* and two galleys.

1762 Capture of Havana by Admiral Sir George Pocock *(Namur)*, Admiral Keppel and his brother, the Earl of Albemarle. [bh]. Ships: *Alcide Belleisle, Cambridge, Centaur, Culloden, Defiance, Devonshire, Dragon, Dublin, Edgar, Hampton Court, Intrepid, Marlborough, Namur, Nottingham, Orford, Pembroke, Ripon, Stirling Castle, Temeraire, Temple, Valiant.* 50's and smaller: *Alarm, Bonetta, Boreas, Centurion, Cerberus, Cygnet, Dover, Echo, Enterprize, Ferret, Glasgow, Lizard, Mercury, Porcupine, Richmond, Sutherland, Trent, Viper.* Bombs: *Basilisk, Grenado, Thunder.* Cutter: *Lurcher.*

1780 *Bienfaisant* and *Charon* captured the French privateer *Comte d'Artois* off the Old Head of Kinsale.

1799 *Crash* and *Undaunted* and boats of *Latona, Juno, Courier, Espiegle* and *Pylades* destroyed the Dutch *Vengeance* and captured a battery on Schiermonnikoog, together with a large row-boat and 12 schuyts. [m]

1810 Landing parties from *Sirius* and *Iphigenia* captured a battery on Île de la Passe, off Mauritius.

1844 Boat of *Hyacinth* captured the Brazilian slaver *Aventureiro* off Little Fish (Mossamedes) Bay, Angola.

1915 *Royal Edward* (transport) sunk by the German UB.14 4 miles South of Kandeliusa, Aegean Sea.

1916 *Lassoo* torpedoed by U-boat off Maas lightvessel.

1917 *Bergamot* sunk by U.84 in Atlantic while serving as Q-ship.

1918 *John Gillman, John Brooker, Miranda II, Viola* and *Florio* sank UB.30 off Whitby.

1940 *Auckland* and *Kimberley* bombarded Italian troops near El Sheik 40 miles West of Berbera.

1942 *Manchester* torpedoed by the Italian MA/SBs 16 and 20 off Kelibia; abandoned and scuttled, albeit prematurely by own crew. Operation Pedestal.

1942 Bombardment of Rhodes (Operation M.G.4) — diversion to facilitate the passage of the 'Pedestal' convoy. Ships: *Arethusa, Cleopatra; Javelin, Kelvin, Sikh, Zulu.*

1943 *Aurora, Penelope, Jervis* and *Paladin* bombarded Vibo Valentia, Calabria.

1943 *Unbroken* torpedoed the Italian cruisers *Bolzano* (CTL) and *Muzia Attendolo.*

14th AUGUST

1697 *Torbay, Defiance, Devonshire, Restoration* and *Betty* fought Commodore Baron de Pointis *(Sceptre),* with five ships, 200 miles S.W. of the Scilly Islands. An unsuccessful chase was maintained for two days after the action.

1779 *Raisonnable, Blonde, Galatea, Greyhound, Camilla* and *Virginia* captured or destroyed an American force of 17 ships and 24 transports in the Penobscot River, Maine.

1781 *Camelion* destroyed a Dutch dogger 18 miles N.W. of the Texel.

1782 David Tyrit (Navy Office spy) executed on Southsea Common.

1803 *Lord Nelson* Indiaman taken by the French privateer *Bellone* in the approaches to the Bay of Biscay.

1804 Boats of *Galatea* repulsed in an attempt to cut out the French *Général Énouf* (ex-British *Lily*) in Anse à Mire, The Saints.

1813 *Pelican* captured the American *Argus* 15 miles West of St. Davids Head, St. George's Channel. [m, bh]

1900 Relief of the Peking Legations by Allied forces. Naval Brigade from *Aurora, Centurion, Endymion, Barfleur. Fame, Phoenix, Terrible.*

1916 *Rembrance (Lammeroo,* Q-ship) sunk by U.38 in the Aegean.

1917 *First Prize* (Q.21) sunk by the German UB.48 N.W. of Ireland.

1917 VC: Skipper Thomas Crisp, RNR *(Nelson).* (Posthumous). *Ethel and Millie* and *Nelson* sunk by UC.63 off Mabelthorpe, Lincolnshire.

1940 *Malcolm* and *Verity* engaged 3 German E-boats and 6 trawlers off the Texel, sinking one E-boat and one trawler. Operation P.O.

1943 *Aphis, Cockchafer* and *Flores* (Neth) bombarded the coast road at Taormina, Sicily. *Dido, Panther* and *Sirius* bombarded Scaletta, Italy.

1943 *Saracen* sunk by the Italian corvette *Minerva* off Bastia.

1944 *Duckworth, Essington* and Liberator G/53 sank U.618 in Bay of Biscay.

Capture of *Lord Nelson* **by French Privateer** *Bellone*

14th AUGUST

Operation Pedestal

Operation Pedestal consisted of a convoy of 14 merchant ships protected by 3 forces of warships; Force Z consisted of *Nelson, Rodney, Eagle, Indomitable* and *Victorious* with 3 cruisers and 14 destroyers; Force X consisted of *Nigeria, Kenya, Manchester* and *Cairo* (cruisers) and 11 destroyers; the remaining force consisted of 8 submarines.

A number of diversionary attacks were also arranged. In spite of losing 9 of the 14 merchant ships, one aircraft carrier, 2 cruisers and one destroyer sunk, and one aircraft carrier and 2 cruisers badly damaged, the arrival of 5 of the merchant ships (including the tanker *Ohio* — almost sinking) enabled Malta to survive the siege. Two Italian cruisers were torpedoed by submarines and one Italian submarine sunk. Operation Pedestal was considered to be a victory for allied arms.

Leading Seaman Bill Stroud's Story

"As we steamed through the Western Med, I was in charge of a twin 4in mounting in the *Manchester*. We were part of the August Malta convoy. I pointed out my old ship *Eagle* to the lads. "With that old lady over there", I said, "we're safe as houses". That moment we heard 3 loud thumps and she started to list. Within a few minutes she was gone.

From then on it was "action stations" non-stop. We lived on sandwiches, slept at our gun, and used a bucket as our "heads".

We had no idea of time as attacks by aircraft and submarines went on and on. Soon after midnight on the 13th we were attacked by a squadron of Italian E-boats. They came at us from 45^0 on the bow and we fired everything we had at them. Two of them broke away and passed astern out of our line of fire. Seconds later the torpedo hit us in the engine room.

The hydraulics went off so we carried on training and elevating the turrets by hand. It was just as well that Nobby Grant, our "training number", was a Navy athlete. After a while we were listing so much we couldn't get the gun round. We were stopped and helpless. We were being attacked all the time so the Captain ordered us to abandon ship and scuttle her. We were off Cape Bon and he told us to keep together in the water and try to get ashore to the right of the lighthouse, which was Vichy French territory.

Some destroyers came back to pick us up, but they were being strafed by aircraft all the time and only managed to get 250 of us. Some of us in the water were hit during the strafing; then the scuttling charges blew and *Manchester* settled down stern first. We got ashore after about 9 hours in the sea and were interned by the French in a Spahi camp in the Sahara. We were all starving then and we had bugs and "desert feet". Only the Red Cross parcels kept us going. In November there was an enemy air-raid and our guards ran off, so we smashed up the camp and burnt it down. Next day an American armoured column came with some buses to get us. By the next Spring I was back in the Med in the *Anthony* as a Petty Officer, getting some of my own back off Sicily".

Bill Stroud 1943

Bombardment of Kagoshima 1863

230

15th AUGUST

1416   Battle of Harfleur. Admiral Sir Walter Hungerford and Prince John, Duke of Bedford, defeated a Franco-Genoese fleet and relieved the town of Harfleur.

1660   First Royal Yacht presented to King (*Mary*).

1761   *Bellona* captured the French *Courageux*. *Brilliant* fought the French *Hermione and Malicieuse*. Both actions to the south-westward of Cape Finisterre. [bh]

1805   *Goliath* captured the French *Faune* 250 miles West of La Rochelle.

1805   Entry, pay and pension of Masters regulated by Order in Council.

1805   Establishment of Fourth RM Division at Woolwich (proceeded 11th September).

1807   *Comus* captured the Danish *Frederikscoarn* between Vinga Beacon and The Skaw. [m, bh]

1809   Boats of *Otter* cut out two French vessels at Rivière Noire, Mauritius.

1853   RN Coast Volunteers formed: abolished 1873.

1863   Bombardment of the Kagoshima forts, Japan, by Vice-Admiral Augustus Kuper (*Euryalus*). Ships: *Argus, Coquette, Euryalus, Perseus, Racehorse; Havock, Pearl*. Five of the squadron carried between them 21 Armstrong breech-loaders. These had 28 accidents in firing 365 rounds, ie one for 13 rounds, which led to a return to muzzle loading.

1918   *Scott* and *Ulleswater* torpedoed by U-boat off Dutch coast.

1918   Concept of a single Imperial Navy rejected by Dominion Prime Ministers.

1938   *Sheffield* fitted with first RN Radar.

1943   *Aphis, Brocklesby* and *Soemba* (Neth) bombarded the East coast road to Messina, in support of the right flank of the Army.

1943   GC: Dudley William Mason, Master, *Ohio*. s.s. *Ohio*, a fast American tanker on charter, eventually reached Grand Harbour, Malta: the culmination of Operation Pedestal. The fuel she carried enabled air strikes to be resumed from Malta — itself awarded the GC — as Rommel was preparing his final offensive against Alexandria.

1944   Landing of U.S. and French troops in South France begins. [bh]. Operation Dragoon. (British Carrier Force withdrawn on 27th). Ships: *Ailsa Craig, Ajax, Aldenham, Antares, Antwerp, Aphis, Arcturus, Argonaut, Aries, Atherstone, Attacker, Aubrieta, Aurora, Bardolf, Barford, Barholm, Barmond, Beaufort, Belvoir, Bicester, Black Prince, Blackmore, Borealis, Brave, Brecon, Brixham, Bruiser, Bude, Caledon, Calm, Calpe, Catterick, Cleveland, Clinton, Colombo, Columbine, Crowlin, Delhi, Dido, Eastway, Eggesford, Emperor, Farndale, Foula, Haydon, Highway, Hunter, Keren, Khedive, Kintyre, Larne, Lauderdale, Liddesdale, Lookout, Mewstone, Nebb, Oakley, Octavia, Orion, Polruan, Prince Baudouin, Prince David, Prince Henry, Prins Albert, Prinses Beatrix, Product, Pursuer, Ramillies, Rhyl, Rinaldo, Rosario, Rothesay, Royalist, Satsa, Scarab, Searcher, Sirius, Skokholm, Spanker, Stalker, Stormcloud, Stornoway, Stuart Prince, Teazer, Tenacious, Termagant, Terpsichore, Thruster, Troubridge, Tumult, Tuscan, Tyrian, Ulster Queen, Welfare, Whaddon, Zetland*. FAA Sq.: Hellcat 800 (*Emperor*), Seafire 807 (*Hunter*), 809 (*Stalker*), 879 (*Attacker*), 899 (*Khedive*), Wildcat 881 (*Pursuer*), 882 (*Searcher*) MBs 2009, 2022, 2026, 2027, 2171, 2172. MLs: 121, 273, 299, 336, 337, 338, 451, 456, 458, 461, 462, 463, 469, 471, 555, 557, 559, 560, 562, 563, 564, 567, 576, 581.

Convoys were sailed from Naples, Taranto, Brindisi, Malta, Palermo and Oran. 86,575 men; 12,520 vehicles and 46,140 tons of stores were landed over the beachhead in the 64 hours following the first landing. The Navy was called upon to provide gunfire support, and much ammunition was used, the cruiser *Argonaut* alone firing 394 rounds of 5.25 in ammunition.

15th AUGUST

1944 *Orchis* sank U.741 off Fécamp. (Convoy FTC.68)

1944 *Mauritius, Iroquois* (RCN) and *Ursa* attacked a convoy between Sables d'Olonne and La Pallice, driving several of the escort and convoy ashore.

1945 Japanese surrender. End of World War II.

"From C.-in-C. Fifth Fleet to Fifth Fleet Pacific.
The war with Japan will end at 1200 on 15th August. It is likely that Kamikazes will attack the fleet after this time as a final fling. Any ex-enemy aircraft attacking the fleet is to be shot down in a friendly manner."

15th August 1945
As the combined US and British fleet sailed for Tokyo to achieve the surrender of the Japanese, strikes were launched into the Tokyo area. During the last strikes of the war on 15th August the Fleet Air Arm aircraft were attacked by a dozen Japanese aircraft. Eight of the attacking aircraft were shot down and the rest damaged. One Seafire was shot down in the Tokyo area. The pilot, Sub-Lieutenant F.C.Hockley, RNVR, bailed out and was taken prisoner: he was executed by his captors, who were subsquently convicted as War Criminals.

The British Pacific Fleet
By the end of the war in August 1945 the Fleet Air Arm consisted of 59 carriers, 3,700 aircraft and more than 72,000 officers and men. Of those aircraft carriers 34 were operational in the Far East on VJ Day.

A Whale, an invasion pier for the unloading of supplies and transport

16th AUGUST

1652 Captain Sir George Ayscue *(Rainbow)*, with 40 ships, fought Rear-Admiral de Ruyter *(Neptune)*, in charge of a Dutch convoy, to the southward of Plymouth.

1778 *Isis* fought the French *César* 60 miles E. by S. of Sandy Hook. Regiment: the light company of the 23rd.

1801 Second unsuccessful boat attack by the squadron under Vice-Admiral Lord Nelson *(Medusa)* on the Boulogne invasion flotilla. Boats of: 1st Div. *Eugenie, Jamaica, Leyden.* 2nd Div. *Medusa, Minx, Queensborough* cutter. 3rd Div. *Discovery, Explosion, Express, Ferriter, Gannet, Providence, York. Hunter* and *Greyhound* (Revenue cutters). Royal Artillery in Howitzer boats.

1805 *Goliath* captured the French *Torche* off Cape Prior.

1846 Boats of *Iris* and *Phlégethon* (Ben. Mar.) destroyed the pirate stronghold of Haji Samon in the Sungei Membakut, Borneo.

1854 Bombardment and reduction of Bomarsund by Vice-Admiral Sir Charles Napier *(Duke of Wellington)*, Rear Admiral Charles Penaud *(Trident)* and British and French troops. Ships: *Ajax, Amphion, Arrogant, Belleisle, Blenheim, Bulldog* (flag for attack), *Driver, Duke of Wellington, Edinburgh, Gladiator, Hecla, Hogue, Leopard, Penelope, Pigmy, Valorous; Lightning.* Troops: Marine Battalion. French ships: *Asmodée, Cocyte, Darien, Duperre, Phlégeton, Trident.* French Troops: Chasseurs.

1861 Moorsom percussion fuze introduced into RN.

1915 *Inverlyon* (armed smack) sank UB.4 3 miles N. by E. of Smith's Knoll spar buoy (52° 46'N., 2° 10'E.), hitting her with first shot.

1915 Harrington, near Whitehaven, shelled by a German submarine.

1917 *Saros* (Q-ship) sunk in Straits of Messina.

1940 GC (ex-EGM): Lieutenant John Niven Angus Low and Able Seaman Henry James Miller, *Unity* (Posthumous) for saving lives of others by giving their own when their submarine was sunk in collision with a neutral merchantman in the N Sea.

Bombardment of Bomarsund 1854

17th AUGUST

1779   *Ardent* taken by a French fleet 18 miles S.S.E. of Plymouth.

1796   Vice-Admiral the Hon. Sir George Elphinstone, later Lord Keith (*Monarch*), received the surrender of Rear-Admiral Engelbertus Lucas (*Dordrecht*) and his squadron in Saldanha Bay, S. Africa.

1801   *Guachapin* captured the Spanish letter of marque *Teresa* between Martinique and St. Lucia.

1804   *Loire* captured the French privateer *Blonde* 240 miles to the westward of the Scilly Islands.

1875   Reed succeeded as Chief Constructor by his brother-in-law, Nathaniel Barnaby who became first DNC.

1895   Capture of M'baruk ibn Raschid's town of M'wele by Naval Brigade from *Barrosa, Phoebe, Racoon, St. George, Thrush, Widgeon*; *Blonde* was also awarded the medal. Troops: 24th and 26th Bombay Native Infantry, East Africa Protectorate Force, Zanzibar Government Army, Indian Native Field Hospital (B Section). Medal: Ashantee — M'wele 1895 (or 1895-6) engraved on the rim.

1940   Bombardment of Bardia and Fort Capuzzo. Operation M.B.2., Ships: *Kent, Malaya* (Rear Admiral H. D. Pridham-Wippell), *Ramillies, Warspite* (Admiral Sir Andrew Cunningham).

1943   *Euryalus, Penelope, Jervis* and *Paladin* bombarded Scalea.

17 August — 30 August 1941
HMS *Manxman*, fast minelayer, left England on 17th disguised as a French cruiser. After passing Gibraltar she hoisted the Tricolour and her crew dressed in French uniforms. During the night of 25th, she removed her disguise, laid mines in the Gulf of Genoa off Leghorn and then retired at high speed, resuming her disguise again to reach Gibraltar. She was back in England on 30th.

Officers and men of a Naval Brigade in Africa, late nineteenth-century.

18th AUGUST

1665 Establishment of Sheerness yard "And thence to Sheernesse, where we walked up and down, laying out the ground to be taken in for a yard to lay provision for cleaning and repair of ships; and a most proper place it is for that purpose" Samuel Pepys' Diary.

1759 Admiral the Hon. Edward Boscawen *(Namur)* defeated Commodore de La Clue Sabran *(Ocean)* off Lagos, Portugal. [bh]. Ships: *America, Conqueror, Culloden, Edgar, Guernsey, Intrepid, Jersey, Namur, Newark, Portland, Prince, St. Albans, Swiftsure, Warspite.* Frigates, etc.: *Active, Ambuscade, Etna, Favourite, Gibraltar, Glasgow, Gramont, Lyme, Rainbow, Salamander, Shannon, Sheerness, Tartar's Prize, Thetis.* Captured: *Centaure, Modeste, Téméraire.* Burnt: *Ocean, Redoutable.*

1798 *Leander* taken by *Généreux* 5 miles West of Gavao Island S.W. of Crete.

1811 *Hawke* captured the French *Héron* and three transports; drove ashore and wrecked twelve more of the convoy and three of the escort about 4 miles N.E. of Pointe de la Percée, North coast of France. [m]

1813 Boats of *Undaunted, Redwing* and *Espoir* and boats of the squadron blockading Toulon stormed the batteries at Cassis, between Marseilles and Toulon, capturing 3 gunboats and 25 coasters.

1857 First party of *Shannon's* Naval Brigade (Captain William Peel) left the ship at Calcutta for Allahabad, proceeding by river steamer and flat.

1915 E.13 stranded on Saltholm, wrecked by German gunfire, interned by Danes and sold for scrap in 1919.

1917 Flying boat 9860 sank UB.32 off Cape Barfleur.

1919 VC: Commander Claude Congreve Dobson (CMB 31) and Lieutenant Gordon Charles Steele (CMB 88). *Vindictive* and CMBs attack on Kronstadt, sinking the Russian *Andrei Pervozanni*[1], *Pamiat Azov*[2] and *Petropavlovsk*[1]. CMBs.: 4, 23[3], 31. 62[3], 72, 79[3], 86,88. RAF: 8 aircraft. [1]Sunk by 31,88. (67 foundered whilst on passage out to the Baltic. [2]Sunk by 79. [3]Sunk in action.

1919 *Kent's* detachment reached Vladivostok, from service in the Urals 4,500 miles West.

1923 L.9 foundered at Hong Kong: salvaged but scrapped.

1941 P.32 sunk by mine off Tripoli whilst attacking a convoy.

1943 Hudson 0/200 and Wellington HZ/697 (Fr) sank U.403 off Gambia in 14° 11' N., 17° 40' W.

1944 *Ottawa, Chaudière* and *Kootenay* (all RCN) sank U.621 and Sunderland W/201 sank U.107 in Bay of Biscay.

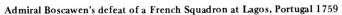

Admiral Boscawen's defeat of a French Squadron at Lagos, Portugal 1759

235

19th AUGUST

1702   Vice-Admiral John Benbow *(Breda)* began to fight Captain Jean Ducasse *(Heureux)* 6 leagues N. by W. of Santa Marta, Colombia. Ships: *Breda, Defiance, Falmouth, Greenwich, Pendennis, Ruby, Windsor.* French: *Ann Galley, Apollon, Heureux, Prince-de-Frise.* Captains Kirby and Ware subsequently shot for cowardice. Captain Ducasse agreed with this sentence: see 23rd August.

1711   Edward Boscawen born.

1782   *Duc de Chartres* captured the French *Aigle* 36 miles S.E. by S. of Cape Henry, Virginia.

1801   *Sybille* captured the French *La Chiffone* in Mahe Roads, Seychelles.

1812   *Guerriere* taken by the American *Constitution* about 500 miles S.E. of Halifax.

1840   *Druid, Hyacinth, Larne* and *Enterprize* (Ben. Mar) destroyed a Chinese fort outside Macao. Troops: Bengal Volunteer Regiment.

1844   Boats of *Dido* destroyed six war prahus and the town of Karangan, Borneo.

1845   Boats of *Agincout, Cruizer, Daedalus, Vestal, Vixen* and *Wolverine, Nemesis* and *Pluto* (Ben. Mar.) destroyed the pirate stronghold of Seriff Osman in the Sungei Malloodoo (Marudu).

1915   GC (ex-AM): Chief Petty Officer M.S. Keogh, *Ark Royal,* for saving life of pilot of crashed and burning aircraft.

1915   *Baralong* (Q-ship) sank U.27 in SW Approaches.

1916   E.23 torpedoed German battleship *Westfalen* off Terschelling. E.1 torpedoed *Moltke* in the Gulf of Riga.

1916   *Nottingham* sunk by U.52 off the Farnes. She and *Falmouth* (see next day) were among the screen for the Grand Fleet as it went South to intercept the High Seas Fleet, known to be at sea: this was its main sortie after Jutland and before surrender. It intended to bombard Sunderland but E.23's success caused its withdrawal.

1941   *Bath* (Nor) sunk by U.201 in S W Approaches. (Convoy OG. 71)

1941   *Aquilla* sunk with loss of 21 WRNS Cypher Officers and Senior Rates.

1942*   Raid on Dieppe by Captain J Hughes-Hallett *(Calpe)* and Major-General J H Roberts (2nd Canadian Division). [bh]. Ships: *Albrighton, Alresford, Berkeley, Bleasdale, Brocklesby, Calpe, Duke of Wellington, Fernie, Garth, Glengyle, Invicta, Locust, Prince Charles, Prince Leopold, Prins Albert, Princes Astrid, Princes Beatrix, Queen Emma.* 9th Minesweeper: *Bangor, Blackpool, Bridlington, Bridport, Rhyl, Sidmcuth, Tenby.* 13th Minesweeper: *Blyth, Clacton, Eastbourne, Felixstowe, Ilfracombe, Polruan, Stornoway.* MGBs: 50, 51, 312, 315, 316, 317, 320, 321, 323, 326, MLs 114, 120, 123, 171, 187, 189, 190, 191, 193, 194, 208, 214, 230, 246, 291, 292, 309, 343, 344, 346, SGBs 5, 6, 8, 9, Polish: *Slazak. Berkeley* sunk by own forces after being bombed. Operation Jubilee.

The raid on Dieppe was mounted :

a.) To give Canadian troops newly arrived in UK battle experience, b.) To gain experience of assault techniques, and c.) To try out new equipment that was being developed. Dieppe offered many targets, including a radar station, a fighter airfield, gun batteries and port installations. It was also within range of UK shore-based fighter aircraft. The final plan incorporated a main assault on the harbour, and attacks on each flank. 237 naval vessels were used, 4961 Canadian Army personnel, 1057 Commandos and a small number of US Rangers were landed, and 67 squadrons of aircraft were in support. The assault started early on 19th. No 4 Commando achieved complete success on the Western Flank, but the reverse was true on the Eastern Flank where the enemy were alerted by the assault force meeting a coastal convoy. In the main assault even the beach was not fully secured, and evacuation was delayed until 1100 hours by too rigid a timetable. By 1230, 1000 men had been recovered from the beach, but one destroyer *(Berkeley)* was damaged by air attack and had to be sunk, and another *(Calpe)* was also hit.
33 landing craft were also lost, and there were 3363 Canadian casualties and 247 Commando casualties. The Germans lost only 600 men from all services, and 48 aircraft. British aircraft losses were 106.
The enemy were jubilant, and criticised the raid for 'too much precision and detailed arrangement'. However, the British learnt many lessons, e.g. the need for heavy gunfire support even with air cover. Many lives were saved in the bigger operations that followed such as in Normandy.
19th August is the *Memorable Date of 40 Commando RM.*

1943   *Tui* (RNZN) and U.S. aircraft of VS/57 sank the Japanese s/m 1.17 in South Pacific.

20th AUGUST

1702 Vice-Admiral Benbow continued to fight Captain Ducasse. (See 19th August).

1765 Harrison explained his fourth chronometer to Board of Longitude.

The Board of Longitude.

British seamen beginning to explore and chart the world could establish their latitude with ease, but longitude could only be achieved by measuring the difference of time between the meridian altitude of the sun and its meridian altitude at Greenwich. In 1714, at the instigation of the Admiralty, a Board of Longitude was set up, offering an award of £20,000 for the construction of a chronometer within a set degree of accuracy. A number of clock-makers took up the challenge, which was eventually won by John Harrison with his fourth chronometer. Captain Cook took a number of these chronometers on his voyages.

1799 *Clyde* captured the French *Vestale* 20 miles W. by N. of Cordouan lighthouse.

1800 *Seine* captured the French *Vengeance* in the Mona Passage. [m, bh]

1824 Boats of *Icarus* captured the pirate schooner *Diableto* at Cayo Blanco, Cuba.

1864 *Royal Sovereign,* only turret ship built of wood and first ship in RN to carry her main armament outside her hull, completed.

1896 First RN Wireless transmission *(Defiance).*

Defiance, a wooden ship of the line, at Devonport, was the first ship to receive a morse transmission. Her Captain, Captain H. B. Jackson, developed the device, and later worked with Marconi in his trials. Marconi's first major trials of radio in Britain were not carried out until the autumn of that year. On 20th May, 1897, the radio was demonstrated at ranges up to 2 miles by the *Defiance,* at anchor, and *Scourge,* under way.

1914 German cruiser *Magdeburg's* code books captured.

During an engagement between Russian and German warships off the Gulf of Finland (20th Aug 1914) the German light cruiser *Magdeburg* ran aground in fog. As the Russian fleet approached the German Captain sent a ship's officer in a rowing boat to drop the naval code books in the deep water. The officer was swept into the sea. After the Russians had finished off the *Magdeburg,* the Russian Captain ordered as many as possible of the German bodies in shallow water to be recovered for burial. Virtue had its own reward. Among the bodies recovered was that of a petty officer with the lead covers of the code books in his arms. The Russians sent down divers and recovered the code books, which they passed to the British. Thereafter German signals were deciphered by the Naval Intelligence Department in Room 40 in the Admiralty, until the codes were changed.

1916 *Falmouth* sunk after four torpedo attacks, the last by U.63 7½ miles South of Flamborough Head. (First torpedoed on the 19th by U.66, 65 miles off the Humber). See previous day.

1917 *Vala (Q.8)* sank UB.54 S.W. of the Scilly Islands.

1917 E.47 lost in N Sea.

1917 *Acton (Q.34)* sank the German UC.72 in Bay of Biscay.

1940 *Cachalot* sank U.51 in Bay of Biscay.

1943 Catalinas C/259 and N/265 sank U.197 off S. Madagascar (28° 40'S., 42° 36'E.).

1944 *Forester, Vidette* and *Wensleydale* sank U.413 off Brighton.

1944 *Chaudière, Kootenay* and *Ottawa* (all RCN) sank U.984 off Ushant.

Convoy forcing its way through frozen seas

21st AUGUST

1702	Vice-Admiral Benbow still fighting Captain Ducasse. (see 19th August)
1740	Admiral Vernon, nicknamed 'Old Grog' because of the grogram material in his boat-cloak, ordered watering of sailors' rum (called Grog thereafter). See 23rd March.
1797	*Penguin* captured the French privateer *Oiseau* and her prize 100 miles West of Ushant.
1798	*Hazard* captured the French *Neptune* 440 miles N.W. by W of Cape Finisterre.
1801	Boats of *Fisgard, Diamond and Boadicea* cut out the Spanish *Neptuno,* a gun boat and a merchant vessel from Coruna.
1810	Two unarmed boats of *Sirius* recaptured the ex-British East Indiaman *Windham* off Rivière Noire, Mauritius.
1860	British and French forces under Admiral Sir James Hope captured the Taku forts, China. Ships: *Chesapeake, Imperieuse, Coromandel* (tender). Gunboats: *Algerine, Clown, Drake, Forester, Havock, Janus, Opossum, Staunch, Woodcock.* French: *Impératrice-Eugénie.* Troops: Royal Artillery, Royal Engineers, RMLI Bn., 3rd, 44th and 67th Regiments; Madras Artillery.

1910	*Bedford* wrecked in Korean Sea.
1915	Crew of *Ruel,* whilst in their boats, fired on by U.38, (S.S.W. of Bishop Rock) first authenticated case of such behaviour.
1916	E.54 sank UC.10 E.S.E. of the Schouwen Bank lightvessel (51° 42' N., 3° 17' E.).
1917	Sopwith Pup N6430 (*Yarmouth*) destroyed Zeppelin L.23 near Lodbjerg Danish coast (56° 35' N., 7° 49' E.).
1917	UC.41 destroyed by trawlers off Tay estuary, having exploded one of her own mines.
1940	*Kylemore* sunk by German aircraft at Harwich.
1941	Start of convoys to North Russia.
1944	*Kite* sunk by U.344 N of Jan Mayen Island. (Convoy JW.59)
1944	*Alberni* (RCN) sunk by mine off St. Catherine's Point (50° 18'N., 0° 51'W.). Operation Neptune.
1944	*Orchis,* mined and beached off Normandy, pronounced CTL.

A King George V class battleship in rough seas.

The deck of a cruiser in the Northern seas

22nd AUGUST

1702 Vice-Admiral Benbow continued to fight Captain Ducasse. (see 19th August).

1778 *Minerva* taken by the French *Concorde* to the northward of Haiti.

1795 *Stag* captured the Dutch *Alliantie* off Jedder (Jeaderen), Norway.

1798 *Alcmene* captured the French *Légère* 12 miles to the westward of Alexandria.

1916 E.16 mined in Heligoland Bight.

1940 3 Swordfish of 824 Sq. (*Eagle*) sank a depot ship, a destroyer and the s/m *Iride* in the Gulf of Bomba, bound for a 'chariot' raid on Alexandria.

1943 *Easton* and *Pindos* (Greek) sank U.458 off Scilly. (Convoy MKF.22)

1944 *Nabob* and *Bickerton* torpedoed by U.354 off Hammerfest (71° 42'N., 19° 11' E.). *Bickerton* sunk by *Vigilant*. (Convoy JW.59)

1944 Swordfish C/825 (*Vindex*) sank U.344 off N Norway. (Convoy JW.59)

1944 *Loyalty* (ex-*Rattler*) sunk by U.480 near E3 buoy off the Nab (50° 09' N., 0° 41'W.). Operation Neptune.

1944 *Spiteful* bombarded the oil tanks at Christmas Island, Pacific.

Anson short-range (radius of 250 miles) shore-based aircraft

23rd AUGUST

1702 Vice-Admiral Benbow in the fifth day of his inconclusive action with Captain Ducasse. (see 19th August). Recapture of *Anne* Galley.

Letter from Captain Ducasse to Admiral Benbow after the battle:
"Sir,
I had little hope on Monday but to have supped in your cabbin (sic); but it pleased God to order it otherwise. I am thankful for it. As for those cowardly captains who deserted you, hang them up, for by heaven, they deserve it."

1794 *Flora* and *Arethusa* drove the French *Espion* and *Alerte* ashore in Audierne Bay, *Alerte* becoming a total wreck. *Diamond, Artois, Diana* and *Santa Margarita* drove the French *Volontaire* ashore off Penmarc'h Point, where she was abandoned and destroyed.

1796 *Galatea* and *Sylph* drove ashore and destroyed the French *Andromaque* near Arcachon.

1798 *Naiad* captured the French *Décade* off Cape Finisterre.

1806 *Arethusa* and *Anson* captured the Spanish *Pomona* under the guns of Morro Castle, Havana, and destroyed nine gunboats and drove three others ashore. [m]

1810 *Nereide* taken by the French *Bellone* in Grand Port, Mauritius.

1853 *Surprise* and two boats of *Cambrian* captured or destroyed 28 pirate junks at Lingting Island.

1854 *Miranda* destroyed the defences and burnt the town of Kola, White Sea.

1883 Royal Corps of Naval Constructors established by Order in Council.

1914 *Kennet* fought the German S.90 off Tsingtau.

1937 *Codrington* and *Repulse* procured release of British ship taken by Spanish republican cruiser *Miguel de Cervante*.

1940 *Hostile* mined off Cape Bon (36° 53' N., 11° 19' E.); sunk by *Hero*.

1941 P.33 sunk by mine off Tripoli.

1941 *Zinnia* sunk by the German U.564 off Oporto (40° 25' N., 10° 40' W.). (Convoy OG.71)

239

24th AUGUST

1217 Battle of Sandwich: Hubert de Burgh's victory over Eustace the Monk off Dover.

Louis of France had invaded England and occupied London on the death of King John. There he was besieged, and a large fleet was gathered at Calais to relieve him. Hubert de Burgh was governor of Dover Castle at the time, and he gathered 16 Cinque Port ships and 20 others to attack the French Fleet. It was a small fleet, and the people were at first unwilling to fight. De Burgh said, "You shall suffer me to be hanged before ye surrender this castle; for it is the key to England".
The fleet sailed out against the 80 French ships, gained the weather gauge, and grappled and fought the enemy ships at will. 65 were captured after a savage fight. De Burgh was made Lord High Admiral for this service.

1702 Vice-Admiral Benbow stopped fighting Captain Ducasse. (see 19th August).

1806 Boats of *Alexandria* and *Gracieuse* destroyed two Spanish vessels at La Hacha, Colombia.

1810 *Magicienne* burnt by own crew to avoid capture at Grand Port, Mauritius.

1831 RN Long Service and Good Conduct medal introduced.

1939 Home Fleet and all ships in Home Ports proceeded to War Stations.

1940 Bombardment of seaplane base at Bomba, N Africa. Ships: *Diamond, Ilex, Juno, Waterhen.* (10th DF)

1940 *Ladybird* and *Waterhen* attacked shore targets at Bardia, N Africa. Operation M.B.1.

1940 *Penzance* sunk by U.37 in N Atlantic (56° 16'N., 27° 19'W.). (Convoy SC.1)

First Long Service and Good Conduct Medal

1941 Raid on Spitzbergen by Rear-Admiral P Vian *(Nigeria).* Ships: *Antelope, Anthony, Aurora, Nigeria; Empress of Canada.* Operation Gauntlet.

1943 *Nubian, Tartar* and *Tumult* bombarded Lucri.

1943 Wellington J/179 sank U.134 off Portugal.

1944 *Louis* sank U.445 in the Bay of Biscay.

1944 Carrier air strikes on the German battle-ship *Tirpitz* in Altenfjord, to synchronise with the passage of Convoy JW.59. Operation Goodwood — repeated on the 29th. *Tirpitz* hit, but not seriously damaged. FAA Sq.: Barracuda 826, Corsair 1841, 1842 — *(Formidable),* Seafire 801; Barracuda 827 — *(Furious),* Barracuda 820; Seafire 887, 894; Firefly 1770; Hellcat 1840 — *(Indefatigable).*

1944 *Indomitable* (Rear-Admiral C Moody) and *Victorious* launched air strikes on Emmahaven and on the cement works at Padang, Sumatra. Operation Banquet. FAA Sq.: Barracuda 815, 817; Hellcat 1839, 1844 — *(Indomitable),* Barracuda 831, Corsair 1834, 1836 — *(Victorious).*

1944 *Keppel, Loch Dunvegan, Mermaid, Peacock,* and Swordfish M/825 *(Vindex)* sank U.354 off Murmansk. (Convoy JW.59)

1946 GC (ex-AM): Lieutenant E.W.K. Walton for saving life during Antarctic survey.

FAA Barracudas on their way to attack the *Tirpitz*: 3rd April

240

25th AUGUST

1553   *Henry Grace à Dieu* burnt.

1707   *Nightingale,* escorting a convoy of 36 sail, taken by six French galleys off Harwich. The convoy escaped.

1795   *Venerable, Repulse, Minotaur* and *Venus* captured the French *Suffisante* off the Texel.

1795   *Spider* captured the French *Victorieuse* off the Texel. [m]

1800   *Success* captured the French *Diana* 50 miles to the northeastward of Malta.

1803   *Seagull* recaptured *Lord Nelson* Indiaman 300 miles W.S.W. of Ushant.

1810   *Sirius* burnt by own crew to avoid capture at Grand Port, Mauritius.

1811   *Diana* and *Semiramis* destroyed the French *Pluvier* and recaptured the ex-British *Teazer* off the mouth of the Gironde: their boats captured all five of a French convoy in the river.

1914   RM and RNAS units landed at Ostend; withdrawn 31st August.

1941   *Vascama* and Catalina J/209 sank U.452 in N Atlantic (61° 30' N., 15° 30'W.).

1942   *Marne, Martin* and *Onslaught* sank the German *Ulm* 100 miles East of Bear Island.

1942   *Aldenham* and *Eridge* bombarded the Daba area, Egypt.

1942   Battle of Eastern Solomons between U.S. and Japanese forces. Present: *Australia, Hobart* (both RAN).

1943   *Orion* bombarded the Calabrian coast.

1943   *Wallflower* and *Wanderer* sank U.523 in Atlantic (42° 03'N., 18° 02'W.). (Convoy KMS24/OG.92)

1944   French troops entered Toulon after bombardment by *Aurora, Black Prince* and US and French Ships.

1944   *Warspite* bombarded Brest.

1972   RN Museum Portsmouth formed from the Victory Museum and the McCarthy Nelson collection.

Quarterdeck of HMS *Royal Sovereign*

1780 Lord Hawke wrote to Geary "for God's sake, if you should be so lucky as to get sight of the enemy, get as close to him as possible. Don't let them shuffle with you by engaging at a distance but get within musket shot if you can: that will be the only way to gain great honour and to make the victory decisive".

1780 *Fame* privateer captured four French letters of marque — *Deux Frères, Univers, Nancy Pink* and ex-British *Zephyr* sloop — off Cap de Gata.

1795 Boats of *Agamemnon, Ariadne, Inconstant, Meleager, Tartar, Southampton* and *Speedy* cut out the French *Résolue, République Constitution, Vigilante* and five other vessels at Alassio and Laigueglia, Italy.

1799 *Tamar* captured the French *Républicaine* 80 miles to the north-westward of Surinam, Guiana.

1808 *Implacable* and *Centaur* captured the Russian *Sevolod* off Rogervik, Gulf of Finland, and burnt her next day. [m, bh]

1841 Capture of Amoy, China by Rear-Admiral Sir William Parker *(Wellesley)* and Lieutenant-General Sir Hugh Gough. Ships: *Algerine, Bentinck, Blenheim, Blonde, Columbine, Cruizer, Druid, Modeste, Pylades, Wellesley; Rattlesnake,* transport. Steamers: *Sesostris* (I.N.); *Nemesis, Phlegethon, Queen* (Ben. Mar). Troops: Royal Artillery, 18th, 26th, 49th and 55th Regiments; Madras Artillery, Madras Sappers and Miners.

1858 *Magicienne, Inflexible, Plover* and *Algerine* destroyed 100 pirate vessels. in the neighbourhood of Hong Kong and to the S.W. of Macao. (Operations lasted until 3rd September).

1914 *Highflyer* sank the German *Kaiser Wilhelm der Grosse* off Rio de Oro, Spanish West Africa, only ten days out from Bremen.

U570; the first intact German prize of the World War 2. 1941

27th AUGUST

1793   Occupation of Toulon by Lord Hood — held for six months.

1809   Boats of *Amphion* cut out six Venetian gunboats and destroyed a fort at Cortellazzo. [m]

1813   Capture of the island of Santa Clara, during the seige of San Sebastian, by boats of squadron and a detachment of the 9th Regiment. [m]. Ships: *Ajax, President, Revolutionnaire, Surveillante; Isabella* and *Millbank* transports.

1816   Bombardment of Algiers by Admiral Lord Exmouth *(Queen Charlotte)* and a Dutch squadron under Vice-Admiral Baron Theodorus van Capellen *(Melampus)*. [m, bh]. Ships: *Albion, Glasgow, Granicus, Hebrus, Impregnable, Leander, Minden, Queen Charlotte, Severn, Superb, Britomart, Cordelia, Heron, Mutine, Prometheus, Hecla, Beelzebub, Fury, Infernal,* Gunboats Nos. 1, 5, 19, 28, 24, *Falmouth* lighter and rocket boats. Dutch: *Amstel, Dageraad, Diana, Eendracht, Frederica, Melampus.* Troops: The Rocket Troop, RHA, Royal Sappers and Miners.

The Barbary coast of North Africa had long been the centre of piracy in the Mediterranean, and its corsairs had ventured as far afield as Scandinavia. After the defeat of Napoleon in 1815, the British government resolved to deal with the matter. Lord Exmouth with the Mediterranean fleet and a Dutch squadron went to Tunis, Tripoli and Algiers and offered treaties to the Deys prohibiting the taking of Christian slaves. The Dey of Algiers refused. A punitive expedition was mounted and the fleet anchored off Algiers 27th August 1816. The Port was very well defended with forts and guns. The defences of Algiers were destroyed by a furious bombardment. 1,200 Christian slaves were freed.

Letter from a 15 year old midshipman in *Severn:*
" ... Our sides, mast, yards, sails and rigging were as completely riddled as anything you ever saw, but notwithstanding we had next to the *Queen Charlotte* the very worst situation there, I suppose we have fewer men killed than any ship in the fleet, only 5 killed and 33 wounded. At 12 after we had expended every grain of powder in the ship we were obliged to hold off and luck it was that the Admiral had just made the signal to that effect, so we all anchored again within about 4 miles of the town. The next morning, what a sight there was, boat loads of dead going to be hoved over board and we could distinguish the dead piled up in heaps on shore. ... I don't think that in Algiers which is — was the strongest place next to Gibraltar in the world there are 3 guns left mounted upon the whole place and this time tomorrow there won't be so many stones one upon another." (1816).

Hudson medium-range (500 miles) aircraft

1896   Rear-Admiral Sir Harry Rawson (*St. George*) bombarded the Sultan's palace at Dar-es-Salaam, Zanzibar and sank his gunboat *Glasgow*. Ships: *St. George, Racoon, Philomel, Thrush* and *Sparrow.*

1917   *Hyderabad* launched; only vessel designed and built as a Q-ship.

1919   GC (ex-AM): Commander H. Buckle *(Tiger)* for saving life at Invergordon.

1940   *Dunvegan Castle* sunk by U.46 off Tory Island, N.W. of Ireland (55° 05'N., 11° 00'W.).

1941   Hudson S/269 (RAF) captured U.570 off Ireland: brought in by *Kingston Agate* and *Northern Chief*. 'Cypher machine captured intact'. Commissoned as HMS *Graph:* see 20th March.

1943   *Egret* sunk by glider bomb off Vigo (42° 10' N., 9° 22' W.).

1944   *Salamander* wrecked and *Britomart* and *Hussar* sunk by RAF Typhoon aircraft off Cap d'Antifer (49° 41'N., 0° 05'E.). (Operation Neptune).

Scimitar belonging to Dey of Algiers presented by him to Lord Exmouth as a token of his surrender.

243

28th AUGUST

1652 Captain Richard Badiley *(Paragon)* escorting a convoy of four sail, fought a Dutch squadron under Captain Johan van Galen 2 leagues South of Leghorn, near Montecristo. [bh]. Ships: *Paragon, Phoenix, Constant Warwick, Elisabeth.* Captured: *Phoenix.* The convoy escaped. (A partial engagement began during the afternoon of the 27th).

1799 Admiral Viscount Duncan *(Kent)* received the surrender of the Dutch fleet at the Texel. Ships: *Circe, Isis, Kent.* Wrecked: *Blanche, Contest, Lutine, Nassau.*

1810 *Iphigenia* taken by the French *Bellone, Minerve, Victor* and three other frigates at Grand Port, Mauritius.

1844 Capture of Colonia, Uruguay: Ships: *Gorgon, Satellite, Philomel.*

1914 Start of naval operation in West Africa with arrival of *Cumberland* and *Dwarf* at Lome.

1914 Battle of the Heligoland Bight.[bh]. Ships: *Lion, Queen Mary, Princess Royal, Invincible, New Zealand, Badger, Beaver, Jackal, Sandfly.* 1 LCS: *Birmingham, Falmouth, Liverpool, Lowestoft, Nottingham, Southampton.* Cruiser Force C: *Aboukir, Amethyst, Bacchante, Cressy, Euryalus, Hogue.* 1 DF: *Acheron, Attack, Hind, Archer, Ariel, Lucifer, Llewellyn, Ferret, Forester, Druid, Defender, Goshawk, Lizard, Lapwing, Phoenix.* 3 DF: *Lookout, Leonidas, Legion, Lennox, Lark, Lance, Linnet, Landrail, Laforey, Lawford, Louis, Lydiard, Laurel, Liberty, Lysander, Laertes, Arethusa,* S/Ms.: *D.2, D.8, E.4, E.5, E.6, E.7, E.8, E.9; Lurcher, Firedrake.* German ships sunk: *Ariadne, Köln, Mainz,* V.187. British War Medal: clasp "Heligoland 28 Aug 1914" approved but not issued.

Although close blockade by the Battle Fleet became obsolete as the mine, submarine and torpedo were introduced, the Grand Fleet still determined to exercise its supremacy of the sea. In August 1914, the light cruiser force from Harwich made a sweep into the Heligoland Bight, tempting German forces out to the guns of the Battle Cruisers under Beatty. The plan succeeded, and three German cruisers and one destroyer were sunk.

Rear-Admiral Richard Kempenfelt (1718-1782)

*Of Swedish extraction, Kempenfelt served in the Caribbean under Vernon and for a considerable period of time in the Far East. He was considered one of the most thoughtful officers of his time, and is remembered for his transformation of the Fleet signalling system, used to great effect by Howe at Gibraltar (1782), and for his introduction of the divisional system. He was drowned when the *Royal George* capsized at Spithead. He has been quoted as writing, "there is a vulgar notion that our seamen are braver than the French. Ridiculous to suppose courage is dependent upon climate. The men who are best disciplined, of whatever nationality they are, will always fight the best ... it is a maxim that experience has ever confirmed, that discipline gives more force than numbers."

1918 *Ouse* and aircraft B.K. 9983 sank UC.70 off Whitby.

1940 First German acoustic mine dropped.

1941 Landing party from *Triumph* demolished the railway bridge near Caronia, N. Sicily.

1942 *Oakville* (RCN) and U.S. VP/92 sank U.94 in Caribbean, S of Haiti.

1943 *Ultor* sank the Italian t.b. *Lince* off Punta Alice (39° 24' N., 17° 01' E.).

1960 Admiral of the Fleet Sir Charles Forbes died.

29th AUGUST

1350	Battle of L'Espagnols sur Mer. Edward III (*Thomas*) defeated the Spanish fleet under Don Carlos de la Cerda off Winchelsea. (First battle in which cannon were used at sea).
1572	Matthew Baker appointed Master Shipwright.
1583	*Delight* lost with all hands off Nova Scotia.
1782*	*Royal George* capsized and sank at Spithead, with loss of Admiral Kempenfelt and most of her crew.
1800	Boats of *Renown, Impetueux, London, Courageux, Amethyst, Stag, Amelia, Brilliant* and *Cynthia* cut out the French privateer *Guêpe* near Redondela, Vigo Bay. [m]
1807	*Plantagenet* captured the French privateer *Incomparable* 50 miles S by W of Lizard Head.
1810	*Dover* and detachments of the Madras European Regiment and Madras Coast Artillery captured Ternate, Moluccas. [bh]
1810	*Queen Charlotte* fought a large French cutter (ex British Revenue cutter *Swan*) 10 miles N.N.E. of Alderney.
1814	Destruction of Fort Washington and capitulation of Alexandria, Potomac River. [m]. Ships: *Seahorse, Euryalus, Devastation, Aetna, Meteor, Erebus, Fairy, Anna Maria*.
1877	Alfred Dudley Rogers Pound born.
1918	UB.109 sunk in controlled minefield off Folkstone.
1939	Admiralty ordered mobilisation of Fleet.
1942	*Arunta* (RAN) sank the Japanese s/m Ro.33 off New Guinea (9° 36'S., 147° 06'E.).
1960	Admiral of the Fleet Sir Charles Lambe died.

HMS *New Zealand*

30th AUGUST

1779	*Boreas* captured the French *Compas* to the eastward of Montserrat.
1799	Admiral Mitchell (*Isis*) received further Dutch surrenders: see 28th.
1806	Boats of *Bacchante* cut out three Spanish vessels at Santa Marta, Colombia.
1806	*Pike* captured a Spanish schooner off Isla de Pinos, Cuba.
1854	Preliminary attack on Petropavlovsk, Kamchatka. Ships: *President, Pique, Virago*, French ships: *Forte, Eurydice, Obligado*. Suicide of Rear-Admiral Price, C in C of British Pacific squadron.
1943	*Stonecrop* and *Stork* sank U.634 in N Atlantic (40° 13'N., 19° 24'W.). (Convoy SL.135/MKS.22). First attacked on 29th.

Experimental firing of a Torpedo, 1870's

245

31st AUGUST

1591	*Revenge* taken by a Spanish fleet under Don Alonzo de Bazan off the Azores. [bh]

The *Revenge*, under Sir Richard Grenville, was at Flores in the Azores with other British ships when a superior force of Spanish ships was sighted. The *Revenge* stayed to recover sick men onshore, and was engaged by the Spanish when she set sail. She fought for 15 hours against no less than 53 enemy ships, and was boarded 15 times, repulsing each attack. Finally she was forced to surrender after sinking 4 enemy ships, and with Sir Richard Grenville mortally wounded.

1607 *Psyche* captured the Dutch *Scipio*, *Ceres* and *Resolutie* 9 miles West of Samarang, Java, and destroyed two Dutch merchant vessels at Samarang.

1782 Fall of Trincomalee.

1810 *Repulse* and *Philomel* fought a French squadron off Hyères.

1817 Admiral Sir John Duckworth died.

1855 VC: Boatswain Joseph Kellaway (*Wrangler*). Destruction of Russian stores at Lyapina, near Mariupol', Sea of Azov, by *Wrangler* and rocket boats of *Vesuvius*.

1870 First unsuccessful RN trial of Whitehead torpedo (*Oberon*).

1877 *Temeraire* launched, having largest spars ever carried (115 ft).

1939 Admiralty ordered general mobilisation of naval Reserves.

1940 *Esk* sunk by mine N.W. of the Texel (53° 25' N, 3° 48' E.).

1940 Swordfish aircraft of 812 Sq. FAA (disembarked) bombed oil tanks at Rotterdam.

1943 *Nelson*, *Rodney* and *Orion*, in Messina Strait, bombarded the Calabrian coast. Operation Hammer.

HMS *Temeraire*; became *Indus II* in 1904, *Akbar* in 1915, b/u 1921; she was the last armoured ship in the RN to enter harbour under sail alone (1891). Nickname "The Great Brig"

246

1st SEPTEMBER

1781   *Chatham* captured the French *Magicienne* 9 miles East of Boston lighthouse.

1812   Boats of *Bacchante* cut out the French *Tisiphone*, two gunboats and all seven of a convoy in the Canale di Leme. [m]

1814   *Avon* sunk by the American *Wasp* 230 miles W.S.W. of Ushant.

1859   *Pearl's* Naval Brigade at Dhebrahia, with detachments of 13th Light Infantry, Bengal Yeomanry, 6th Madras Light Cavalry and 27th Madras Native Infantry.

1867   Launch of *Cerebus*: first ship to dispense with sail and to have fore and aft guns.

1870   First successful RN firing of Whitehead torpedo.

1875   *Iron Duke* rammed and sank *Vanguard* during a thick fog in the Irish Sea, near the Kish lightvessel (53° 13' N, 5° 46' W.): first RN capital ship lost in collision and an inadvertent demonstration of power of the ram.

1898   Bombardment of Omdurman, Sudan (Captured on the 2nd). Gunboats: *Abu Klea, Fateh, Melik, Metemmeh, Nasr, Sheikh, Sulan Tamai.*

1919   *Vittoria* torpedoed by Bolshevik submarine *Pantera* in Gulf of Finland.

1940   *Ivanhoe* mined off the Texel (53° 25' N, 3° 48' E.): sunk by *Kelvin.*

1940   Nine Skua aircraft of 800 and 803 Sq. *(Ark Royal)* attacked Elmas airfield, Sardinia. Operation Smash.

1944   *Hurst Castle* sunk by U.482 off Tory Island NW of Ireland (55° 27' N, 8° 12' W.).

1944   *St. John* and *Swansea* (both RCN) sank U.247 off Land's End (49° 54' N, 5° 49' W.).

1944   *Malaya* bombarded the batteries on Cezembre Island, off St. Malo.

1958   First fishery dispute began with Iceland over her unilateral extensions of fishing zone.

1968   FOAC became FOCAS.

HMS *Agamemnon* **in dry dock at Malta, 1887, showing her ram.**

2nd SEPTEMBER

1762   *Lion* captured the French *Zephyr* 100 miles S.S. by W. of Ushant.

1762   *Aeolus* destroyed the Spanish *San Jose* at Aviles, N.W. Spain.

1801   *Pomone, Phoenix* and *Minerve* drove ashore the French *Succès* on Vada shoal, and *Bravoure* 4 miles South of Leghorn. *Succès* was captured and refloated; *Bravoure* became a total loss.

1801   Capitulation of Alexandria (Egypt) to the forces under Admiral Lord Keith *(Foudroyant)* and Lieutenant-General Sir John Hutchinson. The French *Justice* and five other ships captured. [m]

1801   *Victor* fought the French *Flèche* to the north-eastward of the Seychelles Islands.

1807   Bombardment of Copenhagen by the fleet under Admiral James Gambier *(Prince of Wales)* and shore batteries erected by Lieutenant-General Lord Cathcart. Ships: *Agamemnon, Alfred, Brunswick, Captain, Centaur, Defence, Dictator, Ganges, Goliath, Hercule, Inflexible, Leyden, Maida, Mars, Minotaur, Nassau, Orion, Pom-* *pee, Prince of Wales, Resolution, Ruby, Spencer, Superb, Valiant, Vanguard.* Frigates: *Africaine, Comus, Franchise, Nymphe, Sybille,* Gunbrigs: *Desperate, Fearless, Indignant, Kite, Pincher, Safeguard, Tigress, Urgent.* Bombardment Flotilla: *Aetna, Cruizer, Hebe* (hired), *Mutine, Thunder, Vesuvius, Zebra.*

1917   *s.s. Olive Branch* torpedoed by U.28 off Hammsfort. Gunfire from the U-boat exploded the ammunition carried in No 4 hold and *Olive Branch* blew up. U.28 was wrecked by the explosion and sank.

1918   VC: Chief Petty Officer George Prowse, DSM, RNVR, Drake Battalion RND, France: for gallantry in attack on the Hindenburg Line. Last award on blue ribbon.

1919   Caspian flotilla mission accomplished.

1944   *Keppel, Mermaid, Peacock, Whitehall* and Swordfish A/825 *(Vindex)* sank U.394 off Lofoten Is.

1944   *Glenavon* foundered in Seine Bay.

1945   Japanese delegates signed surrender in *USS Missouri*, Tokyo Bay.

Admiral Sir Bruce Fraser signing the Japanese surrender documents in USS *Missouri*

3rd SEPTEMBER

1780   *Vestal* captured the American packet *Mercury* 620 miles South of Newfoundland.

1782   Fourth battle between Vice-Admiral Sir Edward Hughes *(Superb)* and Commodore Chevalier de Suffren *(Heros)* off Trincomalee. [bh]. Ships: *Exeter, Isis, Hero, Sceptre, Burford, Sultan, Superb, Monarch, Eagle, Magnanime, Monmouth, Worcester.* Frigates, etc.: *Active, Coventry, Medea, Seahorse, San Carlos, Combustion* (F.S.). Troops: 78th Highlanders, 98th Regiment. See 17th February, 12th April and 6th July.

1800   Boats of *Minotaur* and *Niger* cut out the Spanish *Esmeralda* (alias *Concepcion*) and *Paz* at Barcelona.

1806   Landing party from *Superieure, Stork, Flying Fish* and *Pike* captured a fort and six privateers at Batabano, Cuba.

1814   Four boats, under Lieutenant Miller Worsley, cut out the American schooner *Tigress* in the Detour Passage, Lake Huron. Troops: Royal Artillery, Royal Newfoundland Fencible Infantry. [m]

1912   Holland s/m No. 4 foundered.

1914   *Speedy* sunk by mine off the Humber, 12 miles N.N.E. of Outer Dowsing lightvessel.

1918   *Seagull* sunk in collision in Firth of Clyde.

1939   War declared against Germany.

1939   *Plover* laid first British minefield, off Bass Rock in Firth of Forth, and remained in commission for twenty-one years.

1939   Donaldson liner *Athenia* sunk by U.30 in N Western Approaches. First British merchant ship to be sunk in the Second World War.

1939   *Ajax* captured and sank the German *Olinda* in the Plata area.

1939   *Somali* captured the German *Hannah Boge* in N Atlantic (58° 35' N, 20° 11' W.).

1942   *Racoon* sunk by U.165 in the St. Lawrence River.

1942   *Pathfinder, Quentin* and *Vimy* sank U.162 off Trinidad.

1942   Whitley V/77 sank U.705 in Bay of Biscay.

1943   Bombardment support to 8th Army crossing Messina Strait. Operation Baytown. Ships: *Mauritius, Orion; Loyal Offa, Piorun* (Pol), *Quail, Queenborough, Quilliam.* Monitors: *Abercrombie, Erebus, Roberts; Aphis, Scarab.*

An escort carrier in high seas during World War 2

4th SEPTEMBER

1777   *Druid, Camel* and *Weazle* (escorting a convoy) fought the American *Raleigh* 1,100 miles to the eastward of New York.

1782   *Rainbow* captured the French *Hébé* 6 miles North of Île de Bas.

1854   Continuation of the attack on Petropavlosk, which was repulsed. (See 31st August).

1915   E.7 caught in nets and depth charged in the Dardanelles; scuttled by own crew.

1916   British forces captured Dar-es-Salaam. Ships: Inshore Sq.: *Mersey, Severn, Thistle, Helmuth* (armed tug). Main Sq.: *Challenger, Hyacinth, Talbot, Vengeance; Charon, Childers, Echo, Fly, Manica, Pickle, Styx, Trent.* Also: *Himalaya, Prattler, Rinaldo, Salamander.*

1919   *Verulam* mined in Gulf of Finland.

1922   Concentration of HM ships at Smyrna to protect British interests.

1939   *Ajax* captured and sank the German *Carl Fritzen* off Uruguay.

1940   Swordfish aircraft of 812 Sq. (disembarked) attacked invasion barges at Terneuzen.

1940   *Sydney, Dainty* and *Ilex* bombarded Makri Yalo airfield, Scarpanto; *Orion* bombarded Pegadia. *Ilex* sank two MTBs and damaged a third off Pegadia. Pegadia.

1940   Eight Swordfish aircraft of 815 and 819 Sq *(Illustrious)* attacked Callato airfield, Rhodes; twelve Swordfish of 813 and 824 Sq. *(Eagle)* attacked Maritza airfield, Rhodes. Operation M.B.3.

HMS *Sultan* **in 1896**

5th SEPTEMBER

1781 Rear-Admiral Thomas Graves *(London)* fought Vice-Admiral Comte de Grasse *(Ville de Paris)* with 24 ships, 12 miles E.½ N. of Cape Henry, Virginia. Ships: *Shrewsbury, Intrepid, Alcide, Princess, Ajax, Terrible, Europe, Montagu, Royal Oak, London, Bedford, Resolution, America; Centaur, Monarch, Barfleur, Invincible, Belliqueux, Alfred.* Frigates, etc.: *Adamant, Fortunee, Nymphe, Orpheus, Richmond, Santa Monica, Salamander, Sibyl, Solebay* a most disappointing encounter, dominated by adherence to the Line, and partly responsible for the fall of Yorktown.

1782 *Hector* fought the French *Aigle* and *Gloire* 400 miles to the eastward of New York.

1800 Capitulation of Malta to Major-General Henry Pigot after naval blockade. Captain, later Admiral, Ball became Governor.

1801 *Victor* destroyed the French *Flèche* in Mahe Roads, Seychelles.

1810 Boats of *Surveillante* cut out a French brig at St. Gilles sur Vie.

1813 *Boxer* taken by the American *Enterprise* 6 miles East of Portland, Me.

1864 Allied squadron, under Vice-Admiral Sir Augustus Kuper *(Euryalus)* bombarded and destroyed the Japanese batteries at the entrance to Shimonoseki Kaikyo at the W. end of the Inland Sea. Ships: *Argus, Barrosa, Bouncer, Conqueror, Coquette, Euryalus, Leopard, Perseus, Tartar.* French: *Dupleix, Sémiramis, Tancrède.* Dutch: *Amsterdam, D'Jambi, Medusa, Metalen Kruis.* USA: *Takiang* and party from Jamestown. Troops: Royal Engineers, Royal Marine Battalion.

1902 Boats of *Lapwing* captured two pirate dhows outside the bar off Fao, Persian Gulf.

1914 *Pathfinder* sunk by U.21 10 miles S.E. of May Island. First U-boat success against warship in World War I.

1926 Wanhsein incident on Yangtze: *Widgeon* and *Cockchafer* with naval brigade from *Despatch, Scarab* and *Mantis.*

1939 *Neptune* sank the German *Inn* off Para, Brazil.

1939 *Jersey* intercepted the German *Johannes Molkenbuhr,* whose crew scuttled her off Bergen (62° 00' N, 3° 44' E.).

1940 US transferred 50 destroyers and 10 escorts to RN, in return for lease of of West Indian bases.

Action in the Strait of Shimonoseki, 1864

6th SEPTEMBER

1776	*Turtle* (first American submarine) attacked Howe's flagship in New York harbour.
1781	*Savage* taken by the American *Congress* 30 miles to the eastward of Charleston.
1808	*Recruit* fought the French *Diligente* 200 miles E.N.E. of Antigua.
1814	*Tigress* captured the American *Scorpion* on Lake Huron. [m]. Troops: Royal Artillery and Royal Newfoundland Fencible Infantry detachments. (see 3rd September).
1864	VC: Midshipman Duncan Gordon Boyes, Thomas Pride (Captain of the Afterguard) and Ordinary Seaman William Henry Harrison Seeley, (*Euryalus*) for "great intelligence and daring" while leading advance of naval brigade, and carrying its colour under very heavy fire, in attack on stockaded barracks at Shimonoseki, Japan. See 5th September.
1898	VC: Surgeon William Job Maillard (*Hazard*) during landing at Candia,

Crete, for attempts to rescue wounded men under a hail of fire.

1914	*Dwarf* began operations in Cameroons, cutting out four lighters: thwarted three attacks by improvised torpedoes.
1919	Admiral Lord Charles Beresford died.
1935	s.s. *Atreus* commissioned as a controlled mining ship for use in Abyssinian war.
1940	*Godetia* sunk in collision with *s.s. Marsa* off Altacarry Head, N. Ireland (55° 18' N, 5° 57' W.).
1943	*Puckeridge* sunk by U.617 off Europa Point (36° 06' N, 4° 44' W.).
1945	Japanese forces in New Guinea, New Britain and Solomons surrendered in *Glory*.

First Convoys of World War II.

These ran from the Thames to the Firth of Forth and vice versa. The first oceanbound convoys sailed on 7th. Despite opposition to the convoy system on the grounds that it was too "defensive-minded", the system proved to be the most effective means of not only protecting the merchantmen (only 4 of 5756 properly convoyed ships were lost in 1939 to submarines) but of deploying the few escorts against enemy submarines. Losses among ships sailing independently were high, and these sailings were stopped as soon as possible (110 were lost to submarines in 1939).

The Naval Brigade and Marines storming the stockade at Shimonosecki, Japan

252

7th SEPTEMBER

1807 Admiral James Gambier *(Prince of Wales)* received the surrender of the Danish fleet at Copenhagen. Seventy Danish ships surrendered: 18 ships of the line, 10 frigates, 16 corvettes, 26 smaller.

1830 *Primrose* captured the Spanish slaver *Velos Passagera* 90 miles W.N.W. of Akassa, Nigeria, with 555 slaves.

1834 *Imogen, Andromache* and *Louisa* engaged the Bogue forts, Canton River.

1854 *President* and *Virago* captured the Russian *Sitka* and *Anadir* respectively off Petropavlovsk.

1870 *Captain* capsized and sank off Finisterre (last ship to combine turret guns with full sailing rig).

1914 Naval operations against Duala, Cameroons, begun. [bh]. Ships: *Astraea, Challenger, Cumberland, Dwarf.* Niger Flotilla: *Alligator, Balbus, Crocodile, Ivy, Moseley, Porpoise, Remus, Vampire, Vigilant, Walrus.*

1941 *Aurora* and *Nigeria* engaged the escort to a German convoy off Porsanger Fjord (71° 46' N, 21° 30' E.): the German *Bremse* and a trawler were sunk and two other escort vessels damaged.

1943 *Shakespeare* sank the Italian s/m *Velella* in Gulf of Salerno.

1943 Wellington W/407 (RCAF) sank U.669 in Bay of Biscay.

1959 Closure of East Indies station.

8th SEPTEMBER

1656 *Speaker* and two consorts captured six out of eight Spanish ships of the West Indies convoy off Cadiz.

1797 *Dryad* sank the French privateer *Cornelie* 150 miles S.W. by W. of Cape Clear.

1798 *Phaeton* and *Anson* captured the French *Flore* 30 miles West of Cordouan lighthouse.

1811 *Hotspur* sank one French brig and drove two others on shore among the Calvados Rocks, S.E. of Cape Barfleur.

1813 Capture of San Sebastian by Lieutenant-General Sir Thomas Graham. Seamen from the squadron manned some of the breaching batteries. [bh]. Ships: *Ajax, Andromache, Arrow, Beagle, Challenger, Constant, Despatch, Freija, Holly, Juniper, Lyra, Magicienne, President, Revolutionnaire, Sparrow, Surveillante, Stork, Racer, Trio, Reindeer, Goldfinch* and Gunboats 14, 16, 19, 20 and 22. [m]

1849 Boats of *Medea* captured and burnt five pirate junks at Tinpak.

1855 Capture of Sevastopol by British and French forces.

1914 *Oceanic* wrecked off Shetlands.

1918 *Nessus* lost in collision with *Amphitrite* in N Sea.

1940 *Aurora* bombarded Boulogne.

1941 *Croome* sank the Italian s/m *Maggiore Baracca* off Azores.

1943 MTB 77 sunk by aircraft off Vibo Valentia.

1943 Italy surrendered and signed armistice.

The "beef screen" or mess meat store on deck at the start of the 20th century. Traditionally, a ship's butcher was a marine. Messes cooked their own meat.

9th SEPTEMBER

1583 *Squirrel* lost with all hands returning from Newfoundland.

1681 *James Galley* and *Sapphire* captured the Algerine *Half-Moon* 135 miles S.W. by W. of Cape Spartel.

1803 Boats of *Sheerness* captured two French chasse-marees near Audierne, Brittany.

1806 *Leda* destroyed a Spanish brigantine under Yeguas Point, near Montevideo.

1943 Salerno landing. Operation Avalanche. [bh]. Ships: *Abercrombie, Acute, Albacore, Alynbank, Antwerp, Atherstone, Attacker, Aurora, Battler, Beaufort, Belvoir, Blackmore, Blankney, Blencathra, Boxer, Brecon, Brittany, Brixham, Brocklesby, Bruiser, Bude, Cadmus, Calpe, Catterick, Charybdis, Circe, Clacton, Cleveland, Coverley, Delhi, Derwentdale, Dido, Dingledale, Dulverton, Echo, Eclipse, Eggesford, Ensay, Espiegle, Euryalus, Exmoor, Farndale, Faulknor, Felixstowe, Fly, Formidable, Fury, Gavotte, Glengyle, Hambledon, Haydon, Hengist, Hilary, Holcombe, Hunter, Ilex, Illustrious, Inglefield, Intrepid, Jervis, Laforey, Lamerton, Ledbury, Liddesdale, Lookout, Loyal, Mauritius, Mendip, Minuet, Mousa, Mutine, Nelson, Nubian, Offa, Orion, Palomares, Panther, Pathfinder, Penelope, Penn, Petard, Pirouette, Polruan, Prince Charles, Prince Leopold, Prins Albert, Prinses Astrid, Prinses Beatrix, Prinses Josephine Charlotte, Quail, Quantock, Queenborough, Quilliam, Raider, Reighton Wyke, Rhyl, Roberts, Rodney, Rothesay, Royal Scotsman, Royal Ulsterman, St Kilda, Scylla, Shakespeare, Sheffield, Sheppey, Sirius, Stalker, Stella Carina, Stornoway, Tango, Tartar, Tetcott, Thruster, Troubridge, Tumult, Tyrian, Uganda, Ulster Monarch, Ulster Queen, Unicorn, Valiant, Visenda, Warspite, Whaddon, Wheatland.* BYMS: 11, 14, 24, 209, HDML: 1242, 1246, 1247, 1253, 1254, 1258, 1270, 1271, 1297, 1301. M.L.: 238, 273, 280, 283, 336, 554, 555, 556, 557, 559, 560, 561, 562, 564, 566. MMS.: 5, 133, 134. MSML.: 121, 126, 134, 135. FAA Sq.: 820, 888 893 *(Formidable)* (Albacore, Fulmar/Martlet). 810, 878, 890, 894 *(Illustrious)* (Barracuda, Wildcat). 809, 887, 897 *(Unicorn)* (Seafire). 879, 886 *(Attacker)* (Seafire). 807, 808 *(Battler)* (Seafire). 834, 899 *(Hunter)* (Seafire). 880 *(Stalker)* (Seafire).

9th September is the Memorable Date of 41 Commando Royal Marines

During the operations against the Germans in Italy in 1943, it was decided to carry out an amphibious assault in the area of Salerno on the West coast as the first step towards the capture of Naples. Early on the 9th September 41 Commando landed and surprised the town of Vietri. For four days the unit was involved in heavy fighting against elements of five crack German divisions.

1944 *Helmsdale* and *Portchester Castle* sank U.743 in N W Approaches (55° 46' N, 11° 41' W.).

1944 *Hespeler* and *Dunver* (both RCN) sank U.484 off the Hebrides.

HMS *Nelson*

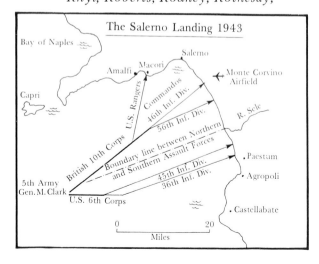

The Salerno Landing 1943

10th SEPTEMBER

1677 *Sapphire* fought the Algerine *Golden Horse* in the Mediterranean.

1759 Vice-Admiral George Pocock *(Yarmouth)* fought Commodore Comte d'Ache *(Zodiaque)*, with 11 ships, 25 miles S.E. of Porto Novo. [bh] . Ships: *Cumberland, Elizabeth, Grafton, Newcastle, Salisbury, Sunderland, Tiger, Weymouth, Yarmouth*. Frigate: *Queenborough*. This third action was in itself inconclusive but concluded a campaign in our favour. See 29th April and 3rd August.

1778 *Fox* taken by the French *Junon* 120 miles S.S.W. of Ushant.

1813 Defeat of the British Lake Squadron by the American Lake Squadron on Lake Erie. Ships: *Chippeway, Detroit, Hunter, Lady Prevost, Little Belt, Queen Charlotte*. Troops: 41st Regiment, Royal Newfoundland Fencible Infantry. American: *Ariel, Caledonia, Lawrence, Niagara, Porcupine, Scorpion, Summers, Tigress, Trip.* (Second *Little Belt* taken by U.S.).

1840 Start of operations which continued until 9th December against Mehemet Ali. [m, bh] . Bombardment of Beirut and landing of troops in d'Jounie (Juniye) Bay. Ships engaged during the operations: *Bellerophon, Benbow,* *Edinburgh, Ganges, Hastings, Princess Charlotte* (Admiral the Hon. Sir Robert Stopford), *Powerful, Revenge, Rodney, Thunderer, Vanguard.* Others: *Asia, Cambridge, Implacable.* Frigates, etc.: *Carysfort, Castor, Dido, Hazard, Pique, Talbot, Wasp, Sabre.* Others: *Daphne, Magicienne.* Steamers: *Cyclops, Gorgon, Hydra, Medea, Phoenic, Stromboli, Vesuvius.* Others: *Hecate.* Austrian: *Guerriera, Lipsia, Medea* (Rear-Admiral Franz, Baron Bandiera). Turkish: *Mookuddimay-I-Hive* (Rear-Admiral Baldwin Walker Bey). Troops: Royal Artillery, Royal Sappers and Miners.

1918 *Ophelia* sank UB.83 off Pentland Firth.

1934 Professor Geoffrey Callender appointed first Director of the National Maritime Museum.

1939 *Oxley* sunk in error by *Triton* off Obrestad (Montrose-Obrestad patrol) in 58° 30' N, 5° 24' E.

1941 *Chambly* and *Moosejaw* (both RCN) sank U.501 off Greenland. (Convoy SC.42)

1943 *Abdiel* sunk by mine off Taranto (40° 29' N, 17° 15' E.). Operation Slapstick.

1944 *Erebus* and *Warspite* bombarded Le Havre.

HMS *Warspite*

255

11th SEPTEMBER

1781	*Iris* and *Richmond* taken by the French squadron under Commodore Comte Barras in Chesapeake Bay.
1793	Nelson *(Agamemnon)* met Lady Hamilton at Naples.

Lady Hamilton

1809	*Diana* captured the Dutch *Zefier* off Menado, Celebes. [m, bh]
1814	Second Battle of Lake Champlain: the British Lake Squadron defeated by the American Lake Squadron in Plattsburg Bay. Ships: *Confiance, Linnet, Chub, Finch* and 10 gunboats. American: *Saratoga, Eagle, Preble, Ticonderoga* and 10 gunboats.
1886	*Rattlesnake,* first Torpedo Gunboat, launched.
1896	*Zafir* burst her boiler on the White Nile much to the chagrin of Kitchener, before Dongola; repaired and in action again on 23rd.
1914	*Emden's* first sinking of British merchant ship.
1917	*British Transport* rammed and

	sank U.49 in Atlantic (46° 17' N, 14° 42' W.).
1921	Admiral of the Fleet Prince Louis of Battenberg died.

Dover Barrage, 1939
The minelayers *Adventure* and *Plover,* augmented by requisitioned train ferries *Shepperton* and *Hampton,* laid over 6000 mines in the Dover Area between 11th September and 23rd October. This barrage achieved the object of preventing U-boats passing through the straits. Only one succeeded, on the night 11/12th September before the barrage was really started. In October, 2 others blew up on mines and a third ran aground on the Goodwins.

1941	*Leamington* and *Veteran* sank the U.207 in N Atlantic (63° 59' N, 34° 48' W.).(Convoy SC.42)
1942	*Charlottetown* (RCN) sunk by U.517 in the St. Lawrence River (49° 12' N, 66° 48' W.). (Convoy QS.33).
1943	*Haarlem, Hyacinth, Woolongong* (RAN) and Wellingtons J/179 and P/179 sank U.617 in the Straits of Gibraltar (U-boat beached on the 12th in 35° 38' N, 3° 29' W in Spanish Morocco)
1943	The surrendered Italian battlefleet arrived at Malta. 'Be pleased to inform Their Lordships that the Italian Fleet now lies at anchor under the guns of the fortress of Malta' — Admiral Sir Andrew Cunningham to the Secretary of the Admiralty.
1944	X.24 laid two charges under the floating dock at Laksvaag, Bergen: dock broken in two. Operation Heckle.

Midget Submarine Attack — Bergen
X.24 had been towed by the submarine *Sceptre* to Bergen and carried out an attack on shipping there on 14th April. She had planned to damage the 8000 ton floating dock, but had been deflected on her approach. She had managed to blow up the 7800 ton ship *Barenfels* and put the coaling wharf out of action for the remainder of the war.
On 11th September, she again entered Bergen harbour, having been towed to the position off Norway by *Sceptre.* X.24 used the mast of the *Barenfels* as a marker, the only part of the ship still showing above water, and placed charges under the floating dock. The X.24 then made her way down the fjord and made contact with *Sceptre* that evening. Four of the six sections of the floating dock were damaged beyond repair, the other two sections were damaged, and so were two ships secured alongside the dock at the time of the attack.
These attacks were carried out very skilfully and caused considerable damage; brought about delays in the harbour's routine and brought up extra troops in security operations.

12th SEPTEMBER

1747 *Amazon* fought the French *Renommée* 120 miles S.S.W. of Ushant.

1757 *Southampton* captured the French *Éméraude* 12 miles W.N.W. of Ushant, the ships foul of one another and in a flat calm. [bh]

1782 *Warwick* captured the French *Sophie* off the Delaware.

1808 *Laurel* taken by the French *Canonnière* off Port Louis, Mauritius.

1840 Abortive attack by *Carysfort, Cyclops* and *Dido* on Jebeil Castle, Syria. [m]

1846 Work began on Keyham Steam yard.

1857 First party of *Pearl's* Naval Brigade (Captain E.S. Sotheby) left the ship at Calcutta for operations against the mutineers in India, proceeding by river steamer and flat.

1914 U.13 sunk in N Sea.

12 September 1916 — Mis-information.

During the First World War the Naval Intelligence Department under Admiral Hall was considered one of the most effective instruments Britain possessed in winning the war. Its activities extended well beyond the strict bounds of naval intelligence. As an example, the Daily Mail of 12th September 1916 reported large troop concentrations at Harwich and Dover in such a way that German agents in Holland were convinced that vital news had leaked to the Daily Mail before being cleared by the censor. As a result the Germans moved a large detachment of their forces to the Belgium coast, thereby relieving the main battle field. The origin of the report was Room 40 at the Admiralty.

1917 D.7 sank U.45 in NW Approaches.

1931 Mutiny at Invergordon over pay cuts.

Extract from petition of Invergordon mutineers

"We the loyal subjects of HM The King do hereby present my Lord's commissioners of the Admiralty our representations to implore them to amend the drastic cuts in pay that had been inflicted on the lowest paid men on the lower deck.
It is evident to all concerned that this cut is the forerunner of tragedy, misery and immorality amongst the families of the lower deck and unless we can be guaranteed a written agreement from Admiralty confirmed by Parliament stating that our pay will be revised we are still to remain as one unit, refusing to serve under the new rates of pay."

1941 Swordfish aircraft of 830 Sq. FAA (Malta) and Blenheims of 105 Sq.

RAF attacked an escorted Tripoli convoy South of Lampione: several ships sunk or damaged.

1942 *Faulknor* sank U.88 off Bear Island. (Convoy PQ.18)

Convoy PQ.18 to Russia, 1942

Convoy PQ.18 comprised 40 merchant ships and 6 minesweepers and auxiliaries, together with a substantial escort comprising:
    17 ships as close escort (including 2 submarines)
    An escort carrier, cruiser and 18 destroyers
    — with the convoy.
    2 battleships, 4 cruisers and 5 destroyers —
    in 2 covering forces.
    Submarines on patrol and oilers and escorts
    in support.
The operation was controlled by the Commander-in-Chief in the battleship *King George V*.
The route chosen for the convoy was long, as the ice had moved North, and all warships other than the close escort were to escort the next return convoy from Russia (QP.14) before returning to harbour.
The main body sailed from Loch Ewe on 2nd September, with a Western Approaches escort which was relieved by the close escort on 7th in the Denmark Strait. On 9th, the cruiser *Scylla* and 9 destroyers joined, and by 13th the escort was at full strength with all the escorts having fuelled from oilers lying at Spitzbergen.
On 12th the destroyer *Faulknor* sank U.88, and on 13th there were other U-boat attacks. Two ships were lost to U-boats, and then 8 more were lost during a massed air attack by 40 torpedo bombers. 5 aircraft were shot down that day and 22 the next day, when there was a series of attacks during which one merchant ship was lost. The destroyer *Onslow* and a Swordfish from the carrier *Avenger* sank U.589. On 15th the aircraft again attacked in large numbers and 12 U-boats were in contact with the convoy, but the escort held them off. On 16th the destroyer *Impulsive* sank U.457, and that afternoon all but the close escort left PQ.18 and joined QP.14. Ten merchant ships had been lost, but the Germans had lost 41 aircraft and 3 U-boats, and 36 ships reached Russia safely.
The Germans attributed their failure to achieve better results to the steadfastness of the convoy in maintaining formation despite the intensity of the attacks.

1943 Bisley J/13 sank the Italian s/m *Topazio* off Sardinia, after she failed to identify herself.

1944 *Furious* and *Trumpeter*, escorted by *Devonshire* and six destroyers of 26th D.F., laid mines in Aramsund Channel: one German escort vessel sunk. Operation Begonia. FAA Sq.: 801, 880; 827, 830 (Seafire, Barracuda) (*Furious*), 846, 852 (Avenger) (*Trumpeter*). This was the last Home Fleet operation in which *Furious* took part before reducing to reserve.

13th SEPTEMBER

1747   *Dover* captured the French *Renommée* 144 miles S.E. of Ushant.

1759   Capture of Québec by Major-General James Wolfe and Vice-Admiral Charles Saunders (*Neptune*). [bh] . Ships: *Alcide, Bedford, Captain, Centurion, Devonshire, Diana, Dublin, Echo, Eurus, Fowey, Hind, Hunter, Lizard, Lowestoffe, Medway, Neptune, Nightingale, Northumberland, Orford, Pembroke, Porcupine, Prince Frederick, Prince of Orange, Princess Amelia, Richmond, Royal William, Scarbourgh, Scorpion, Sea Horse, Shrewsbury, Somerset, Squirrel, Stirling Castle, Sutherland, Terrible, Trent, Trident, Vanguard, Zephyr.* Bombs: *Baltimore, Pelican, Racehorse.* Fireships: *Boscawen, Cormorant, Halifax, Stromolo, Vesuvius.* Cutter: *Rodney.* Storeship: *Crown.*

The Seven Year's War was started as a result of the French settlers in Canada fortifying a number of posts against the advance of English settlers. The French city of Québec was the key to the conquest of Upper Canada. The city stood far up the St. Lawrence river and the tortuous channel was believed to be impassable by anything larger than a frigate. The French therefore believed that Québec was safe from attack by sea.

However a British fleet under Vice-Admiral Sir Charles Saunders, aided by the brilliant Master (later Captain) James Cook sailed up the St. Lawrence river with an army embarked. During the attack on Québec the fleet dominated the river, preventing supplies from reaching the defence, and landed the 17,000 men at the assault position below the plains of Abraham. Seamen of the fleet also landed guns and hauled them up the Heights of Abraham.

1782   Repulse of the Spanish attack on Gibraltar, all ten Spanish battering ships being destroyed. Seamen from *Brilliant* reinforced the garrison.

1799   *Arrow* and *Wolverine* captured the Batavian Republic *Draak* and *Gier* in Vliestroom. [m]

1810   *Africaine* taken by the French *Iphigénie* and *Astrée* off Réunion. Recaptured by *Boadicea, Otter* and *Staunch.* Troops: Detachments of 86th Regiment in *Africaine;* 1/69th in *Otter* and *Staunch*; 89th, in *Boadicea.*

1858   *Pearl's* Naval Brigade, with 13th Light Infantry and 6th Madras Light Cavalry, at Domariaganj.

1882   Battle of Tel-el-Kebir, Sudan. Two battalions of Royal Marines were present.

1914   E.9 sank the German *Hela* 6 miles S.W. of Heligoland.

1947   *Warrnambool* (RAN) mined off Queensland.

1958   *M.V. Melika* and *M.V. Fernand Gilbert* salvaged, after collision and fire in Gulf of Oman, by an RN force including *Bulwark, Puma, Loch Killisport, St. Bride's Bay* and RFA *Wave Knight.*

Russian Convoy PQ 18

14th SEPTEMBER

1650	Admiral Robert Blake *(George)* captured seven ships of the Portuguese Brazil fleet.
1779	*Pearl* captured the Spanish *Santa Monica* 18 miles S. by E. of Corvo Island, Azores. [bh]
1801	Combined attack on the French siege batteries at Port Ferrajo, Elba. Ships: *Renown, Vincejo.*
1805	Vice-Admiral Viscount Nelson sailed from Portsmouth for the last time.
1807	*Blonde* captured the French privateer *Hirondelle* 400 miles to the eastward of Barbados.
1814	Unsuccessful bombardment of fort McHenry by squadron under Rear-Admiral Cochrane led to the composition of the Star-spangled Banner, the American National Anthem on the deck of a British warship.
1909	*Viking* launched at Palmers: the only six funnelled ship the RN has had.
1914	*Carmania* sank the German *Cap Trafalgar* off Trinidad Island, South Atlantic. [bh]. War Medal: clasp 'Cap Trafalgar, 14 Sep. 1914' approved but not issued.
1917	GC (ex-AM): Ordinary Seamen G.F.P. Abbott and R.J. Knowlton. RNR,

for rescuing pilot in aircraft crashed 100 feet up a mast.

1939	*Faulknor, Firedrake* and *Foxhound* sank U.39 off the Hebrides. First U-boat sunk in World War II.
1942	*Coventry* damaged by aircraft off Tobruk (32° 50' N, 28° 15' E.): sunk by *Zulu. Zulu* sunk by German aircraft off Tobruk (32° 30' N, 28° 43' E.). *Sikh* sunk by shore batteries at Tobruk (32° 04' N, 24° 00' E.). Operation Agreement.
1942	*Ottawa* (RCN) (ex-*Crusader*) sunk by U.91 E of Newfoundland. (Convoy ON.127)

Convoy ON.127 (10-14 September 1942)
This convoy consisted of 32 merchant ships. It was attacked by a wolf pack of 13 U-boats, each of which was able to make an attack; the first time in the battle of Atlantic that this had happened. 12 freighters and one destroyer were sunk. Only one U-boat was damaged.

1942	*Dido; Javelin, Jervis, Pakenham* and *Paladin* bombarded the Daba area, Egypt.
1942	*Onslow* and a Swordfish from *Avenger* sank U.589 off Bear Island. (Convoy PQ.18)
1942	Sunderland R/202 sank the Italian s/m *Alabastro* off Algiers.
1942	GC (ex-AM): Chief Officer J.A. Reeves, MN for saving life at sea in convoy.

HMS *Onslow*

259

15th SEPTEMBER

1744 Navy Board proposed RN Hospitals at Portsmouth, Plymouth and Chatham; Haslar established by Order in Council.

1782 *Vestal* and *Bonetta* captured the French *Aigle* off the Delaware.

1797 *Aurora* captured the French privateer *Espiegle* 40 miles to the westward of Cape Roxent (da Roca).

1803 Rear-Admiral Sir James Saumarez *(Cerberus)*, with two bombs, bombarded Granville.

1871 Herbert William Richmond born.

1899 *Alexandra, Europa* and *Juno* fitted with first operational wireless.

1909 Volunteer Reserve Decoration instituted.

1915 E.16 sank U.6 4 miles S.W. of Karmo Island, off Stavanger.

1939 *Sturgeon* (submarine) attacked *Swordfish* (submarine) but fortunately missed.

1940 *Dundee* sunk by U.48 in N Atlantic (56° 45' N, 14° 14' W.). (Convoy SC.3)

1942 Whitley Q/58 sank U.261 S. of Faeroes.

1943 *Valiant* and *Warspite* bombarded enemy positions near Salerno, restoring the Allied situation on shore.

Operation Avalanche – Salerno

The Naval Commander's report on the landings at Salerno stated that 'the margin of success in the landings was carried by the naval guns', and the Germans attributed their failure to break through to the beaches to the devastating effect of the naval gunfire. The battleships *Valiant* and *Warspite* were involved in the bombardments. Of 62 rounds of 15 in shells, 35 fell on target, and another 8 were within 100 yards. *Warspite* was hit by a radio-controlled bomb on 16th, which exploded in No 4 Boiler Room and went out through the bottom. A second bomb landed close alongside and blew a hole in the water-line. The ship had lost all power in five minutes, and was flooding steadily. She was towed to Malta, and then went to Gibraltar where large cofferdams were built on her bottom, and was able to take part in the bombardment during the Normandy landings.

1950 Invasion of Inchon.

The US 10th Corps with over 70,000 men was landed at Inchon from 550 landing craft with the aim of re-capturing Seoul and cutting the enemy forces' supply routes. The landings were a totally American affair, but the British cruisers *Jamaica* and *Kenya* operated with the Gun Fire Support Group, carrying out off-shore patrols and maintaining the blockade. During these operations *Jamaica* became the first United Nations' ship to shoot down an enemy aircraft, on 17 September. During the operations she fired 1290 rounds of 6 inch. and 393 of 4 in, while *Kenya* fired 1242 rounds of 6 in and 205 of 4 in shells.

1966 *Resolution* launched, the first RN Polaris submarine.

HMS *Resolution*

16th SEPTEMBER

1681	*Adventure* captured the Algerine *Two Lions* off Larache, Morocco. [bh]
1719	*Weymouth* and *Winchester* destroyed two Spanish warships (one the ex-British *Greyhound*) and a battery at Ribadeo, and captured a merchant-man.
1795	Capture of the Cape of Good Hope by Vice-Admiral Sir George Elphinstone, later Lord Keith, (*Monarch*) and General Alfred Clarke. [bh] . A Naval Brigade was landed. Ships: *America, Jupiter, Monarch, Ruby, Sceptre, Stately, Tremendous, Trident.* Frigates, etc.: *Crescent, Echo, Hope, Moselle, Rattlesnake, Sphinx.*
1801	*Champion* recaptured the ex-British *Bulldog* at Gallipoli, Gulf of Taranto.
1813	Boats of *Swallow* captured the French *Guerrière* near Porto d'Anzio.
1914	*Dwarf* rammed by, but sank, the German *Nachtigal* in Bimbia River, W. Africa.
1917	G.9 accidentally sunk by *Petard* off Norway.
1918	UB.103 sunk in Dover Barrage.

1918   GC (ex-AM): Sub-Lieutenant D.H. Evans (*Glatton*) for saving life when ship caught fire and had to be sunk in Dover harbour.

1919   M.25 and M.27 blown up in Dvina River, N. Russia, to prevent their capture as they could not cross the bar: end of second Archangel River Expeditionary Force.

1942   *Talisman* sunk, possibly by mine, between Gibraltar and Malta in Sicilian Channel.

1942   *Impulsive* sank U.457 NE of Murmansk. (Convoy PQ.18)

Flight Deck Operations.

To the naval flyer the perils of battle are not over when the battle zone is left. He then has to find the aircraft carrier whence he came, often in poor weather conditions and in wartime generally without the aid of radio and navigation systems. Having found his ship he then has to land on her. The Salerno landings in the Autumn of 1943 are a good example: during 3½ days of carrier-based flying two enemy aircraft were shot down and 4 damaged. No Seafire was lost through enemy action. However 42 were lost or became write-offs through deck-landing accidents and many others were made unserviceable.

A Seafire of 887 Squadron upset on *Unicorn* off Salerno

17th SEPTEMBER

1797   *Pelican* sank the French privateer *Trompeuse* 30 miles N.N.E. of Cape St. Nicolas Mole, Haiti.

1797   *Unite* captured the French privateer *Brunette* to the south-westward of Île de Ré.

1812   Boats of *Eagle* captured 2 gunboats and 21 out of a convoy of 23 sail off Cape Maistro (Majestro), Adriatic. [m]

1840   *Castor, Pique* and the Ottoman *Dewan* captured Caiffa (Haifa). [m]

1917   *Stonecrop* sank U.88 in N Atlantic.

1936   *Esk* rescued eighty one refugees in final evacuation of Bilbao in Spanish Civil War.

1939   *Courageous* sunk by U.29 in the SW Approaches (50° 10' N, 14° 50' W.).

1940   *Janus* and *Juno* bombarded Sidi Barrani. *Juno* and *Ladybird* bombarded Sollum and the escarpment road.

1940   Swordfish of 815 and 819 Sq. (*Illustrious*) mined Benghazi har- bour and bombed the ships inside: the Italian destroyers *Aquilone* sunk by mine and *Borea* by bombing.

1942   *Waterfly* sunk by German aircraft off Dungeness.

1942 Doenitz orders no rescues by U-boats

U.156 sank the troop ship *Laconia*, carrying 1800 Italian prisoners of war, in the South Atlantic. The U-boat radioed for assistance and other U-boats, French warships and a British Merchant ship came to the rescue. But a USAF bomber escorting the British ship did not understand the signals and attacked U.156, and Admiral Doenitz ordered that in future U-boats should attempt no further rescues.

1944   Liberator S/206 sank U.865 off Norway (62° 20' N, 2° 20' E.).

1944   Air strike on Sigli, Sumatra. Operation Light. Ships: *Indomitable, Victorious, Howe, Cumberland, Kenya, Racehorse, Rider, Rapid, Redoubt, Relentless, Rocket, Rotherham.* FAA Sq.: 815, 817; 1839, 1844 (Barracuda, Hellcat) (*Indomitable*). 822, 1834, 1835 (Barracuda, Corsair) (*Victorious*).

1955   *Vidal* annexed Rockall for Great Britain.

A Sea King helicopter from HMS *Tiger* visiting Rockall to service the beacon, 1974

18th SEPTEMBER

1708	Capture of Minorca. Ships: *Centurion, Dunkirk, Milford.*
1714	George, Elector of Hanover, landed at Greenwich to become King George I.
1740	Commodore Anson in *Centurion* sailed with six ships from Plymouth: four years later he returned with *Centurion* alone. See 14th June.
1804	*Centurion* fought the French *Marengo, Atalante* and *Sémillante* in Vizagapatam Roads. [m]
1810	*Ceylon* taken by the French *Venus* and *Victor. Boadicea,* with *Otter* and *Staunch* captured *Venus* and recaptured *Ceylon.* [m]. Troops: 1/69th and 86th Regiments *(Ceylon)* 89th Regiment *(Boadicea),* 1/69th Regiment *(Otter* and *Staunch).*
1811	Reduction of Java by Rear-Admiral the Hon. Robert Stopford *(Scipion)* and Lieutenant-General Sir Samuel Auchmuty. [m, m*, bh]. Ships: *Akbar, Barracouta, Bucephalus, Caroline, Cornelia, Dasher, Doris, Harpy, Hecate, Hesper, Hussar, Illustrious, Leda, Lion, Minden, Modest, Nisus, Phaeton, Phoebe, President, Procris, Psyche, Samarang, Scipion, Sir Francis Drake.*
1812	Boats of *Bacchante* captured a convoy and its escort near Vasto, Adriatic.
1855	VC: Lieutenant George Fiott Day *(Recruit).* Reconnaissance at Genitchi, Sea of Azov.
1855	*Bittern* and *s.s. Paoushun* destroyed 22 pirate junks in Shih pu harbour.
1857	Second party of *Shannon's* Naval Brigade (Lieutenant J.W. Vaughan) left the ship for Allahabad, proceeding by river steamer and flat (See 18th August).
1901	*Cobra,* one of first two turbine-driven destroyers, lost in storm in N. Sea.
1917	*Stonecrop (Glenfoyle)* sunk by U.151 in N W Approaches.
1917	*Contest* torpedoed by U-boat in SW Approaches.
1941	*Unbeaten, Upholder, Upright* and *Ursula* torpedoed three large escorted Italian transports off Tripoli (32° 58' N, 14° 40' E.), sinking two and damaging a third. *Upholder* sank both *Neptunia* and *Oceania.*

19th SEPTEMBER

1777	*Alert* captured the American *Lexington* 45 miles S.W. by W. of Ushant. [bh].
1896	Action at Hafir, Sudan. Gunboats: *Abu Klea, Metemmeh, Tamai.*
1914	Royal Marines landed at Dunkirk.
1914	AE1 (RAN) foundered off Bismarck archipelago, Pacific.
1935	Royal Marines exercised their inherited "ancient privilege and right to march through the City of London with bayonets fixed and flags flying" for the first time since 1746, in honour of Silver Jubilee of King George V.
1941	*Levis* (RCN) sunk by U.74 in N Atlantic (60° 07' N, 38° 37' W.). (Convoy SC.44)
1943	Liberator A/10 (RCAF) sank U.341 in Atlantic (58° 40' N, 25° 30' W.). (Convoy ONS.18)

Convoys ONS.18 and ON.202
Slow convoy ONS.18 of 27 merchant ships and an escort of 8 under *Keppel* sailed from Milford Haven on 12th. Fast convoy ON.202, of 42 ships, left Liverpool on 15th with 6 escorts led by the Canadian *Gatineau.* On 18th the convoys were 120 miles apart, and ONS.18 was diverted to avoid U-boats. On 19th U-341 was sunk by a Liberator aircraft some 160 miles from ONS.18, which was under attack by U-boats. That day the *Escapade's* hedgehog (see 7th August) had a premature explosion, and she had to return to harbour. On the morning of the 20th, the convoys were 30 miles apart, and U-boats sank 2 merchantmen at 0300. The frigate *Lagan* was damaged by an acoustic torpedo and had to be towed home, but a Liberator sank U.338 with an aerial acoustic torpedo. At noon the convoys joined, and the 9th Escort Group reinforced the escorts. Eight U-boats were in the vicinity of the convoys, but two were damaged, one by the surface escort and the other by aircraft. During that night three U-boat attacks were frustrated for the loss of two escorts, the *St Croix* and the *Polyanthus.* The next night the U-boats attacked again, but with no success, and the *Keppel* sank U.229 by ramming after running down a wireless bearing. The following night the frigate *Itchen* was sunk, with only three survivors. Unfortunately she had been carrying survivors of the *St Croix* and *Polyanthus.* In the morning three merchant ships were sunk and one damaged by U-boats. The damaged vessel had to be abandoned later. However, the U-boats ceased their attacks that evening. 19 U-boats had attacked the convoys over five days. Six merchant ships had been lost together with three escorts, but three U-boats had been sunk and another three damaged. Exaggerated claims by the U-boats misled U-Boat Command into believing that the U-boats had been more successful.

1944	*Terpsichore, Troubridge* and *Garland* (Pol) sank U.407 off Crete (36° 27' N, 24° 33' E.) last enemy submarine to be sunk in the Mediterranean.
1944	A/c of 224 Sq. sank U.867 off S.W. Norway.
1944	GC: T/Lieutenant Leon Verdi Goldsworthy DSC, GM, RANVR, Mine Disposal (*Gazette* date).

19th SEPTEMBER

Sea Vixen of 890 Sq.: all-weather fighters — flight refuelling (1961)

HMS *Fittleton* 1976

1725	Antigua Dockyard opened: in use until 1889.
1799	*Rattlesnake* and *Camel* fought the French *Preneuse* in Algoa Bay.
1803	*Princess Augusta* fought the Dutch *Union* and *Wraak* 16 miles N. by W. of Terschelling.
1808	Masters given status of Lieutenants by Order in Council.
1811	*Naiad* fought the Boulogne invasion flotilla off Boulogne.
1873	Boats of *Thalia* and *Midge* destroyed three pirate junks and a fort in the Larut River, Perak.
1914	*Pegasus* sunk by the German *Königsberg* at Zanzibar.
1939	*Forester* and *Fortune* sank U.27 60 miles W. of the Hebrides (58° 35' N, 9° 02' W.).
1941	Gibraltar harbour attacked by Italian s/m *Scire* with chariots — see 3rd January.
1942	*Leda* sunk by U.435 off Spitzbergen (75° 48' N, 5° 00' E.).
1942	*Somali* torpedoed by U.703 off Jan Mayen Is. (75° 40' N, 2° 00' W.). (Convoy QP.14)
1943	*Polyanthus* and *St. Croix* (RCN) sunk by U.952 (or U.641) and U.305 in N Atlantic.
1943	Liberator F/120 sank U.338 in N Atlantic (57° 40' N, 29° 48' W.). (Convoy ONS.18)
1944	German hospital ship *Rostock* escorted to Plymouth.
1976	*Fittleton* sunk in collision with *Mermaid*. 12 lives lost, including RNR under training.

1801	*Thames* captured the Spanish privateer *Sparrow* off Condan Point (Punta Candor).
1803	Rear-Admiral Bryan Marlin (*Creole*) reported to Admiral Lord Keith a remark by the Duke of Wellington: "If anyone wishes to know the history of this war, I will tell them that it is our maritime superiority gives me the power of maintaining my army while the enemy are unable to do the same."
1809	Successful combined attack on Saint Paul, Bourbon (Réunion), and capture of the French *Caroline*, *Grappler* and the ex-British Indiamen *Streatham* and *Europe*. Ships: *Boadicea, Nereide, Otter, Raisonnable, Sirius* and *Wasp* (Bombay Marine). Troops: 1/56th Regiment, 2/2nd Bombay Native Infantry.
1811	*Naiad, Rinaldo, Redpole, Castilian* and *Viper* fought the Boulogne invasion flotilla off Boulogne: capture of the French *Ville de Lyon*.
1811	Boats of *Victory* captured two Danish privateers in Wingo Sound (Vinga Sand). [m]
1867	The first 'time and percussion fuze' introduced.
1941	Martlet aircraft of 802 Sq (*Audacity*) shot down a Focke-Wulf aircraft attacking Convoy OG.74. First success by an auxiliary aircraft carrier.
1941	*Vimy* sank the Italian s/m *Alessandro Malaspina* in N Atlantic.
1943	*Unseen* sank *Brandenburg* (ex-French *Kita*) N.E. of Corsica.

Convoy QP 14 From Russia

QP.14 left Archangel on 13th, escorted by 2 AA ships and 11 corvettes. It was joined by the escort from PQ. 18 on 17th. On 20th a U-boat sank a merchant ship and the minesweeper *Leda*. However, the air threat had passed and *Avenger, Scylla* and 3 destroyers were detached. Just afterwards the destroyer *Somali* was torpedoed. *Ashanti* took her in tow, but a gale sprang up, and *Somali* broke in two and sank on 24th. On 22nd 3 merchant ships were sunk by U.435, but the next day a Catalina sank U.253, and on 26th the 12 surviving ships reached Loch Ewe. Convoys PQ.18 and QP.14 were decisive, and the enemy never again attacked in such strength by air in the far North.

22nd SEPTEMBER

1798   Mutineers delivered *Hermione* to Spanish.

1811   *Leveret* captured the French privateer *Prospère* 200 miles E.N.E. of Flamborough Head.

1812   *Saracen* captured the French privateer *Courrier* 7 miles S. by E. of Beachy Head.

1910   *Temeraire* commissioned as RN PT School.

1914   *Aboukir*, *Cressy* and *Hogue* sunk by the German U.9 off the Maas lightvessel. *Cressy* and *Hogue* were stopped for *Aboukir* survivors. (52° 18' N, 3° 41' E.)

1914   Madras bombarded by the German *Emden*.

1917   Seaplane 8695 bombed and sank UC. 72 in the Channel.

1940   *Janus*, *Jervis* (D.14), *Juno* and *Mohawk* bombarded airfield and troop concentration at Sidi Barrani.

1940   *Osiris* sank the Italian destroyer *Palestro* off Durazzo (41° 16' N, 18° 36' E.).

1943   *Keppel* sank U.229 in N Atlantic (54° 36' N, 36° 35' W.). (Convoy ONS.18/ON.202)

1943   VC: Lieutenant Basil Charles Godfrey Place (X.7). Lieutenant Donald Cameron, RNR (X.6). Attack by midget submarines on the German battleship *Tirpitz* in Altenfjord. [bh]

Midget Submarine attack on the Tirpitz
The German heavy warships in Northern Norway were a constant threat to the convoys being run to and from Russia. It was decided that the *Tirpitz* and *Scharnhorst* should be attacked by midget submarines. These submarines were of 35 tons, carried 2 detachable charges of 2 tons each and were manned by a crew of four. Six midget submarines were towed by S and T Class submarines to a position off Altenfjord. X9 was lost on passage and X8 had to be scuttled. The four remaining midget submarines set off on the evening of 20th, and entered Kaa Fjord on 22nd. X6 (Lieutenant D Cameron RNR) dropped her charges blind as her periscope and compass were out of action. The crew abandoned the submarine and were taken prisoner. *Tirpitz* then started to shift berth. Meanwhile X7 (Lieutenant B C G Place) attacked and placed her charges under the *Tirpitz*. She became caught in the nets while trying to escape and was damaged by the explosions as the charges went off. Lieutenant Place and another officer escaped, but the other two crew were lost. X5 disappeared, and was believed sunk by the Germans. X10, which had been sent to attack *Scharnhorst* nearby, lost her compass and periscope, and returned to sea and was recovered by one of the larger submarines, but sank on tow to UK. In fact *Scharnhorst* had sailed and was not in the fjord. The *Tirpitz* was unfit for sea until April, 1944.

1943   *Itchen* sunk by U.952 (or U.260) in N Atlantic (53° 25' N, 39° 42' W.). (Convoy ONS.18/ON.202)

Commander Cameron, VC

Lieutenant Place, VC

23rd SEPTEMBER

1779 *Serapis* and *Countess of Scarborough* escorting a Baltic convoy, taken by the American *Bonhomme Richard* (Captain John Paul Jones) off Flamborough Head. The convoy escaped and the American ship sank on the 25th. [bh]

1796 *Pelican* fought the French *Medée*, 25 miles N.W. by W. of Deseads (Desirade).

1797 *Espiegle* captured the Dutch *D'Ondeilbaarleid* off Vlieland.

1940 *Ladybird* bombarded Sidi Barrani.

1940 Abortive attack on Dakar (Operation Menace); ceased at midnight 25th/26th. Ships: *Barham* (Vice-Admiral J H D Cunningham), *Resolution*[1], *Renown* Vice-Admiral Sir James Somerville), *Ark Royal*, *Australia* (RAN), *Cornwall*, *Cumberland*, *Delhi*, *Devonshire*, *Dragon*, *Echo*, *Eclipse*, *Encounter*, *Escapade*, *Faulknor*, *Foresight*, *Forester*, *Fortune*, *Fury*, *Greyhound*, *Griffin*, *Hotspur*, *Inglefield*, *Velox*, *Vidette*, *Wishart*, *Bridgewater*, *Milford*, *Quannet*. Free French force, under General Charles de Gaulle: *Président Houduce, Savorgnan de Brazza, Commandant-Duboc, Commandant-Domine*. Vichy-French ships sunk: *Ajax, L'Audacieux* (badly damaged), *Persée*. Torpedoed on 25th. FAA Sq.: Skua 800, 803; Swordfish 810, 814*, 818, 820.
* Lent from *Hermes*.

1941 GC: Henry Herbert Reed, Gunner, DEMS s.s. *Cormount*.

1942 Catalina U/210 sank U.253 off N Norway (68° 19' N, 13° 50' E). (Convoy QP.14).

1942 *Voyager* (RAN) beached in Betano Bay, Timor (9° 11' S, 125° 43' E.) after air attack: blown up by own crew.

1943 *Trenchant* sank U.859 off Penang (5° 46' N, 100° 40' E.).

HMS *Warspite*

24th SEPTEMBER

1568   John Hawkins and Francis Drake at San Juan d'Ulloa. Ships: *Jesus of Lubeck, Judith, Minion.*

1758   *Southampton* captured the French privateer *Caumartin* 150 miles to the south westward of Cape Clear.

1797   *Phaeton* and *Unite* captured the French privateer *Indien* and her prize *(Egmont)* in the vicinity of the Plateau de Rochebonne.

1809   Boats of *Blonde, Fawn* and *Scorpion* destroyed a French vessel at Basse Terre, Guadeloupe.

1840   *Castor* and *Pique* captured Tyre. [m]

1911   *Mayfly* — an unfortunate name for the RN's effort to emulate the Zeppelin — wrecked leaving her shed. She never flew and her accident had a profound effect on the development of British rigid airships.

1915   *Baralong* sank U.41 90 miles West of Ushant, the Q-ship's second success in five weeks.

1916   Destruction of Zeppelin L32 yielded new German naval signal book.

1922   *Speedy* lost in collision with tug in Sea of Marmora.

1942   *Somali* sank whilst in tow of *Ashanti* off Jan Mayen Is. (69° 11' N, 15° 32' W.) after being torpedoed by U.703 on the 20th (q.v.).

1943   MMS 70 sunk by mine off Gallipoli, Italy.

1944   Liberator A/224 sank U.855 off Bergen (61° 00' N, 4° 07' E.).

Sea Service Pistols — French Wars

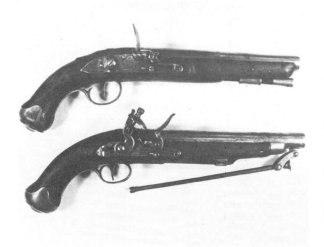

25th SEPTEMBER

1493   Treaty of Tordesilles (Papal Bull) inter Cactera: division of global sphere of influence between Spain and Portugal conditioned British and Spanish privateering activities.

1806   *Centaur, Mars* and *Monarch* captured the French *Armide, Glorie, Infatigable* and *Minerve* off Chassiron lighthouse.

1840   Abortive attack by *Benbow, Carysfort* and *Zebra* on Tortosa, Syria. [m]

1925   X1, largest s/m in RN at the time, commissioned.

1939   First war use of air warning radar at sea *(Rodney* and *Sheffield* during Luftwaffe attack).

1940   *Hereward, Hyperion, Juno* and *Mohawk* bombarded an M.T. concentration West of Sidi Barrani.

1940   French air raid on Gibraltar: *Stella Sirius* sunk.

1945   U.1407 commissioned in RN, and named *Meteorite* in 1947.

Attack on Tortosa, 1840

26th SEPTEMBER

1580 Return of Francis Drake *(Golden Hind, ex- Pelican)* from circumnavigating the World (see 4 October).

1748 Cuthbert Collingwood born.

1801 *Sylph* fought a French frigate 120 miles North of Cape Penas. [m].

1805 *Calcutta,* escorting a convoy of six sail, taken by the French *Magnanime* of the Rochefort Squadron 180 miles W.N.W. of Ushant. Five of the convoy escaped.

1814 Boats of *Plantagenet* and *Rota* attempted to cut out the American privateer *General Armstrong* in Fayal Roads, Azores.

1827 Granting of the Globe, 'Gibraltar' and George IV cypher to be borne on Royal Marines' colours.

1840 Royal Marines and Turkish troops, under Commodore Charles Napier, stormed Sidon. [m]

1904 *Chamois* foundered in Gulf of Patras, pierced by her own screw.

1917 P.61 rammed and sank UC.33 in SW Approaches.

1939 First German aircraft destroyed in World War II shot down by Skuas of Home Fleet.

1940 *Prince Robert* captured the German *Weser* off Manzanillo, Mexico.

1942 *Veteran* sunk by U.404 in N Atlantic. (Convoy RB.1)

1944 Fortress P/220 sank U.871 in N Atlantic.

The Hydrographic Service

The Hydrographer of the Navy is responsible for producing and updating the nautical charts and navigational publications for the RN and for all Government departments: his work is still heavily relied on by most seafarers and many of those concerned with the use of the seabed. Much distinguished but mainly individual and localised work was done in the 17th and 18th centuries by pioneers such as Collins, Mackenzie and Cook. It was not until the Navy started to lose more ships through navigational misadventure than in action with the enemy at the start of the French wars that the first Hydrographer, Dalrymple, was appointed in 1795. Although a civilian — the only one to hold the appointment — he had served the Hon. East India Company as a marine surveyor. By 1820 there were twelve surveying ships in commission, each commanded by a specialist: they and their replacements, one named after Dalrymple, led the world until the formation of an international organisation in 1922. During that intervening century the development of the submarine cable and of the submarine itself hastened the development of sounding machines: since then, Sonar has improved the vertical and Radar the lateral aspects of position finding and surveying.

The development of larger, nuclear-powered submarines, capable of diving deeper and for longer periods than the original submersibles; the doubling of the draught of merchant ships from 13 to 26 metres in the fifties; the. construction, towage and siting of off-shore platforms with four times that draught — all have forced further developments. There are 14,000 wrecks in UK coastal waters; more than half have had to be re-surveyed.

The Hydrographic Department, one of the oldest and smallest in the service, still upholds the tradition — and the standards — whereby a sailor 'can put his trust in God or the Admiralty chart', even though the latter has surrendered the fathom to the metre.

Surveying Ships HMS *Fox* **and** *Swan*

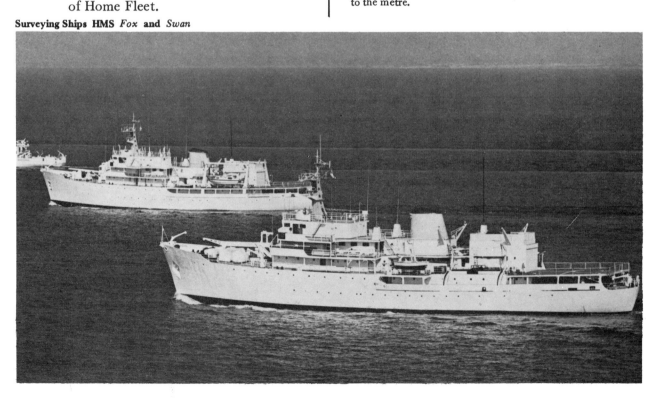

1598	Robert Blake baptised.	1940	GC (ex-AM): Second Hand J.R. Mitchell, RNR, for saving life at sea.

1598   Robert Blake baptised.

1778   *Experiment* and *Unicorn* fought the American *Raleigh* in Penobscot Bay, Maine.

1814   *Carnation* attacked and burnt the American privateer *General Armstrong.* (See 26th September).

1858   VC: A/Second Master George Bell Chicken, No. 3 Detachment I.N., whilst serving as a volunteer with Indian Cavalry against the Indian mutineers at Suhejni.

1873   Ernle Chatfield born.

1914   Allied forces captured Duala, Cameroons. Ships: *Challenger, Dwarf.* Niger Flotilla: *Ivy, Porpoise, Remus.*

1940   GC (ex-AM): Second Hand J.R. Mitchell, RNR, for saving life at sea.

1941   *Trident* sank the German UJ.1201 in Soroysund, Norway.

1941   *Springbank* sunk by U.201 in N Atlantic (49° 09' N, 20° 10'W.). (Convoy MG.73)

1941   *Upright* sank the Italian t.b. *Albatros* off Cape Rasocolmo, N. Sicily.

1943   Halifax B/58 sank U.221 in Atlantic (47° 00' N, 18° 00' W.).

1943   *Eclipse* sank German TA 10 (ex-Italian FR42, ex-French *Pomone).*

1943   *Intrepid* sunk by German aircraft at Leros (37° 07' N, 26° 51' E.). (Attacked on 26th, capsized on 27th).

1944   *Rockingham* sunk by mine (56° 29' N, 0° 57' W.) off Arbroath.

HM Submarine *Trident* **at her launching 7th December 1938**

270

28th SEPTEMBER

1652 Admiral Robert Blake *(Resolution)* defeated the Dutch fleet under Vice Admiral de With *(Prins Willem)* off the Kentish Knock. [bh]. Ships: *Andrew, Diamond, Garland, Greyhound, Guinea, James Longon, Nightingale, Nonsuch, Pelican, Resolution, Ruby, Sovereign, Speaker.*

1677 *Charles* and *James* captured the Algerine *Rose* in Gibraltar Strait.

1778 Boats of *Experiment* captured the American *Raleigh* in Penobscot Bay, where she had been run ashore after being engaged by the *Experiment* and *Unicorn* on previous day.

1806 *Despatch* captured the French *Président* 180 miles West of Ushant.

1810 Boats of *Caledonia, Valiant* and *Armide* cut out three French brigs and captured a shore battery in Basque Roads. [m]

1849 *Inflexible* paid off after first circumnavigation under steam.

1915 VC: Lieutenant-Commander Edgar Christopher Cookson *(Comet)* in an attempt to relieve Kut-al'Amara. When the river was blocked by dhows he took his ship to the centre one and chopped at her cables with an axe until shot dead. Vessels: *Comet, Shaitan, Sumana.*

1917 Curtis flying boat 8676 sank UC.6 in N Sea.

1941* *Hermione* and destroyers bombarded Pantellaria, diversion to Operation Halberd.

1941 *Hyacinth* sank the Italian s/m *Fisalia* off Jaffa in Eastern Mediterranean.

Operation Halberd.

On 24th a convoy of nine 15-knot ships (81,000 tons and 2600 troops) sailed for Malta escorted by the battleships *Nelson, Rodney* and *Prince of Wales*, the carrier *Ark Royal*, 5 cruisers and 8 destroyers. On 27th, air attacks developed and the *Nelson* was hit by a torpedo, but later attacks failed to get past the destroyer screen. By 1900, 27th, the convoy reached the 'Narrows' and the cruisers and destroyers went ahead with the convoy. They turned North to avoid mines, but were unable to throw off the aircraft because of a bright moon. One transport was hit and had to be sunk after the troops had been transferred. At 1130, 28th, the cruisers entered Malta, and at 1330 the convoy arrived. Meanwhile, the Fleet in the Eastern Mediterranean and submarines had been causing diversions, and 3 empty merchantmen were sailed to Gibraltar. An Italian submarine, the *Adua*, was sunk by escorting destroyers on the passage back.

This was the third convoy to Malta from the West in 1941; 39 merchant ships had been convoyed, and only one lost.

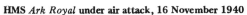

HMS *Ark Royal* under air attack, 16 November 1940

29th SEPTEMBER

1653	Commission for Sick and Wounded formed.
1690	Capture of Cork by the Joint Admirals, Sir Richard Haddock, Henry Killigrew and Sir John Ashby (*Kent*) and the Duke of Marlborough. Ships: *Grafton, Kent, Sovereign, Breda, Charles Galley.*
1758	Horatio Nelson born.
1795	*Southampton* fought the French *Vestale* off Genoa.
1795	*Vanguard* captured the French *Superbe* 50 miles to the eastward of Deseada (Desirade).
1803	*Leda* destroyed two gunboats of the Boulogne invasion flotilla off Boulogne.
1808	*Maria* taken by the French *Departement des Landes* to the north-eastward of Antigues Point, Grand-Terre.
1812	British and Russian gunboats occupied Mittau, Riga, and captured enemy personnel. [m]. Crews provided from *Aboukir* and *Ranger*.
1849	Boats of *Columbine* destroyed a pirate junk in Hong hai Bay.
1917	*Sylvia* and *Tirade* sank the German UC.55 off the Shetlands.
1918	*Ouse* and *Star* sank UB.115 in N Sea: the last U-boat to leave Zeebrugge to attack shipping.
1939	*Calypso* intercepted the German *Minden* which was scuttled 330 miles N.W. of Cape Wrath.
1939	*Caledonia* (ex-*Majestic*) destroyed by fire at Rosyth.
1942	*Nizam* (RAN) and SAAF aircraft intercepted the Vichy *Amiral Pierre* off Lourenco Marques, where she was scuttled on the 30th (26° 04' S, 34° 54' E.).

Burnham Thorpe Rectory-- Nelson's Birthplace

Vice-Admiral Horatio, Viscount Nelson (1758 — 1805)

Born the son of a Norfolk rector in 1758, Nelson joined the Royal Navy in his twelfth year and was posted Captain in his twenty-first. He is still regarded by many as Britain's greatest naval hero. His career at sea was distinguished by bold decisions, usually taking offensive action against the enemy and often exposing his ship to heavy enemy fire. He lost the sight of an eye at Corsica and an arm at Tenerife. With Jervis's fleet at the Battle of Cape St. Vincent in 1797, it was his audacious manoeuvre against the Spanish line that led to their defeat. Against the French at the Battle of the Nile in 1798, his fleet was numerically inferior yet he all but annihilated the enemy squadron. During the attack on the anchored Danish fleet at Copenhagen, again sailing through dangerous waters, he pounded the enemy into submission. On that occasion when signalled to withdraw, he raised his telescope to his blind eye with the remark, "I really do not see the signal." He inspired his men and taught his captains well. It was at Trafalgar in 1805, however, when he made his famous signal, "England expects that every man will do his duty", that set the seal on his fame. In a brilliant tactical victory he won the battle but lost his life, struck down by a bullet from a sharpshooter in the rigging of the French *Redoutable*.

He typified all that was best in the sea officers of the period, being a great fighting man, but much loved by his officers and men. He had a grasp of tactics and strategy which was exceptional even by the standards of his day. After Trafalgar his body was brought home, and amid national mourning was buried with great ceremony in St. Paul's Cathedral.

1780	*Pearl* captured the French *Espérance* 120 miles S.W. by W. of Bermuda.
1822	*Eliza* captured the slaver *Firme Union* off Guajara (Cayo Guajaba), Cuba.
1858	*Pearl's* Naval Brigade at Mau, with detachments of the 13th Light Infantry, Bengal Yeomanry, 6th Madras Light Cavalry, 27th Madras Native Infantry, and Sikh Police Force.
1863	*Britannia* arrived at Dartmouth.
1900	*Pigmy* received the surrender of six Chinese forts at Shanhaikwan, N. China.
1909	Launch of tenth *Neptune,* first HM ship with superimposed turret and first Dreadnought able to fire all main armament in broadside.

1918	*Seagull* sunk in collision in Firth of Clyde.
1940	*Erebus,* with *Garth* and *Vesper,* bombarded Calais. Operation M.W.
1940	*Stuart* (RAN) and Sunderland L.2166 (230 Sq.) sank the Italian s/m *Gondar* off Alexandria (31° 33' N, 28° 33' E.), preparing for a chariot raid.
1941	*Gurkha* and *Legion* sank the Italian s/m *Adua* off Alicante (37° 10' N, 0° 56' E.).
1942	Unsuccessful coastal force action off Terschelling: four MTB and an MGB lost, German ss *Thule* sunk.
1944	Swordfish F/813 (*Campania*) sank U.921 in Arctic (72° 32' N, 12° 55' E.). (Convoy RA.60)

Royal Marines "black-up" before a night patrol in Cyprus, 1956

1748	Rear-Admiral Charles Knowles *(Cornwall)* fought Vice-Admiral Don Andres Reggio *(Africa)* 12 miles N.E. of Havana. Ships: *Tilbury, Strafford, Cornwall, Lenox, Warwick, Canterbury, Oxford.*
1807	*Windsor Castle* packet captured the French privateer *Jeune Richard* 100 miles N.E. by E. of Barbados.
1841	Capture of Ting-Hai, Chusan, by Rear-Admiral Sir William Parker *(Wellesley)* and Lieutenant-General Sir Hugh Gough. Ships: *Wellesley, Blenheim, Blonde, Modeste, Cruizer, Columbine, Bentinck, Sesostris* (I.N.); *Phlegethon, Nemesis, Queen* (Ben. Marine); *Jupiter* and *Rattlesnake* troopships. Troops: Royal Artillery, 18th, 49th and 55th Regiments; Madras Artillery, Madras Sappers and Miners, 36th Madras Native Infantry (rifle coy.). Seamen and Marines were landed.
1849	*Columbine* and *Fury*, with a party from *Hastings,* destroyed 26 junks and the pirate stronghold in Tai Pang harbour, Bias Bay.

1858	*Pearl's* Naval Brigade at Amorha (4th action), with detachments of 13th Light Infantry, 6th Madras Light Cavalry, 27th Madras Native Infantry and Sikh Police Force.
1900	Electrical Departments of Dockyards instituted.
1918	Allied net barrage established across Otranto Strait.
1919	WRNS disbanded.
1923	*Vernon* established ashore, on the old Gunwharf at Portsmouth.
1946	Reconstitution of RNVR.
1946	*Demetrius,* Supply and Secretariat School, renamed *Ceres.*
1960	Royal Marines Forces Volunteer Reserve (RMFVR) became Royal Marines Reserve (RMR).
1971	Announcement of PWO doctrine.

Holland Boat No. 1, 1901

2nd OCTOBER

1699	Half-pay limited by Order in Council to nine Flag officers, 51 captains, 100 Lieutenants and 30 Masters.
1758	*Lizard* captured the French *Duc d'Hanovre* off Brest. A second ship, *Heroine,* was engaged but escaped.
1779	*Apollo* captured the French *Mutin; Jupiter* and *Crescent* captured the French *Pilote* 30 miles S. by W. of Lizard Head.
1786	Admiral Viscount Keppel died.
1805	*Egyptienne* captured the French *Acteon* off La Rochelle.
1836	*Beagle* arrived Falmouth having sailed from Devonport 27th Dec. 1831.
1840	Boats of *Edinburgh* and *Hastings* destroyed an ammunition store at Beirut. [m].
1901	HM first s/m launched at Barrow-in-Furness; a Holland boat with neither name nor number until she became No. 1.

1905	*Dreadnought* keel laid (see 3rd Oct).
1917	*Drake* torpedoed by U.79 in the North Channel; sank later in Church Bay, Rathlin Island.
1917	*Begonia* (Q.10) sunk in collision with U.151 off Casablanca.
1918	Bombardment of Durazzo. Ships: *Dartmouth, Glasgow, Gloucester, Lowestoft* (S.O.), *Weymouth.* Destroyers: *Acheron, Acorn, Badger, Cameleon, Fury, Goshawk, Jackal, Lapwing, Nereide, Nymphe, Ruby, Shark, Swan, Tigress, Tribune* (D.5), *Warrego.*
1934	Royal Indian Marine became Royal Indian Navy. (Bombay Marine 1863-1877).
1940	*Hasty* and *Havock* sank the Italian s/m *Berillo* off Egypt.
1940	*Orion* and *Sydney* (RAN) bombarded Maltezana area, Stampalia.
1942	*Curaçoa* sunk in collision with RMS *Queen Mary* in NW Approaches (55° 50' N, 8° 38' W.).

HM Submarine *A3* in Portsmouth Harbour, 1901. The officer in command is Admiral Sir Charles Little as a Lieutenant, in which role he took over from the Royal Engineers Fort Blockhouse, commission as HMS *Dolphin.*

3rd OCTOBER

1799 *Speedy* destroyed four Spanish coasters near Cape Trafalgar.

1806 Boats of *Minerva* cut out two Spanish gunboats in Arosa Bay.

1808 *Carnation* taken by the French *Palinure* 150 miles to the north eastward of the Virgin Islands.

1857 First party of *Shannon's* Naval Brigade arrived at Allahabad. (See 18th August).

1906 *Dreadnought* began sea trials. (See 2nd October).

1914 First units of the Royal Naval Division (RM Brigade) arrived at Antwerp.

1915 D.5 sunk by mine two miles South of South Cross Sand buoy, Yarmouth.

1915 First German merchant ship *(Svionia)* sunk by British submarine (E.19), in the Baltic. (54° 35' N, 13° 41' E.).

1917 UC.14 sunk by mine off Zeebrugge.

1918 L.10 sunk by German destroyer S.33, which she torpedoed, off Texel.

A little known job for the Wrens — coaling ship, working alongside men, wielding a shovel with the best of them

1941 *Kenya* sank U-Boat supply ship *Kota Pinang** in North Atlantic. (*ex-Dutch)

1943 *Usurper* sunk by the German UJ.2208 in the Gulf of Genoa.

1952 Ships expended in atomic tests at Monte Bello, including *Plym*.

A group of RM Artillerymen from the Royal Naval Division filling water bottles, Belgium 1914

4th OCTOBER

1780 *Phoenix* lost in West Indies.

1797 *Alexandria* captured the French privateer *Epicharis* 20 miles East of Barbados.

1805 *Princess Charlotte* captured the French (ex-British) *Cyane* to the eastward of Tobago. The French *Naiade* was also engaged, but escaped.

1813 Boats of *Furieuse* cut out two gunboats and fourteen of a French convoy, and sank two more of the convoy, at Santa Marinella.

1824 Boats of *Sybille* cut out the Greek *San Nicolo*, *Polyxenes* and *Bella Poula* at Nauplia, Greece.

1854 *Sidon* and *Inflexible* and the French *Cacique* and *Caton* attacked Fort Nikolaev (Pervomaiskaya).

1872 Roger Keyes born.

1912 B.2 sunk in collision with ss *Amerika* off Dover.

1918 *Snapdragon* and *Cradosin*, with s.s. *War Queen*, *Myrmidon* and *Queensland* sank UB.68 in Central Mediterranean (35° 56' N, 16° 20' E.). Her captain, Doenitz, became Grand-Admiral in World War II.

1941 *Lady Shirley* sank U.111 (27° 15' N, 20° 27' W.). W.S.W. of Teneriffe.

The trawler *Lady Shirley* (470 tons-10 knots) was on patrol off the Canary Islands. An object was sighted on the surface and then it disappeared. She closed and gained asdic contact at 1800 yards, dropped a pattern of 5 depth charges and a U-boat (U.111, 740 tons) surfaced and opened fire, hitting the trawler. The submarine's gun exploded as the tampion had not been removed before firing, and the trawler returned the fire, hitting the submarine nine times with 4 in shells. The submarine sank stern first, and the *Lady Shirley's* crew of 30 took 45 prisoners, and then headed for Gibraltar, four days steaming away.

1943 Liberator X/120 sank U.279 in N Atlantic (60° 51' N, 29° 26' W.).

1944 *Chebogue* (RCN) torpedoed by U.1227 in (49° 20' N, 24° 20' W.). (Convoy ONS.33). Foundered in tow: beached on Mumbles, 11th Oct.

1966 First and last Type 82 destroyer, *Bristol,* ordered from Swan Hunter.

HMS *Bristol, 1973.*

1804   *Indefatigable, Lively, Medusa* and *Amphion* captured the Spanish *Medea, Clara* and *Fama* and sank *Mercedes* 27 miles S.W. of Cape de Santa Maria, off Cadiz.

1813   *Edinburgh, Imperieuse, Resistance, Eclair, Pylades* and *Swallow* captured a French convoy of 29 sail and destroyed the batteries at Porto d'Anzio.

1813   *Fantome* captured the American privateer *Portsmouth Packet* (ex-Canadian *Liverpool Packet*) 21 miles S.E. of Matinicus Island.

1942   Hudson N/269 sank U.582 in N Atlantic.

1943   Hudson F/269 sank U.389 in N Atlantic. (Convoy ONS.19). (A squadron anniversary)

1944   *Zwaardvisch* (Neth) sank U.168 off Java.

1944   *Aurora* and *Catterick* bombarded Levitha Island, in the Dodecanese, and landed a party to whom the island surrendered later that day.

1719   Capitulation of Vigo to a combined force under Vice-Admiral James Mighells and Colonel Viscount Cobham *(Ipswich)*. Ships: *Bideford, Enterprize, Ipswich, Kingsale, Speedwell Bomb.*

1762   Capture of Manila by Rear-Admiral Samuel Cornish *(Norfolk)* and Colonel William Draper. Ships: *America, Elizabeth, Grafton, Lenox, Norfolk, Panther, Weymouth.* 50's and smaller: *Argo, Falmouth, Seaford, Seahorse, Southsea Castle* storeship.

1779   *Quebec* blew up in action with the French *Surveillante* 45 miles North of Ushant. *Rambler* fought the French *Expedition* in the same area.

1810   Boats of *Pallas* captured two Danish privateers 30 miles S.W. of Stavanger.

1811   *Rolla* captured the French privateer *Espoir* 3 miles N.W. of Fecamp.

1914   E.9 sank the German S.116 off the Western Ems. First sinking by one of HM submarines.

1915   *Brighton Queen* mined off Nieuport, Belgium.

Navy anti-aircraft gunners with a Lewis gun (World War 2)

1747   *Dartmouth* blew up in action with the Spanish *Glorioso* 20 miles W. by N. of Cape St. Vincent. The *King George* and *Prince Frederick* privateers also engaged *Glorioso*.

1760   Boats of Rear-Admiral Charles Steeven's squadron cut out the French *Hermione* and *Baleine* at Pondicherry.

1769   Captain James Cook discovered New Zealand.

1782   *Mutine* captured the French privateer *Comte de Valentinios* six miles N.E. by E. of the Casquets.

1795   *Censeur* and 15 sail of a convoy taken by the superior squadron of Captain Joseph de Richery *(Jupiter)* 150 miles W. by N. of Cape St. Vincent. *Bedford*, *Fortitude* and 32 others of the convoy escaped.

1943   *Unruly* attacked with gunfire a German convoy of 6 L/C, 1 ammunition ship and 1 trawler which was later destroyed by *Faulknor*, *Fury*, *Penelope* and *Sirius* off Stampalia.

1944   *Termagant* and *Tuscan* sank the German TA.37 (ex-Italian t.b. *Gladio*) off Skiathos E. of Greece (39° 49' N, 23° 17' E.).

1667   Capture of Surinam by Rear-Admiral Sir John Harman *(Lion)*. Ships: *Bonaventure*, *Lion*, *Portsmouth* ketch.

1746   *Weazle* captured the French privateers *Jeantie* and *Fortune* off the Isle of Wight.

1747   *Russell* captured the Spanish *Glorioso* off Cape St. Vincent.

1806   Rocket attack on Boulogne by RN (First rocket bombardment).

1808   *Modeste* captured the French *Iena* in the Bay of Bengal.

1884   *Rodney* launched: last battleship with figure head.

1914   RNAS Sopwith Tabloid destroyed the Zeppelin LZ.25 in her shed at Dusseldorf.

1939   U.12 sunk by mine in Dover Strait.

1942   *Active* sank U.179 off Cape Town.

1943   Liberator R/86 sank U.419, Liberators Z/86 and T/120 sank U.643 and Sunderland J/423 (RCAF) sank U.610 in North Atlantic. (Convoy SC.143). *Orkan* (Pol) sunk by U.610.

1943   *Unruly* sank the German *Bulgaria* (ex-*Bulgarian*) in Aegean.

1944   *Mulgrave* (RCN) mined in Channel: CTL.

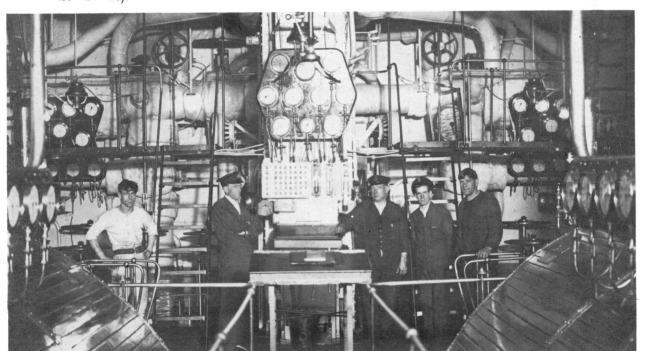

Engine Room of HMS *Royal Sovereign*, 1922

9th OCTOBER

1799	*Lutine* wrecked off Holland: bell recovered and now in use at Lloyds.
1805	Vice-Admiral Lord Nelson wrote the Trafalgar memorandum, now in British Museum — 'no captain can do wrong if he places his ship alongside that of an enemy."
1810	*Rhin* captured the French privateer *Contesse de Montalevèt* 90 miles W.S.W. of the Scilly Islands.
1812	*Briseis* (escorting a convoy) captured the French privateer *Petit Poucet* in Hano Sund.
1813	*Thunder* captured the French privateer *Neptune* off the Owers. [m]
1834	Admiral Lord Saumarez died.
1852	Capture of Prome by a combined force under Major-General Henry Godwin and Commodore George Lambert *(Fox)*. *Fire Queen* (Ben.Mar.) and boats of *Fox, Hastings, Sphinx* and *Winchester.*
1862	VC: Able Seaman George Hinckley, *(Sphinx)* for twice covering 150 yards of ground under enemy fire to rescue wounded men. British and French landing parties, assisted by Chinese troops, repulsed the Taiping rebels and captured the city of FungWha, above Ningpo. Ships: *Hardy, Flamer; Déroulède* and *Confucius* (Fr.). and seamen and Marines of *Encounter* and *Sphinx.*
1939	*Belfast* captured the German *Cap Norte* to the north westward of the Faeroes.
1943	*Panther* sunk by German aircraft in the Scarpanto Channel (35° 43' N, 27° 36' E.).
1943	*Carlisle* damaged beyond repair by German aircraft in Aegean.

HMS *Agincourt* leading the 4th Battle Squadron into Scapa Flow 1915

10th OCTOBER

1707	*Cumberland, Chester* and *Ruby* (escorting a convoy) taken by the superior French squadrons of Commodore Comte de Forbin *(Mars)* and Captain Rene Duguay-Trouin *(Lys); Devonshire* blew up in action S.W. of Dodman Point.
1806	Boats of *Galatea* cut out four Spanish schooners at Barcelona, Venezuela.
1814	Boats of *Endymion* attempted to take the American privateer *Prince de Neufchatel* off Nantucket.
1865	Suppression of Jamaican rebellion: *Wolverine, Onyx* and *Nettle.*
1878	*Vulture* captured 20 pirate dhows near Ras Tinnorah, Persian Gulf.
1917	GC (ex-AM): A.W. Newman, Mate, for disposing of burning ammunition.
1943	*Trooper* sunk by mine in the Aegean: Leros area.
1946	Formation of Torpedo and Anti-Submarine branch.

The impressive sight of First World War Battle Squadrons at Sea. Less elegant but no less awe-inspiring than their wooden predecessors were the capital ships of the first half of this century — coal, then oil-fired battleships and battle cruisers. Their role was taken over by the aircraft carrier in the Second World War and thereafter by the Polaris-firing nuclear-powered submarine, but their power reached its zenith in Operation ZZ, when the Grand Fleet, consisting of 5 Battle Squadrons and 2 Battle Cruiser Squadrons (supported by 6 Cruiser Squadrons and 8 Destroyer Flotillas) received the surrender of the German High Seas Fleet.

HMS *Canada* and part of the 1st Battle Squadron, 1918

11th OCTOBER

1746   *Nottingham* captured the French *Mars* 70 miles to the south westward of Cape Clear.

1776   First battle of Lake Champlain. The British Lake Flotilla fought the American Lake Flotilla. (See 11th September and 13th October).

1780   *Amazon* in a hurricane in the West Indies.

1782   Relief of Gibraltar by Lord Howe; the transformed signalling system of Rear-Admiral Kempenfelt was used with great effect (see 12th December).

1797   Battle of Camperdown. [m*, m, bh]. Admiral Adam Duncan *(Venerable)* defeated the Dutch fleet under Vice-Admiral Jan de Winter *(Vrijheid)*. Ships: *Russell, Director, Montagu, Veteran, Monarch, Powerful, Monmouth, Agincourt, Triumph, Venerable, Ardent, Bedford, Lancaster, Belliqueux, Adamant, Isis.* Frigates, etc.: *Beaulieu, Circe, Martin; Rose, Active, King George, Diligent, Speculator.*

1811   *Imperieuse* captured two French gunboats, sank a third and destroyed a fort at Positano.

1854   *Beagle* and *Firebrand* rescued an Austrian storeship which had run ashore under the Russian batteries near Sevastopol.

1855   VC: Commander John Edmund Commerell and William Thomas Rickard, quartermaster *(Weser)*. Destruction of Russian stores up the Salgir River, Sea of Azov, by landing party from *Weser*.

1914   *Nusa* captured the German *Komet* near Talassia, New Britain — added to RAN as *Una*.

1923   Order in Council confirmed AFO of 22nd June for the amalgamation of the RMA and RMLI.

1940   MTBs 22, 31 and 32 sank two German trawlers off Calais (51° 02' N, 1° 48' E.).

1940   *Revenge*, 7 destroyers and 6 MTBs. bombarded Cherbourg. Covering force: *Cardiff, Emerald, Newcastle* and 6 destroyers. Operation Medium.

1943   *Hythe* sunk by U.371 off Bougie (37° 04' N, 5 °00' E.).

1944   4 MGBs of 57 Flotilla destroyed two German coastal convoys off Vir in Adriatic.

Admiral Adam Viscount Duncan (1731-1804)

Duncan joined the navy at the age of 15 in 1745, was promoted Lieutenant in 1755 and Commander in 1759. He was made post captain in 1761 and commanded the 74 gun *Valiant* under Keppel at Belleisle and Havana. He commanded the *Monarch* at St Vincent in 1780. He was promoted Admiral in 1795 and placed in command of the North Sea squadron. In 1797, while Duncan was responsible for blockading the Dutch fleet, the mutiny broke out at the Nore amongst his fleet. With only the *Venerable, Adamant,* and the frigate *Circe,* Duncan continued the blockade by making signals to the frigate on the horizon who pretended to pass them on to a fleet below the horizon. When the mutiny had been quelled, it says much for Duncan's brilliance as an Admiral that he was able to take his fleet out and inflict the crushing defeat on the Dutch at Camperdown which restored the morale of his fleet.

12th OCTOBER

1702 Admiral Sir George Rooke (*Somerset*)* and the Dutch Vice-Admiral Gerard Callenburgh (*Hollandia*) destroyed the French fleet and treasure-ships under Vice-Admiral Conte de Chateaurenault (*Fort*) in Vigo Bay. [bh]. Ships: *Association, Barfleur, Bedford, Berwick, Cambridge, Essex, Grafton, Kent, Mary, Monmouth, Northumberland, Orford, Pembroke, Ranelagh, Somerset, Swiftsure, Torbay*.
Fireships: *Griffin, Hawk, Hunter, Lightning, Phoenix, Terrible, Vulture*. Dutch ships: *Alkmaar, Dordrecht, Gouda, Hollandia, Katwijk, Muyde (?Muiden), Reigersbergh, Unie, Zeluwe, Zeven Provincien* and three fireships.
*His usual flagship was the *Royal Sovereign*, which was not engaged.
17 French warships and 17 Spanish treasure ships taken or sunk.

1798 Commodore Sir John Warren (*Canada*) defeated Commodore Jean Bompard (*Hoche*) 15 miles N.N.E. of the Rosses, Donegal Bay reducing threat of French aid to Irish rebellion, [m, bh]. Ships: *Canada, Foudroyant, Robust*. Frigates: *Amelia, Anson, Ethalion, Magnanime, Melampus*. Captured: *Bellone, Coquille, Embuscade, Hoche*.

1800 Boats of *Montagu* and *Magnificent* cut out a convoy at Port Danenne, Lorient.

1803 First four of eventually ten Trinity House volunteer artillery vessels manned: paid off after Trafalgar.

1817 *Trincomalee* launched (now *Foudroyant* in Portsmouth Harbour).

1857 Second party of *Pearl's* Naval Brigade (Lieutenant S.W.D. Radcliffe) left the ship. (see 12th September).

1897 *Canopus* launched: first battleship with watertube boilers. Fitted with Krupp armour. Grounded as coast defence ship at Port Stanley 1914: a richochet from a solid shot, loaded in secret anticipation of a competitive gun drill, was the first hit on von Spee's squadron.

1940 *Ajax* sank the Italian t.bs. *Airone* and *Ariel* in Central Mediterranean (35° 37' N, 16° 42' E.), in a night action and damaged the Italian destroyer *Artigliere* which was sunk later in the day by *York* (35° 47' N, 16° 25' E.).

1942 Liberator H/120 sank U.597 in N Atlantic (56° 50' N, 28° 05' W.). (Convoy PNS.136)

Typical control room layout of the submarine G7 (First World War) On the right of the hatch is the Captain's area (cabin). The two large handwheels to the fore are the hydroplane controls. Note the carbines (rifles) to the left. G7 was lost in the North Sea in 1918.

13th OCTOBER

1665 *Merlin,* escorting a convoy, taken by the Dutch *Karel,* to the southward of Cadiz. Three of the convoy were also taken by four other Dutch ships.

1776 The British Lake Flotilla defeated the American Lake Flotilla on Lake Champlain. [bh]. Ships and vessels: *Carleton, Inflexible, Loyal Convert, Maria, Thunderer.* Troops: Royal Artillery.

1796 *Terpsichore* captured the Spanish *Mahonesa* midway between Cartagena and Cape de Gata. [m, bh]

1804 *Thetis, Ceres* and *Penelope* letters of marque fought the French privateer *Bonaparte* 105 miles to the eastward of Barbados.

1805 *Jason* captured the French *Naiade* 350 miles East of S.Lucia.

1813 *Telegraph* destroyed the French *Flibustier* 3 miles off the mouth of the River Adour.

1841 Occupation of Ningpo by Rear-Admiral Sir William Parker *(Modeste)* and Lieutenant-General Sir Hugh Gough. Seamen and Marines were landed. Ships: *Modeste; Nemesis, Phlegethon* (Ben. Mar.) Boats of *Blenheim* and *Welles-ley.* Troops: Royal Artillery, 18th, 49th, 55th (light coy); Madras Artillery, Madras Sappers and Miners, 36th Madras Native Infantry.

1899 Vice-Admiral Philip Colomb died.

1922 Supply Branch established by Order in Council.

1939 U.40 sunk by mine in Dover Strait.

1939 *Ilex* and *Imogen* sank U.42 in Western Approaches.

1939 GC (ex-EGM): James Gordon Melville Turner, Radio-officer, MN (s.s. *Manaar*) *(Gazette* date).

1940 *Ashanti, Cossack* (D.4), *Maori* and *Sikh* sank convoy of 3 ships and its 2 escorts in N Sea.

1940 Air strike by 15 Swordfish aircraft of 815 and 819 Sq. *(Illustrious),* with 2 cruisers and 4 destroyers, on Port Laki, Leros.

1940 *Ladybird* and a Bombay aircraft of 216 Sq. bombarded Sidi Barrani.

1943 *Laforey, Lookout* and *Flores* (Neth) bombarded positions North of the Volturno River, in conjunction with landing of tanks from 4 LCTs. Operation Avalanche.

HMS *Renown* at Portsmouth, late 19th century

1726   Charles Middleton born.

1747   Rear-Admiral Edward Hawke *(Devonshire)* defeated Commodore the Marquis de L'Étanduère *(Tonnant)*, escorting a large convoy. (Ushant, E. by N. 200 miles). [bh] . Ships: *Defiance, Devonshire, Eagle, Edinburgh, Gloucester, Kent, Lion, Monmouth, Nottingham, Portland, Princess Louisa, Tilbury, Windsor, Yarmouth, Weazle.* French ships captured: *Fougueux, Monarque, Neptune, Severne, Terrible, Trident.* The convoy escaped.

1795   *Mermaid* captured the French *Républicaine* 25 miles West of Grenada.

1798   *Melampus* captured the French *Résolue* in Donegal Bay.

1810   *Briseis* captured the French privateer *Sans-Souci* 50 miles W. by S. of Horns Rev. [m]

1859   Eight officers of *Assaye* (Indian Navy) and *Lynx* assisted in the defeat of a rebel force at Zanzibar.

1935   Naval Radio Direction Finding development started at HM Signal School, Portsmouth.

1939   *Royal Oak* sunk by U.47 in Scapa Flow (185° 1.7 miles from Scapa Pier light).

1939   *Icarus, Inglefield, Intrepid* and *Ivanhoe* sank U.45 S.W. of Ireland.

1941   *Fleur-de-Lys* sunk by U.206 in Gibraltar Strait (36° 00' N, 6° 30' W.).

1942   MTB 236 sank the German disguised raider *Komet* (Schiff 45) off Cap de La Hogue. An escorting R-boat was also sunk, and two other escorts set on fire. Operation Bowery. Ships: *Albrighton, Brocklesby, Cottesmore, Eskdale, Fernie, Glaisdale, Krakowiak* (Pol), *Quorn, Tynedale.* MTBs: 49 52, 55, 56, 84, 86, 95, 229, 236.

1711   *Edgar* blew up at Spithead.

1795   *Pomone* captured the French *Eveille* off Île d'Yeu.

1799   Boats of *Echo* cut out a Spanish and a French brig in Aguadilla Bay, Puerto Rico. The actions were a.m. and p.m. respectively.

1914   *Hawke* sunk by U.9, 60 miles East of Kinnairds Head, Aberdeen.

1918   J.6 accidentally sunk by Q-ship *Cymric* off Blyth.

1940   *Rainbow* sunk by the Italian s/m *Enrico Toti* off Calabria.

1940   *Triad* sunk off the Libyan coast, cause unknown.

1941   *Torbay* bombarded Apollonia.

1942   *Viscount* sank U.619 and Liberator H/120 sank U.661 in N Atlantic. (Convoy SC.104)

1944   Re-occupation of Athens by force under Rear-Admiral J.M. Mansfield (15th C.S.). Operation Manna. Ships: *Ajax, Aurora, Black Prince, Orion, Sirius.* LSI(M): *Prince David, Prince Henry.* LST: *Bruiser, Thruster.*

1958   *Eagle, Sheffield, Albion* and *Bulwark* in emergency operations off Lebanon and Jordan.

1965   Admiral of the Fleet Sir Henry Oliver died, aged 101.

A flight deck accident on HMS *Eagle* 1940

16th OCTOBER

1778	Capture of Pondicherry by Major-General Hector Munro after a close blockade by Commodore Sir Edward Vernon *(Ripon)*. Ships: *Ripon, Coventry, Seahorse, Cormorant; Valentine* (H.E.I.C.).
1798	*Kangaroo* fought the French *Loire* off Blacksod Bay, Ireland.
1799	*Ethalion* captured the Spanish *Tetis* off Cape Finisterre.
1918	L.12 torpedoed and sank UB.90 in Skagerrak.
1939	GC (ex-EGM): Commander Richard Frank Jolly *(Mohawk)* (posthumous).
1940	*Dundalk* mined off Harwich (51° 57' N, 1° 27' E.): sank in tow next day.
1940	*Erebus*, with 3 destroyers, bombarded Dunkirk.

1940	11 Swordfish and 3 Skua aircraft of 816 and 801 Sq. *(Furious)* bombed the oil tanks and seaplane base at Tromso. Operation Dhu.
1941	*Gladiolus* sunk by U.568 in Western Approaches.
1942	*Fame* sank U.353 in Western Approaches. (Convoy SC.104)
1943	Liberators S/59 and L/86 sank U.844, Liberators C/59, E/120 and Z/120 sank U.470 and *Sunflower* sank U.631 in N Atlantic. (Convoy ON.206)
1943	Liberator Y/86 sank U.964 in N Atlantic. (Convoy ONS.20)
1943	Bisley aircraft E/244 and H/244 sank U.533 in Gulf of Oman.
1944	*Annan* (RCN) sank U.1006 off the Faeroes.

Sea Hawk aircraft of 898 Squadron, HMS *Eagle,* over Malta, 1959

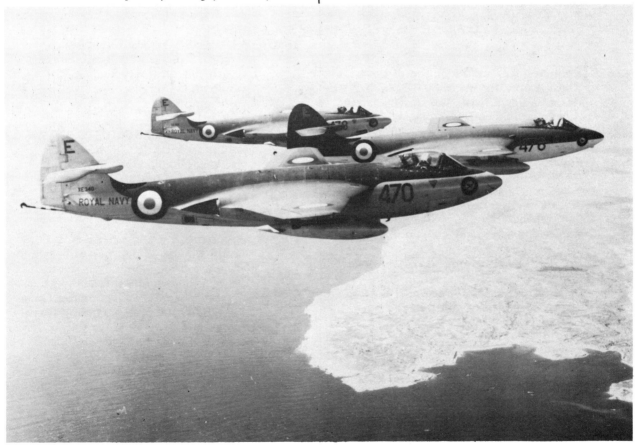

285

17th OCTOBER

1781   Admiral of the Fleet Lord Hawke died.

1782   *London* and *Torbay* fought the French *Scipion* and *Sibylle* in Samana Bay, San Domingo. *Scipion* wrecked. *Badger* in company though not engaged.

1798   *Mermaid* fought the French *Loire* off the SE coast of Ireland.

1799   *Alcmene, Naiad, Ethalion* and *Triton* captured the Spanish *Brigida* and *Thetis* in the entrance to Muros Bay.

1804   *Cruizer* captured the French privateer *Contre-Amiral Magon* after a chase of 97 miles that started with their engagement off Ostend.

1854   First Bombardment of Sevastopol by the Allied Fleet. Ships: *Terrible, Albion, Arethusa, Sampson, London, Sans Pareil, Agamemnon, Sphinx, Tribune, Lynx, Queen, Bellerophon, Rodney, Vengeance, Trafalgar, Britannia.* Towed or lashed alongside larger vessels: *Firebrand, Niger, Triton; Vesuvius, Furious, Retribution, Highflyer, Spitfire, Spiteful, Cyclops.* French: *Napoléon, Henri Quatre, Valmy, Ville de Paris, Jupiter, Friedland, Marengo, Montebello, Suffren, Jean Bart, Charlemagne.* Turkish: *Mahmudieh.*

1855   Bombardment and reduction of the Kinburn forts by British and French fleets. Ships: *Royal Albert, Algiers, Agamemnon, Princess Royal, St Jean D'Acre, Curaçao, Tribune, Sphinx, Hannibal, Dauntless, Terrible; Odin, Spitfire, Valorous, Furious, Sidon, Leopard, Gladiator, Firebrand, Stromboli, Spiteful.* Bomb vessels: *Raven, Magnet, Camel, Hardy, Flamer, Firm.* Gun vessels: *Lynx, Arrow, Viper, Snake, Wrangler, Beagle.* Gunboats: *Boxer, Clinker, Cracker, Fancy, Grinder.* French: *Montebello, Asmodée, Cacique, Sane.* Floating batteries: *Devastation, Lave, Tonnante.* (First armoured ships in action).

1884   Sick Berth branch formed by Order in Council.

1914   *Undaunted, Lance, Lennox, Legion* and *Loyal* sank the German destroyers S.119, S.115, S.117 and S.118 in the Broad Fourteens, 40 miles S.W. of the Texel.

The Screw
The superiority of the screw over the paddle was proved in May 1845 when the steam sloop *Rattler*, screw-driven, competed with the paddle-sloop *Alecto* of similar power and size. *Rattler* won the races easily, and when the two vessels were connected stern to stern and attemped to out-tow each other *Rattler* after some time was able to pull the *Alecto* astern at 2½ knots. Despite this demonstration the early steam warships with screw propulsion remained essentially sailing ships with auxiliary engines. Funnels were telescoped and propellers hoisted up out of the water when under sail. In 1848, the RN commissioned its first screw frigates, the *Dauntless* and the *Arrogant.* The first screw ship-of-the-line was launched in 1850, a 91 gun three-decker, the *Agamemnon.* She proved her worth being one of two vessels able to bombard Sevastopol effectively, because of their ability to manoeuvre regardless of the wind.

1917   *Strongbow* and *Mary Rose,* escorting a Scandinavian convoy, sunk by the German light cruisers *Bremse* and *Brummer* in Norwegian Sea (60° 06' N, 1° 06' E.). [bh]

1917   C.32 grounded and blown up in Gulf of Riga.

1918   Ostend retaken by Allied Forces.

1939   *Iron Duke* bombed in Scapa Flow: grounded but remained in commission.

1940   CG: Jack Maynard Cholmondeley Easton, Sub-Lt. RNVR and Bennett Southwell, Ordinary Seaman, for bomb and mine disposal; the latter posthumously.

1943   Liberators D/59 and H/120 sank U. 540 in N Atlantic (58° 38' N, 31° 56' W.). (Convoy ON.206)

1943   *Byard* sank U.841 in N Atlantic, off Cape Farewell. (Convoy ONS.20)

1944   Bombardment and air strike by Force 63 on Nicobar. Operation Millet. Ships: *Renown* (Vice-Admiral Sir Arthur Power); *Indomitable* (Rear-Admiral C Moody), *Victorious; London* (Rear-Admiral H T C Walker, C.S.5), *Cumberland, Phoebe, Suffolk,* 9 destroyers, including *Norman* and *Van Galen* (Neth). FAA Sq: 815, 817 (Barracuda), 1839, 1844 (Hellcat); 1834, 1836 (Corsair).

1948   GC (ex-AM): A.R. Lowe, Boy, for saving another member of crew of liberty boat capsized in gale at Portland.

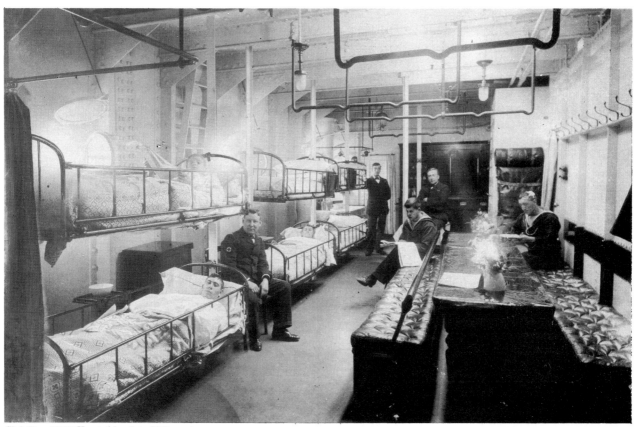

Sick Bay, HMS *Hampshire,* late 19th century

HMS *Terrible* at Sevastopol 1854

18th OCTOBER

1652 First recorded dockyard strike when no pay was available on pay day.

1746 *Severn,* escorting a convoy, taken by the French *Terrible* 450 miles W.S.W. of Ushant. The convoy, with *Woolwich,* escaped.

1760 *Boreas* captured the French *Sirene; Lively* captured *Valeur; Hampshire* drove ashore *Prince Edouard* and *Fleur-de-Lys* (burnt by own crews) off Tortuga.

1778 Surrender of Pondicherri after Vernon's blockade.

1798 *Anson* and *Kangaroo* captured the French *Loire* S.W. of Ireland.

1806 *Caroline* captured the Dutch *Zeerob* between Middleburg and Amsterdam Islands, and *Maria Reygersbergen* in Batavia Roads. The Dutch *Phoenix,* three corvettes and eight merchant vessels ran themselves ashore.

1812 *Frolic,* escorting a convoy, taken by the American *Wasp* 240 miles to the northward of Bermuda. *Poictiers* took both ships.

1854 Boats of *Spartan* recaptured the cargo of the wrecked *Caldera* barque to the southward of Macao; also destroyed 20 junks, 3 villages and a battery at Sam Hoi Chuk.

1854 VC: Captain William Peel and Midshipman Edward St. John Daniel

(*Diamond*) (See 5th November and 18th June). Batteries before Sevastopol.

1881 Completion of the third *Inflexible,* a milestone in British naval architecture with first armoured citadel and with an armoured deck as well as armoured sides.

1914 First bombardment of Ostend. (Continued until the 21st). Ships: *Attentive, Foresight, Humber, Mersey, Severn, Amazon, Mohawk, Nubian.*

1914 E.3 sunk by U.27 off the Ems (first RN submarine sunk in action).

1924 Admiral Sir Percy Scott died.

1940 H.49 sunk by the German UJ.116 and UJ.118 off the Dutch coast.

1940 Seven U-Boats attacked convoy SC.7 and sank seventeen of thirty-four ships; six U-Boats attacked Convoy HX.79 and sank fourteen of forty-nine.

1940 *Firedrake, Wrestler* and London flying boats of 202 Sq, sank the Italian s/m *Durbo* E of Gibraltar.

1941 *Broadwater* sunk by U.101 in N Atlantic. (Convoy SC.48)

1944 *Geelong* (RAN) sunk in collision with the US tanker *York* off New Guinea.

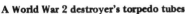

A World War 2 destroyer's torpedo tubes

19th OCTOBER

1797   *Anson* and *Boadicea* captured the French privateer *Zephyr* 45 miles S.W. by W. of Belle Île.

1799   *Stag* captured the French letter of marque *Heureux* 130 miles W. by S. of Cordouan lighthouse.

1799   *Cerberus* fought five Spanish frigates and two brigs, escorting a large convoy, 40 miles N.N.E. of Cape Penas.

1917   E.45 sank UC.62 in N Sea.

1918   Zeebrugge and Bruges retaken by Allied forces.

1918   *Plumpton* mined off Ostend.

1939   *Rawalpindi* intercepted the German *Gonzenheim* which scuttled herself in Iceland-Faeroes gap (63° 25' N, 12° 00' W.).

1939   *Scotstoun* captured the German tanker *Biscaya* off Reykjavik (66° 30' N, 23° 00' W.).

1940   *Venetia* sunk by mine off the East Knob lightvessel in the Thames Estuary (51° 33' N, 1° 10' E.).

1941   *Mallow* and *Rochester* sank U.204 in Strait of Gibraltar.

1942   P.37 (*Unbending*) sank the Italian destroyer *Giovanni da Verazzano* off Lampedusa.

1944   *Termagant* and *Tuscan* drove ashore and destroyed the German TA.18 (ex-Italian t.b. *Solferino*) in the Gulf of Saloniki.

1944   Continuation of attacks on Nicobar and on Nancowry. (See 17th October).

Battle of Navarino (20th October 1827)

289

20th OCTOBER

1778   *Jupiter* and *Medea* fought the French *Triton* off Cape Villano, Spain.

1779   *Charon, Lowestoffe, Pomona, Porcupine, Racehorse,* with the Loyal Irish Volunteers, captured *San Fernando de Omoa* and two Spanish privateers.

1779   *Proserpine* captured the French *Alcmene* 80 miles East of Martinique.

1782   Admiral Viscount Howe *(Victory)* fought the Franco-Spanish fleet 45 miles W. by S. of Cape Spartel. Ships: Van: *Goliath, Ganges, Royal William, Britannia, Atlas, Ruby; Panther, Foudroyant, Edgar, Polyphemus, Suffolk, Vigilant.* Centre: *Courageux, Crown, Alexander, Sampson, Princess Royal, Victory; Blenheim, Asia, Egmont, Queen, Bellona.* Rear: *Raisonnable, Fortitude, Princess Amelia, Berwick, Bienfaisant; Dublin, Cambridge, Ocean, Union, Buffalo, Vengeance.*

1793   *Crescent* captured the French *Réunion* 4 miles E. by N. of Cherbourg. [m, bh]. Captain James Saumarez knighted.

1798   *Fisgard* captured the French *Immortalité* 60 miles W. by N. of Ushant. [m, bh]

1827   Battle of Navarino. (The last sea fight of the sailing Navy). [m, bh]. Vice-Admiral Sir Edward Codrington *(Asia)* destroyed the Turko-Egyptian fleet in Navarino Bay and hence the Turkish hegemony over Greece. Ships: *Albion, Asia, Genoa; Brisk, Cambrian, Dartmouth, Glasgow, Hind Cutter, Mosquito, Philomel, Rose, Talbot.* French: *Alcyone, Armide, Breslaw, Daphne, Scipion, Sirène, Trident.* Russian: *Alexander, Nevski, Azof, Castor, Constantin, Elena, Gangoot, Provornyi, Yezekeyeel.*

1849   *Columbine, Fury, Phlegethon* (Ben. Mar), with a party from *Hastings*, destroyed 58 pirate junks in the Kua Kam, Indo-China. [bh]

1857   Second party of *Shannon's* Naval Brigade arrived at Allahabad. (See 18th September).

1914   First British merchant ship (*Glitra*) to be sunk by a German submarine torpedoed by U.17 14 miles W.S.W. of Skudenaes — until then the submarine had been regarded as mainly a military weapon.

1918   Belgian coast completely recaptured by Allied forces. M.21 mined off Ostend.

1927   L.4 rescued *s.s. Irene* from pirates off Hong Kong.

1939   *Transylvania* captured the German *Bianca* in Denmark Strait (67° 29' N, 22° 15' W.).

1939   First German magnetic mine exploded by magnet sweep (Bosun's nightmare).

1940   *Gallant, Griffin* and *Hotspur* sank the Italian s/m *Lafolé* E. of Gibraltar.

1940   *Triad* overdue and presumed lost off Alexandria.

1941   *Ajax, Galatea* and *Hobart* (RAN) bombarded batteries E. of Tobruk.

1942   Liberator H/224 sank U.216 in Bay of Biscay (48° 21' N, 19° 25' W.).

1943   *Aurora* and *Miaoules* (Greek) bombarded Rhodes.

R34; the last operational airship at the end of 1919

21st OCTOBER

Trafalgar Day: A Memorable Date observed by the Royal Marines.

1757 *Augusta, Dreadnought* and *Edinburgh* fought a superior French squadron of seven ships under Captain Kersaint (*Intrépide*) 30 miles N.N.E. of Cape François, Haiti and severely damaged them. [bh]

1794 *Artois* captured the French *Révolutionnaire* off Ushant. [bh]

1805 Battle of Trafalgar. (Cadiz, N.28° E. 8 leagues.) [m*, m, bh]. Vice-Admiral Viscount Nelson (*Victory*) died of his wound after defeating the Franco-Spanish fleet of 33 sail of the line under Vice-Admiral Pierre Villeneuve (*Bucentaure*) and Admiral Don Federico Gravina (*Principie de Asturias*), of which 16 were destroyed and 4 captured. Ships: *Victory, Temeraire, Neptune, Conqueror, Leviathan, Britannia, Ajax, Orion, Agamemnon, Minotaur, Spartiate, Africa, Royal Sovereign, Belleisle, Mars, Tonnant, Bellerophon, Colossus, Achille, Revenge, Prince, Swiftsure, Polyphemus, Dreadnought, Defence, Defiance, Thunderer.* Frigates: *Euryalus, Naiad, Phoebe, Sirius.* Cutter: *Entreprenante.* Schooner: *Pickle.*

Nelson's Prayer before Trafalgar.

May the great God whom I worship grant to my country, and for the benefit of Europe in general, a great and glorious victory, and may no misconduct in anyone tarnish it; and may humanity after victory be the predominant feature in the British fleet. For myself individually I commit my life to him that made me; and may his blessing alight on my endeavours for serving my country faithfully. To him I resign myself, and the just cause which is entrusted to me to defend.

Amen, Amen, Amen.

Nelson's last main signal:
Made at 1155 — "Engage the enemy more closely"

1813 *Royalist* captured the Franco-Batavian *Weser* off Ushant. [bh]

1813 *Achates* fought the Franco-Batavian *Trave* 150 miles S.W. of Ushant.

1854 Admiral of the Fleet Sir Thomas Byam Martin died. First occasion when the senior Admiral was not automatically promoted, but he was eighty-nine years old, had been on the retired list for forty-five years and had never flown his flag.

1912 *Queen Elizabeth* laid down. First oil fuelled capital ship, first to be armed with 15 in guns, and first to exceed 24 knots.

1915 M.15 and M.28, supported by *Theseus*, bombarded Dedeagatch in Bulgaria.

1917 *Marmion* lost in collision with *Tirade* in N. Sea.

1918 Last British merchant ship *(St. Barchan)* sunk by German submarine in Home Waters in World War I, off St. John's Point, Co. Down.

1928 The Duke of York laid the foundation stone of the Royal Hospital School at Holbrook, which eventually vacated the Queen's House at Greenwich for the National Maritime Museum.

1939 *Sheffield* captured the German *Gloria* off Iceland (65° 30' N, 22° 05' W.).

1939 *Transylvania* intercepted and sank the German raider *Poseidon* off Iceland (66° 25' N, 20° 19' W.).

1940 *Kimberley* drove ashore and wrecked the Italian destroyer *Francesco Nullo* on Harmil Island in the Red Sea (16° 29' N, 40° 13' E.). (Convoy BN.7)

1941 *Jervis, Jupiter* and *Kandahar* bombarded Bardia. *Gnat* torpedoed by U.79 in Mediterranean.

1943 *Chedabucto* (RCN) sunk in collision with *Lord Kelvin* in St. Lawrence River (48° 14' N, 69° 16' W.).

1943 Admiral of the Fleet Sir Dudley Pound died.

1960 *Dreadnought* launched: RN's first nuclear-powered submarine and first true submarine as opposed to submersible.

HMS *Queen Elizabeth* in Firth of Forth 1918

21st OCTOBER

Nelson's signal at Trafalgar: "England expects that every man will do his duty."
Collingwood's reaction was: "I do wish Nelson would stop signalling: we all know perfectly well what is required of us."
A model of Collingwood's division breaking the Franco-Spanish line at Trafalgar (model in the RN Museum Portsmouth)

22nd OCTOBER

Admiral Sir Cloudisley Shovell, 1650–1707

Although he is generally best known for the manner of his death when his flag-ship the *Association,* together with *Romney* and *Eagle,* struck on the Scilly Isles on 22nd Oct 1707, Shovell was quite remarkable for being one of the very few senior officers before this century to have risen in the service entirely on his own merit. He was first reported by Sir John Narborough for gallant behaviour under fire and was later knighted for his conduct at Bantry in 1689. He was an Admiral in 1690 at Beachy Head and at Gibraltar and Malaga in 1704. He was returning from an expedition to Toulon in 1704, which was an attempt to acquire a Mediterranean base for the Fleet, when one of the storms which made such a base so important caused his death.

1683   First officials appointed to open Jamaica Dockyard: closed 1905.

1707   *Association* lost on Scilly Isles. Admiral reputedly killed by looters.

1793   *Agamemnon* fought the French *Melpomène,* three other frigates and a brig corvette 15 miles to the eastward of Cape San Lorenzo, Sardinia.

1800   *Indefatigable* and *Fisgard* captured the French *Venus* 90 miles N. by W. of Cape Belem (Veo).

1809   *Plover* captured the French privateer *Hirondelle* 18 miles S.E. by S. of Lizard Head.

1821   *Rising Star* built for Chilean Navy sailed, first British-built steam warship to cross Atlantic.

1853   British and French fleets passed the Dardanelles, precipitating war between Russia and Turkey.

1870   Slow burning 'pebble powder' introduced in RN.

1926   *Valerian* foundered in hurricane off Bermuda.

1940   *Margaree* (RCN) sank in collision with *s.s. Port Fairy* in Atlantic (53° 24' N, 22° 50' W.). (Convoy OL.8)

1942   Wellington B/179 sank U.412 in Norwegian Sea (63° 55' N, 0° 24' W.).

1943   *Hurworth* sunk by mine off Kalimno Island (36° 59' N, 27° 06' E.).

1943   *Adrias* (Greek), ex-*Border,* mined in Mediterranean; CTL.

1946   *Saumarez* and *Volage* mined off Corfu.

The Corfu Incident
With the War in Europe over for some eighteen months the Mediterranean Fleet of 2 carriers, 5 cruisers, 18 destroyers, 9 frigates together with a submarine and minesweeping flotilla and their attendant depot ships were cruising and visiting in the Greek Islands which included Corfu. The cruisers *Mauritius* and *Leander* with the destroyers *Saumarez* and *Volage* were detached to negotiate the channel between Corfu and Albania where six months before *Orion* and *Superb* had been fired on from the Albanian shore. On passage through the channel the *Saumarez* struck a mine which killed 36 of the ship's company and damaged the ship so badly that she was subsequently scrapped. *Leander* and *Mauritius* cleared the channel immediately leaving *Volage* to tow the stricken *Saumarez* back to Corfu. One and half hours later *Volage* in turn struck a mine which killed eight men, but she was still able to tow over the bow even though it had been blown off, and she proceeded to tow *Saumarez* while steaming astern. Subsequently the International Court of Justice decided that the mines had been laid after the end of hostilities in Europe and awarded Great Britain £1,000,000 in compensation. This has not yet been paid.

1951   Greece and Turkey joined NATO.

HMS *Victorious* on steaming trials 1958

23rd OCTOBER

1702 *Dragon* fought a French 60 gun ship 36 miles West of Cape Finisterre.

1753 RNH Haslar admitted first patients.

The Royal Naval Hospital at Haslar is the oldest naval hospital in the modern sense of the word. It was not built for merely humanitarian reasons, however, but to nurse sick sailors when there was a desperate shortage of trained naval manpower.
Comparatively few men were killed by the enemy. The mortality rate for sailors ran at 1:30¼, compared with a ratio ashore of 1:80. The main killers were scurvy, yellow fever, ship fever, accidents (often caused by drink). It is clear from these figures, allied to the desperate shortage of men to fight the wars, that a hospital which could rehabilitate at least some of them was a sensible investment. At first the hospital was run entirely by doctors, but the desertion rate was so high that post Captains were soon appointed in command.

1762 *Brune* captured the French *Oiseau* 30 miles E.S.E. of Cape Palos, Spain.

1809 *Pomone* burnt five sail of a French convoy in the Gulf of Lyons.

1813 *Andromache* captured the Franco-Batavian *Trave* 45 miles W. by N. of Pointe du Raz, Brittany.

1865 *Bulldog* sank the rebel Salnavist *Voldrogue* and a schooner at Cap Haitien. *Bulldog* ran aground and was finally blown up by her own crew.

1903 *Neptune,* on way to breakers, rammed *Victory.*

1915 E.8 sank the German cruiser *Prinz Adalbert* 20 miles West of Libau, which led to withdrawal of German heavy units from the Baltic.

1916 *Genista* sunk by U.57, 120 miles West of Cape Clear.

1917 *Melampus* sank UC.16 off Selsey Bill.

1941 *Cossack* torpedoed by U.563. (See 27th October).

1942 *Unique* sunk by unknown cause to the westward of Gibraltar Strait whilst on passage from the U.K.

1943 *Duncan, Vidette* and Liberator Z/224 sank U.274 S.W. of Iceland. (Convoy ON.207)

1943 *Cromarty* sunk by mine in Bonifacio Strait, Sardinia (41° 23' N, 9° 12' E.).

1943 *Charybdis* sunk by the German t.bs. T.23 and T.27 off Triagoz Island, France (48° 59' N, 3° 39' W.). *Limbourne* torpedoed by the German t.bs. T.22 and T.24 in the same position: sunk by *Talybont* and *Rocket.* Operation Tunnel. Ships: *Charybdis, Grenville, Limbourne, Rocket, Stevenstone, Talybont, Wensleydale.* Dead washed ashore on Channel Islands buried by islanders despite German occupation.

1944 Battle of Leyte Gulf (20th - 27th October) between US 3rd and 7th Fleets and the Japanese battle fleet, resulting in the defeat of the latter. [bh]. RAN ships present with 7th fleet: *Arunta, Ariadne, Australia, Gascoyne, Warramunga, Shropshire. Australia* was damaged by five Kamikaze bombers on the 21st and had to withdraw, escorted by *Warramunga.*

1954 West Germany joined NATO.

HMS Submarine *Dreadnought* launched 21st October 1960

24th OCTOBER

1793 *Thames* fought the French *Uranie* 130 miles S.W. of Ushant. Whilst still disabled the *Thames* struck to the French *Carmagnole* and two other frigates.

1797 *Indefatigable* captured the French privateer *Hyène* to the westward of Cape de Sines.

1798 *Sirius* captured the Dutch *Furie* and *Waakzaamheid* to the north-westward of the Texel.

1811 *Guadeloupe* captured the French privateer *Sirène* 9 miles N. by W. of Dragonera Island, Majorca.

1862 British and French forces recaptured Kading. Naval Brigade from *Euryalus, Imperieuse, Pearl, Starling* and *Vulcan.* Troops: Royal Artillery, Royal Engineers, 31st and 67th Regiments; 5th Bombay Native Light Infantry.

1877 *Lightning,* RN's first Torpedo Boat, commissioned.

1917 C.32 grounded in the Gulf of Riga, Baltic; blown up by own crew.

1939 U.16 mined in Channel (51° 09' N, 1° 28' E.). (Stranded later on the Goodwin Sands).

1940 Fourteen Swordfish aircraft disembarked from *Illustrious* and *Eagle* bombed Tobruk and mined the entrance of the harbour. FAA Sq.: 815, 819, 824.

1942 Liberator G/224 sank U.599 in SW Approaches (46° 07' N, 17° 40' W.). (Convoy KX.2)

1943 Wellington A/179 sank U.566 in the Bay of Biscay.

1943 *Eclipse* sunk by mine off Kalimno Island in the Aegean (37° 01' N, 27° 11' E.).

1944 Mines laid by aircraft of 852 and 846 Sq. *(Campania* and *Trumpeter),* escorted by *Devonshire* and 6 destroyers in Lepsorev and Harrhamsfjord (62° 36' N, 6° 12' E.); W/T stations on Vigra and Hanoy attacked. Operation Hardy.

A Walrus aircraft being catapulted from a cruiser in World War 2

25th OCTOBER

1694   Royal Hospital Greenwich founded by Charter of William and Mary.

1704   Leake's first relief of Gibraltar.

1747   *Hampshire* captured the French *Castor* 200 miles South of Cape Clear.

1796   *Santa Margarita* captured the French privateer *Vengeur* off the South coast of Ireland; her boat captured the privateer's prize, *Potomah*.

1799   Boats of *Surprise* cut out the Spanish *Santa Cecilia* (ex-British *Hermione*) at Porto Cavallo. [m*, m, bh] : renamed *Retaliation* and then *Retribution*.

1803   Boat of *Osprey* captured the French privateer *Resource* off Tobago.

1807   Boats of *Herald* cut out the French privateer *César* from under the guns of a fort at Otranto.

1812   *Macedonian* taken by the American *United States* 600 miles W.S.W. of Madeira.

1915   *Velox* mined off the Nab lightvessel.

1939   *Delhi* captured the German *Rheingold* in Iceland- Faeroes gap (64° 00' N, 11° 40' W.).

1940   *Aphis* bombarded enemy concentrations 15 miles East of Sidi Barrani.

1941   *Ajax* bombarded Bardia.

1941   *Lamerton* and Catalina A/202 sank the Italian s/m *Ferraris* in Atlantic (37° 07' N, 14° 19' W.). (Convoy HG.75)

1941   *Latona* sunk by German aircraft off Bardia (32° 15' N, 25° 14' E.).

1944   *Skeena* (RCN) wrecked in a gale at Reykjavik (64° 09' N, 21° 50' W.).

1944   *Aurora, Tetcott* and *Tyrian* bombarded Milos (and on the 26th).

The sword awarded to Captain Hamilton for the recapture of *Hermione* 25th October 1799

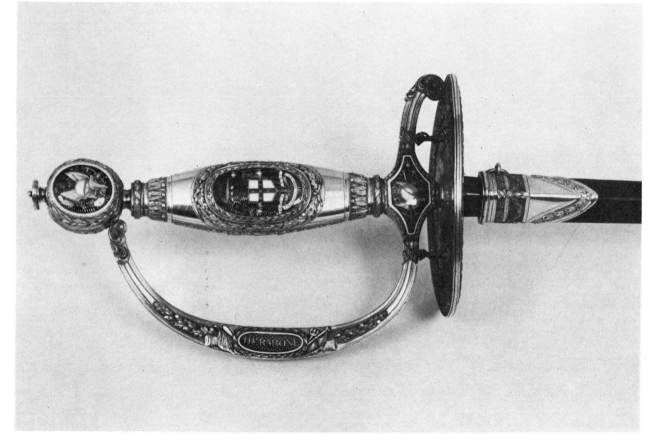

26th OCTOBER

1781   *Hannibal* captured the French *Necker* off the Cape of Good Hope.

1854   VC: Acting Mate William Nathan Wrighte Hewett (*Beagle*), for heroic action when manning a gun before Sevastopol. See 5th November.

1858   *Pearl's* Naval Brigade at the unsuccessful action at Jagdispur.

1916   German destroyer raid in Dover Strait. (night of 26/27). Ships: *Viking, Amazon Nubian*[1], *Tartar, Mohawk, Cossack*[2], *Kangaroo, Gipsey,* P.21; *Swift, Laforey, Liberty, Lucifer, Laurel, Syren, Racehorse, Falcon, Myrmidon; Lawford, Lance, Lochinvar, Lark; Flirt*[4], P.34, P.23; *Zulu,* T.B.15. Aux vessels: *Ombra, Dragon, H.E. Stroud.* Drifters: *Eskburn, South Tyne, East Holme, Girl Norah, Pleasants, Roburn*[3], *Paradox, Spotless Prince*[3], *Waveney*[3], *Gleaner of the Sea*[3],

Datum[3], *Young Crow, E.B.C. Ajax II*[3], *Launch Out*[3], *Mishe Nahma, I.F.S.; Devon County, Girl Annie, F.H.S., New Spray, Broadland, Roulette.*
[1] Torpedoed on 27th. [2] Not engaged. [3] Sunk on 26th. [4] Sunk on 27th.

1943   Liberator A/10 (RCAF) sank U.420 in N Atlantic (45° 49' N, 41° 01' W.). (Convoy ON.207)

1944   *Rose* (Nor.) sunk in collision with *Manners* in Atlantic (45° 10' N, 39° 40' W.).(Convoy ON.260)

1944   *Implacable* (Admiral Sir Henry Moore), *Mauritius* and six destroyers of 26th DF successfully attacked shipping ; between Bodo and Rorvik (and on 27th and 28th). Operation Athletic. FAA Sq.: 828, 841, Barracuda; 1771, Firefly; 887, 894, Seafire.

1944   Accountant Branch retitled Supply and Secretariat Branch, and prefix 'Paymaster' abolished.

HMS *Jupiter* (see 17th January and 21st October); HMS *Saumarez* in background

1651	'General at Sea' Blake defeated the Royalist fleet under Prince Rupert.
1758	Admiral the Hon Edward Boscawen *(Namur)* fought five French ships under Captain Comte du Chaffault *(Dragon)* in the Soundings. Ships: *Bienfaisant, Namur, Royal William, Somerset.* Frigates: *Boreas, Echo, Trent.*
1800	Boats of *Phaeton* cut out the Spanish *San Jose* at Fuengirola, near Malaga. [m]
1810	*Orestes* captured the French privateer *Loup Garou* 120 miles West of Ushant.
1890	Capture of Witu by Naval Brigade from *Boadicea, Brisk, Conquest, Cossack, Humber, Kingfisher, Pigeon, Redbreast* and *Turquoise.* Troops: Detachment of East African Protectorate Forces and Zanzibar Government Army.
1914	*Audacious* sunk by mine 18 miles N.3° E. of Tory Island, NW of Ireland.
1916	*Flirt* torpedoed by German destroyers off Dover and *Nubian* off Folkestone: (*Zubian* created from salvaged parts of *Nubian* and *Zulu*).
1927	*Wild Swan* repulsed Chinese attack on mission hospital at Swatow, China.
1940	Eight Swordfish aircaft of 813 and 824 Sq. *(Eagle)* bombed Maltezana airfield, Stampalia.
1941	*Cossack* sank whilst in tow after being torpedoed by U.563 off Cape St. Vincent on the 23rd. (Convoy HG.75)
1942	Fortress F/206 sank U.627 in N Atlantic (59° 14' N, 22° 49' W.).
1944	Firefly aircraft of 1771 Sq. *(Implacable)*; Halifax D/502, T/502, and Liberators H/311, Y/311 (Czech) sank U.1060 off Norwegian coast (65° 24' N, 12° 00' E.).

1664	A Memorable Date observed by the Royal Marines. King Charles II sanctioned the formation of the Duke of York and Albany's Martime Regiment of Foot, the first regiment to be formed specially for service afloat, and the colour of whose uniform is remembered in the yellow of the Corps' colours.
1801	*Pasley* captured the Spanish *Virgin del Rosario* 60 miles E.S.E. of Cape de Gata. [m]
1914	*Undaunted, Legion, Loyal, Lennox* and *Lance* sank four German tb's off the Texel.
1915	*Argyll* wrecked on Bell Rock, E. coast of Scotland.
1918	UB.116 sunk in the controlled minefield guarding Hoxa Boom, Scapa Flow.
1918	G.2 sank U.78 in Skagerrak (56° 02' N, 5° 08' E.).
1944	Two "Chariots" from *Trenchant* sank one merchant ship and damaged another in Phuket harbour, Siam.

1664 – The Birth of the Royal Marine Corps

"That twelve hundred land souldjers be forthwith raysed, to be in readiness, to be distributed into his Mats Fleets prepared for Sea Service". So read the report of the Proceedings of a Meeting of the Privy Council held on 28th October, which authorised the formation of the first regiment specially for service afloat. Styled the Duke of York and Albany's Maritime Regiment of Foot or Admiral's Regiment, it was recruited mainly from the Trained Bands of the City of London. It is from this origin that the Royal Marines derive their privilege of marching through the City with Colours flying, drums beating and bayonets fixed.

In a report after the particularly fierce Battle of Solebay in 1672, one of the early actions of the new regiment, a ship's Captain wrote "Those Marines of whom I soe oft have wrote behaved themselves stoutly". This is also the first reference to the title 'Marine'.

After the taking of Belle Île (Isle) on 7th June, 1761, Admiral Keppel praised the part played by the Marines when he requested "that his Majesty may be informed of the goodness and spirited behaviour of that Corps". A contemporary account of the action stated "The Marines have gained immortal glory and as a reward have been appointed to every post of honour". The laurel wreath in the badge worn today is believed to have been awarded in commemoration of their conduct.

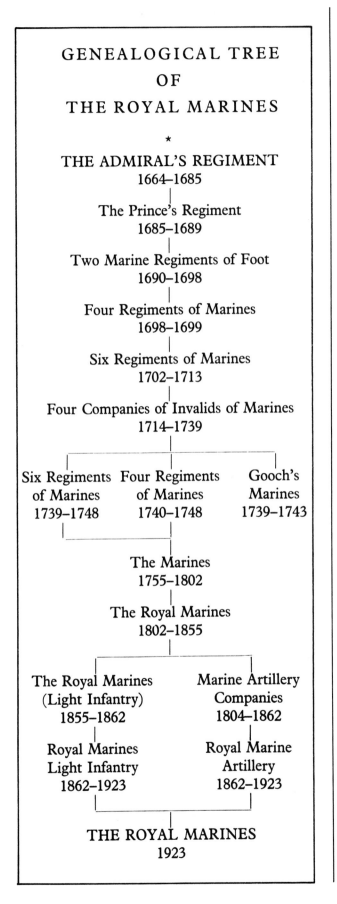

GENEALOGICAL TREE
OF
THE ROYAL MARINES

★

THE ADMIRAL'S REGIMENT
1664–1685

The Prince's Regiment
1685–1689

Two Marine Regiments of Foot
1690–1698

Four Regiments of Marines
1698–1699

Six Regiments of Marines
1702–1713

Four Companies of Invalids of Marines
1714–1739

Six Regiments of Marines 1739–1748 | Four Regiments of Marines 1740–1748 | Gooch's Marines 1739–1743

The Marines
1755–1802

The Royal Marines
1802–1855

The Royal Marines (Light Infantry) 1855–1862 | Marine Artillery Companies 1804–1862

Royal Marines Light Infantry 1862–1923 | Royal Marine Artillery 1862–1923

THE ROYAL MARINES
1923

1704 Vice-Admiral Sir John Leake *(Nottingham)* destroyed a French squadron in Gibraltar Bay. Ships: *Nottingham, Swallow.*

1746 *Eagle* captured the French privateer *Shoreham* 90 miles to the westward of the Scilly Islands.

1807 *Louisa* fought a French lugger privateer to the southward of Cork. [m]

1813 Capitulation of the French forces at Trieste. Ships: *Eagle, Elizabeth, Milford, Tremendous, Weazle, Wizard.* Troops: 21st Regiment; Austrian, under Major-General Count Nugent. Naval siege batteries were landed.

1856 Capture of a portion of Canton by Rear-Admiral Sir Michael Seymour *(Coromandel).* Ships: *Barracouta, Bittern, Calcutta, Comus, Coromandel, Encounter, Nankin, Sampson, Sybille, Winchester,* U.S. Ships: *Levant, Portsmouth.* Naval Brigade was landed, with Royal Artillery.

1915 *Hythe* lost in collision with *Sarnia* off Cap Helles.

1916 *Picton, Grafton,* M.18, M.28, M.32 and, occasionally, *Raglan* began bombardment of Turkish forts in Macedonia.

1918 *Ulysses* lost in collision in Firth of Clyde.

1940 First German accoustic mine recovered by Lt. S. Baker, RNVR and Sub-Lt. P.A. Cummins, RNVR in R. Ogmore near Porthcawl: stripped and identified 3rd November in *Vernon* by L. Walden, Esquire.

1943 *Duncan, Sunflower* and *Vidette* sank U.282 in N Atlantic (55° 28' N, 31° 57' W.). (Convoys HX.263 and ON.208)

30th OCTOBER

1757	Admiral Edward Vernon died.
1809	*Surveillante* captured the French *Milan* 60 miles S.W. of Ushant.
1824	Capture of Martaban by combined forces under Lieutenant-Colonel Henry Godwin (41st Regiment) and Lieutenant Charles Keele *(Arachne)*. Ships: *Arachne, Sophie.* Troops: 41st Regiment; Bengal and Madras Artillery, 3rd Madras Native Light Infantry.
1828	Bombardment and capture of Morea Castle, Patras, by combined British and French forces. Ships: *Blonde, Aetna; Conquerant, Armide, Didon, Duchesse de Berry.* Ships landed guns for the bombardment. French troops under General Schneider.
1844	*Gorgon* refloated, having been aground since 10th May near Montevideo.
1899	*Powerful's* Naval Brigade at Lombard's Kop, Ladysmith.
1917	M.15, M.29, M.31 with occasionally M.32 and *Raglan,* and *Ladybird, Aphis, Comet, Staunch* and *City of Oxford,* began bombardment of Gaza coast: ended 11th November with loss of M.15 and *Staunch.*
1918	L.10 sunk by German S.33 off the Texel.
1939	*Mercury* commissioned.
1940	*Sturdy* wrecked in a gale on Tiree Island, W. Scotland. (Convoy SC.8.)
1940	*Harvester* and *Highlander* sank U.32 in NW Approaches (55° 37' N, 12° 20' W.).
1942	Liberator X/10 (RCAF) sank U.520 (47° 47' N, 49° 50' W.) and Hudson Y/145 (RCAF) sank U.658 in Atlantic (50° 32' N, 46° 32' W.).(Convoy SC.107)
1942	GC: Lieutenant Francis Anthony Blair Fasson and Able Seaman Colin Grazier *(Petard)* for attempting to salvage cypher machine from sinking prize. (Both posthumous)
1942	*Dulverton, Hero, Hurworth, Pakenham, Petard* and Wellesley aircraft of 47 Sq sank U.559 in E Mediterranean (32° 30' N, 33° 00' E.).
1943	*Ultimatum* sank U.431 off Toulon.

31st OCTOBER

1762	*Panther* and *Argo* captured the Spanish *Santissima Trinidad* off Kapul Island, Phillipines.
1803	*Admiral Mitchell* drove ashore two French invasion vessels at Patel (Le Portel).
1808	*Circe* captured the French *Palinure* at Cape Solomon, Martinique.
1860	Admiral of the Fleet Thomas Cochrane, tenth Earl of Dundonald, died.
1914	*Hermes* sunk by U.27 off the Outer Ruytingen Shoal, Dover Strait, while employed as a seaplane carrier.
1914	The German cruiser *Königsberg* located in the Rufigi River, East Africa.
1915	*Louis* wrecked in Suvla Bay.
1943	*Douglas, Imperialist* and *Loch Oskaig* sank U.732 in Gibraltar Strait (35° 54' N, 5° 52' W.).
1943	*Geranium* and *Whitehall* sank the U.306 in Atlantic (46° 19' N, 20° 44' W.). (Convoy SL.138/MKS.28)

Purser: a Rowlandson print of 1799

1st NOVEMBER

A Memorable Date observed by the Royal Marines

1757	*Tartar* recaptured the British *Princess Amelia* 360 miles to the N.W. of Ushant.
1806	Boats of *Pique* destroyed a battery and cut out a Spanish gunbrig in Cabaret Bay, Puerto Rico.
1808	*Cruizer* fought twenty Danish gunboats, and captured the Danish privateer *Rinaldo* 15 miles S.S.W. of Vinga Beacon, Kattegat. [m]
1809	Boats of squadron cut out four and burnt seven French vessels in Rosas Bay. [m]. Ships: *Tigre, Renown, Cumberland, Apollo, Volontaire, Topaze, Philomel, Scout, Tuscan.*
1811	*Imperieuse* and *Thames* and troops destroyed the batteries and captured 12 gunboats and 22 feluccas at Porto Palinuro. Troops: 62nd Regiment.
1857	*Shannon's* Naval Brigade at Kudjwa. Troops: Royal Engineers, 53rd, 64th and 84th Regiments, 93rd Highlanders; 1st Bengal Fusiliers, 1st Madras Fusilier Regiment, 5th Bengal Artillery (E Coy). 4,000 enemy defeated and two guns captured.
1914	Vice-Admiral Sir Christopher Cradock *(Good Hope)* defeated by Vice-Admiral Graf von Spee *(Scharnhorst)* off Coronel. Ships: *Good Hope*, Mon-*

mouth*, Glasgow, Otranto. *Sunk. (Wireless used in battle by RN for the first time).

1917	E.52 sank UC.63 in Channel (51° 23' N, 2° 00' E.).
1918	G.7 lost in N. Sea.
1921	Emperor Karl of Austria-Hungary abdicated after second unsuccessful coup, and surrendered to S.N.O. Danube in *Glowworm,* escorted by *Ladybird,* drafting and signing his own parole until transferred to *Cardiff.*
1940	East Oaze lightvessel sunk by German aircraft.
1941	Advanced shore training for Supply Officers, instituted: *President V* commissioned.

Mr Nipcheese

The Bursar (later Purser), now "Pusser", of a King's ship has been a member of the crew from the earliest days of the Navy. In 1623, Slops (clothing shops) were established "to avoyde nastie beastlyness by continuall wearing of one suite of clothes, and therbie boddilie diseases and unwholesome ill smells". The "Slop Room" still exists today.

In 1683 the Purser was officially paid by making "savings", a euphemism for cheating the sailor of his rations, and this persisted until the Spithead Mutiny in 1797. By 1808 he had become a warrant officer of wardroom rank and by 1843 a commissioned officer. In 1852 he became salaried, and was no longer paid on a percentage basis. On 1st January 1956 the Supply Officer became a General List Officer. He is now an expert on logistics and administration as well as taking a full part in the fighting of his ship.

1st NOVEMBER

1943   *Active, Fleetwood, Witherington* and Wellingtons R/179 and W/179 sank U.340 in Gibraltar Strait.

1944   Successful assault on Walcheren. Operation Infatuate 1 and 2. [bh]. Ships: *Erebus, Roberts, Warspite, Kingsmill.* No 4 Army and 41, 47 and 48 RM Commandos. About 180 landing craft of a wide range of types took part.

Walcheren 1944
The attacking allied armies in Europe were slowed down by the lack of a sufficient port to supply them with ammunition, fuel, food etc. It was therefore resolved to take Antwerp, and for this it was necessary to capture the heavily fortified island of Walcheren. On the 1st November 1944 the bombers allocated for softening up the defences were fog bound in England. The naval support vessels therefore sailed close in shore and attacked enemy defences with a heavy bombardment. Of these vessels 9 were sunk with 372 men killed. General Eisenhower said of this bombardment "credit for the success of the amphibious operations is largely due to the support craft of the British Navy which unhesitatingly and in the highest tradition of the service attracted to themselves the point blank fire of the land batteries, thus permitting the commandos and assault troops to gain the shore . . ."
The Royal Marine Commandos stormed the shore and in the face of stout resistence and with little support from the air took the island after 2 days of hard fighting. The German batteries were silenced, thus enabling the Scheldt and the Port of Antwerp to be opened for the support of the Allied Armies in Flanders. Of this operation Sir Winston Churchill wrote, "the extreme gallantry of the Royal Marines stands forth," and its anniversary is a Memorable Date observed by the Royal Marines.

1948   Recruiting began for the Royal Marines Forces Volunteer Reserve.

1956   *Newfoundland* and *Diana* sank Egyptian frigate *Domiat* (Suez campaign).

1958   RNR and RNVR combined to form the present Royal Naval Reserve.

In 1853 a Naval Volunteer Act allowed for the recall of naval pensioners in time of emergency. This Act has been used as recently as 1956. At the same time a Coastal Volunteer Force was formed.
Continuing anxiety over the numbers of trained men led to the Royal Naval Reserve (Volunteers) Act in 1859 which allowed for a reserve of trained merchant seamen. The rapid German armament led to the institution of the Royal Naval Volunteer Reserve, consisting of civilian volunteers, in 1903.
Both the RNR and RNVR served with great distinction in both major wars and in many ships formed the majority of the crew.
On 1st November 1958 the RNR and RNVR were combined under the title RNR and are now active in MCMVs and Maritime Headquarters. They are largely responsible for the Naval Control of Shipping in war and undertake many specialist tasks.

The Scene at Walcheren

2nd NOVEMBER

1757 *Antelope* captured the French privateer *Moras* 100 miles to the westward of Cape Finisterre.

1757 *Tartar* captured the French privateer *Mélampe* 360 miles N.W. of Ushant.

1758 *Antelope* captured the French *Belliqueux* off Ilfracombe.

1762 *Terpsichore* captured the French letter of marque *Marquis De Marigny* 100 miles W. by S. of Île de Ré.

1780 *Zephyr* captured the French *Sénégal* in the Gambia River.

1917 Raid by British light forces in the Kattegat.

1854 Boats of *Winchester* and *Spartan* destroyed nine pirate junks in Tynmoon Bay, near Hong Kong.

1918 Last two British merchant ships (*Murcia* and *Surada*) to be sunk in World War I torpedoed by UC.74 off Port Said.

1940 *Antelope* sank U.31 in N.W. Approaches (56° 26' N, 10° 18' W.). (Convoy OB.237). A third anniversary for the name.

1941 *Tetrarch* sunk by a mine in Sicilian channel on passage from Malta to Gibraltar.

1944 *Avon Vale* and *Wheatland* sank the German TA.20 (ex-Italian *Audace*, ex-Japanese *Kawakaze*, built Yarrow), UJ.202 (ex-Italian *Spingada*) off Pag UJ.208 Adriatic (44° 35' N, 14° 36' E.).

1944 *Shalimar* bombarded Malacca, Nicobar.

Experimental submarine of the interwar period; *M1* with a 12 in gun

3rd NOVEMBER

1758   *Buckingham* fought the French *Florissant*, *Bellone* and *Aigrette* between Guadeloupe and Montserrat.

1778   *Maidstone* captured the French *Lion* 190 miles S.S.E. of Cape Henry.

1839   *Volage* and *Hyacinth* defeated a flotilla of Chinese war junks in the Bogue, Canton River.

1840   Bombardment of Acre. [m]. (See 4th November).

1854   *Encounter, Barracouta, Queen* (U.S. hired steamer) and boats of *Spartan* destroyed 17 pirate junks at Tai ho, Lantao.

1914   Bombardment by Anglo-French squadron of the outer forts at the Dardanelles. Ships: *Indefatigable, Indomitable; Vérité, Suffren.*

1914   "I drink to the memory of a gallant and honourable foe" — Von Spee in reply to a German civilian who proposed the toast "Damnation to the British Navy" at Valparaiso.

1914   British coast (near Gorleston, Norfolk) raided by German battle cruisers for the first time. HM Ships: *Halcyon, Leopard, Lively.*

1917   C.15 sank UC.65 in Channel (50° 28' N, 0° 17' E.).

1940   U.99 sank *Laurentic* (54° 09' N, 13° 44' W.) and *Patroclus* (53° 43' N, 14° 41' W.) in NW Approaches.

1941   *Trident* sank German UJ.1213 off north coast of Norway.

1942   GC: Lieutenant John Stuart Mould, GM, RANVR, for mine recovery and disposal. (*Gazette* date).

1956   First RN loss of Suez campaign: Wyvern from *Eagle* shot down.

HM Submarines *A5*, *A6* and *C3* leaving Portsmouth Harbour, 1907. *C3* was used during the Zeebrugge raid (23rd April 1918) where she was blown up. The warship to the left is either HMS *Centurion* or *Barfleur*; to the rear HMS *Queen*.

4th NOVEMBER

1650	*Black Prince* burnt by Parliamentarians.
1803	Launch of *Blanche* captured a French armed schooner in the Caracol Passage, Haiti. [m]
1805	Captain Sir Richard Strachan (*Caesar*) with *Hero*, *Namur* and *Courageux* took the French *Formidable* (Rear-Admiral Dumanoir Le Pelley), *Scipion*, *Mont Blanc* and *Duguay-Trouin* 260 miles West of Rochefort. These were the first survivors of Trafalgar to be captured, and the exuberant wording of his despatch earned Strachan the nickname "Delighted Sir Dicky". [m*, m, bh]
1810	Boats of *Blossom* captured the French privateer *César* 100 miles S. by W. of Cape Sicie. [m]
1840	Capture of Acre by Admiral the Hon. Sir Robert Stopford and Commodore Charles Napier (*Princess Charlotte*). [m, bh] . Ships: *Bellerophon, Benbow, Edinburgh, Powerful, Princess Charlotte, Revenge, Thunderer, Carysfort, Castor, Hazard, Pique, Talbot, Wasp,*

Gorgon, Phoenix, Stromboli, Vesuvius. Austrian: *Guerriera, Lipsia, Medea.* Turkish: *Mookuddimay-I-Hive.* (Flag of Sir Baldwin Walker). Troops: Royal Artillery, Royal Sappers and Miners. 7059 claims for the Naval General Service medal were made in connection with the Syrian operations which began on 10th September and which were the last for which that medal was awarded.

1855	Destruction of the Russian stores in the Gheisk Estuary, Sea of Azov. Ships:

Vesuvius, Ardent, Curlew, Weser. Gunboats: *Boxer, Clinker, Cracker, Grinder, Recruit.*

1914	German cruiser *Karlsruhe* sunk in the Atlantic about 300 miles off Barbados, by internal explosion (10° 7' N, 55° 25' W.).
1914	German cruiser *Yorck* sunk by British mine in Schillig Roads.
1914	*Bustard* and *Excellent* bombarded Lombartzyde, near Nieuport.

HMS *Newcastle*, type 42 Destroyer

5th NOVEMBER

1650	Blake destroyed the Royalist fleet under Prince Rupert off Carthagena.
1803	Boat of *Blanche* cut out the French *Albion* at Monte Christi, Haiti.
1813	Inconclusive engagement off Toulon between Vice-Admiral Sir Edward Pellew (*Caledonia*) and Vice-Admiral Comte Emeriau (*Imperial*).
1854	Battle of Inkerman. V.C: Captain William Peel and Midshipman Edward St. John Daniel *(Diamond)**. Lieutenant William Nathan Wrighte Hewett *(Beagle)+*. Seamen Thomas Reeves, James Gorman, Mark Scholefield. Corporal John Prettyjohn, RMLI. *See 18th October and 18th June. + See 26th October. Prettyjohn, having been cut off with his party by a strong Russian column and having run out of ammunition, drove off the Russians by heaving stones down the hill at them. Reeves, Gorman and Scholefield repulsed a Russian attack at Inkerman, exposing themselves to heavy fire.
1914	Rear-Admiral Troubridge's court-martial began.
1915	*Tara* sunk by U.35 off Sollum. The Egyptian coastguard cruisers *Abbas* and *Nur El Bahr* sunk and damaged respectively at Sollum by U.35.
1918	*Campania* sunk in collision with *Revenge* and *Glorious* in Scapa Flow.
1940	VC: Captain Edward Stephen Fogarty Fegen (*Jervis Bay*). *Jervis Bay* sunk by *Admiral Scheer* whilst defending Convoy HX.84 in Mid Atlantic (52° 41' N, 32° 17' W.). [bh]
1942	Liberator H/120 sank U.132 in N Atlantic (58° 08' N, 33° 15' W.). (Convoy SC.107)
1943	*Aldenham* and *Miaoules* (Greek) bombarded Kos.
1946	GC: Lieutenant-Commander Patrick Albert O'Leary, D.S.O. Work in connection with the escape of Allied prisoners of war. (*Gazette* date).
1956	Carriers withdrew from Suez assault zone having destroyed Egyptian aircraft and sunk 4 MTBs.
1962	The RN Mine Watching Service, formed in 1952, renamed Royal Naval Auxiliary Service (RNXS); announced in the House of Commons.

Convoy HX.84, of 37 ships escorted by the Armed Merchant Cruiser *Jervis Bay* (Captain E.S.F. Fegen) was homeward bound from Halifax. The German pocket battleship *Admiral Scheer* (6 x 11 in guns, 8 x 5.9 in guns) encountered the convoy in mid-Atlantic. The convoy was scattered immediately, while the *Jervis Bay* closed the battleship and engaged her. The *Jervis Bay* was overwhelmed, but she gave the convoy time to make smoke and scatter, and only 5 ships were sunk.

One vessel in the convoy was the British tanker *San Demetrio*, which was set on fire and abandoned. The men in one of her lifeboats later sighted her, re-embarked, brought the fire under control and, despite the lack of navigational aids, brought her to port with most of her cargo intact.

HMS *Campania* sinking

6th NOVEMBER

1794   *Alexander* taken by a French squadron under Rear-Admiral Joseph Nielly *(Tigre)* 100 miles West of Ushant.

1799   *Speedy* fought fifteen Spanish gunboats off Europa Point. [m].

1856   *Barracouta* and *Coromandel*, with boats of *Calcutta, Encounter, Sampson, Sybille* and *Winchester*, captured French Folly, Canton River, and destroyed 21 war junks.

1860   Admiral Sir Charles Napier died: "It is seamen, not ships, that constitute a navy".

1914   *Bustard* and *Humber* bombarded Westend and Lombartzyde, Belgium.

1914   Start of naval operations on R. Tigris. *Odin* and *Espiegle*, joined by *Comet, Shaiton, Sumana* and *Lewis Pelly;* reinforced by Fly and Insect class gunboats.

1915   E.20 sunk by the German UB.14 in the Dardanelles.

1917   *Peveril (Puma)* (Q.36) sunk by U.63 off Cadiz (35° 44' N, 6° 48' W.).

1943   *Kite, Starling* and *Woodcock* sank U.226 in N Atlantic (44° 49' N, 41° 13' W.), and *Starling* and *Wild Goose* sank U.842 (43° 42' N, 42° 08' W.).

1956*   Helicopter assault in Whirlwind and Sycamore aircraft by 45 RM Commando launched from *Ocean* and *Theseus* on Suez. (First major helicopter borne assault from ships).

Early August — *Bulwark, Theseus* sailed from Portsmouth, latter with 13th Indep Para Brigade Gp Devonport.
Ocean sailed from Devonport, also with troops and some craft including LCTs brought forward from reserve and hastily refitted by the Dockyard.
30 Oct —war broke out between Israel and Egypt
31 Oct — Egyptian destroyer *Ibrahim Ah Ahwal* (ex-*Mendip*) was captured by Israel, and Britain and France intervened in hostilities.
 1 Nov – *Newfoundland* and *Diana* sank Egyptian frigate *Domiat* (ex-*Nith*).
 6 Nov - Assault at Suez, involving more than 100 RN and French ships including 6 carriers (*Eagle, Albion, Bulwark, Ocean, Theseus* and *Lafayette*).

Ocean and *Theseus* carried RM Commandos and helicopters. RN aircraft flew about 2000 sorties, 1600 of them by Seahawks and Wyverns. 400 sorties were made by Whirlwind and Sycamore helicopters over the beaches in the airborne assault. No 3 Commando Brigade were landed by LST/LCT — with 45 Commando by air all in 91 minutes. Naval bombardment also took place; little damage was done to the town, except to strong points of resistance. No guns larger than 6 in were used and wanton damage was carefully avoided.

1969   *Amazon*, first Type 21 frigate and ninth of the name, laid down at Vospers.

Six helicopters carrying men of 45 Commando, Royal Marines, passing two LCAs manned by RM crews in the assault on Port Said, 6th November 1956. Taken from HMS *Sallyport,* a landing craft H.Q. ship of the Deputy to Commodore, Amphibious Warfare.

7th NOVEMBER

1803 Cutter of *Blanche* captured a French armed schooner in Manchineal (Manzanillo) Bay, Haiti.

1807 Boats of *Renommée* and *Grasshopper* cut out a Spanish brig and a French tartan under Torre de Estacio, near Cartagena.

1914 Japanese forces captured Tsingtau.

1915 E.19 sank the German light cruiser *Undine* in the Baltic, 22 miles off Trolleborg, Sweden.

1918 Last attack (unsuccessful) by a German submarine on a British merchant ship, (*Sarpedon*), in World War I.

1940 *Milford* and Walrus aircraft of *Devonshire* (700 Sqdn) engaged the French s/m *Poncelet,* which scuttled herself in Gulf of Guinea (0° 20' S, 8° 50' E.).

* Merchant Ship Losses 1914-18

Year	Merchant Ships	Fishing Vessels	Total Tonnage (thsds)	Lives Lost
1914	64	45	248	164
1915	278	192	880	2,601
1916	396	141	1,251	1,255
1917	1,197	213	3,751	6,521
1918	544	84	1,670	4,180
War Totals	2,479	675	7,800	14,721*

*Official War History quotes 15,313

A Sea Harrier during landing trials on HMS *Hermes*, November 1978. The Harrier on the flight deck is the manufacturer's demonstration aircraft

8th NOVEMBER

1709   *Defiance* and *Centurion* fought two French third rates between Almeria and Malaga.

1723   Hon. John Byron born.

1810   Boats of *Quebec* cut out the French privateer *Jeune Louise* at Vliestroom.

1813   Boats of *Revenge* cut out a French privateer at Palamos.

1848   *Polyphemus* recaptured the British *Three Sisters* at Cala Tramontana, Riff coast.

1907   Kaiser's visit to Channel Fleet provoked "paintwork v gunnery" signal.

1910   Esquimalt first used as RCN base: arrival of *Rainbow*.

The 'Paintwork v. Gunnery' Controversy

Sir Percy Scott was the great exponent of naval gunnery during the 1890s and 1900s. His training devices for gunlayers, his insistence of frequent gunnery practice and his introduction of prize shooting at realistic long ranges did much to improve gunnery standards in the Royal Navy. However, his abrasive personality and his unorthodox methods often brought him into conflict with senior officers and his most publicised clash occurred with Lord Charles Beresford in 1907.

Beresford was himself a colourful and dashing personality, having first won fame when he attacked a huge Egyptian fort in his tiny gunboat *Condor* during the bombardment of Alexandria in July 1882. But he was also a strong traditionalist and was very suspicious of the reforms that were being introduced by his great rival, Fisher, and other younger men such as Percy Scott.

Rear-Admiral Sir Percy Scott

Lord Charles Beresford, then a Vice-Admiral

In 1907, Beresford was in command of the Channel fleet with Scott, then a Rear-Admiral, commanding the First Cruiser Squadron under him. The Kaiser was due to visit the fleet at Spithead and Beresford ordered all his ships to prepare themselves by painting and cleaning. Permission was asked for one of Scott's cruisers, HMS *Roxburgh*, to complete her firing practice before beginning work, but Beresford refused, whereupon Scott made his now-famous signal: "SINCE PAINTWORK APPEARS TO BE MORE IMPORTANT THAN GUNNERY YOU MUST REMAIN IN HARBOUR AND MAKE YOURSELF LOOK PRETTY"

Such a signal was certainly insubordinate but Beresford over-reacted badly by publishing the full text and publicly reprimanding Scott. As a result, the incident was exaggerated out of all proportion and has come to be seen as a symbol of the old reactionary attitude to gunnery practice. In fact, Beresford had a very good reason for his decision and was, under normal circumstances, in favour of effective training.

1916   *Zulu* mined off Dunkirk (51° 04' N, 2° 04' E.); stern blown off. Fore part later joined to after part of *Nubian*, the composite destroyer being named *Zubian*. See 4th February and 27th October.

1918   Paymaster, Instructor and Medical officers took executive ranks and branch title, e.g. Paymaster-Captain.

1940   *Havelock* sank the Italian s/m *Commandante Faà di Bruno* in N Atlantic.

8th NOVEMBER

1941 Martlet aircraft of 802 Sq *(Audacity)* shot down two Fockewulf FW200 in Atlantic (41° 27' N, 15° 18' W.). (Convoy OG.76)

Operation Torch – Landings in N Africa
Admiral Sir Andrew Cunningham was in command of the naval aspects of the landings in North Africa. Three main landings were planned, the Royal Navy covering those at Oran and Algiers, with the USN covering that at Casablanca. The co-ordination and planning required can be judged by the convoy sailings for the initial assaults. These convoys involved nearly 400 merchant ships and 170 escorts, and started on 2nd October from the Clyde (slow) and 1st November (fast) with some convoys sailing from America. A long series of follow up convoys were planned and run for the re-supply of the 70,000 troops landed.
The assaults took place early on 8th. During the attack at Algiers one airfield was captured by Martlet FAA fighters under Lt B H C Nation of *Victorious*. This was probably the first time a shore airfield had been captured by Naval aircraft.
Naval losses during the assault were the destroyer *Broke*, after breaking through the boom at Algiers to land troops in the harbour area, and the ex-US Coast Guard Cutters *Walney* and *Hartland*, during the assault on the harbour at Oran. The cruiser *Aurora* and destroyers engaged French destroyers off Oran, sank one, drove one ashore and the third returned to harbour.

1942 VC: Captain Frederick Thornton Peters *(Walney)*, Oran Harbour.
Landing in North Africa. Operation Torch. [bh]. Ships: *Aberdeen, Achates, Acute, Alarm, Albacore, Algerine, Alynbank, Amazon, Antelope, Arctic Ranger, Argonaut, Argus, Ashanti, Aubrietia, Aurora, Avenger, Avon Vale, Bachaquero, Banff, Beagle, Bermuda, Bicester, Bideford, Biter, Blean, Boadicea, Boreas, Bradford, Bramham, Brilliant, Brixham, Broke*[1]*, Bude, Bulldog, Bulolo, Burke, Cadmus, Calpe, Cava, Charybdis, Clacton, Clare, Clyne Castle, Coltsfoot, Convolvulus, Coreopsis, Coriolanus, Cowdray, Cumberland, Dasher, Delhi, Deptford, Dianella, Duke of York, Eastbourne, Eday, Egret, Elbury, Empyrean, Enchantress, Erne, Eskimo, Exe, Farndale, Felixstowe, Filey Bay, Fleetwood, Fluellen, Formidable, Foula, Furious, Gardenia, Geranium, Glengyle, Goth, Hartland*[2]*, Horatio, Hoy, Hunda, Hussar, Ibis, Ilfracombe, Imperialist, Inchcolm, Inchmarnock, Jamaica, Jonquil, Juliet, Jura, Karanja, Keren, Kerrera, Kingston Chrysolite, Kintyre, Lamerton, Landguard, Largs, Laurel, Leith, Leyland, Linnet, Loch Oskaig, Londonderry, Lookout, Lord Hotham, Lord Nuffield, Lotus, Lulworth, Lunenburg, Maidstone, Malcolm,*

HMS *Aurora* **in 1942**

8th NOVEMBER

Marigold, Martin, Meteor, Milne, Misoa, Mull, Negro, Nelson, Norfolk, Offa, Onslow, Opportune, Oribi, Othello, P.45, P.48, P.51, P.54, P.217, P.219, P.221, P.222, P.228, Palomares, Panther, Partridge, Pathfinder, Pelican, Penn, Pentstemon, Philante, Polruan, Poppy, Pozarica, Prescott, Prinses Beatrix, Puckeridge, Quality, Queen Emma, Quentin, Quiberon, Renown, Returno, Rhododendron, Rhyl, Roberts, Rochester, Rodney, Ronaldshay, Rother, Rothesay, Rousay, Royal Scotsman, Royal Ulsterman, Ruskholm, Rysa, St. Day, St. Mellons, St. Nectan, Samphire, Sandwich, Scarborough, Scottish, Scylla, Sennen, Sheffield, Shiant, Sirius, Speedwell, Spey, Spirea, Starwort, Stork, Stornoway, Stroma, Stronsay, Sturgeon, Swale, Tartar, Tasajera, Tribune, Tynwald, Ulster Monarch, Ursula, Vanoc, Vansittart, Velox, Venomous, Verity, Vetch, Victorious, Vienna, Violet, Walney[2], Westcott, Westray, Wheatland, Wilton, Wishart, Wivern, Woodstock, Wrestler, Zetland. Abbeydale, Brown Ranger, Derwentdale,

Dewdale, Dingledale, Ennerdale, Hengist, Ithuriel, Jaunty, Nasprite, Porcupine, Restive, Viscol, Weyburn. FAA Sqdns. Albacore, 817, 832 *(Victorious);* 820 *(Formidable);* 822 *(Furious).* Fulmar, 809, 882 *(Victorious);* 888 *(Formidable).* Martlet, 893 *(Formidable).* Sea Hurricane, 800 *(Biter).* 802, 883 *(Avenger);* 804, 891 *(Dasher).* Seafire 801, 807 *(Furious);* 880 *(Argus)* 884 *(Victorious);* 885 *(Formidable).* Swordfish, 833 *(Avenger and Biter).* HDML: 1127, 1128, 1139, M.L.: 238, 273, 280, 283, 295, 307, 336, 338, 433, 444, 458, 463, 469, 471, 480, 483.
[1] Sank on 9th, in 37° 00' N, 0° 46' E., whilst in tow off Zetland, after damage by shore batteries at Algiers. Operation Terminal.
[2] Sunk by shore batteries during attack on Oran harbour. Operation Reservist.

1943   *Grenville, Tumult, Tyrian* and *Piorun* (Pol) bombarded enemy positions in the Gulf of Gaeta, in support of the 5th Army.

HMS *Rodney* **about to open fire**

9th NOVEMBER

1806 *Dart* and *Wolverine* captured the French privateer *Jeune Gabrielle* 140 miles to the eastward of Barbados.

1807 *Skylark* captured the French privateer *Renard* in Dover Strait.

1865 *Galatea* and *Lily* destroyed the insurgent batteries at Cape Haitien.

1914 *Sydney* (RAN) destroyed the German cruiser *Emden* at the Cocos Islands. [bh]. War Medal: clasp 'Emden, 9 Nov 1914' approved but not issued.

1916 *Fair Maid* mined near Cross Sand buoy.

1918 Alexandretta occupied by allied naval forces.

1918 *Privet* (Q.19) and ML155 sank U.34 in Gibraltar Strait (35° 56' N, 5° 25' W.).

1918 GC (ex-AM): Lieutenant H.M.A. May, RMLI for saving life when *Britannia* was sunk by UB.50 off Cape Trafalgar (35° 56' N, 5°58' W.), the last major RN ship to be sunk in World War I.

1939 *Isis* captured the German *Leander* off Cape Finisterre (42° 32' N, 12° 46' W.).

1940 *Aphis* bombarded Sidi Barrani.

1940 Fulmar, Skua and Swordfish aircraft (*Ark Royal*) attacked Elmas airfield, Sardinia. Operation Crack. FAA Sqds: 810, 818, 820.

1941 *Aurora, Penelope; Lance* and *Lively* destroyed two escorted convoys in Mediterranean (36° 50' N, 18° 07' E.) The Italian destroyers *Fulmine* and *Libeccio*[1] and 10 merchant ships sunk.
[1] Sunk by *Upholder*.

1942 *Gardenia* sunk in collision with *Fluellen* off Oran (35° 49' N, 1° 05' W.). (Operation Torch).

1942 *Cromer* sunk by mine off Mersa Matruh (31° 26' N, 27 ° 16' E.).

1942 P.247 (later *Saracen*) sank the Italian s/m *Granito* off Cape San Vito, Sicily. (38° 34' N, 12° 09' E.).

1943 Fortress J/220 sank U.707 in N Atlantic (40° 31' N, 20° 17' W.). (Convoy MKS.29A)

An RN task group during the Central Treaty Organisation (CENTO — Britain, Iran, Pakistan, Turkey, USA) exercise 'Mudlark' in the Indian Ocean, November 1974.

10th NOVEMBER

1337   Sacking of Cadzand by Henry, Earl of Derby, and Sir Walter Manny; virtually the start of the Hundred Years' War.

1808   *Amethyst* captured the French *Thétis* off Isle de Groix. [m*, m, bh]

1811   *Skylark* and *Locust* defeated a French flotilla of twelve gunvessels off Calais and took a brig. [m]

1813   Boats of *Undaunted* and *Guadeloupe* stormed the batteries at La Nouvelle, South coast of France, captured two vessels and destroyed five more.

1833   *Nimble* captured the Spanish slaver *Joaquina* 7 miles off Isla de Pinos, near Cuba.

1914   Collier (*Newbridge*) sunk to block *Königsberg* in Rufigi River.

1914   British forces bombarded and stormed Sheikh Sa'id (S. Arabia) and destroyed the defences. Ship: *Duke of Edinburgh*. Troops: 29th Indian Infantry Brigade under Brigadier-General H.V. Cox.

1918   *Ascot* torpedoed by UB.67 off the Farnes; last RN ship sunk in World War I

1942   *Martin* sunk by U.431 off Algiers (37° 53' N, 3° 57' E.).

1942   *Ibis* sunk by torpedo aircraft off Algiers (37° 00' N, 3° 00' E.).

1942   *Lord Nuffield* sank the Italian s/m *Emo* off Algiers (36° 50' N, 2° 50' E.).

1943   Liberator D/311 (Czech) and US Liberators E/103 and E/110 sank U.966 off Bay of Biscay (44° 30' n, 10° 30' W.).

1944   *Hydra* mined in Channel: CTL.

1944   *Assiniboine* (RCN) (ex-*Kempenfelt*) wrecked on Prince Edward Island.

From the flight deck; a Royal Navy Phantom is tailing a Russian Badger intruder streaking low over the aircraft carrier HMS *Ark Royal*, NATO exercise, September 1970. The aircraft on deck are a Gannet (left) and a Buccaneer (right) with wings folded.

313

11th NOVEMBER

1755 *Orford* captured the French *Espérance* 240 miles S.S.W. of Lizard Head.

1779 *Tartar* captured the Spanish *Santa Margarita* off Cape Ortegal.

1794 Mutiny in *Windsor Castle* in Mediterranean.

1804 *Cyane* captured the French privateer *Bonaparte* between Desirade and Marie Galante, West Indies.

1858 Detachments of the *Pearl's* Naval Brigade, 13th Light Infantry and Bengal Yeomanry dispersed the Indian rebels at Phanpur .

1914 *Niger* sunk by U.12 off Deal.

1917 *Staunch* and M.15 torpedoed and sunk off Gaza by UC.38.

1918 Hostilities with Germany ceased.

1940* Fleet Air Arm attack on Italian battleships at Taranto by two squadrons from *Illustrious* and two lent from *Eagle*. [bh] . Ships: *Illustrious; Berwick, Glasgow, Gloucester, Hasty, Havock, Hyperion, Ilex, York.* Cover: *Barham, Malaya, Valiant, Warspite, Gallant, Greyhound, Griffin, Hereward, Hero.* F.A.A. Sqdns: 813*, 815, 819, 824*. (*From *Eagle*). Seriously damaged: *Conte di Cavour, Caio Duilio, Littorio.* Operation Judgment.

1942 *Unbeaten* sunk in error by British aircraft in the Bay of Biscay (46° 50' N, 6° 51' W.).

The Italian Battleship *Conte di Cavour* after Taranto

1942 *Hecla* torpedoed by U. 505 off Cape St Vincent sank the next day.

1942 *Tynwald* sunk by Italian s/m *Argo* off Bougie.

1942 *Bengal* (RIN) and the Dutch tanker *Ondina* attacked by two Japanese armed merchant cruisers in the Indian Ocean (19° 45' S, 92° 45' E.). The *Hokoku Maru* was sunk and *Aikoku Maru* made off. [bh]

The RIN Fleet Minesweeper *Bengal* (735 tons, 1 x 12 pounder gun) was escorting the Dutch tanker *Ondina* (1 x 4 in gun) from Fremantle to Diego Garcia. Two Japanese raiders, the *Hokoku Maru* and *Aikoku Maru* (each with 6 x 6 in guns. topedoes and aircraft), appeared. The *Bengal* told the *Ondina* to act independently, and then attacked the enemy. Just after noon, the enemy opened fire, but the *Bengal* (or *Ondina*) managed to hit the *Hokoku Maru* and set her on fire. The *Bengal* then made smoke and, as *Ondina* was seven miles away and escaping and apparently safe, retired. The damaged raider blew up at 1312, but the other raider continued the action and hit the *Ondina* with shells and two torpedoes. The crew abandoned the tanker, but survivors re-embarked, put out the fires and brought her safely to Fremantle.

1943 *Beaufort, Faulknor* and *Pindos* (Greek) bombarded Kos.

1943 *Rockwood* bombed by German aircraft in Aegean: CTL.

1944 *Venturer* sank U.771 off Tromsö (69° 17' N, 16° 28' E.). Both vessels submerged at the time.

1944 *Kenilworth Castle, Launceston Castle, Pevensey Castle, Portchester Castle* sank U.1200 off Cape Clear (50° 24' N, 9° 10' W.).

*Taranto

The carrier *Illustrious* mounted an air strike against the Italian Fleet at Taranto. The *Eagle* was to have been in company, but suffered damage just before the strike while in action off Calabria. Some of *Eagle's* aircraft were transferred to *Illustrious* for the operation. 21 aircraft in 2 waves flew off from *Illustrious* at 2040 and 2100 on 11th. They achieved complete surprise and sank three battleships at their moorings. All but two aircraft returned safely to *Illustrious*. Letter from Admiral Cunningham. "The 11th and 12th November 1940 shall be remembered for ever as having shown once and for all that in the Fleet Air Arm the Navy has a devastating weapon. In a total flying time of about 6½ hours carrier to carrier 20 aircraft inflicted more damage upon the Italian fleet than was inflicted upon the German High Seas Fleet in the daylight action at the Battle of Jutland."

All vessels welcomed the returning *Illustrious* with the hoist "*Illustrious* manoeuvre well executed".

12th NOVEMBER

1595   John Hawkins died.

1684   Edward Vernon born.

1781   Capture of Negapatam by Vice-Admiral Sir Edward Hughes *(Superb)* and Major-General Sir Hector Munro. Ships: *Burford, Eagle, Exeter, Monarca, Superb, Worcester.* Frigates, etc.: *Active, Nymph, Combustion.* H.E.I.Co's ships: *Essex, Expedition, Neptune, Panther, Rochford, Royal Admiral.* Seamen and Marines were landed.

1806   Boats of *Galatea* captured the French *Réunion* 15 miles to the north-eastward of Guadeloupe.

1854   *Tribune, Highflyer* and *Lynx* destroyed a Russian tower 10 miles N.W. of Anapa.

1856   Capture of the Bogue forts, Canton River. Ships: *Barracouta, Calcutta, Coromandel, Hornet, Nankin.*

1920   *Tobago* mined off Malta and sold there.

1925   M.1 (ex-K.18) sunk in collision with Swedish ss *Vidar* off Start Point.

1931   *Petersfield*, yacht of C in C China station, wrecked on Tung Yung Island: Admiral Kelly's long-estranged brother, another Admiral, was moved to signal 'glad you're safe' which produced the perhaps typical reply "glad you're glad".

1939   *Delhi* intercepted the German *Mecklenburg*, which scuttled herself off Faeroes (62° 37' N, 10° 26' W.).

1940   7th C.S., (Vice-Admiral H.D. Pridham-Wippell) *(Orion)* sank one ship and set two on fire in an escorted convoy of four ships off Valona (40° 48' N, 19° 18' E.). Operation Judgment.

Pre-war picture of HMS *Argus*

1942   *Lotus* and *Starwort* sank U.660 in Mediterranean (36° 07' N, 1° 00' W.). (Convoy TE.3)

1944   *Kimberley* bombarded an enemy battery on Alimnia, Dodecanese.

1944   Lancaster bombers of No. 5 Group, Bomber Command, sank the German battleship *Tirpitz* at Tromso. Operation Catechism.

1970   FONAC moved from *Daedalus* (Lee-on-Solent) to *Heron* (Yeovilton).

World War I Warship Losses.

	RN	Allied	Enemy
Capital Ships	16	12	6
Cruisers	25	17	28
Submarines	54	35	207
Others	159	90	172
Totals	254	154	413

Casualties	HM Ships	RN Division	Total
Killed In Action) or Died of Wounds)	22,811	7,924	30,735
Died — other causes	11,843	666	12,509
Wounded	4,510	20,165	24,675
Injured — other causes	648	—	648
	39,812	28,755	68,567

12/11/18 From Admiralty

"The Lords Commissioners of the Admiralty desire heartily to congratulate officers and men of the Royal Navy and Royal Marines upon the triumph of the Allied cause, in realisation of which they have played so splendid a part, adding lustre throughout to the great tradition of the Service to which they belong.

Their Lordships feel that after four years of ceaseless vigilance a relaxation of war conditions cannot but be eagerly desired by officers and men: they may be relied upon to grant leave and modify routine immediately when circumstances permit. For the present however with German submarines possibly still at sea ignorant of the Armistice, with the work of escorting ships to be surrendered or interned devolving largely on British Navy and with the full capacity of the mine-sweepers required for sweeping the seas it is plain that no officer or man can be spared from their duties until the safety of the country at sea is assured.

The Navy had in time of Peace to be ready for War in a sense which land forces cannot be. Now that Peace is again in prospect, it may prove that even after the troops in the field are enjoying a relief from tension the Navy must for a time continue its war routine. If so their Lordships are confident that this will be cheerfully accepted as being at once the burden and the privilege of the Empire's first line of defence."

13th NOVEMBER

1705 *Orford, Warspite* and *Litchfield* captured the French *Hasardeux* 90 miles W.N.W. of Ushant.

1797 Launch of *Fairy* captured the French privateer *Épervier* in Whitesand Bay, near Calais.

1798 *Argo* recaptured the Spanish (ex-British) *Peterel* South of Majorca.

1800 *Milbrook* fought the French privateer *Bellone* off Oporto.

1809 *La Chiffone, Caroline* and six Bombay Marine cruisers, *Ariel, Aurora, Fury, Mornington, Nautilus, Prince of Wales,* destroyed the Joasmi pirate stronghold at Ras Al Khaimah.

1838 *Experiment, Cobourg* and *Queen Victoria* (manned from *Niagara*) repulsed an attack on Prescott, Canada, during Papineau's rebellion. Troops: 23rd Regiment.

1854 *Barracouta, Encounter, Styx,* the P. & O. *Canton* and *Sir Charles Forbes, Amazona, Queen* (hired) and boats of *Spartan* destroyed 48 pirate junks and 2 batteries of Ty-loo (Kau lan).

1866 Admiral of the Fleet Sir William Parker died.

1917 *Firedrake* sank UC.51 in N Sea.

1918 Battle squadron reached Constantinople: *Temeraire, Superb, Lord Nelson* and *Agamemnon.*

1939 *Blanche* sunk by mine off the Tongue lightvessel in Thames estuary.

1939 *Newcastle* intercepted the German *Parana* which scuttled herself off Iceland (65° 41' N, 25° 22' W.).

1940 *Aphis* bombarded Maktila.

1941 *Ark Royal* torpedoed by U.81 off Gibraltar (36° 03' N, 4° 45' W.) whilst returning from Operation Perpetual: sank on the 14th.

1942 *Lotus* and *Poppy* sank U.605 off Algiers (37° 4' N, 2° 55' E.). (Convoy TE.3)

1943 *Dulverton* sunk by German glider bomb off Kos (36° 50' N, 27° 30' E.).

1943 *Taurus* sank the Japanese s/m I.34 in Malacca Strait (5° 17' N, 100° 05' E.).

1944 *Bellona, Kent* (Rear-Admiral R.R. McGrigor, C.S.1); *Algonquin* (RCN), *Myngs, Verulam* and *Zambesi* attacked an escorted convoy off S. Norway (58° 14' N, 6° 12' E.). Operation Counterblast. Sunk: 6 out of 7 of convoy, 3 out of 4 escorts.

1978 First deck landing by a Sea Harrier, on *Hermes.*

HMS *Ark Royal* **sinking after being torpedoed whilst returning from Operation Perpetual, 1941**

316

14th NOVEMBER

1797   *Majestic* captured the Spanish *Bolador* 25 miles W.N.W. of Cape St. Vincent.

1807   *Carrier* captured the French privateer *Actif* off Cromer. [m].

1808   Boats of *Polyphemus* captured the French *Colibri* off San Domingo.

1918   *Cochrane* wrecked in Mersey estuary.

1941   *Talisman* and *Torbay* landed a party of Commandos near Apollonia to raid Rommel's headquarters.

1942   Hudsons F, K, L, W and X/500 sank U.595 off SW Spain.

1944   *Brocklesby* and *Wheatland* bombarded Bar, Adriatic.

1944   *Kimberley* destroyed two landing craft in Lividia Bay.

1967   Order for first Type 42 GMD placed with Vickers: *Sheffield.*

'Making Smoke', HMS *Kimberley* World War 2

HM Submarine *Opossum* in the Arctic pack ice, 1965

15th NOVEMBER

1798   Capture of Minorca by Commodore John Duckworth (*Leviathan*) and troops under General the Hon Charles Stuart. [bh]. Ships: *Argo, Aurora, Centaur, Constitution, Cormorant, Leviathan, Peterel.* Seamen and Marines were landed.

1799   *Crescent* captured the Spanish *Galgo* 50 miles to the north-eastward of Puerto Rico.

1808   Defence by *Excellent's* Marines of Fort Trinidad, Rosas, assisted by *Excellent* and *Meteor.*

1875   Boats of *Thistle* and *Fly* with detachments of Royal Artillery and the 1/10th Regiment, captured the stockades of a rebel chief at Passir Salat, Perak River.

1918   VC: Commander Daniel Marcus William Beak DSO, MC, RNVR for heroic leadership including a single handed attack on a machine gun nest in France at Logeast Wood (*Gazette* date). First recipient of cross on crimson ribbon.

1942   *Avenger* sunk by U.155 W of Gibraltar (36° 15' N, 7° 45' W.), and *Wrestler* sank U.411 off Gibraltar (36° 09' N, 7° 42' W.). (Convoy MKF.1Y)

1942   Hudson S/500 sank U.259 off Algiers (37° 20' N, 3 ° 05' E.).

1942   *Algerine* sunk by the Italian s/m *Ascianghi* off Bougie (36° 47' N, 5° E.).

1967   Admiral of the Fleet Lord Chatfield died.

16th NOVEMBER

1294   Edward I ordered construction of twenty galleys, each of 120 oars, for use against the French.

1693   Bombardment of St. Malo by Captain John Benbow (*Norwich*) with a squadron of fourth rates and bombs.

1810   *Phipps* captured the French privateer *Barbier de Séville* off Calais. Enemy foundered shortly afterwards.

1857   VC: Lieutenant Nowell Salmon and Able Seaman John Harrison, and Lieutenant Thomas James Young and William Hall (*Shannon*) for gallantry at Lucknow during the Indian Mutiny.

1858   Armstrong rifled breech-loaded gun adopted.

1863   *Bustard* captured three pirate junks in Meichow Wan.

1926   *Bluebell* rescued s.s. *Sunning* from pirates off Hong Kong.

1940   *Swordfish* sunk off Ushant: cause unknown.

1941   *Marigold* sank U.433 off Gibraltar (36° 13' N, 4° 42' W.).

1943   Liberator M/86 sank U.280 in N Atlantic (49° 11' N, 27° 32' W.). (Convoy HX.265)

First British Submarine, 1879

The first submarine to be designed and built in England was the Reverend George Garrett's *Resurgam.* Built in Liverpool in 1879; she was powered by steam when on the surface and by latent heat from the boiler when submarged. She had no weapons and was bad at depth-keeping because of inefficient diving planes fitted amidships. But it was to be a Holland Type VI — the successful design of American John P. Holland that had been accepted by the US Navy — which was built under licence for the Royal Navy to become HM Submarine No. 1. See 2nd October.

17th NOVEMBER

1797 *Anson* and *Boadicea* captured the French privateer *Railleur* 100 miles S.W. of Yeu Island.

1800 Boats of *Captain* and *Magicienne*, and *Nile* cutter, cut out and destroyed the French *Réolaise* and two merchant vessels at Port Navalo, Morbihan.

1803 Boats of *Blenheim* with *Drake* and *Swift*, cut out the French privateer *Harmonie* and captured a battery at Marin, Martinique.

1809 *Royalist* captured the French privateer *Grand Napoléon* in Dover Strait. [m]

1809 *La Chiffone, Caroline* and six Bombay Marine cruisers, *Ariel, Aurora, Fury, Mornington, Nautilus, Prince of Wales*, destroyed the Joasmi pirate stronghold at Lingeh.

1849 Boats of *Castor* and *Dee* destroyed a slave vessel and the shore defences of the Arab slavers up the river from Porto de Angoche, Portuguese East Africa.

1857 *Shannon's* Naval Brigade at the relief of the Residency, Lucknow. Indian Mutiny Medal: clasp "Relief of Lucknow".

1871 Completion of *Hotspur,* first British warship to be built as a ram and the only one to have a fixed turret.

1917 VC: Ordinary Seaman John Henry Carless, (*Caledon*) (posthumous). Light cruiser action off Heligoland. Ships: 1 CS: *Nerissa; Umpire, Urchin, Ursa.* 6 LCS: *Calypso, Caradoc, Cardiff, Ceres; Valentine, Vanquisher, Vehement, Vimier.* 1 LCS: *Caledon, Galatea, Inconstant, Royalist; Medway, Vendetta.* 1 BCS: *Lion, New Zealand, Princess Royal, Repulse, Tiger, Champion, Nepean, Obdurate, Oriana, Petard, Telemachus, Tower, Tristram, Verdun.*

1917 K1 sank after collision with K4 off Danish Coast.

1918 Occupation of Baku.

1942 Walrus of 700 Sq., Albacore of 820 Sq. (*Formidable*) and Hudsons C, L and Z/500 sank U.331 in E Mediterranean (37° 08' N, 2° 24' E.).

1944 *Eggesford* and *Lauderdale* bombarded enemy positions at Cristofora, Rab Island, Admiralty Islands.

A battery manned by European sailors of the Indian Navy, 1849

17th NOVEMBER

Coastal Forces: MTBs returning from patrol

Coastal Forces, 19 November 1941

Three MGBs were ordered to sea as a result of reports of activity by German E boats. They set out for the Hook of Holland in a calm sea, but one had to return to harbour because of engine defects. At 0200 on 20th they reached their position and waited. At 0445 they heard the enemy approaching and closed to intercept them. They found five S boats, and in a close action suffered no serious damage themselves, but sank one enemy, badly damaged two and inflicted light damage on the other two. Three S boats were sunk by the RAF on their return to harbour. Lt-Cdr R P Hitchens was in command of this operation. He served with distinction in Coastal Forces, being awarded the DSO and bar, DSC and two bars and being mentioned in despatches three times before being killed in action on 13th April 1943.

Vice-Admiral Richard Bell-Davies VC (see 19th November)

A Nieuport Scout aircraft; 1st World War

320

18th NOVEMBER

1705   *Montagu* fought two French ships off Cape St. Nicolas Mole, Haiti.

1793   *Latona* fought two French frigates 90 miles West of Ushant.

1861   *Kestrel* defeated a superior force of Chinese pirates and dismounted the guns in their shore battery at Ching Keang, Chu san.

1917   *Marsa* lost in collision in Harwich harbour.

1917   P.57 rammed and sank UC.47 in N. Sea (54° 01' N, 0° 22' E.).

1917   *Candytuft (Pavitt)* (Q-ship) sunk by U.39 off Bougie (36° 59' N, 4° 41' E.).

1939   *California* captured the German *Borkum* and *Eilbek* off Iceland: *Borkum* despatched by U.33 on 23rd.

1940   *Dorsetshire* bombarded Zante, Italian Somaliland.

1941   *Euryalus* and *Naiad* bombarded Halfaya area in support of the 8th Army in the Western Desert.

1942   *Montbretia* (Nor) sunk by U.624 in N Atlantic (53° 37' N, 38° 15' W.). (Convoy ONS.144)

1942
Arethusa, light cruiser, was escorting a convoy to Malta in Operation Stoneage. Air attacks started at 0600 18th, and at 1800 *Arethusa* was torpedoed. She was towed stern first back to Alexandria, having to battle with raging fires and a rising gale. She reached Alexandria on the evening of 22nd, with 155 men dead. She was the last serious casualty of the famous 15th Cruiser Squadron. In 1944, *Arethusa* led the bombarding forces at Normandy and later carried King George VI over the Channel to visit forces in Normandy.

1943   *Chanticleer* damaged beyond repair by U.238 W. of Portugal.

Hunting a U-Boat. Two destroyers drop depth charges while an Anson keeps look out.

19th NOVEMBER

1791   *Phoenix* captured the French *Resolue* off Mangalore.

1804   *Donegal* captured the Spanish *Anfitrite* off Cape Kantin, Morocco.

1893   *Adventure* and *Pioneer* with troops, destroyed the stronghold of Makanjira, a slave trading chief on Lake Nyassa.

1915   VC: Squadron-Commander Richard Bell-Davies, RNAS, at Ferrijik Railway junction, Bulgaria, for landing during an air attack behind enemy lines to rescue a colleague who had been shot down, while under heavy fire.

1918   First (twenty) U-boats surrendered at Harwich.

1935   Admiral of the Fleet Earl Jellicoe of Scapa died.

1941   *Sydney* (RAN) engaged the German disguised raider *Kormoran* (Schiff 41) off the West coast of Australia (26° 34' S, 111° 00' E.). Both ships sunk. [bh]

The German raider *Kormoran*, disguised as a merchant ship, was off the West Australian Coast. The light cruiser, *Sydney*, with about the same armament, sighted her and closed to investigate. She closed to within a mile before the raider revealed her identity by opening fire and hitting the cruiser heavily around the bridge and torpedoing her. The after turrets of *Sydney*, in local control, managed to continue the action for an hour before the *Sydney* drifted away, a flaming wreck. The *Kormoran* had to be abandoned and scuttled, and 315 of the 400 crew were rescued by searchers for the *Sydney*.

1942   Hudson G/608 sank U.98 in the Western Approaches to Gibraltar Strait.

1943   Wellington F/179 sank U.211 in N Atlantic (40° 15' N, 19° 18' W.). (Convoy SL.139/MKS.30)

20th NOVEMBER

1759 Battle of Quiberon Bay. Admiral Sir Edward Hawke *(Royal George)* defeated Admiral le Comte de Conflans *(Soleil Royal).* [bh] . Ships: *Burford, Chichester, Defiance, Dorsetshire, Duke, Dunkirk, Essex*, Hercules, Hero, Intrepid, Kingston, Magnanime, Mars, Montague, Namur, Resolution*, Revenge, Royal George, Swiftsure, Temple, Torbay, Union, Warspite.* Captain Robert Duff's squadron *Rochester, Chatham, Coventry, Falkland, Maidstone, Minerva, Portland, Sapphire, Vengeance, Venus.*
* Wrecked. 11 French ships captured or destroyed out of 21.

Sir Edward Hawke chased the French Fleet, under Conflans, in the teeth of a gale into the shoal waters of Quiberon Bay, on a lee shore. 11 French ships were lost, and others only escaped by throwing overboard their guns and weapons to lighten themselves and cross the shoals. Only 2 British vessels were lost. This was a decisive victory, as close blockade of the French was no longer required, and the French had to withdraw their army from Hanover. From this victory, and the taking of Québec two months before, comes the toast 'May our Officers have the eye of a Hawke and the Heart of a Wolfe.'

"Where there is a passage for the enemy there is a passage for me. You have done your duty in showing me the danger: now obey my orders and lay me alongside the *Soleil Royal*".

1779 *Hussar* (escorting a convoy) captured the Spanish privateer *N.S. Del Buen Consejo* 100 miles S.W. by W. of Cape Roxent (da Roca).

1806 Boats of *Success* cut out the French privateer *Vengeur* at Hidden Port (Puerto Escondido) Cuba.

1807 *Ann* captured the Spanish privateer *Vincejo* 90 miles S.W. of Cape Finisterre. [m] . (See 24th November)

1845 Anglo-French squadron cut the boom and captured the Argentine batteries at Obligado. British ships: *Gorgon, Firebrand, Philomel, Comus, Dolphin, Fanny.* French Ships: *San Martin, Fulton, Expeditive, Pandour, Procida.* The Argentine *Republicano* set on fire by her own crew and blew up.

The Battle of Quiberon Bay 1759

20th NOVEMBER

1863	Attack on the Maori position at Rangariri by Commodore Sir William Wiseman (*Curaçoa*) and Lieutenant-General Duncan Cameron. Gunboats, etc.: *Ant, Avon, Chub, Flirt, Midge* and *Pioneer* (Colonial steamer). Landing parties from *Curacoa, Eclipse, Harrier, Miranda.* Troops: Royal Artillery, 40th and 65th Regiments.
1939	*Chitral* intercepted the German *Bertha Fisser* which scuttled herself off Iceland (64° 10' N, 15° 14' W.).
1939	*Sturgeon* sank the German trawler *Gauleiter Telschow* 30 miles N.W. of Heligoland: first RN submarine success in World War II.
1942	*Potentilla* (Nor.) sank U.184 off Newfoundland. (49° 25' N, 45° 25' W.). (Convoy ONS.144)
1943	*Nene, Snowberry* and *Calgary* (all RCN) sank U.536 in N Atlantic (43° 50' 19° 39' W.). (Convoy SL.139/MKS.30)
1944	Minelaying air strike at Haugesund. Operation Handfast. Ships: *Diadem, Premier, Pursuer, Onslaught, Scorpion, Scourge, Zealous.* FAA 8 Avenger aircraft of 856 Sq. (*Premier*): 16 Wildcat aircraft of 881 Sq. (*Pursuer*).

The River Gun Boat *Pioneer* in the Maori wars. Built at Sydney in 1863, she was an iron flat-bottomed stern wheel paddle steamer (300 tons), armour-plated, with cupolas pierced for 12-pounder guns and for rifle fire.

21st NOVEMBER

1652 Boats of *Leopard, Constant Warwick* and *Bonaventure* cut out the Dutch (ex-British) *Phoenix* at Leghorn.

1757 *Unicorn* captured the French *Hermione* 180 miles N.W. of Cape Finisterre.

1797 *Jason* captured the French privateer *Marie* off Belle Île.

1852 Capture of Pegu. Ships: Bengal Marine steamers *Mahanuddy, Nerbudda, Damooda,* and *Lord William Bentinck* and boats of *Fox* and *Sphinx.* Troops: 1st Bengal Fusiliers, 1st Madras Fusilier Regiment, 5th Madras Native Infantry, Bengal Artillery, Madras Sappers and Miners.

1868 *Hercules* (fifth of the name) completed, first battleship to have cables led onto the upper instead of into the main deck, and first with three-calibre main armament.

1914 RNAS attacked the Zeppelin sheds at Friedrichshavn.

1918 German High Seas Fleet surrendered off May Island and arrived at Rosyth en route for internment at Scapa Flow. "Didn't I tell you they'd have to come out?" (Beatty) Operation ZZ.
"The German ensign will be hauled down at sunset today, Thursday, and will not be hoisted again without permission."

1939 *Gipsy* sunk by mine in the entrance to Harwich.

1939 *Transylvania* intercepted the German *Tenerife,* which scuttled herself to the West of Iceland.

1939 *Bayonet* sunk by British mine in South Inchkeith Channel.

1939 *Belfast* severely damaged by German mine in the Firth of Forth.

1940 *Rhododendron* sank U.104 in NW Approaches (56° 28' N, 14° 13' W.). (Convoy OB.244)

1941 *Utmost* torpedoed and severly damaged the Italian cruiser *Luigi di Savoia Duca Degli Abruzzi* in the Mediterranean.

1942 Albacore I/817 (*Victorious*) sank U.517 in N. Atlantic (46° 16' N, 17° 09' W.).

1943 *Crane* and *Foley* sank U.538 in N. Atlantic (45° 40' N, 19° 35' W.). (Convoy SL.139/MKS.30)

1947 P.511 foundered at her moorings in Kames Bay.

Scuttled German warships at Scapa, 1918

324

22nd NOVEMBER

1718 Lieutenant Robert Maynard *(Ranger and Jane)* killed the pirate Edward Teach ("Blackbeard") and captured all his crew in Ocracoke Inlet, Pamlico Sound.

1739 Vice-Admiral Edward Vernon *(Burford)* captured Porto Bello. [bh]. Ships: *Burford, Hampton Court, Norwich, Princess Louisa, Strafford, Worcester.*

1812 *Southampton* captured the American *Vixen* off the Bahamas.

1847 Boats of *President* and *Eurydice,* with Portuguese boats, destroyed an Arab slaver's stockade up the river from Porto de Angoche. The Portuguese *Juan De Castro* captured an American gun-running brig.

1857 VC: Midshipman Arthur Mayo, Indian Navy (received award while an undergraduate at Oxford). No. 4 Detachment, Indian Navy, defeated and dispersed a superior force of sepoy mutineers at Dacca.

1888 Charles Forbes born.

1914 British forces captured Basra, Mesopotamia. Ships and vessels: *Espiegle, Ocean, Odin, Lawrence,* (RIN) *Comet, Lewis Pelly* (RIN), *Sirdar-I-Naphte.*

1915 Battle of Ctesiphon, Mesopotamia. River gunboat and Vessels: *Firefly, Comet, Messoudieh, Shaitan, Shushan, Sumana.*

1916 E.30 lost in N. Sea.

1918 G.11 wrecked off Howick, Northumberland.

1939 *Laurentic* intercepted the German *Antiochia* which scuttled herself in Atlantic (52° 12' N, 15° 08' W.).

1941 *Devonshire* sank the German disguised raider *Atlantis* (Schiff 16) in S Atlantic (4° 15' S, 18° 34' W.).

1943 *Hebe* sunk by mine off Bari (41° 08' N, 16° 53' E.).

1944 *Stratagem* sunk by Japanese destroyer in Malacca Strait.

Devonshire sighted the German Raider *Atlantis* (armed as a light cruiser) in the South Atlantic. *Atlantis* had sunk or captured 145,697 tons of allied shipping, and was disguised as a merchantman. *Devonshire* stood off until it was confirmed that *Atlantis* could not be the vessel she pretended to be, and then sank her. *Atlantis'* survivors were rescued by U-boat, transferred to a supply ship, which was sunk just over a week later by *Devonshire's* sister ship *Dorsetshire.* Again the survivors were rescued by U-boats and made an epic journey of 5000 miles to Biscay ports.

Capture of Porto Bello, 1739

1757   *Hussar* and *Dolphin* sank the French *Alcyon* 220 miles N.N.W. of Cape Finisterre.

1757   *Chichester* captured the French *Abenakise* 100 miles S.W. of Ushant.

1799   *Courier* captured the French privateer *Guerrier* 20 miles S.E. of Lowestoft. [m]

1799   *Solebay* captured the French *Egyptien, Éole, Levrier* and *Vengeur* 10 miles W.N.W. of Cape Tiburon, Haiti.

1810   Bomb and mortar vessels of Rear–Admiral Sir Richard Keats' squadron attacked the French gunboats in Puerto de Santa Maria, near Cadiz. [m]

1865   *Grasshopper* captured two pirate lorchas and destroyed a third at Port Matheson.

1914   *Russell* and *Exmouth* bombarded Zeebrugge.

1914   *Garry* and *Dorothy Gray* rammed U.18 trying to enter Scapa Flow: scuttled by own crew.

1939   *Rawalpindi* sunk by the *Scharnhorst* in Iceland-Faeroes gap (63° 40' N, 11° 31' W.).

The AMC *Rawalpindi* (Captain E C Kennedy) was on the Northern Patrol when she sighted the new German battlecruiser *Scharnhorst* at dusk. The enemy was attempting to break out into the Atlantic to attack merchant ships with her sister, *Gneisenau*. *Rawalpindi* reported the enemy and despite the disparity in armament, managed to hit *Scharnhorst* in the quarter of an hour before she was sunk. The cruiser *Newcastle*, which was the next ship in the patrol line, closed and sighted the battle cruisers' lights as she picked up survivors. However, she lost them in the dark and rain squalls. The battle cruisers decided to return to base, without attacking shipping, as they had been damaged and their position was known.

1939   *Calypso* captured the German *Konsul Hendrik Fisser* North of the Faeroes (63° 00' N, 7° 00' W.).

1939   First German magnetic mine located at Shoeburyness: rendered safe by Lt-Cdr J.G.D. Ouvry and Chief Petty Officer C.E. Baldwin, assisted by Lt-Cdr R.C. Lewis and Able Seamen A.L. Vearncombe, on 24th: dissected at *Vernon* by Dr A.B. Wood.

1943   *Bazely, Blackwood* and *Drury* sank U.648 in Atlantic (42° 40' N, 20° 37' W.). (Convoy OS.59/KMS.33)

Wrens after a flight in an RN Oxford, World War II

1807   *Anne* fought ten Spanish gunboats off Tarifa and took three. [m]

1812   Boats of *Narcissus* captured the American privateer *Joseph and Mary* 20 miles S.E. of Cape Tiburon, Haiti.

1875   Purchase of controlling interest in Suez Canal, by Disraeli.

1885   Irrawaddy flotilla and troops defeated the Burmese at Myingyan, Upper Burma. Boats of *Bacchante, Turquoise, Woodlark* and *Mariner* with the Indian Marine *Irrawaddy*.

1917   *Gipsy* and five trawlers attacked U.48 which had stranded on the Goodwin Sands, where she blew up (51° 17' N, 1° 31' E.).

1941   *Dunedin* sunk by U.124 in Mid Atlantic (3° N, 26° W.).

The German magnetic mine recovered in 1939

A Buccaneer aircraft of 809 Sq taking off from HMS *Hermes*

Oil rig patrol HMS *Ashanti* **in Forties Field, 1975**

25th NOVEMBER

1793   *Penelope* and *Iphigenia* captured the French *Inconstante* 12 miles to the westward of Leogane, Haiti.

1851   *Niger, Bloodhound* and boats of *Vulcan, Harlequin, Waterwitch* and *Philomel* attacked Lagos consequent on a flag of truce being fired on, but had to withdraw.

1868   *Algerine* captured the Amping and Zealandia forts of Taiwan (Formosa).

1899   Battle of Graspan, South Africa, Naval Brigade of *Doris, Monarch* and *Powerful*.

1914   D.2 sunk by German patrol craft off Western Ems.

1940   Three accoustic mines exploded in Thames: first use of technique developed since 29th October.

1941   *Barham* sunk by U.331 off Sidi Barrani (32° 34' N, 26° 24' E.)

1942   *Utmost* sunk by the Italian t.b. *Groppo* off Marettimo, W of Sicily (38° 31' N, 12° 01' E.).

1943   *Bazeley* and *Blackwood* sank U.600 in N Atlantic (41° 45' N, 22° 30' W.).

1944   *Shawinigan* (RCN) sunk by U.1228 in Cabot Strait (47° 34' N, 59° 11' W.).

1944   *Ascension* and Sunderland G/330 (Nor) sank U.3222 in Shetland/Faeroes Gap (60° 18' N, 4° 52' W.).

1960   Royal Marines, except recruits and bandsmen, empowered to wear the green beret of the Commandos.

26th NOVEMBER

1703   Great storm destroyed 13 warships and the Eddystone light. 1500 seamen drowned. "This was such a storm as never was known before" — Defoe.

1799   *Amphion* captured the Spanish letter of marque *Asturiana* 120 miles W.N.W. of Cape Catoche, Gulf of Mexico.

1806   Rear-Admiral Sir Edward Pellew's squadron captured the Dutch *Maria Wilhelmina* off Banten. (see 27th November).

1813   Boats of *Swiftsure* captured the French privateer *Charlemagne* 10 miles W.N.W. of Cape Rouse (Rosso), Corsica.

1858   *Pearl's* Naval Brigade at Domariaganj (2nd Action).

1914   *Bulwark* destroyed by internal explosion at Sheerness.

1914   *Friedrich Karl* mined in Baltic.

1916   Second German raid on Lowestoft.

1918   "Nothing, nothing in the world, nothing that you may think of or dream of, or anyone else may tell you: no argument, however seductive, must lead you to abandon that naval supremacy on which the life of our country depends".   W.S. Churchill

1940   15 Swordfish aircraft of 815 and 819 Sq. (*Illustrious*) bombed Port Laki, Leros.

1943   *Orion, Paladin, Teazer* and *Troubridge* bombarded enemy positions North of Garigliano River.

Boiler Room of HMS *Royal Sovereign,* **1922**

27th NOVEMBER

1762   Samuel Hood born.

1806   Rear-Admiral Sir Edward Pellew (*Culloden*) destroyed a Dutch squadron and twenty merchantmen at Batavia, (Djakarta). Ships: *Belliqueux, Culloden, Powerful, Russell, Seaflower, Sir Francis Drake, Terpsichore.*

1809   *La Chiffonne* and the Hon E I Co's cruisers *Fury, Mornington, Nautilus* and *Ternate* destroyed the Joasmi pirate stronghold at Laft.

1811   *Eagle* captured the French *Corcyre* off Brindisi.

1857   *Shannon's* Naval Brigade at the defence of Cawnpore.

1916   R.9 made first successful flight by an RNAS rigid airship.

1940   Action off Cape Spartivento, Sardinia (36° N, 8° 30' E.). Vice-Admiral Sir James Somerville (*Renown*) fought the Italian Fleet. [bh]. Ships: *Ark Royal, Berwick, Coventry, Defender, Despatch, Diamond, Duncan, Encounter, Faulknor, Firedrake, Forester, Fury, Gallant, Gloxinia, Greyhound, Hereward, Hotspur, Hyacinth, Jaguar, Kelvin, Manchester, Newcastle, Peony, Ramillies, Renown, Salvia, Sheffield, Southampton, Vidette, Wishart.* FAA Sq: 700 (Walrus); 800 (Skua), 808 (Fulmar), 810, 818, 820 (Swordfish). *(Ark Royal).* RAF: Sunderland flying-boat.

A convoy was passing from Gibraltar to Alexandria. The Italians determined to stop it, and sailed 2 battleships, seven 8 in cruisers and 16 destroyers from Naples and Messina. Admiral Somerville, in command of Force H covering the convoy, decided that the best defence for the convoy was a determined attack by his inferior escort. The battlecruiser *Renown*, one eight in gunned cruiser, 3 six in gun cruisers and one four in (AA) cruiser together with the aircraft carrier *Ark Royal* raced to attack the Italian Fleet. In the action which followed, one British cruiser was damaged, but the enemy withdrew and the convoy passed safely.

1940   *Port Napier* destroyed by fire in Loch Alsh (57° 17' N, 5° 44' W.).

1941   *Parramatta* (RAN) sunk by U.559 off Tobruk (32° 20' N, 24° 35' E.).

28th NOVEMBER

Leading Seaman Bateman, one of the first rating pilots to be trained before the First World War, beside his Avro biplane at Upavon, 1912

1803   *Ardent* drove ashore and destroyed the French *Bayonnaise* near Cape Finisterre.

1808   Boats of *Heureux* fought shore batteries and seven vessels in Mahault harbour, Guadeloupe. [m].

1914   VC: Commander Henry Peel Ritchie (*Goliath*), at Dar-es-Salaam during search and destroy operation. Ships: *Fox, Goliath, Duplex* and *Helmuth:* three German ships disabled, and harbour installations wrecked.

1916   RNAS aircraft destroyed the Zeppelin L.21, 8 miles East of Lowestoft.

1917   WRNS instituted by Admiralty announcement in office memorandum No. 245.

1941   O.21 (Neth) sank U.95 off Gibraltar. (36° 24' N, 3° 20' W.).

1942   *Quentin* and *Quiberon* (RCN) sank the Italian s/m *Dessie* N of Bone (37° 04' N, 7° 45' E.).

1942   *Ithuriel* beached, CTL, in Bone Harbour after air attack.

1943   Wellington L/179 sank U.542 in N. Atlantic (39° 03' N, 16° 25' W.). (Convoy SL.140)

1959   HM Dockyard Hong Kong closed.

1970   Admiral of the Fleet Sir Michael Le Fanu died: "cultivate courage".

1682	Prince Rupert died.
1779	*Proserpine* captured the French *Sphinx* 12 miles S.E. by W. of Montserrat.
1805	Boats of *Serpent* cut out the Spanish *San Cristobal Pano* in Truxillo Bay, Honduras.
1811	*Alceste, Active, Acorn* and *Unite* captured the French *Pomone* and *Persanne* 15 miles N.E. of the Pelagos Islands, Dalmatia. [m, bh]. A third French frigate *Pauline,* escaped.
1883	Max Kennedy Horton born.
1915	Withdrawal from Ctesiphon, near Baghdad, to Kut-al'Amara. River gunboats and vessels; *Butterfly, Firefly, Comet, Massoudieh, Shaitan*[1], *Shushan, Sumana.* [1] Destroyed by enemy.
1915	*Duchess of Hamilton* mined off Longsand.
1939	*Icarus, Kashmir* and *Kingston* sank U.35. E. of Shetland. (60° 53 'N, 2° 47' E.).
1940	*Leander* bombarded Mogadishu.
1944	MMS 101 sunk by mine in the Gulf of Salonica.
1945	First RN Helicopter air sea rescue (Sikorski R.5).

Air-Sea Rescue

1612	*Dragon* and *Osiander* (H.E.I. Co.) fought a Portuguese squadron off Surat.
1652	Admiral Robert Blake *(Triumph)* fought Admiral Maerten Tromp *(Brederode)* off Dungeness. Ships: *Bonaventure*[1], *Garland*[1], *Happy Entrance*[2], *Hercules*[2], *Nimble, Sapphire* [2], *Ruby* [2], *Triumph* [1], *Vanguard, Victory.* [1] Captured. [2] Sunk.
1803	*Bellerophon* and *Hercule* at the evacuation by the French of San Domingo (Haiti). Captured: *Cerf, Clorinde, Sémillante, Vertu.*
1808	Captain Lord Cochrane's defence of Fort Trinidad, Rosas.
1811	*Rover* captured the French privateer *Comte Regnaud* (ex-British *Vincejo*) 250 miles S.W. by W. of the Scilly Islands.
1851	Second punitive expedition against Lagos.
1916	*Penshurst* (Q.7) sank UB.19 18 miles N.W. of the Casquets (49° 56' N, 2° 45' W.).
1940	GC: Lieutenant Harold Reginald Newgass, RNVR for mine disposal at Garston Gasworks, Liverpool.
1941	Whitley B/502 sank U.206 in the Bay of Biscay (46° 55' N, 7° 16' W.). First RAF U-boat kill.
1944	Launch of *Vanguard,* twelfth of the name and our last battleship afloat.
1945	*Merrittonia* (RCN) wrecked on coast of Nova Scotia.
1950	Battle of the Chosin Reservoir, Korea. 41 Independent Commando RM present, under command of 1st U.S. Marine Division; later awarded the Presidential Unit citation.

The team of people involved in an air sea rescue operation

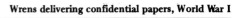

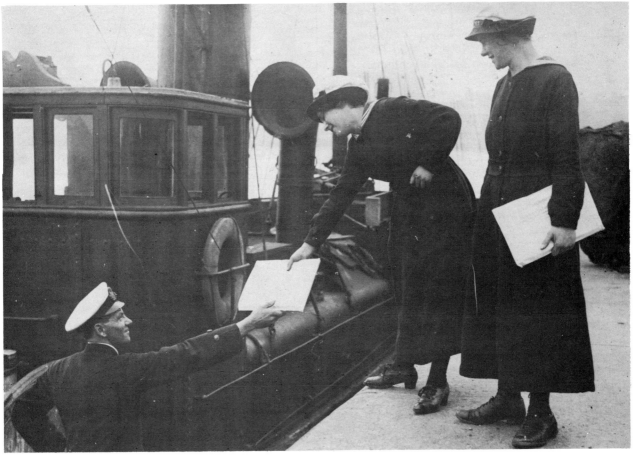

1st DECEMBER

1588 Chatham Chest founded for relief of distressed seamen.

The Chatham Chest was a pension fund founded in the sixteenth century to help disabled sailors by deducting sums from seamen's pay. The Chest had five locks, with five different keys held by five different officers. Despite this there was severe mismanagement of funds. Pepys set up a Commission to inspect its administration.

1744 *Rose* captured the Spanish *Concepcion* 100 miles to the eastward of Havana.

1781 William Parker born.

1811 Boats of *Colossus* and *Conquestador*, with *Arrow*, captured one vessel of a French convoy, burnt three more and drove three others ashore near La Rochelle.

1915 Withdrawal from Ctesiphon. Action at Umm-at-Tubul. River gunboats and vessels: *Butterfly, Firefly*,[1] *Comet*[1], *Massoudieh, Shusham, Sumana*.
1 . Disabled and abandoned.

1916 E.37 lost in N Sea.

1940 GC (ex-AM): Able Seaman A. Miles, (*Saltash*). For saving life at sea.

1941 *Dorsetshire* sank the German supply ship *Python* in S. Atlantic (27° 50' S. 3° 55' W.) See 22nd November.

1941 *Aurora, Penelope* and *Lively* sank the Italian destroyer *Alvise da Mosto* off Kerkenah Bank (33° 45' N., 12° 30' E.).

1942 *Armidale* (RAN) sunk by Japanese torpedo aircraft off Darwin (10° 00' S, 128° 00' E.).

1942 *Jasper* sunk by German t.b. flotilla off Start Point.(Convoy PW.256)

1943 *Paladin, Teazer* and *Troubridge* bombarded the Minturno area, Gulf of Gaeta.

HMS *Broadsword*, 1979

HMS *Vanguard* launched by Princess Elizabeth on December 1st, 1944

2nd DECEMBER

1793   *Antelope* packet captured the French privateer *Atlanta* off Jamaica.

1796   *Quebec* captured the French *Africaine* 20 miles to the southward of Cape Bainet, Haiti.

1796   *Southampton* captured the Spanish privateer *Corso* off Cape delle Mele.

1825   Defeat of the Burmese at Pagoda Point, above Prome. *Diana* and boats of the Irrawaddy flotilla captured 300 warboats.

1917   P.32 sank UB.81, mined off Isle of Wight.

1940   *Forfar* sunk by U.99 in Western Approaches (54° 35' N, 18° 18' W.).

1942   *Argonaut, Aurora, Sirius, Quentin* and *Quiberon* (RAN) sank the Italian destroyer *Folgore* and destroyed an escorted convoy of 4 ships off Skerki Bank, (37° 39' N. 10° 50' E.).

1942   *Quentin* sunk by torpedo aircraft off Bone (37° 32' N., 8° 32' E.).

1949   *Implacable,* (ex-*Duguay-Trouin*), scuttled off the Owers. The oldest warship then afloat, she took a good deal of sinking. Captured on 4 November 1805 she had been in private hands since 1912 but could not be maintained.

Early Navigation equipment. (top) Back staff, c.1740, (left) Octant and (right) Sextant, both c.1810

1794	Mutiny in *Culloden*.
1796	*Lapwing* captured the French *Decius* and destroyed *Vailiante* at Anguilla, West Indies. [m]
1799	*Racoon* captured the French privateer *Intrépide* in Dover Strait.
1807	*Curieux* fought the French privateer *Revanche* 120 miles to the eastward of Barbados.
1807	Pellew's destruction of Dutch squadron at Grisee, Java.
1810	Capture of Île de France (Mauritius) by Vice-Admiral Albemarle Bertie (*Africaine*) and Major-General the Hon John Abercromby. Ships: *Africaine, Illustrious, Boadicea, Nisus, Cornwallis, Clorinde, Cornelia, Doris, Nereide, Psyche, Ceylon, Hesper, Hecate, Eclipse, Emma, Staunch, Egremont, Farquhar, Mouche, Phoebe, Actaeon.* Regiments: Royal Artillery, 12th, 14th, 22nd, 33rd, 56th, 59th, 84th, 87th, 1st Bengal Volunteers, 2nd Bombay Native Infantry, Madras Artillery, Madras Pioneers.
1858	*Pearl's* Naval Brigade at Bururiah (Baunrihar).
1916	*Perugia* (Q.1) sunk by U.63 in the Gulf of Genoa.

1942	*Janus, Javelin, Jervis* (D. 14) and *Kelvin* sank the Italian t.b. *Lupo* off Kerkenah Bank (34° 34' N, 11° 39' E.).
1942	*Penylan* sunk by the German S.115 off Start Point (50° 08' N., 3° 39' W.). (Convoy PW.257)
1945	First deck landing of jet aircraft by Lt. Cdr. E. M. Brown a Sea Vampite onto *Ocean,* off the Isle of Wight.
1946	*Middlesex* (RCN) wrecked on Bald Island Point, near Halifax.

View in mirror landing sight

The 'batsman' had controlled deck landings in the Royal Navy for 15 years, but his usefulness had declined as aircraft approach speeds increased, and he was replaced from 1954 by the mirror deck landing system. By aligning the reflection of a spotlight with reference marks on either side of a large polished steel mirror set at the side of the landing area, the pilot could make an approach at a steady angle of descent which was so accurate that a single arrester wire could be designated as the 'target wire', although at least three other wires were provided to cater for slight inaccuracies in flying. Within 10 years, the mirror was replaced by a projector sight, using narrow beams of direct light instead of a single reflected source but working on the same principle.

4th DECEMBER

1775	*Fowey* captured the American *Washington* 50 miles to the south-eastward of Cape Ann, Mass.
1799	*Atalante* captured the French privateer *Succès* off Dungeness.
1811	Boats of *Sultan* captured the French *Languedoc* and *Castor* off Bastia, Corsica. [m]
1856	*Encounter, Barracouta* and boats of squadron destroyed French Folly, Canton River.
1939	*Salmon* sank U.36 in North Sea, S.W. of Stavanger (57° N, 5° 10' E.).
1939	*Nelson* severely damaged by mine in the entrance to Loch Ewe.
1941	*Aphis* bombarded the Derna-Tobruk road (and on 7th and 8th).
1944	*Aurora, Marne, Meteor* and *Musketeer* bombarded shipping at Rhodes.
1967	*Plover* paid off, having been in continuous commission since 27th September 1939.

5th DECEMBER

1578	Drake sacked Valparaiso.
1797	*Diana* captured the French privateer *Mouche* 500 miles West of Lands End.
1804	Rank of Sub-Lieutenant established by Order in Council.
1808	*Magnet* captured the Danish privateer *Paulina* off Bornholm.
1859	J.R. Jellicoe born.
1866	Start of naval operations against the Fenians in S. Ireland: *Helicon, Vestal* and *Black Prince;* also in Canadian waters by N. American Squadron.
1918	*Cassandra* sunk by German mine in the Baltic (58° 29' N, 21° 11' E.). in operations against the Bolsheviks.
1940	*Cameron* sunk by German aircraft at Portsmouth.
1940	Inconclusive action between *Carnarvon Castle* and the German disguised raider *Thor (Schiff 10)* in 31° 00' S., 43° 15' W.
1950	Evacuation of troops from Chinnampo, Korea.

HMS *Ceylon* in 1956

The Chinese Forces intervened in the Korean War at the end of November 1950 and it became necessary to withdraw forces southward. The cruiser *Ceylon*, destroyers HMCS *Cayuga, Sioux* and *Athabaskan* and HMAS *Warramunga* and *Bataan* with one American destroyer, and with air cover from the carrier *Theseus*, safely escorted transports from Chinnampo. 1800 troops of the US 8th Army and the Navy Port personnel together with 5900 RoK troops were taken off, and military supplies, oil tanks and dock installations remaining were demolished.

6th DECEMBER

1608	George Monck born.
1672	First attempt, by Order in Council, to introduce retired pay as opposed to half pay.
1768	*Chaleur,* RN's first schooner, sold out of the service.
1782	*Ruby* captured the French *Solitaire* 120 miles East of Barbados.
1799	*Speedwell* captured the French privateer *Heureux Speculateur* off the Channel Islands.
1809	*Royalist* captured the French privateer *Heureuse Étoile* South of Beachy Head. [m]
1810	Ceylon retaken for third and last time from the French.
1856	*Sampson* destroyed five pirate junks at Stonecutters Island.
1857	*Shannon's* Naval Brigade at the defeat of the Gwalior Contingent of mutineers at Cawnpore.
1916	*Ariel* sank UC.19 in Channel.
1917	GC (ex-AM): Leading Seaman T. N. Davis for disposing of burning ammunition in burning and drifting tug at Halifax, N.S.
1940	*Regulus* sunk by unknown cause in Otranto Strait. (approx. date).
1941	*Perseus* sunk by mine seven miles N of Zante (37° 54′ N, 20° 54′ E.): one survivor, from 170 feet, who swam ten miles to Cephalonia.
1942	*Tigris* sank the Italian s/m *Porfido* S. of Sardinia. (38° 10′ N, 8° 35′ E.).
1944	*Bullen* sunk by U.775 off Cape Wrath. (58° 30′ N, 5° 03′ W.).
1944	*Loch Insh* and *Goodall* sank U.297 off Orkneys. (58° 44′ N, 4° 29′ W.).
1951	Admiralty decided to establish Mine-watching Services, forerunner of RN Auxiliary Service.

7th DECEMBER

1809	*Rinaldo* captured the French privateer *Maraudeur* in Dover Strait.
1824	Repulse of the Burmese attack on Kemmendine. Ships: *Teignmouth* (Bombay Marine), *Sophie, Powerful.* Troops: 26th Madras Native Infantry.
1842	Boats of *Persian* captured the Portuguese slaver *Maria Segunda* 40 miles E.S.E. of Whydah.
1858	*Bustard, Firm* and boats of *Fury* destroyed two pirate junks in the Estuary of the Broadway.
1878	Completion of *Northampton,* named after First Lord's parliamentary constituency, and last ship to have main armament between decks and on the broadside.
1939	*Jersey* torpedoed by the German destroyer *Erich Giese* near the Haisborough lightvessel.
1939	First German Type B magnetic mine rendered safe in Thames estuary by Lt. J.E.M. Glenny and Lt. R.S. Armitage of *Vernon.*
1941	*Windflower* (RCN) sunk in collision with ss *Zypenberg* a ship of the convoy off Newfoundland. (Convoy SC.53). (46° 19′ N, 49° 22′ W.).
1942	RM Boom Patrol Detachment (Canoeist raiders) from *Tuna* attacked German blockade runners in the Gironde — the "Cockleshell heros" — Operation Frankton.
1944	Minelaying strike by 12 Avenger aircraft of 856 Sq. (*Premier*) and 14 Wildcat aircraft of 881 Sq. (*Trumpeter*), escorted by *Diadem* and 8 destroyers, in Salhusstrommen, Norway (59° 22′ N, 5° 24′ E.). Operation Urbane.

A Wildcat aircraft landing on a Carrier, 1944

8th DECEMBER

Vice-Admiral Sir Doveton Sturdee

As a result of the Battle of Coronel on 1st November, the First Sea Lord ordered two battle-cruisers to the area. The *Invincible* and *Inflexible*, under Admiral Sturdee, arrived at the Falklands to coal on 7th December, having kept radio silence since 18th November. On 8th December the German force was sighted off the Falklands, and the British squadron sailed immediately. During the running battle, the crew of *Kent* was mustered on the quarterdeck to give extra speed by forcing the propellers deeper into the sea.

1780   Boats of squadron under Vice-Admiral Sir Edward Hughes *(Superb)*, covered by *Drake* and *Eagle* (Bombay Marine), destroyed a number of armed vessels in Mangalore Roads.

1798   *Cambrian* captured the French privateer *Cantabre* 50 miles North of Cape Peñas.

1803   *Medusa* captured the French privateer *Espérance* and destroyed *Sorcier* off Cabrita (Carnero) Point, Gibraltar Bay.

1858   Boats and landing party of *Bustard*, *Firm* and *Fury* destroyed ten pirate junks in the Estuary to the Broadway.

1900   *Espiegle* launched at Sheerness: last ship with a figurehead.

1914   Battle of Falkland Islands. Vice-Admiral Sir Doveton Sturdee *(Invincible)* defeated Vice-Admiral Graf von Spee *(Scharnhost)* off the Falkland Islands. [bh]. Ships: *Bristol, Caernarvon, Cornwall, Glasgow, Inflexible, Invincible, Kent, Macedonia*. Sunk: *Gneisenau, Leipzig, Nürnberg, Scharnhorst*. Escaped: *Dresden*. War Medal: clasp 'Falkland Islands 8 Dec 1914' approved but not issued.

Survivors of the German cruiser *Gneisenau* being picked up by HMS *Inflexible*, Battle of the Falkland Islands, 1914

8th DECEMBER

1918   Action between British and Bolshevik light forces in the Caspian.

1929   *Sterling* and *Sirdar* rescued *Hai Ching* from pirates off Chilang Point, S. China.

1941 Siege of Tobruk raised
Transported by RN to Tobruk during the 242 day siege 12th April to 8th December 1941: 72 tanks, 92 guns, 34,000 tons of stores, 32,667 men replaced by 32,113 fresh troops, 7,516 wounded withdrawn, 7,097 prisoners withdrawn. Cost to RN — 25 ships sunk, 9 seriously damaged; cost to MN — 5 sunk, 4 seriously damaged.

1941   *Peterel* sunk by Japanese *Idzuma* at Shanghai.

1942   Liberator B/120 sank U.254 in Atlantic (57° 25' N, 35° 19' W.). (Convoy HX.217)

1942   *Traveller* sunk by mine in the Gulf of Taranto.

1944   Continuation of Operation Urbane (See 7th). 12 Firefly of 1771 Sq (*Implacable*) and 9 Wildcat aircraft of 881 Sq. (*Trumpeter*) bombed two merchant ships and set them on fire off Stavanger (59° 43' N., 5° 24' E.).

1968   Closing ceremony of *St. Vincent*, boys training establishment at Gosport.

A Phantom aircraft landing on *Ark Royal*

338

9th DECEMBER

1677	*Guernsey* fought the Algerine *White Horse* 20 miles East of Cape Palos.
1798	*Boadicea* captured the French privateer *Invincible Bonaparte* 500 miles West of Ushant.
1809	*Redpole* captured the French privateer *Grand Rodeur* off Beachy Head.
1819	Destruction of the Joasmi pirate stronghold at Ras al Khaimah. Ships: *Liverpool, Curlew, Eden* (Bombay Marine). *Aurora, Nautilus,* and 3 others. Troops: 47th and 65th Regiments; 1/3rd, 1/11th and flank coy of 1/2nd Native Infantry.
1856	Capture of the Persian fort at Reshire (Rishahr). Ships: *Assaye, Semiramis, Ferooz, Ajdaha, Victoria, Falkland, Berenice* (Indian Navy).

1914	British forces captured Qurra, Mesopotamia. Ships and vessels: *Espiegle, Ocean, Odin, Lawrence, Lewis Pelly, Miner, Shaitan.*
1914	U.11 mined and sunk in Channel.
1914	Launch of *Ark Royal*, purchased for conversion to seaplane carrier.
1917	*Ben Lawer* rammed and sank UB.18 in Channel.
1942	*Porcupine* torpedoed by the German U.602 off Cape Ferrat (36° 40' N., 0° 04' W.); reached Gibraltar, but scrapped later.
1942	*Marigold* sunk by Italian torpedo aircraft W of Algiers. (Convoy MKS.3Y)
1944	*Bamborough Castle* sank U.387 off Murmansk (69° 41' N, 33° 12' E.). (Convoy RA.62)

The second *Ark Royal*, 1914

339

10th DECEMBER

1809   *Royalist* captured the French privateer *Beau Marseille* 4 miles S.S.E. of Dungeness. [m]

1810   *Rosario* captured the French privateer *Mameluk* off Dungeness.

1856   Capture of Bushire. Ships: *Assaye, Semiramis, Ferooz, Ajdaha, Victoria Falkland, Berenice* (Indian Navy).

1917   UB.75 mined and sunk off Flamborough Head.

1936   Formation of RNVSR.

1941   *Prince of Wales* and *Repulse* sunk by Japanese torpedo aircraft off the East coast of Malaya (3° 33.6' N, 104° 28.7' E. and 3° 45' N., 104° 24' E. respectively).

Royal Marine detachments from the two ships were rescued and went on to join the Argyll and Sutherland Highlanders to form the 'Plymouth Argylls' in the defence of Singapore.

1941   *Naiad* bombarded Derna.

Sinking of *Prince of Wales*

340

11th DECEMBER

1798 *Perdrix* captured the French privateer *Armée d'Italie* 21 miles East of Virgin Gorda.

1799 *Tremendous* destroyed the French *Preneuse* at the mouth of the Tombeau River, Mauritius.

1807 *Grasshopper* captured the Spanish *San Jose* under Cape Negrete.

1941 *Farndale* sank the Italian s/m *Ammiraglio Caracciolo* off Bardia (32° 09' N, 25° 19' E.). (Convoy TA.2)

1941 *Truant* sank the Italian t.b. *Alcione* off Suda Bay, Crete.

1941 *Bluebell* sank U.208 W. of Gibraltar.

1942 *Blean* sunk by U.443 W. of Oran (35° 55' N., 1° 50' W.).

Ammunitioning a submarine (World War 2)

1962 L Company, 42 Commando landed at Limbang, Brunei.

1968 *Cochrane* commissioned at Rosyth.

The painting by Terence Cuneo of the assault on Limbang by 'L' Company, 42 Commando during the Brunei Revolt, in 1962.

341

12th DECEMBER

1721   Alexander Selkirk, Master's Mate in *Weymouth* and Defoe's inspiration for Robinson Crusoe, died.

1724   Samuel Hood born.

1779   *Salisbury* captured the Spanish privateer *San Carlos* 20 miles W. by N. of Punta de la Sal, Gulf of Honduras.

1781   Rear-Admiral Richard Kempenfelt (*Victory*) captured 20 sail of a French convoy 160 miles S.W. by W. of Ushant [bh]. Ships: *Agamemnon, Alexander, Britannia, Courageux, Duke, Edgar, Medway, Ocean, Queen, Renown, Union, Valiant, Victory.* Frigates, etc: *Arethusa, Monsieur, Prudente, Tartar, Tisiphone.*

1782   *Mediator* captured the French *Alexandre* and *Menagère* off Ferrol.

1809   *Thetis, Achates, Attentive, Bacchus* and *Pultusk* captured the French *Nisus* and destroyed a battery at Deshayes, Guadeloupe. [m]

1810   *Entreprenante* fought four French privateers between Malaga and Almeria.

1849   Boats of *Centaur, Teazer* and the French *Rubis* recaptured the *British Grant* up the Mansoa River, Gambia. Troops: 2nd and 3rd West India Regiments.

1917   *Partridge* (escorting a Scandinavian convoy) sunk and *Pellew* damaged by German destroyers G.101, G.103, G.104 and V.100 in 59° 48' N, 3° 53' E. off Norwegian coast. [bh]

HMS *Campania* a seaplane carrier of the 1st World War period

Admiral Samuel, Viscount Hood (1724-1816)

Joined, promoted Lieutenant and made Post in the same years as his younger brother Alexander (see 23rd June). Employed during the peace between the Seven Years' War and the War of American Independence, and appointed Commissioner at Portsmouth in 1778. Distinguished service in American waters as a Flag Officer — at the Chesapeake (5th September) and the Saints (12th April): made an Irish peer for the latter. C in C Portsmouth: then a member of the Board of Admiralty 1778-1795. C in C Mediterranean 1793-1794, during which period he occupied Toulon for a time and did much damage on its evacuation. Politics procured his recall — though he was then over seventy — much to Nelson's disgust: "Oh miserable Board of Admiralty: they have forced the first office of the service away from his command." But he became Governor of Greenwich Hospital, for twenty years, and his monument describes him rightly as "an officer of the highest distinction among the illustrious men who rendered their own age the brightest period in the naval history of their country."

1917   *Wolverine* lost in collision with *Rosemary* off N.W. Ireland.

1939   *Duchess* sunk in collision with *Barham* off the Mull of Kintyre (55° 19' N., 6° 06' W.).

1940   *Aphis, Ladybird* and *Terror* bombarded enemy positions on the Egyptian frontier.

1941   *Moth* sunk in action by Japanese aircraft at Hong Kong.

1942   P.222 sunk by the Italian t.b. *Fortunale* in the Gulf of Naples.

1943   *Holcombe* and *Tynedale* sunk by the U.593 off Bougie (37° 20' N., 50' E. and 37° 10' N., 6° 05' E. respectively). (Convoy KMS.34)

1944   *Tunsberg Castle* (Nor) (ex-*Shrewsbury Castle*) sunk by mine off Sandstabben light (70° 44' N, 30° 09' E.).

13th DECEMBER

1710	*Breda* captured the French *Maure* 100 miles West of Lisbon.
1796	*Terpsichore* captured the French *Vestale* 60 miles West of Cadiz. Retaken by the prisoners.
1806	*Halcyon* captured the Spanish *Neptune Dios de los Mares* off Cape San Martin.
1808	Destruction of the French *Cygne* and two schooners off St. Pierre, Martinique. [m]. Ships: *Circe, Amaranthe, Stork, Épervier, Express, Morne Fortunée.* Troops: Royal York Rangers.
1809	*Junon* taken by the French *Renommée* and *Clorinde* 270 miles E. by N. of Guadeloupe.
1810	Boats of *Kent, Ajax, Cambrian, Minstrel* and *Sparrowhawk* destroyed a French convoy at Palamos, Catalonia.
1914	VC: Lieutenant Norman Douglas Holbrook (B.11) for passing through the Turkish minefield at the entrance to the Dardanelles and sinking the Turkish *Messoudieh*.
1916	*Landrail* sank UB.29 in W. Channel; first sinking by depth charge.
1917	U.75 mined and sunk off Borkum.
1939	*Salmon* torpedoed the German cruisers *Leipzig* and *Nürnberg* 130 miles West of Jutland.

The *Salmon*, on patrol in the North Sea, sighted an enemy force on the morning of 13th. At 1030, three enemy cruisers were in a position to be attacked, and *Salmon* hit both the *Leipzig* and the *Nürnberg*. The *Leipzig* remained under repair for a year, and then was employed on training duties; the *Nürnberg* took six months to repair. Nine days before, the *Salmon* had sunk U.36 in the same area, the first successful submarine versus enemy submarine attack in the war. For this patrol Lt-Cdr Bickford was promoted and awarded the DSO.

1939	Commodore H.H.Harwood (*Ajax*) engaged the *Admiral Graf Spee* off the River Plate (34° 28' S. 49° 05' W.) and drove her into Montevideo, where she was scuttled on the 17th. [bh]. Ships: *Ajax, Achilles* (RNZN), *Exeter*. FAA Sq: Seafox 700 (*Ajax*).

The German battleship *Graf Spee* had been commerce raiding in the South Atlantic. Various naval units were searching for her; Force G, under Commodore Harwood, was off the River Plate. On 13th December the squadron sighted smoke, and action with the *Graf Spee* opened at 0614 at 9½ miles. The *Exeter* was hit heavily, but continued to fight with only one turret working by hand, on emergency steering and using the after conning position passing orders to the steering position by a line of sailors. *Graf Spee* also hit *Ajax* and *Achilles*, but finally turned for Montevideo to make repairs. After the permitted 72 hours in a neutral port *Graf Spee* sailed, and then scuttled herself, having been given the impression that superior forces were outside the harbour, when in fact they were 48 hours steaming away.

1941	*Legion, Sikh, Maori,* and *Isaac Sweers* (Dutch) sank the Italian cruisers *Alberico da Barbiano* and *Alberto di Giussano* off Cape Bon (37° 04' N., 11° 47' E.). [bh]
1942	*Enchantress* sank the Italian s/m *Corallo* off Bougie (37° 00' N., 5° 09' E.). (Convoy ET.5)
1943	Liberator B/53 sank U.391 in the Bay of Biscay (45° 45' N, 9° 38' W.).
1943	*Calpe* and the USS *Wainwright* sank U.593 in W. Mediterranean (37° 38' N., 5° 58' E.). (Convoy KMS.34)
1944	Swordfish L/813 and Q/813 (*Campania*) sank U.365 in Arctic (70° 43' N., 8° 07' E.). (Convoy RA 62)

HMS *Ajax*

Lieutenant Holbrook VC (standing 3rd from left) and the crew of submarine B11, 1914

The *Graf Spee* burning after being scuttled by her crew, 1939

14th DECEMBER

1624	Lord Howard of Effingham died.
1775	Thomas Cochrane born.
1798	*Ambuscade* taken by the French *Bayonnaise* off the mouth of the Gironde.
1809	*Melampus* captured the French *Béarnais* 80 miles N.N.E. of Barbuda.
1814	Boats of fleet captured five American gunboats and a sloop on Lake Borgne. [m]
1852	Relief of Pegu, Burma. Ships (Bengal Marine) *Nerbudda, Mahanuddy*. Boats of: *Fox, Sphinx* and *Moozuffer* (Indian Navy).
1860	Landing party from *Nimrod* captured six pirate junks in Taune Bay.
1864	*Bombay* destroyed by fire off Montevideo.
1939	*Ursula* sank the German escort F.9 and an R-boat off Heligoland (54° 08' N., 7° 55' E.).
1939	*Kelly* badly damaged by mine 13 miles off the mouth of the Tyne.
1940	Eight Swordfish aircraft of 830 Sq. (Malta) bombed Tripoli.
1940	*Hereward* and *Hyperion* sank the Italian s/m *Naiade* off Bardia (32° 03' N., 25° 56' E.).
1941	*Galatea* sunk by U.557 off Alexandria (31° 17' N., 29° 13'E.).
1944	*Aldenham* sunk by mine off Pola (44° 30' N., 14° 50' E.).
1944	*Diadem, Mauritius* and 4 destroyers attacked shipping off Stadtlandet.
1944	Bombardment of the Arakan coast in the neighbourhood of St. Martin's Island (13 bombardments during the next 9 days). Ships: *Napier, Nepal* HDML: 1275, 1303. ML 438, 439, 440, 441, 447, 847, 855.

15th DECEMBER

1379	Sir John Arundel's squadron destroyed by storm on coast of Ireland.
1778	Rear-Admiral the Hon Samuel Barrington (*Prince of Wales*) fought Vice-Admiral Comte d'Estaing at St. Lucia. [bh]. Ships: *Boyne, Centurion, Isis, Nonsuch, Preston, Prince of Wales, St. Albans*. Frigates, etc: *Ariadne, Aurora, Barbados, Carcass, Ceres, Pelican, Snake, Venus, Weazle*.
1824	Attack on a flotilla of Burmese war boats in the Panhlaing River by *Diana*, boats of *Arachne* and *Sophie* and the Bombay Marine *Prince of Wales*.
1841	*Charybdis* captured the Colombian Federal *Marcellino* and five Federal schooners in Zapote Bay.
1899	Battle of Colenso. Naval Brigade of *Terrible, Forte, Tartar, Philomel* and Natal Naval Volunteers.
1917	*Arbutus* torpedoed by UB.65 in the entrance to the Bristol Channel (51° 38.5' N., 6° 00' W.). Sank 16th.
1940	*Cameron* capsized in Portland harbour after attack by German aircraft.
1940	*Thunderbolt* sank the Italian s/m *Capitano Tarantini* in Bay of Biscay. (45° 25' N., 9° 12' W.).
1941	*Nestor* (RAN) sank U.127 off Cape St. Vincent.
1942	GC (ex-AM): Petty Officer Cook C. H. Walker, for saving life in Malta Harbour. (*Gazette* date).
1942	*Petard* and *Queen Olga* (Greek) captured the Italian s/m *Uarsciek* S. of Malta (35° 10' N., 14° 25' E.); s/m sank later in tow.
1946	Admiral Sir Herbert Richmond, founder of the *Naval Review* and Master of Downing College, Cambridge, died.

16th DECEMBER

1796   *Cleopatra* captured the French privateer *Hirondelle* 500 miles to the westward of Ushant.

1808   *Naiad* and *Narcissus* captured the French privateer *Fanny* off Noirmoutier.

1812   Saving of *Magnificent* in a violet gale off Île de Ré in Bay of Biscay.

1914   Scarborough, Hartlepool and Whitby bombarded by German battle cruisers. Ships: *Patrol, Doon, Waveney, Test.*

1917   *Arbutus* foundered in heavy weather in St. Georges Channel, after being torpedoed by U.B. 65 whilst serving as a Q-ship.

1941   *Thracian* beached at Hong Kong and captured by Japanese forces; recaptured in September 1945.

1942   *Firedrake* sunk by U.211 in N Atlantic (50° 50' N., 25°15'W.). (Convoy ON.153)

Royal Marines on a jungle patrol in Borneo, 1963

1957   *Thorough* returned to *Dolphin* after first circumnavigation by a submarine.

Borneo 1962–1966

In December 1962 the Brunei rebellion marked the beginning of an attempt by Indonesia to infiltrate the remaining countries in Borneo. Strong guerilla patrols operated out of Indonesian territory deep into Sarawak, Saba and Brunei.

42 Commando, Royal Marines was flown in to Brunei town from Singapore. The British resident and other hostages including 2 women were held by the rebels at Limbang. Two old landing craft were commandeered and manned by seamen of *Chawton* and *Fiskerton.* They embarked L company of 42 Commando, and at dawn on 12th December, under a heavy fire from the shore, the landing craft went into the beach at Limbang. The Royal Marines stormed ashore, drove off the rebels, and rescued the hostages moments before they were due to be executed. The rebels were later hunted down by helicopters and river patrols. During this attack 5 Royal Marines were killed and 5 wounded.

For 3½ years British troops including Royal Marines operated in the jungles of Borneo and were supported by 845 and 846 FAA helicopter squadrons from *Albion* and *Bulwark.* These squadrons, operating out of tiny clearings and on the limits of their aircrafts' capabilities, achieved a very high level of operational readiness. For example in 1963, 846 squadron of Whirlwinds carried out 3,750 operational sorties, and in 1964 845 squadron aircraft of Wessex helicopter carried out 10,000 operational flying hours in support of the Army and Royal Marines.

17th DECEMBER

1619   Prince Rupert born.

1706   *Romney* captured a French privateer in Malaga Bay.

1810   *Rinaldo* sank the French privateer *Vieille Josephine* off the Owers.

1834   *Buzzard* captured the Spanish slaver *Formidable* 20 miles to the northward of Cape Bullen, West Coast of Africa.

1857   Rear-Admiral Sir Francis Beaufort died.

1915   German cruiser *Bremen* sunk in E. Baltic by RN submarine: E.9 sank the German V.191.

1940   *Acheron* sunk by mine off the Isle of Wight (50° 31 N., 1° 31' W.).

1940   *Aphis* bombarded the Bardia area.

1941   *Blankney, Exmoor, Penstemon, Stanley, Stork* and Martlet aircraft of 802 Sq. (*Audacity*) sank U.131 W of Gibraltar (34° 12' N, 13° 35' W.). (Convoy HG.76)

1941   First Battle of Sirte. Passage of *Breconshire* from Alexandria to Malta and partial engagement with Italian battlefleet off the Gulf of Sirte (34° 00' N., 18° 30' E.). Ships: *Euryalus, Naiad* (Rear-Admiral Vian — C.S.15) *Decoy, Havock, Jervis* (D.14), *Kimberley, Kipling, Nizam* Force K: *Aurora, Penelope, Lance, Legion, Lively, Maori, Sikh, Isaac Sweers* (Neth).

1942   *Splendid* sank the Italian destroyer *Aviere* off Bizerta (38° 00' N., 10° 05' E.).

1944   *Nyasaland* sank U.400 off Cape Clear (51° 16' N, 8° 05' W.).

18th DECEMBER

1677   Qualifying examination introduced for Lieutenants, RN.

1779   Rear-Admiral Hyde Parker (*Princess Royal*) captured nine sail of a French convoy and burnt ten more off Fort Royal, Martinique, and engaged the escort. Ships: *Albion, Centurion, Conqueror, Elizabeth, Preston, Princess Royal, Vigilant* and *Boreas*.

1793   Vice-Admiral Lord Hood (*Victory*) at the evacuation of Toulon. Ships: *Britannia, Princess Royal, Robust, Terrible, Victory, Windsor Castle* and boats of fleet. Frigates, etc.: *Arethusa, Pearl, Topaze, Alert, Swallow* (tender). Gunboats: *Union, Wasp, Jean Bart, Petite Victoire*. Expended: *Vulcan* and *Conflagration* fireships. Captured or destroyed: 14 French ships of the line, 19 frigates and corvettes.

1809   Capture and destruction of the French *Seine* and *Loire* in Barque Cove, Guadeloupe; two batteries stormed and captured. [m]. Ships: *Blonde, Castor, Cygnet, Elizabeth, Freija, Hazard, Ringdove, Sceptre, Thetis*.

1810   *Royalist* captured the French privateer *Adventurier* 15 miles N.N.W. of Fecamp.

1914   U.15 mined and sunk off Belgian coast.

1940   *Triton* sunk by Italian t.b. *Clio* in the South Adriatic.

1940   Swordfish aircraft of 815 and 819 Sq. (*Illustrious*) attacked Stampelia.

1941   *Blankney* and *Stanley* sank U.434 off Azores.(Convoy HG.76)

1942   *Partridge* sunk by U.565 off Oran (35° 50' N, 1° 35' W.).

1943   *Felixstowe* sunk by mine off Cape Ferro, Sardinia (40° 09' N, 9° 36' E.).

HM Submarine *Onslaught* in the 1960s

19th DECEMBER

1664	Captain Thomas Allin *(Plymouth)* and squadron fought the Dutch Smyrna convoy in Gibraltar Strait. Ships: *Advice, Antelope, Crown, Leopard, Milford, Oxford, Plymouth, Portsmouth.*
1681	*Calabash* captured the Algerine *Red Lion* off Majorca.
1796	*Minerve* captured the Spanish *Sabina* 25 miles S.W. of Cartagena — retaken by Spanish reinforcements. *Blanche* forced the Spanish *Ceres* to strike, but was unable to take possession. [m]. Regiment: Detachment of the 11th.
1804	*Fisgard* captured the French privateer *Tiger* 200 miles West of Cape St. Vincent.
1809	*Rosamond* captured the French *Papillon* 12 miles S.S.E. of St. Croix, West Indies.
1811	*Royalist* captured the French privateer *Rodeur* in Dover Strait.

1914	*Doris* harassed Turkish coast near Alexandretta.
1915	Evacuation of Anzac and Suvla beachheads begun at Gallipoli: successfully completed by 21st.
1917	UB.56 sunk in Dover Barrage.
1941	*Neptune* and *Kandahar* mined off Tripoli (33° 15' N., 13° 30' E. and 33° 15' N., 13° 12' E. respectively): *Neptune* sank, and *Kandahar* despatched next day by *Jaguar*.
1941	*Stanley* sunk by U.574 East of Azores (38° 12' N., 17° 23' W.) (Convoy HG.76): *Stork* sank U.574.
1941	*Queen Elizabeth* and *Valiant* severely damaged by Italian two-men torpedoes at Alexandria: *Jervis* damaged.
1942	*Snapdragon* sunk by German aircraft off Benghazi (32° 18' N, 19° 54' E.).
1943	*Simoom* sunk by mine off the Dardanelles.

His Majesty King George presenting the first Naval Honours of the war in HMS *Vernon*, 19th December 1939 for the recovery, dismantling and examination of a German magnetic mine. (see 24th November)

Top row: Chief Petty Officer Charles E. Baldwin, D.S.M.; Able Seaman Archibald L. Vearncombe, D.S.M.
Bottom row: Lieutenant-Commander John Ouvry, D.S.O.; Lieutenant-Commander Roger Lewis, D.S.O.; Lieutenant John Glenny, D.S.O.

20th DECEMBER

1666   *Adventure* fought four French men-of-war off Lands End.

1782   *Diomede* and *Quebec* captured the American *South Carolina* 50 miles to the eastward of Cape May.

1799   Boats of *Queen Charlotte* and *Emerald* recaptured *Lady Nelson* in Gibraltar Bay. [m]

1896   John G. Lang born.

1900   Charles Lambe born.

1939   *Hyperion* intercepted the German *Columbus,* which scuttled herself off the coast of Florida.

1940   Ten Swordfish aircraft of 830 Sq. FAA (Malta) bombed Tripoli and mined the harbour.

1940   GC: Lieut-Commander Richard John Hammersley Ryan,* Sub-Lieutenant Peter Victor Danckwerts, RNVR, C.P.O. Reginald Vincent Ellingworth*. *(Posthumous) (*Gazette* date). All for bomb and mine disposal.

1944   Force 67 made an unsuccessful attack on the harbour and oil installations at Medan, Sumatra. Carriers: *Indomitable*[1], *Illustrious*[2]. Cover: *Argonaut, Black Prince, Newcastle, Kempenfelt* (D.27), *Wager, Wakeful, Wessex, Whelp, Whirlwind, Wrangler.* FAA Sqs: 854, 857 (Avenger)[1]. 1830, 1833 (Corsair)[2]. 1839, 1844 (Hellcat)[1]. Operation Robson.

HMS *Whelp* 1944. Part of Force 67. The Duke of Edinburgh was her First Lieutenant

21st DECEMBER

1779	*Suffolk* and *Magnificent* captured the French *Fortunêe* and *Blanche* respectively to the north-westward of St. Lucia.
1797	*Phoebe* captured the French *Nerêide* 180 miles West of Ushant. [m, bh] .
1916	*Hoste* and *Negro* sunk in collision (depth charges exploded) 10 miles off fair Island.
1917	*Lady Ismay* mined near the Galloper.
1940	Nine Swordfish aircraft of 815 and 819 Sq. *(Illustrious)* sank two of an Italian convoy off Kerkenah Island, Tunisia (34° 44′ N, 11° 58′ E.)
1941	Swordfish A/812 (*Audacity*) sank U.451 off Gibraltar. (35⁰ 55′ N., 6ᵘ 08′ W). First night sinking by aircraft.

1941   *Audacity* sunk by U.751 (44° 00′ N, 20° 00′ W.) and *Deptford* and *Samphire* sank U.567 in Atlantic (44° 02′ N, 20° 10′ W.). (Convoy HG.76)

This convoy sailed from Gibraltar on 14th December, escorted by 17 ships, including *Audacity* (ex-German liner *Hanover* — the first escort carrier) and Cdr F. J. Walker's 36th Escort Group. They were attacked by 9 U-boats, and by Focke Wolfe aircraft. Two merchant ships were sunk, together with the *Audacity* and an escort. However, 4 U-boats were sunk, and two FW were shot down. The relatively safe passage of the convoy showed how a well trained escort group aided by air support could counter attacks by U-boats.

1941   *Cicala* sunk by Japanese aircraft at Hong Kong.

Gun Room in HMS *Jupiter*, 1895

22nd DECEMBER

1813   *Helicon* captured the French privateer *Revenant* 6 miles West of Bolt Tail.

1940   15 Swordfish aircraft of 815 and 819 Sq. (*Illustrious*) bombed Tripoli.

1940   *Hyperion* damaged by mine off Cape Bon (37° 04' N., 11° 31' E.) ; sunk by *Janus*.

1943   *Niobe* (German, ex-*Yugoslav*) sunk by MTBs in Adriatic.

The Aircraft Carrier

The Royal Navy has led the way in the development of aircraft carriers at every stage. The First World War, however, came too soon in the development of the aeroplane for any real advances in tactical thinking within the RN. Between the wars the Navy's air service and that of the Army were combined in the Royal Air Force, and the resultant lack of naval influence over the types of planes to be designed and how to use them, left the Fleet Air Arm when it was reformed just before the Second World War equipped with absurdly outdated aircraft. The Carriers themselves, however, were well-designed and remained better equipped to meet even Kamikaze attacks than their US equivalents.

The Navy was quick to learn the use of the Air Arm. The Taranto attack is a classic episode. After the war, as aeroplanes became bigger and faster, the Royal Navy led the world in the development of the angled deck, the steam catapult and the mirror (later projector) sight. Without these inventions in the early fifties, the huge USN carrier fleet would never have been possible. Financial constraints have affected the Fleet Air Arm savagely. The "through deck-cruiser", the "jump jet aircraft" and the "ski jump" are the most recent British innovations.

23rd DECEMBER

1796   *Minerve* captured the French privateer *Maria* 30 miles S.W. by W. of Cape Spartivento, Sardinia.

1796   *Polyphemus* captured the French *Justine* 90 miles to the westward of Cape Clear.

1812   *Phoebe* captured the American privateer *Hunter* 300 miles to the north-westward of Corvo Island, Azores.

1858   *Pearl's* Naval Brigade at Tulsipur.

1915   Start of naval operations on Lake Tanganyika, East Africa.

1917   *Tornado, Torrent* and *Surprise* sunk by mines off Maas lightvessel.

1927   GC(ex-EGM): Sto.P.O. Herbert John Mahoney (*Taurus*) for gallantry in a boiler room explosion. (*Gazette* date)

1941   *Hasty* and *Hotspur* sank U.79 S of Crete (32° 15' N, 25° 19' E.). (Convoy AT.5)

HMS *Ark Royal*, **February 1978**

Royal Marines during Arctic training, 1962

HMS *Invincible*, early 1979

1757	*Augusta* captured eight sail of a French convoy off Île de la Petite Gonave, Haiti.
1777	Captain Cook discovered Christmas Is.
1787	*Bounty* sailed on her last voyage.
1805	*Loire* and *Egyptienne* captured the French *Libre* 21 miles S.S.W. of Île d' Yeu.
1810	Boats of *Diana* destroyed the French *L'Elise* driven ashore to the northward of Tatihou. [m]
1811	*Defence* wrecked on coast of Jutland.
1814	Vice-Admiral Sir Samuel Hood died.
1917	*Penshurst* (Q.7) torpedoed by the German U.110 in the entrance to the Bristol Channel (51° 32' N., 5° 48' W.).
1940	*Borde* detonated first electrically swept German mine.
1941	H.31 sunk by unknown cause in the Bay of Biscay.
1941	*Salvia* sunk by U.568 N.E. of Mersa Matruh (31° 46' N, 28° 00' E.).

The Trawler *Rolls Royce* swept her 100th mine, the first minesweeping trawler to score a century — in 1941 over 36 million tons of shipping went in and out of the Thames for the loss of about ½% of the total.

1943	*Hurricane* torpedoed by U.415 in Atlantic (45° 10' N., 22° 05' W.): sunk by own forces. USS *Leary* sunk at the same time by U.275 Operation Stonewall.
1944	*Clayoquot* (RCN) sunk by U.806 off Halifax (44° 25' N., 63° 20' W.).

1652	Articles of War first formulated.
1666	*Warspite, Jersey, Diamond, St. Patrick, Nightingale,* and *Oxford* captured the Dutch *Cleen Harderwijk, Leijden* and *Els* off the Texel.
1781	*Agamemnon* captured five sail of a French convoy 130 miles S.W. of Ushant.
1797	*Niger* captured the French privateer *Delphine* 6 miles S.W. by W. of Bolt Head.
1809	*Weazle* captured the French privateer *Éole* off Palmas Bay, Sardinia.
1811	*St. George* and *Defence* wrecked off Jutland.
1914	RNAS seaplane raid on Cuxhaven. Ships: *Arethusa, Undaunted; Empress, Engadine, Riviera; Lurcher,* D.6, E.11. Seaplanes: Nos: 119, 120, 135, 136, 811, 814, 815.
1917	P.56 and *Buttercup* rammed and sank U.87 in Irish Sea (52° 56' N, 5° 07' W.).
1923	*Capetown* up Coatzocoales River, Mexico to protect British interests.
1940	*Berwick* and *Bonaventure* escorting Convoy WS.5A drove off the German cruiser *Admiral Hipper* in Atlantic (43° 39' N., 25° 08' W.).
1941	Hong Kong surrendered to Japanese forces. *Robin* scuttled to avoid capture.
1942	P.48 sunk by the Italian t.b. *Ardente* off Bizerta (37° 17' N., 10° 32' E.).

Admiral Sir Bruce Fraser

As Third Sea Lord and Controller from March 1939 — May 1942, Fraser was responsible for the expansion of the Royal Navy. In 1943 he became Commander-in-Chief of the Home Fleet, with responsibility for protection of Russian convoys. He refused the post of First Sea Lord in September 1943, commenting that Cunningham would be a more appropriate choice. When *Scharnhorst* sailed to attack a convoy in the winter of 1943, Fraser from his Flag Ship *Duke of York* directed the forces which crippled the German raider and sank her by torpedo attack. In 1944 he became CinC Eastern Fleet and then CinC of the British Pacific Fleet which played a vital part in the final defeat of Japanese forces. He signed the Japanese surrender document on behalf of Britain on board USS *Missouri*.

King George VI and Admiral Sir Bruce Fraser, on the quarter deck of HMS *King George V*

26th DECEMBER

1799 *Viper* captured the French privateer *Furet* off Dodman Point. [m].

1807 *Seine* captured the French privateer *Sibylle* 100 miles to the south-westward of the Scilly Islands.

1811 Boats of *Volontaire* cut out the French privateer *Décidée* at Palamos.

1851 Start of final reduction of Lagos, complete by 29th.

1857 *Pearl's* Naval Brigade at Sohanpur.

1915 *Mimi* and *Toutou* captured the German *Kingani* on Lake Tanganyika, East Africa.

1915 E.6 mined and sunk in N Sea.

1927 *Keppel* sailed from Shanghai to protect British interests in Chingwangtao.

1939 *Triumph* severely damaged by German mine in North Sea (56° 44' N., 5° 00' E.). 18 feet of fore end blown off.

1942 *Hesperus* and *Vanessa* sank U.357 in NW Approaches (57° 10' N, 15° 40' W.). (Convoy HX.219)

HMS *Duke of York*

1943 Admiral Sir Bruce Fraser *(Duke of York)* sank the German battlecruiser *Scharnhorst* off North Cape (72° 16' N, 28° 41' E.). [bh]. Ships: *Duke of York; Belfast, Jamaica, Norfolk, Sheffield; Matchless, Musketeer, Opportune, Virago; Saumarez, Savage, Scorpion, Stord* (Nor).

The battleship *Duke of York*, cruiser *Jamaica* and 4 destroyers provided a close cover for convoys JW55B and RA55A, with 3 cruisers (*Belfast, Norfolk* and *Sheffield*) acting as a further cover. At dusk on Christmas Day, the German battlecruiser *Scharnhorst* and 5 destroyers sailed from Norway. Heavy seas caused the German destroyers to fall astern, and they never rejoined the battlecruiser. The 3 cruisers detected *Scharnhorst* on radar at 0840 on Boxing Day; they engaged, and *Scharnhorst* turned away at 30 knots. The cruisers followed, using radar, and *Duke of York* started to close at 24 knots in a gale. The cruisers again opened fire at 1205 when *Scharnhorst* re-approached the convoy; *Norfolk* was hit by *Scharnhorst*, but the latter turned for her base. *Duke of York* intercepted her, and hit her on 'A' turret with her first salvo of 14 in shells. The *Scharnhorst* was hit by at least 13 fourteen in shells, 12 eight in shells and 11 torpedoes before sinking. There were only 36 survivors.

1944 *Capel* sunk by U.486 off the Isle of Wight (49° 50' N., 1° 41' W.).

1945 Admiral of the Fleet Lord Keyes of Zeebrugge died.

1707   *Ludlow Castle* captured the French *Nightingale* off the Long Sand.

1742   *Pulteney* beat off two Spanish xebecs off Europa Point.

1805   Body of Lord Nelson laid in Painted Hall Greenwich.

1807   *Resistance* captured the French privateer *Aigle* off the Ower.

1831   *Beagle* sailed on five year circumnavigation carrying Charles Darwin, author of 'Origin of Species'.

1914   *Success* wrecked off Fife Ness.

1939   *Wishart* intercepted the German *Glucksberg* which ran herself ashore near Chipiona light, S.W. Spain.

1940   GC: Lieutenant Robert Selby Armitage, RNVR, Sub-Lieut. (Sp) Richard Valentine Moore, RNVR and Sub-Lieut. (Sp) John Herbert Babington, RNVR (*Gazette* date). All for bomb and mine disposal.

1941   Raid on Vågso, Norway. Operation Archery. Ships: *Kenya; Chiddingfold, Offa, Onslow, Oribi; Tuna, Prince Charles, Prince Leopold.* 3 Commando, two troops of 12 Commando, and Norwegian troops. RAF: 7 Hampden aircraft.

1942   *Battleford, Chilliwack, Napanee* and *St. Laurent* (all RCN) sank U.356 in Atlantic (45° 30' N., 25° 40' W.). (Convoy ONS.15)

1944   *St. Thomas* (RCN) sank U.877 in Atlantic (46° 25' N., 36° 38' W.). (Convoy HX.327)

Surface Action, 1943

Two groups of enemy destroyers sailed from France to cover the arrival of the blockade runner *Alsterufer*. She was sunk on 27th, and the cruisers *Glasgow* and *Enterprise* were despatched to intercept the German destroyers. At 1100 on 28th the Germans joined forces and turned back for France. The cruisers were proceeding at 28 knots in rough weather and opened fire on the ten destroyers at 18,000 yards at 1335. The Germans retaliated with torpedoes and glider bombs, but did no damage. The German forces then split, and the cruisers increased to 30 knots and by 1600 had sunk the Z27, T25 and T26. Because the *Glasgow* was low on ammunition and the *Enterprise* was suffering from defects, the cruisers did not chase the second enemy force, but retired to Plymouth, which they reached safely on the evening of 29th, despite further enemy air attacks.

1756   Court Martial of Admiral Byng began (lasted 29 days).

1793   *Blanche* captured the French *Sans-Culotte* 6 miles W. by S. of Guave Island (Goyave Islets).

1805   *Favourite* captured the French privateer *Général Blanchard* off the mouth of the Pongo River.

1814   *Leander, Newcastle* and *Acasta* captured the American privateer *Prince de Neufchâtel* 450 miles S. E. by E. of Sable Island.

1857   Admiral Sir Michael Seymour bombarded Canton in Second Chinese War.

1922   *Rodney* and *Nelson* laid down: nicknamed the Cherrytrees because they were cut down by Washington (Naval treaty): only British ship to mount 16 in guns, and to carry main armamant in triple turrets.

1939   *Barham* torpedoed by U.30 N of Hebrides (58° 47' N, 8° 05' W.).

1941   *Kipling* sank U.75 off Mersa Matruh (31° 50' N, 26° 40' E.).

1943   *Enterprise* and *Glasgow* engaged and pursued ten German destroyers 270 miles S.W. of Ushant (46° 33' N, 12° 30' W.). [bh]. German ships sunk: T.25, T.26, Z.27.

A Wren radio mechanic in World War II

29th DECEMBER

1669   *Mary Rose* drove off seven Algerine pirates between Sali and Tangier, while escorting a convoy. [bh]

1709   *Pembroke* and *Falcon* taken by three French ships between Toulon and Corsica.

1758   Capture of Gorée by Commodore the Hon. Augustus Keppel *(Torbay)* and Lieut-Colonel Worge. Ships: *Dunkirk, Fougueux, Nassau, Torbay*. 50's and smaller: *Experiment, Prince Edward, Roman Emperor, Saltash*. Bombs: *Firedrake, Furnace*. Troops: Royal Artillery.

1797   *Anson* recaptured the French *Daphné* off Archachon, S of Bordeaux.

1807   *Anson* wrecked in Mounts Bay.

1812   *Royalist* captured the French privateer *La Ruse* 6 miles West of Dungeness. [m]

1812   *Java* taken by the American *Constitution* 30 miles East of Bahia.

1837   Commander Andrew Drew cut out and destroyed the pirate steamer *Caroline* by sending her over Niagara Falls.

1857   British and French forces occupied Canton. Ships: *Acteon, Coromandel, Sans Pareil*. French: *Capricieuse, Némésis*.

1860   Naval Brigade of *Pelorus* at Kairau, New Zealand.

1860   *Warrior*, first British seagoing ironclad ship launched at Blackwall: reduced to fuelling hulk, Pembroke Dock.

1915   Durazzo raided by Austrian light forces which were brought to action but escaped. Ships: *Dartmouth, Weymouth*. Italian: *Quarto, Nino Bixio; Abba, Nievo, Pilo, Mosto*.

1916   *Ludlow* mined off Shipwash lightvessel.

1917   GC (ex-AM): Deckhand J.G. Stanners, RNR for fighting fire in magazine, ML.289.

HMS *Warrior*, the first 'iron-clad', armour-plated screw ship, 1860

30th DECEMBER

1756   Capture of Fort Budge-Budge, Calcutta. Ships: *Bridgewater, Kent, Kingfisher, Salisbury, Tiger.*

1778   Capture of St. Lucia. Ships: *Boyne, Nonsuch, Preston, Prince of Wales, Centurion, Isis, St. Albans.* Frigates, etc: *Ariadne, Aurora, Carcass, Pearl, Venus.*

1780   *Bellona* captured the Dutch *Princess Carolina* off the Goodwin Sands.

1820   Bombardment and destruction of the defences of Mocha. Ships: *Topaze* and *Antelope, Benares, Thames* (all Bombay Marine).

1893   *Havoc* commissioned: first TBD.

1915   *Natal* destroyed by internal explosion in Cromarty Firth.

1917   *Attack* torpedoed by UC.34 off Alexandria.

1941   *Ajax* and *Aphis* bombarded Bardia.

1944   Wellington L/407 (RCAF) sank U.772 in Channel (50° 05' N, 2° 31', W.).

Cook; a Rowlandson print of 1799

31st DECEMBER

1666   *Adventure* fought three Flushing men-of-war in the English Channel.

1796   *Polyphemus* captured the French *Tartu* 140 miles West of Cape Clear.

1811   *Egeria* captured the Danish privateer *Alvor* 80 miles to the eastward of St. Abbs Head.

1813   *Venerable* captured the French privateer *Jason* 760 miles N.E. of Madeira.

1823   Dock renamed Devonport.

1847   Last signal to Spithead from Admiralty by Semaphore Tower. (The electric telegraph in service).

1861   Boats of *Falcon* with *Dover*, first RN steam vessel, destroyed four towns up the Rokel River. (Operations lasted four days).

1942   VC: Captain Robert St. Vincent Sherbrooke (*Onslow*) in defence of Convoy JW.51B (14 ships) against *Lützow, Admiral Hipper* and 6 destroyers 140 miles N.N.E. of North Cape (73° 18' N, 30° 06' E.). [bh]. Close escort: *Achates*[1], *Bramble*[1], *Hyderabad, Northern Gem, Obdurate, Obedient, Onslow, Oribi, Orwell, Rhododendron.* Force R: *Sheffield* (Rear-Admiral R.L. Burnett), *Jamaica.* German casualties: *Friedrich Eckoldt* (sunk by *Sheffield*), *Admiral Hipper* (damaged). 1. Sunk.

1942   P.311 (*Tutenkhamen*) sunk by mine off Maddalena, Sardinia.

1943   *Clacton* sunk by mine off the East coast of Corsica.

Convoy JW.51B
The convoy sailed for Russia on 22 December, the escort being led by Captain R. St. V. Sherbrooke in *Onslow*. On 28th December a gale scattered the convoy, and the next few days were spent gathering the ships together again. Two cruisers (*Sheffield* and *Jamaica*) were covering the convoy after delivering convoy JW.51A. On 31st, the German heavy cruiser *Hipper* was sighted, and the destroyer escort beat her off using smoke and gunfire, though the *Onslow* was badly hit and her Captain severely wounded. The German pocket battleship *Lützow* then attacked the convoy from a different direction, while *Hipper* reapproached. The destroyers made a torpedo attack, which turned the *Hipper* away and into the fire of the two covering cruisers which were closing at speed. The destroyers then turned *Lützow* away. 5 destroyers had held a battleship and heavy cruiser and 6 large destroyers at bay for 3 hours, till 2 light cruisers arrived and drove them off.

HONOURS, AWARDS AND REWARDS

We have not space enough to include the many honours, decorations and other forms of recognition that have come the way of the navy. Prize money and promotion were the earliest, the most tangible and probably the most acceptable. Personal and individual recognition of a wider but less remunerative sort began when the Commonwealth Parliament awarded medals to those who had helped to defeat the Dutch.

In the French wars honours went mainly to the officers. Theirs were the larger shares in prize money, theirs most of the promotions: theirs were the much coveted, even solicited, crimson ribbon of the Bath. George III relieved the situation, but only slightly, by conferring a gold medal, but only on Admirals and Captains, and for only the most notable actions between 1794 and 1815. (These awards are designated m* in the text)

Further recognition was given, and to a wider range of people, by private awards such as those of Davison, Nelson's prize agent and Boulton, the Birmingham industrialist who bestowed medals on the survivers of the Nile and Trafalgar. Lloyds of London established a Patriotic Fund from which awards of decorated swords, vases or pieces of plate were made to successful senior officers. Groups of individuals might choose to commission private medals to honour, usually posthumously, some individual whose patronage or interest they had enjoyed and whose reputation they wished to perpetuate, as did an anonymous company who commissioned Mills to design and make a medal, in silver and in bronze, "dedicated by his followers to their illustrious leader, Admiral Sir J. T. Duckworth, Bart., GCB." But again, it was almost entirely the officers who participated.

In 1842, the East India Company, which had issued awards to all its forces, including natives, since 1784 proposed to award a medal for operations in the First Chinese War. As a number of regular troops and some of HM ships had been involved, H M Government decided that it would take over the award. Thus almost by chance began the tradition of campaign medals. Equity required that the survivors of the Great War — the last century's name for the long Revolutionary and Napoleonic wars with France — should not linger unrecognised, and in 1847, ten years after Victoria became Queen and more than thirty since the finally defeated Napoleon sailed for St. Helena in 1815, the Naval General Service Medal was issued. Individual ribbons could be adorned by clasps to recognise particular actions: 231 were authorised, 228 to commemorate events up to 1815. There were 7059 applications for the last, issued for the Syrian operations in 1840. The most worn by one man

was seven: only one recipient qualified for the three in honour of Nelson's greatest victories. Some were awarded for boat actions and others for larger engagements. (Almost all are denoted in the text by [m]).

But these were medals, awarded on a large scale, and not individual decorations: as Melville said, albeit of the Garter, there was "no damn' nonsense about merit." Gallantry and distinguished service merited special recognition, a sentiment particularly appropriate in Victorian times, and the Victoria Cross was instituted by Royal Warrant in 1856. It was followed by the George Cross, instituted by her great-grandson in 1940. We have recorded all naval holders of each cross, including the recipients of the Albert Medal and the Empire Gallantry Medals who survived to exchange their decorations for the G.C. in accordance with subsequent royal warrants. We have had to draw the line there, though we are conscious of the great numbers of meritorious men and women who have received lesser but still distinguished decorations — and those, equally deserving, who have escaped or missed recognition.

The second great war, or World War I, involved the mobilisation of more individuals than its predecessors, but two basic medals were issued to most participants, with a third for those engaged in 1914-15. The Admiralty intended to award clasps for services covered by seven categories, but though approved, these were never issued. In World War II there were more individuals and more medals and area stars, with additional clasps for a few services. But these were more trumpery in finish, struck in baser metals and alloys and not inscribed with the names and numbers of the recipients as were those received by their fathers and uncles after 1918.

So much for the metallurgy of money, of swords and medals for individuals. Collective recognition for service, by a ship's company or a unit, has been recognised by the award of battle honours (signified by [bh] in the text). These were codified by AFO 2565 in October 1954: this lists 155 fleet actions or campaigns between 1588 and 1945, and 40 single ship or boat actions, denoted by the name of the enemy engaged and not by a place name. Both lists have enjoyed subsequent additions.

The Royal Marines are content with only one battle honour — Gibraltar — but they have the globe itself as their badge. The Corps recognises six Memorable Dates and celebrates them annually, publishing in daily orders a brief citation beforehand and on the anniversary mounting a guard which presents arms to a ceremonial fanfare. Ten more Memorable Dates are recognised

by individual units and celebrated by them with appropriate ceremony.

Army units engaged at naval victories have received due recognition and are noted in the text. It is good to know that other regiments, not specifically honoured, nevertheless demonstrate their naval association by playing "Rule, Britannia" before their own regimental march on ceremonial occasions.

BIBLIOGRAPHY

SELECT BIBLIOGRAPHY

Anything approaching a comprehensive bibliography of the Royal Navy would need a book to itself. Our aim is to guide you to a few but reliable — and readable — sources from which you may start off.

All the books listed were published in London unless otherwise stated: in each case their date of publication is given. Volumes published by the Navy Records Society are distinguished by an *.

If you aim and are able to browse, the *Naval Chronicle*, published periodically and bound annually from 1799—1818 is enormously attractive: Forester revealed in his 'Hornblower Companion' that it was his favourite source. The *Illustrated London News* is good, especially for the latter half of the nineteenth century; the *Mariner's Mirror*, the quarterly journal of the Society for Nautical Research, covers many aspects of nautical history since the first syllable of recorded time. Its index will give you a good fix on particular subjects.

Other general works are *Janes' Fighting Ships*, first published in 1897 and virtually each year since, and for the more memorable officers of the classic period, Ralfe's *Naval Biography* in four volumes, (1828), and Marshall's in twelve (1823).

GENERAL

Broome, J.E. *Make a signal* (1955)
Bush, E. *The flowers of the sea — an anthology* (1962)
Frere-Cook, G. *Guinness history of sea warfare* (1975)
Graham, G.S. *The politics of naval supremacy* (1965)
Hamilton, *Naval administration* (1846)
Kemp, P. *The Oxford companion to ships and the sea* (1976)
Kennedy, P. *The rise and fall of British naval mastery* (1976)
Lewen, M. *The navy of Britain — a historical portrait* (1948)
Lloyd, C. *The nation and the navy* (1954)
Manning, T.D. *British warship names* (1959)
Marcus, G.J. *A naval history of England, Vols I and II* (1961-1971)
Marcus, G.J. *Heart of Oak* (1975)
Mathew, D. *The naval heritage* (1945)
Mathew, D. *British seamen* (1943)
Oppenheim, M. *The administration of the Royal Navy* (1896)
Richmond, H.W. *Statesmen and seapower* (1946)
Roskill, S.W. *The strategy of sea power* (1962)
Warner, O. *Battle honours of the Royal Navy* (1956)
Warner, O. *The British navy — a concise history* (1975)
Webb, W. *Coastguard* (1976)
Williamson, J.A. *A short history of British expansion* (New York 1967)
Winton, J. *The Victoria Cross at sea* (1978)

HISTORICAL PERIODS

Medieval
Brooks, F.W. *English naval forces, 1199-1272* (1933)

Tudors and Stuarts
Bevan, B. *The great seamen of Elizabeth I* (1971)

Corbett, J.S. *Drake and the Tudor navy* (1912)
Froude, J.A. *English seamen of the 16th century* (Oxford 1894)
Mattingley, G. *The defeat of the Spanish Armada* (1959)
Penn, C.D. *The navy of the early Stuarts* (1920)
Rowse, A.L. *The expansion of Elizabethan England* (1975)
Williamson, J.A. *The age of Drake* (1936)

Commonwealth and Restoration
Ehrman, J. *The navy in the war of William III* (1953)
*Merriman, R.D. *Sergison papers* (1949)
Merriman, R.D. *Queen Anne's navy* (1961)
Ollard, R. *Man of War: Holmes and the Restoration navy* (1969)
Powley, E.P. *The English navy in the Revolution of 1688* (1928)
Rogers, P.G. *The Dutch in the Medway* (Oxford 1970)
Tedder, A.W. *The navy of the Restoration* (Cambridge 1916)
Wilcox, L.A. *Mr Pepys' navy* (1966)

William III, Anne and the first Hanoverians
Aubrey, P. *The Defeat of James Stuart's Armada 1692* (Leicester 1979)
Baugh, D.A. *British naval administration in the age of Walpole* (Princeton 1965)
*Baugh, D.A. *Naval administration, 1715-1750* (1977)
Gibson, J.S. *Ships of the '45* (1967)
Richmond, H.W. *The Navy in the war of 1739-48* (three vols) (1920)

The French Wars

The Seven Years War
Corbett, J.S. *England in the Seven Years War* (1907)
Marcus, G.J. *Quiberon Bay* (1960)

The War of American Independence
Gardener, A. *Naval history of the American Revolution* (Boston 1913)
James, W.M. *The British Navy in adversity* (1926)
Mackesy, P. *The war for America* (1964)
Richmond, H.W. *The navy in India 1762-1783* (1931)

The Revolutionary and Napoleonic Wars
Bryant, A. *The Years of Endurance, 1793-1802* (1942)
Bryant, A. *The Years of Victory, 1802-1812* (1944)
Bryant, A. *The Age of Elegance, 1812* (1950)
Corbett, J.S. *The Trafalgar campaign* (1910)
Lloyd, C. *St. Vincent and Camperdown* (1963)
Lloyd, C. *The Nile campaign* (Newton Abbot 1973)
Marcus, G.J. *The age of Nelson* (1971)
Mackesy, P. *The war in the Mediterranean, 1803-1810* (1957)
Masefield, J. *Sea life in Nelson's time* (3rd edition, 1971)
Parkinson, C.N. *Britannia rules!* (1977)
Pope, D. *The Black Ship* (the mutiny in *Hemione*, her surrender and recapture) (1963)
Warner, O. *The Glorious First of June* (1961)

The American War 1812-1815
Forester, C.S. *The age of fighting sail* (1956)
Roosevelt, T. *The naval war of 1812* (New York 1894)

Pax Brittanica

Bartlett, C.J. *Great Britain and seapower 1815-1853* (Oxford 1963)
Churchill, W.S. *The River War* (1933)
Colomb, P.H. *Slave catching in the Indian Ocean* (1873)
Fleming, P. *The siege at Peking* (1959)
Holt, E. *The Boer War* (1958)
Holt, E. *New Zealand — the strangest war* (1962)
Lloyd, C. *The Navy and the slave trade* (1949)
Marder, A.J. *British naval policy 1880-1905* (1941)
Preston, A. and Major, J. *Send a gunboat* (1967)
*Rowbotham, W.B. *Naval Brigade in the Indian Mutiny* (1947)
Schurman, D. *The education of a navy:* (the development of British naval strategic thought, *1867-1914* (1965)
Waley *The Opium War through Chinese eyes* (1958)
Woodhouse, C.M. *The battle of Navarino* (1965)

World War I

Bennett, G. *Coronel and the Falklands* (1962)
Bennett, G. *The battle of Jutland* (1964)
Bennett, G. *Cowan's war — the Baltic 1918-1920* (1964)
Bennett, G. *Naval battles of World War I* (1968)
Churchill, W.S. *World Crisis* (1938 ed)
Corbett, J.S. and Newbolt, H. *Naval Operations (the official history)* (1920)
Gibson, R.H. *The German submarine war, 1914-1918* (1931)
Grant, R.M. *U-boats destroyed* (1964)
Grant, R.M. *U-boat intelligence* (1969)
Hough, R. *The pursuit of Admiral von Spee — a study of loneliness and bravery* (1969)
Irving, J. *The smokescreen of Jutland* (1966)
James, R.R. *Gallipoli* (1968)
Jellicoe, J.R. *The Grand Fleet* (1919)
Jellicoe, J.R. *The crisis of the naval war* (1920)
Marder, A.J. *Dreadnought to Scapa Flow* (five vols) (1961-1970)

World War II — see also 'Intelligence'

Marder, A.J. *From the Dardanelles to Oran — 1915-1940* (1974)
Roskill, S.W. *Naval policy between the wars* (two vols) (1968, 1976)
Schofield, B.B. *British sea power* (1967)

Churchill, W.S. *The Second World War* (six vols (1948-1954)
Costello, J. and Hughes, T. *The battle of the Atlantic* (1977)
Creswell, J. *Sea warfare 1939-1943* (1968)
Grenfell, R. *Main fleet to Singapore* (1951)
Gretton, P. *Former Naval Person — Winston Churchill and the Royal Navy* (1968)
Harling, R. *The Steep Atlantick Stream* (1946)
Hitchens, R.P. *We fought them in gunboats* (1944)
Hough, R. *The hunting of Force Z* (1967)
Macintyre, D. *The naval war against Hitler* (1971)
Macintyre, D. *The battle of the Atlantic* (1961)
Macintyre, D. *The battle for the mediterranean* (1964)
Marder, A.J. *Operation Menace (Dakar and Admiral North)* (1976)
Middlebrook, M. *Battleship* (1978)
Middlebrook, M. *Convoy* (1976)
Pack, S.W.C. *The battle of Matapan* (1961)
Pope, D. *73 North* (1958)
Roskill, S.W. *Churchill and the Admirals* (1977)
Roskill, S.W. *The Navy at War, 1939-1945* (1960)
Roskill, S.W. *The War at Sea* (official history) (three vols) (1954-1961)
Scott, P. *The battle of the narrow seas* (1945)
Winton, J. *The forgotten Fleet* (the British Pacific Fleet) (1969)
Winton, J. *Freedom's battle: the war at sea* (an anthology) (1967)

BIOGRAPHY

Anson	Heaps, L. *Log of the 'Centurion'* (1973)
	Pack, S.W.C. *Admiral Lord Anson* (1960)
	*Williams, G. *Anson's Voyage, 1740-1744* (1967)
Beatty	Chalmers, W.S. *Life and letters of ...* (1951)
Beaufort	Friendley, A. *Beaufort of the Admiralty* (1977)
Beresford	Bennet, G. *Charlie B* (1968)
Blake	Powell, J.R. *Robert Blake* (1972)
Bligh	Kennedy, G. *Bligh* (1978)
Broke	Padfield, P. *Broke of the 'Shannon'* (1968)
	Pullen, H. *The 'Shannon' and the 'Chesapeake'* (Toronto 1970)
Byng	Pope, D. *At 12 Mr Byng was shot* (1962)
Byron	Shankland, P. *Byron of the 'Wager'* (1975)
Chatfield	Chatfield, Lord *The Navy and Defence* (1942)
	Chatfield, Lord, *It might happen again* (1946)
Cochrane	Lloyd, C. *Lord Cochrane* (1947)
	Mallalieu, J.P.W. *Extraordinary Seaman* (1957)
	Thomas, D. *Cochrane* (1978)
Collingwood	*Hughes, E. *Correspondence of Lord Collingwood* (1957)
	Warner, O. *Vice-Admiral Lord Collingwood* (1968)
Cook	Beaglehole, J.C. *Life of Captain James Cook* (1974)
	Campbell, C. *Captain Cook* (1936)
	Villiers, A. *Captain Cook, the seaman's seaman* (1967)
	Syme, *Travels of Captain Cook* (1971)
Cornwallis	Cornwallis-West, G. *Life and letters of ...* (1927)
Cunningham	Cunningham, A.B. *A Sailor's odyssey* (1951)
	Warner, O. *Cunningham of Hyndehope* (1967)
Dewar	Dewar, K.G.B. *The Navy from within* (1939)
Drake	Mason, A.E.W. *The life of Francis Drake* (1941)
	Williamson, J.A. *Sir Francis Drake* (1938)
Duncan	Camperdown, Earl of *Admiral Duncan* (1898)
Fisher, Lord	Bacon, R. *Life of Lord Fisher* (1929)
	Hough, R. *First Sea Lord* (1969)
	*Kemp, P. (ed) *Papers* (1960, 1964)
	Mackay, R.F. *Fear God and Dreadnought (1952-1959)*
	Marder, A.J. *Fisher of Kilverstone* (1973)
Fisher, Sir W.	James, W.M. *Admiral Sir William Fisher* (1943)
Hall	James, W.M. *The eyes of the Navy* (1955)
Hawke	Mackay, R.F. *Admiral Hawke* (1965)
Hood	Hood, D. *The Admirals Hood* (n.d.)
Horton	Chalmers, W.S. *Max Horton and the Western Approaches* (1954)
Hoste	Pocock, T. *Remember Nelson* (1977)
Jellicoe	Bacon, R. *Life of Earl Jellicoe* (1936)
	Temple Patterson, A. *Jellicoe* (1969)
	*Temple Patterson, A. (ed) *Jellicoe Papers* (1966, 1968)
Jervis	Berckman, E. *Nelson's dear Lord* (1962)
	Brenton, P. *Life and correspondence ...* (1838)
	James, W.M. *Old Oak (1950)*
	Tucker, (ed) *Memoirs ...* (1844)
Lamb	Warner, O. *Admiral of the Fleet* (1969)
Le Fanu	Baker, R. *Dry ginger* (1977)
Monck	Warner, O. *Hero of the restoration* (1936)
Nelson	Bennett, G. *Nelson's battles* (1965)
	Bennett, G. *Nelson the commander* (1972)
	Forester, C.S. *Nelson* (1929)
	Grenfell, R. *Nelson the sailor* (1944)
	Howarth, D. *Trafalgar, the Nelson touch* (1969)
	James, W.M. *The durable monument* (1948)
	Kennedy, L. *Nelson's band of brothers* (1951)
	Oman, C. *Nelson* (1947)
	Pocock, T. *Nelson and his world* (1968)
	Pope, D. *England expects* (1959)
	Warner, O. *Nelson* (1975)
Peel	Verney, E.H. *'Shannon's' brigade in India* (1862)
Pellew	Parkinson, C.N. *Viscount Exmouth* (1934)
Pepys	Bryant, A. *Saviour of the Navy* (1933, 1935, 1938)
	Ollard, R. *Pepys* (1974)
	Pepy, S. (ed) R.S. Latham: *Diary 1660-1669* (1970-1976)
Richmond	Marder, A.J. *Portrait of an Admiral* (1952)
Rodney	Mackintyre, D. *Admiral Rodney* (1962)
	Spinney, D. *Rodney* (1969)
Saumarez	Ross, J. *Memoirs ...* (1838)
Scott, Percy	Scott, P. *Fifty years in the Royal Navy* (1919)
	Padfield, P. *Aim straight* (1966)
Scott, R.F.	Pound, R. *Scott of the Antarctic* (1966)
Smith, S.	Barrow, J. *Life and letters of ...* (1838)
Tyrwhitt	Temple Patterson, A. *Tyrwhitt of the Harwich Force* (1973)
Vernon	Harteman, C.H. *The angry Admiral* (1957)
Vian	Vian, P. *Action this day* (1960)
Walker	Robertson, T. *Walker, RN* (1956)
Weston	Weston, Agnes *My life among the bluejackets* (1911)

SOCIAL

Mutiny
Bullocke, J.G. *Sailors' rebellion — a century of naval mutinies* (1938)
Divine, D. *Mutiny at Invergordon* (1970)
Dobree and Manwaring *The Floating Republic* (1935)
Dugan, J. *The Great Mutiny* (1966)
Edwards, K. *The Mutiny at Invergordon* (1937)

Health
Allison, R.S. *Sea diseases* (1943)
Keevil, J.J. *Medicine and the Navy, 1200-1900* (1957-1967)
Lloyd, C. **Health of Seamen* (1965)
Plumridge, J. *Hospital ships* (1975)

Dockyards and ports
Lipscomb, F.W. *Heritage of seapower: Portsmouth* (1967)
Presnail, J. *Chatham* (Chatham) (1952)
Sparks, H.J. *Naval history of Portsmouth* (Portsmouth) (1912)

General
Baynham, H. *From the lower deck, 1780-1840* (1969)
Baynham, H. *Before the mast* (1971)
Baynham, H. *The men from the Dreadnought* (1976)
Cresswell, W. *Close to the wind* (1965)
Kemp, P. *The British sailor* (1970)
Jarrett, D. *British Naval dress* (1960)
Laffin, J. *Jack Tar* (1969)
Lewis, M. *England's Sea Officer* (1934)
Lewis, M. *The social history of the Royal Navy 1793-1815* (1960)
Lewis, M. *The navy in transition* (1965)
Lloyd, C.C. *The British seaman* (1968)
Penn, G. *Snotty* (1957)
Penn, G. *Up funnel, down screw* (1955)
Taylor, G. *The sea chaplains* (1978)
Winton, J. *Hurrah for the life of a sailor* (1977)

SHIPS AND WEAPONS

Archibald, E. *The wooden fighting ship* (1968)
Archibald, E. *The metal fighting ship* (1971)
Browne, D. *The floating bulwark* (1963)
Cowburn, P. *The warship in history* (1966)
Henderson, J. *The Frigates* (1970)
Henderson, J. *Sloops and Brigs* (1972)
Hough, R. *Dreadnought* (1965)
Kemp, P. *HM destroyers* (1956)
Lewis, M. *Armada guns* (1961)
Macintyre, D. *The thunder of the guns* (1959)
Padfield, P. *Guns at sea* (1973)
Padfield, P. *The great naval race* (1974)
Parkes, O. *British battleships* (1957)

Aircraft
Brown, D. *Carrier operation in World War II* (1974)
Hezlet, A. *Aircraft and seapower* (1970)
Higham, R. *The British rigid airship, 1908-1931* (1961)
Macintyre, D. *Wings of Neptune* (1963)
Nicholls, G.W. *The Supermarine Walrus* (1966)
Price, A. *Aircraft versus submarine* (1973)
Thetford, O. *British naval aircraft* (1958)

Submarine warfare
Bargess, R.F. *Ships beneath the sea* (1975)
Cowie, J. *Mines, minelayers and minelaying* (1949)
Dorling, *Swept channels* (1925)
Hezlet, A. *The submarine and seapower* (1962)
Jameson, W. *The most formidable thing* (history of submarine to 1918) (1965)
Kemp, P. *HM Submarines* (1952)
Lipscomb, F.W. *The British submarine* (1954)
Macintyre, D. *U-boat killer* (1961)
Waldron, T. *The Frogmen* (1950)
Warren, C. *Above us the waves* (1953)
Young, E. *One of our submarines* (1953)

THE ROYAL MARINES

Blumberg, H.E. *Britain's sea soldiers III* (Devonport 1927)
Field, C. *Britain's sea soldiers I and II (Liverpool 1974)*
Graver, C. *Short History of the Royal Marines* (Aldershot 1959)
Moulton, J.L. *The Royal Marines* (1972)
Saunders, H. S.J. *The green beret* (1944)
Smith, P.C. *Per mare, per terram* (Cambridge 1974)

THE WRNS

Laughton Mathews, V. *Blue Tapestry* (1948)
Mason, U. *The WRNS, 1917-1977* (1977)
Spain, N. *Thank you, Nelson (n.d.)*

RESERVES AND AUXILIARIES

Bowen, F.C. *History of the Royal Naval Reserve* (1926)
Kerr, J.L. and Granvill, W. *The RNVR: a record of achievement* (1957)
Sigwart, E.E. *The Royal Fleet Auxiliary, 1600-1968* (1968)

INTELLIGENCE

Beesley, P. *Very Special Intelligence* (1978)
Hinsley, F.H. et al *British Intelligence in the Second World War* Volume 1 (1979)
Johnson, B. *The Secret War* (1978)
Jones, R. V. *Most secret war* (1978)
Lewin, R. *Ultra goes to war* (1978)
McLachlan, D. *Room 39 - Naval intelligence in action* (1967)
Montagu, E. *The man who never was* (1953)

FICTION

'Bartimeus'	*Naval occasions* (1916)
	The Navy eternal (1918)
Cooper, Duff	*Operation Heartbreak* (1950)
	(see Operation Mincemeat)
Forrester, C.S.	*The Hornblower Companion* (1964)
	Lieutenant Hornblower,
	Hornblower and the 'Atropos'
	Hornblower and the 'Hotspur'
	The Happy Return
	Ship of the Line } republished as 'Captain RN'
	Flying Colours
	The Commodore
	Lord Hornblower
Fullerton, A.	*One man's mistress* (1955)
Griggs, C.P.	*The readiness is all* (1945)
	(Coastal Forces)
Machardy, C.	*Send down a dove* (1968)
	(Submarine service)
Mallalieu, J.P.W.	*Very ordinary seaman* (1944)
	(Lower deck, W.W.II)
Marryat, F.	*Frank Mildmay* (1827)
	The King's Own (1830)
	Peter Simple (1834)
	Mr Midshipman Easy (1836)
Morgan, C.	*The Gunroom* (1919)
O'Brian, P.	*Master and Commander* (1970)
	Post Captain (1972)
	HMS Surprise (1973)
Parkinson, C.N.	*Life and times of Horatio Hornblower* (1970)
	(so successful a spoof biography that it was hard to exclude it from that section)
Winton, J.	*We joined the Navy* (1959)
	We saw the sea (1960)
	Down the hatch (1961)
	Good enough for Nelson (1977)

GENERAL INDEX

(The page numbers of illustrations are printed in italic)

INDEX OF BRITISH AND COMMONWEALTH
SHIPS AND NAVAL ESTABLISHMENTS

366

367

369

370

373

377

FOREIGN SHIPS

378

379

382

GERMAN SUBMARINES

520 300
521 32
522 48
523 241
528 126
529 39
531 104, 120
533 285
534 119
535 184
536 323
538 324
540 286
542 329
545 34
548 121
551 76
556 177
557 345
559 300, 329
561 192
562 45
563 149, 294, 298
564 165, 239
565 64, 347
566 295
567 350
568 145, 227, 285, 354
570 *242*, 243
571 22
573 115
575 61, 67
577 7
578 225
581 27
582 278
585 78, 81
587 78
588 213
589 257, 259
592 25
593 342, 343
594 156
595 317
597 282
599 295
600 328
601 50
602 339
605 316
607 193
608 224
610 279
614 210
616 131
617 26, 252, 256
618 229
619 284
621 235
623 47
624 31, 321
625 62
627 298
628 182
629 162
630 118
631 285
632 89
633 59
634 245
635 89
636 103
638 104, 119
640 131
641 15, 265
643 279
644 89
646 131
648 326
651 178
652 74, 77, 153
653 69
654 32
655 76
658 300
660 315
661 284
663 121
665 75
666 34
667 222
669 253
671 219
672 198
674 116
675 139
678 185
683 65
698 42
701 64
703 265, 268
705 249
707 312
710 108
711 42, 118
713 49
714 68
715 165
716 74
719 176
722 80
731 129
732 300
734 33
736 220
740 163
741 232
742 198
743 254
744 58
751 199, 350
752 138
754 213
755 145
757 7
761 49
762 32
764 46, 166
765 120
767 166, 169
771 314
772 357
774 90
775 336
804 91
806 353
821 163
841 286
842 307
843 91
844 285
845 62
846 118
852 117
855 268
859 267
864 33
865 262
867 263
871 269
877 355
878 71, 92
905 74
921 273
927 49
952 265, 266
954 134
955 161
956 50
959 116
960 134
961 81
962 90
964 285
965 78
966 313
968 113
970 161
971 175
973 58
974 101
976 77
979 116
980 164
981 227
984 237
987 166
988 178
989 38
990 140
992 37
1001 90
1003 74
1004 48
1006 285
1008 120
1014 30
1017 113
1018 51
1021 82
1024 94
1051 21
1060 298
1063 97
1065 91
1105 110
1106 81
1172 21
1191 176
1195 89
1199 16
1200 314
1201 270
1208 46
1210 117
1213 304
1222 191
1225 175
1227 277
1228 328
1274 98
1276 86
1278 42
1279 28
1302 59
1407 268
2106 172
2201 81
2204 81
2208 276
2213 129
2336 121
2338 118
2359 116
2365 119
2503 118
2521 119
2524 117
2534 120
2540 117
3030 117
3032 117
3503 119
3523 119
4712 118
6075 110
6078 163

UB Boats

4 233
6 115
8 146
13 109
14 228, 306, 307
16 125
17 50
18 109, 339
19 330
20 210
22 15
26 88
27 210
29 343
30 228
31 116
32 235
33 93
35 21
37 11
39 131
48 229
50 312
52 138
54 64, 237
55 105
56 348
58 62
65 345, 346
66 15
67 313
68 277
69 7
70 123
71 104
72 127
73 178
74 141
75 340
78 124
80 211
81 333
82 99
83 255
85 114
90 285
103 261
107 208
109 245
110 199
115 272
116 298
124 200

UC Boats

1 204
2
3 143
5 110
6 271
7 184
10 238
14 276
16 294
18 45
19 336
26 124
29 161
33 269
34 357
36 136
38 314
39 32
41 238
43 62
46 32
47 321
48 229
49 222
50 30
51 316
55 272
61 186
62 289
63 229, 301
65 207, 304
66 164
68 88, 277
70 244
71 222
72 237, 266
74 202, 303
75 119, 149

INDEX OF PEOPLE

Abbott, Lt. E.G. 219
Abbott, Ord. G.F.P. 259
Abercromby, Major-General the Hon. J. 334
Abercrombie, Lt.-General Sir Ralph 43, 139
Agar, Lt. later Commodore A.W.S. 168
Albemarle, first Duke of: *see* G. Monck
Alexander, Captain T. 85
Alexandra, Queen *222*
Allin, Captain T. 348
Amherst, Major-General J. 207
Anderson, Chief ERA F.C. 206
Anson, Admiral of the Fleet George, first Baron Anson G. 117, *158*, 165, 171, 263
Arbuthnot, Admiral M. 70, 126
Armitage, Lt. R.S. 336, 355
Armytage, Lt. R.W. 138
Arundel, Sir John 76, 345
Ashby, Sir John 272
Auchinleck, General Sir Claude 90
Auchmuchty,-Lt.-General Sir Samuel 28, 263
Austen, Rear-Admiral C.J. 96
Auten, Lt. H., RNR 211
Ayscue, Admiral Sir George 164, 233
Babington, Sub-Lt. J.H., RNVR 355
Badiley, Admiral R. 244
Bagot, Lt. A.G. RNVR 94
Baird, Major-General Sir David 8
Baker, M. 245
Baldwin, CPO C.E. 326, *348*
Bamford, Captain E., RMLI 106
Bandiera, Rear-Admiral Franz, Baron 255
Barham, Admiral Lord, *see* Middleton
Barker, Lt.-Cdr. J.F. 162
Barlow, Capt Sir Robert 45
Barnaby, N. 234
Barras, Commodore le Comte 256
Barrington, Admiral the Hon. Samuel 345
Barton, A., pirate 217
Bateman, L/S *329*
Bazan, Don Alonso de 246
Beak, Commander D.N.W., RNVR 318

INDEX OF PLACES

389

390

ARMY UNITS

2nd Army 198
5th Army 311
8th Army 75, 227, 231, 249, 321
RHA 243
Royal Artillery 6, 9, 22, 51, 84, 86, 99, 111, 115, 117, 119, 120, 121, 127, 131, 132, 134, 137, 140, 158, 161, 168, 177, 180, 182, 202, 207, 226, 233, 238, 242, 252, 255, 274, 283, 295, 299, 305, 318, 323, 334, 356
Royal Engineers 9, 57, 115, 127, 131, 176, 177, 226, 238, 251, 295, 301
Royal Sappers & Miners 9, 86, 119, 120, 137, 243, 255, 305
King's Dragoon Guards 22
Royal Inniskilling Dragoon Guards 71
16th Light Dragoons 161
Commando Brigade 10, 17, 18, 57, 115, 236, 302, 317, 328, 341, 346
Airborne Division *158*

Foot Regiments
1st Foot 207
2nd/1st 38
2nd 150
3rd 161, 238
4th 185
5th 129, 185
9th 161, 243
10th 51, 318
11th 38, 68, 137, 193, 348
12th 334
13th 15, 20, 99, 109, 112, 163, 169, 247, 258, 273, 274, 314,
14th 138, 213, 334
15th 207
16th 119
17th 207
18th 38, 62, 69, 86, 88, 96, 132, 140, 202, 225, 242, 274, 283
19th 161
20th 177
21st 22, 161, 299
22nd 134, 207, 334
23rd 134, 233, 316
25th 68, 137, 150, 176, 193
26th 6, 51, 62, 69, 132, 139, 140, 202, 242

27th 176
28th 20, 207, 220
29th 150, 193
30th 68, 137, 161, 193, 225
31st 115, 127, 131, 295
33rd 187, 334
35th 207
36th 161
38th 15, 36, 130
40th 28, 177, 185, 207, 323
41st 15, 134, 254, 300
43rd 112
44th 238
45th 207
46th 185
47th 15, 207, 339
48th 207
49th 6, 51, 62, 69, 132, 140, 202, 242, 274, 283
50th 38, 50, 193, 208
51st 38, 96, 134, 225
53rd 301,
55th 62, 132, 202, 242, 274, 283
56th 187, 223, 265, 334
58th 9, 22, 51, 134, 180
59th 226, 334
60th 22, 51, 119, 207
62nd 207, 301
63rd 99
64th 83, 119, 301
65th 339
67th 115, 127, 131, 161, 238, 295
68th 111
69th 20, 38, 68, 94, 137, 150, 161, 187, 193, 258, 263
71st 177
75th 161
76th 161
78th 83, 249
80th 88, 96, 156
84th 301, 334
85th 161
86th 168, 174, 186, 193, 258, 263
87th 15, 94, 129
89th 15, 213, 258, 263
90th 38, 161
2nd 90th 174, 193
92nd 51
93rd 301
96th 63

97th 161, 174, 193, 219
98th 42, 94, 161, 185, 202, 249
99th 9, 99, 115, 131
118th 168, 174
Dalzell's 44
De Wattevilles 120
Wessex 80
Glengarry FLI 120
Hampshire 103
Handasyd's 57, 144
Hertfordshire 84
Invalids 121
Irish Guards 138
Maritime 180
Plymouth Argyles 340
Queens 150
Royal Green Jackets 84
Royal Regt of Wales 94
Royal York Rangers 343
Scotch Bde 54, 340
Welsh Guards 138
Worcestershire & Sherwood Foresters 150

Colonial and Commonwealth Forces
6th Australian Div 128
7th Australian Div 180
East African Protectorate Forces 234, 298
King's African Rifles 10
Niger Coast Protectorate Forces 48
Royal Newfoundland Fencibles 249, 252, 254
St Helena Artillery 177
St Helena 177
Ward's Chinese 99
1st West India 44, 47, 76
2nd West India 7, 14, 44, 47, 191, 342
3rd West India 342
6th West India 119
Zanzibar Army 234, 298

Indian Army
26th Indian Div 116
1st Assam 51
Assam Local Artillery 51
Bengal Artillery 15, 88, 96, 134, 300, 301, 324

Bengal Engineers 15
Bengal Foot Artillery 163
Bengal Volunteers 6, 51, 140, 202, 236, 334
Bengal Yeomanry 58, 99, 109, 112, 163, 247, 273, 314
1st Bengal 42, 46, 58, 99, 109, 112, 163, 301, 324
22nd Bengal 99, 115, 127, 131
40th Bengal 96
67th Bengal 30, 156
Bombay Artillery 15, 39, 77
Bombay Artillery Pioneers 187
1st Bombay 15
2nd Bombay 28, 265, 334
5th Bombay 99, 115, 127, 131, 295
24th Bombay 15, 234
26th Bombay 234
Guraknath 58,
Gurkhas 42, 46, 58, 99, 109, 112
Burakh Gurkhas 58
Madras Artillery 15, 51, 62, 69, 132, 139, 140, 170, 184, 238, 242, 245, 274, 283, 300, 334
Madras Europeans 42, 223, 245
Madras Pioneers 15, 334
Madras Sappers & Miners 69, 88, 96, 132, 134, 140, 156, 202, 242, 274, 283, 324
1st Madras 301, 324
2nd Madras 202
3rd Madras 300
5th Madras 324
6th Madras 163, 187, 202, 247, 258, 273, 274
9th Madras 96, 134
12th Madras 187, 226
14th Madras 202
18th Madras 15
26th Madras 88, 336
27th Madras 247, 273, 274,
28th Madras 15
35th Madras 96
36th Madras 69, 132, 202, 274, 283
37th Madras 6, 51, 140
41st Madras 202
42nd Madras 86
43rd Madras 15
Sikh Police Force 273, 274

AIRCRAFT AND SQUADRONS

AIRSHIPS AND ZEPPELINS
see General Index

ALBACORE *60*
817 61, 189, 211, 311, 324
820 189, 191, 254, 311, 319
822 311
826 27, 37, 47, 54, 79, 103, 136, 142
827 121, 211
828 211
829 27, 37, 47, 79, 103, 136, 142
831 121
832 61, 311

ANSON (RAF) *239*

AVENGER *114, 131*
820 19, 77, 94, 95, 119
828 166
846 83, 86, 118, 257
848 119
849 4, 19, 77, 119
851 130, 227
852 257
853 118
854 19, 77, 349
856 323, 336
857 4, 19, 77, 119, 349

BARRACUDA *86, 240*
810 101, 172, 254
815 240, 262, 286
817 240, 262, 286
820 240
822 262
826 240
827 86, 110, 240, 257
828 297
829 86
830 86, 257
831 86, 206, 240
841 297
847 101, 172

BEAUFIGHTER
236 117, 118, 152
254 117, 118

BEAUFORT (RAF)
42 36
86 36
217 36

BISLEY (RAF)
15 42, 257
244 285

391

TH
O